ILLEGAL IMMIGRATION IN AMERICA

A Reference Handbook

Edited by
David W. Haines
and
Karen E. Rosenblum

Greenwood Press
Westport, Connecticut • London

Library of Congress Cataloging-in-Publication Data

Illegal immigration in America : a reference handbook / edited by
David W. Haines and Karen E. Rosenblum.
    p. cm.
  Includes bibliographical references and index.
  ISBN 0–313–30436–X (alk. paper)
  1. Illegal aliens—United States. 2. Illegal aliens—Government
policy—United States. I. Haines, David W. II. Rosenblum, Karen
Elaine.
  JV6483.I53   1999
  325.73—dc21   99–13705

British Library Cataloguing in Publication Data is available.

Library of Congress Catalog Card Number: 99–13705
ISBN: 0–313–30436–X

First published in 1999

Greenwood Press, 88 Post Road West, Westport, CT 06881
An imprint of Greenwood Publishing Group, Inc.
www.greenwood.com

Printed in the United States of America

The paper used in this book complies with the
Permanent Paper Standard issued by the National
Information Standards Organization (Z39.48–1984).

10 9 8 7 6 5 4 3 2 1

For our students

Contents

PART III.   THE RESPONSES

PART IV.   ILLEGAL IMMIGRATION IN PERSPECTIVE

Preface

This volume is partly accidental in origin. In a previous reference volume on refugees, one of us (Haines, *Refugees in America in the 1990s*, Greenwood Press, 1996) decided ultimately to restrict the book's coverage to those formally accepted into the United States as refugees. There are a number of reasons for that kind of restriction, but the net result was to exclude a large number of people who—although not formally designated as refugees—met most of the accepted criteria for being refugees. That omission, especially of Central Americans, was not a happy one. Thus the suggestion by Cynthia Harris at Greenwood Press of preparing a volume on undocumented immigration raised the possibility of remedying that limitation and, at the same time, highlighting the broader experience of those who struggle with the problems of being "illegal" in their country of refuge. This book, unlike many others on the subject, thus begins with the observation that many of the illegal shouldn't be illegal, wouldn't be if they had happened to come from a different country at a different time, and often won't be as their legal cases are resolved or additional legislation brings them within the borders of legality.

Although the experience of the undocumented deserves attention in its own right, illegal immigration as a social and political issue is as much about the way immigration is structured, conceived, and legislated as it is about the undocumented immigrants themselves. Thus, we were also interested in how the subject of illegal immigration throws light on other aspects of contemporary American society. That broader framework connects to several of our other areas of research, especially the structure of governance (Haines' work on the analysis of federal and state organizational structures and processes), work itself (in which we both have a strong interest), and the construction of difference in America (particularly Rosenblum's work with Toni Travis on race, gender, and class). Our interest in immigration also draws strength from where we work—George Mason University—and its distinctive mix of foreign students, immigrants, and the children of immigrants. These students have been a pleasure to know, a test of our assumptions, and a frequent source of new understanding.

The result is an approach to illegal immigration that emphasizes the range of people involved on both sides of the equation, those who—for various reasons—end up being illegal for at least some period of time and those who respond to illegal immigration as a topic and to illegal immigrants as people. As varied as the immigrants themselves are, it is possible that the range of the responses is even greater: from the nativist sentiments seen in Proposition 187, to the commitment to being illegal on behalf of the illegal seen in the sanctuary movement; from government protestations about controlling our borders, to legislative actions that directly encourage illegal border crossing; from concern about the general abuse of human rights that occurs with labor trafficking, to a concern about how particular families reconstitute themselves as they alternately correct and ignore their legal status.

In developing this volume, we have incurred many debts: particularly to Cynthia Harris for suggesting the effort and to Steve Gold, Linda Gordon, and David Howell for especially wise counsel on potential chapter authors. Appreciation for helpful comments along the way also goes to Leo Chavez, Josh DeWind, Nancy Foner, David Gutiérrez, David Heer, Carlos Vélez-Ibáñez, Evelyn Jacob, Johanna Lessinger, Sarah Mahler, Susan Martin, Rubén Rumbaut, and Roger Waldinger. Two sessions organized at professional meetings over the past two years have been helpful in thinking through immigration issues, and appreciation thus goes to Carol Mortland as coorganizer of one of those sessions and to the participants: Janet Benson, Ted Downing, Ruth Krulfeld, Jeffery MacDonald, Lance Rasbridge, Ann Rynearson, Alex Stepick, and Nancy Wellmeier. Since we bridge the disciplines of anthropology and sociology, we would also like to acknowledge the invaluable work of both the American Sociological Association's International Migration Section and the American Anthropological Association's Committee on Refugees and Immigrants. In the production of the book we are indebted to Betty Pessagno, our production editor, Carol Lucas, our copyeditor, and the staff at Greenwood Press.

Reference volumes have a particular goal in providing an introduction to a subject: to be balanced and accessible yet relatively detailed. The standard for a reference volume is that it be the single best place to begin an inquiry on a particular subject—whatever the political, social, or academic inclination of the person doing that inquiry. We hope we have at least approached that standard.

Introduction: Problematic Labels, Volatile Issues

David W. Haines and Karen E. Rosenblum

Illegal immigration is a difficult issue. Few subjects are so fraught with misinformation and lack of information, complexity and paradox, political interest and governmental neglect, social concern and human callousness, careful economic analysis and fiscal incertitude. In addressing this subject, this volume aims to shed light on the variety of migrants and migrations that fall within the category of illegal immigration and on the ever-shifting legal frameworks that cause some people to be ''legal'' and others to be ''illegal.'' Indeed, many people shift between those two legal statuses as they move to America, live in America, and return—temporarily or permanently—to the countries from which they came. This chapter provides an introduction to the problems posed by ''illegal immigration'' as a label and then discusses five distinct social and political issues to which that label nevertheless points. The chapter concludes with a brief overview of the volume as a whole.

PROBLEMATIC LABELS

There are, by the most common estimates, some 5 million people in the United States who lack, as Lucy Cohen refers to it in her chapter, ''proper papers.'' That number appears to be increasing by roughly a quarter of a million persons each year. There are three conventional breakdowns of the overall numbers. The first is by the ''how'' of illegality. At least two-fifths—and perhaps more—of these people came to the United States with legal documents but subsequently stayed beyond the provisions of those documents. These are the ''visa-overstayers.'' Visa-overstayers, of course, are not literally illegal immigrants; they are legal migrants (nonimmigrants in Immigration and Natural- ization Service [INS] parlance) who simply outlast their temporary legality. The larger portion of the illegal population entered the country without inspection and are thus conventionally noted as "EWIs" (entered without inspection). Un- counted in either of these are the significant numbers of nonimmigrants (e.g., tourists and students) who may be legally in the country but then work, usually violating the conditions of their visas. These last are thus perfectly legal in arrival and departure but perfectly illegal in their actions while in the United States.

The second conventional breakdown is the "where from" of illegality. Roughly half of the undocumented are from Mexico, reflecting a long history of labor migration that has been encouraged by U.S. employers and often le- gitimated by the U.S. government. The next largest set of illegal immigrants— around 15 percent—are from Central America. Here, the motivations are mixed, but a large number reflect political turmoil and civil war, reflecting long-term U.S. political and economic involvement in the regions. But there are other origins as well: the Caribbean, South America, Asia, and Europe each contribute 5 percent to 7 percent of the total estimated illegal population.

The third conventional breakdown is the "where to" of illegal immigration. The latest figures suggest that nearly half of the undocumented reside in Cali- fornia, with another 30 percent accounted for by Texas, New York, and Florida (see Passel's more detailed figures in Chapter 3). But again, there is considerable diversity here, too. The undocumented appear in a variety of other states, and even where their overall numbers may be modest, their impact may be signifi- cant when they constitute a major segment of the labor force in selected indus- tries (several in rural areas) or a significant presence in localities where their number and newness create a demand for services ranging from health, to trans- lation, to education.

In the simplest sense and the one most active in the public mind, the overall issue of illegal immigration might be roundly condensed into that of illegal border crossers from Mexico into California—clearly the single major cluster of illegal immigrants, even though only a minority of the total. That California, indeed, bears the brunt of the issue is seen in the strong responses there to illegal immigration, particularly the 1994 passage of Proposition 187. Ironically, the subsequent reaction against the often-draconian controls specified in that proposition appeared to be a significant factor in the resurgence of the Demo- cratic Party in California in the 1998 elections, with potential repercussions for the country as a whole.

Even if we were to limit our view to illegal border crossers from Mexico, complexities remain. Many illegal border crossers are directly recruited by U.S. employers; those employers remain relatively immune from any sanctions for such recruitment. Many of the border crossers are circular migrants—so their illegal residence in the United States is temporary, and they may on former trips have been legal border crossers. Many are family members of people who are legal residents in the United States; often they come to join relatives who are now legal because of amnesties of the late 1980s. Many of these undocumented border crossers are thus quite clearly drawn across the border by economic and political inducements; they may be participants in an illegal system but are hardly its creators or controllers. They are simply the ones who get caught. Nor is the Mexican border crossed by Mexicans and Central Americans alone. Increasingly, global trafficking networks use that border as one option for delivering their clients into the United States.

Furthermore, many of those drawn across the Mexican border are not labor migrants at all. Especially during the 1980s, large numbers of Central Americans came across the border fleeing civil wars and government repression in Guatemala, El Salvador, and Nicaragua. Since the government did not recognize them as refugees and thus as eligible for resettlement in the United States, their only choice was to cross the border illegally and then seek asylum once inside the United States. That quest has led to multiple asylum applications, a variety of legal suits, and, finally in 1997, legislation to make it easier—if far from automatic—for them to legalize their status.

Thus, even with a focus only on the illegal crossing of the Mexican border, four distinct groups emerge: labor migrants who are a part of long-established and encouraged routes between Mexico and the United States, labor brought and trafficked from farther away as part of new channels into the United States, those seeking asylum in the United States from political repression in other countries, and a variety of people whose motivation to cross is largely to reunite with relatives in the United States, who, in turn, may be in various legal statuses.

Broadening the perspective and moving away from the Mexican border to include the rest of the undocumented, the picture expands further. Origin countries increase, and transit paths become more complex. Labor migrants from the Caribbean, for example, aim directly for the continental United States or for the shores of Puerto Rico, from which it is easier to reach the United States. Labor migrants from China are trafficked by a variety of means, including ships dropping their human cargo in the New York City area. Others seek asylum as they emerge elsewhere at airports, on beaches, or in ships. Those with more credible bank accounts arrive with tourist visas, only to overstay them and move into the ranks of the undocumented.

There are thus multiple reasons for being undocumented, and there are multiple paths by which this happens. There are also multiple histories afterward. Many of the undocumented eventually are legalized. Asylum applicants, for example, may adequately prove their case and have their legal status adjusted on that basis. Undocumented workers may find a sponsoring employer who helps them gain legal status through normal immigration channels. Relatives who are illegally in the country may eventually be legally sponsored and have their status adjusted with full recognition that they have been residing in the country without proper documents. Finally, the U.S. government may provide an amnesty that directly allows the undocumented to become legal residents.

The major example was the 1986 Immigration Reform and Control Act, but a variety of other legislation over the years has singled out particular groups for special consideration, most recently Central Americans and Eastern Europeans (Nicaraguan Adjustment and Central American Relief Act of 1997) and Haitians (Omnibus Appropriations Bill of 1998).

Illegal immigrants thus look much like regular immigrants: some seek work, and others seek refuge; some come for money, and others come for family; some are welcomed, and others become a focus for nativist reactions. Some were once regular, documented migrants, and others will be in the future or have a strong case in U.S. or international law for being so now. Many live in households with legal spouses and with children who may be citizens. The phrase "illegal immigrant" does a poor job of grasping the meaning of these disparate people's lives. But the alternatives are not much better. The common preference now is usually to call these people undocumented, but that has problems: many of the illegal do have documents—they just aren't the right ones for where they are living and what they are doing. It also seems a weak term considering the stress placed on those without documents. Certainly, as the INS expands its enforcement functions, the sense of a mere misdemeanor indiscretion seems out of place. Other words have problems as well. The more internationally used term "irregular migration" poses a different set of problems, as it implies that regular migration is, in fact, very regular (it is not) or that irregular migration is not often extremely orderly (it often is). "Unlegal" and "nonlegal" seem a bit forced; "clandestine" misses the point that much of this migration is far from hidden. We have here continued to use the terms "illegal," "undocumented," and occasionally, "unauthorized" because they are the conventional ones; they are of some limited descriptive use, and to fabricate a new term could only add to the existing confusion. These words may be poor choices in reference to the people, but they do point clearly toward a set of very volatile social and political issues.

VOLATILE ISSUES

The inadequacy of the label "illegal immigration" is matched by the volatility of the subject as a social and political issue. The attempt to see illegal immigration as a single issue is immediately undermined by the diversity of the people and situations to which it refers. It is necessary to recognize that there are multiple issues. We think five are most important: issues of borders, labor, queuing, asylum, and impact. We discuss each of these briefly, less to resolve them than to provide an introductory framework. Each is a difficult issue in its own right; the collation of all of them within the greater issue of illegal immigration helps explain much of the confusion in the public debate on the subject.

Borders. Borders are an integral aspect of state systems. Whether as imaginary lines across a desert or in the middle of a river or as actual fortified walls (such as the Great Wall of China or the fence that is being constructed along key portions of the U.S. border with Mexico), borders serve practically and symbolically to mark those who are outside and those inside a particular state. But it is rare that borders are not meant to be crossed by people (both temporarily and more permanently) and by goods. In particular, there are often socially and economically integrated regions that span borders and that are thus dependent on relatively free movement across those borders.

Therein lies the dilemma in border control: a state must control a border as much to facilitate movement as to restrict it. This is perhaps clearest with the physical U.S. border with Mexico, where the U.S. government is attempting both to speed up border crossing (to avoid delays for those who are authorized to cross) but also, with a sharp increase in funding, to decrease illegal movements across the border. The problem is compounded when many of those who might cross the border illegally either are, in fact, wanted on the other side (e.g., as seasonal agricultural labor) or may turn out to be "legal" in terms of international or U.S. refugee law. This problem of land borders is compounded with that of air travel to the United States, the need for internal monitoring of people who may now be "illegal" by having outstayed or violated their initial legal entry, and the strong evidence that efforts to control a border at one point often simply displace border crossings to other areas—and may force simple border crossers into the same channels as more criminal trafficking in labor and goods. The situation is rendered yet more complex since much "border" control does not actually take place at the country's actual physical borders: INS raids on businesses, for example, are a form of border control, as are more routine adjustments of legal status for those already within the country. In its raids, the INS, in effect, brings the border to the workplace to again screen out those who should have been apprehended at the "real" border.

Labor.   Many U.S. employers rely on undocumented labor. As various chapters in this book note, the flow of undocumented Mexican workers to the United States has its origin in legal flows of workers, including the bracero program that ended in 1964. That employer interest is seen throughout U.S. immigration legislation, particularly in the special agricultural worker (SAW) legalization program of the 1986 Immigration Reform and Control Act (IRCA). That pattern of desired labor is far from limited to Mexican border issues. Mexican and Central American undocumented labor is moving farther to the north and east, and a variety of other nationalities are being drawn into the undocumented workforce, whether Chinese in the garment industry or Irish in the seasonal tourist industry.

Not all of this labor is low-wage, nor is all of it as vital to economic interests as may be argued by employers. Nevertheless, as a labor issue, undocumented immigration raises difficult questions about the structure of the American economy and how it continues to seek low-wage labor and to avoid extraneous labor costs such as health benefits, retirement packages, worker protection from injury in dangerous work, and worker protection from disability in debilitating jobs. The undocumented thus raise questions about the viability of an American economic system in which employers cannot afford to provide a normal employment contract in many industries. The desperation with which workers from other countries will nevertheless accept such conditions is an equally damning indictment of the existing efforts to spread development and some measure of prosperity more broadly throughout the world.

Queuing. Many of the undocumented are on their way to being documented. They are in the United States to be with relatives or to work in jobs for which they may have either U.S. experience or U.S. education. Many of the undocumented are thus queued up to be documented; they simply wait out their period in the queue in the United States rather than in their country of origin. This is actually two separate issues, and although they may seem to pale in comparison to the other aspects of illegal immigration noted here, they merit some mention. First is the general issue of undocumented residence. At a time when even legal immigrants are subject to deportation for previous criminal behavior (often of a minor nature), it is troubling to some that one set of people suffers no sanction for undocumented residence. Indeed, the government passed legislation allowing them to simply pay a fine at the time their papers finally came through without even leaving the country, thus effectively buying themselves out of any culpability for their illegal residence (see Section 245[i] of the Immigration and Nationality Act).

Second is the question of whether undocumented residence in the United States in fact increases people's opportunities to become legal residents. Certainly, if people have lived in the United States for a long period of time, can call upon an employer to help them obtain legal status of one kind or another, or—even better—lay a claim to having been somehow legal at the time of entry, then length of time in the country may increase their individual argument for special consideration. It may also make them eligible for some kind of amnesty program that depends on their being illegally within the United States. Simply put, by spending queuing time in the United States itself, people not only can move more quickly to be with family and perhaps in better jobs but may well find that, having waited in one queue, they are simultaneously in another, faster moving one.

Asylum. The United States has for two decades admitted well over 50,000 people annually as refugees and, in many years, over 100,000. Although the Refugee Act of 1980 brought the U.S. definition of refugees in line with international conventions, it has never succeeded in creating a refugee determination process that has been independent of U.S. foreign policy interests. The extent to which the U.S. refugee numbers have been composed of Cuban, Southeast Asian, and Soviet (now largely Russian) refugees underlines that point. The numbers remaining for other parts of the world have thus been very limited.

The result has been that for many people from many other countries the only available mechanism either for temporary protection or long-term resettlement is to travel illegally to the United States. Once within the country, they can either remain undocumented or apply for asylum, arguing that their individual situation indeed resembles that of those formally admitted into the country as refugees. In some cases, changes in governments in the home country may place people already in the United States in a similar position: unable to return home, they overextend or violate their current visa status and thus become undocumented and possible asylum applicants. At times, other legal statuses may become available (e.g., temporary protected status may be extended to people whose home country is in turmoil), but these are, indeed, temporary delays in resolving the long-term issue of legal status. Perhaps no other aspect of illegal immigration has drawn such a strong and broad-spectrum response from Americans, yet such humanitarian concern has not kept the U.S. government from interdicting asylum seekers on the high seas (before they can set foot on U.S. territory and thus become "persons" with access to the U.S. legal system) or, in more recent years, from trying to impose an expedited removal process that would also keep arriving asylum applicants from having full access to the U.S. legal system. These so-called court-stripping provisions of the 1996 Illegal Immigration Reform and Immigrant Responsibility Act came under immediate legal attack, although the Supreme Court let a central element stand in an early 1999 ruling (*Reno v. American-Arab Anti-Discrimination Committee*).

Impact. With about 5 million illegal immigrants in the United States and an annual net increase of perhaps .25 million, there is, indeed, impact. Although the number is small as a percentage of the overall U.S. population, the localization of illegal immigrants in particular regions (especially the Southwest) and in particular cities (Los Angeles, New York) and industries (certain agricultural sectors, the garment industry, construction) magnifies the effect. Some of the impact is positive, particularly if the employers complain that without such labor they would go out of business. Some of that impact is negative: the world of labor trafficking feeds into criminal activities, competition for low-wage jobs may drive wages even lower, the unexpected appearance of many children (either undocumented themselves or the offspring of undocumented immigrants) may challenge school systems, and use of hospital emergency rooms by those with no access to other kinds of health care may strain resources.

Given the unresolved debate about the overall direction and degree of the impact from *all* immigrants, it is unlikely that any definitive statement about impact is possible. Enrico Marcelli in his chapter on Los Angeles goes to great lengths to utilize a particularly good set of data on the undocumented to address this question statistically; the results suggest that the undocumented complement, rather than compete with, other segments of the labor force, but he is cautious in his conclusions. The more important conclusion may well be the lack of evidence showing competition. Beyond that, for every example of negative impact, there is probably one of positive contribution. If good immigrants are, after all, expected to be hardworking and law-abiding, illegal immigrants fit that bill very well—indeed, sometimes more so than legal immigrants. The issue of impact, perhaps the single item that most drives the public debate on illegal immigration, may thus be the one that is murkiest.

STRUCTURE OF THE BOOK

This book aims to illuminate the subject of illegal migration in the United States as broadly as possible. It thus stresses the variety of migration experiences that are, in at least some ways, illegal and the varied public responses to the overall issue of illegality and to the specific groups who end up for one reason or another as illegal. The attempt at that range results in the four parts of this book.

"Part I: Concepts, Policies, and Numbers" introduces the basic ideas and data that are most central to the issue of illegal immigration. In this introduction, we have attempted a brief reconnaissance of the major concepts and issues involved in understanding illegal immigration, but in the next chapter, Karen Woodrow-Lafield focuses in more detail on illegal immigration as a component of overall immigration, noting, for example, how the debate about the impact of immigration seems to focus so strongly on the illegal segment of it. She then introduces the theoretical frameworks used to look at immigration and the specific legal categories that shape the migration process—and sort it into legal and illegal streams. Jeffrey Passel then takes on the daunting task of "the numbers." One of the results of being undocumented is that one doesn't leave a very good statistical trail. Passel provides a succinct background of illegal immigration to the United States and then provides a detailed introduction to the task of counting the undocumented. He emphasizes the need for residual estimates: working from censuses and surveys that include all immigrants (both documented and undocumented) and then accounting for all the documented people, thus leaving, as the residue, the number of the undocumented.

With the numbers thus established, Katharine Donato and Rebecca Carter in the succeeding chapter focus on what has traditionally been the core of illegal immigration, Mexican border crossers. They review the general history of Mexican–U.S. border policies (from both sides of the border) and address in particular detail what is probably the major watershed in U.S. policy: IRCA. Their description of the amnesty provisions of the law shows clearly how government policy, while claiming to attempt to reduce illegal immigration, often has the opposite effect. The political and economic struggles that underlie U.S. immigration legislation become painfully clear.

"Part II: The Migrants and the Work" begins with four chapters focusing on the work that illegal immigrants do. Philip Martin describes how three specific agricultural niches are structured (apples, oranges, and grapes), including how employers assess the relative merits of automation versus use of low-wage, often undocumented laborers. David Griffith and Janet Benson in the two following chapters provide similar insight into the poultry and meatpacking industries. Both represent a new industrialization of food processing and a significant niche for undocumented labor, either in processing itself or in the jobs supporting it. Enrico Marcelli then takes a more quantitative look at whether

illegal workers in urban areas (Los Angeles is the specific case) actually displace other workers. Emphasizing undocumented workers from Central America, who typically receive much less attention than undocumented Mexicans, his general conclusion is that they do not, raising questions about policies or policy pronouncements that suggest that illegal immigration is damaging to other components of the labor force.

The next set of chapters looks more at the specific channels of illegal immigration, aiming to expand understanding beyond the usual emphasis on Mexican immigration. Cecilia Menjívar begins with the largest set of the undocumented after those from Mexico. She notes the mixed origins and motivations of those from El Salvador and Nicaragua and their diverging fates as their legal fortunes have ebbed and flowed—finally with the promise for many of legalization under the 1997 Nicaraguan Adjustment and Central American Relief Act (NACARA). The final three chapters of Part II turn to other parts of the world and to groups whose migration tends to be more economic in motivation. Elzbieta Gozdziak addresses the significant amount of illegal immigration from Europe, giving both an Eastern European example (the Poles) and a Western European example (the Irish). Sam Martínez examines the complicated migration patterns within the Caribbean, the end results of which are major streams of legal and illegal immigration to the United States and an abiding controversy about the refugee determination process. Finally, Ko-lin Chin turns to a relatively new, undocumented population, the mostly trafficked Chinese in New York City. His pathbreaking survey work with this population provides an invaluable snapshot of the work they do, the costs of being undocumented in America, and how they evaluate their future lives—including whether those future lives should be in the United States or in China.

"*Part III: The Responses*" introduces the social, legal, and moral challenges raised by illegal immigration and the way Americans have responded to those issues. Victoria Rader begins by describing the origins and development of the sanctuary movement in response to the flight of refugees from Central America. As she notes, the sanctuary movement involved a complex web of people collectively thinking through not only issues of assistance to refugees but the overall structure of their social responsibilities as people and as citizens of the world. Haines then writes on the ways in which undocumented labor is exploited and can be protected, and Rosenblum writes on Proposition 187 in California, which marked not only a high point for nativist reaction against immigration but also a galvanizing moment for the political participation of Latinos in California. In the succeeding chapter, Lucy Cohen provides two case studies of the way families respond to shifting patterns of legal status. The two families she describes are now legal, but the complexity and duration of the processes that made them so have caused gaps in family relationships that cannot be undone. Finally, Duncan Earle brings the discussion full circle and back to the Mexican border, where he finds both a region that spans the border and a variety of control strategies toward the Mexican origin population on the U.S. side of the border. Here "control"—the root concept in efforts to "combat" illegal immigration—takes on a harsher meaning.

"*Part IV: Illegal Immigration in Perspective*" provides some different vantage points from which to assess illegal immigration. Norman Buchignani and Doreen Indra provide a comprehensive look at illegal immigration to Canada (which is far more tilted toward asylum seekers than labor migrants) and note how the issue is defined more in terms of public sentiments than in terms of the actualities of illegal immigration. Deborah Altamirano turns to the situation in Europe, where the dictates of the European Union are putting additional pressure on individual countries to control illegal immigration. Her two case studies, Greece and Italy, show the tension between those two levels of governance. Keiko Yamanaka then provides a general portrait of illegal immigration in Asia and a focused case study of the Nepalese in Japan, where they work in the multilayered contracting system of Japanese industry. All three chapters help highlight what is common in national concerns about controlling illegal immigration and also how a country's individual history can shape a more distinctive set of issues.

The book concludes with a selected set of annotations to the rapidly growing literature on illegal immigration in the United States, providing an opportunity to sample the issues and approaches out of which the discussion on the politics and actualities of illegal immigration has been constructed, with an emphasis on the 1990s. An abbreviated list of immigration legislation from 1980 (the Refugee Act) through 1998 is also included, not only for the detail on illegal immigration legislation in particular but to illustrate how much legislative tinkering there has been and how much of that is directly or indirectly related to illegal immigration. For example, the determination of who is a refugee determines the nature of the pool of those who will have to cross U.S. borders to seek asylum, thereby usually becoming "illegal." The structure of legal temporary worker programs delineates the labor pool for illegal workers now and shapes the migration paths of other illegal immigration in the future. After all, the determination of who the legal immigrants are (whether long-term or short-term) largely sets in place the channels through which others may come—sometimes as legal immigrants and sometimes as illegal ones.

PART I

CONCEPTS, POLICIES, AND NUMBERS

2

Labor Migration, Family Integration, and the New America

Karen A. Woodrow-Lafield

The topics of illegal immigration and legal immigration are inexorably inter-twined. Overall, immigration is more clearly discernible statistically than either of its components of illegal (or unauthorized) and legal (or authorized) immi-gration. Public concern has tended to dwell on unauthorized immigration, es-pecially the portion involving illegal border crossing. Even societal implications of immigration in general are often recast or expressed specifically to the illegal or unauthorized segment. This chapter confronts four issues surrounding the twin topics of authorized and unauthorized immigration. First is the recent debate about immigration and its impacts, an area in which the illegal component seems to bear the burden of the argument despite its relatively modest magnitude and in which, more generally, the data are not convincing as to either any great magnitude of effect or its character as positive or negative. Second is the range of current general theories of immigration and types of immigrants, irrespective of authorization status. Third is the immigration policy that has defined the categories within which immigration channels have evolved, resulting in the authorized (legal) resident population. There is also a residue of individuals seeking to live in the United States for whom the immigration system fails to offer an appropriate category or mechanism, and, from that population base, an illegal immigration flow results for which the settled portion can be measured as a residual from the foreign-born population and the authorized population. Fourth is the general magnitude and momentum of current immigration, partic-ularly the interplay of unauthorized immigration, legalization, naturalization, and authorized immigration. Overall, it is likely that immigration to the United States has become perpetual and contributes to the essential definition of America; illegal immigration may well be as perpetual as its lawful counterpart.

THE DEBATE ABOUT IMPACT

Within America of recent decades, there has been a continuing sensitivity to immigration impacts, especially undocumented immigration. A major concern is immigration's impact on wages and job opportunities for natives. A second concern is whether these effects are especially disadvantageous for certain groups, African Americans in particular. A third concern is about the relative usage of public services for natives and immigrants. Addressing these concerns is not simple. Indeed, these points have been the focus of numerous studies seeking to inform public policy, yet following the report on the demographic, economic, and fiscal effects of immigration (Smith and Edmonston 1997) from the National Academy of Sciences' National Research Council, the overall questions remain unresolved, much less the more specific question as to the effects of the illegal (or undocumented or unauthorized) components.

These concerns about impact have several aspects ranging from general to specific—the economy, the multiplicity of social problems, the "welfare state" status, public perception, and organized movements. As a leader among the movements, the Federation for American Immigration Reform (FAIR) seeks to restrain immigration as protection for the environment against the added acceleration to the momentum of U.S. population growth. The high visibility of immigration policy reinforces the existence of such organizations (Espenshade and Belanger 1998). Public attitudes about immigration are ambivalent and tend to be unfavorable toward contemporary streams of immigrants (Simon 1985; Simon and Alexander 1993; Espenshade and Calhoun 1992; Espenshade and Belanger 1998). The contexts of the economy, social problems, and welfare state are relevant nationally, subnationally, and locally with differential salience for specific subgroups.

Although the overall effect of immigration may be small, there are specific, negative effects for areas with large immigrant communities, and there are adverse effects for wages of certain types of native workers. This was the conclusion of the National Research Council (NRC) Study (Smith and Edmonston 1997). Those workers most affected are those lacking a high school education, with whom recent immigrants may have promoted wage and job competition. Although one is tempted to generalize this finding to groups for which educational achievement levels are low, that could be misleading. Nor could the NRC study attribute that portion of the negative effects due to the presence of illegal immigrants for whom illegal status could restrict occupational mobility. In their study of immigration's impacts within California, McCarthy and Vernez (1997) noted the importance of distinguishing these influences from illegal immigration, but they could merely surmise.

Yet such refinements would be critical for telling the degree, if any, to which illegal immigration may be worsening the problem of income inequality within America (Levy 1987, 1995). The U.S. economy has shifted from an industrial, manufacturing economy to a postindustrial economy within which the lesser educated are faring worse and worse over time. Greater and greater numbers of persons became distanced from the top earning category over the 1970s, 1980s, and early 1990s. Within a systemic analysis, in a sense, income shares shifted in an upward direction through the social class structure. Those at the bottom of the economic ladder are disproportionately African-American, Hispanic, female, and unskilled. For many located in central cities, the notion of economic migration is distant, despite economic theories of the nation as a marketplace with locales alternately attracting and disattracting workers. The possibility of a persistent underclass has evoked heated debates about causes and ameliorative strategies (Wilson 1987, 1998; Massey 1996). Concomitant with this debate is an awareness that new immigrants having low levels of human capital, especially illegal immigrants, might become additions to an underclass or lower economic echelon. In the late 1990s, income inequality seems to have plateaued (U.S. Bureau of the Census 1998a). The long-term prospects for the income gap may not be bright if recent monetary policies contributed to dropping unemployment rates to the lowest levels in four decades, which then may have led to higher wages for the lower-earning workers (Galbraith 1998).

A systems orientation is suitable for considering immigrants as labor and human capital exchanges from developed and developing nations to the United States and certain other receiving nations. World inequality is increasing in the aggregate as the more developed nations hold an ever greater share of income and wealth (United Nations Development Programme 1998). Nations at lower levels of development have generally showed high levels of population growth and deepening poverty. There are now positive signs of bringing population growth under control in the mid-twenty-first century (Johnson 1994; United Nations Population Division 1998). Despite the quality of life for large population segments in the developing world, migration is not commensurately sought. Real barriers prevent leaving one's home and community. Taken as a whole, international migration may be at unprecedented levels (Miller 1994), or it may not be increasing on a relative basis (United Nations ACC Task Force on Basic Social Services for All [BSSA] 1998).

The immigration debate continues even as the full force of events in the late 1980s reaches fruition. In endeavoring to stop illegal immigration and to diminish the accumulated effect of illegal immigration over two decades, the U.S. Congress passed the Immigration Reform and Control Act of 1986 (IRCA), which held provisions for beginning sanctions against employers who hired undocumented workers, increased enforcement activities at the border, and extended amnesty to formerly undocumented workers in agriculture and other long-term residents. This legislation resulted from years of careful consideration, beginning with the Select Commission on Immigration and Refugee Policy (SCIRP) (Greenwood and McDowell 1985). Congress later passed the Immigration Act of 1990, with provisions redesigning the immigration preference system and creating the U.S. Commission on Immigration Reform to undertake another comprehensive review of immigration's impacts. These reforms were concomitant with a redirected focus of RAND from defense to domestic issues such as immigration and the emergence of other think tank organizations such as the Public Policy Institute of California and the Center for Immigration Studies.

Unanticipated or unintended consequences are apparently the sequelae to immigration legislation if history can be taken as predictive. The evolution of major migration streams from Latin America and Asia, for example, was not foreseen at the time of the Immigration and Nationality Act of 1965 (Reimers 1985). The contemporary immigration debate is thus influenced by the specifics of prior policies, including amnesty programs that have affected the lives of millions, steering them and their families in the path to becoming lawful permanent residents and Americans.

KINDS OF IMMIGRANTS; THEORIES OF IMMIGRATION

A typology of migrants or immigrants may help point to underlying explanations for social behavior or even be a "valid intellectual exercise" (Portes 1997: 806), but a typology is not sufficient as a theoretical explanation. Some typologies, as will be noted, are not specific as to authorization status for the migrant, although there may be more substantive relevance as to societal institutions of the economy, labor, and the family. Portes (1997) refers to typologies based on administrative categories, including authorization status (U.S. Immigration and Naturalization Service 1998; Edmonston 1996: 15–17; U.S. Commission on Immigration Reform and Mexican Ministry of Foreign Affairs 1997: xi–xii; Woodrow-Lafield 1998). Outside of the administrative or legally defined categories for authorized migrants, there is the category referred to as unauthorized, undocumented, illegal, informal, irregular, clandestine, nonlegal, or unofficial (see Hill 1985). Within this category, there are frequently differentiations on the basis of mode of actual U.S. entry between the major categories of visa-overstayers and border crossers, or those entering without inspection.

One frequently overlooked issue is that of future mode of admission for permanent residence, for the unauthorized population includes persons for whom there is not, nor ever will be, a visa petition but also includes persons for whom there is currently, or will be, a visa petition. Therefore, unauthorized migrants have a certain probability of becoming eligible to receive an immigrant visa for admission as lawful, permanent residents. At that point, individuals may return to their embassy to receive their visa or, alternatively, may apply at an Immigration and Naturalization Service (INS) office to receive their visa without traveling to the country of application, as allowed under Section 245(i) of the Immigration and Nationality Act since 1995.

Portes and Rumbaut (1996) suggest a different typology as having greater theoretical bearing, as "building blocks" for theories, in its four categories of manual labor immigrants, professional immigrants, immigrant entrepreneurs, and political refugees. Other typologies delve into aspects of immigrant incorporation and adjustment, including distinctions along lines of ethnicity or generational status. There are interconnections between such theoretical categories and more administrative or legalistic typologies. Indeed, the principal bases of the official immigration system are labor or employer sponsorship, family sponsorship, humanitarian reasons, and diversity criteria. However, individual motivations may deviate from the umbrella under which admission for lawful, permanent residence is granted.

Portes (1997) also provides a useful classification scheme for theories of immigration: the origins of immigration, the directionality and continuity of migration flows, the utilization of immigrant labor, and the sociocultural adaptation of immigrants (cf. Portes and Bach 1985). Furthermore, microlevel and macrolevel approaches are equally warranted. Massey and comembers of the IUSSP Committee on South-North Migration (1993, 1994) endeavored to establish a comprehensive, theoretical framework for studying the initiation and perpetuation of international migration, and promising empirical work is to follow. The major theories explaining the initiation of international migration are neoclassical economics (macrolevel and microlevel), the new economics of migration, dual labor market theory, and world systems theory. They posit a cumulative causation process theory for explaining the perpetuation of migration, drawing from network theory and institutional theory.

The individual has multiple points of reference before actually immigrating: origin family, origin household, origin community, origin country, coresident family, U.S. community, and the United States. Neo-classical theory explains international migration as the result of individuals' cost-benefit decision making to maximize expected income, whether for the individual or for the household, through a move to a destination country. There is ample evidence that relative wage differentials, unemployment rates, and differentials in expected wages are important for variation among countries' emigration flows (Massey et al. 1993). The new economics of migration is complementary in recognizing the role of the family network or household as the key unit in international migration (Massey et al. 1993; Tilly 1990). Individual members of households may emigrate for economic advantages for the household unit in the origin community, with their remittances critical for both investment and consumption. Migrants either return to their families or households in the origin community, bring family members to the new settlement community, or form families in this new place, thus tracing the chain or path between labor migration and family migration (Tilly 1990; MacDonald and MacDonald 1974).

A complementary third theory posits that immigration is induced by demand for unskilled workers for a secondary labor market, where there are limited returns to education, skills, and experience. Some conclude that U.S. labor markets appear to be segmented such that immigrants are selectively excluded from the primary labor market and that immigrants are found disproportionately in secondary labor markets (Massey et al. 1994). Finally, the globalization of the market economy and concomitant creation of global cities as central in the management of production with high-wage areas involved in capital-intensive operations and low-wage areas involved in labor-intensive operations lead to specific international migration exchanges. Low-wage areas are generally experiencing unfavorable demographic or agricultural conditions, so that new modes of subsistence are more desirable even at the expense of familial lifestyles.

These migration experts elaborate on the special case of the North American migration patterns, but Massey et al. (1994: 739) note the serious limitations in translating results from Mexico–United States studies into the contexts of other prominent sending countries. Their assessment leads them to retain each of the four major theories as having importance for explaining the initiation and perpetuation of migration within North America. In the Mexico–United States Binational Study on Migration, Escobar Latapi et al. (1998) examine types of migrants (economic or noneconomic) in a framework of demand–pull factors, supply–push factors, and network and other factors influencing the decision to migrate. These experts found explanations for Mexico-to-United States migration to be primarily within the United States as a consequence of historical patterns of migration from an accumulating set of sending communities. However, demand–pull factors operate toward the influx of Mexican unskilled labor, and supply–push factors function toward the same outcomes. Various social networks are informative and conductive to the perpetuation of labor migration into settled, family migration, leading to the statement that "migration to the U.S. has become a way of life" in some portions of west-central Mexico (Escobar et al. 1998: 167). This might seem surprising if one considers the vast resources expended at the southern border to prevent northward migration and the concentrated enforcement focus. One noted scholar (Bustamante 1997) contrasts views from opposite sides of the southern border as emphasizing movement for economic migration rather than for more permanent reasons, as from the Mexican side, versus a criminality emphasis divorced from structural factors, including dependence of the U.S. economy on cheap labor. More optimistically, the Binational Study anticipated an ebb in Mexico–United States migration, with greater retention of Mexicans as a result of lessened demographic pressures and economic restructuring.

The mix of labor, family, and other bases for migration is not easy to disentangle. Mexican migration is a singular case in magnitude and history. For some, the decision to immigrate stems from forces inherent in neo-classical, new economics, segmented market, or world systems theories. For others, the decision to migrate stems from the aftereffects of an ongoing international migration stream. As immigrant communities develop, social networks facilitate the exchange of information with the origin community about employment, living situations, education, medical services, and recreation. Specialized institutions or special programs emerge for immigrant assistance. Whereas the initiating forces may help sustain a migration stream, both as to new migrants and as to minimizing return migrants, social networks and institutions play special roles in the perpetuation of international migration via cumulative causation (Massey et al. 1993).

LEGAL CATEGORIES: LABOR MIGRATION AND FAMILY REUNIFICATION

In addition to such theories about the initiation and perpetuation of international migration, discrete categories in the immigration system itself circumscribe authorized admissions without necessarily reflecting those underlying motivations and intentions. Apart from influences on individuals' decisions to emigrate that initiate international migration, individual circumstances of immigration depend on whether the individual can be accommodated within the four principles of the U.S. legal immigration system: family unification, labor requirements, diversity, and humanitarian considerations. Given the role of family preferences in the U.S. legal immigration system, most migration to the United States is based in a social network structure that integrates families, households, and communities.

Numerically limited preference categories for family or labor migration were established in the Immigration and Nationality Act Amendments of 1965. As of 1990, for the annual restricted total of 270,000 immigrant visas, the largest numbers were set aside for second preference (26 percent), fifth preference (24 percent), and first preference (20 percent) for uniting immigrants with certain family members—spouses, children, and adult siblings with dependents. Among these preferences, the only one under which permanent resident aliens might submit petitions for family members is second preference. The remaining amount (30 percent) was allocated equally among third preference (professional workers), fourth preference (adult sons and daughters with dependents), and sixth preference (skilled or unskilled workers). U.S. citizens, whether native-born or naturalized, have greater capability for sponsoring a family member as a legal immigrant. Any unused or residual visa numbers would become available on a nonpreference basis.

The Refugee Act of 1980 placed refugee admissions outside the preference system and established procedures for annual consultation with Congress on the numbers of refugees to be admitted in each fiscal year. The term ''refugee'' was defined to conform to the 1967 United Nations Protocol on Refugees, with a distinction between refugee and asylee status. In addition, the act established a comprehensive program for domestic resettlement of refugees (Office of Refugee Resettlement within the Department of Health and Human Services) and provided for adjustment to permanent residence status of refugees physically present in the United States for at least one year and of asylees one year after granting of asylum.

The Immigration Act of 1990 established a new preference system that took effect October 1, 1991, the first day of fiscal year (FY) 1992. Although these changes entailed increases for most visa categories, the overall family-sponsored preferences total was established at no more than 226,000, and the employment-based preference total was 140,000. Although the act set a theoretical cap on immigration, at 700,000 for FY 1992–1994 and at 675,000 thereafter, the cap is "pierceable" because immigration by immediate relatives of U.S. citizens remained numerically exempt. Maintaining family-sponsored, labor-sponsored and humanitarian bases, the 1990 law provided for a new diversity-based track. The impacts of the diversity-based immigration have been gradual in that this program was introduced during 1992–1994 by allowing at least 40,000 "transitional" visas. Aliens qualified as natives of an "adversely affected" nation "not contiguous to the United States and that was identified as an adversely affected foreign state for purposes of section 314 of the Immigration Reform and Control Act of 1986" (Sec. 132), for example, the NP-5 transitional diversity program of 1988–1989. A total of thirty-four countries were identified as being adversely affected by the 1965 immigration amendments as evidenced by a decrease in total immigration after 1965. From FY 1995 on, there were 55,000 "diversity" visas annually for persons from countries not among those principal source countries of current immigrants.

The system by which individuals seek to lawfully immigrate to the United States may appear well defined, regularized, and, from a client perspective, sluggish. It is laden with complexity, and successful navigation of immigration channels is testimony to the effectiveness of the social network's transmission of such information. Of those not fitting these categories, some may choose to expedite physical reunification by entry as unauthorized with the hope of later changing to an authorized status, especially lawful, permanent resident. Two data sources highlight the inadequacy of the immigration system: (1) numbers of U.S. resident and nonresident and immigration-intending family members of legalized immigrants under general provisions and (2) waiting-list counts attributed to petitions from these individuals as well as legalized immigrants under agricultural provisions. There is a unique set of migration dynamics at the close of this century with the possibility of significant population crossovers from unauthorized into authorized status.

THE MAGNITUDE AND MOMENTUM OF IMMIGRATION

The trend of increasing levels of immigration has been noted in Massey's (1995) review of legislative shifts and changing migration streams for the "classical era," the "long hiatus," and the "new regime" over the twentieth century. Immigration levels in the new regime are rivaling those of the classical era, and the composition of new arrivals implies an evolving mix of racial, ethnic, and generational identities. The foreign-born population now exceeds 26 million (U.S. Bureau of the Census 1998b), having increased by one-third since 1990.

Despite an emphasis on controlling immigration amid laborious debate about the labor force and economic consequences of immigration (Cornelius, Martin, and Hollifield 1994; Calavita 1994), admissions of lawful, permanent residents increased pursuant to key legislation over 1980–1990, and unauthorized immigration persists. Drawing from household surveys in seventeen Mexican communities and U.S. communities, Donato (1994) noted growing representation of women, first with their children and later with or without their children, for successive Mexican migrant entry cohorts over 1942–1992. With legislative impetus, immigration to the United States has become characteristically family-oriented in tandem with individual-level labor or economic orientation. Based on the regularities and inconsistencies observed for U.S. and Mexican transnational migration (and somewhat within the Caribbean and Latin America), Massey, Goldring, and Durand (1994) set forth a migration theory of cumulative causation for which the community-specific prevalence of migration is a key variable. As communities differ in the prevalence of migration or percentage of adult community members who have ever been to the United States, kinship ties to U.S. migrants are greater, demographic diversity is greater, and the migration stream exhibits less selectivity as to socioeconomic backgrounds. Increasing heterogeneity and less selectivity among Mexican migrants were also suggested by the Mexico–United States Binational Study (Bustamante et al. 1998).

Corresponding with the increasing magnitude of the foreign-born population, the quantity of net authorized immigration for the post-1960 entry period increased from 3.3 million in 1970, to 7.2 million in 1980, to at least 14.6 million in 1990, and to at least 18.2 million in 1996, according to estimates shown in Woodrow-Lafield (1998). Conservatively, the upper bound on net authorized or legal immigration may be 18.5 million, but more than 19 million is a plausible figure. The upward trend in legal immigration to the United States and the focused impact of IRCA's amnesty programs account for an increasing authorized immigrant presence since 1980. The margin of increase over 1990 is probably between 20 and 40 percent. Net authorized Mexican migration as of 1996 was at least 4.7–4.9 million (Woodrow-Lafield 1998; Bean et al. 1998; U.S. Commission on Immigration Reform 1997). With alternative accounting for uncertainties stemming from family migration pursuant to both the general legalization and the agricultural legalization, lawful residents from Mexico may reach 5.5 million, considerably more than in 1990 (3.8–4.0 million) or in 1980 (1.4 million). Agricultural legalization beneficiaries probably began to settle here in 1990, but some, perhaps many, may still live in Mexico or elsewhere. For those legalized beneficiaries having settled in the United States, their family members may be seeking authorized status and yet already live in the United States.

Mounting uncertainty about net authorized immigration means there is also more uncertainty about the residual amount of net unauthorized immigration, or the number of unauthorized, undocumented, or illegal immigrants living in the United States. Most of the rhetoric about demographic and economic impacts associated with the "illegal immigration problem" fails to properly recognize the elusiveness of accurate statistical information on the population stock. There are signs of an unauthorized presence posing a dilemma for researchers given that some individuals may be considered as "marginally authorized-unauthorized persons." The unknown numbers in calculations of authorization status hinge upon unknowns as to nonspecific sources of authorized immigration, especially related to the behavior of those legalized in applying to naturalize, timing of naturalization outcomes, and sponsorship petitioning, as well as their family members' characteristics and migration behavior. Significant increases in naturalizations over 1996–1998 and an accumulated backlog of 2 million applicants suggest a present and imminent possibility of a "hump" in legal immigration under provisions for immediate relatives and increases to preference category waiting lists. As many as 1.3 million relatives of generally legalized immigrants intended to live here as of 1992, including some already present without authorization (Woodrow-Lafield 1994, 1995). Given that generally legalized immigrants had already experienced substantial family unification over a decade of settlement, sponsorship levels of agriculturally legalized immigrants could be markedly greater.

A NEW AMERICA

The influences of historical patterns of European migration on the racial-ethnic composition of the American population are diminishing (Edmonston and Passel 1994; Gibson 1992; Bean et al. 1997; U.S. Bureau of the Census 1996). One hundred years hence, America will have a different demographic profile than now, just as the one today differs from that at the close of the nineteenth century. As the white population that is not Hispanic decreases in population share, the Hispanic and Asian shares are increasing. Simultaneously, there are demonstrable trends toward "balkanization," spatial patterns of population growth by race, status, and age that are explicable by industrial restructuring, immigration, and segmented redistribution (Frey 1995). The extension of this scenario into the long run is disturbing when weighed against concerns about income inequality and hypersegregation.

Immigration to America may now be perpetual. Certainly, contraindications are lacking. Through social networks effectively providing knowledge about mechanisms for migrating and adapting within American society, families are dominating U.S. immigration flows. Family integration is a persistent reason and viable mechanism (whether formal or informal) for coming to America. Labor motivations remain as overt and underlying bases for entry. The distinction between authorized and unauthorized statuses is perhaps becoming more troublesome to delineate conceptually and empirically. The politics of American immigration signify that the country has entered an era of frequent modification to immigration policies that further contributes to the complex taxonomy as to authorized and unauthorized statuses. For example, changes proposed in 1995

(U.S. Commission on Immigration Reform 1995) would have deleted the new diversity category and markedly decreased family-based immigration by eliminating immigration of adult, married or unmarried sons and daughters and U.S. citizens' siblings. One commissioner (Leiden 1995) dissented as to another proposed change: introduction of numeric limits on spouses and minor children of U.S. citizens and parents of U.S. citizens. Such changes would radically alter lawful family unification for legalized immigrants under the Immigration Reform and Control Act of 1986, greatly lengthening waiting periods until family members can join them with an authorized status. More recent immigrant entry cohorts might then be more likely than earlier ones to have family members present whose unauthorized status jeopardizes family stability.

The problem of illegal immigration is essentially without a clear domain for resolution. The very immigration policies intended to limit the problem of illegal immigration seem to have been thwarted repeatedly, possibly because these policies inappropriately deal with the complexities as to economic development, social behavior, world system dynamics, and the immigration system's dynamics. One can only wonder at the insights to be gained about the contemporary debate from the vantage point of the end of the twenty-first century.

REFERENCES

Bean, Frank D., Rodolfo Corona, Rodolfo Tuiran, and Karen A. Woodrow-Lafield
1998   The Quantification of Migration between Mexico and the United States. In *Migration between Mexico and the United States: Binational Study*. Vol. 1: *Thematic Chapters. Mexico–United States Binational Migration Study*. Mexican Ministry of Foreign Affairs and U.S. Commission on Immigration Reform. Pp. 1–90.

Bean, Frank D., Robert G. Cushing, Charles W. Haynes, and Jennifer V. W. Van Hook
1997   Immigration and the Social Contract. *Social Science Quarterly* 78 (June): 249–268.

Bustamante, Jorge
1997   Mexico–United States Labor Migration Flow. *International Migration Review* 31 (Winter): 1112–1121.

Bustamante, Jorge A., Guillermina Jasso, J. Edward Taylor, and Paz Trigueros Legarreta
1998   Characteristics of Migrants. In *Migration between Mexico and the United States: Binational Study*. Vol. 1: *Thematic Chapters. Mexico–United States Binational Migration Study*. Mexican Ministry of Foreign Affairs and U.S. Commission on Immigration Reform. Pp. 91–162.

Calavita, Kitty
1994   U.S. Immigration and Policy Responses: The Limits of Legislation. In *Controlling Immigration: A Global Perspective*. Edited by Wayne A. Cornelius, Philip L. Martin, and James F. Hollifield. Stanford: Stanford University Press. Pp. 56–82.

Cornelius, Wayne A., Philip L. Martin, and James F. Hollifield
1994   Introduction: The Ambivalent Quest for Immigration Control. In *Controlling Immigration: A Global Perspective*. Edited by Wayne A. Cornelius, Philip L. Martin, and James F. Hollifield. Stanford: Stanford University Press. Pp. 3–42.

Donato, Katharine M.
1994   U.S. Policy and Mexican Migration to the United States, 1942–92. *Social Science Quarterly* 75 (December): 705–729.

Edmonston, Barry, Editor
1996   *Statistics on U.S. Immigration: An Assessment of Data Needs for Future Research.* Report of the National Research Council, Committees on National Statistics and Population. Washington, D.C.: National Academy Press.

Edmonston, Barry, and Jeffrey S. Passel, Editors
1994   *Immigration and Ethnicity: The Integration of America's Newest Arrivals.* Washington, DC: Urban Institute Press.

Escobar Latapi, Agustin, Philip Martin, Paul S. Davies, Gustavo Lopez Castro, and Katharine Donato
1998   Factors That Influence Migration. In *Migration between Mexico and the United States: Binational Study.* Vol. 1: *Thematic Chapters.* Mexico–United States Binational Migration Study. Mexican Ministry of Foreign Affairs and U.S. Commission on Immigration Reform. Pp. 163–250.

Espenshade, Thomas J., and Maryann Belanger
1998   Immigration and Public Opinion. In *Crossings: Mexican Immigration in Interdisciplinary Perspectives.* Edited by Marcelo M. Suarez-Orozco. Cambridge: Harvard University Press. Pp. 365–403.

Espenshade, Thomas J., and Charles A. Calhoun
1992   Public Opinion toward Illegal Immigration and Undocumented Migrants in Southern California. Working Paper No. 92–2. Princeton, New Jersey: Princeton University, Office of Population Research. March.

Frey, William H.
1995   Immigration and Internal Migration "Flight" from U.S. Metropolitan Areas. *Urban Studies* 32 (4/5): 733–757.

Galbraith, James K.
1998   *Created Unequal: The Crisis in American Pay.* New York: Free Press.

Gibson, Campbell
1992   The Contribution of Immigration to the Growth and Ethnic Diversity of the American Population. *Proceedings of the American Philosophical Society* 136 (2): 157–175.

Greenwood, Michael J., and John M. McDowell
1985   U.S. Immigration Reform: Policy Issues and Economic Analysis. *Contemporary Policy Issues* 3 (Spring): 59–75.

Hill, Kenneth
1985   Illegal Aliens: An Assessment. In *Immigration Statistics: A Story of Neglect.* Report of the Panel on Immigration Statistics. Edited by Daniel B. Levine, Kenneth Hill, and Robert Warren. Washington, D.C.: National Academy Press. Pp. 225–250.

Johnson, Stanley P.
1994   *World Population—Turning the Tide: Three Decades of Progress.* The Hague: Kluwer Law International.

Leiden, Warren R.
1995   Dissenting Statement from Commissioner Warren R. Leiden. In *Legal Immigration: Setting Priorities.* U.S. Commission on Immigration Reform, 1995 Legal Immigration Report to Congress. Washington, D.C.: U.S. Government Printing Office. June. Pp. 227–245.

Levy, Frank
1987   *Dollars and Dreams: The Changing American Income Distribution.* New York: Russell Sage Foundation.
1995   Incomes and Income Inequality. In *State of the Union: America in the 1990s.* Vol. 1: *Economic Trends.* Edited by Reynolds Farley. New York: Russell Sage Foundation. Pp. 1–58.
MacDonald, John S., and Leatrice D. MacDonald
1974   Chain Migration, Ethnic Neighborhood Formation, and Social Networks. In *An Urban World.* Edited by Charles Tilly. Boston: Little, Brown. Pp. 226–236.
Massey, Douglas S.
1995   The New Immigration and Ethnicity in the United States. *Population and Development Review* 21 (September): 631–652.
1996   The Age of Extremes: Concentrated Affluence and Poverty in the Twenty-First Century. *Demography* 33 (November): 395–412.
Massey, D. S., J. Arango, G. Hugo, A. Kouaouci, A. Pellegrino, and J. E. Taylor
1993   Theories of International Migration: A Review and Appraisal. *Population and Development Review* 19 (1): 431–466.
Massey, D. S., J. Arango, G. Hugo, A. Kouaouci, A. Pellegrino, and J. E. Taylor
1994   An Evaluation of International Migration Theory: The North American Case. *Population and Development Review* 20 (1): 699–752.
Massey, Douglas S., Luin Goldring, and Jorge Durand
1994   Continuities in Transnational Migration: An Analysis of Nineteen Mexican Communities. *American Journal of Sociology* 99 (May): 1492–1533.
McCarthy, Kevin F., and Georges Vernez
1997   *Immigration in a Changing Economy: California's Experience.* Santa Monica: RAND.
Miller, Mark J.
1994   Preface, Strategies for Immigration Control: An International Comparison. *The Annals* 532 (July): 8–18.
Portes, Alejandro
1997   Immigration Theory for a New Century: Some Problems and Opportunities. *International Migration Review* 31 (4) (Winter): 799–825.
Portes, Alejandro, and Robert L. Bach
1985   *Latin Journey: Cuban and Mexican Immigrants in the United States.* Berkeley: University of California Press.
Portes, Alejandro, and Rubén Rumbaut
1996   *Immigrant America.* Berkeley: University of California Press.
Reimers, David M.
1985   *Still the Golden Door: The Third World Comes to America.* New York: Columbia University Press.
Simon, Rita J.
1985   *Public Opinion and the Immigrant: Print Media Coverage, 1880–1980.* Lexington, Massachusetts: Lexington Books, D. C. Heath.
Simon, Rita J., and Susan H. Alexander
1993   *The Ambivalent Welcome: Print Media, Public Opinion and Immigration.* Westport, Connecticut: Praeger.
Smith, James P., and Barry Edmonston, editors.
1997   *The New Americans: Economic, Demographic, and Fiscal Effects of Immigration.* Panel on the Demographic and Economic Impacts of Immigration, Committee on

Population and Committee on National Statistics, National Research Council, Washington, D.C.: National Academy Press.

Tilly, Charles
1990   Transplanted Networks. In *Immigration Reconsidered: History, Sociology, and Politics*. Edited by Virginia Yans-McLaughlin. New York: Oxford University Press. Pp. 79–95.

United Nations ACC Task Force on Basic Social Services for All (BSSA)
1998   Technical Symposium on International Migration and Development, June 29–July 3. Summarized in *Migration News* 5 (10) (October).

United Nations Development Programme
1998   *Human Development Report 1998*. New York: Oxford University Press.

United Nations Population Division
1998   *World Population Projections to 2150*. Department of Economic and Social Affairs. New York: United Nations Secretariat.

U.S. Bureau of the Census
1996   *Population Projections of the United States by Age, Sex, Race, and Hispanic Origin: 1995–2050*. Washington, D.C.

1998a   *Money Income in the United States: 1997*. Current Population Reports, P60–200. Washington, D.C.: U.S. Government Printing Office.

1998b   *Poverty in the United States: 1997*. Current Population Reports, P60–201. Washington, D.C.: U.S. Government Printing Office.

U.S. Commission on Immigration Reform
1995   *Legal Immigration: Setting Priorities*. Legal Immigration Report to Congress. Washington, D.C.: U.S. Government Printing Office. June.

U.S. Commission on Immigration Reform and Mexican Ministry of Foreign Affairs
1997   *Migration between Mexico and the United States: Binational Study. A Report of the Binational Study on Migration*. Mexico–United States Binational Migration Study.

U.S. Immigration and Naturalization Service
1998   *1996 Statistical Yearbook of the U.S. Immigration and Naturalization Service*. Washington, D.C.: U.S. Government Printing Office.

Wilson, William Julius
1987   *The Truly Disadvantaged: The Inner City, the Underclass, and Public Policy*. Chicago: University of Chicago Press.

Wilson, William Julius
1998   *When Work Disappears*. New York: Alfred Knopf.

Woodrow-Lafield, Karen A.
1994   Post-Legalization Household Change and Potential Family Reunification. Revised (March 1995) version of paper presented at the 1994 annual meeting of the Population Association of America, Miami.

1995   *Potential Sponsorship by IRCA-Legalized Immigrants*. U.S. Commission on Immigration Reform. Washington, D.C.

1998   Estimating Authorized Immigration. In *Migration between Mexico and the United States: Binational Study*. Vol. 2: *Research Reports and Background Materials*. Mexico–United States Binational Migration Study. Mexican Ministry of Foreign Affairs and U.S. Commission on Immigration Reform. Mexico City and Washington, D.C. Pp. 619–682.

3

Undocumented Immigration to the United States: Numbers, Trends, and Characteristics

Jeffrey S. Passel

Illegal immigration to the United States remains a serious problem. Current estimates suggest that both the the stock of illegal immigrants (in excess of 5 million) and the net annual flow (200,000–300,000) are at historical peaks, with no workable control mechanisms in sight. The continuation of illegal immigration despite legislative, administrative, and enforcement initiatives over the last two decades represents a clear failure of national sovereignty and economic security objectives of U.S. immigration policy. Because illegal immigrants in the United States are concentrated geographically, their demographic, social, and fiscal impacts tend to be felt most strongly in a limited number of geographic areas and among similarly situated immigrants, both legal and illegal (Fix and Passel 1994).

Since developing sound policies requires sound data, measurement issues concerning the numbers of undocumented immigrants, their characteristics, and their impacts remain vexing problems for demographers, economists, and policymakers alike. This chapter presents new estimates of the size of the undocumented alien population of the United States in 1990 and 1995. It includes detailed analyses by country of birth and period of entry, plus estimates for states. The chapter also reviews existing evidence regarding the numbers of illegal aliens living in the United States, placing the measurement issues in historical context and assessing the quality of the various estimates.

The chapter has four main sections: The first section summarizes the major findings. It also provides background information on current immigration trends to the United States and reviews the historical roots of contemporary undocumented migration to the United States. The second major section is devoted to describing the size, growth, and geographic distribution of the undocumented population, with particular attention to measurement concerns and data. This section reviews the existing estimates made through 1996 and assesses the overall quality of the estimates.

The third section presents the methods used to develop the new estimates for 1995 and 1990. The fourth section then presents the new estimates and compares them with the most widely accepted estimates currently available—those developed by the Immigration and Naturalization Service (INS). This fourth section describes the size of the undocumented population living in the United States, the growth rate, the major sources of illegal immigration to the United States, and the numbers living in major receiving states. The chapter closes with a summary of major results and some inferences regarding control strategies.

MAJOR FINDINGS

Undocumented Immigrant Population—1995

- There were 5.102 million undocumented aliens living in the United States in October 1995. This estimate uses residual-based methods and the Current Population Survey (CPS). The estimate differs by 377,000 or 8 percent, from the INS estimate of 4.725 million for the same date.

- About 58 percent of undocumented aliens, or 3.0 million, entered the United States since 1990; about one-quarter had been in the country for ten years or more, a decrease from the equivalent percentage in 1990.

- About 43 percent of all immigrants coming since 1990 are undocumented, or roughly the same percentage as was found for 1985–1990 entrants in 1990. However, because there has been no legalization program in the 1990s, all remained as undocumented in 1995, but only three-quarters remained so in 1990.

- Mexico accounts for 54 percent of the undocumented population in the 1995 CPS, or 2.7 million persons. The INS estimate for the same date is 184,000 less, or about 7 percent less.

- A very high percentage of current immigration from Mexico is undocumented—90 percent of 1990s arrivals. This figure is only about ten percentage points higher than for earlier periods. However, for these earlier cohorts in both 1990 and 1995, the percentage remaining undocumented is less because the legalization programs of the 1980s reduced this population.

- Central America accounts for another 767,000 undocumented aliens, or about 15 percent of the total, with 282,000 from El Salvador. Only three other individual countries exceed 100,000—Haiti (138,000), India (126,000), and China (124,000).[1]

- Other source regions of undocumented aliens in 1995 are:
  Central America—15.0 percent, or 767,000;
  Caribbean—6.1 percent, or 309,000;
  South America—4.8 percent, or 247,000;
  Middle East—1.3 percent, or 69,000;

South and East Asia—6.8 percent, or 346,000;
Europe—5.1 percent, or 263,000;
Africa—1.5 percent, or 77,000.

- About 57 percent of Central American arrivals in the 1990s remain undocumented. This percentage represents a reduction from the roughly 70 percent of Central Americans who arrived illegally in the late 1980s.

- We estimate a *net* annual inflow for the 1990–1995 period of 296,000 per year; the INS estimate is 278,000.

- About 95 percent of the undocumented immigrant population is represented in the 1995 CPS, or about 4,829,000 undocumented aliens. The principal states where these undocumented aliens live are as follows (INS figures are shown in parentheses):
California—2,174,000, or 45 percent (1,901,000);
Texas—606,000, or 13 percent (657,000);
New York—429,000, or 9 percent (507,000);
Florida—381,000, or 8 percent (330,000);
New Jersey—166,000, or 3 percent (127,000);
Illinois—118,000, or 2 percent (274,000);
Other states—956,000, or 20 percent (929,000).

Undocumented Immigrant Population—1990

- There were 3,471,000 undocumented aliens living in the United States in 1990, according to residual-based estimates based on the 1990 Census. The conventional residual estimate shows that about two-thirds of these, or 2.3 million, are represented in the 1990 Census.

- Just under half of the 3.5 million illegal aliens in 1990 entered in the five years before the census; about one-third are estimated to have been in the country for ten years or more.

- About 40 percent of recent entrants (i.e., 1985–1990 entrants) came as undocumented immigrants; for Mexico, almost 80 percent of recent entrants came as undocumented immigrants. The Immigration Reform and Control Act's (IRCA) legalization programs reduced the percentage undocumented substantially by 1990.

- Mexico accounts for 41 percent of the undocumented population in 1990, or 1,445,000 aliens. This estimate is about 14 percent lower than the INS figure of 1,768,000 for the same date.

- The next three largest sources are from Central America—El Salvador (257,000), Nicaragua (127,000), and Guatemala (114,000)—representing 14 percent of the total. After Central America (578,000 or 17 percent), the principal source regions are Asia (371,000, or 11 percent); the Caribbean (210,000, or 6 percent); Europe (209,000, or 6 percent); and South America (199,000, or 6 percent). Africa (63,000) and the Middle East (47,000) are estimated to send smaller numbers. These overall estimates are similar to the INS estimates.

- Only 43 percent of the undocumented aliens in the 1990 Census are male, according to the conventional residual estimates (Passel 1998a). The sex distribution appears to be a legacy of IRCA, which legalized many more males than females and, thus, left the majority as female in the remaining illegal population.

• Our conventional residual estimates show that 28 percent of the undocumented population is under age fifteen (Passel 1998a). For the 1985–1990 entrants, an even higher percentage are children, 39 percent under age fifteen. This pattern may not be generalizable to the 1990s, however. IRCA legalized mainly adults; their children, especially very young ones, could not meet IRCA's residency requirements. Thus, it appears that some of the IRCA legalized population were joined by undocumented children as of the 1990 Census.

• Few undocumented immigrants are over age thirty—only 576,000, or 25 percent of the total; virtually none are over age forty-five—40,000, or 2 percent. Among the recent arrivals (i.e., those coming in 1985–1990), an even smaller percentage were over age thirty—6 percent of all undocumented immigrants and 1 percent of Mexicans (Passel 1998a).

Background

Roots of Contemporary Illegal Immigration. Although there are some references to concerns with illegal immigration in the early part of the twentieth century (Bloch 1928) through the 1950s (INS 1991), these related mainly to movement of farm labor from Mexico to the United States. The "Bracero Program" was begun during World War II to supply farm labor for agriculture in the southwestern United States. Several million Mexican men worked as braceros on a temporary basis in U.S. agriculture from 1942 until 1964, when the program ended.

Although the purpose of the Bracero Program was to provide growers with a substantial labor force, its lasting impact came from the access it afforded to U.S. labor markets for Mexican laborers. The braceros gained familiarity with U.S. labor markets, made contacts with employers, and acquired U.S.-specific work skills (e.g., a small, working knowledge of English). The end of the official program was supposed to mean a shift by growers to a native labor force and more mechanized agriculture. However, the easy access to former braceros meant that growers substituted illegal labor for the formerly legal bracero labor (Calavita 1994).

Settlement Patterns. Immigration between Mexico and the United States, especially illegal migration, has followed a clear pattern historically that is still in evidence today and that can be seen in other flows (Massey et al. 1994). The migration starts out with "pioneer" immigrants, usually young males, often working in agriculture or other low-wage, low-skill jobs. Over time, these pioneers make multiple trips and accumulate experience in the U.S. labor force and knowledge of the new country. With this experience, more of these illegal *migrants* settle in the United States and become illegal *immigrants*.

After the pioneer males settle in the United States, family unification proceeds as they bring wives, children, and more distant relatives to the United States.

The maturation of the migrant stream also opens it to friends and acquaintances in Mexico as the benefits of migration become apparent to a larger circle in the migrants' home cities and towns. In addition, for many, illegal entry is simply a prelude to *legal* migration.

Postbracero Illegal Immigration. The bracero explanation works well for explaining the stream from Mexico, but other illegal streams have been spurred by the internationalization of the U.S. economy and global integration. The 1965 Immigration Act opened the U.S. labor market to Asians and Latin Americans. The post-1965 period has also witnessed substantial increases in international trade, travel, and tourism.

The increased immigration led to networks of legal immigrants and U.S. citizens with ties to many different countries. These new U.S. residents provide information and network connections that could facilitate further immigration. Although some of the network immigration occurs through legal channels, not all of it does. Thus, with increased mobility and improved global communications came increased immigration, and a significant proportion of this new immigration occurred, and still occurs, illegally.

The sheer magnitude of flows of non-U.S. citizens through the United States provides ample opportunities for would-be illegal migrants. Over 300 million land crossings are monitored by the Immigration and Naturalization Service annually across the U.S.–Mexican and U.S.–Canadian borders (INS 1994). In addition, over 20 million noncitizens are admitted for temporary purposes every year. These "nonimmigrants" include students, diplomats, and aliens in transit, but by far the largest number—in excess of 90 percent—includes temporary visitors for business and pleasure (e.g., tourists).

Against this backdrop of large-scale international movement and intense border activity, even small percentages of "leakage" (i.e., clandestine entries or visa-overstayers) can result in fairly sizable numbers of illegal immigrants.

MEASURES OF UNDOCUMENTED IMMIGRATION THROUGH 1996

Two generalizations stand out in reviewing the studies purporting to measure the size of the undocumented immigrant population: First, estimates based on *data* are smaller than speculative ones. This is true today as in the past. Second, throughout the 1970s and 1980s, as the size of the illegal immigrant population grew steadily, the estimates declined so that at the beginning of the 1990s, the most widely accepted estimates were generally accurate. However, in the mid-1990s, the absence of detailed, empirically based estimates brought the first generalization into play again as more and more speculative estimates were beginning to be used by politicians and advocates. However, the existence of widely accepted, empirically based estimates has narrowed the range of discourse. Further, the continued growth of the undocumented population in the

United States has brought some of the more speculative estimates within reach of the empirical numbers; rhetoric and reality have converged.

Early (Pre-IRCA) Estimates

In the mid-to-late 1970s, the size of the undocumented alien population began to be of political concern. One of the earliest recorded conjectures was by INS commissioner Raymond Farrell, who testified that there were 1 million illegal aliens in the country. Although this figure was apparently just a guess, unsupported by empirical work, subsequent research (e.g., Warren and Passel 1987) suggests he may have been reasonably close. This figure was not accepted at all. By 1976, the next INS commissioner placed the number at 4–12 million (Chapman 1976), again without empirical support.

In the late 1970s, speculative estimates and "conventional wisdom" generally placed the number of illegal aliens in the United States at between 6 and 12 million. This range included the notorious "Lesko" estimate of 8.2 million derived by the so-called Delphi technique,[2] which represented little more than guessing dressed up as science. The magnitude of the estimate and the width of the range asserted were often tied to the position of the guesser. Thus, Commissioner Chapman, who advocated massive increases in funding to expand the Border Patrol against the threat posed by high levels of illegal immigration, guessed 4–12 million, whereas the next INS commissioner, Leonel Castillo (1978), who did not perceive immigration from Mexico to be a threat to the United States, guessed 3–6 million.

To bring some rationality to policy discussions, the Select Commission on Immigration and Refugee Policy (SCIRP) called on Census Bureau analysts to examine the available estimates and assess the size of this clandestine population. Siegel, Passel, and Robinson (1980) concluded that there were "certainly" fewer than 6 million undocumented aliens in the country at the time, "possibly" *only* 3.5 to 5 million. The accepted range quickly became 3–6 million. As we will soon see, even this range proved to be too high.

The most detailed measurement of the undocumented population and their characteristics to date was completed in 1983 by Warren and Passel (1987). They compared the 1980 Census count of the foreign-born population with an estimate of legal foreign-born residents based on the number of aliens who registered with the post office in 1980 and INS data on naturalized citizens. Warren and Passel estimated that there were 2.1 million undocumented aliens *counted* in the 1980 Census.

Since the Warren–Passel estimate is based on the 1980 Census and does not represent those missed by the census, it is obviously less than the total number. Using data from the 1980 Census of Mexico and various other information, Passel (1985) concluded that there were 2.5–3.5 million undocumented aliens in the country in 1980. Other analysts arrived at similar estimates (Bean, King, and Passel 1983; Hill 1985; Levine, Hill, and Warren 1985), and the accuracy of these assessments became apparent after the implementation of the legalization programs of IRCA in the late 1980s (see later).

Starting from this research, Census Bureau analysts conducted a number of studies during the 1980s using data from special supplements to the Current Population Survey to measure growth in the illegal alien population. They applied the residual technique of Warren–Passel to data from April 1983, June 1986, and June 1988. This new research placed the annual increment to the illegal population at 100,000–300,000 per year, with 200,000 annual growth becoming the generally accepted and most widely used figure (Passel and Woodrow 1987; Woodrow, Passel, and Warren 1987; Woodrow and Passel 1990). Thus, *on the eve of the passage of the Immigration Reform and Control Act in November 1986, the illegal alien population in the United States numbered between 3 and 5 million* (see Figure 3.1).

IRCA's Legalization Programs

The Immigration Reform and Control Act of 1986 attempted to apply a carrot-and-stick approach to solve the problem of illegal immigration. The "stick" was employer sanctions, which, for the first time, imposed penalties on U.S. employers for hiring illegal immigrants. Also included were contemplated increases in the Border Patrol. The "carrot" was two separate legalization programs: the first to permit those illegal aliens who had lived in the United States for some time and built up significant equities in the United States to acquire legal status and the second to alleviate anticipated shortages of agricultural labor by legalizing some agricultural workers.

Under the first program (the so-called I-687 or LAWs [legally authorized workers] program), illegal aliens who had lived in the country for five years or longer (i.e., since January 1, 1982) in an illegal status and who met certain other criteria could become legal temporary residents. They could then become legal permanent residents within a few years by meeting some other, not terribly onerous, criteria. Almost 1.8 million applications were filed under this program, and more than 95 percent were eventually approved (INS 1992a). About 70 percent, or more than 1.2 million, were from Mexico; El Salvador at 143,000, or 8 percent, was second; Guatemala with 53,000, or 3 percent, was third. The group was about 57 percent male; 80 percent were between ages fifteen and forty-four, with 9 percent under age fifteen.

The agricultural worker program, known by the acronym SAW (for special agricultural worker), generated almost 1.3 million applications. The program required only that the illegal immigrant have worked ninety days in qualifying agricultural activities over a three-year period. Fraud proved to be rampant in the SAW program since the burden of proof as to the accuracy of the application was placed on the INS, not the applicant. One measure of the degree of fraud is that the entire qualifying alien labor force (legal and illegal) was thought to number only 300,000 or so (Martin and Taylor 1988), but more than four times

Figure 3.1
Undocumented Population Returns to Pre-IRCA Levels

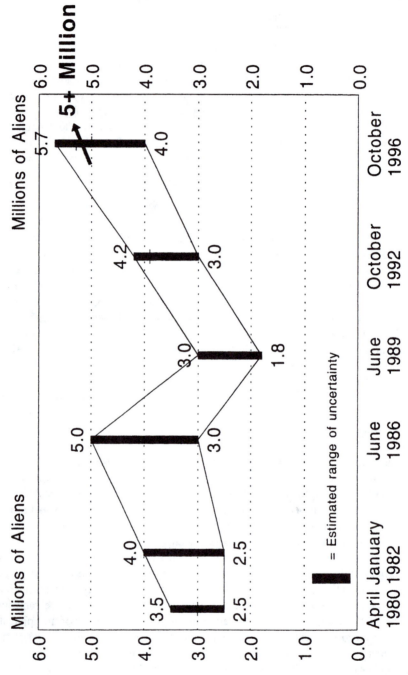

Millions of Aliens

as many *illegal* workers applied. In an interesting twist to the SAW program, residence in the United States was not necessary to qualify for legalization; only time spent in U.S. agriculture mattered. Thus, many persons qualified for legal immigration status who had never treated the United States as a principal residence.

Eventually, more than 1 million SAW applicants were approved for temporary and then permanent residence in the United States. Over 80 percent of the SAWs were from Mexico; Haiti at 3 percent and El Salvador at 2 percent were second and third. The SAWs had quite different characteristics from those of the LAWs. Over 80 percent of the SAWs were male; although 80 percent were also aged fifteen to forty-four years, none of the SAWs were under age fifteen.

IRCA's implementation had two significant impacts on the illegal alien population. First and foremost, the legalization programs dramatically reduced the size of the illegal population and also changed its composition. Second and clearly of relevance mainly to the demographers dealing with this issue, the legalization programs served to validate the estimates that had been done at the Census Bureau. Specifically, the number and characteristics of illegal aliens who took advantage of IRCA's amnesty programs were consistent with the census-based estimates in terms of total number, origins, age-sex distribution, and geographic distribution (Baker 1990).

As a consequence of IRCA, more than 2.7 million formerly illegal aliens acquired legal status, so that *the post-IRCA illegal alien population dropped to about 2.2 million in 1987* (Warren 1994). Because more than 2 million Mexican-born illegal aliens legalized, the number of illegal Mexicans and their proportion in the undocumented population dropped dramatically. Because so many of the legalizations were in California and Texas, the geographic distribution of the remaining illegal population also changed dramatically.

Post-IRCA Estimates of the Undocumented Population

We discuss here the three major, empirically based, original estimates of the size of the undocumented population for 1990 or later: (1) INS estimates using nonimmigrant entry data by Warren (1990, 1994, 1997); (2) estimates of the undocumented Mexican population produced using a combination of data from both countries produced for the Binational Study of Migration between Mexico and the United States (Bean et al. 1997); and (3) new residual estimates derived using the 1990 Census and CPS data for 1995–1997 (Passel 1998a, b). Other estimates (Fernandez and Robinson 1994; Center for Immigration Studies 1994; and General Accounting Office 1993) are based strictly on extrapolation or rely principally on unsubstantiated assumptions.

This section of the chapter presents the highlights of Binational and INS estimates and summarizes the estimation methods. Detailed descriptions of the estimates and methods can be found in the original sources (Warren 1997; Bean et al. 1997). A more thorough discussion of the INS estimates is presented later in conjunction with the new residual estimates for 1995.

INS Estimates of the Undocumented Alien Population in 1996—Methods. The INS estimates are the sum of the two components—visa-overstayers plus clandestine entrants, or "entries without inspections," which are called EWIs in INS parlance—calibrated with an estimate of the number of undocumented aliens who failed to take advantage of the various legalization programs offered under IRCA. Visa-overstayers are estimated with data from the INS Nonimmigrant Information System (NIIS). (See Warren 1997 for a description of the current methodology; Warren 1990, 1994 and GAO 1995 describe the methods used in previous INS estimates and recommendations for updates.) The NIIS system incorporates data from the two-part I-94 form, which nonimmigrant aliens submit upon arrival in the United States. One part of the form is collected at entry, and the other is stapled to the alien's passport. When the alien departs, the second part of the form is collected. The two parts are linked together in the INS processing system. Incoming forms without corresponding departure forms at the end of a year fall into one of four groups:

1. aliens who are "in status," that is, not required to have departed;
2. aliens who have "adjusted their status" to some other legal status, usually permanent resident alien or asylee, that allows the alien to remain in the United States legally;
3. aliens who actually departed, but the second half of the form was lost, was not collected, or could not be matched; and
4. aliens who should have departed but remain in the United States, usually in violation of their admission terms.

The crucial part of the INS estimation process involves estimating the magnitude of the first three components so as to derive the fourth, the number of visa-overstayers. The number of aliens currently "in status," the first category, can be determined directly from the NIIS database. The second category, the number adjusting status (principally to legal permanent residents), is also determined directly from INS data sets.[3] In addition, departures from the country by nonimmigrants who entered in previous years are enumerated in INS systems and subtracted at this step.

The most difficult and problematic component to estimate is the third group—those who departed but whose arrival forms could not be accessed or matched; this component is called "system error." Warren (1990) estimates this component by first identifying countries that have sent virtually no unauthorized immigrants to the United States. The "apparent overstay rate" for this group of countries is taken as the measure of the system error rate and is used for other countries as well. After subtracting apparent overstays, Warren is left with actual estimated overstays, or the net undocumented immigration through visa-overstays. Refinements of the basic method have been introduced since 1990, but the estimates have proved to be quite robust and thus have not changed much (Warren 1994; GAO 1995).

In estimating EWIs, Warren (1997) draws on a number of studies conducted throughout the 1980s that have measured changes in the undocumented population. These studies rely generally on the 1980 Census and supplements to the Current Population Survey for selected dates throughout the decade (Passel and Woodrow 1987; Woodrow, Passel, and Warren 1987; Woodrow and Passel 1990; Woodrow 1991). For the 1982–1988 period, Warren uses these CPS-based estimates, corrected for undercount. For 1988–1992, the EWI estimates are adjusted downward slightly to reflect the apparent reduction in flow for the first few years following the passage of IRCA. For EWIs during 1988–1996, the INS estimates draw on data from the annual March supplements to the CPS. The CPS data are used principally for Mexican and Central American EWIs.

The result of the initial estimation process is a set of national estimates of the number of undocumented aliens living in the United States for ninety-nine countries of birth. To derive estimates for states, Warren has used two different methods. In the first estimates released (Warren 1994), the national estimates for each country are distributed according to the state distribution of persons from that country legalizing under IRCA. The results are summed to give state totals. In the later estimates, separate state distributions for EWIs and overstays use INS data on the destinations of beneficiaries of legalized aliens (without regard to country). For both estimates, annual change is taken to be the average change over the 1988–1992 and 1992–1996 periods for countries of birth and for states.

INS Estimates—Results. The INS estimates place the illegal alien population at about 5.0 million living in the country as of October 1996. This population grew by an annual average of 275,000 over the period from October 1992 through October 1996 and by 281,000 for October 1988 through October 1992. The estimate of 3.9 million for October 1992 represents an upward revision from the earlier estimate of 3.4 million, but the rate of annual change has been revised downward.[4] These estimates imply, then, that the illegal alien population is currently greater than the number in the country in 1980 and probably slightly above the number when IRCA was passed in 1986 (Figure 3.1).

The largest number of undocumented immigrants living in the United States as of 1996 is from Mexico (2.7 million), followed by El Salvador (335,000), Guatemala (165,000), Canada (120,000), and Haiti (105,000) (see Table 3.1). No other country has an undocumented population exceeding 100,000, although the Philippines, Honduras, Nicaragua, Colombia, and Poland approach this number. The Mexican undocumented population is estimated to be growing at 154,200 per year with no other country reaching even one-tenth of this growth. The proportion of Mexicans in the undocumented population is estimated at 51 percent in 1988 and 54 percent in 1992 and 1996. These figures are comparable to, but slightly below, the 55 percent Warren and Passel (1987) estimated for 1980. This slight shift in origins occurred largely because of the IRCA legali-

Table 3.1

INS Estimates of Resident Undocumented Population by Country of Citizenship: October 1996

(Populations in thousands)

Area or Country of Birth	Estimate	Pct. of Total	Area or Country of Birth	Estimate	Pct. of Total
All Countries	*5,000*	*100.0*			
Europe	*234*	*4.7*	*Oceania*	*14*	*0.3*
Ireland	30	0.6			
Italy	25	0.5	*Canada*	*120*	*2.4*
Poland	70	1.4			
Portugal	27	0.5	*Mexico*	*2,700*	*54.0*
Fmr. USSR	19	0.4			
Fmr. Yugoslavia	20	0.4	*Central America*	*691*	*13.8*
Other Europe	43	0.9	El Salvador	335	6.7
			Guatemala	165	3.3
Middle East	*78*	*1.6*	Honduras	90	1.8
Iran	25	0.5	Nicaragua	70	1.4
Israel	11	0.2	Panama	12	0.2
Jordan	14	0.3	Belize	11	0.2
Lebanon	20	0.4	Other C. Amer.	8	0.2
Oth. Mid. East	8	0.2			
			Caribbean	*410*	*8.2*
S. & E. Asia	*286*	*5.7*	Bahamas	70	1.4
Bangladesh	13	0.3	Dominican Rep.	75	1.5
China	25	0.5	Haiti	105	2.1
Hong Kong	13	0.3	Jamaica	50	1.0
India	33	0.7	Trinidad & Tob.	50	1.0
Korea	30	0.6	Other Carib.	60	1.2
Malaysia	15	0.3			
Pakistan	41	0.8	*South America*	*199*	*4.0*
Philippines	95	1.9	Bolivia	17	0.3
Oth. S. & E. Asia	21	0.4	Chile	10	0.2
			Colombia	65	1.3
Africa	*117*	*2.3*	Ecuador	55	1.1
Egypt	11	0.2	Guyana	11	0.2
Ghana	10	0.2	Peru	30	0.6
Liberia	11	0.2	Oth. S. Amer.	11	0.2
Nigeria	16	0.3			
Oth. Africa	69	1.4	*Stateless & Unk.*	*151*	*3.0*

Note: Italics denote area totals. Countries with more than 10,000 shown. In all the tables in this chapter, numbers and percentages may not sum exactly due to rounding.

Source: Warren (1997).

Table 3.2
INS Estimates of Resident Undocumented Population by State of Residence:
October 1996

(Populations in thousands)

State	Estimate	Pct. of Total	State	Estimate	Pct. of Total
Total	*5,000*	*100.0*			
California	2,000	40.0	Oregon	33	0.7
Texas	700	14.0	Georgia	32	0.6
New York	540	10.8	D.C.	30	0.6
Florida	350	7.0	Connecticut	29	0.6
Illinois	290	5.8	Nevada	24	0.5
New Jersey	135	2.7	Ohio	23	0.5
Arizona	115	2.3	North Carolina	22	0.4
Massachusetts	85	1.7	Kansas	22	0.4
Virginia	55	1.1	Oklahoma	21	0.4
Washington	52	1.0	Louisiana	20	0.4
Colorado	45	0.9	Other States	169	3.4
Maryland	44	0.9			
Pennsylvania	37	0.7	Territories & Unk.	54	1.1
New Mexico	37	0.7			
Michigan	37	0.7			

Note: States with more than 20,000 shown.

Source: Warren (1997).

zations. Almost three-quarters of all legalization applicants, or more than 2 million persons, were from Mexico. With the legalization of this group, the percentage of Mexicans in the undocumented population dropped from almost 60 percent of the pre-IRCA population in 1988 to 51 percent post-IRCA.

The relative shift away from Mexico as a source country results in a shift in the geographic distribution away from California. Whereas the state had about half of the undocumented population in 1980 (Passel and Woodrow 1984), INS estimated that it had about 40 percent in 1996. Of course, even this figure still represents a very large number of persons, or *more than 2.0 million undocumented residents in California in 1996.* New York, Texas, Florida, Illinois, and New Jersey combine with California to account for 80 percent of this clandestine population, a figure about the same as in the 1980 estimates. (Table 3.2 shows estimates for states.)

The quality of these estimates is assessed in conjunction with the residual estimates later. However, there are three principal sources of error deserving mention. First, there are some definitional issues concerning who is or is not part of the undocumented population. Some visa-overstayers (perhaps many) are authorized to be in the United States on a temporary basis but are not recognized as such in the INS databases. Consequently, these groups are erroneously included as part of the undocumented population. Examples of such groups are asylum applicants whose cases have not been adjudicated and persons who have had temporary protected status (TPS), extended voluntary departure (EVD), or any number of other statuses.[5]

A second issue is that some small countries with very large tourist traffic with the United States appear to have substantially inflated estimates, possibly because of third country nationals entering the United States from one tourist destination and departing to another (or to their home country). Most examples of this phenomenon are small Caribbean countries. Table 3.3 illustrates the import of this issue by comparing the estimated undocumented population living in the United States with the population of the origin country. For example, the 1996 estimate for undocumented migrants from the Bahamas is 70,000. Were this estimate accurate, it would imply that more than 20 percent of the Bahamian-born population is currently in the United States—a figure undoubtedly too high. Several other Caribbean islands have estimates of more than 5 percent in the United States, a very high level. Table 3.4 provides another point of comparison—the 1990 U.S. Census count of the foreign-born from a country versus the interpolated INS estimate of undocumented aliens from that country in 1990. The INS estimate for the Bahamas exceeds the number of Bahamians counted in the 1990 Census. Other countries exhibit high percentages, but none this high.

A third issue affecting the accuracy of the INS estimates is measurement of clandestine entrants from countries other than Mexico. While the CPS can provide some information here, the sample sizes may be too small to provide reliable figures. There does not appear to be a good data source for making estimates such as these. Our residual-based estimates imply much larger numbers of EWIs from China, for example, than do the INS estimates. Given that there are myriad press stories about ships from China or smuggling rings working through Latin America, the INS figure of 22,000 undocumented Chinese seems too small.

Binational Study Estimates of Undocumented Migration from Mexico. The Commission on Immigration Reform created the Binational Study of Migration between Mexico and the United States to address issues particular to the very large flows between the countries. Scholars on both sides of the border were recruited to research specific issues, one of which was the magnitude of the flow. The group working on quantification of the flow conducted a detailed review of existing estimates and produced its own estimate (Bean et al. 1997; Van Hook and Bean 1997a, b).

Studies conducted in Mexico have provided some useful information on the nature of the migratory flow and place some limits on the magnitude of the flow without providing precise estimates of the numbers living in the United States. The Mexican studies document a large-scale circulatory flow of temporary workers who do not intend to reside permanently in the United States; at any time, large numbers may be in the United States, however. Household surveys conducted in Mexico over the last several decades document a steadily increasing flow northward since the 1960s. Further, indirect measurements place some limits on the numbers migrating to the United States permanently. In the 1960s, the total annual flow (including legal and undocumented Mexicans) amounted to 22,000–24,000 per year; in the 1970s, 100,000–130,000. By the 1980s, the annual flow grew to 175,000–220,000, and in the 1990s, the annual number may have reached 275,000. Since annual legal immigration from Mexico to the United States now exceeds 100,000 per year, the binational estimate implies an annual undocumented flow similar to Warren's estimate.

In producing its consensus estimate of the number of undocumented Mexicans living in the United States (in 1996), the binational group turned to the residual estimation technique. It delineated four important issues that affect such estimates: (1) the presence of nonimmigrants in the United States, including temporary workers; (2) the magnitude of emigration; (3) the number of SAWs (special agricultural workers) actually residing in the United States; and (4) the flow effects of IRCA in generating continuing migration. The binational group's estimates for 1996 are a legally resident, Mexican-born population in the United States of 4.8 million, including about 700,000 SAWs; and 2.35 million undocumented Mexicans.

The binational study's estimate for the undocumented population is slightly lower than the INS estimate and our new residual estimate. However, the binational study's estimate for legal Mexicans is substantially higher than ours, notwithstanding the fact that ours includes a somewhat larger number of SAWs. The sum of these discrepancies suggests that the binational estimate of undocumented Mexicans in the United States is too small, but of approximately the correct magnitude. We address these issues in more detail later.

CENSUS OR SURVEY-BASED RESIDUAL METHODOLOGY

Estimation Methods

Conceptually, the residual estimation technique is very simple: we subtract an estimate of the legally resident, foreign-born population from the survey or census measure of the same population. The difference is taken to represent undocumented immigrants included in the census. In our estimates, we disaggregate the various data sets by age (a), sex (s), period of entry to the United States (p), and country of birth (c). Thus, we can write the essential relationship as:

$$I_{a,s,c,p}^{199x} = C_{a,s,c,p}^{199x} - L_{a,s,c,p}^{199x} \tag{1}$$

where

Table 3.3
1996 Population of Country and INS Estimate of U.S. Undocumented Population, by Country

(Populations in thousands)

Country or area	1996 Country Pop.	U.S. Undoc. Est.	Pct. of Pop.	Country or area	1996 Country Pop.	U.S. Undoc. Est.	Pct. of Pop.
WORLD	*5,505,875*	*5,000*	*.09*				
EUROPE AND THE NEW INDEPENDENT STATES	*799,589*	*234*	*.03*	*AFRICA*	*731,538*	*117*	*.02*
Western Europe	*386,600*	*105*	*.03*	Cameroon	14,262	1	.01
Denmark	5,211	2	.04	Cape Verde	449	6	1.34
France	58,317	6	.01	Cote d'Ivoire	14,762	2	.01
Greece	10,719	5	.05	Ethiopia	57,172	8	.01
Ireland	3,563	30	.84	Ghana	17,698	10	.06
Italy	57,460	25	.04	Kenya	28,177	3	.01
Malta	372	1	.13	Liberia	2,110	11	.52
Netherlands	15,532	0	.00	Nigeria	103,912	16	.02
Portugal	9,865	27	.27	Senegal	9,093	4	.04
Spain	38,853	2	.01	Sierra Leone	4,793	9	.19
Sweden	8,861	1	.01	South Africa	41,743	3	.01
United Kingdom	58,715	7	.01	Sudan	31,065	3	.01
				Uganda	20,158	2	.01

Eastern Europe	*120,190*	*109*	*.09*
Bulgaria	8,613	7	.08
Former Czechoslovakia	15,695	3	.02
Hungary	10,003	3	.03
Poland	38,643	70	.18
Romania	21,657	6	.03
Former Yugoslavia	22,329	20	.09
New Independent States	*292,799*	*19*	*.01*
Other Europe	*122,382*	*2*	*.00*
NEAR EAST	*157,333*	*53*	*.03*
Iraq	21,422	1	.00
Israel	5,215	11	.21
Jordan	4,212	14	.33
Lebanon	3,776	20	.53
Syria	15,609	3	.02
Turkey	62,484	1	.00
Yemen	13,483	2	.01
Other Near East	31,132	(x)	(x)
Algeria	29,183	1	.00
Egypt	63,575	11	.02
Morocco	29,779	2	.01
Other Africa	263,607	27	.01
ASIA	*3,270,944*	*311*	*.01*
Afghanistan	22,664	2	.01
Bangladesh	123,063	13	.01
Burma	45,976	1	.00
China	1,231,471	25	.00
Hong Kong	6,305	13	.21
India	952,108	33	.00
Indonesia	206,612	1	.00
Iran	66,094	25	.04
Japan	125,450	2	.00
Malaysia	19,963	15	.08
Pakistan	129,276	41	.03
Philippines	74,481	95	.13
South Korea	45,482	30	.07
Sri Lanka	18,553	9	.05
Other Asia	234,578	7	.00

Table 3.3 (continued)

(Populations in thousands)

Country or area	1996 Country Pop.	U.S. Undoc. Est.	Pct. of Pop.	Country or area	1996 Country Pop.	U.S. Undoc. Est.	Pct. of Pop.
LATIN AMERICA AND THE CARIBBEAN	*488,608*	*3,996*	*.82*	*South America*	*323,659*	*199*	*.06*
				Argentina	34,673	3	.01
Lesser Antilles	*2,241*	*112*	*5.01*	Bolivia	7,165	17	.24
Antigua & Barbuda	66	4	6.06	Brazil	162,661	3	.00
Bahamas, The	259	70	27.03	Chile	14,333	10	.07
Barbados	257	6	2.33	Colombia	36,813	65	.18
Dominica	83	7	8.43	Ecuador	11,466	55	.48
Grenada	95	6	5.79	Guyana	712	11	1.54
Neth. Antilles	209	2	.81	Paraguay	5,504	2	.03
Saint Kitts & Nevis	41	6	13.41	Peru	24,523	30	.12
Saint Lucia	158	7	4.11	Uruguay	3,239	2	.05
St. Vin. & Grenadines	118	6	5.08	Venezuela	21,983	2	.01
Other Lesser Antilles	955			Other S. America	587		

44

Region / Country			
Greater Antilles	28,422	238	.84
Cuba	11,007	8	.07
Dominican Republic	8,089	75	.93
Haiti	6,732	105	1.56
Jamaica	2,594	50	1.93
Trinidad and Tobago	1,272	50	3.93
Central America	33,321	691	2.07
Belize	219	11	5.02
Costa Rica	3,463	8	.24
El Salvador	5,829	335	5.75
Guatemala	11,278	165	1.46
Honduras	5,605	90	1.61
Nicaragua	4,272	70	1.64
Panama	2,655	12	.45
Mexico	95,772	2,700	2.82
Other Latin America	1,542	6	.36
NORTH AMERICA	28,948	124	.43
Bermuda	62	4	6.45
Canada	28,821	120	.42
OCEANIA	28,915	14	.05
Australia	18,261	0	.00
Fiji	782	4	.47
New Zealand	3,548	0	.01
Tonga	106	5	4.25
Western Samoa	214	4	1.78
Other Oceania	6,004	2	.03
Other	(x)	151	(x)

(x)—not applicable.

Sources: Bureau of the Census (1997); Warren (1997).

Table 3.4
1990 U.S. Census Population and 1990 INS Estimate of U.S. Undocumented Population, by Country

(Populations in thousands)

Area or Country of Birth	1990 U.S. Census	1990 Undoc (INS)	Pct. of Census	Area or Country of Birth	1990 U.S. Census	1990 Undoc (INS)	Pct. of Census
WORLD	*19,682*	*3,196*	*16.2*				
LATIN AMERICA AND THE CARIBBEAN	*8,641*	*2,492*	*28.8*	*South America*	*1,057*	*124*	*11.8*
Lesser Antilles	*140*	*57*	*41.0*	Argentina	96	3	3.2
Bahamas, The	22	24	108.3	Bolivia	31	7	24.3
Barbados	42	5	12.1	Brazil	83	2	2.0
Dominica	18	6	32.9	Chile	57	4	7.5
Other Lesser Antilles	58	23	39.1	Colombia	295	46	15.5
				Ecuador	144	33	22.5
Greater Antilles	*1,683*	*134*	*8.0*	Guyana	119	13	11.1
Cuba	765	7	1.0	Peru	147	13	9.1
Dominican Republic	361	35	9.7	Venezuela	42	1	3.2
Haiti	225	61	27.2	Other South America	41	2	4.8
Jamaica	332	31	9.3				
				Mexico	4,474	1,678	37.5
Trinidad and Tobago	117	26	22.0	Canada	744	69	9.3
Other Latin America	15	8	48.9				

Central America	*1,154*	*465*	*40.3*
Belize	31	9	29.0
Costa Rica	45	3	7.3
El Salvador	482	262	54.3
Guatemala	230	87	37.7
Honduras	109	38	34.3
Nicaragua	172	60	34.8
Panama	85	7	8.3

AFRICA	*370*	*78*	*21.0*
Cape Verde	16	3	17.1
Ethiopia	36	6	17.4
Ghana	21	7	33.1
Liberia	11	9	83.4
Nigeria	57	13	22.9
Sierra Leone	7	5	71.6
South Africa	35	3	9.1
Egypt	69	9	13.1
Other Africa	119	22	18.9

Table 3.4 (*continued*)

(Populations in thousands)

Area or Country of Birth	1990 U.S. Census	1990 Undoc (INS)	Pct. of Census	Area or Country of Birth	1990 U.S. Census	1990 Undoc (INS)	Pct. of Census
EUROPE AND THE NEW INDEPENDENT STATES	*4,369*	*203*	*4.6*	*NEAR EAST*	*405*	*34*	*8.4*
Western Europe	*2,083*	*85*	*4.1*	Iraq	44	1	2.6
France	121	2	2.0	Israel	106	10	9.5
Greece	176	7	3.7	Jordan	31	5	15.0
Ireland	172	31	18.2	Lebanon	89	13	14.4
Italy	579	12	2.0	Syria	38	3	7.3
Netherlands	95	0	.4	Turkey	54	2	3.1
Portugal	215	25	11.5	Other Near East	43	1	2.3
Spain	79	2	2.8				
United Kingdom	646	5	.8	*ASIA*	*4,727*	*226*	*4.8*
				Afghanistan	28	2	7.7
Eastern Europe	*739*	*107*	*14.5*	Bangladesh	22	4	18.9
Hungary	111	2	2.2	China	958	27	2.8
Poland	394	88	22.2	India	471	19	4.1
Romania	95	3	3.6	Iran	212	31	14.8
Former Yugoslavia	139	14	9.7	Japan	298	2	.8
				Malaysia	33	8	23.0
New Independent States	397	4	.9	Pakistan	87	19	22.2
				Philippines	940	89	9.4
Other Europe	1,151	8	.7	South Korea	581	10	1.8
				Sri Lanka	14	5	32.8
				Other Asia	1,085	10	.9

OCEANIA	*105*	*12*	*11.5*
Australia	41	0	.7
Other Oceania	63	12	18.6
Other	321	82	25.5

Note: Totals shown in italics.

Source: Author's tabulations from 1-percent Public Use Microdata Sample (PUMS) and interpolated from Warren (1997).

$I^{199x}_{a,s,c,p}$ = the residual estimate of undocumented aliens in a census or survey of 199x for age group a, sex s, country c, and period of entry p;

$C^{199x}_{a,s,c,p}$ = census count or survey estimate of foreign-born persons in 199x for the same group; and

$L^{199x}_{a,s,c,p}$ = the legally resident, foreign-born population in the group as of 199x, the date of the census or survey (e.g., as of April 1, 1990, for the 1990 Census or October 1, 1995, for our 1995 estimates).

For ease of presentation and discussion, we drop the subscripts for age, sex, period of entry, and country of birth in subsequent equations but note that all estimates are prepared with the full detail, which provides some data on trends as well as additional information for assessing the quality of the estimates.

While the underlying logic of the method is straightforward, there are a number of issues to be dealt with in deriving the estimates. The estimate of legal, foreign-born residents is built up from administrative data on components of the immigrant population that correspond to different routes of entry into the United States—admission for permanent residence (i.e., ''normal'' immigration), humanitarian admission of refugees and asylees, legalization of formerly undocumented immigrants under the provisions of IRCA, and admission for temporary residence as a ''nonimmigrant.'' Each of these groups presents special difficulties, but the most problematic are the special agricultural workers or SAWs admitted for legalization under IRCA. We discuss all of the groups later.

After figuring out the number of immigrants entering the United States legally, we next use demographic techniques to carry the populations forward from the time they enter the country until the date of the estimate (i.e., 1995). The two demographic components that must be dealt with are mortality and emigration (migration out of the country).[6] Of these, the most problematic is emigration because there are no official measures of emigration. We use estimates developed by Ahmed and Robinson (1994) with some modifications.

To accurately measure undocumented immigration, we want to know the total number in the country, not the number included in the census. Obviously, the census misses people, so our residual estimate will understate the number of undocumented immigrants. Unfortunately, the problem is greater than simply not knowing how many undocumented aliens are missed in the census—the issue is complicated because of undercoverage of *legal*, foreign-born residents. Accordingly, we define three variants of the residual estimate, and, by returning to the estimation equation, we can clarify the coverage issue.

Conventional Residual Estimate. The first variant is the conventional residual estimate as defined and implemented by Warren and Passel (1987). The estimate, denoted as I^{199x}_{conv}, is the one represented as in Equation (1):

$$I^{199x}_{conv} = C^{199x} - L^{199x} \tag{2}$$

The estimate of legal, foreign-born residents, L^{199x}, is conceptually defined to include all legal residents, not just those counted in the survey.[7] This group is, in essence, assumed to be completely covered in the survey. However, the survey population, C^{199x}, is not complete and omits both legal and undocumented immigrants. These omissions lead to an underestimate of undocumented immigrants by exactly the number of foreign-born residents left out of the survey or census, without regard to their legal status. Consequently, we would expect the conventional residual estimate to be smaller than other estimates, such as the INS estimate for each country. As we shall see later, this pattern generally holds; when our estimate is higher than the INS estimate, the difference is indicative of potential problems in one estimate or the other.

Residual Estimate of Undocumented Aliens Covered in a Survey or Census. The second variant corrects the conventional residual estimate for undercount of *legal* immigrants in the survey or census to produce an estimate of the number of undocumented aliens covered. There are a number of options for implementing this variant. In the estimates presented here, we explicitly correct the estimate of the legal immigrant population, L^{199x}, for undercoverage in the survey or census by applying a correction factor, f_L, to the estimated legal, foreign-born population from the previous equation:

$$I^{199x}_{covered} = C^{199x} - f_L * L^{199x} \tag{3}$$

where

$I^{199x}_{covered}$ = the residual estimate of undocumented aliens covered in the census or survey of 199x;

f_L = the coverage rate for legal immigrants in the census or survey, defined as 1.0 minus the undercount rate, u_L.

We deal more explicitly later with how the coverage factor is estimated. The estimate of undocumented aliens covered in the survey or census can be very informative. For example, it measures the most visible segment of this hard-to-measure population. In addition, knowing the number of undocumented aliens covered in a survey, together with the number of legal immigrants covered, is a first step toward partitioning the population by legal status.

Residual-Based Estimate of Undocumented Aliens in the Country. The final variant is an estimate of the *total* number of undocumented aliens in the country, not just those covered in the survey. We derive this estimate by correcting the estimate of undocumented aliens included in the survey (Equation 3) for undercount in the survey, specifically:

$$I^{199x}_{total} = \frac{I^{199x}_{covered}}{(1.0 - u_l)} \tag{4}$$

where

I_{total}^{199x} = the residual-based estimate of the total number of undocumented aliens in the country in 199x;

u_I = the undercount rate for illegal immigrants in the census or survey.

A critical factor for this estimate is obviously the undercount rate for undocumented aliens. Little is actually known about this factor, so it generally must be assumed.

The range of estimates can be assessed with our estimates for 1995, using an average of the March 1995 and 1996 Current Population Surveys. Our conventional residual estimate is 4,696,000 undocumented aliens. Since the CPS is already corrected for general undercoverage, the only additional correction needed for f_L in Equation (3) is undercount of legal immigrants in the CPS in excess of the undercount for their age-sex-race/Hispanic group. We assume that this excess undercount is relatively small for most immigrant groups, so that the residual estimate of undocumented aliens *included in the CPS* for 1995 is 4,823,000. Finally, with an assumption that undocumented aliens are missed at three times the rate of legal aliens, we estimate the total undocumented population for 1995 at 5,102,000. The INS estimate for the same date is 7 percent smaller at 4,725,000.

For the 1990 Census, the estimates show a similar pattern. The conventional residual estimate of the number of undocumented aliens is 2,283,000. Because the 1990 Census is not corrected for undercount (in contrast to the CPS), the number of undocumented aliens counted in the 1990 Census is estimated to be 3,034,000. To estimate the total number of undocumented aliens, we assume that the excess omission rate for undocumented aliens is also three times that of legal immigrants. The estimated total undocumented alien population for 1990 is thus 3,471,000. The INS estimate for 1990 is 3,197,000, or a figure 8 percent smaller. For all of the estimates, Mexico and Central America are the principal sources of undocumented immigration. Following are more detailed results and comparison with the INS estimates.

Components of Demographic Estimate

The legally resident immigration component for 1995 (or 1990) in Equations (1)–(4), $L^{1995\ (1990)}$, is built up from six immigration (or population) components:

- Legal, foreign-born residents as of the 1980 Census—called ''1980 legal residents'';
- Aliens attaining legal permanent resident (LPR) status in 1980 or later, called ''LPRs''; this group excludes those LPRs who had first legalized under IRCA, persons who entered the country as refugees, and those who acquired LPR status through the asylum process; the LPR group does include those adjusting from other legal statuses;
- Persons acquiring LPR status by adjusting from refugee or asylee status, plus those granted refugee or asylee status who had not adjusted to LPR by October 1, 1995 (or April 1, 1990, for the 1990 estimates)—called ''refugees'',

- Aliens approved for temporary residency under the general legalization provisions of IRCA—called "LAWs";

- Aliens approved for temporary residency under IRCA as special agricultural workers—called "SAWs"; and

- Nonimmigrants living in the United States who consider themselves to be, or who would be considered under standard definitions to be, U.S. residents; we consider only those nonimmigrants who are included in the CPS (or the 1990 Census)—called "non-immigrants" or "census nonimmigrants."

The estimation process entails constructing an estimate, usually from administrative records, of the number of immigrants in the category (by age, sex, period of entry, and country of birth). We then estimate the mortality and emigration experienced by the cohort from entry until the date of the estimate.

The final piece of the estimate is the foreign-born population in the 1995 CPS or the 1990 Census population, $C^{1995(1990)}$. For 1995, we use a combination of CPS data from the March supplements for 1995–1997; for 1990, the 5 percent public-use microdata sample (PUMS) from the 1990 Census. For both dates, some modifications to the census/survey data are required.

We compile all of the data using the same categories, to the extent possible. If necessary, cases with unknown values are imputed or otherwise assigned to categories when possible. We generate the estimates for a set of twenty-five countries of birth or residual areas in 1995.[8] Because of problems concerning the accuracy of reporting of data of entry and in the interests of making the estimates interpretable and accessible, we collapsed the period of entry categories to 1990–1995, 1985–1989, 1980–1984, and before 1980.[9]

The demographic components use a variety of data sources. In addition, each requires specific adjustments and assumptions to deal with anomalies and shortcomings in the data. The next few sections present the main data sources and describe the resulting estimates for each of the components. More detail on the estimation procedures is provided in other sources (Passel 1998a, b; Passel and Clark 1998).

Legal Permanent Resident Aliens Admitted, 1980–1990. Most legally admitted, foreign-born residents come to the United States as "legal permanent residents." Fortunately, this group is well counted by the Immigration and Naturalization Service. Further, the INS provides access to individual records of LPR admissions through public-use tapes, which we use for fiscal years 1980 through 1995 to develop counts of LPR admissions. For this estimate, persons adjusting to LPR status from refugee or asylee status are excluded from the LPR category.

The tabulations are based on year of nonimmigrant entry, rather than the year the immigrant receives LPR status. This choice is thought to better approximate year of entry as reported in the CPS and census. However, the accuracy of tabulating and reporting of year of entry does not affect the total magnitude of either the estimated legally resident population derived from these data or the estimate of the number of undocumented aliens included in the census. Rather, this reporting issue affects the period of entry in which the undocumented are assumed to have arrived. We discuss this issue further in our evaluation of the estimates and point out some cases where our adjustments do not appear to correspond to the reporting patterns of persons in the CPS or census.

Tables 3.5 and 3.6 show the number of LPRs in 1995, net of emigration and mortality. The 1980–1995 LPRs represent a very large component of the legal, foreign-born population in 1995 at 7.4 million. Mexicans are by far the largest group at 1.1 million. Other sizable LPR populations are from China[10] (704,000), the Philippines (673,000), India (394,000), the Dominican Republic (373,000), and Korea (334,000).

Refugees and Asylees. Individuals admitted to the United States as refugees and individuals granted asylum in the United States do not immediately become LPRs. There is usually a lag of one to two years between arrival (or granting asylee status) and conversion to LPR status. We use the INS public-use data files for LPRs to tabulate refugees and asylees as they adjust to LPR status. We also estimate the number who had not adjusted by 1995 (or 1990), using data from INS and the Office of Refugee Resettlement (ORR) in the U.S. Department of Health and Human Services.

By 1995, 1,843,000 refugees and asylees were admitted during 1980–1995, net of emigration and mortality (Tables 3.5 and 3.6); this figure represents an average of about 120,000 per year. There were almost as many admissions in the 1990s as in the 1980s. Refugees from Southeast Asia (Vietnam, Cambodia, Laos) account for almost half of refugees and asylees (867,000).[11] The other two large sources of refugees are the former Soviet Union (353,000) and Cuba (249,000).

1980 Legal, Foreign-Born Residents. For the 1980 legal population, we use estimates made by Warren and Passel (1987), using information on aliens registering with the Post Office, naturalizations during 1960–1980, and admissions January–March 1980. We used unpublished detailed data by age, sex, and period of entry for about forty countries separated for aliens and naturalized citizens.

The legal, foreign-born population of 1980 surviving to 1995 is, by a small amount, the largest of any component, representing 7.4 million persons (Table 3.5) or slightly more than the number of 1980–1995 LPR admissions. However, since this group is considerably older than post-1980 legal immigrants, in the future, the group of pre-1980 legals will continue to decrease in size, principally from mortality.

Mexico is also the largest source for this group at 1.1 million (Table 3.5). Since the 1980 legal population represents the cumulation of twentieth-century immigration, there are a very large number of Europeans (2.4 million), Asians (1.5 million), and persons from the Caribbean (900,000). Specific other countries with more than 200,000 pre-1980 legal immigrants include Cuba (489,000), Canada (449,000), the Philippines (380,000), China (344,000), the United Kingdom (323,000), and the former Soviet Union (210,000).

Aliens Legalizing under IRCA: LAWs.   For the two groups of aliens legalizing under the Immigration Reform and Control Act of 1986, INS provides public-use data sets with information on the individual characteristics of legalizing aliens. For the LAWs (persons who had been living in the United States in an illegal status since before January 1, 1982), we tabulated the microdata by age, sex, country of birth, and year of entry for all persons whose applications for legal status were eventually approved. We adjusted the year-of-entry distribution with data from a survey of about 7,000 legalizing aliens done by INS, which collected more detailed information on the process of migration by this group (INS 1992b).

The LAW program was the larger of the two legalization programs, with almost 1.7 million LAWs eventually being approved for permanent residence. By 1995, we estimate that 1,550,000 remained in the United States. About 70 percent of the LAWs, or 1,092,000, were from Mexico (Table 3.5). Another 129,000, or 8 percent, came from El Salvador.

Aliens Legalizing under IRCA: SAWs.   The SAWs program legalized far more aliens than had been anticipated (Martin and Taylor 1988). Minimal documentation was required, and the SAWs did not have to live in the United States to apply. As a result, the question of how many SAWs actually live in the United States is difficult, but crucial, for the residual estimates. (See Woodrow and Passel 1990; Bean et al. 1997; Van Hook and Bean 1997a for detailed discussion of this question.)

For 1990, the available evidence suggests that many SAWs, particularly from Mexico, were not living in the United States (Passel 1998a). Accordingly, we excluded many from our tabulations. However, by the mid-1990s, there appears to have been a shift in their residency decisions. Specifically, many of the SAWs had been working in the United States but living in Mexico. They participated in a circular labor flow and did not maintain full-time residence in the United States. As a result, we estimated a SAW population in the United States in 1990 of about 750,000 (Passel 1998a). However, by 1995, several pieces of evidence suggest that many of these migrants dropped out of the circular flow to settle in the United States (Martin, Taylor, and Fix 1997; Bean et al. 1997; Passel 1998a). Accordingly, for our 1995 estimates we include all approved SAWs in the estimation process (but used high emigration rates).

The surviving resident SAW population for 1995 is 1.0 million (Table 3.5). Mexicans are most of this group with 825,000. This number and derivation process are consistent with the estimates of Bean et al. (1997). Their range of estimates is 670,000–810,000, with a preferred estimate about 100,000 lower than our SAW population. If the Bean et al. figure is correct, then our residual estimate of undocumented aliens would be higher by this amount.

Nonimmigrants in the CPS and 1990 Census.   Nonimmigrants are aliens admitted to the United States for limited time periods and for specific purposes. More than 20 million nonimmigrants are admitted to the United States every year; by far the largest number are tourists (INS 1994). Some nonimmigrants

Table 3.5
Components of Legal Foreign-Born Population and Conventional Residual Estimate of
Undocumented Aliens in 1995 CPS, by Detailed Country of Birth and Period of Entry

(Populations in thousands)

Country of Birth and Period of Entry	Immigration Component (Net)					CPS Non-Immig	Legal Foreign-Born Pop.	1995 CPS F-B Pop.	Undocumented	
	Regular LPRs '80-'95	Refu-gees '80-'95	LAWs	SAWs	Pre-80 Legals				CPS minus Legals	INS 1995
All Countries	7,397	1,843	1,550	1,006	7,410	613	19,819	24,515	4,696	4,725
1990-95	2,755	834	0	0	0	607	4,196	6,876	2,680	
1985-89	2,515	465	0	674	0	6	3,660	4,465	805	
1980-84	1,872	522	610	301	0	0	3,306	3,800	495	
Pre-1980	255	23	940	31	7,410	0	8,658	9,373	716	
Europe, total	820	469	27	3	2,433	103	3,855	4,102	247	228
1990-95	367	323	0	0	0	103	793	904	111	
1985-89	236	106	0	2	0	0	345	369	24	
1980-84	193	39	11	1	0	0	244	330	86	
Pre-1980	24	0	16	0	2,433	0	2,473	2,499	26	
Poland	138	36	13	0	182	8	378	450	71	71
1990-95	81	10	0	0	0	8	99	98	-1	
1985-89	28	18	0	0	0	0	46	75	30	
1980-84	26	8	5	0	0	0	39	79	40	
Pre-1980	4	0	8	0	182	0	194	197	3	

United Kingdom	185	0	4	0	323	24	536	577	41	6
1990-95	69	0	0	0	0	24	93	109	16	
1985-89	59	0	0	0	0	0	59	56	-3	
1980-84	53	0	2	0	0	0	54	57	3	
Pre-1980	5	0	3	0	323	0	330	355	25	
Former USSR	61	353	0	0	210	0	623	693	69	17
1990-95	37	269	0	0	0	0	306	365	59	
1985-89	17	64	0	0	0	0	81	77	-4	
1980-84	2	19	0	0	0	0	21	57	35	
Pre-1980	5	0	0	0	210	0	215	194	-21	
Europe, bal.	437	80	9	2	1,718	71	2,317	2,383	66	133
1990-95	180	43	0	0	0	71	294	332	38	
1985-89	133	24	0	2	0	0	159	160	1	
1980-84	113	12	4	1	0	0	129	137	8	
Pre-1980	11	0	6	0	1,718	0	1,734	1,753	19	
Middle East	351	92	16	3	198	38	699	760	61	75
1990-95	107	50	0	0	0	38	195	234	39	
1985-89	114	31	0	2	0	0	147	119	-29	
1980-84	91	12	3	1	0	0	107	119	12	
Pre-1980	39	0	13	0	198	0	250	289	39	
Iran	109	61	11	0	46	11	239	260	21	26
1990-95	17	29	0	0	0	11	56	64	8	
1985-89	32	28	0	0	0	0	61	36	-25	
1980-84	31	5	1	0	0	0	37	41	3	
Pre-1980	29	0	10	0	46	0	85	120	35	

Table 3.5 (continued)

(Populations in thousands)

Country of Birth and Period of Entry	Immigration Component (Net)						Legal Foreign-Born Pop.	1995 CPS F-B Pop.	Undocumented	
	Regular LPRs '80-'95	Refu-gees '80-'95	LAWs	SAWs	Pre-80 Legals	CPS Non-Immig			CPS minus Legals	INS 1995
Mid.East, bal.	242	31	5	3	152	28	460	500	40	50
1990-95	90	21	0	0	0	28	139	169	30	
1985-89	82	3	0	2	0	0	87	83	-4	
1980-84	60	7	2	1	0	0	70	78	9	
Pre-1980	10	0	3	0	152	0	165	169	5	
S & E Asia, total	2,638	886	52	45	1,543	316	5,480	5,762	283	274
1990-95	1,005	289	0	0	0	312	1,607	1,900	293	
1985-89	965	257	0	33	0	3	1,258	1,142	-116	
1980-84	619	317	21	12	0	0	969	1,111	142	
Pre-1980	49	23	31	0	1,543	0	1,646	1,610	-36	
China	704	14	13	2	344	99	1,178	1,296	119	36
1990-95	258	6	0	0	0	97	361	397	35	
1985-89	262	3	0	1	0	2	268	293	25	
1980-84	170	5	5	1	0	0	182	236	55	
Pre-1980	14	0	8	0	344	0	366	370	4	
India	394	1	5	14	177	25	616	733	117	31
1990-95	160	1	0	0	0	25	186	251	65	
1985-89	134	0	0	11	0	0	145	136	-9	
1980-84	95	0	2	3	0	0	101	129	29	
Pre-1980	5	0	3	0	177	0	185	218	32	

Korea	334	0	4	4	191	47	581	556	-25	27
1990-95	84	0	0	0	0	47	131	170	39	
1985-89	149	0	0	3	0	0	152	113	-39	
1980-84	97	0	2	1	0	0	100	133	33	
Pre-1980	3	0	3	0	191	0	197	140	-58	
Philippines	673	4	17	8	380	12	1,093	1,118	25	95
1990-95	253	1	0	0	0	12	267	272	6	
1985-89	237	2	0	5	0	0	243	221	-22	
1980-84	167	1	7	3	0	0	178	186	8	
Pre-1980	16	0	10	0	380	0	405	439	33	
S&E Asia, bal.	533	867	13	17	450	132	2,012	2,059	47	84
1990-95	250	281	0	0	0	131	662	810	148	
1985-89	183	253	0	13	0	1	450	379	-71	
1980-84	90	311	5	3	0	0	409	426	18	
Pre-1980	11	23	8	0	450	0	491	443	-48	
Canada	159	0	6	0	449	32	646	589	-57	111
1990-95	65	0	0	0	0	32	97	108	11	
1985-89	50	0	0	0	0	0	50	60	10	
1980-84	39	0	3	0	0	0	42	44	2	
Pre-1980	5	0	2	0	449	0	456	377	-79	

Table 3.5 (*continued*)

(Populations in thousands)

Country of Birth and Period of Entry	Immigration Component (Net)						Legal Foreign-Born Pop.	1995 CPS F-B Pop.	Undocumented	
	Regular LPRs '80-'95	Refu-gees '80-'95	LAWs	SAWs	Pre-80 Legals	CPS Non-Immig			CPS minus Legals	INS 1995
Mexico	1,098	0	1,092	825	1,127	16	4,158	6,671	2,513	2,548
1990-95	362	0	0	0	0	14	377	2,015	1,638	
1985-89	368	0	0	549	0	1	919	1,469	551	
1980-84	311	0	371	246	0	0	928	950	22	
Pre-1980	56	0	721	30	1,127	0	1,935	2,237	303	
Cent.Am., total	451	36	212	41	213	4	956	1,681	726	653
1990-95	157	32	0	0	0	4	192	393	201	
1985-89	160	4	0	27	0	0	190	500	310	
1980-84	119	1	125	14	0	0	259	356	97	
Pre-1980	14	0	87	0	213	0	314	432	118	
El Salvador	180	5	129	20	42	1	377	637	261	324
1990-95	78	4	0	0	0	1	84	138	55	
1985-89	61	1	0	12	0	0	74	176	102	
1980-84	38	0	76	8	0	0	122	165	43	
Pre-1980	2	0	53	0	42	0	97	158	61	
Cent.Am., bal.	271	31	83	20	171	3	579	1,044	465	330
1990-95	78	27	0	0	0	3	108	255	147	
1985-89	100	3	0	14	0	0	117	325	208	
1980-84	81	1	49	6	0	0	137	191	54	
Pre-1980	12	0	34	0	171	0	217	274	57	

Caribbean, total	970	299	47	52	898	19	2,285	2,570	284	382
1990-95	384	106	0	0	0	19	509	578	68	
1985-89	295	53	0	35	0	0	382	385	3	
1980-84	259	141	25	17	0	0	442	485	43	
Pre-1980	32	0	22	0	898	0	952	1,122	170	
Cuba	58	249	1	0	489	0	798	821	24	8
1990-95	17	85	0	0	0	0	102	119	18	
1985-89	16	24	0	0	0	0	40	46	6	
1980-84	15	140	0	0	0	0	156	155	-1	
Pre-1980	10	0	0	0	489	0	499	500	1	
Dom. Rep.	373	0	13	6	138	2	532	558	27	69
1990-95	207	0	0	0	0	2	209	182	-27	
1985-89	109	0	0	5	0	0	114	109	-6	
1980-84	52	0	6	1	0	0	59	90	31	
Pre-1980	4	0	7	0	138	0	149	177	29	
Haiti	132	49	13	39	41	0	275	407	133	99
1990-95	39	21	0	0	0	0	60	114	54	
1985-89	24	28	0	25	0	0	76	78	2	
1980-84	66	0	8	14	0	0	88	107	19	
Pre-1980	4	0	6	0	41	0	51	108	57	

Table 3.5 (*continued*)

(Populations in thousands)

Country of Birth and Period of Entry	Immigration Component (Net)						Legal Foreign-Born Pop.	1995 CPS F-B Pop.	Undocumented	
	Regular LPRs '80-'95	Refu-gees '80-'95	LAWs	SAWs	Pre-80 Legals	CPS Non-Immig			CPS minus Legals	INS 1995
Jamaica	242	0	10	4	126	5	388	440	52	47
1990-95	75	0	0	0	0	5	80	88	8	
1985-89	90	0	0	3	0	0	93	96	3	
1980-84	70	0	6	1	0	0	77	79	2	
Pre-1980	6	0	5	0	126	0	137	177	39	
Caribbean, bal.	165	1	10	3	104	12	294	343	49	160
1990-95	46	0	0	0	0	12	58	74	16	
1985-89	55	1	0	2	0	0	58	56	-2	
1980-84	55	0	6	1	0	0	62	53	-8	
Pre-1980	8	0	4	0	104	0	116	159	44	
S.Amer., total	625	4	68	25	402	26	1,150	1,376	226	187
1990-95	211	3	0	0	0	26	240	406	166	
1985-89	232	1	0	20	0	0	252	247	-5	
1980-84	162	1	39	6	0	0	207	258	51	
Pre-1980	20	0	29	0	402	0	451	465	14	
Colombia	158	1	24	7	109	4	303	357	54	63
1990-95	48	0	0	0	0	4	53	74	21	
1985-89	61	0	0	5	0	0	67	70	4	
1980-84	44	0	14	2	0	0	59	83	24	
Pre-1980	5	0	10	0	109	0	124	130	5	

Peru	96	1	12	6	38	1	154	210	56	28
1990-95	39	1	0	0	0	1	40	57	16	
1985-89	34	0	0	5	0	0	39	48	9	
1980-84	19	0	7	1	0	0	27	37	10	
Pre-1980	4	0	5	0	38	0	47	68	21	
S.Amer., bal.	370	2	32	12	255	22	694	809	115	97
1990-95	124	1	0	0	0	22	147	275	129	
1985-89	136	0	0	10	0	0	146	128	-18	
1980-84	99	1	18	3	0	0	120	138	17	
Pre-1980	12	0	14	0	255	0	280	268	-13	
Africa	228	56	26	9	103	45	467	531	64	111
1990-95	77	31	0	0	0	45	153	214	61	
1985-89	75	13	0	6	0	0	94	93	-1	
1980-84	63	12	10	3	0	0	88	87	-1	
Pre-1980	13	0	16	0	103	0	131	137	6	
Other & Unk.	57	1	4	2	45	15	124	472	348	156
1990-95	19	0	0	0	0	14	33	125	92	
1985-89	19	0	0	1	0	1	21	80	59	
1980-84	17	0	1	1	0	0	20	62	42	
Pre-1980	2	0	2	0	45	0	50	205	155	

Table 3.6
Components of Legal Foreign-Born Population and Conventional Residual Estimate of Undocumented Aliens in 1995 CPS, by Country of Birth

(Populations in thousands)

Country of Birth	Immigration Component (Net)						Legal Foreign-Born Pop.	1995 CPS F-B Pop.	Undocumented	
	Regular LPRs '80-'95	Refu-gees '80-'95	LAWs	SAWs	Pre-80 Legals	CPS Non-Immig			CPS minus Legals	INS 1995
All Countries	7,397	1,843	1,550	1,006	7,410	613	19,819	24,515	4,696	4,725
1990-95	2,755	834	0	0	0	607	4,196	6,876	2,680	(x)
1985-89	2,515	465	0	674	0	6	3,660	4,465	805	(x)
1980-84	1,872	522	610	301	0	0	3,306	3,800	495	(x)
Pre-1980	255	23	940	31	7,410	0	8,658	9,373	716	(x)
Europe, total	820	469	27	3	2,433	103	3,855	4,102	247	228
Poland	138	36	13	0	182	8	378	450	71	71
United King.	185	0	4	0	323	24	536	577	41	6
Former USSR	61	353	0	0	210	0	623	693	69	17
Europe, bal.	437	80	9	2	1,718	71	2,317	2,383	66	133
Middle East	351	92	16	3	198	38	699	760	61	75
Iran	109	61	11	0	46	11	239	260	21	26
Mid.East, bal.	242	31	5	3	152	28	460	500	40	50
S & E Asia, tot.	2,638	886	52	45	1,543	316	5,480	5,762	283	274
China	704	14	13	2	344	99	1,178	1,296	119	36
India	394	1	5	14	177	25	616	733	117	31
Korea	334	0	4	4	191	47	581	556	-25	27
Philippines	673	4	17	8	380	12	1,093	1,118	25	95
S&E Asia, bal.	533	867	13	17	450	132	2,012	2,059	47	84

Canada	159	0	6	0	449	32	646	589	-57	111
Mexico	1,098	0	1,092	825	1,127	16	4,158	6,671	2,513	2,548
1990-95	362	0	0	0	0	14	377	2,015	1,638	
1985-89	368	0	0	549	0	1	919	1,469	551	
1980-84	311	0	371	246	0	0	928	950	22	
Pre-1980	56	0	721	30	1,127	0	1,935	2,237	303	
Cent.Am., tot.	451	36	212	41	213	4	956	1,681	726	653
El Salvador	180	5	129	20	42	1	377	637	261	324
Cent.Am., bal.	271	31	83	20	171	3	579	1,044	465	330
Caribbean, tot.	970	299	47	52	898	19	2,285	2,570	284	382
Cuba	58	249	1	0	489	0	798	821	24	8
Dom. Rep.	373	0	13	6	138	2	532	558	27	69
Haiti	132	49	13	39	41	0	275	407	133	99
Jamaica	242	0	10	4	126	5	388	440	52	47
Carib., bal.	165	1	10	3	104	12	294	343	49	160
S.Amer., total	625	4	68	25	402	26	1,150	1,376	226	187
Colombia	158	1	24	7	109	4	303	357	54	63
Peru	96	1	12	6	38	1	154	210	56	28
S.Amer., bal.	370	2	32	12	255	22	694	809	115	97
Africa	228	56	26	9	103	45	467	531	64	111
Other & Unk.	57	1	4	2	45	15	124	472	348	156

are permitted to work in the United States, while others are not. For the purpose of the census or a survey such as the CPS or for population estimates, the key feature of nonimmigrants is whether they can be considered U.S. residents. For our estimates of the legally resident, foreign-born population, we consider a nonimmigrant to be a U.S. resident if he or she appears in the census and meets one of the criteria described later.

The procedures used for our estimates attempt to match the characteristics of aliens in the census or CPS with the criteria used to award nonimmigrant visas. Our estimates for the 1990 Census are from Word (1995), who developed them from microdata for the full census sample. For our 1995 estimates, we developed our own procedures based on Word's procedures. We made modifications to allow for more detail in the CPS and other differences between the CPS and the 1990 Census.[12] Our methods are set forth in detail in Passel and Clark (1998). The first criterion is that the nonimmigrant must have come to the United States within the last three years. Next, if an alien's spouse is a U.S. citizen (either native or foreign-born), or the alien's parent or grandparent is in the household, the alien is not assigned to be a nonimmigrant. Beyond these procedures, the individual's age, income, occupation, and other household characteristics come into play.

Our procedures are not designed to identify every nonimmigrant in the census, but merely those most likely to be nonimmigrants. For estimating undocumented aliens in the census, however, an estimate of nonimmigrants in the census is extremely useful. Returning to Equations (1)–(4), the estimate of *all* legal residents, L^{199x}, is subtracted from the foreign-born population *counted* in the census, C^{199x}. But, if nonimmigrants are removed from consideration in the census and the estimate of legal residents, the estimates of undocumented immigrants included in the census will be improved. To eliminate the nonimmigrants, it is necessary to know the number of nonimmigrants *counted* in the census, not the total number.

The estimated 613,000 nonimmigrants in the 1995–1996 CPS come from many different countries, with less concentration than was found for the other components (Table 3.5). The largest number (99,000) come from China, mainly as students and scholars. Japan (not shown) provides the next largest number as intracompany transfers and students. Korea, India, and Canada are the only other countries with as many as 20,000 each.

Mortality and Emigration. The incoming immigrants and refugees, 1980 legal population, and legalized aliens must be "carried forward" to the estimate dates in 1990 and 1995. We apply age-sex-specific mortality and emigration rates, using as the base year the immigrants' year of admission (not the year of arrival), 1980, or year of legalization, points at which the immigrants are known to be alive. The survival rates are calculated from life tables (by sex and race-ethnicity) that are used in recent population projections from the Bureau of the Census (1995, 1996). The survival rates are specified for race/ethnic populations (white, black, Asian/Pacific Islander, American Indian, Hispanic), and the choice of life table for a particular country is determined by the race/ethnicity of the majority of immigrants from the country.

Estimating emigration is more problematic than mortality because of the paucity of data. For these estimates, we developed a set of annual age-sex-specific emigration rates by race consistent with the estimates of Ahmed and Robinson (1994). We use three sets of emigration rates: full and half exposure rates for the 1980s calculated by Ahmed and Robinson as smoothed with our fitting procedure; and for legal immigrants entering before 1970, residual estimates calculated from 1980 and 1990 Census data. Lower exposure rates (i.e., lower emigration rates) are used for Hispanic countries in our estimates, consistent with the estimates and observations of Ahmed and Robinson. The lower exposure rates are also used for naturalized citizens and refugees, groups with greater attachment to the United States and weaker ties to their home countries.

There are few benchmarks available for assessing emigration estimates. Our estimate of 1.7 million foreign-born emigrants during the 1980s (Passel 1998a) exceeds the numbers used in official Census Bureau population estimates for the 1980s by almost 30 percent. This difference is, however, consistent with Ahmed and Robinson's (1994) conclusions, revisions to the bureau's emigration assumption, and some studies done with innovative techniques and the CPS around 1990 (cited in Bean et al. 1997).

Foreign-Born Population in the CPS and Census. The logical population to use for comparison with our estimates of legal residents is the foreign-born population in October 1995. The CPS data used for analytic work come from the annual March Socio-Economic Supplements. Thus, we could use the average of data from the March CPS supplements for 1995 and 1996 to develop an October 1995 "CPS" population. However, because of the relatively small sample size of the CPS compared with the 1990 Census (50,000 households versus more than 5 million), we would like to use data from more years, such as 1994–1997. There are, however, some problems with several of the years that limit our options.

The first problem we identified was incorrect weighting in the 1994 and 1995 March CPS supplements (Passel 1996; Schmidley and Robinson 1998). We have fixed the weighting problem (Passel and Clark 1998), but another problem we have identified calls for an alternative approach. The public-use version of the 1994 CPS identifies only twenty-two specific countries and places all other foreign-born persons into a single, large residual "other countries" category. This problem renders the 1994 data unusable for our estimates. A slight vestige of this problem continues to afflict the 1995 CPS data, but to a lesser degree that can be remedied.

Accordingly, our approach is to use the data from the March 1995–1997 CPSs in an averaging process. We get the total CPS foreign-born population as of October 1995 as an average of the March 1995 and 1996 totals; the result is 24,515,000. The distribution by country of birth is derived from an average of the 1996 and 1997 CPSs, adjusted to the previously derived U.S. total. This procedure eliminates the residual "other country" problem. The period of entry data use all three years for each country. Sampling error continues to affect these averages, and, in our analysis, we point out several groups that appear to have 1995 populations further above or below the 1990 Census counts than would be expected on the basis of demographic change.

The CPS data in the 1990s have one major advantage over the 1990 Census data—the CPS is corrected for undercoverage. That is, the control totals used in weighting the CPS take into account the persons missed in the 1990 Census. Although the corrections are not made explicitly for the foreign-born population, they do take into account race and Hispanic origin categories. Thus, the conventional residual estimate for 1995 needs less correction to estimate covered illegals in the CPS than the 1990 Census-based estimates.

Our 1990 Census population comes from the 5 percent public-use microdata sample (PUMS), tabulated by age, sex, period of entry, and country of birth. The 1990 Census has 19.7 million foreign-born persons, including about 805,000 foreign-born individuals with no country of birth reported, representing 4.1 percent of the immigrant population. We assigned countries of birth to 484,000 of these on the basis of reported race, Hispanic origin, and ethnicity characteristics that suggest specific countries of birth. For example, foreign-born persons with no country of birth reported but of Mexican or Cuban origin were assigned to Mexico or Cuba, respectively.

ESTIMATES OF UNDOCUMENTED ALIENS IN 1990 AND 1995

Conventional Residual Estimates

The residual estimates show 4.7 million undocumented aliens in the 1995 CPS (Tables 3.5 and 3.6), a slightly higher figure of 4.8 million with adjusted CPS estimates (Tables 3.7 and 3.8), and 2.3 million in the 1990 Census (Tables 3.9 and 3.10). In 1995, about 57 percent, or 2.7 million, had entered the United States since 1990—a slight increase in the percentage of recent immigrants over those found in the 1990 Census (52 percent). Just over one-quarter had been in the country for ten years or more in 1995, a decrease from the 31 percent in 1990. According to the conventional residual estimate, about 39 percent of all immigrants coming since 1990 are undocumented—2.7 million undocumented out of 6.9 million who entered in the 1990s (Table 3.5). In 1990, roughly the same percentage of recent immigrants came as undocumented immigrants (i.e., 1.7 million undocumented out of 4.8 million entrants during 1985–1990). However, in 1990, only 25 percent of the cohort, or 1.2 million recent entrants, remained undocumented because IRCA's legalization program had made 500,000 of the recent entrants legal. Because there has been no legalization program in the 1990s, all of 2.7 million illegal entrants during the 1990s remain undocumented in 1995.

Mexico accounts for 53 percent of the conventional residual estimate of un-documented aliens in the 1995 CPS, or 2.5 million persons. Central America accounts for another 726,000 undocumented aliens, or about 15 percent of the total, with 261,000 from El Salvador.[13] Only three other individual countries exceed 100,000 in the conventional residual estimates—Haiti with 133,000, China with 119,000, and India with 117,000.

For 1990, the principal sources follow roughly the same pattern, with a few exceptions. Mexico accounts for 899,000, or only 39 percent of the total (Tables 3.9 and 3.10). Mexico's percentage of the total is lower in 1990 because IRCA removed more Mexicans from the undocumented population than from any other country. Central America accounts for another 411,000, or 18 percent. The larg-est Central American sources are El Salvador (185,000), Nicaragua (99,000), and Guatemala (81,000). The only other countries accounting for more than 50,000 are China (79,000) and the Philippines (57,000).

Correction for Undercoverage of Legal Immigrants. As discussed earlier, the conventional residual estimates understate the numbers of undocumented aliens included in the CPS or census by the number of legal immigrants missed in the survey. To account for this omission, we introduce corrections for un-dercoverage. As noted earlier, the CPS is already adjusted for race and Hispanic undercounts. However, the corrections are not specific for immigrants and make no allowance for the supposedly higher-than-average undercount rates of the foreign-born population. Further, the 1990 Census is not adjusted for any un-dercount. Accordingly, we introduce two sets of undercount adjustments—one for general undercount in the 1990 Census and one for ''excess'' undercount suffered by immigrants in both the 1990 Census and the 1995 CPS.

For census undercount adjustments, we follow the work of Schmidley and Robinson (1998). We use the official estimates of undercount rates by race. For each country of birth, we choose the rate pertaining to the largest race/ethnic group from the country. The undercount rates for the 1990 Census are as fol-lows: Hispanic origin, 5.9 percent; black, 5.7 percent; Asian and Pacific Islander, 1.9 percent; white, 0.6 percent.[14]

Additional adjustments for immigrants are more problematic because of an almost complete lack of data. The estimates made for the Binational Study (Bean et al. 1997) attempt to address just this issue for the CPS and census. They estimate that legal immigrants from Mexico are subject to a 4.0 percent under-count in addition to the usual census undercount. We use this figure as a bench-mark for our additional adjustments beyond those for overall census undercount. Specifically, for Mexican legal immigrants in 1990 who entered the United States in 1985–1990 and 1980–1984, we assume a further undercount of 4.0 percent. For those who had been in the country for more than ten years, we assume that the coverage disadvantage is reduced by half because of their greater exposure to the country; thus, we assume an additional undercount of 2.0 per-cent. We applied these same factors to other countries with high census under-count rates, that is, countries sending black and Hispanic immigrants. We scaled

Table 3.7
Residual Estimates of Undocumented Aliens in 1995, Counted in the CPS and Total
(Assuming Additional Undercount of Legal Immigrants), by Detailed Country of Birth and Period of Entry

(Populations in thousands. Undocumented alien undercount factor assumed to be 3.0 times undercount of legals)

Country of Birth and Period of Entry	Legal Immigration (Net)					Legal F-B in 1995 CPS	1995 CPS F-B Pop.	Undocumented Aliens		
	Total Legal Immig.	Assumed Add'l Undercount Pct.	Amt.	Counted Legal Immig.	CPS Non-Immig.			Counted in 1995 CPS	Total, w/ Under-Count	INS 1995
All Countries	19,206	0.7%	127	19,079	613	19,692	24,515	4,823	5,102	4,725
1990-95	3,589	2.1%	76	3,513	607	4,120	6,876	2,756	2,989	
1985-89	3,654	1.1%	41	3,613	6	3,619	4,465	846	889	
1980-84	3,306	0.3%	10	3,295	0	3,295	3,800	505	509	
Pre-1980	8,658		0	8,658	0	8,658	9,373	716	716	
Europe, total	3,752	0.3%	10	3,742	103	3,845	4,102	257	263	228
1990-95	690	1.2%	8	682	103	785	904	120	124	
1985-89	345	0.4%	2	344	0	344	369	25	26	
1980-84	244	(x)	0	244	0	244	330	86	86	
Pre-1980	2,473		0	2,473	0	2,473	2,499	26	26	
Poland	370	0.6%	2	368	8	376	450	73	74	71
1990-95	91	2.0%	2	89	8	98	98	1	1	
1985-89	46	1.0%	0	45	0	45	75	30	31	
1980-84	39	(x)	0	39	0	39	79	40	40	
Pre-1980	194		0	194	0	194	197	3	3	

United Kingdom	512		0	512	24	536	577	41	41	6
1990-95	69	(x)	0	69	24	93	109	16	16	
1985-89	59	(x)	0	59	0	59	56	-3	-3	
1980-84	54	(x)	0	54	0	54	57	3	3	
Pre-1980	330	(x)	0	330	0	330	355	25	25	
Former USSR	623		7	617	0	617	693	81	76	17
1990-95	306	1.1%	6	300	0	300	365	69	65	
1985-89	81	2.0%	1	81	0	81	77	-3	-3	
1980-84	21	1.0%	0	21	0	21	57	35	35	
Pre-1980	215	(x)	0	215	0	215	194	-21	-21	
Europe, bal.	2,246		1	2,246	71	2,317	2,383	66	66	133
1990-95	223	0.0%	0	223	71	294	332	38	38	
1985-89	159	0.1%	0	159	0	159	160	2	1	
1980-84	129	0.1%	0	129	0	129	137	8	8	
Pre-1980	1,734	(x)	0	1,734	0	1,734	1,753	19	19	
Middle East	661		5	656	38	694	760	69	66	75
1990-95	157	0.7%	3	153	38	192	234	44	42	
1985-89	147	2.0%	1	146	0	146	119	-27	-27	
1980-84	107	1.0%	0	107	0	107	119	12	12	
Pre-1980	250	(x)	0	250	0	250	289	39	39	
Iran	228		2	227	11	238	260	23	23	26
1990-95	45	0.7%	1	45	11	55	64	10	9	
1985-89	61	2.0%	1	60	0	60	36	-24	-24	
1980-84	37	1.0%	0	37	0	37	41	3	3	
Pre-1980	85	(x)	0	85	0	85	120	35	35	

Table 3.7 (continued)

(Populations in thousands. Undocumented alien undercount factor assumed to be 3.0 times undercount of legals)

Country of Birth and Period of Entry	Legal Immigration (Net)					Legal F-B in 1995 CPS	1995 CPS F-B Pop.	Undocumented Aliens		
	Total Legal Immig.	Assumed Undercount Pct.	Amt.	Counted Legal Immig.	CPS Non-Immig.			Counted in 1995 CPS	Total, w/ Under-Count	INS 1995
Mid.East, bal.	432	0.7%	3	429	28	457	500	43	45	50
1990-95	111	2.0%	2	109	28	136	169	33	35	
1985-89	87	1.0%	1	86	0	86	83	-3	-3	
1980-84	70	(x)	0	70	0	70	78	9	9	
Pre-1980	165		0	165	0	165	169	5	5	
S & E Asia, total	5,164	0.8%	41	5,123	316	5,439	5,762	324	346	274
1990-95	1,295	2.1%	27	1,268	312	1,580	1,900	320	342	
1985-89	1,255	1.0%	12	1,243	3	1,246	1,142	-104	-103	
1980-84	969	0.2%	2	967	0	967	1,111	144	144	
Pre-1980	1,646		0	1,646	0	1,646	1,610	-36	-36	
China	1,078	0.4%	4	1,075	99	1,174	1,296	123	124	36
1990-95	265	1.0%	3	262	97	359	397	38	39	
1985-89	266	0.5%	1	265	2	267	293	26	27	
1980-84	182	(x)	0	182	0	182	236	55	55	
Pre-1980	366		0	366	0	366	370	4	4	
India	591	0.8%	5	586	25	611	733	122	126	31
1990-95	160	2.0%	3	157	25	182	251	68	73	
1985-89	145	1.0%	1	143	0	143	136	-7	-7	
1980-84	101	(x)	0	101	0	101	129	29	29	
Pre-1980	185		0	185	0	185	218	32	32	

Korea	533		0	533	47	580	556	-24	-24	27
1990-95	84	0.1%	0	84	47	131	170	39	40	
1985-89	152	0.5%	0	152	0	152	113	-39	-39	
1980-84	100	(x)	0	100	0	100	133	33	33	
Pre-1980	197	(x)	0	197	0	197	140	-58	-58	
Philippines	1,081		17	1,065	12	1,077	1,118	42	44	95
1990-95	255	1.6%	10	244	12	257	272	16	18	
1985-89	243	4.0%	5	238	0	238	221	-17	-17	
1980-84	178	2.0%	2	176	0	176	186	9	10	
Pre-1980	405	1.0%	0	405	0	405	439	33	33	
S&E Asia, bal.	1,880		15	1,865	132	1,997	2,059	62	75	84
1990-95	531	0.8%	11	520	131	651	810	158	172	
1985-89	449	2.0%	4	444	1	445	379	-66	-66	
1980-84	409	1.0%	0	409	0	409	426	18	18	
Pre-1980	491	(x)	0	491	0	491	443	-48	-48	
Canada	614		0	613	32	645	589	-56	-56	111
1990-95	65	0.1%	0	65	32	97	108	11	12	
1985-89	50	0.5%	0	50	0	50	60	10	10	
1980-84	42	0.3%	0	42	0	42	44	2	2	
Pre-1980	456	(x)	0	456	0	456	377	-79	-79	

Table 3.7 (continued)

(Populations in thousands. Undocumented alien undercount factor assumed to be 3.0 times undercount of legals)

Country of Birth and Period of Entry	Legal Immigration (Net)					Legal F-B in 1995 CPS	1995 CPS F-B Pop.	Undocumented Aliens		
	Total Legal Immig.	Assumed Add'l Undercount Pct.	Amt.	Counted Legal Immig.	CPS Non-Immig.			Counted in 1995 CPS	Total, w/ Under-Count	INS 1995
Mexico	4,142	0.7%	29	4,113	16	4,129	6,671	2,542	2,732	2,548
1990-95	363	3.0%	11	352	14	366	2,015	1,649	1,812	
1985-89	917	1.5%	14	904	1	905	1,469	564	591	
1980-84	928	0.5%	5	923	0	923	950	26	27	
Pre-1980	1,935	0.5%	0	1,935	0	1,935	2,237	303	303	
Cent.Am., total	952	1.0%	9	943	4	946	1,681	735	767	653
1990-95	188	2.9%	5	183	4	186	393	207	224	
1985-89	190	1.4%	3	188	0	188	500	313	326	
1980-84	259	0.5%	1	258	0	258	356	98	100	
Pre-1980	314	0.5%	0	314	0	314	432	118	118	
El Salvador	376	1.6%	6	370	1	371	637	267	282	324
1990-95	83	4.0%	3	79	1	80	138	58	66	
1985-89	74	2.0%	1	72	0	72	176	104	110	
1980-84	122	1.0%	1	121	0	121	165	44	45	
Pre-1980	97	1.0%	0	97	0	97	158	61	61	
Cent.Am., bal.	576	0.6%	3	573	3	576	1,044	469	485	330
1990-95	106	2.0%	2	103	3	106	255	149	158	
1985-89	117	1.0%	1	116	0	116	325	209	215	
1980-84	137	(x)	0	137	0	137	191	54	54	
Pre-1980	217		0	217	0	217	274	57	57	

Caribbean, total	2,266	0.8%	19	2,248	19	2,267	2,570	303	309	382
1990-95	490	2.6%	13	478	19	496	578	81	87	
1985-89	382	1.3%	5	377	0	377	385	8	8	
1980-84	442	0.2%	1	441	0	441	485	44	45	
Pre-1980	952		0	952	0	952	1,122	170	170	
Cuba	798	0.1%	1	797	0	797	821	24	24	8
1990-95	102	0.5%	1	101	0	101	119	18	18	
1985-89	40	0.3%	0	40	0	40	46	6	6	
1980-84	156	(x)	0	156	0	156	155	-1	-1	
Pre-1980	499		0	499	0	499	500	1	1	
Dom. Rep.	530	2.1%	11	519	2	521	558	38	39	69
1990-95	207	4.0%	8	199	2	201	182	-19	-19	
1985-89	114	2.0%	2	112	0	112	109	-4	-4	
1980-84	59	1.0%	1	59	0	59	90	31	32	
Pre-1980	149		0	149	0	149	177	29	29	
Haiti	275	0.7%	2	273	0	273	407	135	138	99
1990-95	60	2.0%	1	58	0	58	114	55	59	
1985-89	76	1.0%	1	75	0	75	78	3	3	
1980-84	88	(x)	0	88	0	88	107	19	19	
Pre-1980	51		0	51	0	51	108	57	57	

Table 3.7 (*continued*)

(Populations in thousands. Undocumented alien undercount factor assumed to be 3.0 times undercount of legals)

Country of Birth and Period of Entry	Legal Immigration (Net)					Legal F-B in 1995 CPS	1995 CPS F-B Pop.	Undocumented Aliens		
	Total Legal Immig.	Assumed Undercount Pct.	Add'l Amt.	Counted Legal Immig.	CPS Non-Immig.			Counted in 1995 CPS	Total, w/ Under-Count	INS 1995
Jamaica	383	1.1%	4	379	5	384	440	56	57	47
1990-95	75	3.0%	2	73	5	78	88	10	11	
1985-89	93	1.5%	1	91	0	91	96	4	5	
1980-84	77	0.5%	0	77	0	77	79	2	2	
Pre-1980	137	0.5%	0	137	0	137	177	39	39	
Caribbean, bal.	282	0.3%	1	281	12	293	343	50	51	160
1990-95	46	1.0%	0	46	12	58	74	16	17	
1985-89	58	0.5%	0	58	0	58	56	-2	-2	
1980-84	62	(x)	0	62	0	62	53	-8	-8	
Pre-1980	116	(x)	0	116	0	116	159	44	44	
S.Amer., total	1,124	0.8%	9	1,116	26	1,142	1,376	234	247	187
1990-95	214	2.2%	5	209	26	235	406	171	183	
1985-89	252	1.2%	3	249	0	249	247	-2	-2	
1980-84	207	0.6%	1	206	0	206	258	52	52	
Pre-1980	451		0	451	0	451	465	14	14	
Colombia	299	1.0%	3	296	4	300	357	57	60	63
1990-95	49	3.0%	1	47	4	51	74	23	25	
1985-89	67	1.5%	1	66	0	66	70	5	5	
1980-84	59	0.8%	0	59	0	59	83	24	25	
Pre-1980	124		0	124	0	124	130	5	5	

Peru	153	0.4%	1	153	1	153	210	57	57	28
1990-95	40	1.0%	0	40	1	40	57	17	17	
1985-89	39	0.5%	0	39	0	39	48	10	10	
1980-84	27	(x)	0	27	0	27	37	10	10	
Pre-1980	47		0	47	0	47	68	21	21	
S.Amer., bal.	672	0.8%	5	667	22	688	809	121	130	97
1990-95	125	2.3%	3	122	22	144	275	131	140	
1985-89	146	1.2%	2	145	0	145	128	-16	-16	
1980-84	120	0.6%	1	120	0	120	138	18	18	
Pre-1980	280		0	280	0	280	268	-13	-13	
Africa	422	1.3%	5	416	45	461	531	70	77	111
1990-95	108	3.0%	3	105	45	150	214	64	71	
1985-89	94	1.5%	1	93	0	93	93	1	1	
1980-84	88	0.8%	1	87	0	87	87	-1	0	
Pre-1980	131		0	131	0	131	137	6	6	
Other & Unk.	109	(x)	0	109	15	124	472	348	348	156
1990-95	19	(x)	0	19	14	33	125	92	92	
1985-89	20	(x)	0	20	1	21	80	59	59	
1980-84	20	(x)	0	20	0	20	62	42	42	
Pre-1980	50		0	50	0	50	205	155	155	

Table 3.8
Residual Estimates of Undocumented Aliens in 1995, Counted in the CPS and Total (Assuming Additional Undercount of Legal Immigrants), by Country of Birth

(Populations in thousands. Undocumented alien undercount factor assumed to be 3.0 times undercount of legals)

Country of Birth	Legal Immigration (Net)					Legal F-B in 1995 CPS	1995 CPS F-B Pop.	Undocumented Aliens		
	Total Legal Immig.	Assumed Add'l Undercount Pct.	Amt.	Counted Legal Immig.	CPS Non-Immig			Counted in 1995 CPS	Total, w/ Under-Count CPS	INS 1995
All Countries	19,206	0.7%	127	19,079	613	19,692	24,515	4,823	5,102	4,725
1990-95	3,589	2.1%	76	3,513	607	4,120	6,876	2,756	2,989	
1985-89	3,654	1.1%	41	3,613	6	3,619	4,465	846	889	
1980-84	3,306	0.3%	10	3,295	0	3,295	3,800	505	509	
Pre-1980	8,658	0.3%	0	8,658	0	8,658	9,373	716	716	
Europe, total	3,752	0.3%	10	3,742	103	3,845	4,102	257	263	228
Poland	370	0.6%	2	368	8	376	450	73	74	71
United King.	512	(x)	0	512	24	536	577	41	41	6
Former USSR	623	1.1%	7	617	0	617	693	76	81	17
Europe, bal.	2,246	0.0%	1	2,246	71	2,317	2,383	66	66	133
Middle East	661	0.7%	5	656	38	694	760	66	69	75
Iran	228	0.7%	2	227	11	238	260	23	23	26
Mid.East, bal.	432	0.7%	3	429	28	457	500	43	45	50
S & E Asia, tot.	5,164	0.8%	41	5,123	316	5,439	5,762	324	346	274
China	1,078	0.4%	4	1,075	99	1,174	1,296	123	124	36
India	591	0.8%	5	586	25	611	733	122	126	31
Korea	533	0.1%	0	533	47	580	556	-24	-24	27
Philippines	1,081	1.6%	17	1,065	12	1,077	1,118	42	44	95
S&E Asia, bal.	1,880	0.8%	15	1,865	132	1,997	2,059	62	75	84

Canada	614	0.1%	0	613	32	645	589	-56	-56	111
Mexico	4,142	0.7%	29	4,113	16	4,129	6,671	2,542	2,732	2,548
1990-95	363	3.0%	11	352	14	366	2,015	1,649	1,812	
1985-89	917	1.5%	14	904	1	905	1,469	564	591	
1980-84	928	0.5%	5	923	0	923	950	26	27	
Pre-1980	1,935		0	1,935	0	1,935	2,237	303	303	
Cent.Am., tot.	952	1.0%	9	943	4	946	1,681	735	767	653
El Salvador	376	1.6%	6	370	1	371	637	267	282	324
Cent.Am., bal.	576	0.6%	3	573	3	576	1,044	469	485	330
Caribbean, tot.	2,266	0.8%	19	2,248	19	2,267	2,570	303	309	382
Cuba	798	0.1%	1	797	0	797	821	24	24	8
Dom. Rep.	530	2.1%	11	519	2	521	558	38	39	69
Haiti	275	0.7%	2	273	0	273	407	135	138	99
Jamaica	383	1.1%	4	379	5	384	440	56	57	47
Carib., bal.	282	0.3%	1	281	12	293	343	50	51	160
S.Amer., total	1,124	0.8%	9	1,116	26	1,142	1,376	234	247	187
Colombia	299	1.0%	3	296	4	300	357	57	60	63
Peru	153	0.4%	1	153	1	153	210	57	57	28
S.Amer., bal.	672	0.8%	5	667	22	688	809	121	130	97
Africa	422	1.3%	5	416	45	461	531	70	77	111
Other & Unk.	109	(x)	0	109	15	124	472	348	348	156

Table 3.9
Legal Foreign-Born Population and Undocumented Aliens in 1990, INS Estimates and
Alternative Census-Based Estimates, by Detailed Country of Birth

(Populations in thousands)

Country or Area of Birth	Census Non-Immig.	1990 Legal Immig.	Pct. Under-Count	1990 Population			1990 Undocumented			
				Legals Cnted.	Total Legals	Census F-B	Convent. Resid.	Counted Resid.	Total Undoc.	INS
Total	536	16,862	4.5%	16,648	17,399	19,682	2,283	3,034	3,471	3,197
1985-1990	536	3,125	6.8%	3,449	3,662	4,848	1,187	1,399	1,658	
1980-1984	0	3,388	6.1%	3,180	3,388	3,776	388	596	682	
Pre-1980	0	10,349	3.2%	10,019	10,349	11,058	709	1,039	1,131	
N & C Amer.	65	6,840	7.0%	6,423	6,905	8,328	1,423	1,904	2,268	2,437
Canada	22	692	0.7%	710	715	744	29	34	34	69
Mexico	17	3,558	8.7%	3,264	3,576	4,474	899	1,210	1,445	1,678
1985-1990	17	664	5.9%	615	681	1,331	650	716	872	
1980-1984	0	844	5.9%	761	844	910	66	150	183	
Pre-1980	0	2,051	5.9%	1,889	2,051	2,233	182	344	391	
Central Amer.	10	749	8.9%	692	759	1,170	411	478	578	468
Guatemala	2	147	9.1%	135	149	230	81	95	114	87
El Salvador	0	297	9.2%	270	297	482	185	213	257	262
Belize	0	25	8.8%	23	26	31	5	7	9	9
Honduras	2	74	9.2%	69	75	109	34	41	49	38
Nicaragua	2	72	8.9%	67	73	172	99	105	127	60
Costa Rica	2	34	8.7%	32	35	45	10	13	15	3
Panama	2	70	8.6%	66	72	85	12	18	21	7
Oth. N&C Am.	0	30	5.4%	29	30	15	-15	-13	-13	3

	15	1,840	5.4%	1,757	1,856	1,940	84	183	210	222
Caribbean, tot.										
Bahamas	1	14	8.6%	14	15	22	7	8	10	24
Cuba	0	752	0.6%	747	752	765	13	17	18	7
Jamaica	4	312	8.8%	289	316	332	16	44	51	31
Haiti	2	199	9.2%	183	201	225	24	42	48	61
Dom. Republic	3	349	9.0%	321	352	361	9	40	47	35
Dominica	0	8	9.4%	7	8	18	11	11	13	6
Barbados	0	32	8.7%	30	32	42	10	12	14	5
Trinidad & Tobago	2	76	4.0%	76	79	117	38	41	43	26
Other Carib.	2	98	9.1%	92	101	58	-43	-34	-34	27
	40	892	5.8%	881	932	1,057	125	176	199	124
S. America, tot.										
Colombia	5	245	4.0%	240	250	295	45	55	59	46
Venezuela	3	41	3.9%	43	45	42	-2	-1	0	1
Guyana	1	121	9.2%	111	122	119	-3	8	11	13
Ecuador	1	129	8.7%	119	130	144	14	26	30	33
Peru	9	111	4.1%	115	119	147	28	33	35	13
Bolivia	1	24	8.9%	23	25	31	6	8	10	7
Brazil	13	57	8.8%	65	70	83	13	18	22	2
Argentina	4	82	3.7%	83	86	96	10	13	14	3
Chile	2	52	3.9%	52	54	57	3	5	6	4
Oth. S. Amer.	1	30	3.9%	30	31	41	10	11	12	2

Table 3.9 (*continued*)

(Populations in thousands)

Country or Area of Birth	Census Non-Immig.	1990 Legal Immig.	Pct. Under-Count	1990 Population			1990 Undocumented			
				Legals Cnted.	Total Legals	Census F-B	Convent. Resid.	Counted Resid.	Total Undoc.	INS
Asia, tot.	*304*	*4,604*	*3.6%*	*4,744*	*4,909*	*5,132*	*223*	*388*	*418*	*261*
Middle East, tot.	*33*	*554*	*2.8%*	*572*	*588*	*617*	*29*	*44*	*47*	*65*
Turkey	3	54	3.4%	55	57	54	-3	-1	-1	2
Syria	2	36	3.7%	36	38	38	0	1	2	3
Lebanon	3	72	1.1%	74	75	89	14	15	15	13
Israel/Palestine	6	83	1.0%	88	89	106	17	18	18	10
Jordan	2	42	4.0%	42	43	31	-13	-11	-11	5
Iraq	1	38	3.5%	38	39	44	5	6	7	1
Iran	9	192	3.8%	193	201	212	11	18	19	31
Other Mid-East	8	38	1.0%	46	46	43	-3	-2	-2	1
S & E Asia, tot.	*271*	*4,050*	*3.7%*	*4,172*	*4,321*	*4,515*	*194*	*344*	*371*	*195*
Afghanistan	0	29	2.5%	29	29	28	-1	0	0	2
Pakistan	7	91	7.5%	91	98	87	-11	-4	-4	19
India	25	433	6.8%	429	459	471	12	42	45	19
Bangladesh	2	21	8.0%	21	23	22	-1	1	1	4
Sri Lanka	2	10	6.6%	11	12	14	2	3	3	5
Korea	28	539	2.3%	555	567	581	14	26	27	10
Japan	96	185	2.0%	277	281	298	17	20	22	2
China+	63	815	2.6%	857	878	958	79	101	107	27

Philippines	17	866	3.9%	849	883	940	57	91	98	89
Thailand	7	93	3.6%	97	100	108	8	11	12	0
Cambodia	0	127	3.9%	122	127	121	-6	-1	0	0
Laos	0	202	3.9%	194	202	179	-23	-15	-15	0
Vietnam	0	550	3.6%	530	550	586	37	57	61	0
Malaysia	11	14	2.4%	25	25	33	7	8	8	8
Oth. S&E Asia	14	73	2.2%	85	87	90	4	5	5	11
Europe, tot.	*82*	*4,122*	*0.8%*	*4,170*	*4,204*	*4,369*	*165*	*199*	*209*	*203*
Scandinavia	9	149	0.6%	156	157	161	4	5	5	3
United Kingdom	19	596	0.6%	611	615	646	31	35	36	5
Ireland	3	160	0.7%	161	163	172	10	11	11	31
Netherlands	3	91	0.6%	94	95	95	0	1	1	0
France	9	106	0.6%	114	115	121	6	6	7	2
Germany	11	694	0.6%	701	706	714	9	13	13	0
Portugal	1	189	0.6%	188	189	215	26	27	27	25
Spain	5	66	0.6%	70	71	79	8	9	9	2
Italy	3	566	0.6%	566	569	579	10	14	14	12
Greece	2	171	0.6%	172	173	176	2	4	4	7
Poland	6	351	1.3%	353	357	394	37	41	46	88
Hungary	2	116	0.9%	117	118	111	-7	-6	-5	2
Romania	0	90	1.9%	89	90	95	5	6	7	3
Fmr. Yugoslavia	2	130	1.0%	130	131	139	8	9	9	14
Former USSR	0	386	1.7%	379	386	397	11	18	20	4
Other Europe	8	262	0.6%	268	270	275	5	7	7	5

Table 3.9 (continued)

(Populations in thousands)

Country or Area of Birth	Census Non-Immig.	1990 Legal Immig.	Pct. Under-Count	1990 Population			1990 Undocumented			
				Legals Cnted.	Total Legals	Census F-B	Convent. Resid.	Counted Resid.	Total Undoc.	INS
Africa, tot.	*24*	*309*	*5.8%*	*315*	*333*	*370*	*36*	*55*	*63*	*78*
Egypt	3	61	4.1%	61	64	69	5	8	8	9
Other N. Africa	2	30	4.0%	30	31	35	3	4	5	2
Cape Verde	0	11	7.6%	10	11	16	5	6	6	3
Sierra Leone	0	6	7.5%	5	6	7	1	2	2	5
Liberia	0	10	7.3%	10	11	11	0	1	1	9
Ghana	1	19	7.4%	18	20	21	1	2	3	7
Nigeria	3	52	7.1%	51	54	57	3	7	9	13
Ethiopia	2	31	8.0%	31	33	36	3	6	7	6
South Africa	3	24	1.0%	27	27	35	7	8	8	3
Other Africa	10	67	6.9%	72	77	84	7	12	15	20
Oceania, tot.	*6*	*93*	*1.6%*	*97*	*99*	*105*	*6*	*8*	*8*	*12*
Australia	4	40	0.6%	44	44	41	-3	-2	-2	0
Other Oceania	2	53	1.9%	53	55	63	9	10	10	12
All Other	*15*	*1*	*0.6%*	*16*	*16*	*321*	*305*	*305*	*307*	*82*

the additional undercount adjustments proportionately based on the overall census undercount rates. For example, legal immigrants from European countries received an overall census adjustment of only 0.6 percent, so the most recent entry cohort received an additional adjustment of 0.5 percent, and earlier cohorts received none.

For the CPS, we assumed that the additional undercount is slightly less than in the census because of the use of trained interviewers. Accordingly, we assume the additional undercount rates are half to three-quarters of those assumed for the census. We again reduce the rate of additional undercount for those cohorts who have been in the United States longer. Thus, those entering during 1985–1989 suffer half the rate of additional undercount of those entering during the 1990s; those entering during 1980–1984, one-quarter the rate; and those entering before 1980, no additional undercount.

Residual Estimates of Covered Undocumented Aliens (Adjusted for Undercount of Legal Immigrants)

The adjustment for undercount of legal immigrants raises the estimate of undocumented aliens included in the 1995 CPS by 127,000, or 2.7 percent, from 4.7 million to 4.8 million (Tables 3.7 and 3.8). The new estimate differs by 100,000 from the interpolated INS estimate for the same date. The new estimate of undocumented aliens counted in the 1990 Census is 3.0 million (Tables 3.9 and 3.10). The increase over the conventional residual estimate is 751,000 or 33 percent. The change from the conventional estimate is much greater in 1990 than in 1995 because the undercount rate for legal immigrants in the 1990 Census is much greater than in the 1995 CPS.

The percentage of undocumented aliens arriving in the five years before the estimate date also increases in the adjusted estimates, principally because this group is assumed to have higher undercounts. In 1995, about 58 percent, or 3.0 million, had been in the United States for less than five years, and 24 percent for more than ten years. With the adjustment, the distribution for 1990 changes in similar ways, with 46 percent in the United States for less than five years and 34 percent for more than ten years.

Mexico and Central America remain the principal sources of illegal immigration for both dates. Mexico still accounts for 53 percent of the illegals in the 1995 CPS, 2.5 million persons. Central America accounts for another 735,000 undocumented aliens, or still about 15 percent of the total. For 1990, the share from these two areas changes only slightly. Mexico now accounts for 1.2 million, or 40 percent of the total undocumented population in the 1990 Census. Central America now accounts for another 478,000, or 16 percent.

Correction for Undercoverage of Undocumented Immigrants. There is even less information available for assessing the undercoverage of undocumented aliens in the CPS and census than for legal immigrants. Bean et al. (1997) conclude that the excess undercount of undocumented aliens in the CPS is 12

Table 3.10
Legal Foreign-Born Population and Undocumented Aliens in 1990, INS Estimates and
Alternative Census-Based Estimates, by Country of Birth

(Populations in thousands)

Country or Area of Birth	Census Non-Immig.	1990 Legal Immig.	Pct. Under-Count	1990 Population			1990 Undocumented			
				Legals Cnted.	Total Legals	Census F-B	Convent. Resid.	Counted Resid.	Total Undoc.	INS
Total	536	16,862	4.5%	16,648	17,399	19,682	2,283	3,034	3,471	3,197
1985-1990	536	3,125	6.8%	3,449	3,662	4,848	1,187	1,399	1,658	
1980-1984	0	3,388	6.1%	3,180	3,388	3,776	388	596	682	
Pre-1980	0	10,349	3.2%	10,019	10,349	11,058	709	1,039	1,131	
N & C Amer.	65	6,840	7.0%	6,423	6,905	8,328	1,423	1,904	2,268	2,437
Canada	22	692	0.7%	710	715	744	29	34	34	69
Mexico	17	3,558	8.7%	3,264	3,576	4,474	899	1,210	1,445	1,678
Central Amer.	10	749	8.9%	692	759	1,170	411	478	578	468
Guatemala	2	147	9.1%	135	149	230	81	95	114	87
El Salvador	0	297	9.2%	270	297	482	185	213	257	262
Honduras	2	74	9.2%	69	75	109	34	41	49	38
Nicaragua	2	72	8.9%	67	73	172	99	105	127	60
Oth. N&C Am.	4	159	8.1%	151	164	176	12	25	32	22
Caribbean, tot.	15	1,840	5.4%	1,757	1,856	1,940	84	183	210	222
Cuba	0	752	0.6%	747	752	765	13	17	18	7
Jamaica	4	312	8.8%	289	316	332	16	44	51	31
Haiti	2	199	9.2%	183	201	225	24	42	48	61
Dom. Republic	3	349	9.0%	321	352	361	9	40	47	35
Other Carib.	6	228	7.3%	217	234	257	22	39	46	88

	40	*892*	*5.8%*	*881*	*932*	*1,057*	*125*	*176*	*199*	*124*
S. America, tot.	40	892	5.8%	881	932	1,057	125	176	199	124
Colombia	5	245	4.0%	240	250	295	45	55	59	46
Guyana	1	121	9.2%	111	122	119	-3	8	11	13
Ecuador	1	129	8.7%	119	130	144	14	26	30	33
Peru	9	111	4.1%	115	119	147	28	33	35	13
Oth. S. Amer.	24	287	5.2%	296	311	351	40	55	63	20
Middle East, tot.	33	554	2.8%	572	588	617	29	44	47	65
Iran	9	192	3.8%	193	201	212	11	18	19	31
Iraq	1	38	3.5%	38	39	44	5	6	7	1
Other Mid-East	24	324	2.1%	341	348	361	13	19	21	33
S & E Asia, tot.	271	4,050	3.7%	4,172	4,321	4,515	194	344	371	195
China+	63	815	2.6%	857	878	958	79	101	107	27
India	25	433	6.8%	429	459	471	12	42	45	19
Korea	28	539	2.3%	555	567	581	14	26	27	10
Philippines	17	866	3.9%	849	883	940	57	91	98	89
Oth. S&E Asia	138	1,396	3.7%	1,482	1,534	1,566	32	84	94	50
Europe, tot.	82	4,122	0.8%	4,170	4,204	4,369	165	199	209	203
United Kingdom	19	596	0.6%	611	615	646	31	35	36	5
Portugal	1	189	0.6%	188	189	215	26	27	27	25
Poland	6	351	1.3%	353	357	394	37	41	46	88
Romania	0	90	1.9%	89	90	95	5	6	7	3
Former USSR	0	386	1.7%	379	386	397	11	18	20	4
Other Europe	56	2,510	0.7%	2,550	2,567	2,622	55	72	73	78
Africa (x-Ethiopia)	22	279	5.6%	285	300	334	33	49	56	71
Ethiopia	2	31	8.0%	31	33	36	3	6	7	6
Other & Unknown	21	94	1.6%	114	115	426	311	312	315	94

percent versus 4 percent for legal immigrants. We follow their assumption by assuming that the additional adjustment required for undercount of undocumented aliens is three times the rate used for undercount of legal immigrants. For 1990, this undercount rate must be added to the assumption regarding general undercount.

Residual-Based Estimates of the Total Undocumented Alien Population (Fully Adjusted for Undercount of Legal and Illegal Immigrants)

The final adjustment for undercount of illegal immigrants yields an estimate of 5.1 million undocumented aliens in the country in 1995. This estimate is 406,000 higher than the conventional residual estimate and 377,000 or 8.0 percent greater than the INS estimate of 4.7 million for the same date (Tables 3.5 and 3.6). The residual-based estimate implies an excess undercount rate of 5.4 percent. The effect of this final adjustment on the 1990 estimates is even greater. The final estimate for 1990 is almost 3.5 million undocumented aliens, a figure that exceeds the INS estimate of 3.2 million by 274,000, or 8.6 percent.

Mexico accounts for 54 percent of the undocumented population in 1995, or 2.7 million persons. Central America accounts for another 767,000 undocumented aliens, or 15 percent of the total, with 282,000 from El Salvador. Only three other individual countries exceed 100,000—Haiti (138,000), India (126,000), and China (124,000)—although Nicaragua and Guatemala would undoubtedly exceed this mark if separate estimates were available. After Mesoamerica, the source regions of undocumented aliens in 1995 are well distributed around the world: South and East Asia (346,000, or 6.8 percent), the Caribbean (309,000, or 6.1 percent), Europe (263,000, or 5.2 percent), and South America (247,000, or 4.8 percent).

With these new data, it is possible to assess the composition of the foreign-born population with regard to legal status at entry because we now have estimates for the entire population (Table 3.11). Overall, undocumented immigrants accounted for 21 percent of the foreign-born population in 1995. For those entering in the 1990s, fully 43 percent are undocumented.

For Mexican immigrants, the percentages undocumented are about double the overall figures, with undocumented aliens accounting for 41 percent of the Mexican-born population and 90 percent of those entering during the 1990s. The percentage undocumented has increased over the last five years. For the 1985–1989 entry cohort of Mexicans, 40 percent are undocumented. However, another 37 percent acquired legal status through IRCA. The analysis of 1990 data (not shown) supports this result, as 56 percent of the 1985–1990 entrants were undocumented in 1990, but 79 percent were either undocumented or legalized.

The Central American immigrants have a very different pattern. About 57 percent of Central American arrivals in the 1990s remain undocumented (not shown separately). However, for the 1985–1989 arrival cohort, about 65 percent are undocumented, and another 5 percent of the cohort are legalized. Thus, the earlier cohort has a higher percentage undocumented, according to our estimates. This pattern reflects two phenomena. First, the improved political situation in Central America appears to have led to a decrease in undocumented migration, possibly augmented by return migration. Second, our methodological treatment of applicants for asylum, of whom there are large numbers from Central America, leads to higher estimates for periods when the applicants arrived. Specifically, we do not include asylum applicants in our estimate of legal residents. However, they cannot be deported while their applications are pending and are not technically "undocumented" or illegal. As a result, our estimates of the undocumented population are too high, as are the INS estimates for the same reason.

Evaluation of the Residual-Based Estimates

1990 Estimates. The patterns shown by the residual estimates are generally consistent with "conventional wisdom" regarding undocumented immigrants, in terms of the origins, entry patterns, and age-sex structure. In this section, we conduct a more systematic evaluation by comparing the estimates with the INS estimates for 1990 and by examining the residual estimates for internal inconsistencies and anomalies. Any internal contradictions may identify estimation errors or other data problems. Differences with INS could be attributable to errors in either set of estimates.

One overall issue affecting the census-based residual estimates is the large estimated number of undocumented immigrants for the "other & unknown" category—305,000, or 13 percent of the total. This large figure is almost entirely attributable to the 1990 Census population, which has more than 300,000 persons with no country of birth reported, even after allocating those with some codable information. The census foreign-born actually belong in specific countries. Were they properly classified, the residual estimates of undocumented aliens would be higher for some of the specific countries.[15] This reporting problem should be kept in mind when evaluating the estimates.

A second general issue concerns the estimates of negative numbers of undocumented aliens. These estimates occur when the 1990 Census figure is smaller than the estimated legally resident population. Small negative estimates can arise just by chance; that is, both the 1980 data used for the legal population and the 1990 Census data are from samples and thus are subject to sampling error. When the "true" estimate for a cell (e.g., country-period) is no undocumented aliens, half of the time the residual estimate will be negative because of random variability, *even* if our demographic estimate is completely accurate. Second, if "adjacent" estimates offset one another (e.g., age groups or period-of-entry groups with negative and positive errors), the pattern indicates possible classification problems in the census data or in the estimates. This type of error could arise, for example, if persons arriving in the United States in late 1984

Table 3.11
Legal Status of the Foreign-Born Population in 1995, Corrected for CPS Undercoverage, by Country of Birth

(Populations in thousands. Undocumented alien undercount factor assumed to be 3.0 times undercount of legals)

Country of Birth	Net Legal Immigration							1995	Percent Distribution by Status						
	Reg. LPRs 80-95	Refu-gees 80-95	LAW	SAW	Pre-'80 Legal Immig	Non-Legal Immig	Undoc. Aliens (Tot.)	F-B Pop. (Sum)	Reg. LPRs 80-95	Refu-gees 80-95	LAW	SAW	Pre-'80 Legal Immig	Non-Legal Immig	Undoc. Aliens (Tot.)
All Countries	7,397	1,843	1,550	1,006	7,410	613	5,102	24,921	30%	7%	6%	4%	30%	2%	20%
1990-95	2,755	834	0	0	0	607	2,989	7,185	38%	12%	x	x	x	8%	42%
1985-89	2,515	465	0	674	0	6	889	4,548	55%	10%	0%	15%	x	0%	20%
1980-84	1,872	522	610	301	0	0	509	3,815	49%	14%	16%	8%	x	x	13%
Pre-1980	255	23	940	31	7,410	0	716	9,373	3%	0%	10%	0%	79%	x	8%
Europe, total	820	469	27	3	2,433	103	263	4,118	20%	11%	1%	0%	59%	3%	6%
Poland	138	36	13	0	182	8	74	453	30%	8%	3%	0%	40%	2%	16%
United King.	185	0	4	0	323	24	41	577	32%	0%	1%	0%	56%	4%	7%
Former USSR	61	353	0	0	210	0	81	704	9%	50%	0%	0%	30%	x	11%
Europe, bal.	437	80	9	2	1,718	71	66	2,384	18%	3%	0%	0%	72%	3%	3%
Middle East	351	92	16	3	198	38	69	768	46%	12%	2%	0%	26%	5%	9%
Iran	109	61	11	0	46	11	23	262	42%	23%	4%	0%	18%	4%	9%
Mid.East, bal.	242	31	5	3	152	28	45	505	48%	6%	1%	1%	30%	5%	9%
S & E Asia, tot.	2,638	886	52	45	1,543	316	346	5,826	45%	15%	1%	1%	26%	5%	6%
China	704	14	13	2	344	99	124	1,302	54%	1%	1%	0%	26%	8%	10%
India	394	1	5	14	177	25	126	742	53%	0%	1%	2%	24%	3%	17%
Korea	334	0	4	4	191	47	-24	557	60%	0%	1%	1%	34%	8%	x
Philippines	673	4	17	8	380	12	44	1,138	59%	0%	1%	1%	33%	1%	4%
S&E Asia, bal.	533	867	13	17	450	132	75	2,087	26%	42%	1%	1%	22%	6%	4%

Canada	159	0	6	0	449	32	-56	590	27%	0%	1%	0%	76%	5%	x
Mexico	1,098	0	1,092	825	1,127	16	2,732	6,890	16%	0%	16%	12%	16%	0%	40%
1990-95	362	0	0	0	0	14	1,812	2,188	17%	0%	x	x	x	1%	83%
1985-89	368	0	0	549	0	1	591	1,510	24%	0%	x	36%	x	0%	39%
1980-84	311	0	371	246	0	0	27	955	33%	0%	39%	26%	x	x	3%
Pre-1980	56	0	721	30	1,127	0	303	2,237	3%	x	32%	1%	50%	x	14%
Cent.Am., tot.	451	36	212	41	213	4	767	1,723	26%	2%	12%	2%	12%	0%	45%
El Salvador	180	5	129	20	42	1	282	659	27%	1%	20%	3%	6%	0%	43%
Cent.Am., bal.	271	31	83	20	171	3	485	1,064	25%	3%	8%	2%	16%	0%	46%
Caribbean, tot.	970	299	47	52	898	19	309	2,595	37%	12%	2%	2%	35%	1%	12%
Cuba	58	249	1	0	489	0	24	822	7%	30%	0%	0%	60%	x	3%
Dom. Rep.	373	0	13	6	138	2	39	571	65%	0%	2%	1%	24%	0%	7%
Haiti	132	49	13	39	41	0	138	413	32%	12%	3%	9%	10%	x	33%
Jamaica	242	0	10	4	126	5	57	445	54%	x	2%	1%	28%	1%	13%
Carib., bal.	165	1	10	3	104	12	51	344	48%	0%	3%	1%	30%	4%	15%
S.Amer., total	625	4	68	25	402	26	247	1,398	45%	0%	5%	2%	29%	2%	18%
Colombia	158	1	24	7	109	4	60	363	44%	0%	7%	2%	30%	1%	17%
Peru	96	1	12	6	38	1	57	211	46%	0%	5%	3%	18%	0%	27%
S.Amer., bal.	370	2	32	12	255	22	130	823	45%	0%	4%	1%	31%	3%	16%
Africa	228	56	26	9	103	45	77	543	42%	10%	5%	2%	19%	8%	14%
Other & Unk.	57	1	4	2	45	15	348	472	12%	0%	1%	0%	10%	3%	74%

reported that they arrived in the country in 1985. Many negative estimates do indicate estimation problems, usually with emigration or mortality estimates.

The origins shown by the INS and census-based estimates are also generally consistent. Each set has the same first two countries (Mexico and El Salvador), with the estimate for Mexico being lower in the census-based estimate (Table 3.8). Of the top ten countries, seven overlap between the INS and census-based estimates. Of the three countries that the residual-based estimates place in the top ten that the INS estimates do not, one (China) is probably an underestimate by the INS, another (Vietnam) is an error in the residual estimates related to inconsistencies in the country-of-birth data and problems with refugee data, and the third (Jamaica) missed the INS top ten by only 7,000. The three in the INS top ten, but not in the residual-based, include Haiti and Poland, which rank eleventh and thirteenth, respectively, in the residual ranking, and Canada, which appears to have some coverage issues in the 1990 Census. This degree of agreement is actually very close, given the extremely detailed nature of the calculation (i.e., eighty-one different countries or groups). The regional patterns from the two sets also exhibit a great deal of consistency.

To the extent that there are differences between the two, many can be traced to specific problems with one estimate or the other. The four countries of Southeast Asia appear to present some reporting problems within the residual estimates. Using the 1990 Census, Vietnam is estimated to have 61,000 illegal immigrants, or the ninth largest number (Table 3.9). This figure seems incongruous since most Vietnamese are admitted as refugees, and illegal entry is quite difficult. The source of potential estimation problems comes into focus when we note that some of the refugee data are classified by country of chargeability or country of citizenship rather than country of birth and that governmental jurisdiction over parts of Southeast Asia changed often. Paired with the large estimate for Vietnam is a large negative estimate for Laos ($-15,000$) and a smaller one for Cambodia ($-1,000$). Also, we can note that many children admitted as Southeast Asian refugees with their parents were born in refugee camps in Thailand but are "charged" to other countries. In addition, our method of correcting for undercount seems to exacerbate some problems when initial estimates are negative. Thus, if we aggregate the uncorrected estimates for the four countries (Vietnam, Laos, Cambodia, and Thailand), we get a conventional residual estimate of only 16,000 in the 1990 Census compared with a total estimated legal population of 994,000. This difference of 1.6 percent is well within the accuracy of our estimates and should, thus, be considered equivalent to the INS estimate of zero.

Canada, the Dominican Republic, Jamaica, and Haiti all illustrate a similar issue: there are simply too few recent immigrants in the 1990 Census to give an estimate as high as the INS figures. For Canada, the 1990 Census includes 126,000 persons entering in the 1980s. We estimate a legal population for this cohort of 116,000 (to give a conventional residual estimate of 10,000). Thus, there simply aren't enough people in the census to come close to the INS estimate of 69,000. Either the estimate of census coverage of recently arrived Canadians or the INS estimate of visa-overstays is too high by several percentage points. Another possibility is a large number of Canadians residing temporarily in the United States and not showing up in the census. This explanation seems very reasonable given the seasonal patterns of vacation/temporary migration between Canada and the United States; many of these persons may be only temporarily resident in the United States as illegals.

Haiti and the Dominican Republic present a somewhat different set of issues. There are actually fewer Haitians in the 1990 Census arriving in the 1980s than there are in the legal arrival data for the period (148,000 versus 135,000); the same is true of Dominicans (200,000 versus 193,000). The overall residual estimates of 24,000 and 9,000 come principally from pre-1980 illegals. The INS estimates of 61,000 and 35,000 are difficult to reconcile with the census data. As with other countries, poor census coverage is always possible. For Haiti, the difficulty of accounting for refugee arrivals by sea and the possibility of clandestine arrivals may contribute to the large differences. Another possibility is related to other Caribbean countries.

The principal sources of nonrefugee migration from the Caribbean all exhibit patterns of circular migration (Pessar 1994). These patterns could lead to significant reporting problems whereby immigrants granted legal status in the 1970s moved back and forth a number of times before eventually settling in the United States. If circular migrants report their year of immigration as their most recent move (in the 1980s), we would see just the pattern captured in the data, because the INS data record them as migrating much earlier. In addition, substantial movement back and forth between the Caribbean countries and the United States increases the possibility of overestimating overstays with the INS methodology because a significant portion of the flow is repetitive movement, not unique individuals. Much higher levels of immediate return migration than are in the estimates could also contribute to the observed pattern.

China is another large source of both legal and illegal immigration, but the census-based estimate of undocumented migration (107,000) is much higher than the INS estimate (27,000). Our analysis of the data suggests that the higher estimate is probably correct. The INS estimate explicitly excludes foreign students, who make up a significant proportion of the Chinese population in the United States. Overstayers from this population could certainly contribute to the undocumented Chinese population. Further, Chinese undocumented immigrants are known to be a part of the EWI stream both through Mexico and on ships, such as the *Golden Venture*, which ran aground in New York Harbor in 1993. These sources of Chinese undocumented migration are known to be only partially captured by the INS methods, so that the higher residual estimates appear to be reasonable.

1995 Estimates. The sources of undocumented aliens and their arrival patterns in 1995 are very similar to the results for 1990. Our evaluation is somewhat more limited for 1995 because we have fewer country-specific estimates to compare with the INS estimates. The evaluation does investigate internal contradictions and search for anomalies resulting from the smaller CPS sample.

The period-of-entry data show some minor inconsistencies with the 1990 estimates. For the same entry cohort observed at five years apart, we would expect to have significantly fewer undocumented immigrants in 1995 than in 1990 from the combination of return migration and individuals progressing to legal status. We find this pattern for the 1985–1990 cohorts: the number of undocumented Mexicans decreased from 872,000 in 1990 to 591,000 in 1995; for non-Mexicans the drop was greater, from 786,000 to 298,000 (Tables 3.7 and 3.9). However, for the pre-1980 arrivals, while the non-Mexicans did decrease substantially (from 740,000 to 413,000), the number of undocumented Mexicans hardly changed (from 391,000 to 303,000). One possibility for explaining this pattern is that coverage of undocumented Mexicans in this cohort may have improved since they have an additional five years in the United States. Otherwise, the 1995 measure of total immigrants in this cohort may be too high just by chance, or the reporting of date of entry may be erroneous. The same pattern can also be found for non-Mexican undocumented immigrants arriving during 1980–1984, where the number decreased by a very small amount, from 499,000 in 1990 to 486,000 in 1995.

The 1995 estimate for the Caribbean shows the same pattern found in 1990—a majority of the undocumented immigration comes from cohorts that have been in the United States for a long time (i.e., since before 1980). Haiti is a slight exception, as we do show 59,000 undocumented aliens from Haiti arriving during 1990–1995. Unusual patterns of return migration, as noted earlier, may explain these estimates.

Sampling anomalies loom large for some countries. Our estimate for Canada, −56,000, is totally implausible. Examination of the detailed data shows that our estimate for the pre-1980 entry cohort is −79,000; in other words, the CPS figure is 79,000 less than the estimate for legal residents. The figure for pre-1980 Canadians dropped considerably in the 1997 CPS and contributed to a low estimate for 1995. Were we to use the average of 1995 and 1996 for this cohort, the estimate of undocumented aliens would be close to zero. Likewise, Korea shows a large and unusual drop in the CPS populations versus the 1990 Census for the 1985–1990 cohort in 1996 and 1997 and for the pre-1980 cohort in 1996.[16] The residual estimates for these two cohorts are large negative numbers, consistent with the idea that the CPS figures represent sampling anomalies.

Comparison of the residual-based estimates of the total undocumented population with the INS figures for 1995 shows extreme consistency on the numbers of undocumented immigrants and broad agreement on their origins, as was found in 1990. To the extent that there remain differences, some of the same patterns and issues are repeated from the 1990 estimates. The total number of undocumented aliens is 8 percent higher than the INS estimate; for Mexico, the 1995 estimate exceeds the INS figure by 184,000, or 7 percent, unlike 1990, when the INS estimate was higher. The largest three sources—Mexico, other Central

Table 3.12

Major Sources of Undocumented Immigration, 1995: CPS Residual-Based Total and INS Estimates

(Populations in thousands)

Country of Birth	Estimated Total Undocumented Population						Difference CPS minus INS	
	CPS Residual-Based Total			INS				
	Number	Pct.	Rank	Number	Pct.	Rank	In Amt.	In Pct.
All Countries	*5,102*	*100.0*	*(x)*	*4,725*	*100.0*	*(x)*	*377*	*(x)*
Mexico	2,732	53.5	1	2,548	53.9	1	184	-0.4
Oth. C. Amer.	485	9.5	2	334	7.1	2	151	2.4
El Salvador	282	5.5	3	324	6.9	3	-41	-1.3
Haiti	138	2.7	4	99	2.1	8	40	0.6
Oth. S. Amer.	130	2.5	5	97	2.1	9	32	0.5
India	126	2.5	6	31	0.7	18	95	1.8
China	124	2.4	7	36	0.8	17	88	1.7
Former USSR	81	1.6	8	17	0.3	22	64	1.2
Africa, balance	77	1.5	9	111	2.4	7	-34	-0.8
Oth S&E Asia	75	1.5	10	84	1.8	11	-9	-0.3
Poland	74	1.5	11	71	1.5	12	3	0.0
Other Europe	66	1.3	12	133	2.8	5	-67	-1.5
Colombia	60	1.2	13	63	1.3	14	-3	-0.1
Peru	57	1.1	14	28	0.6	19	30	0.5
Jamaica	57	1.1	15	47	1.0	16	11	0.1
Other Carib.	51	1.0	16	156	3.3	4	-105	-2.3
Oth. Mid-East	45	0.9	17	50	1.0	15	-4	-0.2
Philippines	44	0.9	18	95	2.0	10	-51	-1.1
United King.	41	0.8	19	6	0.1	24	35	0.7
Domin. Rep.	39	0.8	20	69	1.5	13	-30	-0.7
Cuba	24	0.5	21	8	0.2	23	17	0.3
Iran	23	0.5	22	26	0.5	21	-2	-0.1
Korea	-24	-0.5	23	27	0.6	20	-51	-1.0
Canada	-56	-1.1	24	111	2.4	6	-167	-3.5
Other & Unk.	348	6.8	(x)	156	3.3	(x)	192	3.5

America, and El Salvador—represent 68.5 percent of the CPS-based estimates and 67.9 percent in the INS estimates (Table 3.12), percentages from Mexico having risen since 1990 (see Table 3.13). Haiti, other South America, and Africa are in the top ten sources in both. India and China are much higher in the CPS-based estimates; Canada and other Caribbean are much lower. The regions also tend to be very close in percentages (Table 3.14):

Central America—15.0 percent in the CPS-based estimates versus 13.9 in INS;

Caribbean—6.1 versus 8.0 percent;

South America—4.8 versus 4.0 percent;

Middle East—1.3 versus 1.6 percent;

Table 3.13

Major Sources of Undocumented Immigration, 1990: Census Residual-Based Total and INS Estimates

(Populations in thousands)

Country of Birth	Estimated Total Undocumented Population						Difference Census minus INS	
	Census Residual-Based Tot.			INS				
	Number	Pct.	Rank	Number	Pct.	Rank	In Amt.	In Pct.
All Countries	*3,471*	*100.0*	*(x)*	*3,197*	*100.0*	*(x)*	*274*	*(x)*
Mexico	1,445	41.6	1	1,678	52.5	1	-232	-10.8
El Salvador	257	7.4	2	262	8.2	2	-5	-0.8
Nicaragua	127	3.7	3	60	1.9	8	67	1.8
Guatemala	114	3.3	4	87	2.7	5	27	0.6
China	107	3.1	5	27	0.8	17	81	2.3
Philippines	98	2.8	6	89	2.8	3	10	0.1
Vietnam	61	1.8	7	0	0.0	76	61	1.8
Colombia	59	1.7	8	46	1.4	9	13	0.3
Jamaica	51	1.5	9	31	1.0	15	20	0.5
Honduras	49	1.4	10	38	1.2	10	11	0.2
Haiti	48	1.4	11	61	1.9	7	-13	-0.5
Dom. Republic	47	1.4	12	35	1.1	11	12	0.3
Poland	46	1.3	13	88	2.7	4	-42	-1.4
India	45	1.3	14	19	0.6	23	26	0.7
Trinidad & Tob.	43	1.2	15	26	0.8	18	17	0.4
United Kingdom	36	1.0	16	5	0.2	45	30	0.9
Peru	35	1.0	17	13	0.4	25	22	0.6
Canada	34	1.0	18	69	2.2	6	-35	-1.2
Ecuador	30	0.9	19	33	1.0	12	-2	-0.1
Portugal	27	0.8	20	25	0.8	19	3	0.0
Iran	19	0.6	26	31	1.0	13	-12	-0.4
Ireland	11	0.3	40	31	1.0	14	-21	-0.7
Bahamas	10	0.3	43	24	0.7	20	-14	-0.5
Other Caribbean	-34	-1.0	80	27	0.9	16	-61	-1.8
Other & Unk.	307	8.9	(x)	82	2.6	(x)	225	6.3

South and East Asia—6.8 versus 5.8 percent;

Europe—5.1 versus 4.8 percent;

Africa—1.5 versus 2.4 percent.

As with the 1990 estimates, all of the CPS-based estimates for the specific areas should probably be a little bit higher because the residual "other and unknown" category has too many CPS respondents.

China has a larger number of undocumented aliens in the CPS estimates (124,000) than in the INS figures (36,000). This situation is consistent with the previous discussion in that the INS figure omits student overstayers and understates EWIs. As in 1990, the "other Caribbean" is much lower in the CPS-

Table 3.14

Total Undocumented Alien Population in 1995, by Country of Birth: CPS Residual-Based Total and INS Estimates

(Populations in thousands)

Country of Birth	Population			Estimated Undocumented Population				Difference: CPS Total minus INS	
	1990 Census	1995 CPS F-B	1995 Legal Est.	Residual-Based		INS			
				Pop.	Pct.	Pop.	Pct.	Amount	Pct.
All Countries	*19,682*	*24,515*	*19,819*	*5,102*	*100.0*	*4,725*	*100.0*	*377*	*8*
Canada	*744*	*589*	*646*	*-56*	*-1.1*	*111*	*2.4*	*-167*	*(x)*
Mexico	*4,474*	*6,671*	*4,158*	*2,732*	*53.5*	*2,548*	*53.9*	*184*	*7*
Central America	*1,170*	*1,681*	*956*	*767*	*15.0*	*657*	*13.9*	*110*	*17*
El Salvador	482	637	377	282	5.5	324	6.9	-41	-13
Oth. C. Amer.	687	1,044	579	485	9.5	334	7.1	151	45
Caribbean	*1,940*	*2,570*	*2,285*	*309*	*6.1*	*378*	*8.0*	*-69*	*-18*
Cuba	765	821	798	24	0.5	8	0.2	17	212
Domin. Rep.	361	558	532	39	0.8	69	1.5	-30	-44
Haiti	225	407	275	138	2.7	99	2.1	40	40
Jamaica	332	440	388	57	1.1	47	1.0	11	22
Other Carib.	257	343	294	51	1.0	156	3.3	-105	-68
South America	*1,057*	*1,376*	*1,150*	*247*	*4.8*	*187*	*4.0*	*60*	*32*
Colombia	295	357	303	60	1.2	63	1.3	-3	-4
Peru	147	210	154	57	1.1	28	0.6	30	109
Oth. S. Amer.	615	809	694	130	2.5	97	2.1	32	33
Middle East	*617*	*760*	*699*	*69*	*1.3*	*75*	*1.6*	*-6*	*-8*
Iran	212	260	239	23	0.5	26	0.5	-2	-9
Oth. Mid-East	405	500	460	45	0.9	50	1.0	-4	-8
S & E Asia	*4,515*	*5,762*	*5,480*	*346*	*6.8*	*274*	*5.8*	*73*	*27*
China	958	1,296	1,178	124	2.4	36	0.8	88	244
India	471	733	616	126	2.5	31	0.7	95	303
Korea	581	556	581	-24	-0.5	27	0.6	-51	-187
Philippines	940	1,118	1,093	44	0.9	95	2.0	-51	-53
Oth S&E Asia	1,566	2,059	2,012	75	1.5	84	1.8	-9	-11
Europe	*4,369*	*4,102*	*3,855*	*263*	*5.1*	*228*	*4.8*	*35*	*15*
Poland	394	450	378	74	1.5	71	1.5	3	4
United King.	646	577	536	41	0.8	6	0.1	35	(x)
Former USSR	397	693	623	81	1.6	17	0.3	64	(x)
Other Europe	2,932	2,383	2,317	66	1.3	133	2.8	-67	-50
Africa	*370*	*531*	*467*	*77*	*1.5*	*111*	*2.4*	*-34*	*-31*
Other & Unk.	*426*	*472*	*124*	*348*	*6.8*	*156*	*3.3*	*192*	*123*

based estimates (51,000) than in the INS estimates (156,000). The INS estimates for the Caribbean are clearly too high for some of the smaller countries (especially notable in 1996 is the Bahamas at 70,000). The INS overstay estimates probably overestimate overstayers because of the sheer volume of traffic from some of these countries. Thus, the CPS-based estimate is surely more accurate.

For Canada and the Philippines, the CPS estimates are substantially lower than the INS estimates. The estimate for Canada is seriously affected by CPS sampling variability, but even if it were not, it would be too low. Similarly, the CPS population for the Philippines may be affected by sampling considerations in 1996 and 1997. For both of these countries, misestimation of mortality and emigration is probably the culprit in yielding lower estimates than does the INS method. Although the INS estimates may be somewhat too high, especially for Canada, the CPS numbers are too small.

Mexican Undocumented Migration. In October 1995, there were 4,157,000 Mexicans living legally in the United States, with 2,732,000 undocumented residents, according to our estimates. Our legal estimate differs considerably from the Binational Study's estimate of 4.8 million legal Mexicans for 1996 (Bean et al. 1997). The source of the difference is not clear from the published materials since our estimate actually has a slightly *larger* SAW population (825,000 versus 727,000). Because of the higher estimate of legal residents, the Binational Study has a smaller figure for undocumented Mexicans—2.3 million. Our CPS-based estimate of undocumented Mexicans is also slightly higher than that of the INS (Warren 1997)—2.5 million—which, in turn, is also higher than the Binational Study estimate. The period-of-entry data and legal population data are more consistent with the INS and residual-based estimates than with the binational figures.

More than four out of every five Mexicans moving to the United States do so as undocumented immigrants. This level has been roughly consistent for the last twenty years. (See Warren and Passel 1987 for 1980 estimates; Table 3.9 in this chapter for 1990 and Table 3.11 for 1995.) During the 1990s, the percentage undocumented appears to have increased somewhat—to nine out of ten. IRCA's legalization programs of the 1980s and return migration have reduced the actual percentage of earlier entry cohorts that remained undocumented in 1995. About 40 percent of 1985–1989 entrants still living in the United States in 1995 were undocumented. For pre-1985 entrants from Mexico, only about 10 percent were still undocumented in 1995.

Annual Flow of Undocumented Immigrants

The residual-based estimates do not provide direct measures of the annual inflow or outflow of undocumented immigrants. However, we can make inferences about recent inflows and net flows over time from the estimates. The residual-based estimate of undocumented immigrants entering in the most recent period before the estimate date is a reasonable approximation of the *inflow* during the period. The data suggest that the inflows are very high recently. In the 1995 estimates, 2,989,000 undocumented immigrants came to the United States during the 1990s. Based on this figure, the average annual inflow for the

1990s is 520,000 per year (Table 3.15). This figure represents an increase over the 1985–1990 period, as measured by our 1990 residual-based estimates; during this period 2,166,000 undocumented immigrants entered and remained in the country in 1990 (1,658,000 of whom remained undocumented, and 508,000 of whom acquired legal status as SAWs). Thus, the average annual inflow of undocumented immigrants over this five-year period was 413,000.[17]

Using this method, the inflow of undocumented Mexicans was 1,812,000 for 1990–1995 and 1,228,000 for 1985–1990; these figures translate to average annual inflows of Mexican undocumented immigrants of 315,000 for 1990–1995 and 224,000 for 1985–1990. It should be noted that the inflow for the earlier period may be underestimated with this method because the residual-based estimate for 1990 is lower than the INS estimate by 233,000. If this underestimate is concentrated in the most recent arrival period, the average annual inflow estimate would be 44,000 higher.

We can measure *net change* in the undocumented population by subtracting the estimated undocumented population at two points in time; the average annual *net undocumented immigration* is then this difference divided by the number of years between the two measures. Using the residual-based estimates for 1990 and 1995, the net change in the undocumented population is 1,631,000 (5,102,000 minus 3,471,000) for the five-and-one-half-year period. Thus, the average annual net undocumented immigration for 1990–1995 is 296,000 (Table 3.15). The figure derived from the INS estimates for the same period is somewhat lower at 278,000.

Examination of the data in Table 3.15 shows that average annual net undocumented immigration tends to be quite similar for the two different measures (i.e., INS versus residual-based) for almost all of the countries. The most glaring exception is the most important country—Mexico. The INS measures imply average annual immigration from Mexico of 158,000 during the 1990s. The figure from the residual-based measures is almost 50 percent higher at 234,000. This particular measure is sensitive to potential errors in the estimates at *both* dates. As noted earlier, there are a number of indications that the undercount corrections for undocumented Mexicans in the 1990 Census may not have been great enough; were they higher, then the estimated undocumented Mexican population in 1990 would be higher, and estimated net undocumented immigration between 1990 and 1995 would be lower. For illustrative purposes, the INS estimate for 1990 and the residual-based estimate for 1995 imply average annual net undocumented immigration from Mexico of 192,000. Regardless of which measures are used, both the inflow and net flow from Mexico are quite high.

Geographic Distribution

We have produced estimates, using the residual method, of undocumented immigrants counted in the 1995 CPS for the major receiving states. The methods

Table 3.15

Average Annual Change in the Undocumented Alien Population, 1990 to 1995, by Country of Birth: Census/CPS Residual-Based Total and INS Estimates

(Populations in thousands)

Country of Birth	Population			Estimated Total Undocumented Population				Average Annual Change, '90-'95	
	1990 Census	1995 CPS F-B	1995 Legal Est.	Residual-Based		INS		Residual-Based	INS
				1995	1990	1995	1990		
All Countries	*19,682*	*24,515*	*19,819*	*5,102*	*3,471*	*4,725*	*3,197*	*296*	*278*
1990s	(x)	6,876	4,196	2,989		(x)	(x)	520	(x)
1985-89	4,848	4,465	3,660	889	1,658	(x)	(x)	-140	(x)
1980-84	3,776	3,800	3,306	509	682	(x)	(x)	-31	(x)
Pre-1980	11,058	9,373	8,658	716	1,131	(x)	(x)	-76	(x)
Canada	*744*	*589*	*646*	*-56*	*34*	*111*	*69*	*-16*	*8*
Mexico	*4,474*	*6,671*	*4,158*	*2,732*	*1,445*	*2,548*	*1,678*	*234*	*158*
1990s	(x)	2,015	377	1,812		(x)	(x)	315	(x)
1985-89	1,331	1,469	919	591	872	(x)	(x)	-51	(x)
1980-84	910	950	928	27	183	(x)	(x)	-28	(x)
Pre-1980	2,233	2,237	1,935	303	391	(x)	(x)	-16	(x)
Central America	*1,170*	*1,681*	*956*	*767*	*578*	*657*	*468*	*34*	*34*
El Salvador	482	637	377	282	257	324	262	5	11
Oth. C. Amer.	687	1,044	579	485	322	334	207	30	23
Caribbean	*1,940*	*2,570*	*2,285*	*309*	*210*	*378*	*222*	*18*	*28*
Cuba	765	821	798	24	18	8	7	1	0
Domin. Rep.	361	558	532	39	47	69	35	-2	6
Haiti	225	407	275	138	48	99	61	16	7
Jamaica	332	440	388	57	51	47	31	1	3
Other Carib.	257	343	294	51	46	156	88	1	12
South America	*1,057*	*1,376*	*1,150*	*247*	*199*	*187*	*124*	*9*	*11*
Colombia	295	357	303	60	59	63	46	0	3
Guyana					0		0	0	0
Peru	147	210	154	57	35	28	13	4	3
Oth. S. Amer.	615	809	694	130	104	97	65	5	6
Middle East	*617*	*760*	*699*	*69*	*47*	*75*	*65*	*4*	*2*
Iran	212	260	239	23	19	26	31	1	-1
Oth. Mid-East	405	500	460	45	28	50	34	3	3
S & E Asia	*4,515*	*5,762*	*5,480*	*346*	*371*	*274*	*195*	*-4*	*14*
China	958	1,296	1,178	124	107	36	27	3	2
India	471	733	616	126	45	31	19	15	2
Korea	581	556	581	-24	27	27	10	-9	3
Philippines	940	1,118	1,093	44	98	95	89	-10	1
Oth S&E Asia	1,566	2,059	2,012	75	94	84	50	-3	6
Europe	*4,369*	*4,102*	*3,855*	*263*	*209*	*228*	*203*	*10*	*4*
Poland	394	450	378	74	46	71	88	5	-3
United King.	646	577	536	41	36	6	5	1	0
Former USSR	397	693	623	81	20	17	4	11	2
Other Europe	2,932	2,383	2,317	66	107	133	107	-7	5
Africa	*370*	*531*	*467*	*77*	*63*	*111*	*78*	*2*	*6*
Other & Unk.	*426*	*472*	*124*	*348*	*315*	*156*	*94*	*6*	*11*

Table 3.16
Undocumented Alien Population in 1995, by State: CPS Estimate of Counted Illegals and INS Estimate

(Populations in thousands)

State of Residence	Population			Undocumented Population				Difference: CPS Counted minus INS	
	Counted Legal Immig.	CPS Non- Immig.	1995 CPS F-B	Counted in 1995 CPS		INS Estimate		In No.	In Pct.
				Number	Pct.	Number	Pct.		
U.S., Total	19,079	613	24,515	4,823	100%	4,725	100%	98	(x)
California	5,853	128	8,153	2,172	45%	1,901	40%	271	5%
Florida	1,718	32	2,131	381	8%	330	7%	51	1%
Illinois	921	22	1,060	117	2%	274	6%	-157	-3%
New Jersey	949	22	1,137	165	3%	127	3%	38	1%
New York	2,721	47	3,196	428	9%	507	11%	-79	-2%
Texas	1,504	21	2,130	605	13%	657	14%	-52	-1%
Other States	5,413	341	6,708	954	20%	929	20%	25	0%

parallel those described earlier for the entire United States, but with two additional steps. First, we assigned each of the immigration components to states using data on destinations and intended residence of incoming LPRs, refugees, LAWs, and SAWs. Then, we estimated internal migration (i.e., migration between states) for each group between their date of entry to the United States and 1995. (See Passel and Clark 1998 for a more complete exposition of the methods used.) We then compared the estimated legal, foreign-born population in each state with the CPS population, after correcting for "excess" undercount of legal immigrants.

Table 3.16 shows the estimates of undocumented immigrants included in the 1995 CPS and INS estimates for six major receiving states. These six states have 80 percent of all undocumented immigrants in the country, according to both sets of estimates. Further, the overall patterns are quite similar. California is estimated to have 2,172,000 undocumented aliens in 1995, or 45 percent of the national total. This estimate is higher than the 1.9 million estimated by INS. The second largest number is the estimate for Texas in both sets of estimates— 605,000, or 13 percent of the total in the CPS-based estimates, and 657,000, or 14 percent in the INS estimate. These are followed in both estimates by New York and Florida, with New York being slightly higher in the INS estimates and Florida slightly higher in the CPS-based estimates.

The major discrepancy between the estimates is found for Illinois, which is estimated by INS to have 274,000 undocumented aliens, or 6 percent of the U.S. total, but only 117,000 in the CPS-based estimates, or 2 percent of the total. The INS estimates use information on relatives of legalized aliens applying for LPR status to ascertain the distribution of undocumented aliens. These data may capture only part of the new undocumented population and so give an inaccurate picture of the geographic distribution. On the other hand, the CPS-based estimates rely on numerous assumptions, particularly regarding internal migration of legal immigrants. As a result, the state-level estimates probably are not extremely precise and may have a significant band of probable error. Thus, the overall agreement of the distributions reinforces the accuracy of both but also suggests that even moderately large differences may not be significant.

CONCLUSION

The undocumented immigrant population of the United States is larger now (and in 1995) than when IRCA was enacted in 1986 to control illegal immigration. Further, the rate of growth has not been curtailed, and the numbers may be increasing faster than during the mid-1980s. The various estimates presented here (INS estimates, CPS-residual estimates, and 1990 Census-based estimates) paint a fairly consistent picture of undocumented immigration in terms of the size of the population, the rate of growth, the countries of origin, and the state-level distribution. A significant majority of undocumented immigrants are from Mexico and Central America. However, there are large and growing numbers from all parts of the world. There are some differences between the two sets of estimates, but these differences are in both directions. Further, investigation of these differences suggests that ''correct'' numbers can be found in each set so that the overall total is relatively unaffected.

Our preferred estimates, the CPS-based estimates of the total undocumented population in 1995, show 5.1 million undocumented aliens in the country as of October 1995. The rate of growth appears to fall in a range of 250,000–300,000 per year. Mexico and Central America account for about 70 percent of the total population and represent the fastest growing component. The INS estimates have slightly lower numbers for the total undocumented population and the amount of annual growth; each of these is 6–8 percent below the census-based estimate. The geographic patterns of origins and destinations are also very similar between the estimates.

Quality of the Estimates

How good are these estimates? They are clearly not definitive, but they appear to be sound and consistent. The INS and CPS/census estimates focus on a fairly narrow range, with around 5 million illegal immigrants in the country as of the mid-1990s, with about half of the total being from Mexico. The INS, binational, and our estimates are empirically based and use relevant, applicable data. Other recent estimates (e.g., Huddle 1993; Simcox 1994) tend to be higher but are speculative, based on little data, and incorporate seriously flawed assumptions. Specifically, these other estimates assume much larger numbers of undocumented aliens who failed to take advantage of IRCA than does Warren (1994, 1997). Such large estimates of unlegalized aliens in 1986 are inconsistent with other evidence from the legalization programs and with data from the 1990 Census and post-1990 CPS (Passel 1994).

The estimates for Mexico appear to be converging on a range around 2.5 million for 1996. The INS, binational, and our estimates are consistent with information from Mexico. Bustamante (1990) and the Mexican government are taking surveys of persons leaving Mexico to estimate the *total* flow to the United States.

New Data, New Trends, and Border Crossers

The March CPSs from 1994 through 1997 provide a unique opportunity to obtain multiple observations on the foreign-born population that can be used to assess trends in the undocumented population. As we note, these CPS data clearly show that undocumented immigration to the United States is continuing at high levels. Other ways of looking at these same CPS data highlight the possibility of newly emerging trends, particularly for Mexican immigration.

In the substantial increase shown in the Mexican-born population since 1990, there is one peculiar, but very interesting and anomalous, result in these data. Specifically, the number of Mexicans in the CPS *who said they came to the United States before 1990* is *greater* than the number of Mexicans counted in the 1990 Census; logically, the CPS figure has to be smaller. This result appears in every year for 1994–1997. One possibility is, of course, the improved coverage in the CPS. However, the increase is greater than can be accounted for by undercount. Another hypothesis for explaining this pattern relates to IRCA's legalizations. Many of the persons who legalized under IRCA (especially the SAWs) did not actually live in the United States when they applied for legal status; rather, they were temporary migrants who lived in Mexico but participated in U.S. agriculture or other low-wage jobs in the United States. After IRCA, these persons acquired an entitlement to settle legally in the United States but were not required to do so. In 1990, many may still have resided in Mexico and so did not participate in the 1990 U.S. Census. By the mid-1990s, however, many of these same persons may have settled in the United States and thus are represented in the March CPS for 1994–1997. In responding to the question of when they came to the United States to stay, these people appear to have given a date before 1990, possibly the date when they acquired legal status or the date of their first trip to the United States.

Another pattern in the CPS is consistent with this explanation and other data (Bustamante 1990). The Mexican-born population entering after 1990 has roughly as many adult women as men, whereas earlier flows contain a much higher proportion of adult men. Also, the proportion under age fifteen among recent entrants is much higher than in previous cohorts. Thus, not only do many of the IRCA legalized aliens appear to be settling in the United States, but they appear to be bringing their wives and families to join them. The Binational Study (Bean et al. 1997) finds similar results.

Flow across the U.S.–Mexico Border.   Although we do not know exactly the magnitude of the flow across our southern border, we have learned a substantial amount about the characteristics of the flow and factors influencing crossings. The main characteristic of the flow is its sheer volume. Every year there are several *hundred million* border crossings (INS 1994). The vast majority are legal and of short duration, being balanced by a very large return flow (Bean et al. 1997). Although there are clearly hundreds of thousands of successful illegal crossings every year, some recent research suggests that there may be as many as 2 million successful *illegal* crossings every year (Espenshade 1990, 1994). There is also clearly a substantial return flow to Mexico of illegal aliens, as many of the illegal aliens enter on a daily or weekly basis to shop or work in border communities (Bean et al. 1994).[18]

With flows this large, even small changes in migrants' propensity to settle in the United States or in the enforcement regimes can result in substantial changes in the number of undocumented aliens residing in the United States. Further, there is a substantial literature supporting the notion that INS enforcement activities, at historical levels, do virtually nothing to deter illegal entry across the U.S.–Mexican border (Massey, Donato, and Liang 1990; Espenshade 1990, 1994; Donato, Durand, and Massey 1992; Kossoudji 1992). The cost of entering is sufficiently low in relation to the potential payoff from working in the United States that the meager penalty for being caught (i.e., being returned across the Mexican border to try entering again) has little or no deterrent effect. The large wage differential between the United States and Mexico makes a successful entry highly lucrative and motivates trips to the United States. However, the principal factor permitting large-scale migration between the United States and Mexico is the established networks of family, friends, and acquaintances built up in the United States over the last thirty or more years (Massey et al. 1994). These networks aid illegal migrants in finding jobs and shelter once in the United States.

Recently, INS has shown that new enforcement strategies can, however, induce some changes in the flow. Operation "Hold the Line" in El Paso saturated the border with Border Patrol officers stationed within sight of one another. This operation has clearly served to reduce what might be termed "casual crossings" (Bean et al. 1994). It also appears that persons heading for points other than El Paso have simply gone around the line in El Paso. Operation "Gatekeeper" in San Diego has added more technology, newer and stronger barriers, and more officers at the border. However, even from early data, this INS operation has forced many potential crossers to shift to Arizona as a port of entry or try a sea route rather than crossing from Tijuana to San Diego. Some apparent reduction in the flow has also been noted. (See Passel 1998c for a discussion of the enforcement strategies.)

This analysis offers an explanation for the phenomenon of a large and rapidly growing undocumented alien population in the face of ever-increasing enforcement and deterrence activities on the part of the INS. Persistent migrants continue to try to enter the United States until they succeed. Once in the country, they are reluctant to leave for fear that a return to the United States will be even more difficult and expensive. The outcome of this scenario is a reduction in circular, temporary migration, but not necessarily a reduction in the inflows to the United States. Survey data also offer support to the notion that increased border enforcement results in longer stays in the United States, but not reductions in the flow. Consistent with this explanation, the Binational Study (Bean et al. 1997) notes that Mexican surveys are finding reductions in return migration. The estimates in this chapter coupled with more detailed analysis of new CPS data showing increased numbers of Mexicans in the CPS and a larger representation of older cohorts are all consistent with this scenario. Clearly, alternative strategies for enforcement and deterrence are required.

NOTES

This is a revised version of a paper presented at a conference on *Managing Migration in the 21st Century: On the Politics and Economics of Illegal Migration* in Hamburg, Germany, on June 21–23, 1998. The conference was sponsored by Universitat Konstanz and the University of California Comparative Immigration and Integration Program with the support of Transcoop Program and the German Marshall Fund of the United States, Edmund Siemers-Stiftung, Europa Kolleg Hamburg. Some of the research reported was conducted under Grant No. 10-P-98348–3-02, "Immigration, Fertility, and the Future American Work Force," from the Social Security Administration with additional funding from the Ford Foundation through the Urban Institute's Program for Research on Immigration Policy. The views expressed are the author's and do not necessarily reflect those of other staff members, officers, or trustees of the Urban Institute, the Ford Foundation, or any other organization financially supporting the researcher's organizations.

1. China includes Taiwan and Hong Kong. We did not make separate estimates for Guatemala or Nicaragua, but these two countries probably have undocumented populations exceeding 100,000.

2. See Edmonston, Passel, and Bean (1990) and Passel (1986) for a review of the various early estimates; Bean et al. (1997) review early estimates for Mexican undocumented migration.

3. For some individuals and groups, the status can be indeterminate, that is neither strictly legal nonimmigrant nor undocumented (illegal). Some examples would include persons whose status may change as a result of judicial decisions or asylum applicants not yet adjudicated. The estimation procedure described does not fully account for this group. Thus, it treats such persons as undocumented, probably overstating the number of illegals.

4. Extrapolation of the earlier INS estimates (Warren 1994) to 1996 would have placed the estimate at 4.6 million versus the 5.0 million in the revised estimate.

5. This problem can affect the other estimates as well; some of these same populations also end up as part of the undocumented population in residual estimates.

6. The other two demographic components—birth and immigration—are not relevant at this stage. The immigrants have already been estimated, and any births that occur are part of the native population.

7. We actually estimate the nonimmigrant population counted in the survey and census, but this definition is dealt with in the estimation process.

8. The selection of countries was guided by the principal countries of origin of undocumented aliens, refugees, and legal immigrants in the six states with the largest numbers of immigrants (California, Florida, Illinois, New Jersey, New York, and Texas). For the 1990 estimates, we used a very detailed set of areas, encompassing eighty-one separate countries of birth or residual areas. Some of the countries have only a few cases in data sources, so that it is necessary to aggregate to regions in some cases to make sense of the estimates.

9. For 1990, we initially produced estimates by period of entry corresponding to the following categories collected in the 1990 Census: 1987–1990, 1985–1986, 1982–1984, 1980–1981, 1975–1979, 1970–1974, 1960–1969, and before 1960. Again, to better interpret the estimates, we collapsed to the periods defined in the text.

10. Includes persons born in Taiwan and Hong Kong. Hereafter, all references to "China" include all three areas.

11. These areas are aggregated in the tabulations because of some issues regarding country of birth. The group also includes a sizable number of children born in refugee camps in Thailand.

12. For 1995, we used an average of the number of nonimmigrants in the March CPSs of 1995–1997.

13. We did not make separate estimates for Guatemala or Nicaragua because of a programming error, but these two countries account for most of the 465,000 undocumented aliens from the rest of Central America.

14. We introduced some minor adjustments, based on the educational attainment and ethnicity of some immigrants. For countries of Southwest Asia and North Africa, we used higher adjustments than those for whites. For South American countries that tend to send highly educated immigrants, we reduced the adjustments slightly from the level used for Hispanics.

15. The remaining "other country" group is unlikely to be from Mexico, Cuba, or other Hispanic countries because individuals with these origins would have been recoded already.

16. Schmidley and Robinson (1998) report on some processing errors that may contribute to this and similar problems.

17. As discussed later, this figure appears to be somewhat too small because of understatement of the undocumented flow from Mexico.

18. In fact, Bean et al. (1994) found that many of the illegal crossers were entitled to enter the United States legally but chose to cross clandestinely because of the lengthy delays at border checkpoints.

REFERENCES

Ahmed, Bashir, and J. Gregory Robinson
1994   Estimates of Emigration of the Foreign-Born Population: 1980–1990. Population Technical Working Paper No. 9. Washington, D.C.: U.S. Bureau of the Census. December.

Baker, Susan González
1990   *The Cautious Welcome: The Legalization Programs of the Immigration Reform and Control Act.* Urban Institute Report 90–9. Washington, D.C.: Program for Research on Immigration Policy, Urban Institute.

Bean, Frank D., Roland Chanove, Robert G. Cushing, Rodolfo de la Garza, Gary Freeman, Charles W. Haynes, and David Spener
1994   Illegal Mexican Migration and the United States/Mexico Border: The Effects of Operation Hold-the-Line on El Paso/Juarez. Report for the U.S. Commission on Immigration Reform. Population Research Center, University of Texas at Austin. July 15.

Bean, Frank D., Rodolfo Corona, Karen Woodrow-Lafield, and Rodolfo Tuiran
1997   *The Quantification of Migration between Mexico and the United States.* Binational Study of Migration between Mexico and the United States. Commission on Immigration Reform: Washington, D.C. July.

Bean, Frank D., Barry Edmonston, and Jeffrey S. Passel, Editors
1990   *Undocumented Migration to the United States: IRCA and the Experience of the 1980s.* Washington, D.C.: Urban Institute Press.

Bean, Frank D., Allan G. King, and Jeffrey S. Passel
1983   The Number of Illegal Migrants of Mexican Origin in the United States: Sex Ratio-Based Estimates for 1980. *Demography* 20 (1):99–110.

Bloch, Louis
1928   Facts about Mexican Immigration before and since the Quota Restriction Laws. *Journal of the American Statistical Association* 50 (March):50–60.

Bureau of the Census
1995   Life Tables for U.S. Population Projections. *Population Division Home Page.* Online, http://www.census.gov.
1996   Population Projections of the United States by Age, Sex, Race, and Hispanic Origin: 1995 to 2050. *Current Population Reports, P25–1130.* Washington, D.C.: U.S. Government Printing Office.
1997   World Population Profile. Appendix Table 4. *Bureau of the Census Home Page.* Online, http://www.census.gov.

Bustamente, Jorge
1990   Undocumented Migration from Mexico to the United States: Preliminary Findings of the Zapata Canyon Project. In *Undocumented Migration to the United States: IRCA and the Experience of the 1980s.* Edited by Frank D. Bean, Barry Edmonston, and Jeffrey S. Passel. Washington, D.C.: Urban Institute Press. Pp. 211–226.

Calavita, Kitty
1994   U.S. Immigration and Policy Responses: The Limits of Legislation. In *Controlling Immigration: A Global Perspective.* Edited by Wayne A. Cornelius, Philip L. Martin, and James F. Hollifield. Stanford: Stanford University Press.

Castillo, Leonel
1978   Statement before the House Select Committee on Population. U.S. House of Representatives. 95th Congress, 2d sess., April 6, 497–515. Washington, D.C.: U.S. Government Printing Office.

Center for Immigration Studies
1994   Immigration-Related Statistics—1994. *Backgrounder* No. 1–94. Washington, D.C. May.

Chapman, Leonard J.
1976   Statement of Leonard J. Chapman. U.S. Senate, Committee on the Judiciary, Subcommittee on Immigration and Naturalization, 94th Cong., 2d sess., March 17. Washington, D.C.: U.S. Government Printing Office.

Clark, Rebecca L., Jeffrey S. Passel, Wendy N. Zimmermann, and Michael Fix
1994   Fiscal Impacts of Undocumented Aliens: Selected Estimates for Seven States. Report to the Department of Justice, September. Washington, D.C.: Urban Institute.

Donato, Katherine M., Jorge Durand, and Douglas S. Massey
1992   Stemming the Tide? Assessing the Deterrent Effects of the Immigration Reform and Control Act. *Demography* 29 (2) (May): 139–157.

Edmonston, Barry, Jeffrey S. Passel, and Frank D. Bean
1990   Perceptions and Estimates of Undocumented Migration to the United States. In *Undocumented Migration to the United States: IRCA and the Experience of the 1980s.* Edited by Frank D. Bean, Barry Edmonston, and Jeffrey S. Passel. Washington, D.C.: Urban Institute Press. Pp. 11–32.

Espenshade, Thomas J.
1990   Undocumented Migration to the United States: Evidence from a Repeated Trials Model. In *Undocumented Migration to the United States: IRCA and the Experience of the 1980s.* Edited by Frank D. Bean, Barry Edmonston, and Jeffrey S. Passel. Washington, D.C.: Urban Institute Press. Pp. 159–182.
1994   Does the Threat of Border Apprehension Deter Undocumented U.S. Immigration? *Population and Development Review 20* (4) (December): 871–892.

Fernandez, Edward J., and J. Gregory Robinson
1994   Illustrative Ranges for the Number of Undocumented Immigrants Residing in the United States: October 1992. Paper presented at California Immigration 1994, a seminar sponsored by the California Research Bureau in Sacramento. Washington, D.C.: U.S. Bureau of the Census. April 29.

Fix, Michael, and Jeffrey S. Passel
1994   *Immigration and Immigrants: Setting the Record Straight.* Washington, D.C.: Urban Institute.

General Accounting Office
1993   *Illegal Aliens: Despite Data Limitations, Current Methods Provide Better Population Estimates.* Program Evaluation and Methodology Division. Report GAO/PEMD-93-25. Washington, D.C. August.
1995   *Illegal Immigration: INS Overstay Estimation Methods Need Improvement.* Program Evaluation and Methodology Division. Report GAO/PEMD-95-20. Washington, D.C. September.

Hill, Kenneth
1985   Illegal Aliens: An Assessment. In *Immigration Statistics: A Story of Neglect.* Edited by Daniel B. Levine, Kenneth Hill, and Robert Warren. Washington, D.C.: National Academy Press. Pp. 225–250.

Huddle, Donald
1993   The Costs of Immigration. Washington, D.C.: Carrying Capacity Network. Revised July 1993.

INS
1991   *Statistical Yearbook of the Immigration and Naturalization Service: 1990.* Washington, D.C.: U.S. Government Printing Office.

1992a Provisional Legalization Application Statistics. Statistics Division. Washington, D.C.

1992b *Immigration Reform and Control Act: Report on the Legalized Alien Population*, M-375. U.S. Department of Justice.

1994 *Statistical Yearbook of the Immigration and Naturalization Service: 1993*. Washington, D.C.: U.S. Government Printing Office.

Kossoudji, Sherrie A.

1992 Playing Cat and Mouse at the U.S.–Mexican Border. *Demography* 29: 159–180.

Levine, Daniel B., Kenneth Hill, and Robert Warren

1985 *Immigration Statistics: A Story of Neglect*. Washington, D.C.: National Academy Press.

Martin, Philip L., and J. Edward Taylor

1988 Harvest of Confusion: SAWs, RAWs, and Farmworkers. Policy Discussion Paper PRIP-UI-4. Washington, D.C.: Program for Research on Immigration Policy, Urban Institute. December.

Martin, Philip L., J. Edward Taylor, and Michael Fix

1997 *Poverty amid Prosperity: Immigration and the Changing Face of Rural California*. Washington, D.C.: Urban Institute Press.

Massey, Douglas S., et al.

1994 An Evaluation of International Migration Theory: The North American Case. *Population and Development Review* 20 (4) (December): 699–751.

Massey, Douglas S., Katharine M. Donato, and Zai Liang

1990 Effects of the Immigration Reform and Control Act of 1986: Preliminary Data from Mexico. In *Undocumented Migration to the United States: IRCA and the Experience of the 1980s*. Edited by Frank D. Bean, Barry Edmonston, and Jeffrey S. Passel. Washington, D.C.: Urban Institute Press. Pp. 183–210.

Passel, Jeffrey S.

1985 Undocumented Immigrants: How Many? In *Proceedings of the Social Statistics Section of the American Statistical Association, 1985*. Washington, D.C.: American Statistical Association. Pp. 65–81.

1986 Undocumented Immigration. *Annals of the American Academy for Political and Social Science* 186 (September): 186–221.

1994 Estimates of the Undocumented Immigrant Population in Seven States: 1992 and Beyond. Chapter 2 in *Fiscal Impacts of Undocumented Aliens: Selected Estimates for Seven States*. Edited by Rebecca L. Clark, Jeffrey S. Passel, Wendy N. Zimmermann, and Michael Fix. Washington, D.C.: Urban Institute.

1996 Problem with March 1994 and 1995 CPS Weighting. Technical memorandum to CPS users. Population Studies Center, Urban Institute: Washington, D.C. November 12.

1998a New Estimates of Undocumented Immigrants in the 1990 Census. Chapter 4 in Passel and Kahn, *Immigration, Fertility, and the Future American Work Force*. Final Report to the Social Security Administration. Washington, D.C.: Urban Institute. March.

1998b Estimates of Undocumented Immigrants in 1995. Chapter 6 in Passel and Kahn, *Immigration, Fertility, and the Future American Work Force*. Final Report to the Social Security Administration. Washington, D.C.: Urban Institute. March.

1998c Impacts of Undocumented Immigration, Control Efforts, and Potential Policy Responses. Chapter 7 in Passel and Kahn, *Immigration, Fertility, and the Future*

American Work Force. Final Report to the Social Security Administration. Washington, D.C.: Urban Institute. March.

Passel, Jeffrey S., Frank D. Bean, and Barry Edmonston

1990   Undocumented Migration since IRCA: An Overall Assessment. In *Undocumented Migration to the United States: IRCA and the Experience of the 1980s.* Edited by Frank D. Bean, Barry Edmonston, and Jeffrey S. Passel. Washington, D.C.: Urban Institute Press. Pp. 11–32.

Passel, Jeffrey S., and Rebecca L. Clark

1998   *Immigrants in New York: Their Legal Status, Incomes, and Taxes.* Washington, D.C.: Urban Institute. April.

Passel, Jeffrey S., and Joan R. Kahn

1998   *Immigration, Fertility, and the Future American Work Force.* Final Report to the Social Security Administration. Washington, D.C.: Urban Institute. March.

Passel, Jeffrey S., and Karen A. Woodrow

1984   Geographic Distribution of Undocumented Immigrants: Estimates of Undocumented Aliens Counted in the 1980 Census by State. *International Migration Review* 18: 642–671.

1987   Change in the Undocumented Alien Population in the United States, 1979–1983. *International Migration Review* 21 (4): 1304–1334.

Pessar, Patricia

1994   Sweatshop Workers and Domestic Ideologies. *International Journal of Urban and Regional Research* 18(1): 127–142.

Schmidley, A. Diane, and J. Gregory Robinson

1998   How Well Does the Current Population Survey Measure the Foreign Born Population in the United States? Technical Working Paper No. 22, Population Division. Washington, D.C.: U.S. Bureau of the Census. April.

Siegel, Jacob S., Jeffrey S. Passel, and J. Gregory Robinson

1980   Preliminary Review of Existing Studies of the Number of Illegal Residents in the United States. Report to the U.S. Select Commission on Immigration and Refugee Policy. Washington, D.C.: U.S. Bureau of the Census. Reprinted in 1981 in *U.S. Immigration Policy and the National Interest: The Staff Report of the Select Commission on Immigration and Refugee Policy.* Washington, D.C.: U.S. Government Printing Office.

Simcox, David

1994   INS Estimate of 4.0 Million Illegals Present in 1994: Estimate Seen as Low. *Immigration Review* 18 (Summer). Washington, D.C.: Center for Immigration Studies.

Van Hook, Jennifer, and Frank D. Bean

1997a Estimating Underenumeration among Unauthorized Mexican Migrants to the United States: Applications of Mortality Analyses. Technical Appendix for Bean et al. (1997), *The Quantification of Migration between Mexico and the United States.* Binational Study of Migration between Mexico and the United States. Commission on Immigration Reform: Washington, D.C. July.

1997b Estimating Unauthorized Mexican Migration to the United States: Issues and Results. Technical Appendix for Bean et al. (1997), *The Quantification of Migration between Mexico and the United States.* Binational Study of Migration between Mexico and the United States. Commission on Immigration Reform: Washington, D.C. July.

Warren, Robert

1990   Annual Estimates of Nonimmigrant Overstays in the United States: 1985 to 1988. In *Undocumented Migration to the United States: IRCA and the Experience of the 1980s*. Edited by Frank D. Bean, Barry Edmonston, and Jeffrey S. Passel. Washington, D.C.: Urban Institute Press. Pp. 77–110.

1994   Estimates of the Unauthorized Immigrant Population Residing in the United States, by Country of Origin and State of Residence: October 1992. Office of Policy and Planning. Washington, D.C.: U.S. Immigration and Naturalization Service.

1997   Estimates of the Undocumented Immigrant Population Residing in the United States: October 1996. Office of Policy and Planning, Immigration. Washington, D.C.: U.S. Immigration and Naturalization Service. August.

Warren, Robert, and Jeffrey S. Passel

1987   A Count of the Uncountable: Estimates of Undocumented Aliens Counted in the 1980 U.S. Census. *Demography* 24: 375–396.

Woodrow, Karen A.

1991   Preliminary Estimates of Undocumented Residents in 1990: Demographic Analysis Evaluation Project D2. Preliminary Research and Evaluation Memorandum No. 75. Washington, D.C.: U.S. Bureau of the Census. May 22.

Woodrow, Karen A., and Jeffrey S. Passel

1990   Post-IRCA Undocumented Immigration to the United States: An Assessment Based on the June 1988 CPS. In *Undocumented Migration to the United States: IRCA and the Experience of the 1980s*. Edited by Frank D. Bean, Barry Edmonston, and Jeffrey S. Passel. Washington, D.C.: Urban Institute Press. Pp. 33–76.

Woodrow, Karen A., Jeffrey S. Passel, and Robert Warren

1987   Preliminary Estimates of Undocumented Immigration to the United States, 1980–1986: Analysis of the June 1986 Current Population Survey. In *Proceedings of the Social Statistics Section of the American Statistical Association, 1987*. Washington, D.C.: American Statistical Association.

Word, David L.

1995   Unpublished estimates of nonimmigrants in the United States in 1990. Personal communication. Washington, D.C.: U.S. Bureau of the Census.

4

Mexico and U.S. Policy on Illegal Immigration: A Fifty-Year Retrospective

Katharine M. Donato and Rebecca S. Carter

Since midcentury, illegal immigration to the United States has emerged as a hotly contested issue. One consequence was passage of the first U.S. legislation designed to curb illegal immigration to the United States. In 1986, the Immigration Control and Reform Act was signed into law; ten years later, Congress passed the Illegal Immigration Reform and Immigrant Responsibility Act (IIR-IRA). Both aimed to curb illegal immigration.

The objective of this chapter is to describe how U.S. and Mexican governments have responded to illegal immigration in recent decades. We begin by describing the historical context that has governed legal and illegal migration to the United States since 1942 and identifying four periods that represent significant changes in migration policy. As we will see, the most recent period marked a notable shift in the migration policies of the U.S. and Mexican governments. Since 1986, as many previously illegal Mexican migrants received legal status in the United States, the two governments have begun a bilateral dialogue that represents a new era in Mexican–U.S. relations. This is likely to have consequences for illegal migration in the future, an issue we discuss in the final section.

POLICY RESPONSES TO MEXICO–U.S. MIGRATION: THE HISTORICAL CONTEXT

Although many came to the United States prior to the twentieth century, Mexicans began to migrate in large numbers in 1910, after the Mexican revolution, attracted by a strong demand for labor, especially in the Southwest.[1] They entered at a time when U.S. residents were increasingly likely to be suspicious of immigrants. Congress responded to xenophobic sentiment by passing legislation that included a national origin quota system to limit immigration from nations in the Eastern Hemisphere and to protect the composition of the U.S. population. Because the new laws exempted Western Hemisphere nations, Mexican migrants were relatively untouched until the early 1930s, when thousands were deported as U.S. unemployment rose sharply. Others returned home, attracted by promises of land reform.

Spurred on by a shortage of agricultural labor during World War II, the first major Mexican migration regime took place after Congress signed the 1942 Bracero Accord, which permitted Mexicans to migrate temporarily for agricultural employment in the United States. It began a twenty-two-year period that legally sanctioned Mexican workers to meet the labor demands of U.S. farmers. By the end of the period, millions of Mexicans had worked as braceros (Galarza 1964), outnumbering legal immigrants during the period. This type of contract labor encouraged seasonality in U.S. migration flows, with movement back and forth across the border corresponding to agricultural opportunities. Migration was often passed down from one generation to the next, especially from fathers to sons, and brothers who were U.S. migrants maintained strong ties with each other (Massey et al. 1987; Reichert and Massey 1979, 1980; Massey and Liang 1989).

To many, the Bracero Accord was different from policy efforts in the past because it represented bilateral cooperation between the Mexican and U.S. governments to temporarily employ Mexicans in agriculture (Weintraub et al. 1998). The two governments shared responsibility for implementation of the temporary worker program, and together they jointly defined the terms of employer–worker agreements, enforcement of the agreements, and transportation of workers. Their efforts also included reducing illegal migration, as the Mexican government pressured the United States to enforce its southern border and adopted its own strategies to discourage illegal emigration. Despite a breakdown between governments in the mid-1950s, when the United States angered Mexico by trying to unilaterally recruit workers, the two governments eventually cooperated in Operation Wetback (which led to 175,000 apprehensions and expulsions in the summer of 1954) (Weintraub et al. 1998: 443).

During the same period, Congress also passed new legislation to govern legal immigration. The Immigration and Nationality Act (INA) of 1952 maintained the national origin quota system. It also contained a five-preference admission system to allocate visas to different types of relatives of permanent residents or U.S. citizens and to workers believed not to have adverse effects on the U.S. labor market. Exempt from the preference system (and its numerical limits) were immediate relatives of U.S. citizens, such as spouses and minor children.

Dramatic changes in recent immigrant policy first appeared in amendments to the INA passed in 1965 and 1981 and governed the next phase of Mexican migration.[2] The 1965 provisions represented the first significant attempt to open immigration policy in the twentieth century. Rather than using national origin quotas, visas were issued on a first-come, first-serve hemispheric basis. The admission system was expanded to seven preferences and included a nonpreference category for applicants who were not eligible under a specific preference. In an effort to be more equitable than U.S. policy had permitted in the past, all nations in the Eastern Hemisphere were limited to 20,000 immigrants per year.

In contrast to Eastern Hemisphere immigrants, all prospective migrants from the Western Hemisphere faced a single queue for visas (Roney 1992). Without a preference system or country restrictions, the admission system permitted these persons to migrate free from eligibility requirements or country numerical limits. As a result, many migrated based on relationships not specified in the seven preferences, including parents of minor children born in the United States; Mexico, because of its proximity and size, dominated these flows.

These changes led to a surge in the size of the legal immigrant population and a shift in their ethnic composition. By the late 1970s, migrants entering the United States rivaled the number of their counterparts entering at the turn of the century. In addition, new immigrants were more likely to enter from Asia and Latin America rather than traditional sending areas in Europe, and the result was increasing immigrant visibility and ethnic diversity in the United States. As the demand for visas grew, huge backlogs were created in the preference system, and undocumented migration to the United States grew. Additional amendments worsened this situation by making visa allocation equitable between the two hemispheres. Beginning in 1977, the same numerical limits and preferences governed legal migration from both hemispheres. The impact was dramatic; legal immigration from Mexico was halved.

Throughout the first half of the 1965–1981 period, bilateral relations between Mexico and the United States were tense. Conflict originally derived from differences in opinions about terminating the Bracero Accord in 1964. For almost ten years, Mexico unsuccessfully pressured the United States to implement a new temporary worker program. Subsequently, without a temporary worker program in place, the Mexican government operated until the mid-1980s with a "no-policy" policy (Garcia y Griego 1988; de la Garza and Szekely 1997).

During the last few years of this period, other legal policy changes—positive and negative—did nothing to shift the bilateral tensions between the two nations. One was related to a judicial decision stemming from a lawsuit (*Silva v. Levi*) that added 145,000 visas to the 120,000 numerical ceiling for the Western Hemisphere. Those benefiting from the Silva decision had been turned down for visas earlier because they had been mistakenly issued to Cuban refugees under numerical limitations. Mexicans constituted the majority of the beneficiaries; almost 80 percent of visas were allocated to persons born in Mexico, and more than half went to women.[3]

The second change occurred when Congress created a global admission policy in late 1978, so that all visas were then allocated through preference categories, and persons in the nonpreference category, primarily Mexican parents of minor

U.S. children, were virtually unable to obtain visas. The third change was the 1980 Refugee Act, which eliminated the seventh preference for the conditional entry of refugees; visas originally allocated to the seventh preference were assigned to the second preference (for spouses and children of permanent residents) to ease one backlog in the U.S. legal admission system.

In general, the pre-Immigration Reform and Control Act (IRCA) (1982–1986) period was significant because of its conflict. The Mexican and U.S. governments took opposing sides on the illegal migration issue. U.S. concerns about illegal immigration grew at a time when "Mexican public opinion was that migration . . . was virtually inevitable and that problems were created by U.S. measures to expel millions of migrants who could not be absorbed by a weak Mexican economy'' (Weintraub et al. 1998: 446). Throughout the period, the U.S. government debated recommendations that emerged from the Select Commission on Immigration and Refugee Policy. Consisting of U.S. migration specialists, the commission recommended that the United States develop policies designed to reduce undocumented migration to the United States. As a result, a long legislative battle ensued in the U.S. Congress. In 1986, it was finally settled. Congress passed IRCA, which increased border enforcement, offered amnesty to migrants already resident in the United States, and established employer sanctions against those who knowingly hired undocumented migrants for work. By 1989, IRCA resulted in more than 2 million Mexican applicants for amnesty (Bean, Vernez, and Keely 1989).

The post-IRCA period (1987–1996) is significant for many reasons. First and foremost, it was a time when Mexico began to privatize its economy and play a more active role in world affairs (Weintrab et al. 1998).[4] At the same time, IRCA mandated that a binational dialogue begin on ways to deter illegal migration.[5] As a result, for the first time, many discussions about binational research emerged between the two nations.

Second, the period was also unusual because it witnessed many immigration debates in the United States. In 1990, legal immigration policy was changed and took the form of the Immigration Act (IMMACT) of 1990. Designed to reduce competition for visas and additional backlogs in the preference system, IMMACT created a new selection procedure by increasing the annual worldwide numerical limit to 366,000 immigrants, revising the visa preference system, and implementing a three-track system based on family ties, employment, and diversity (Yale-Loehr 1991). One key feature was the substantial increase in the number of immigrant workers (from 54,000 to 140,000 immigrants per year). The new law also allocated, in 1992–1994, 55,000 visas to family members of IRCA's newly legalized migrants, and, beginning in 1995, another 55,000 visas were offered to natives from countries that had contributed few immigrants in the previous five-year period.

By middecade, however, debates about illegal migration emerged again and led to the passage of the 1996 Illegal Immigration Reform and Immigrant Responsibility Act (IIRIRA) (Weintraub et al. 1998). That act allocated many more

Table 4.1
Periods of Policy Transition

1942–1964	*Bilateral Cooperation between Mexico and the United States* Mexico–U.S. Bracero Programs Immigration Nationality Act (INA) of 1952
1965–1981	*Conflict between Mexico and the United States: Mexico's No-Policy Policy Begins* 1965 Amendments to INA implemented 1976 Amendments to INA implemented Limits now set on immigration from Western Hemisphere nations Extra visas added to accommodate the *Silva v. Levi* decision
1982–1986	*Conflict between Mexico and the United States: The Divide Continues*
1987–1996	*Convergence and Agreement: New Bilateral Relations* Immigration Reform and Control Act passed in 1986 Illegal Immigration Reform and Immigrant Responsibility Act passed in 1996

resources to border enforcement than did IRCA; strengthened employer sanction provisions that originally appeared in IRCA; expedited the removal of migrants without, or with fraudulent, documents; barred legal admission of persons who had migrated illegally in the past; encouraged cooperation between federal, state, and local enforcement agencies; and levied costs and criminal penalties on illegal immigrants. Together with legislation passed in 1996 on welfare reform and antiterrorism, IIRIRA's passage guaranteed that unauthorized immigrants could not rely on safeguards that protect citizens of the United States.

Despite these more radical measures, the post-1986 period was one of convergence in Mexican and U.S. bilateral relations. Mexico shifted from its "no-policy policy" to one of "increasing engagement" with the United States (Weintraub et al. 1998: 502), whereas the United States recognized that greater cooperation from Mexico was critical to accomplishing its objectives. Thus, since 1986, the two nations have engaged in a new bilateral dialogue about all kinds of migration issues, such as discussions about border enforcement, illegal migration, and human rights. One result is passage of Mexican legislation designed to boost the sanctions against Mexicans who illegally traffic migrants (Weintraub et al. 1998: 459).

Table 4.1 summarizes the salient policy transitions in Mexican–U.S. immigrant policy. It lists the four periods of large-scale Mexican migration to the United States and the legislation governing migration between 1942 and 1996 highlighted earlier. In an analysis later, we consider each period separately to understand the reciprocal relationship between restrictions on legal and illegal immigration and the size and composition of migrant flows. We use two regimes to assess whether and how events in the pre- and post-IRCA periods affected trends in Mexican migration to the United States. The first, 1981–1986, covers the period just prior to IRCA's passage (pre-IRCA), and the second, 1987–1996, represents a period of convergence between Mexico and the United States, culminating with the most radical legislation designed to curb illegal migration in U.S. history.

Organizing information around different migration regimes highlights the role that shifting U.S. migration policy may play in the development of migration from Mexico. An early study by Reichert and Massey (1980) constructed migrant cohorts from the detailed histories of residents in one Mexican town between 1940 and 1978 and found two distinct waves of migration. The earlier wave (1940–1964) was dominated by men who migrated legally as braceros. Only toward the end of this period, when bracero contracts became difficult to obtain, did the proportion of undocumented men begin to increase. In the later phase (1965–1978), women and children, relatives of the former braceros who had become permanent U.S. residents, were likely to migrate.

Although their study is highly suggestive, like many others it relied on data from an isolated community and did not permit generalizations (Durand and Massey 1992). Using data collected from seventeen Mexican communities, Donato (1994) overcame this limitation and found a third migration wave. Begun in the late 1970s, this period witnessed women migrating in large numbers without children and a soaring increase in the number of men and women migrating without legal documents. In this chapter, we build on these studies using data that represent a large sample of migrants (with and without documents), covering the 1942–1996 period.

DATA

This study is based on data collected through representative surveys of fifty communities—most located in the western central Mexican states that have traditionally sent many migrants to the United States, such as Jalisco, Michoacán, Guanajuato, San Luis Potosí, and Nayarit (Dagodag 1975; North and Houstoun 1976; Jones 1988). Within each community, 150 to 200 households were randomly selected and interviewed during December and January in successive years between 1987 and 1996. These months were the best times to locate U.S. migrants in Mexico, since many returned to spend the holidays with their families.

The data were supplemented with a nonrandom survey of out-migrants located in the United States during the summer after the original survey was taken. From the Mexican samples, interviewers found out where in the U.S. migrants had settled permanently and then went to those areas to interview households. Snowball sampling methods were used to compile a sample of twenty out-migrant households from each community. Although these data do not represent all out-migrants, they provide a partial control for biases originating from selective emigration. Mexicans who remain in the United States for prolonged periods tend to be relatively more successful economically than migrants who returned home early (Borjas 1985; Massey 1987).

The survey questionnaire collected information on the social, economic, and demographic characteristics of persons in sample households. It asked whether household members, including the head, spouse, and resident children, had ever been to the United States. If so, the survey obtained information about the first and most recent trip to the United States, including the date of initial entry, duration, occupation, wage, place of destination, and legal status. Although retrospective histories obviously contain some recall error, checks for internal consistency revealed that migrants were able to remember with considerable accuracy the years when they left for the United States (see Massey 1985). For the present chapter, we drew on the year of the migrant's first trip to the United States and created four cohorts, based on more than 14,000 migrants, that represent the different periods of U.S. and Mexican immigration policy.

Our analytic plan in this part of the chapter is as follows. We begin by describing overall trends and patterns in Mexico–U.S. migration by cohort and then examine cohorts separately by legal status. Finally, to understand how and why illegal migration has grown, we examine the legal status and other characteristics of migrants who received amnesty as part of IRCA. In contrast to what is generally thought, our results suggest that many of these migrants illegally received their legal documents or chose not to apply, even though they were eligible. These results raise questions about feasibility of amnesty programs, a topic discussed at the end of this chapter.

OVERALL TRENDS IN MEXICAN–UNITED STATES MIGRATION

Table 4.2 displays cohort characteristics that replicate the three patterns of migration described in Donato (1994). The first is the bracero period (1942–1964), when mostly young men migrated. Approximately half entered with bracero contracts, and two-thirds reported having legal papers[6] and doing agricultural work. Their duration of stay in United States was short (about six months), and most migrated to California (57 percent) or Texas (21 percent). As a result, two-thirds of the migrants in this cohort made more than one U.S. trip, with 4.6 trips on average.

Big differences between the first and second cohort (1965–1981) reveal the emergence of the second migration pattern: more women and children, many more entering without documents and with fraudulent documents,[7] and rising percentages of skilled and unskilled workers, of those bound for California and, to a much smaller extent, Florida and Illinois. Interestingly, the percentage of agricultural workers dropped by slightly more than half, as it did for those having legal documents and those migrating to Texas. Finally, just over half of these migrants made more than two trips, with 2.6 trips on average.

Table 4.2

Characteristics of Migrant Cohorts Leaving Fifty Mexican Communities on a First Trip to the United States, 1942–1996

	1942-64	1965-81	1982-86	1987-96
Demographic attributes				
Percent female	15.1	30.2	27.2	37.4
Percent under age 15	16.9	22.2	15.2	13.1
Average age	20.4	19.6	21.1	22.4
First trip characteristics				
Percent migrating with:				
Legal documents	65.3	25.9	18.5	17.3
Bracero contracts	45.8	0	0	0
No documents	32.8	68.6	75.0	76.3
Fraudulent documents	1.1	4.3	5.4	5.1
Percent employed in:				
Skilled work	5.6	10.6	12.0	14.4
Unskilled work	11.9	30.7	35.7	35.1
Agricultural work	66.8	31.6	25.9	14.1
Not in labor force	7.4	14.6	13.0	22.4
Median trip duration (mo.)	6.0	24.0	24.0	14.0
Percent migrating to:				
California	57.1	68.5	66.3	63.8
Texas	21.2	11.7	13.0	11.8
Florida	0.1	2.9	3.6	2.2
Illinois	4.1	7.4	6.4	8.4
Additional trips	4.6	2.6	1.4	0.5
Percentage with 2+ trips	68.3	52.7	45.4	23.6
Percentage in US sample	14.4	19.8	16.7	14.7
Number of migrants	1,847	6,075	2,587	3,759

In general, patterns found in the pre-IRCA cohort continue the trends begun in the 1965–1981 period, albeit more dramatically in some cases. Three-quarters of this cohort reported having no legal documents, whereas the representation among agricultural workers dropped to just one-quarter of the cohort. One exception refers to the presence of children; it dropped to just 15 percent from 22 percent in the 1965–1981 period, representing the first documented time in U.S. history when the age and sex composition of migrants diverged. The final cohort (1987–1996) differs from earlier ones in that it contained many more women (37 percent female) and more skilled workers. Most migrants remained bound for California, although, increasingly, Illinois was also a popular U.S. destination, and most entered without legal documents.

TRENDS IN LEGAL AND ILLEGAL MIGRATION

Investigating these trends by legal status helps us to understand whether and how legal migrants are different from those without legal status. Table 4.3 shows that women constituted slightly more than half of all legal migrants in 1965–1981 and 1987–1996. No doubt these percentages reflect the large number of

Table 4.3

Characteristics of Legal Migrant Cohorts Leaving Fifty Mexican Communities on a First Trip to the United States, 1942–1996

	1942-64	1965-81	1982-86	1987-96
Demographic attributes				
Percent female	16.2	54.6	46.1	58.7
Percent under age 15	19.6	57.4	58.9	52.2
Average age	20.3	12.6	12.4	16.9
First trip characteristics				
Percent migrating as:				
Permanent residents	16.4	51.9	34.9	22.5
US citizens	11.7	38.7	50.3	46.2
Tourists	1.7	9.1	15.3	32.7
Braceros	70.2	0	0	0
Percent employed in:				
Skilled work	5.4	7.4	5.0	2.9
Unskilled work	9.3	12.4	11.5	6.6
Agricultural work	68.0	18.1	9.4	3.7
Not in labor force	8.1	27.9	26.7	43.0
Median trip duration (mo.)	6.0	120.0	60.0	18.0
Percent migrating to:				
California	58.6	74.4	71.0	71.0
Texas	16.0	5.6	9.0	7.8
Florida	0.1	4.6	5.2	2.3
Illinois	4.4	8.9	6.3	9.2
Additional trips	4.1	2.1	0.6	0.3
Percentage with 2+ trips	66.6	31.9	20.0	13.1
Percentage in US sample	17.1	39.0	42.0	42.2
Number of migrants	1,206	1,573	479	649

wives and parents of permanent residents and U.S.-born children who obtained visas during these periods. Children have constituted the majority of legal migrants since 1965. As their presence declined between 1982–1986 and 1987–1996, their average age grew to seventeen years.

Table 4.3 also documents dramatic changes in legal status and employment. After the bracero period ended, the flow of legal migrants was originally predominated by permanent residents. But by the 1980s, these migrants were most likely to enter as U.S. citizens. Between 1982–1986 and 1987–1996 alone, the percentage of legal tourists doubled (from 15 to 33 percent). Employment trends describe a huge decline in agricultural work among legal migrants after 1964 and an increase in the percentage of legal migrants not in the labor force. The latter corresponds with the large presence of women and children by the early 1990s.

Many studies have documented that the decision to migrate is a family affair (Massey et al. 1987; Reichert and Massey 1980). Decisions to move are usually made by families or households, and migration involves one or more members who remit earnings back to these households. After one family member receives legal documents, others are likely to follow either as legal migrants sponsored by relatives already in the United States or as illegal migrants hoping to change legal status in the future. As a result, trends in legal migration are closely linked to those of illegal migration.

We therefore examine characteristics of illegal migrants in Table 4.4. Since 1942, women's representation among illegal migrants has grown, but that of children has declined. By 1987–1996, 32 percent and 5 percent of illegal migrants were women and children, respectively. A corresponding trend was the rise in the average age of illegal migrants (from twenty-one to twenty-four years).

Among all cohorts, illegal migrants favored leaving Mexico on an initial U.S. trip without documents. After 1964, however, the percentage leaving Mexico on a first trip with fraudulent documents increased and remained at roughly 6 percent of all illegal migrants through 1996. Trends in employment and U.S. destination were consistent with those for legal migrants. In general, there were a gradual trend toward skilled and unskilled work and a trend toward more migrants not in the labor force. The latter was related, in part, to the rising presence of women among illegal migrants. In addition, by the 1987–1996 period, California had attracted two-thirds of illegal migrants, with Texas and Illinois attracting another 20 percent.

Compared to legal migrants, illegals made shorter, yet more, U.S. trips, with at least half making two or more trips prior to 1987. Moreover, the percentages of illegals who were interviewed in the United States were far lower than those for legal migrants. Thus, even though most illegal migrants are no longer agricultural workers, they are more likely than legals to engage in temporary, recurrent movement across the Mexico–U.S. border.

Table 4.4 also shows how the characteristics of illegal first-trip migrants changed by the year of their last trip to the United States. Despite the amnesty provisions in IRCA, across the 1942–1996 period, illegal migrants were less successful obtaining legal papers by the year of their last trip. During the 1942–1964 period, 32 percent were able to adjust their legal status, but by the 1987–1996 period, only 13 percent did so. Among those who were able to obtain legal papers, data on the timing of this adjustment suggest that many did so under IRCA's amnesty provisions. There is also evidence that some illegal migrants were able to change occupations by the year of their last trip. Although there was no clear trend in occupational mobility (upward or downward), by the year of their last trip migrants were slightly more likely to work in skilled, unskilled, and agricultural jobs. Fewer were out of the labor force.

These trends suggest that policies may operate as both the cause and consequence of migrant behavior. Although the Bracero Accord sparked the migration of many Mexicans, who later obtained legal status and sponsored eligible family members, U.S. legal immigration policy after 1965 curtailed this opportunity. After the 1976 amendments were phased in, most Mexicans were unable to

Table 4.4

Characteristics of Illegal Migrant Cohorts Leaving Fifty Mexican Communities on a First Trip to the United States, 1942–1996

	1942-64	1965-81	1982-86	1987-96
Demographic attributes	12.5	21.3	23.0	32.5
Percent female				
Percent under age 15	11.7	9.7	5.1	4.7
Average age	20.7	22.1	23.0	23.5
First trip characteristics				
Percent migrating with:				
No documents	96.6	94.1	93.3	93.8
Fraudulent documents	3.4	5.9	6.7	6.2
Percent employed in:				
Skilled work	6.1	11.7	13.7	16.9
Unskilled work	16.9	37.5	41.6	41.4
Agricultural work	65.6	36.8	30.1	16.5
Not in labor force	5.9	9.8	10.0	18.1
Median trip duration (mo.)	8.0	14.0	18.0	12.0
Percent migrating to:				
California	54.0	66.7	65.4	62.6
Texas	31.5	13.9	14.0	12.6
Florida	0	2.3	3.3	2.2
Illinois	3.7	6.6	6.4	8.3
Additional trips	5.6	2.9	1.6	0.5
Percentage with 2+ trips	72.0	60.4	51.6	25.9
Percentage in U.S. sample	9.3	13.2	11.1	9.0
Number of migrants	626	4,425	2,078	3,059
Legalization attributes				
Average year documents				
were received	1987	1987	1988	1987
Average years between 1st				
trip and receiving docs	30.7	12.2	3.9	0.3
(N)	(9)	(261)	(84)	(10)
Last trip characteristics				
Percent migrating with				
legal documents	32.1	24.5	25.2	13.3
Percent employed in:				
Skilled work	10.9	14.9	17.6	20.5
Unskilled work	24.1	40.1	42.0	42.7
Agricultural work	55.1	35.4	30.6	23.3
Not in labor force	7.1	6.8	6.9	9.5
Median trip duration (mo.)	8.0	10.0	8.0	7.0
(N)	(448)	(2,660)	(1,068)	(791)

obtain legal status. As a result, illegal immigration surged, and debates about this population led to the passage of IRCA and IIRIRA.

DIFFERENCES AMONG IRCA's AMNESTY RECIPIENTS

Because IRCA offered legal status to some 3 million previously illegal migrants, we examine the characteristics of amnesty recipients. Before doing so, however, we review the two types of amnesty programs that IRCA permitted. The first, derived from the legally authorized worker (LAW) program, required that migrants were continuous U.S. residents since 1982 or earlier (Bean, Vernez, and Keely 1989). Approximately 1.7 million long-term, unauthorized migrants applied for amnesty under the LAW program. The second was part of the special agricultural worker (SAW) program; it gave amnesty to illegal migrants who documented having worked in agriculture for at least ninety days each year between 1984 and 1986 and to those who documented having worked in agriculture for at least ninety days in 1986. The SAW program generated approximately 1.3 million applicants. Together, Mexicans made up more than 70 percent of the total immigrant population who legalized under IRCA (Woodrow and Passel 1990).

As IRCA's amnesty programs were implemented, reports surfaced that suggested many migrants illegally became eligible for amnesty (see Mathews 1988). Some suggested that many SAW applicants had never been agricultural workers and that loopholes in IRCA's employer sanction provisions permitted the development of a wide range of fraudulent documents available for sale in many Mexican communities, including letters from U.S. employers that lied about a migrant's agricultural employment experience in the United States.

To help us assess the extent to which persons who reported receiving LAW and SAW amnesty did so legally, in the following text we describe their distributions by legal status. We also provide an estimate of how many migrants could have met eligibility criteria for either type of amnesty but did not apply. Among the 482 LAWs, twenty-seven percent were legitimate applicants—had continuously lived in the nation since 1982—and seventy-three percent were fraudulent.[8] Surprisingly, however, many migrants (N = 752) were able to meet the eligibility criteria but did not apply. (For this analysis, we refer to these persons as potential LAWs.) Among the 487 SAWs, far more were legitimate applicants (60 vs. 27 percent), and fewer were likely to have fraudulently applied for amnesty (40 vs. 73 percent).[9] Interestingly, the number of migrants who could have applied for SAW amnesty because they met the eligibility criteria was much smaller (N = 102) than the number of potential LAWs.

These numbers are surprising because they suggest that (1) less than half of the LAWs and disproportionately more SAWs had a legitimate claim to amnesty; (2) fraudulent LAW documents were either easier and/or more abundant to generate than SAW documents; and (3) many migrants had what was nec-

Table 4.5
Characteristics of Documented and Potential LAWs on a Last Trip to the United States from Forty-eight Mexican Communities, 1942–1996

	Legit	Fraud	Potential
Demographic attributes			
Percent female	15.2	18.8	26.7
Average age	31.4	30.5	22.4
Last trip characteristics			
Percent employed in:			
Skilled work	34.1	27.1	27.5
Unskilled work	58.3	57.7	70.3
Agricultural work	0	8.8	0.5
Not in labor force	6.8	4.6	1.5
Median trip duration (mo.)	30.0	12.0	150.0
Percent migrating to:			
California	77.3	69.4	66.4
Texas	10.6	11.4	10.6
Florida	0	1.7	0
Illinois	7.6	7.1	10.1
Additional trips	4.4	4.2	0.6
Percentage with 2+ trips	78.0	83.4	19.0
Percentage in US sample	53.8	10.8	19.1
Percent who were continuously resident in US 5 or more years	100.0	0	100.0
(N)	132	350	752

essary to meet eligibility criteria for LAW and SAW amnesty but did not apply. Tables 4.5 and 4.6 provide additional information about the migrant groups, and from them, several important findings related to demographic composition, U.S. employment, and migration experience emerge.

Legitimate and fraudulent LAWs were similar in some key respects. Approximately 85 percent were male; on average, they were about thirty-one years old. In addition, at least half were unskilled workers on their most recent U.S. trip, and they made four U.S. trips on average. However, legitimate and fraudulent recipients also differed in notable ways. Disproportionately more legitimate recipients were skilled workers, and more fraudulent recipients were agricultural workers. Morever, migration experience differed for the two groups. More legitimate LAWs had migrated to California by the year of their last U.S. trip than fraudulent recipients (77 vs. 69 percent), whereas more fraudulent LAWs made two or more trips than legitimate LAWs (83 vs. 78 percent). One big difference between legitimate and fraudulent recipients was in the percentage who were interviewed in the United States: 54 percent versus 11 percent, respectively.

Table 4.6

Characteristics of Documented and Potential SAWs on a Last Trip to the United States from Forty-seven Mexican Communities, 1942–1996

	Legit	Fraud	Potential
Demographic attributes			
Percent female	9.0	13.7	1.0
Average age	32.9	28.9	36.9
Percent employed in:			
Skilled work	2.1	17.8	2.9
Unskilled work	9.6	38.6	13.7
Agricultural work	85.5	36.5	83.3
Not in labor force	2.4	4.6	0
Median trip duration (mo.)	7.0	9.0	8.0
Percent migrating to:			
California	40.7	54.3	64.7
Texas	3.8	8.6	10.8
Florida	21.4	15.2	2.0
Illinois	1.4	1.0	2.0
Additional trips	8.0	3.6	5.1
Percentage with 2+ trips	99.0	83.8	83.3
Percentage in US sample	6.6	18.8	3.9
Percent eligible for SAW docs			
In US for each yr 1984-86,			
working in agriculture for 3 or			
more months	66.5	0	41.2
In US working in agriculture			
for 3 or more months in 1986	33.5	0	58.8
(N)	290	197	102

Among those with the potential to receive LAW documents (those who were eligible but did not apply), more were female and younger than other LAW migrant groups. Almost three-quarters reported unskilled work during their most recent U.S. trip, and, on average, remained in the country for much longer durations. Potential LAWs also averaged far fewer U.S. trips and were less likely to have made two or more trips than fraudulent or legitimate LAWs. On the whole, this young female profile suggests to us that potential LAWS were poorer and among the most vulnerable migrants, who were either too scared to apply for amnesty, did not understand the law or know about it (Bean et al. 1989), or did not think it was necessary because they lived with a spouse or head of household who had applied (or already had legal status).

SAWs were quite different, however. SAWs were overwhelmingly male and this was especially true for potential SAWs who met eligibility conditions but did not apply for this type of amnesty. Women's presence was highest among fraudulent SAWs, and we wonder to what extent these women are related to men who legitimately received SAW amnesty. Also among fraudulent SAWs, the percentage of skilled and unskilled workers was highest. As a consequence, only thirty-six percent were agricultural workers (far less than among other groups). In contrast to expectations, however, more fraudulent SAWs were interviewed in the United States than other SAWs.

Although California was the most popular destination for SAWs by the year of their last U.S. trip, almost seventy-seven percent of potential SAWs were concentrated in California and Texas—areas that border Mexico and have attracted many Mexican migrants for decades. This suggests that some migrants chose not to be legal residents of the United States, an idea that, for some anti-immigrant conservatives in the United States, is hard to fathom.

Interestingly, legitimate SAW recipients made more U.S. trips on average than other groups, attesting to the seasonal nature of agricultural work. Moreover, sixty-seven percent of legitimate SAWs met eligibility criteria by being U.S. agricultural workers for ninety days each year in the 1984–86 period, whereas thirty-four percent of legitimate SAWs met the more lenient eligibility criteria by working in U.S. agriculture only in 1986. Among those who could have potentially received SAW amnesty, the percentages were switched. Fewer (41 percent) would have met the three-year requirement had they applied, whereas more (59 percent) would have done so as agricultural workers in 1986.

DISCUSSION

We began this chapter by describing the Mexico–U.S. policy context in which illegal U.S. migration has developed and grown since 1942. Then, using data from the Mexican Migration Project, we have described trends and patterns in Mexico–U.S. migration by period, and separately by legal status. Finally, to understand how and why illegal migration has grown, we examined the legal status of migrants who received amnesty as part of IRCA and their attributes. On the one hand, our results confirm those reported in prior studies: migrants are more likely than those in the past to be older and female, to enter without legal documents, to be skilled and unskilled workers, and to migrate to California, Texas, and Florida.

On the other hand, our findings about documented and potential amnesty recipients are surprising because they suggest that (1) many amnesty recipients—SAWs and LAWs—did not have a legitimate claim to amnesty; (2) fraudulent LAW documents may have been easier to obtain and/or more abundant than SAW documents; and (3) many migrants could have met eligibility criteria for LAW and SAW amnesty but did not apply. Although the first point is consistent with field and media reports immediately after IRCA's passage, the two remaining findings have no immediate explanation.

To our knowledge, no study has yet generated a profile of amnesty recipients as detailed as the one we present here. Our goal in doing so is to show how immigration policy often generates intended *and* unintended consequences. For example, despite the best intentions of policy makers, giving amnesty to millions has resulted in an illegal legal population. Therefore, IRCA's amnesty programs served the needs of many, some of which were not technically eligible. Exactly how these migrants became eligible for, and able to obtain, amnesty is a question that needs to be answered in future research. It requires an enormous effort, however, because many immigrants may be reluctant to tell the truth for fear of deportation.

NOTES

1. This review relies on the following sources: Hoffman (1974), Levine, Hill, and Warren (1985), Reimers (1985), Massey et al. (1987), Jasso and Rosenzweig (1990), Vernez and Ronfeldt (1991), Durand and Massey (1992), Garcia y Griego (1992), and Roney (1992). Some of this information appears in Donato (1994).

2. Although in the first few years of this period the 1965 amendments were unevenly implemented, after 1968 the new amendments were phased in completely.

3. Data on the number of Mexicans benefiting from the Silva decision originate from personal correspondence with Lisa S. Roney at the U.S. Immigration and Naturalization Service (INS), July 1992.

4. These changes were subsequently followed by the passage of the North American Free Trade Agreement (NAFTA).

5. IRCA mandated the formation of the Commission for the Study of International Migration and Cooperative Economic Development, aka Ascencio Commission, named after its chairman (Weintraub et al. 1998: 448).

6. Legal migrants comprise persons leaving on an initial U.S. trip as permanent residents, U.S. citizens, tourists who did not report working in an occupation on their first trip, those receiving Silva visas, and persons who entered as braceros before 1965.

7. Persons entering with fraudulent documents include persons who entered with a tourist visa but reported a U.S. job on their first trip; persons who entered as braceros after 1964 when these programs had terminated; and migrants who had never migrated before their first trip, when they left as newly legalized migrants under IRCA's amnesty provisions.

8. Technically speaking, legitimate LAWs were migrants who lived in the country for at least ten months every year since (or before) 1982. Fraudulent LAWs were migrants who reported receipt of LAW documents but did not qualify as continuous U.S. residents since 1982 or longer.

9. Legitimate SAWs were migrants who worked in U.S. agriculture for at least three months each year between 1984 and 1986 or for at least three months in 1986. Fraudulent SAWs were migrants who reported receipt of SAW documents but did not qualify on the basis of duration and timing of U.S. residence and/or agricultural employment.

REFERENCES

Bean, Frank D., Georges Vernez, and Charles B. Keely
1989 *Opening and Closing the Doors: Evaluating Immigration Reform and Control.* Washington, D.C.: Urban Institute.

Borjas, George J.
1985   Assimilation, Changes in Cohort Quality, and the Earnings of Immigrants. *Journal of Labor Economics* 3: 463–489.

Dagodag W. Tim
1975   Source Regions and Composition of Illegal Mexican Immigration to California. *International Migration Review* 9: 499–511.

Donato, Katharine M.
1994   U.S. Policy and Mexican Migration to the United States, 1942–92. *Social Science Quarterly* 75(4): 705–729.

Durand, Jorge, and Douglas S. Massey
1992   Generalizations about Mexico–U.S. Migration: A Critical Review. *Latin American Research Review* 27(2): 3–42.

Galarza, Ernest
1964   *Merchants of Labor: The Mexican Bracero Story*. Santa Barbara, California: McNally and Loftin.

García y Griego, Manuel
1988   Hacia una nueva vision del problema de los indocumentados en Estados Unidos. In *México y Estados Unidos Frente a la Migración de Indocumentados*. Edited by Manuel García y Griego and Mónica Verea Campos. Mexico City: UNAM-Porrúa. Pp. 123–52.

1992   Policymaking at the Apex: International Migration, State Autonomy, and Societal Constraints. In *U.S.–Mexico Relations: Labor Market Interdependence*. Edited by Jorge A. Bustamante, Clark W. Reynolds, and Raul A. Hinojosa Ojeda. Stanford: Stanford University Press. Pp. 75–112.

de la Garza, Rudolfo, and Gabriel Szekely
1997   Policy, Politics and Emigration: Reexamining the Mexican Experience. In *At the Crossroads: Mexico and U.S. Immigration Policy*. Edited by Frank D. Bean et al. Lanham, Maryland: Rowman and Littlefield.

Hoffman, Abraham
1974   *Unwanted Mexican Americans in the Great Depression: Repatriation Pressures 1929–39*. Tucson: University of Arizona Press.

Jasso, Guillermina, and Mark R. Rosenzweig
1990   *The New Chosen People: Immigrants in the United States*. New York: Russell Sage Foundation.

Jones, Richard C.
1988   Micro Source Regions of Mexican Undocumented Migration. *National Geographic Research* 4: 11–22.

Levine, Daniel B., Kenneth Hill, and Robert Warren
1985   *Immigration Statistics: A Story of Neglect*. Washington, D.C.: National Academy Press.

Massey, Douglas S.
1985   The Settlement Process among Mexican Migrants to the United States: New Methods and Findings. In *Immigration Statistics: A Story of Neglect*. Edited by Daniel Levine, Kenneth Hill, and Robert Warren. Washington, D.C.: National Academy Press. Pp. 255–292.

1987   Understanding Mexican Migration to the United States. *American Journal of Sociology* 92: 1372–1403.

Massey, Douglas S., Rafael Alarcón, Jorge Durand, and Humberto González
1987   *Return to Aztlan: The Social Process of International Migration from Western Mexico*. Berkeley: University of California Press.

Massey Douglas S., and Zai Liang
1989   The Long Term Consequences of a Temporary Worker Program: The U.S. Bracero Experience. *Population Research and Policy Review* 8: 199–226.

Mathews, Jay
1988   Using Fake Papers, Migrants Skirt Law. *The Washington Post*. November 3, A3.

North, David S., and Marion F. Houston
1976   *The Characteristics and Role of Illegal Aliens in the U.S. Labor Market*. Washington, D.C.: Linton.

Reichert, Josh, and Douglas S. Massey
1979   Patterns of Migration from a Mexican Sending Community: A Comparison of Legal and Illegal Migrants. *International Migration Review* 13: 599–623.

1980   History and Trends in U.S. Bound Migration from a Mexican Town. *International Migration Review* 14(4): 475–491.

Reimers, David M.
1985   *Still the Golden Door: The Third World Comes to America*. New York: Columbia University Press.

Roney, Lisa S.
1992   Immigration Policy over the Past Quarter Century—Who Immigrated and Why? Paper presented at the annual meeting of the Population Association of America, Denver.

Vernez, Georges, and David Ronfeldt
1991   The Current Situation in Mexican Immigration. *Science* 251: 1189–1193.

Weintraub, Sidney, Francisco Alba, Rafael Fernández de Castro, and Manuel García y Griego
1998   Responses to Migration Issues. In *Migration between Mexico and the United States: Binational Study*. Vol. 1: *Thematic Chapters*. Washington, D.C.: U.S. Commission on Immigration Reform. Pp. 437–509.

Woodrow, Karen A., and Jeffrey S. Passel
1990   Post-IRCA Undocumented Immigration to the United States: Assessment Based on the June 1988 CPS. In *Undocumented Migration to the United States: IRCA and the Experience of the 1980s*. Edited by Frank D. Bean, Barry Edmonston, and Jeffrey S. Passel. Washington, D.C.: Urban Institute. Pp. 33–76.

Yale-Loehr, Stephen
1991   *Understanding the Immigration Act of 1990*. Washington, D.C.: Federal Publications.

PART II

THE MIGRANTS AND THE WORK

5

Unauthorized Workers in U.S. Agriculture: Old versus New Migrations

Philip L. Martin

The people who work for wages on U.S. farms are generally among the poorest American workers. A few American youth may dream of growing up to be cowboys, but practically no American boys and girls dream of growing up to be seasonal workers on the nation's farms. Most of those who work on U.S. farms are employed for less than ten months, and the combination of seasonality, low hourly earnings, and often hard work has made farmworker an occupation dominated by those with no other U.S. job options, including foreigners in the United States as immigrants, nonimmigrants, and unauthorized workers. Most Americans do not know any farmworkers, and most have no acquaintances who know farmworkers.

About 2.5 million persons are employed on U.S. farms for wages sometime during a typical year. Most are employed for less than twelve months—average annual farmworker employment is about 1 million, suggesting that the average farmworker is employed about five months. Averages can be misleading in an occupation such as farmworker, in which workers tend to be bunched near the extremes of days worked: the fifteen to twenty percent of workers who are year-round contribute about half of all days of farmwork done by hired workers, while perhaps one-third of the seasonal workers do less than one month of farmwork.

In this chapter, farmworker refers, unless otherwise noted, to seasonal hired workers, those employed up to nine months for wages on U.S. farms. Seasonal farmworkers earn about half as much as non-farmworkers, $5 to $7 per hour versus $10 to $14, and work about half the year, giving farmworkers, on average, annual earnings of $5,000 to $7,000, versus more than $20,000 for non-farmworkers.

It is hard to determine how many farmworkers are legally authorized to work in the United States. However, three trends are clear:

1. The share of unauthorized workers is significant—some 40 to 50 percent of U.S. farmworkers may have been unauthorized in 1997–1998.

2. The unauthorized share of farmworkers has been rising, from less than ten percent in 1989–1990, after the Immigration Reform and Control Act of 1986 legalization programs ended in 1987–1988, or by almost 4 percent per year.

3. The unauthorized percentage of farmworkers is highest outside the major farmworker states of California, Florida, and Texas; in ''new'' destinations for foreign farmworkers such as Georgia, Kentucky, and North Carolina, the unauthorized share of the farm workforce exceeded fifty percent in 1997–1998 in many seasonal worker crews.

This chapter reviews the major features of U.S. agriculture that have led to the presence of a high and rising share of unauthorized farmworkers in a workforce whose overall numbers have been stable. We then turn to farmworkers in three representative commodities, Washington apples, Florida oranges, and California raisin grapes, to review in context the organization of farmwork and the alternatives in the event that fewer foreign workers were available. Finally, we review the policy options being considered by Congress to deal with the foreign farmworker issue.

U.S. AGRICULTURE

Agriculture is the oldest and most widely dispersed industry in the United States, but the farmers and farmworkers who produce food and fiber are largely invisible to most Americans. About 2 percent of the nation's 270 million residents live on 2 million farms, and almost 2 percent of the 140 million U.S. wage and salary workers employed sometime during a typical year work for wages on the 800,000 U.S. farms that reported expenditures for labor to the Census of Agriculture in 1992.

Farming is actually the smallest segment of the three-part U.S. food and fiber industry: (1) providing inputs to agriculture, (2) farming, and (3) processing and distributing farm commodities. Input industries such as banks, chemical companies, and equipment manufacturers supply credit, fertilizers, and machinery to farmers, and they employ a workforce that mirrors in skills and characteristics the U.S. labor force. The second sector is farming: the production of crops and livestock. The third and largest part of the food and fiber sector includes the industries that pack and process farm commodities, the transportation companies that move food and fiber products, and the grocery stores and restaurants that distribute them to consumers; most workers in this sector are involved in restaurants and include many immigrants. There were twenty-three million Americans employed in the food and fiber sector of the economy in 1991 (Martin 1996: Chapter 1).

The farmers at the center of the U.S. food and fiber industry were held in high esteem by the founding fathers, especially by Thomas Jefferson, the third president. In his *Notes on Virginia*, Jefferson wrote, ''Those who labor in the earth are the chosen people of God . . . corruption of morals in the mass of cultivators is a phenomenon of which no age or nation has furnished an example'' (Jefferson 1982: 164–165). Jefferson argued that agriculture was the most basic and important industry in the nation, rural life was superior to urban life, and self-sufficient family farmers were the guarantors of democracy.

Farmers continue to be praised as a living link to the founding fathers and as the business operators acknowledged to be among the world's most productive. The most important expression of U.S. agricultural leadership manifests itself at the grocery store: Americans devoted only 8 percent of their personal consumption expenditures to food eaten at home in 1993, versus 15 percent in France and 55 percent in the Philippines (U.S. Bureau of the Census 1997: 841). The United States is also a major food exporter, exporting over one-fourth of the annual $200 billion of farm output, and farming is one of the few sectors of the American economy that has run a trade surplus for decades.

The family farm ideal and the success of U.S. agriculture combined with a third factor—the political clout of farmers—to produce unusual labor policies in agriculture. Farming is dispersed throughout fifty states and 3,100 U.S. counties, and virtually all states and counties have farm bureaus and other organizations that have looked to government to provide assistance to farmers since the 1930s. Farmers have been able to persuade the federal government to not include farmworkers under labor relations (collective bargaining) laws in 1935 and under minimum wage and unemployment insurance laws in 1938 and to permit the entry of Mexican bracero workers between 1942 and 1964 (Craig 1971; Daniel 1981; Galarza 1964; García y Griego 1981; Martin 1996: Chapter 2).

At the dawn of the twenty-first century, there is a sharp contrast between detailed U.S. farm policies—which for fifty years involved the federal government's inducing farmers to reduce the supply of farm commodities in exchange for guaranteed government prices, thus stabilizing and pushing upward farm prices, and the value of agriculture's major asset, land—and the absence of farm labor policies. Instead of farm labor policies that might have increased farm wages or stabilized farm employment, federal policies for farmworkers have sought to remedy the poverty of many farmworkers and to give their children education and training to ''escape'' from seasonal farmwork. The federal government in the mid-1990s was spending about $600 million per year—equivalent to 10 percent of what farmworkers earn—on programs that provide supplemental education, health, and training services for eligible seasonal workers and their children (Martin and Martin 1993).

FARMS AND FVH COMMODITIES

Most U.S. farms are the family operations idealized by Thomas Jefferson: the farm produces crops and livestock so that farmers and their families stay busy year-round, planting and harvesting crops from spring through fall and tending livestock in the winter. Mechanization has enabled most of these family farms to include a person employed in a nonfarm job; so many farm families also have nonfarm jobs that 88 percent of the average farm household's income in 1993 came from nonfarm sources. In the Northeast, Midwest, and Southeast, where family farms predominate, farmers tend to outnumber farmworkers, and both groups are largely non-Hispanic whites.

One farming subsector, however, is different: fruit and nut, vegetable and melon, and horticultural specialty (FVH) farms, such as those that produce flowers and mushrooms. In the fruits, vegetables, and horticulture (FVH) sector of U.S. agriculture, farmworkers outnumber farmers, and the farmworkers tend to be minorities, while the farmers tend to be non-Hispanic whites. FVH farms have been dubbed "factories in the fields" because they are typically larger-than-family-sized operations that depend on hired workers to come for a few weeks and harvest crops (McWilliams 1939).

There are fewer than 100,000 FVH farms throughout the United States that had expenditures for farm labor in 1987, making them about 10 percent of all farm employers, but they accounted for almost 40 percent of all farmers' expenditures on hired labor (Oliveira et al. 1993: 10). These FVH farms are scattered throughout the United States, but the largest FVH farms are in California, the state that accounts for about 40 percent of U.S. FVH sales. Farm labor is thus concentrated in three ways: by crop, geography, and size of farm.

Farm sales and thus FVH employment have been rising: the United States produced $33 billion worth of fruit and nut, vegetable and melon, and specialty crops in 1997 and exported about one-third, or $11 billion, of FVH commodities. In California, farmworker employment rose 22 percent in the 1990s, from an average 352,000 in 1992 to an average 429,000 in 1997 (Figure 5.1).

There have been numerous changes in the technology of producing and marketing fruits and vegetables, but there have been far fewer changes in the characteristics of farmworkers and the manner in which they find jobs. An 1890s California fruit grower would be baffled by today's pesticides and computer-operated irrigation systems but very familiar with bilingual farm labor contractors' recruiting and supervising crews of immigrant farmworkers. The seasonal farmworkers who work on farms have usually been seen by farmers as a temporary addition to the farm operation and the community, but not the source of future farming partners or community leaders.

WASHINGTON APPLES

Washington's 3,500 growers produce about 4 billion pounds of apples worth $1 billion, or about 60 percent of U.S. apples. Production is concentrated: the

Figure 5.1
Farmworkers in California: 1992–1997

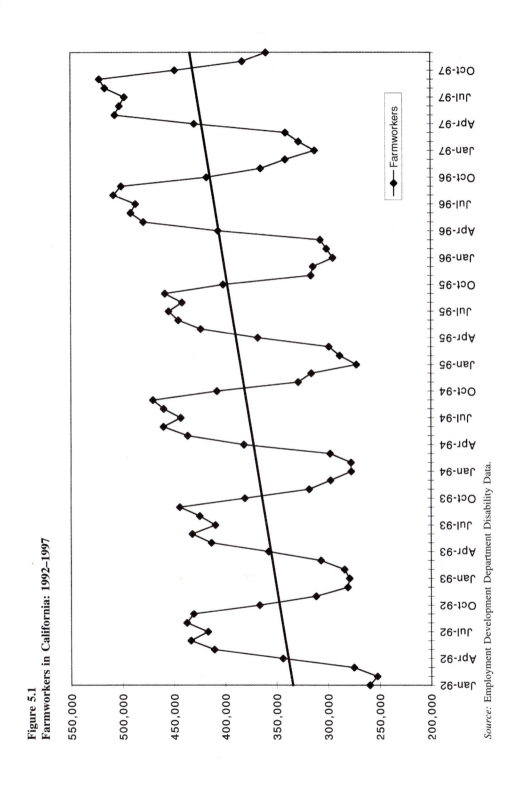

Source: Employment Development Department Disability Data.

largest 7 percent of growers control 53 percent of the state's apple acreage. About 40,000 farmworkers harvest Washington apples each year, and another 15,000 non-farmworkers are employed in apple packing and processing plants. Virtually all farmworkers and packing workers are Hispanic, but the unauthorized share of the field-workers is believed to be larger than the unauthorized share of non-farmworkers (*Rural Migration News*).

Apple pickers receive about $0.01 per pound for picking apples—about $8–10 for filling a 900-pound bin with 5,000 apples. Most pickers earn $7 to $8 per hour and are employed 500 to 800 hours per year, while nonfarm packing workers earn about $7.50 per hour. The state of Washington estimated that apple pickers earned an average $5,750 in 1996, and packinghouse workers earned $11,000. Some pickers can double their earnings by pruning and thinning apples in the winter and spring, but most leave the state after the harvest is over, returning to Mexico or home bases in California or Texas. An estimated 30 to 40 percent of Washington apple pickers are not authorized to work in the United States, about the same as the national average.

In the Northeast, apples are often picked by nonimmigrants admitted with H-2A visas. The H-2A program requires U.S. farm employers to demonstrate to the satisfaction of the U.S. Department of Labor that they tried and failed to find U.S. workers and then provide the H-2A foreign workers with free housing and pay their round-trip transportation. Farmers have to guarantee workers employment for at least 75 percent of a forty-four-hour workweek, or thirty-three hours a week. H-2A workers and any U.S. workers who are employed alongside them are guaranteed an adverse effect wage rate (AEWR), a minimum hourly wage established annually by the U.S. Department of Labor.[1]

FLORIDA ORANGES

U.S. farmworker employment peaks in September. Florida is different: the peak demand is in January. Florida is also different in the characteristics of farmworkers. The farm workforce in Florida changed from U.S.-born blacks and whites in the 1970s to foreign-born Hispanics in the 1980s and 1990s. With the U.S. trade embargo on Cuba and a ready supply of workers in Florida, Florida agriculture has expanded significantly over the past three decades. The Caribbean has traditionally been seen as a competitor in the product market and a source of farmworkers for Florida agriculture, making Florida one of the best examples of trade and migration dilemmas.

Citrus accounts for about 30 percent of Florida's $6 billion annual farm sales and employs 30 percent of the state's 100,000 peak farm employment—the peak is in January, although citrus is harvested from December through April. Florida farmers have traditionally relied on farm labor contractors (FLCs) or crew leaders to recruit and supervise crews of twenty to thirty pickers on their farms—about one-third of Florida's farm labor expenditures are paid to FLCs, the highest percentage of any state. Citrus growers often became joint employers with these FLCs/crew leaders; some testimony suggests that the reason for joint employment was that many of the black crew leaders were not literate.

Florida produces most of the oranges grown in the United States that are processed into orange juice. In 1996–1997, Florida produced 10.4 million tons or 220 million 90-pound boxes of oranges worth $825 million, or $3.70 per box. Citrus is picked into over-the-shoulder bags that weigh 70 to 90 pounds when full; the bags are dumped into field tubs or bins that hold about ten 90-pound boxes or 900 pounds of oranges. Pickers in the early 1990s were paid $0.60 to $0.70 per 90-pound box, up from $0.35 in the late 1960s. Crew leaders typically receive an overhead of 30 percent to cover the cost of payroll taxes, toilets, and supervision, bringing the total cost of harvesting oranges to about $0.91 per box, or $0.01 per pound (Commission on Agricultural Workers Hearing, West Palm Beach, Florida, February 14–16, 1991).

The industry has been shifting from the central part of the state to the southwest in an effort to avoid freezes and to find cheaper land as urban development accelerates in central Florida. The migration of the industry is also affecting the structure of citrus production and the characteristics of farmworkers. Many of the orange groves in the central part of the state were small, family-run operations of 30 to 40 acres each, while those in southwest Florida are often 2,000 to 3,000 acres and owned by corporations or absentee investors. Southwestern Florida has a relatively limited infrastructure to handle a seasonal influx of workers, and thus cities such as Immokalee have become, in one sense, "overgrown labor camps," places where often-unauthorized Mexicans and Guatemalans flock to link up with crew leaders for farm jobs.[2] In the mid-1990s, the Florida farm workforce was estimated to be 50 to 60 percent Mexican and Guatemalan, 20 percent Haitian, and 20 to 30 percent U.S.-born Mexican Americans, blacks, and whites.

Florida sugarcane is a special case in U.S. agriculture and farm labor. Between the 1950s and early 1990s, about half of the legal foreign workers admitted under the H-2/H-2A program were employed in Florida to hand-cut sugarcane, while U.S. sugar policies limited sugar imports from Caribbean islands. There are about 450,000 acres of sugarcane in Florida, producing sugarcane worth $400 million a year. There are perhaps 100 growers of cane, but only four mills to process it, and these mills do the harvesting.

Sugarcane production in southern Florida began in 1931, when GM executives founded U.S. Sugar, obtained swampland cheaply, and persuaded the government to construct dams so that the land draining into the Everglades could be farmed. U.S. Sugar in the early 1990s employed 3,500 H-2A workers from Jamaica to hand-cut cane; they earned, according to U.S. Sugar, about $7.29 in 1990, above the government-set minimum wage, the $5.30 AEWR. However, U.S. Sugar was charged with understating the hours workers work in order to raise the reported hourly earnings of its H-2A workers, and, in 1998, U.S. Sugar agreed to pay $5.6 million to settle suits that it underreported the hours of work of up to 20,000 H-2 workers between 1987 and 1991. U.S. Sugar mechanized cane harvesting in 1995.

CALIFORNIA GRAPES

California had record farm sales of $26.8 billion in 1997, up from $25.3 billion in 1996; number two Texas had farm sales of $15.9 billion in 1997. FVH sales were 60 percent of California farm sales in 1997, including fruits and nuts (worth $7.6 billion), vegetables and melons ($5.9 billion), and horticultural specialties such as nursery and greenhouse products ($2.5 billion). Table, wine, and raisin grapes worth $2.8 billion were the most valuable FVH commodity (*Rural Migration News*, October 1998).

The California grape industry illustrates three different ways of dealing with farm labor issues (Martin 1998). The United States is the world's third largest producer of grapes, after Italy and France. About 90 percent of U.S. grapes are produced in California, and 3 percent each in New York and Washington.

California had a record 744,000 acres of grapes in 1996, including 378,000 acres of wine grapes, 277,000 acres of raisin grapes (about half of the Thompson seedless grapes that are normally grown for raisins are instead sold to wineries and blended into bulk wines, so that only 125,000 to 150,000 acres of raisin grapes are typically harvested for raisins), and 88,000 acres of table grapes.[3] As the wine grape industry expanded, mechanical harvesters replaced hand pickers—between 1975 and 1995, the percentage of wine grapes harvested by machine increased from less than 10 percent to about seventy percent. Four hand harvesters can pick about one acre of grapes per day; a mechanical harvester, which uses a crew of five to harvest around the clock, can harvest ten to twenty acres per day.[4] Hand wine grape harvesters are paid $6 to $8 per hour to pick grapes that may be worth $1,500 per ton, or $0.75 per pound. Many hand harvesters are employed by wineries that want to protect their image, and some are represented by the United Farm Workers union. The percentage of unauthorized workers in the wine grape industry is less than the forty percent average.

About 15 percent of U.S. grapes are consumed fresh as table grapes. California produced a record 80 million twenty-one-pound boxes of table grapes in 1997; farmers received an average $0.36 per pound. Most table grapes are field-packed, which means that workers cut bunches of grapes, put them into plastic tubs, and take fifteen to twenty-five pounds of grapes to the end of each row, where they are packed into boxes and taken to cold storage locations. Table grape harvesters are typically paid $5 to $6 per hour, plus about $0.30 per box of grapes picked and packed. Many of the workers are women, and many are older than typical farmworkers, often in their forties and fifties. Many workers report earning $7 to $10 per hour, and those employed on large farms can obtain 1,000 hours of work between May and October and then draw unemployment insurance benefits. The percentage of unauthorized workers is less than the 40 percent average.

The raisin grape industry is different in seasonality, earnings, and worker characteristics. Some 40,000 to 60,000 workers are involved in what has been described as the single most labor-intensive activity in North American agriculture: harvesting raisin grapes around Fresno, California. The percentage of these workers who are unauthorized has been rising: 35 percent admitted to being unauthorized in 1991 (CAW 1992). If the share of unauthorized farmworkers increases by 3 to 5 percent per year, then in 1998, there were likely 55 to 70 percent unauthorized workers among raisin harvesters.

The raisin industry is characterized by forty-acre vineyards operated by persons in their mid-sixties, which makes the industry more likely to press for continued access to an immigrant workforce than to embrace mechanization or other laborsaving changes; in one early 1990s survey, fewer than one-third of raisin growers were interested in mechanization (Mason 1998). There are three major futures for the raisin industry, and each has different labor and immigration consequences:

1. The option preferred by most of the 4,000 raisin growers is to develop an alternative to the H-2A program, so that currently unauthorized workers could be hired legally without changing wages or working conditions. Between 1986 and 1996, harvest workers were paid $0.16 to $0.18 per 18 to 22 pounds of grapes that are cut and laid on a thirty-inch-square paper tray to dry; about 4.5 pounds of green grapes dry into 1 pound of raisins.

   Piece rate wages rose to $0.19–$0.20 a tray in 1998. On March 1, 1998, California's minimum wage rose to $5.75 an hour; California's minimum wage was $4.25 an hour in September 1996, so that the minimum wage has increased by $1.50 an hour, or 35 percent in fifteen months. If a typical piece rate increased from $0.17 in 1996 to $0.20 in 1998, the piece rate rose eighteen percent, half as fast as the hourly minimum.

   The FLCs who organize most harvest workers into crews are paid an additional 30 to 33 percent, or $0.06 per tray, as a commission to cover payroll taxes, provision of toilets, and supervision. Most workers harvest 300 to 400 twenty-five-pound trays of green grapes per nine-hour day, for daily earnings of $63, or $7 per hour. Workers employed 300 hours of work during the harvest season would earn $2,100 for harvesting raisins.

2. The cooperative that handles 35 percent of the U.S. raisin crop, Sun Maid, has developed a dried-on-the-vine (DOV) system that permits existing vineyards to be retrofitted into separate fruiting (higher vine) and harvesting/drying (lower vine) zones. Canes are trained to grow over guide wires on the southern side of rows planted in an east-west direction. The canes are cut by machine so that the grapes can dry while still in bunches on the vine, and then the raisins are harvested by a machine outfitted with rotating fingers and a catcher, with a blower eliminating most of the leaves. One machine with two operators can harvest about fifteen acres a day, equivalent to what a crew of thirty-five to forty workers can harvest by hand. The southside DOV system is used by a handful of Sun Maid's 1,500 growers on 400 to 500 acres; if it were adopted throughout the industry, the peak number of workers might fall by five-sixths, from 50,00 to 10,000.

3. Simpson Vineyards has designed a high-density DOV vineyard for the mechanical harvesting of raisin grapes. Grape vines grow on so-called pergola trellising that shades the whole vineyard floor much of the summer, and drip irrigation is used to minimize humidity—in this manner, the amount of sunlight on the leaves is maxi-

mized.[5] The advantage of this system, used on about 160 acres of newly planted raisin grapes, is that yields are five to six tons per acre, three times the industry average of two tons per acre. High-density DOV smooths out the demand for labor—about thirty-one hours per ton of raisins are needed versus the usual forty hours—and workers are employed year-round rather than in a four-to-six-week harvest period. If this high-density DOV system were widely adopted, the same quantity of raisins could be produced with one-third of today's raisin grape acreage, and the current peaks and troughs in the demand for labor would be practically eliminated.

Will the raisin industry follow the wine grape industry toward mechanization, which is likely to result in a smaller and more legal workforce? The major factors driving change in the raisin industry are (1) availability of harvest labor and (2) marketing/world competition. In the summer of 1998, there were claims of labor shortages in Fresno County, California, where the raisin industry is concentrated: Manuel Cunha of the Nisei Farmers League claimed that San Joaquin Valley growers were short 80,000 of their usual 230,000 seasonal workers and requested prison inmates, the National Guard, or delayed school starts to help harvest crops such as raisins. However, unemployment rates would seem to belie labor shortage claims: at a time when the U.S. unemployment rate was under 5 percent, all of Fresno County's farmworker cities had unemployment rates that were far, far higher (see Figure 5.2).

There is always a "labor shortage" in the raisin industry because growers want to wait as long as possible to hand-harvest, thereby raising sugar levels and the value of the raisins, but they must have their raisins on the ground by a critical date (e.g., September 20, 1998) if they want to collect insurance payments in case of rain. If there were a sustained labor shortage, growers would likely divide into two groups—those willing to make the investment needed for DOV and those that go out of business. A second factor that might change labor needs in the raisin industry is international competition. The United States is a high-cost producer of raisins. If non-U.S. producers such as Turkey raise the quality of their raisins to U.S. standards, lower-cost imports could force production changes that would have labor implications.

The apple, orange, and raisin industries illustrate that most U.S. growers of FVH commodities do not integrate labor into their planning decisions. Apples and oranges were planted in remote sections of Washington and Florida, where there were few workers and little infrastructure for migrant workers who were expected to arrive when trees were ready to pick. This "field of dreams" mentality permeates many planting decisions—in the past, government has acted to ensure that fruit did not rot on the trees by making immigrant workers available, and farmers assume that government will react in the same manner again.

Raisin grapes represent a second type of farm labor challenge. Much of the industry is not competitive globally, but instead of restructuring the industry to meet tougher international competition, many growers prefer to maximize dependence on labor, which can be laid off at no cost to the grower if imports

Figure 5.2
Unemployment Rates in Fresno County Farmworker Cities: July 1998

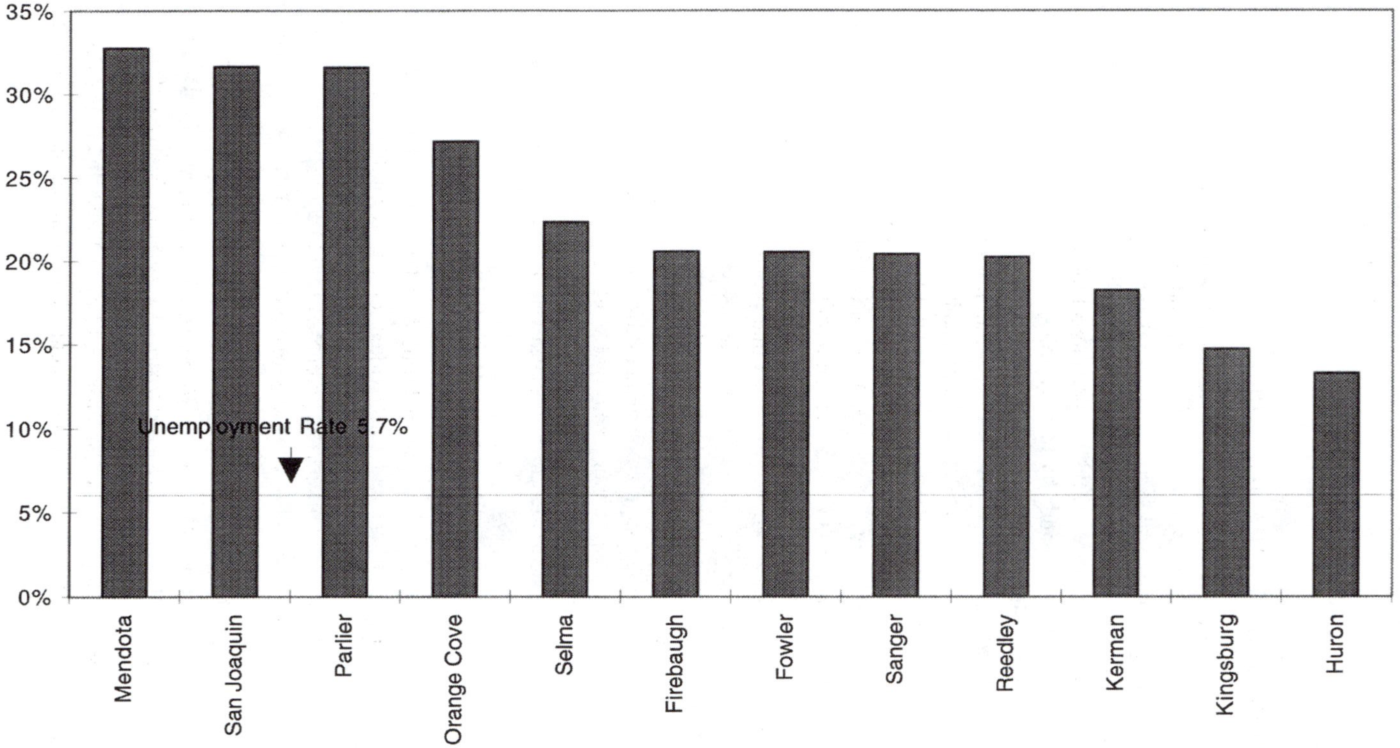

Source: Employment Development Department.

make producing raisins unprofitable. Bank loans to restructure the production methods, on the other hand, must be paid off whether or not farming raisins remains profitable.

FARM LABOR: THE WORKERS

The individuals who work on farms for wages—farmworkers—are diverse; they range from managers, office staff, and equipment operators to irrigators, harvesters, and general laborers. There is no single, reliable source of data that provides an accurate profile of farmworkers. Each source of data on farmworkers can be considered a window that permits a look inside the room. These windows vary from picture windows to peepholes, and their reliability or transparency ranges from almost clear to almost opaque.[6]

Three major sources of data provide information on farmworkers. Most employment data are collected from establishments or employers,[7] and most personal data on U.S. workers come from a household survey, the Current Population Survey (CPS), which is the source of monthly unemployment rate data. Neither establishment nor household surveys fully cover farmworkers, so many profiles of farmworkers are based on administrative data, such as that obtained when farmworkers or their children receive employment and training, health, or education services from the agencies that provide them.

Between the 1950s and the 1990s, the major source of data on the characteristics of hired farmworkers came from supplemental questions attached to the CPS in December; the basic CPS obtained demographic and employment information, and then supplemental questions were asked of those in households that had at least one member who had worked for wages on a farm during the previous twelve months. In the 1980s, about 1,500 households in the CPS reported that someone in the household did farmwork for wages in that year (Oliveira 1989).

The CPS continues to collect data on farmworkers. The 1994 CPS, for example, reported that an average 779,000 workers were employed for wages on the nation's farms by farmers or brought to farms by labor contractors. In addition, 66,000 workers had farmworker jobs as secondary jobs—over half of these workers were in the Midwest. Farmworkers are more likely to be male (84 percent) than all workers (52 percent), more likely to be Hispanic (42 percent vs. 9 percent) and younger (thirty-two years vs. thirty-six years)—about 55 percent of farmworkers were under thirty-five years of age. About 34 percent of farmworkers and 7 percent of all U.S. workers were born abroad. The 266,000 foreign-born farmworkers were 96 percent Hispanic and poorly educated—74 percent completed less than nine years of schooling (Runyan 1997).

There were 342,100 farmworkers in California, according to the March 1997 Current Population Survey (Bugarin and Lopez 1998). In comparison to persons employed in other industries and occupations, California farmworkers tend to be at the extremes of distributions. For example, farmworkers include the highest percentage of Latinos of any major occupation (78 percent in March 1997), the highest percentage of workers without high school diplomas (69 percent), and the highest percentage of workers who do not speak English well (50 percent in 1990). At the other end of the distributions, farmworkers have the lowest median family incomes ($17,700) and median earnings ($9,800) and the lowest percentage of workers employed nine or more months (56 percent).

The National Agricultural Worker Survey (NAWS) has become the most widely cited source of farmworker characteristics in the 1990s (Mines, Gabbard, and Steirman 1997; U.S. Department of Labor 1993a, b). The NAWS is a DOL-funded survey of farmworkers launched to determine entries into, and exits from, the farm workforce between 1989 and 1992. The NAWS interviews 2,500 workers a year employed on U.S. crop farms in 288 counties in twenty-five states; the states are grouped into twelve agricultural regions, with a minimum of four counties in each region (three regions are single states: California, Florida, and Texas). Workers are interviewed during one of three cycles that reflect agricultural activities: a fall cycle, a winter cycle, and a spring/summer cycle.

The NAWS reports that most farmworkers are immigrants and that the percent of immigrant farmworkers not authorized to work in the United States has been rising. About 70 percent of the farmworkers interviewed in 1994–1995 were born abroad, and the percentage of unauthorized workers rose from 7 percent in 1989 to 37 percent in 1995. Almost one in five workers in 1994–1995 was working on U.S. farms for the first time, and 70 percent of those working on U.S. farms for the first time in 1994–1995 were unauthorized.[8] Most farmworkers were young men—80 percent were male, and two-thirds of farmworkers were under age thirty-five in 1994–1995.

California farmworkers interviewed in the NAWS were more likely to be Mexican-born, to be employed by farm labor contractors (30 percent in California) rather than directly by growers, and to live off the farm than workers in other parts of the United States. The percentage of unauthorized farmworkers was about the same in California as in the rest of the United States in the early 1990s and was lower in 1997–1998 as unauthorized workers spread to other parts of the United States. California farmworkers do not speak English (only 11 percent in 1990–1991), and few finished high school (only 13 percent).

Stepped-up U.S. border control operations may be changing migration patterns for farmworkers. In the years between legalization in 1987–1988 until Gatekeeper and similar operations in 1994, many newly legalized married men brought their families illegally to the United States, anticipating eventual immigration visas. However, stepped-up U.S. border control operations have made it more difficult for women and children to illegally enter the United States, and the result in 1997–1998 was a return to a pre-Immigration Reform and Control Act (IRCA)-style solo male and often unauthorized farm workforce, a sort of guest worker program, in the sense that most of the solo men are in the United

States to maximize their earnings and savings. The deaths of migrants in the desert in the summer of 1998 have reportedly discouraged many women and children from attempting illegal entry.

FARM LABOR: EMPLOYERS AND IMMIGRATION

In the nineteenth century, U.S. agriculture in general and California agriculture in particular were considered land-abundant and labor-short. Labor shortages were compounded in California by the dominance of large farms growing fruit and vegetable crops that required large numbers of harvest workers (Fuller 1940; Fisher 1953).

California agriculture began in the 1850s and 1860s with a legacy of large Spanish and Mexican land grants; large tracts of land were necessary for grazing cattle and farming grain without irrigation. These large farms were expected to be broken up into family-sized parcels during the 1870s and the 1880s, when irrigation, advances in agricultural science, and the completion of the transcontinental railroad brought settlers to California and made labor-intensive fruit farming profitable. Since the 1870s, there has been a debate among farm labor reformers over (1) whether to break large farms into family-sized parcels, thus eliminating the need for so many seasonal farmworkers, or (2) whether factories in the fields should be acknowledged, and factory labor and immigration laws applied to agriculture. It now seems clear that large farms will not be broken up, but agriculture retains exemptions under U.S. labor and immigration laws.

The wages and working conditions that immigrant farmworkers were willing to accept largely determined wages and working conditions for all farmworkers. The availability of immigrant workers permitted agriculture to continue to offer seasonal jobs that paid about half of the average manufacturing wages, so farmworkers and their children moved into nonfarm jobs that offered higher wages, better working conditions, and year-round work as soon as they could. These exits from the farm workforce caused farm labor shortages, which were solved by importing more foreign workers, repeating the cycle.

The story is most transparent in California. The first seasonal farmworkers were the 12,000 Chinese workers who had been imported to build the railroad through the Sierra Nevada Mountains. When they were released by the railroad companies in 1870, they were kept out of urban jobs by anti-Chinese movements (Fuller 1940: 19809). Chinese immigration was halted in 1883, and the next wave of immigrant farmworkers was from Japan. Japanese immigration was stopped in 1907, and workers were imported from present-day India and Pakistan. The United States began to restrict immigration after World War I—the 1917 Immigration Act, for example, imposed a head tax on immigrants and excluded immigrants over sixteen who could not read in any language. California farmers asked the U.S. government to suspend the head tax and literacy test for Mexican workers coming to the United States for up to one year to work on U.S. farms, and the government agreed. Thus began U.S. government-approved recruitment of Mexican farmworkers.

Mexican migration for U.S. farmwork was stopped by repatriations during the depression and the arrival in California of dust bowl farmers from the Midwest. In 1942, U.S. government-approved Mexican migration for farmwork resumed and continued until 1964. So-called bracero workers were imported under a number of agreements, but, between 1942 and 1964, more Mexicans were apprehended in the United States than were admitted as legal farmworkers (Figure 5.3); that is, illegal immigration occurred alongside legal migration (Garcia y Griego 1981). Both apprehensions and bracero admissions measure events and not unique individuals—the same person could be apprehended several times, and the same person could be legally admitted as a bracero several times.

The availability of braceros permitted fruit and vegetable production to expand without real farm wages rising significantly. California fruit and nut production rose 15 percent during the 1950s, and vegetable production rose 50 percent. The U.S. Department of Agriculture's estimate of average hourly farmworker earnings rose 41 percent—slightly more than the 35 percent increase in consumer prices—from $0.85 in 1950 to $1.20 in 1960. In contrast, average factory wages in California rose 63 percent, from $1.60 per hour in 1950 to $2.60 in 1960.

After the bracero program ended in 1964, some Mexican workers became U.S. immigrants who commuted seasonally from homes in Mexico to farm jobs in the United States. During the 1960s, Mexicans could become so-called green card commuters by obtaining a letter from a U.S. employer offering a job and certifying that the employer sought and failed to find a U.S. worker to fill it. Most of the 50,000 to 60,000 Mexican immigrants admitted each year in the mid-1960s were believed to be ex-braceros who got U.S. immigrant status as a result of a U.S. farmer's offering them a job.

During the 1970s and early 1980s, U.S. citizens and green card commuters were joined in the fields by unauthorized or illegal alien workers. As IRCA moved toward approval in 1986, California farmers argued strongly that they needed easy access to Mexican and other foreign workers. Farmers "invested" $2 million to $4 million to lobby Congress to preserve access to foreign workers, and their investment was rewarded with the "Schumer" compromise—illegal, alien farmworkers who had done at least ninety days of U.S. farmwork could become immigrants. IRCA's special agricultural worker (SAW) provisions permitted 1 million Mexicans—about one-sixth of the adult men in rural Mexico—to become legal U.S. immigrants.

If there were farm labor shortages in the early 1990s, U.S. farmers could obtain legal foreign workers through two programs. The H-2A program is a nonimmigrant program that admits foreign workers to fill vacant jobs after the U.S. government certifies that the farmer made a good-faith effort but failed to recruit U.S. workers. The replenishment agricultural worker (RAW) program,

Figure 5.3
Mexican Immigration

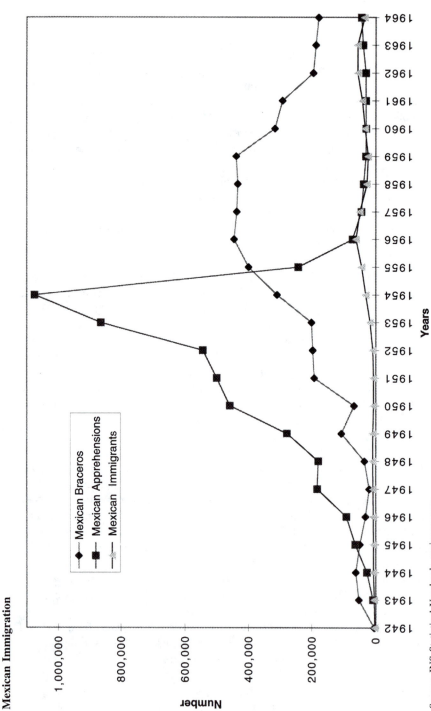

Source: INS Statistical Yearbook, various years.

by contrast, was a four-year safety-valve program. If SAWs left agriculture, and labor shortages developed, then RAW probationary immigrants could be admitted. The U.S. government did not find farm labor shortages in the 1990s, largely because illegal immigration continued, and workers and employers found it easy to use counterfeit documents to satisfy employee verification requirements (Martin et al. 1995). However, SAW workers did not stay in agriculture: as they left, they were replaced by unauthorized workers (see Figure 5.4).

ALTERNATIVE FUTURES: ILLEGALS, GUEST WORKERS, UNIONS, OR MECHANIZATION

At the end of the twentieth century, the percentage of U.S. farmworkers who are not authorized to work in the U.S. is 40 percent and rising. Will twenty-first century farmworkers be unauthorized migrants, legal guest workers, or U.S. workers with other job opportunities who elect to remain in agriculture, or will U.S. farmers offer fewer seasonal farm jobs? These future trajectories are interlinked; for example, easier access to immigrant workers will likely slow both unionization and mechanization.

Illegals/Guest Workers. There is consensus that the farm labor status quo is suboptimal. Farmers are unsure if workers will be available when they are needed, and they fear harvest time Immigration and Naturalization Service (INS) raids that might leave them without a labor force. On the other hand, farmers do not want to obtain legal, nonimmigrant workers through the H-2A program because they fear that required certification from the U.S. Department of Labor will expose them to lawsuits from farmworker advocates and stepped-up labor law enforcement.

To avoid the Hobson's choice between the risk of INS raids and the risk of H-2A-related lawsuits, farm employers have been asking Congress for a free agent guest worker program. The major difference between the H-2A program and the Agricultural Job Opportunity Benefits and Security Act (AgJobs) of 1998, the latest version of the farmers' proposal, is that the H-2A program requires government certification of the farmer's need for workers before the border gates are opened, while AgJobs would permit the farmer to open the border gates by attesting that he tried and failed to find U.S. workers, and the government would enforce regulations for AgJobs only if there were complaints. For a farmer worried about harvest labor shortages, AgJobs is preferred because enforcement, if any, occurs after the work has begun.

The AgJobs program was approved in the U.S. Senate by a lopsided 68–31 vote in July 1998. The heart of AgJobs is a system of farmworker registries to be created and maintained by DOL. Workers would have to apply for inclusion in the registry, and DOL/INS would have to certify the legal status of all workers asking to be registered, so that only legally authorized workers were referred to growers. Farmers seeking workers would apply at the closest registry at least twenty-one days before workers were needed, and if an insufficient number of

Figure 5.4
Legalized SAWs and Unauthorized Farmworkers: 1989–1995

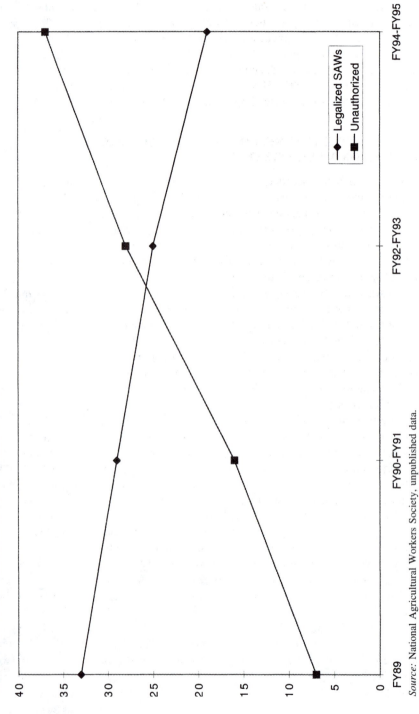

Source: National Agricultural Workers Society, unpublished data.

workers were registered, farmers would be presumed to need foreign workers, who would be admitted to fill the vacant jobs.

Critics had three major objections to AgJobs. First, they argued that AgJobs made it too easy for farmers to reject qualified U.S. workers. Employers could reject U.S. workers who fail "to meet lawful job-related employment criteria" such as the ability to pick fast enough at the piece-rate wage offered to earn the minimum wage. Second, critics noted that the adverse effect wage rate—the government-set minimum wage designed to offset the wage-depressing effects of foreign workers—would be eliminated. Third, AgJobs would eliminate the requirement that employers must provide housing at no cost to U.S. and foreign workers, under the theory that workers entering an area for seasonal farmwork have little time or ability to locate their own acceptable housing.

AgJobs was not included in the FY 1999 budget approved in October 1998; most observers credit strong opposition from Hispanic representatives in the House and a White House veto threat. But farmers promised to make another effort to legalize the farm labor status quo in 1999.

Unions/Mechanization.   There are several alternatives to agriculture's growing dependence on legal or unauthorized farmworkers, including union-inspired changes in wages and working conditions that turn farmwork from a job into a career, mechanization that substitutes a handful of equipment operators for an army of harvest workers, and freer trade that allows the United States to import labor-intensive commodities rather than laborers.

One goal of the United Farm Workers union has been to convert farmwork from a job into a career. During its heyday in the 1970s, the UFW attempted to imitate the longshore unions and make the union the major organizing instrument in the casual farm labor market—the UFW would operate hiring halls and allocate work to union members on the basis of their union seniority. The UFW's hiring halls, operating without computers among workers who preferred to work with family or friends, failed miserably and were dropped from most UFW contracts in the 1980s.

Even if employers continue to select workers, unions could make farmwork an attractive career option by raising wages, improving working conditions and fringe benefits, and establishing job ladders within firms. However, there are fewer union contracts in agriculture in the 1990s than there were in the 1970s, and each new union victory seems offset by a union defeat. Despite a new emphasis on organizing in 1993, after the death of Cesar Chavez, the UFW in California has been able to increase its membership from about 20,000 to only 26,000, one-third of its peak 70,000 members in the 1970s. The Farm Labor Organizing Committee, based in Ohio, has a reported 7,000 members but believes that its wage gains may be undermined by the growth of cucumber production in lower-wage North Carolina.

If unions are unlikely to alter the farm labor market, perhaps mechanization or trade might lead to fewer U.S. farm jobs and farm labor market restructuring. Mechanization usually speeds up when wages are rising relative to machinery costs; the opposite has happened since the 1970s (Figure 5.5). There was a widespread expectation that the North American Free Trade Agreement (NAFTA) would shift farm jobs to Mexico and reduce illegal immigration. This may happen in the long run, but until at least 2005, NAFTA is more likely to increase, than to decrease, Mexican–U.S. migration, reflecting the migration hump that often accompanies closer economic integration.

CONCLUSIONS

At the end of the twentieth century, there are probably more foreign-born workers employed in U.S. agriculture than at any time since 1900, and there is little prospect that the immigrant percentage of the 2.5 million persons who do farmwork for wages will stop rising from its current 70 percent. The major policy issue in the late 1990s is what legal status these workers should have: illegal, nonimmigrant H-2A or guest worker, or legal immigrant.

The status quo is probably not sustainable. As the "face" of U.S. agricultural areas changes with the influx of Hispanic immigrants to do farmwork, the result is a patchwork of poverty amid prosperity: most of the immigrants who do seasonal farmwork have individual and family incomes below the U.S. poverty line, while farm production and sales increase to record levels (Taylor, Martin, and Fix, 1997). The most important agricultural county in the United States, Fresno County, California, illustrates this poverty-amid-prosperity trend. In 1997, Fresno County had farm sales of $3.3 billion, more than half the state's, yet 40 percent of the almost 800,000 residents of the county had incomes below the poverty line, twenty-five percent received some form of public assistance in 1997, unemployment averaged 12 percent, and farmers complained of labor shortages and asked for easier access to guest workers.

The contrast between the two major labor shortage and immigration debates in 1998 illustrates why the immigrant farm labor issue is likely to persist. High-tech employers persuaded Congress to approve in 1998 the American Competitiveness Act, which increased the number of visas available to foreign computer programmers and other professionals by 143,500 over three years. All parties agreed that the United States must train more U.S. citizens to be programmers, and employers were required to pay $500 per visa to provide funding for training and scholarships for Americans.

In agriculture, there was no long-run plan to eliminate the need for foreign workers in the future. Under AgJobs, fees were aimed at inducing migrants to leave the United States, not upgrading jobs to attract Americans: if the attorney general found that a significant number of AgJobs workers were remaining in the United States, 20 percent of their earnings could be deducted by their employers, paid into a U.S. Trust Fund, and returned to the worker only after he surrendered his visa-ID at a U.S. consulate in his country of origin. This difference between the two approaches to resolving labor shortage complaints

Figure 5.5
Ratio of U.S. Farm Wages Index to Index of Farm Machinery Prices, 1945–1990

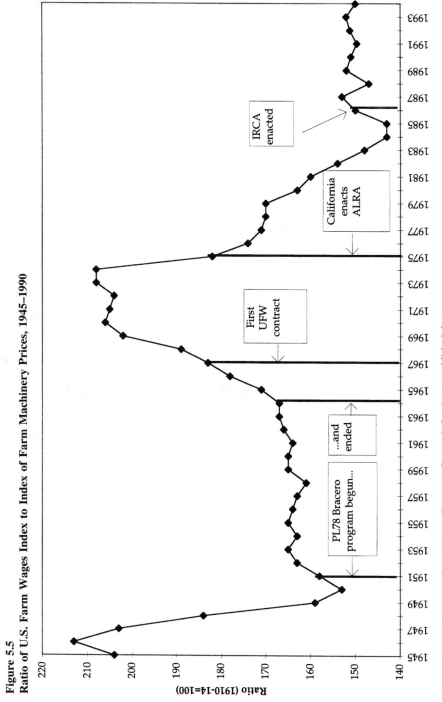

Source: U.S. Department of Agriculture, Economic Research Service, unpublished data.

speaks volumes about the different visions Americans have of the high-tech and the farm labor markets.

NOTES

1. The H-2A program admits temporary foreign workers to the United States under the H-2A program, Section 101(a)(15)(H)(ii)(a) of the Immigration and Nationality Act. The Department of Labor (DOL) reports the number of jobs that it certifies can be filled by foreign H-2A workers. In fiscal year (FY) 1996, DOL certified the need for H-2A workers to fill 19,100 U.S. farm jobs, including 4,900 in North Carolina (mostly tobacco), 3,100 in Virginia (2,700 of them in tobacco), 2,600 in New York (all apples), 1,200 in Kentucky, and 1,100 in Connecticut (851 in tobacco). By commodity, there were 9,800 jobs certified in tobacco, 4,600 in apples, 1,700 in shepherding, and 1,100 in vegetables.

2. The United Farm Workers (UFW) had a collective bargaining agreement covering 600 orange harvesters with the Minute Maid subsidiary of Coca-Cola between 1972 and 1993. In December 1993, Coca-Cola Foods sold 16,000 acres of Florida oranges, ending the contract.

3. Most U.S. grapes by tonnage are processed—85 percent, including 64 percent that are turned into wine, 28 percent into raisins, and 8 percent into grape juice.

4. About 16 percent of U.S. adults consume 88 percent of the wine drunk in the United States. As with most farm products, most of the value-added in wine grapes comes after the grapes leave the vineyard. The cost of the grapes in a $20 retail bottle of Napa chardonnay is about $2.25, while the distributor and retailer markup is $10. On a $7 retail bottle of chardonnay, the grapes cost $1, and the distributor and retailer markup is $3.50.

5. Most raisin growers receive water from the Fresno Irrigation District, which charges a flat price per acre regardless of how much water is applied. For this reason, most growers use flood irrigation.

6. For a review and appraisal of various farm labor data sources, see Martin and Martin (1993).

7. It is easier and cheaper to obtain data from a sample of the 7 million employers in the United States than from a sample of 100 million households, or 140 million workers.

8. NAWS data found that 70 percent of U.S. crop workers were born in Mexico in the 1994–1997 period and that 72 percent of the workers doing farmwork for the first time were Mexicans.

REFERENCES

Bugarin, Alicia, and Elias Lopez
1998   *Farmworkers in California.* California Research Bureau. CRB 98–007. July.
CAW (Commission on Agricultural Workers)
1992   *Report of the Commission on Agricultural Workers.* Washington, D.C.: U.S. Government Printing Office. November.
Craig, Richard B.
1971   *The Bracero Program: Interest Groups and Foreign Policy.* Austin: University of Texas Press.

Daniel, Cletus E.

1981   *Bitter Harvest: A History of California Farmworkers 1870–1941*. Berkeley: University of California Press.

Fisher, Lloyd

1953   *The Harvest Labor Market in California*. Cambridge: Harvard University Press.

Fuller, Varden

1940   The Supply of Agricultural Labor as a Factor in the Evolution of Farm Organization in California. Unpublished Ph.D. dissertation, U.C. Berkeley, 1939. Reprinted in Violations of Free Speech and the Rights of Labor Education and Labor Committee [LaFollette Committee]. Washington, D.C.: Senate Education and Labor Committee. 19778–19894.

Gabbard, Susan, Richard Mines, and Beatiz Boccalandro

1994   *Migrant Farmworkers: Pursuing Security in an Unstable Labor Market*. Washington, D.C.: U.S. Department of Labor, ASP Research Report 5. May.

Galarza, Ernesto

1964   *Merchants of Labor: The Mexican Bracero Story*. Charlotte, North Carolina: McNally and Loftin.

García y Griego, Manuel

1981   The Importation of Mexican Contract Laborers to the U.S., 1941–1964. Program in U.S.–Mexican Studies, UCSD, Working Paper 11.

Jefferson, Thomas

1982   [orig 1787] *Notes on the State of Virginia*. Edited by William Peden. Chapel Hill: University of North Carolina Press.

Martin, Philip L.

1993   *Trade and Migration: NAFTA and Agriculture*. Washington, D.C.: Institute for International Economics. October.

1996   *Promises to Keep: Collective Bargaining in California Agriculture*. Ames: Iowa State University Press.

1998   Immigration and the Changing Face of Rural California. Report of the conference held in Parlier, California. Mimeo. September 10–12, 1998.

Martin, Philip L., and David Martin

1993   *The Endless Quest: Helping America's Farm Workers*. Boulder, Colorado: Westview Press.

Martin, Philip, Wallace Huffman, Robert Emerson, J. Edward Taylor, and Refugio Rochin, Editors

1995   *Immigration Reform and U.S. Agriculture*. Berkeley, California: Division of Agriculture and Natural Resources Publication 3358.

Mason, Bert

1998   The Raisin Grape Industry. Mimeo. August.

McWilliams, Carey

1939   *Factories in the Field*. Boston: Little Brown.

Mines, Richard, Susan Gabbard, and Anne Steirman

1997   *A Profile of U.S. Farmworkers: Demographics, Household Composition, Income and Use of Services*. Washington, D.C.: U.S. Department of Labor. April.

Oliveira, Victor

1989   *Trends in the Hired Farm Work Force, 1945–87*. Washington, D.C.: U.S. Department of Agriculture, Economic Research Service, Agricultural Information Bulletin 561.

Oliveira, Victor, Anne Effland, Jack Runyan, and Shannon Hamm
1993   *Hired Farm Labor Use on Fruit, Vegetable, and Horticultural Specialty Farms.* Washington, D.C.: U.S. Department of Agriculture, Economic Research Service, Agricultural Economics Report 676. December.

Runyan, Jack L.
1997   Profile of Hired Farm Workers, 1994 Annual Averages. U.S.D.A. Economic Research Service Report 748.

Rural Migration News
quarterly   http://migration.ucdavis.edu or rural@primal.ucdavis.edu

Taylor, J. Edward, Philip Martin, and Michael Fix
1997   *Poverty amid Prosperity: Immigration and the Changing Face of Rural California.* Washington, D.C.: Urban Institute Press.

U.S. Bureau of the Census
1997   *Statistical Abstract of the United States.* Washington, D.C.

U.S. Department of Labor
1993a   U.S. Farm Workers in the Post-IRCA Period. Washington, D.C.: Office of the Assistant Secretary for Policy, Office of Program Economics. March.
1993b   California Findings from the National Agricultural Workers Survey. Washington, D.C.: Office of the Assistant Secretary for Policy, Office of Program Economics.

6

Social and Cultural Bases for Undocumented Immigration into the U.S. Poultry Industry

David Griffith

Daily, throughout much of rural America, eighteen-wheeled trucks coming from long, metal chicken houses arrive at chicken-processing factories and sit in the breezes of huge industrial fans until the birds are ready for what poultry workers know as "live-hang." Just six weeks old, within hours of their arrival, the birds will enter the dim light of blue, frosted bulbs in a room where people wearing paper gas masks yank them from yellow and red crates to hang upside down on hooks for a fatal ride through an electrified bath, between spinning pluckers and jets of flame, down along fields of eviscerators, cutters, graders, packagers, and loaders, and, finally, chilled, onto refrigerated trucks to market. The consumer's table is the end point of historical and industrial processes whose development has reached into the genetic design of the chicken as deeply as into land use patterns and labor relations throughout rural America. Over the past fifty years, the poultry industry, for a radius of at least twenty-five miles around each of its plants, has influenced cropping systems, environmental health, ethnic relations, and the social and cultural complexions of labor and housing markets of rural hamlets and neighborhoods throughout hundreds of small towns.

In the most recent chapter of its history, the poultry industry has begun recruiting documented and undocumented immigrant workers, replacing its traditional labor force of female and African-American workers with people from Mexico, Central America, the Caribbean, and various parts of the world where state crises have resulted in large-scale refugee movements and emigration. While it is impossible to estimate the exact number of undocumented immigrants, interviews with both poultry personnel managers and immigrants suggest that undocumented immigrants have had less and less difficulty moving around in rural neighborhoods and labor markets in the southeastern United States, where much of the poultry industry is concentrated (Griffith 1993, 1995). In recent newspaper coverage, immigrants were so complacent about enforcement of immigration laws that they agreed to be photographed and named and gave their places of work for the interview (Andrews 1998). Because the industry's jobs have become subject to high labor turnover, being among some of the most hazardous jobs in the world, the specific character of groups entering and leaving the industry continues to change from year to year and from region to region.

This chapter discusses the industry from the perspective of its ability to absorb documented and undocumented immigrants into its labor force, describing a context in which accessing new immigrants and refugees has become an industry standard. It gives a brief overview of the industry's history, followed by a con- sideration of the ways immigrants have entered and, in some regions, colonized in poultry-processing jobs. I pay particular attention to the relationships that exist among rural labor and housing markets and how these fit into the migration histories of immigrants from Mexico, Central America, the Caribbean, and other areas. The industry's continual need to construct and reconstruct its labor sup- plies from a wide variety of sources has led to the Latinization of many parts of rural America, a process that creates ever more complex social infrastructures and cultural settings capable of incorporating undocumented immigrants.

BACKGROUND: FROM EGG MONEY TO BROILERS

Prior to the 1940s, most poultry production in the United States was con- ducted as a somewhat marginal sideline to market-oriented crop and livestock production, its reputation on farms being primarily of an activity of farm wives, raising hens to sell surplus eggs and birds in nearby urban areas. After World War II and particularly through the 1950s, poultry production changed from a subsidiary farm activity to one that attracted more and more agricultural capital, with ever larger and more integrated producers growing young birds called "broilers" specifically for sale (Griffith 1993: 84–89). The way this industry developed laid the groundwork for today's use of immigrants in four principal ways: (1) industry organization has expanded opportunities for accessing new immigrant and different immigrant groups; (2) subcontracting, common in im- migrant labor markets, has been common in the poultry industry for over half a century; (3) geographical shifts in production locations have put the industry closer to rural neighborhoods of immigrants; and (4) high turnover in poultry- processing plants has created the need for constant supplies of new, disposable workers.

First, the industry has distinct, integrated sectors that have different labor requirements: grow-out farms, consisting of farmers who build chicken houses (often with letters of support from poultry companies) and raise chickens for the processing plants through subcontractual arrangements; hatcheries, where workers sex and debeak the birds; feed mills; and processing plants. Of these sectors, processing plants are the most labor-intensive and today occupy the center of the industry, literally and figuratively.[1] The industry is vertically integrated in the sense that all sectors feed into the processing plants, with the industry rule of thumb being that they locate all within a twenty-five mile radius of the plant. Hatcheries and feed mills tend to be staffed by local workers, although immigrant Koreans used to be used to sex chickens in the hatcheries, a fairly esoteric and painstaking task. While most of the work with chickens on the grow-out farms is handled by farm owners and their family members, often these same farmers grow perishable fruits and vegetables that require large numbers of largely undocumented immigrant workers every season (Griffith and Kissam 1995: Chapter 3). In many regions, this has alerted processing plants to the potential opportunities of using immigrant labor, while also alerting immigrants about the potential opportunities of using the plants to settle out of the migrant stream and stabilize their income and employment.

Second, the subcontracting arrangements that exist between grow-out farmers and the processing plants are similar to the labor subcontracting arrangements that characterize many industries that utilize immigrants, including some, such as farm labor, that are located in rural areas alongside chicken-processing plants. Undocumented immigrants, in particular, rely on labor contractors because they provide (at usually exorbitant rates) housing, transportation, documentation, and other services that enable workers to move around the countryside undetected by authorities. Quite recently, the U.S. Department of Labor expressed concern over farm labor contractors' beginning to increase their presence in the poultry industry. At the same time, several labor organizations in the United States have adopted strong positions toward subcontractual agreements, more commonly known as outsourcing, as the June 1998 United Automobile Workers (UAW) strike demonstrated. For a number of reasons, industries that rely heavily on subcontracting are often among the easiest for undocumented immigrants to penetrate. This is because, over time, the workforce is broken up into several small firms, integrated through a corporate office, each firm hiring workers under its own labor policy. In most cases, the company need not treat these individuals as employees but can treat them as contract workers, similar to those workers who worked for the infamous banana company in Garcia Márquez's *One Hundred Years of Solitude* (1970):

Tired of that hermeneutical delirium, the workers turned away from the authorities in Macondo and brought their complaints up to the higher courts. It was there that the sleight-of-hand lawyers proved that the demands lacked all validity for the simple reason that the banana company did not have, never had had, and never would have any workers in its service because they were all hired on a temporary and occasional basis . . . and by the decision of the court it was established and set down in solemn decrees that the workers did not exist. (1970: 307)

In industries with seasonal shifts in production, breaking up the labor force into small groups enables large firms to expand and contract their labor forces by negotiating subcontracts when the need arises and simply not entering into such agreements when consumer demand for their products is slack.[2]

Third, at the same time that the poultry industry became more vertically integrated, displacing the home production operations, it moved into the southern United States, where land and labor costs were cheaper (Lasley 1980); this had the added advantage of placing poultry firms within reach of populations of Mexican and Mexican-American workers, who began migrating into rural areas of the Southeast as early as the 1950s (Griffith and Kissam 1995). While poultry plants continued to rely primarily on African-American and female labor into the 1980s, Mexican and Central American workers, at first confined largely to Texas plants, diffused through the industry relatively rapidly during the late 1980s and early 1990s (Griffith 1993). In some regions, these immigrants displaced African-American workers, while in others they filled a vacuum as African-American workers left the plants, depending on the character of growth around poultry plants. Some regions of the South during this period became havens for retirees moving in from northern regions of the country, creating opportunities for African Americans in nursing, home health care, domestic and food services, security, and other services connected to the growth of gated communities catering to the elderly. Other regions of the South witnessed influxes of automobile and automobile parts manfacturing, as foreign automakers began producing in the United States and as U.S. automakers began outsourcing production tasks to cheaper, nonunion, southern locations. At the same time, this was a time of industry expansion because of increased consumption of poultry—particularly the labor-intensively produced, specialty boned cuts— throughout the United States, which surpassed beef consumption in 1987 (U.S. Bureau of the Census 1990; Griffith 1995). Thus, as labor available for poultry processing was constricting in some areas, the need for more labor was on the rise. This trend continued into the 1990s, as the country reached nearly full employment by 1996, a key factor in the reelection of a president from the largest poultry-producing state in the nation.[3]

Fourth, as part of the process of vertical integration, industrial growth in poultry involved the transfer of relatively highly paid, skilled butchers' jobs from supermarkets into rural processing plants, replacing jobs that paid between five and eight times the minimum wage with factory jobs paying about one and one-half times minimum wage (Lasley 1980). Instead of staffing stores with butchers, supermarkets now needed only minimum-wage stock boys to unload prepackaged chicken portions. As this occurred, the processing sector became more and more labor-intensive and began to be characterized by higher turnover and more hazardous jobs, creating the need for "disposable" workers (Hackenberg et al. 1996).

High injury rates and the resulting turnover allowed immigrants to shift into processing jobs easily, primarily because of the industry's history of recruiting new workers through the networks of current workers rather than relying on conventional sources such as newspaper ads and radio. While most firms continued to use conventional channels, network recruiting became so institution-alized that many poultry firms offered bonuses to workers who brought new workers into the plant. Once the first immigrants entered the plants, it became relatively easy to fill vacancies opened by injuries and other sources of high turnover with the friends and relatives of immigrants, whether documented or not. For undocumented immigrants in particular, network recruiting was partic-ularly fortuitous, since network recruitment occurred outside conventional chan-nels such as employment services and was based on relations of trust between current and new workers. Bach et al. (1990) report, moreover, that network recruiting became more efficient with the expansion of communications tech-nologies among immigrants, where jobs could be filled quickly through phone calls to immigrants' home villages (see Goldring 1990).

TIME AND SPACE IN THE PRODUCTION OF POULTRY

The four developments just described encouraged widespread use of foreign, primarily Mexican, and largely undocumented workers. Why foreign workers? In his historical work about sugar, Mintz (1983) suggested that the coordination between mill and field necessary on West Indian sugar plantations introduced the time regimen that, later, came to be mistakenly viewed as the offspring of urban factory production. Similarly, Scott Cook (personal manuscript) referred to "industrialization before industrialization" when writing about Mexican stone workers based in rural hamlets in Oaxaca, and Raymond Williams, in a reference to the Industrial Revolution in *The Country and the City*, linked agricultural and industrial production within the intimate contexts of food consumption and so-cial reproduction:

The growth of the industrial working-class must be related also, and perhaps primarily, to the growth of population, itself spectacular, which though primarily related to birth and death rates in the general modernisation of the society, is related also to the increase in agricultural production which was so marked in the eighteenth century: especially in corn, but also in meat; changes themselves related to enclosure and more efficient pro-duction. The crisis of poverty, which was so marked in towns and villages alike in the late eighteenth and early nineteenth centuries, was a result of this social and economic process as a whole, and cannot be explained as the fall of one order and the institution of another. (1973: 98)

Within these observations lie the fundamentals of rural industrialization and the essential cause of the transition from native to foreign labor in the poultry industry: the desire to produce more efficiently by more closely regulating work-ers' time. In the most industrialized of rural industries—after the fashion of law firms or HMOs making salaried lawyers and doctors account for their time in fifteen minute intervals, following the development of the time clock, the timed visit to the rest room, the timed coffee break—breaking up a worker's day into minutes and his or her week into shifts has become so prevalent that the rhythms of production influence his or her leisure time, at the same time influencing the work and nonwork schedules of many others in the community. In rural industries that depend on agricultural products, regulating time extends to the farmers and other producers who supply, say, corn to the mill, tomatoes to the cannery, oranges to the juice plant, or, in the present case, birds to the processing plants.

Regulating time is most efficiently accomplished by regulating space as well, arranging landscapes in ways that encircle production centers or at least reduce transportation time and expense. From a broad geographical perspective, the high values placed on controlling space influenced the early development of the poultry industry and the later development of the beef- and hog-processing industries, initiating the former's move south and the latter's move west and now south. More narrowly, in communities near poultry plants, regulating space involves encouraging housing and transportation arrangements for workers that best suit the production schedules of processing plants.

Attempts to regulate time and rearrange landscapes rarely occur without some resistance from some segment of the native population. Recently, in a community neighboring the town where I live, IBP—one of the world's largest hog producers—tried to push through the zoning to establish a 15,000/day hog-slaughtering facility. The facility would have encouraged the development of hog confinement operations capable of raising 3,000–4,000 head per farm, utilizing less acreage than the average tobacco allotment. North Carolina is courting operations of this sort because the legislature is peppered with hog farmers, because tobacco's demise has hastened the search for alternative production on small spaces, and because raising livestock in confined settings, through subcontractual arrangements, has already been pioneered by the poultry industry. As in the poultry industry, whose gradual development in the East and South through the 1940s and 1950s encouraged ecological transformation from diverse cropping strategies to the production of feed grains and birds, the hog industry will eventually reconfigure landscapes to streamline pork production, surrounding its processing plants with not only confinement operations but farrowing facilities, waste lagoons, and feed mills, as well as furthering the trend to produce feed grains and soybeans that the poultry industry founded. It will, in addition, encourage the growth of immigrant communities around the slaughtering and processing of hogs.

My own community mobilized against IBP primarily around the prophecy of environmental havoc, particularly the hog industry's adverse impacts on water quality. But during the debates and arguments, while IBP managed to convince twelve of thirteen county commissioners of the county's economic need for the slaughterhouse, other arguments against the plant were added to those about water quality, including publicity about attracting new immigrants, stressing rural housing stocks, dealing with high rates of occupational injury, and so forth.

When Upton Sinclair wrote *The Jungle*, the outrage people felt derived less from the workers' conditions than the filth inside the plants and the food safety issues this filth raised. Similarly, this past summer, residents of eastern North Carolina blocked IBP less because of the direct human costs of the plant than the environmental costs. Presumably, food safety and water quality issues affect everyone, but the issues of occupational health, housing insecurity, and ethnic relations are more confined to specific jobs, neighborhoods, and peoples. In rural America, thus, the metaphors of confinement and regulated existence apply not merely to chickens and now hogs but also to people, particularly in the areas of housing and work.

HOUSING AND NEIGHBORHOODS

The development of rural industry, in its demand for labor, usually draws individuals out of other rural occupations, particularly agriculture but also the domestic production segments of the economy. New industries can always count on meeting a portion of their labor needs from the local area—more or less depending on the character of economic growth or decline in the region, distance from population clusters, and ability to encourage commuting. To the extent that new industries utilize local residents—filling gaps in economic opportunity in the wake of plant closures or farm foreclosures—they present no additional strain on existing housing stocks.

Encouraging immigration into a region, however, as often happens with new rural industries, may result in several housing problems, some of which exist in the community and some of which immigrants bring with them. In her work on rural poverty and housing insecurity, Janet Fitchen discusses several housing problems rural communities are likely to be experiencing prior to the arrival of new industries. Most of us are familiar with the low-income rural neighborhoods of the kind Fitchen discusses: "open country neighborhoods of dilapidated farmhouses, isolated trailers, and mixed clusters of houses, trailers, shacks, and makeshift buildings; lower cost trailer parks, either in the countryside or in small communities; and small, economically depressed hamlets and villages where vacant houses and commercial buildings have been divided and converted to cheap apartments'' (1992: 179).

Residents of any of these kinds of neighborhoods may be on the brink of homelessness for several reasons, including under- or unemployment, which new industry may address, but usually because of other reasons related to imbalance between the demand for, and supply of, low-income housing in rural areas. Among the factors Fitchen notes are zoning, rural gentrification (suburban-like development in rural areas), increasingly stringent building codes, and rising housing costs, primary rents, in neighboring urban areas. With large proportions of the rural poor in these kinds of neighborhoods renting instead of owning their dwellings, increasing competition for low-cost housing is likely to result in crowding, sporadic homelessness, increased movement among different forms of temporary housing (shelters and campsites), and shorter-term and perverse housing strategies (sponging, sleeping around, moving in with relatives).

The scope and character of these behaviors will certainly vary from region to region, but ethnographic information from areas that fill with low-income immigrants every year, such as the farming communities of Florida, Texas, and California, provides some means of anticipating problems that are likely to arise. Immokalee, Florida, is a small, inland community in Collier County in the heart of tomato, citrus, gladiolus, and vegetable fields. During much of the year, Immokalee is a sleepy community of 8,000–9,000, inhabited by the descendants of poachers and fishers and a handful of Mexican-American families whose parents and grandparents settled out of the harvest work and established themselves as local businessmen and civic leaders thirty or forty years ago. From late October until March, however, Immokalee's population more than quadruples: the surrounding harvests attract 25,000–30,000 additional residents. They arrive from Mexico, Central America, the Caribbean, and other parts of the United States, as far away as Washington State's Yakima Valley.

The community is always partially prepared for this annual invasion, maintaining a foundation housing stock of labor camps, dormitories, trailers, and other kinds of temporary units (including shelters), but every year demand for housing outstrips supply. What happens to the surplus tenants? They spill over into garages, utility sheds, vacant lots, and farm storage areas. They double and triple up, they share water supplies, they drink themselves into states where they don't care where they sleep, they bathe in restaurant rest rooms, they roam around. Crowding and tolerating unsafe conditions become the rules instead of the exceptions for a good portion of the population, resulting in increased tensions that often take the form of ethnic conflicts. Competition for space exacerbates these conflicts and favors those employers who can offer housing as a part of employment, undermining workers' bargaining powers regarding wages and working conditions at the same time.

One of the adaptive responses to housing shortages that tends not to occur in Immokalee but has been documented in several other locations is the practice of sleeping in shifts, of two or more individuals using a single bed or single room at different times of the day. After a large North Carolina poultry firm began suffering from housing shortages for its workers, it established a trailer park and began assigning housing as though it was just another task. In one case, they assigned a married couple, both Mexican, to a trailer and then assigned two unrelated, unfamiliar to the couple, single Mexican men to the same trailer. As though forcing the couple to live with two unfamiliar men weren't enough, they then assigned one of the men and the husband to the day shift and the other man and the wife to the night shift, expecting the wife to sleep in the trailer with the man during the day.

Anecdotes like this suggest that as rural industries construct labor markets, they also construct neighborhoods. In many of today's rural areas, with the recruitment of many rural factory workers out of the farm labor market, these constructed neighborhoods are likely to be multiethnic in character, including new and old residents from backgrounds as disparate as Port-au-Prince, Haiti, and the Hmong villages of Southeast Asia. While multiethnic neighborhoods can be rich in character, spawning fascinating markets, artistic styles, and other cultural practices, under conditions of poverty and competition for jobs and other resources, interethnic relations (as we know from several infamous cases in Eastern Europe and the former Soviet Union) are more often hostile than benevolent or benign. One of the lessons of a recently completed study of interethnic relations in the urban and rural areas of southern Florida is that competition in poor, multiethnic neighborhoods involves conflicts over public spaces as well as private ones, which further expose groups to the powers of zoning, police, and those agencies and businesses that specialize in organizing and structuring poverty. Spouse abuse shelters replace grocery stores. Pawnshops take over dentists' offices. Liquor tunnels and convenience stores spring up where shoes, clothes, and toys used to be sold. Insurance companies and banks practice redlining. Around such blocks, gradually, communities construct visible barriers to traffic, or residents come to know the boundaries of railroad tracks or busy thoroughfares that only those who live or work in these areas cross. These neighborhoods come to resemble inner cities—at once densely populated and broken up with abandoned buildings and vacant lots, their public spaces up for grabs, less patrolled by the police than occupied by them or, worse, patrolled only along their outskirts, thus abandoning the neighborhoods to their own internal turmoil.

LABOR MARKETS

The sense of fragmentation we derive from examining neighborhoods of the working poor characterizes many of the labor markets that rural industries construct as well. Particularly in high-injury and low-wage, unpleasant industries such as food processing, high labor turnover becomes an institutionalized component of the production process, encouraging plant personnel staff to experiment with methods that either lower turnover or assure steady supplies of replacement workers. Undocumented immigrant workers, with little legal basis for complaint, suit these conditions almost perfectly. In the most progressive plants, personnel managers assess production techniques and wage and benefit packages regularly, eliciting feedback from workers and attempting to influence production managers to modify tasks, line organizations and structures, and interpersonal relations in ways that reduce occupational hazards, reward employees, and generally improve workplace relations. Yet other solutions to high labor turnover are less enlightened, relying on ready supplies of workers with little collective strength or bargaining power concerning the terms of their employment.

Historically, rural industries have addressed the problems associated with high injury and high labor turnover with a combination of methods that are unevenly distributed over their workforces. Loyal workers who enable more effective production and help legitimate current practices tend to migrate to positions within plants that are less hazardous, forming a core of employees who remain in the plant year in, year out, exemplifying desired worker behaviors and teaching new employees about the subtler aspects of survival, getting along, and resistance within the plant. Often this core provides a foundation for recruiting new workers, accessing labor through family and friendship networks.

In most rural areas, this source of labor is limited, particularly with the arrival of new industries or the growth of alternative employment opportunities. Because economic activity in nearly any region of the country fluctuates, labor supplies to unpleasant rural industries are the first to constrict with economic growth and are among those that benefit from the economic problems that periodically harm rural areas: declining or stagnating farm prices, debt crises, natural disasters that affect agricultural output, and the negative economic impacts on support industries. Southeast Asian and Mayan refugees are examples of this on an international scale, where war and terror overseas produced a pliant labor force for industries throughout the rural United States.

Almost by definition, however, rural areas rarely have enough people to staff the new rural industries we see emerging across America. Many of these old agricultural regions of the Midwest have been losing their young, working-age families to the Southeast, West, and South over the past three decades; these trends are exacerbated by rural-to-urban migration within regions. To compensate for these losses, the new rural industries have engaged in several strategies, including various enhanced recruiting techniques, accessing new labor supplies, underwriting housing and transportation development, and subsidizing network recruiting. At the heart of each of these efforts, today, are immigrants and refugees.

The use of immigrants and refugees in food processing is nothing new, but the contemporary contexts surrounding the entry of immigrants and refugees into rural labor markets are quite distinct from the days Upton Sinclair's Jurgis cut meat in turn-of-the-century Chicago. Among the factors distinguishing contemporary immigrants' and refugees' experiences from earlier uses of immigrants, in addition to rural settings, are their transnational and transregional networks and their attempts to pioneer economic alternatives to wage work in the United States, in their sending countries, and in other countries where members of their families and networks are living. They are also more likely than later waves of European immigrants to be ethnically distinct from native community members (particularly if they are peoples of color arriving in the rural Midwest), arriving in areas without fully formed ethnic enclaves. What they share with earlier waves of immigrants is their constant attention to creative consumption habits and creative uses of domestic and reproductive labor, pooling the rights and obligations of household membership in ways that challenge conventional notions of family and household.

Structurally, too, new immigrants and refugees are more likely today than previously to be incorporated into rural labor processes through intermediaries, such as labor contractors, whose responsibilities extend far beyond the simple tasks of those New York labor contractors who, earlier this century, sent fresh Hungarian Jews into the turpentine distilleries of North Carolina or infrastructure projects in Florida's swampy southern cone (Daniel 1972). As rural industries access labor from farm labor markets, they are likely to draw into the labor process the practices currently common among farm labor contractors. This should come as no surprise when the same individuals are acting as labor contractors for agricultural and for food-processing firms. According to an investigator at the Department of Labor (Mike Hancock, personal communication, October 9, 1996), longtime farm labor contractors along the U.S.–Mexican border have begun moving into poultry- and other food-processing labor markets. Those practices of farm labor contractors that are relevant to food-processing firms include controlling housing and transportation, providing false identification, operating as cultural brokers inside processing plants, and engaging in paternal relations with those they recruit. As the farm labor market becomes increasingly dependent on young single males, in part because of the dormitory conditions of more and more labor camps in the principal labor supply regions of the United States, we are likely to see fewer families and more single males in food-processing production centers as well. Each of these behaviors has the potential to further segment a labor force and a community already segmented by racial stereotypes, differences in the expression of ethnic identity, language, and social class. Less common are those practices that involve daily debt schemes related to housing and transportation, which workers resist more effectively—although new immigrants may be indebted to labor contractors for the initial costs of transporting them from Mexico and Central America to production centers throughout rural America.

This partial subcontracting of labor recruiting and labor management, conforming to the growing use of temporary workers and employment agencies that specialize in supplying temps, bears a functional resemblance to the controversial practice of outsourcing, or the business of subcontracting parts of the production process to companies whose production costs are lower, generally due to lower wages and labor costs and relaxed environmental regulations or enforcement. We need not look outside the food industry to find functional equivalents to outsourcing, however, because subcontracting has been a central part of the organization of major food companies since the 1940s. Integration takes place through the contract, not the market, making relations between contractors and integrators logically distinct from simple exchanges between direct and secondary producers. In addition, subcontractors are usually part-time, directing only part of their production energies to growing chickens, hogs, or whatever for the integrators. Subcontractors depend, often quite heavily, on integrators' contracts, commonly using them as negotiating tools for loans and relying on integrators' payments to satisfy cash flow needs while they wait for rises in grain prices or wait for their summer vegetables to mature. Although subcontractors are usually more dependent on the integrator than the other way around, the poultry, hog, and other farmers who provide products to food-processing firms through contracts engage in multiple production strategies, reducing this dependence.

Similarly, workers who are integrated into the production process according to the logic of the subcontract—whether through labor intermediaries or by working for only brief periods, coming and going because of injuries, layoffs, or personal reasons—also often engage in multiple livelihoods. There is growing evidence that what Lambros Comitas (1974) called occupational multiplicity three decades ago, referring to Caribbean survival strategies, and what others have referred to as semiproletarianization (DeJanvry 1981; Griffith, Valdes, and Johnson 1992; Collins 1995) is becoming more common across the rural landscape.

At the same time, engaging in multiple livelihoods is becoming ever more complex, spanning regions and nations in ways that facilitate and encourage transience. Much of the recent work on international labor migration directs attention to the growing complexity of transnationalism: the tendency for international labor migrants to maintain close connections with family and friends in their home countries and in other nations. Migrants from island-nations and small nations with long histories of migration often have family members in three or more nations (Basch, Glick Schiller, and Szanton Blanc 1995). As such, they have long histories of behaviors, such as child sharing, that allow the movement of family and network members among several regions, several economic activities and training programs, and several social and cultural environments. Ever more sophisticated communication, transportation, and shipping technologies have made maintaining transnational social groups easier than ever, creating a fluidity that bears a remarkable likeness to the hypermobility of transnational capital.

CONCLUSIONS

The transience and fragmentation that we witness under conditions of rural industrialization are potentially socially disruptive, often leading to high numbers of occupationally injured workers, higher crime rates, stressed public services such as schools and police, increasing senses of dislocation and culture shock on the part of newcomers and natives, and even increased unemployment when more workers respond to labor demand signals than are needed at the plant or arrive in town and fail to pass drug or other tests necessary for employment. These have been chronicled in the most recent works on food processing, including academic and popular books (Stull, Broadway, and Griffith 1995; Rifkin 1992), journal articles (Durrenberger and Thu 1996; Griffith 1987), and more conventional journalism, including Tony Horwitz's Pulitzer Prize-winning story (1994; see also Zahren 1989; Petroski 1989). What effect rural industrialization is likely to have on local history—on the rootedness and stability we normally associate with rural America—depends on the abilities of communities to anticipate these problems and respond to them quickly and efficiently, holding responsible those interests that foster transience and encourage, willingly or unwillingly, fragmentation.

Yet the influxes of immigrants, the growth of transnational ethnic enclaves, and the increasing importance of multiple livelihoods may also become paths of discovery for rural communities, opening up new niches in the economy and suggesting methods of living and working that build on alternative cultural models and environmentally sensitive practices. Clearly, our nation's urban areas are far richer in experience from the multiculturalism we normally find in places like Miami, Washington, New York, San Francisco, and Seattle. Their great stores of expressive culture and folk knowledge expand our abilities to formulate ideas and pursue new paths toward knowledge. Recognizing cultural and economic activities that explore new opportunities requires an openness similar to the commonly praised, but less commonly utilized, business practice of employers' listening to their employees for ways to improve the productive process. Those activities that may violate current health, housing, business, and licensing codes—extended families living together in shelters they construct themselves, small-scale food production and sales operations, street vending, and so on— may, in fact, represent mechanisms by which families contribute to the diversity of goods and services available within the community and the store of human knowledge about ways of achieving well-being. Criminalizing such behaviors, without first assessing their potential to contribute to community development— development in the most general sense—will only serve the goal of transnational capital: creating people with no vested interest in community, no loyalty, no nation, no home.

NOTES

1. Formerly, feed mills were the center of the industry, using crop subsidy programs to accumulate capital that they converted into chickens and then routed to processing, becoming more and more involved with specialty cuts and less involved with the sole production of whole birds.

2. The growth of subcontracting has been accompanied by the growth of firms that hire out workers on a temporary basis, such as Manpower, and some of these companies depend on large corporations for financial backing. General Motors owns over one-third of all stock in Kelly Services, for example.

3. That President Clinton has had long association with the poultry industry was revealed in one of the many Republican assaults on the presidency and in the observation, by many residents of Washington, D.C., that shortly after the Clinton administration took office, it was hard to find any chicken not produced by Arkansas-based Tyson Foods in the city.

REFERENCES

Andrews, Gigi
1998   Heart without a Home. (*Raleigh, North Carolina*) *News & Observer*, March 8.

Bach, Robert, H. Brill, N. Chinchilla, D. Griffith, J. Hagan, N. Hamilton, J. Loucky, T. Repak, N. Rodriguez, C. Shacter, and R. Waldinger
1990   *The Impact of IRCA on the U.S. Labor Market and Economy*. SUNY Binghamton: Institute on Multiculturalism and International Labor.

Basch, Linda, N. Glick Schiller, and C. Szanton Blanc
1995   *Nations Unbound: Transnational Projects, Postcolonial Predicaments, and Deterritorialized Nation-States*. Luxembourg: Gordon and Breach.

Collins, Jane
1995   Unwaged Labor in Comparative Perspective: Recent Theories and Unanswered Questions. In *Work without Wages: Domestic Labor and Self-Employment within Capitalism*. Edited by Jane Collins and Martha Giminez. Albany: State University of New York Press. Pp. 3–24.

Comitas, Lambros
1974   Occupational Multiplicity in Rural Jamaica. In *Work and Family Life: West Indian Perspectives*. Edited by L. Comitas and D. Lowenthal. Garden City, New York: Anchor Books. Pp. 157–173.

Daniel, Peter
1972   *In the Shadow of Slavery: Debt Peonage in the U.S. South*. Urbana: University of Illinois Press.

DeJanvry, Alain
1981   *The Agrarian Question and Reformism in Latin America*. Baltimore: Johns Hopkins University Press.

Durrenberger, E. Paul, and Kendall Thu
1996   The Industrialization of Swine Production in the United States: An Overview. *Culture and Agriculture* 18 (1):19–23.

Fitchen, Janet
1992   On the Edge of Homelessness: Rural Poverty and Housing Insecurity. *Rural Sociology* 57 (2): 173–193.

Garcia Marquez, Gabriel
1970   *One Hundred Years of Solitude*. Translated by Gregory Rabasa. New York: Alfred Knopf.

Gibson, Janet
1996   Boots, Belts, and Baggage: Taming the American Alligator. *Culture and Agriculture* 18(2): 37–46.

Goldring, Luin
1990   *Development and Migration: A Comparative Analysis of Two Mexican Migration Circuits*. Working Paper 37, Commission for the Study of International Migration and Cooperative Economic Development, Washington, D.C.

Griffith, David
1987   Nonmarket Labor Processes in an Advanced Capitalist Economy. *American Anthropologist* 89 (4): 838–852.
1993   *Jones's Minimal: Low-Wage Labor in the United States*. Albany: State University of New York Press.
1995   Names of Death. *American Anthropologist* 97 (3): 453–456.

Griffith, David, and Ed Kissam
1995   *Working Poor: Farmworkers in the United States*. Philadelphia: Temple University Press.

Griffith, David, Manuel Valdes Pizzini, and Jeffrey Johnson
1992   Injury and Therapy: Proletarianization in Puerto Rico's Fisheries. *American Ethnologist* 19 (1): 53–74.
Hackenberg, Robert, David Griffith, Donald Stull, Lourdes Gouviea, and Michael Broadway
1996   Creating a Disposable Labor Force. *Aspen Institute Quarterly* 5 (2): 78–101.
Horwitz, Tony
1994   9 to Nowhere. *Wall Street Journal*, Thursday, December 1, A: 1, A: 8–9.
Lasley, Floyd
1980   The U.S. Poultry Industry: Changing Structure and Economics. Agricultural Economic Report 502, USDA, ESR, Washington, D.C.
Mintz, Sidney
1983   *Sweetness and Power.* New York: Vintage Books.
Petroski, William
1989   Coming Up Short: Iowa's Working Poor. *Des Moines Register*, Sunday, June 4–Thursday, June 8.
Rifkin, Jeremy
1992   *Beyond Beef.* New York: E. P. Dutton.
Stull, Donald, Michael Broadway, and David Griffith
1995   *Any Way You Cut It: Meat Processing and Small Town America.* Lawrence: University Press of Kansas.
U.S. Bureau of the Census
1990   *Statistical Abstract of the United States.* Washington, D.C.
Williams, Raymond
1973   *The Country and the City.* New York: Oxford University Press.
Wolf, Eric
1982   *Europe and the People without History.* Berkeley: University of California Press.
Zahren, Bill
1989   New IBP Workers Lack Affordable Housing. *Sioux City Journal*, Friday, March 17.

7

Undocumented Immigrants and the Meatpacking Industry in the Midwest

Janet E. Benson

An observant driver following I-70 through Kansas last year and pausing at a Topeka rest stop's fast-food restaurant would have noticed a vending machine labeled in Spanish that dispensed telephone calling cards for Mexico. This new service symbolizes the growing importance of Mexican workers to employers in the United States. U.S. unemployment is at its lowest in more than two decades, and employer demand for workers is high. At the same time, international migration from Mexico continues, as it has for nearly fifty years (Massey et al. 1990: 321). Particularly in the Midwest, meatpacking jobs are a major attraction for Mexican newcomers, although a decreasing proportion of these are held by undocumented immigrants.

The use of undocumented labor in meatpacking is directly related to changes in the industry since the 1960s that place a premium on low-wage labor. Further changes in labor use are currently taking place due to new immigration laws, enforcement procedures, and the availability of immigrant workers. A brief background on the meatpacking industry is followed by a more detailed discussion of meatpacking in southwest Kansas during the 1980s and 1990s, with particular emphasis on the effects of the 1986 Immigration Reform and Control Act (IRCA).

THE MEATPACKING INDUSTRY

Changing Structure

Since the 1960s, packing plants have moved from urban centers to small communities near water and grain supplies; companies have found it cost-effective to build slaughterhouses near local feed yards, avoiding the weight loss that cattle suffer when shipped, and to recruit labor from other locales when necessary. Intense competition has led to cost cutting and mechanization, so that complex tasks performed by skilled (and highly paid) butchers have been reduced to a variety of simpler actions that workers can perform with relatively less training and often even without a knowledge of English (Bjerklie 1995; Broadway 1995; Skaggs 1986; Stanley 1992; Stull and Broadway 1990; Stull, Broadway, and Griffith 1995). Plants have been closed, eliminating unionized jobs, and reopened later with nonunionized (often partly immigrant) workforces, while in some cases worker intimidation hampers unionization efforts. These comments refer to the large beef- and pork-packers, but similar patterns of labor use can be seen in poultry processing today (see Griffith 1995; this volume).

By 1996, following intense industry competition, the largest U.S. meatpacking operations in terms of sales were IBP, Inc.; Excel (a subsidiary of Cargill); ConAgra (which purchased Monfort in the late 1980s); and National Beef (now owned by Farmland). All have plants in southwest Kansas with a current total of approximately 11,400 workers. The first three companies also led the nation in pork packing (Bjerklie 1995: 54; Nunes 1996: 28). Until recently, it has been mainly the largest packers and processors who recruit immigrant labor. For example, IBP, the world's largest fresh meat company with 1995 sales of $12.7 billion, has been very sophisticated in tapping new immigrant populations. IBP established nineteen major facilities between 1980 and 1991 (Kay 1996: 17), during a period of massive refugee influx from Southeast Asia, and supplemented local labor with Vietnamese, Lao, and other Southeast Asian refugees as well as Mexican immigrants. Minority workers were contacted through recruiters employed by IBP who came from the same ethnic groups. More recently, the company (along with other large packers and processors) has also hired Somali, Bosnian, and other refugees.

IBP currently employs some 38,000 workers at twenty-three packing (slaughter) plants in nine states (*Rural Migration News* 1998a) but is rapidly moving into processing as well by acquiring other companies. By July 1998, IBP plants (slaughter and processing together) totaled forty-one. The company recently acquired Foodbrands America, a food processor headquartered in Oklahoma City that owns a number of processing facilities (Nunes 1998: 17, 24). In 1996 the company was expanding its exports and expected to increase its sales to $20 billion by the year 2000, when it planned to kill 11 million cattle and 18 to 20 million hogs per year (Kay 1996: 17–24). Although the Asian economic crisis and dropping exports make this unlikely, the company's profitability remains at least partly dependent on maintaining an adequate, low-cost labor supply.

Due to unpleasant, stressful, and dangerous working conditions for packing plant workers, turnover tends to be very high in this industry. While it is highest when plants first open and becomes more stable once they are well established, rates of over 100 percent turnover per year are not uncommon at some large plants. Workers frequently quit after a few days or months, and large plants may hire 500 or more new workers per year (Bjerklie 1995: 54; U.S. General Accounting Office 1998: 5).

Although plant managers always want sufficient labor to meet production quotas, individual workers become more costly at the point where they gain seniority and receive bonuses, health plans, and extra benefits. Those who show signs of becoming disabled or resisting plant discipline are likely to be fired, as are those who cannot meet production quotas. High turnover is therefore built into the structure of the current work setting. Most established Americans are unwilling to undertake this stigmatized, dangerous, and relatively low-paying work (approximately $6.15 to $8.20 an hour for entry-level wages in 1995–1996, or an average of $415 per week) (U.S. General Accounting Office 1998: 3).[1]

While meatpacking does provide employment opportunities for immigrants, single parents, or disadvantaged local populations that would find it difficult to earn a similar wage elsewhere, the pay is not high enough to support most families at more than a poverty level. Without a secure job and several wage earners in the household, it is difficult to own a home, pay for medical insurance, or afford more than minimal housing. Pregnant women usually cannot pay for prenatal care and may be fired if the plant discovers they are pregnant, since pregnancy is considered a "preexisting condition." According to worker accounts, women who admit they are pregnant will not be hired (Benson 1994). There is a waiting period of four to six months, depending on the company, before workers can apply for medical insurance. Many employees do not work that long; they may be injured, then quit or be fired before they are eligible for medical benefits. Also, while medical plans cover the individual worker, they may not include the worker's spouse and children without extra payments, which most families cannot afford. Even if they have insurance, workers may not be able to pay the deductibles required when they do seek medical attention. This means that workers and their families, including children, often go without medical and dental care. Plants provide limited on-site treatment for work-related injuries and refer patients to off-site doctors in some cases.

Immigrant workers are attractive labor sources for packing plants, as they are for certain other employers. Initially at least, immigrants will tolerate low wages and poor working conditions because they have relatively few options. Unfamiliar with the country, insecure because of their legal status (or lack of it), and not yet fluent in English, they are less likely to protest and to openly resist plant practices than their established American counterparts. While an American citizen might seek legal counsel, a noncitizen is less likely to do so.

It is important to emphasize that most packing plant workers are American citizens or legal residents. Although labor practices of personnel managers and companies vary, plant workforces include local people from the small towns where most large plants are located and established Americans from other communities and states, in addition to members of new refugee and immigrant populations. Even in the case of foreign-born workers or those who speak only

Spanish, it is not easy to determine legal status. Newcomers may hold work permits or may be temporary or permanent residents or citizens with full rights to employment in the United States. On the other hand, they may be undocumented or may have family members who are undocumented.

Invisible Workers

The undocumented workers in meatpacking are generally from Central America and Mexico, including such overlooked minorities as German-speaking Mennonites and Guatemalan Mayans. Due to political problems in their own countries, Central Americans have fled to Mexico first and then to the United States, where several hundred thousand have lived since the 1980s.[2] The Salvadorans and Guatemalans in southwest Kansas have migrated from Texas or Florida in search of jobs in meatpacking and constitute about 10–20 percent of local immigrants and perhaps 5–6 percent of the workforce in some southwest Kansas plants. Some have been in the area since the early 1980s, while others are recent arrivals.

The term "refugee" used here (e.g., in relation to Southeast Asians) refers to people who have come to the United States under legal refugee status, which confers the right to work and certain other initial benefits. Although some newcomers from Central America might also be considered refugees, only a portion of them are usually classified this way by the Immigration and Naturalization Service (e.g., more commonly Nicaraguans than Guatemalans). Persons who have not been given the legal status of "refugee," although they may, in fact, have fled due to political persecution, may or may not be authorized to work in the United States. If not authorized, they will be disadvantaged relative to legal immigrants and apt to take the worst jobs, for example, at the companies that clean the slaughterhouses during the night. Some of them live in rented farmhouses out in the country to escape detection. Members of some refugee groups such as Somalis, Bosnians, Salvadorans, and others working for packers have been given temporary permission to remain in the country and work until conditions change at home (Fix and Passel 1994: 85).

An act passed by Congress in late 1997 (the Nicaraguan Adjustment and Central American Relief Act, NACARA) will allow only a small proportion of the Central Americans in southwest Kansas to stay, although by this time many have been in the country more than ten years and have developed strong ties to the United States (see Chavez and Flores 1988).

Sojourners and Settlers

Both legal and undocumented immigrant workers must also decide whether they wish to remain in the United States or return home. This alternation between sojourner and settler patterns goes back to the very early use of migrant labor in the southwest (Chavez 1988; Portes and Rumbaut 1996: 273–274).

Many newcomers from Mexico come only to work for varying periods of time before returning to their homes and kin and have no intention of staying permanently. This is particularly true of men and women who travel without their families. They come to work as hard as they can, earn and save as much as possible, and then go home. Earnings are either sent back to Mexico to support relatives or are used for consumer goods or capital investments, for example, to start a business. These labor migrants have little interest in acquiring legal status since they intend to return to Mexico.

Some people, on the other hand, have always ''settled out'' from this stream of migrants; for example, southwest Kansas has established Mexican-American families in its comunities whose ancestors came in the first decade of this century to work on the railroad and in the sugar beet fields. Studies show that people are more likely to remain and to identify with the United States when their families are with them; for one thing, the longer the children stay in the United States, the more Americanized they become, and the more ties parents develop with local communities (Chavez and Flores 1988). While the general public is apt to mistake all newcomers for settlers, there is often no clear point at which one becomes the other. Migrants retain close ties with relatives in Mexico and visit whenever they can; proximity to the border and ease of travel for legalized immigrants (permanent residents or holders of so-called green cards) mean that people may not decide to settle permanently for years. On the other hand, recent public policy changes that reduce services to noncitizens are prompting more naturalization by Latino newcomers. Packers' use of these immigrants and others has changed over time depending on employer needs and changes in immigration laws. The following discussion relates primarily to southwest Kansas, a major meatpacking region of the United States, but also refers to other states in the Midwest.

MEATPACKING IN SOUTHWEST KANSAS

Labor Patterns in the 1980s

Meatpacking companies engaged in fierce competition during the 1980s, with IBP initiating the struggle to cut costs and increase market share. The company's 1981 opening of the second shift at its new plant in Holcomb, Kansas—the world's largest meatpacking plant—attracted potential employees from throughout the United States. Plant officials made it clear from the outset that local labor would not be sufficient, and new arrivals could be expected. By the mid-1980s, a sizable component of IBP's workforce in Kansas consisted of Southeast Asian refugees (primarily Vietnamese and Lao) as well as Mexicans and Mexican Americans, Central Americans, Anglos (whites), a few African Americans, and workers of other ethnic origins (Stull et al. 1990).

Other companies in southwest Kansas during the 1980s included Monfort (now owned by ConAgra), a Colorado-based company with a plant in Garden

City (also home to most of IBP's Holcomb plant employees). Out of 1,449 Monfort workers in 1988, about fifty-six percent were ''Hispanics,'' a little less than 2 percent ''Asian'' (down from five percent the previous year), less than one percent Native American, and forty percent ''white'' (Stull et al. 1990: 96). These are official government terms for ethnic groups and not very useful in determining which ''Hispanics'' or Latinos were established U.S. citizens (Mexican Americans) and how many might have been recent newcomers, legal or illegal, from Mexico or Central America. What these figures indicate, however, is that ''Hispanic'' (Latino) workers of both types were important to the plant. Packing plants in the neighboring towns of Liberal and Dodge in southwest Kansas employed a similar variety of workers.

IRCA and Labor Patterns in the 1990s

By the late 1980s and early 1990s, many Vietnamese and Lao were moving out of southwest Kansas (and beef packing) and being replaced by additional Mexican and Mexican-American newcomers. The Southeast Asian refugee flow was ending, and individuals who had worked initially at meatpacking were ready for different occupations.[3] As this was happening, rural communities were beginning to feel the impact of IRCA. In 1992, IBP's personnel manager at Holcomb estimated that fifty percent of his workers were Hispanic (Latino), twenty-five percent Anglo, and twenty-five percent ''mixed'' (Vietnamese, Lao, and others) (Benson 1993). By 1998, 75 percent of the workers at Dodge City's two largest meatpackers, Excel Corp. (a Cargill subsidiary) and National Beef (now owned by Farmland), out of a total of 3,800 workers, were estimated to be Latino; the same was true of Garden City and Liberal (*Rural Migration News* 1998b). Latino employees dominate the packers' workforce not only in Kansas but throughout the Midwest.

IRCA and Employer Sanctions

IRCA was the first piece of U.S. legislation designed to reduce the level of illegal immigration by sanctioning employers who knowingly use such workers. However, it also had an amnesty provision that permitted the legalization of undocumented immigrants who already had work histories in the United States. Before IRCA, illegal migrants could be arrested at any time, but their employers could not. Since IRCA's passage, employers are required to fill out an I-9 form verifying that they have seen documents establishing an applicant's identity and authorization to work; they are subject to fines or imprisonment if they can be shown to make a regular practice of hiring undocumented workers (Donato, Durand, and Massey 1992: 95).

Two kinds of migrants received amnesty under this bill: those who had lived continuously in the United States since January 1, 1982 (legally authorized workers, or LAWS), and those who could document work in agricultural jobs during 1984–1986 (special agricultural workers, or SAWS). The SAW provision was created due to lobbying by growers in California and Texas who feared losing their workforce (Donato, Durand, and Massey 1992: 95–96; Martin 1990). While meatpacking did not qualify as an agricultural job, many agricultural workers who became legalized as SAWS then moved into meatpacking. Nearly 3 million people applied for legalization under these two provisions (1.7 million LAW and 1.3 million SAW) (Baker 1997: 10). The result was continued immigration, both legal and illegal.

Effects on Families

Many of the newly legalized Mexican migrants were married but had previously left their families at home. By the early 1990s, these workers (primarily males) were bringing wives and children to live with them in the United States (see Passel, Bean, and Edmonston 1991: 206, 208). Older married men had typically made numerous trips, returning after a year or two each time to visit their families in Mexico. Women and children who accompanied men to the United States in the 1990s usually lacked documentation, which meant that families included (and still often include) both documented and undocumented members.

Most Mexican men legalizing in southwest Kansas got official residency in December 1990, which meant that they could apply for citizenship by December 1995 (usually requiring a fifteen-month wait in the Kansas Immigration and Naturalization Service [INS] district). Husbands who are legal residents can petition for wives and children, though it is faster for those with citizenship. The situation is difficult for families because Mexico's quota is limited; for example, during May 1998 the INS was still processing petitions for legal residence submitted in 1993. If the marriage took place after 1990, wives have to wait even longer for legalization. The main problem is that IRCA's authors did not anticipate the large number of petitions by legalized people (disproportionately male) for family members. Many of the men considered "single males" by established Americans actually have families in Mexico or other U.S. communities. According to local estimates, eighty-five percent of the Mexican men legalized in southwest Kansas had wives and children.

Because of these factors, undocumented immigration decreased only temporarily (because of the large numbers of people legalized) after IRCA. Families followed legalized men, and the flow of first-time immigrants, both male and female, continued. Most studies do not indicate that the passage of IRCA had the intended effect of slowing illegal immigration (Baker 1997; Donato, Durand, and Massey 1992; Massey et al. 1990). As packers expanded their production in the 1990s, the big plants continued to attract Mexican workers, some of whom became settlers. Towns in southwest Kansas have rapidly increased theirLatino populations since the late 1980s; for example, the Garden City schooldistrict's minority (mostly Latino) population has been growing by two to three percent per year, and by September 1998 the Hispanic share of the student population had reached 52 percent (nearly sixty-six percent at the elementary school level) (Benson 1997; USD 457: 1998).[4] A similar phenomenon is taking place in rural communities throughout the Midwest wherever meatpackers are found (Gouveia and Stull 1995).

CASE STUDIES: ILLEGAL TO LEGAL

The following case studies are of individuals and families interviewed during the early 1990s in southwest Kansas.[5] Although this was not a representative sample, since it consisted largely of newcomers who chose to legalize rather than those who did not, these cases are useful in illustrating the migration process, the effects of IRCA, and the gradual effects of employer sanctions. By the 1990s, the possession of documents was becoming increasingly important for formal employment in meatpacking and other occupations. The data also show that illegal immigration continues. All personal names are pseudonyms, and it is unlikely that the people mentioned here will still be living in the community where they were initially interviewed.

Case 1: Continuing Undocumented Migration among Singles

Francisco and Ernesto were two young, single males, both undocumented. Francisco, from Jemenez, Chihuahua, Mexico, was twenty when we interviewed him and had already worked in several locations in the United States, including California and Texas. He had been in southwest Kansas a year and three months. Ernesto was twenty-one and also came from Chihuahua, though a different community. While Francisco had left school after the ninth grade, Ernesto had studied business administration in Mexico for two years. He had previously been employed in construction in Texas and picking apples in Colorado. Ernesto had been in southwest Kansas for about a year and a half. Both worked at the local packing plant, which they had heard of from a female cousin when she visited Mexico. They shared a rented house trailer with her and two other friends. Both men wanted to improve their English and continue their education. Francisco hoped for a ''good job,'' perhaps as an engineer, while Ernesto, an exceptional student, wanted to enter law. He definitely did not plan to be cutting beef in the future. Francisco felt that the town needed more housing because of increased family migration from Mexico. He also said that an immigrant's greatest need was for papers (documents).

Case 2: Becoming Documented

Rafael, a native of Durango, Mexico, was young (twenty-eight) and still unmarried when we met him. Rafael first came to the United States (California) in 1979, at his parents' insistence, when he was about sixteen. Rafael worked there in a variety of service-type occupations for about nine years. Finally, he got some documents "because to be illegal is very sad [*muy triste*] here." Companies no longer wanted to hire people without documents. He knew some California companies that were heavily fined because they employed so many undocumented workers.

Rafael had moved to his present location (the second southwest Kansas town in which he had lived) one month before and filled out the application form for the local packing plant. He hoped that he would find work because he had his documents. Meanwhile, he was studying English at a community center.

Case 3: A Married Man Traveling Alone

Like many of the packing plant workers, Enrico was young, only twenty-four. He was born in San Angel, Durango, Mexico, and completed secondary school there, making him more educated than many Mexican migrants. After he graduated, he worked as a farm laborer in San Angel. On his first trip to the United States in 1983, he was employed on a ranch in a small town near Amarillo, Texas. When we interviewed him, he had been working in a packing plant in southwest Kansas for two years, his first experience in meatpacking. He came because his cousin, who was employed there, told him that the wages were a little better at the plant than at the ranch, where he earned $800 a month. Although he still performed line work (cutting meat with knives), he had achieved a semisupervisory position that could lead to promotion if he improved his English. After staying with his cousin for two months, he was followed by his sister and brother-in-law, who decided to work in meatpacking also. He had lived with them and their four children ever since. His wife was in Mexico, in San Angel, with his two children, ages six and four.

According to Enrico, many men with wives in Mexico left their jobs and went home because the work was very hard. Almost no one brought families initially since they needed to be sure of job security. Visiting Mexico was more common than previously because by the early 1990s, many people had become legalized and could travel freely. Enrico had often considered bringing his family to the United States but knew that setting up a household here would be expensive. Enrico's situation illustrates a stage in the "settling out" process in which an individual has become somewhat established but has not yet decided to bring his family to live permanently in the United States.

Case 4: Mixed Legal Statuses in a Reunited Family

Juan Portes was born in Chihuahua, Mexico, in 1948, as was his wife, Leandra. He did not really have any education, while Leandra had attended only first grade. Juan was a day laborer in Mexico, working in both rural and urban areas: his wife ran a small store from her house. He first worked in California during

1968 on a work permit that allowed him to be there for seven or eight months. His wife (his fiancée at the time) then came, and they got married. She lived in California for three consecutive years, and one of their daughters was born there. Then they returned to Mexico for about eleven years, though he worked in the United States occasionally. One of their sons was born in El Paso, Texas. Juan first came to southwest Kansas in June 1989, when friends invited him to join them in working on the kill floor at a meatpacking plant. (The kill floor refers to the area where cattle are stunned with a stun gun, their throats cut, and the initial "disassembly" process begun. This is one of the dirtiest and most dangerous areas of the plant, although jobs here are relatively highly paid and apt to be staffed with recent immigrants.) Juan explained that, initially, he came by himself because he was not familiar with the situation and did not know whether he could support his family.

After saving for some months (probably living with friends meanwhile), he was able to buy a small, run-down, secondhand house trailer. His wife and four children joined him because, he said, "it's our custom to remain together always." They lived in the first home for a year and eight months before selling it to buy a second, new one. He said this had been an economic challenge for them, since they had to make monthly payments. Local housing was very expensive in relation to his income, and since he had injured himself in the plant, he did not want to commit himself to a mortgage in case he had to move. His family had decided to stay for a time because at this point they had two incomes from an older daughter and a son who worked in the plant. These were probably the two children (out of four) who had been born in the United States and were therefore citizens. Previously, he was the only wage earner in the family. Juan was in the process of becoming, or had been recently, legalized under IRCA. His wife, who was not working outside the home, probably was undocumented, as were the children not born in the United States.

The family did not plan to stay in southwest Kansas indefinitely. Because Leandra's relatives lived in El Paso and Juarez, she thought one of these cities might be their next destination. The two younger children might pursue higher education in either Mexico or the United States (one daughter had already taken a course in Mexico but was currently in high school in Kansas). Leandra saw their future as being either in the United States or in Mexico.

Case 5: Another Reunited Family

Anita was born in Cuernavaca, Morelos, Mexico, in 1967, making her twenty-four at the time she was interviewed (1991). Her education stopped after sixth grade. The only kind of work she had done in Mexico was clerking in a clothing store, and she had not been employed outside the home since coming to Kansas a year ago. Her husband had worked at the plant for two years this time but had made previous short trips to the same location when they were both younger and not yet married (the oldest of her two daughters was seven). She came because the "father of my daughters was here all the time and my daughters missed him."

At the time of the interview, they lived in an older house divided into four apartments and occupied by three other families. A friend of Anita's husband had lived in their apartment previously and had left it for them when he returned to Mexico. Cockroach-infested and lacking air-conditioning, it cost them $200 per month plus the utilities.

Anita explained that she was not working because she did not have legal documentation. Her husband had applied for her, and they were waiting. When asked what they would be doing in five years, she assumed that they would be in southwest Kansas if her husband still had a job at the packing plant. She wanted to work as a sales clerk; however, without knowing English this will be impossible, and she lacked transportation to attend classes at the Adult Learning Center.

Case 6: A Central American Immigrant

Miguel was a thirty-six-year-old Salvadoran who may or may not have been documented at the time he was interviewed. Although he had attended high school, his education had been interrupted by the war in his country. Miguel first came to Garden City in 1980 as part of a crew hired by a maintenance company; he had previously worked for them in Iowa. At that time IBP was new and had only one shift. He worked twelve to fourteen hours at a time cleaning up after the construction work. He considered himself lucky because the maintenance company provided trailers for workers (eight men lived in his trailer), deducting twenty dollars a week from each paycheck. After that he worked in construction, finally returning to the maintenance company. He shared a house with a Mexican friend who was purchasing it. Then he applied to IBP and worked there for six and a half years, from 1982 to 1989 (he married during this period and bought a small house trailer). After that he was employed at Monfort between 1989 and 1991, quitting about a month before he was interviewed. He was unemployed in 1991 and attending vocational classes at the community college; he said that he didn't want to work in plants again and was hoping to become an auto mechanic.

His wife had been born in Cuernavaca, Mexico, in 1967, but her family came to the United States when she was a child, and she studied through the ninth grade in Garden City. Then she married Miguel and dropped out. They had three children, ranging from three to seven years of age. She had worked in a plant, on the kill floor, for just one month about two years before the interview but stopped because she became dizzy and nauseated. Since then, she had not worked outside the home. The family lacked medical insurance. Miguel had family coverage when at IBP, but at Monfort he had it only for himself, as it was too expensive to cover the family. He noted that at the plants, people who were sick or injured were required to be present even when they should see a doctor (to avoid having to report injuries—cf. Griffith 1995).

Analysis

The preceding accounts illustrate several points: the uncertainty of the job situation, the tendency for families to reunite (whatever the cost or difficulty) once adult members are legalized, and the probability of mixed legal statuses within immigrant families. It also illustrates transnationalism, that is, long-established habits of moving back and forth across the border, as families maintained strong ties with both Mexico and the United States. From the viewpoint of immigrant Latinos, the significance of the green card (permanent resident status) is that it allows holders to travel freely between the two countries. Immigrants were more interested in being able to cross the border without harassment than in staying permanently in the United States. Another point that emerged from systematic questioning was that many women were not working in the packing plants because they did not have legal documents. Immigrants agreed that when women had the documents to do so, and when families needed the money, wives also worked.

IRCA'S AFTERMATH

Still Undocumented

The case studies show workers in the process of legalizing. However, not all undocumented newcomers took advantage of this opportunity. Some did not intend to stay and did not feel legalization was necessary; others did not trust the INS and were afraid to petition since some family members were undocumented. Not everyone could pay the application fees, which were relatively expensive for low-wage workers with large families. Women who have entered into common-law marriages with legalized men cannot petition for legal resident status and remain undocumented. Also, because most of the Central Americans arrived after the first cutoff date (January 1, 1982), they were not included in IRCA's legalization provisions (Chavez and Flores 1988). Recent legislation[6] may benefit a few, but the majority are subject to deportation at present if identified by the INS.

Informal accounts by residents of southwest Kansas communities, as well as published discussions of labor practices by packing plants in other midwestern states (U.S. General Accounting Office 1998; Hedges 1996; Hedges and Hawkins with Loeb 1996: 45; Cohen 1998), indicate that the flow of undocumented newcomers has not stopped. However, fewer of them are likely to be working in meatpacking plants today (though they may well be employed in plant-related occupations such as cleaning companies and feed yards). Estimates of the percentage of undocumented immigrant meatpacking workers in the Midwest vary from 15 percent to 25 percent according to state and source (see U.S. General Accounting Office 1998).

Imposing Employer Sanctions

. The Immigration Reform and Control Act of 1986 called for sanctions on employers using undocumented immigrants; these have been phased in gradually over the last few years. Because of its heavy use of immigrant labor, meat-packing has been targeted by the INS as one of fifteen industries to receive top priority in efforts to discourage the employment of undocumented workers (U.S. General Accounting Office 1998: 15). Until recently, meatpackers have not been strongly motivated to identify undocumented immigrants and, according to some accounts, have deliberately recruited them. Like other employers in competitive industries, meatpackers focus on maintaining an adequate labor supply and cutting costs in any way possible. In one southwestern Kansas case, a plant personnel manager was arrested and sentenced to prison for recruiting undocu-mented Mexican workers. More commonly, companies use independent brokers to recruit for them, paying a "finder's fee" but publically denying the practice (*Rural Migration News* 1998a; Hedges 1996: 36). IBP maintains an office in Mexico City, supposedly for the purpose of attracting legal permanent residents who are home visiting but plan to return to the United States. Recruitment in all the larger plants takes place along lines of kinship and friendship, since migrants prefer to move into a community where they know others and can receive initial economic and social support (Benson 1990, 1993; Griffith 1995).

Some of the workers recruited in this manner have false documents. Whenever possible, the INS arrests entrepreneurs who manufacture documents, but to little effect; as INS technology becomes more sophisticated, so does that of the coun-terfeiters. In some plants, personnel staff reject obviously false documents; in others, the same applicant may be hired. Until recently, meatpackers could argue that they had asked for verification of work authorization as required under IRCA and that it was not their fault if they could not identify false or fraudulent identification. Personnel managers and line supervisors are constantly concerned about maintaining a sufficient labor supply to keep up production and fill orders. Some individuals in midwestern plants have clearly been more concerned about this imperative than screening for undocumented immigrants. On the other hand, it has been difficult for employers to check, since by law job applicants can submit a wide variety of documents, and it is illegal to discriminate against prospective employees simply on the grounds of their appearance or presumed legal status.

Until recently, although the INS could check documents of noncitizens against its database (e.g., to see if workers were, indeed, legal permanent residents), it was not possible to check Social Security numbers for citizens. Undocumented workers simply claimed citizenship status and borrowed or purchased Social

Security numbers from others. In some cases plant personnel, acting on their own account, have sold the Social Security numbers of departing employees to new, undocumented workers. Up until now, the American public has resisted the idea of having a photo-bearing national identity card, and a wide variety of documents can be used for identification by citizens. The problem is matching the individual appearing before an employer with the Social Security number. INS staff assert that regardless of verification problems with documents, someone among packing plant personnel is always aware if workers with false documentation are being employed and that the company is therefore responsible.

To encourage meatpacker compliance with law, the INS occasionally undertakes "operations," or raids, which are very disruptive to plants since they remove needed laborers from the workforce, shutting down production. A disgruntled employee usually contacts the INS to report unauthorized workers. The INS has carried out "operations" at meatpacking plants in Colorado, Illinois, Iowa, Nebraska, and Kansas during the last few years. In addition to slowing or halting production, these operations can have disruptive effects on entire communities. A raid on a plant in Garden City, Kansas, during 1996 angered local people since the INS apprehended, embarrassed, and inconvenienced citizens and legal residents as well as undocumented newcomers (sixty-one of whom were apprehended). The school district lost funding (based on student counts before a cutoff date) because parents, fearing deportation, withdrew their children from classes.

In some cases, suspecting a problem with undocumented workers, plants provide the INS with information so that it can conduct its "operation" with relatively less disruption to the company (which conducts advance hiring of additional workers). Most apprehensions of undocumented foreigners take place during crime investigations or routine traffic checks rather than at the plants. According to INS officials, their efforts are currently directed more at criminals than at plant employees. However, plant raids still occur. For example, the INS raided IBP's Joslin, Illinois, plant in June 1997 and removed 130 of 2,100 employees (*Rural Migration News* 1998a).

Assuming a good-faith effort to hire people legally authorized to work, identifying false documentation has been difficult until recently. Until 1996, there was no easy way for employers to verify the accuracy of employee documents. As one INS investigator explained:

All I need is a name, a Social Security number, and a date of birth. With these [using a Social Security number belonging to another individual], I get a drivers' license and put my photo on it. When I go to an employer, I fill out the I-9 form and use the Social Security number. The employer runs the Social Security number and it comes back o.k. The problem is, you don't know who you're dealing with.

This situation, however, may be changing.

The Basic Pilot Program

The Immigration and Naturalization Service is authorized to carry out demonstration projects ("pilots") of changes in the way employment authorization is verified. Starting in 1992, several pilots were initiated in different locations with a small number of companies. Meatpackers began to participate in the Employment Verification Pilot (EVP) during 1996, starting with the larger companies.[7]

Several other pilots followed. Under the Illegal Immigration Reform and Immigrant Responsibility Act of 1996 (IIRIRA), the INS is required to conduct three distinct pilot programs, each of four years' duration only, in the high-immigration states of California, Texas, New York, Florida, and Illinois. The one relevant to meatpacking is called the Basic Pilot. Companies may participate if they have plants in any of these states; enrollment is voluntary (Cassie Booth, personal communication 1998). Employers are not allowed to be selective but must verify all new employees. At first the INS could verify documents only of noncitizens (aliens or permanent residents), since it had access only to its own system of tracking; some prospective workers evaded detection by falsely claiming citizenship. Now it utilizes the Social Security Administration's database to verify both citizens and noncitizens under the Basic Pilot program (Elaine Schaming, personal communication 1998; U.S. INS n.d.).

The Basic Pilot started in April 1996, and again the larger meatpackers quickly signed agreements with the INS.[8] As of May 1998, most large meatpackers and processors had signed up for the Basic Pilot program, which continues to recruit. By that date the program covered 121,628 workers in meat- and poultry-processing and related food industries at 163 sites in twenty-one states and Puerto Rico (INS 1998). Companies do not necessarily include all their plant locations, just the ones in which they think they have a "problem" with undocumented workers.

Some job applicants still submit false documents to employers but are now apt to be fired after a few days if their legal status cannot be verified. For example, an individual claiming to be a citizen must have a name, a Social Security number, and a date of birth that match the other two pieces of information. Most undocumented applicants do not have complete information. If it does not match, the employee must contact the Social Security Administration within eight days. The employer sends a second query in ten days. If the irregularity has not been cleared up, the employer is required to fire the employee (U.S. INS n.d.; Schaming 1998).

Because this program is so new, it is not clear whether it will be consistently implemented by all companies or in all plants covered by a particular company's memorandum of understanding. While some authorities feel that it will function effectively, others do not. Packers can point to participation as evidence of their good-faith efforts to follow the law, and it will probably relieve some of the unwelcome attention they have received from the INS. Compliance will vary, and some undocumented immigrants will continue to work in meatpacking. However, once undocumented workers know about the verification system, they are likely to leave, or not apply for, jobs with some companies or plants. This does not necessarily mean that they will leave the country; the tendency is to apply at less compliant plants or to "go underground" into the informal economy.

IMPLICATIONS OF UNDOCUMENTED STATUS FOR IMMIGRANTS

Not having legal status has many implications for people. In the case of families in which husbands are legalized, but wives are not, women without documents are at a disadvantage. They cannot obtain packing plant jobs, which would help move the family above the poverty line, but can work only as maids, baby-sitters, or other employees in the informal economy for low pay in very insecure working conditions. While not prime targets for deportation, particularly if they are not working or have not committed any crime, the possibility always exists and adds to their insecurity. The 1998 changes in minimum income requirements for sponsoring family members ($20,562 for a family of four) will make it virtually impossible for male packing plant workers to petition for wives in the future, since this amount exceeds the average worker's wage.[9] If undocumented wives and their children follow husbands to the United States, they will be disadvantaged due to their lack of legal status. Recent changes in immigration law have increased application fees, making it more difficult for undocumented wives to legalize. Service providers in southwest Kansas currently advise women to return to Mexico to wait in order to avoid paying the $1,000 fee charged illegal residents. A number of women have gone home, but other families have paid the price—up to $5,000 in certain cases. In the future, undocumented couples will be unable to legally marry, and children will not receive Social Security numbers if the parents cannot prove their legal status.

Some women also face abusive domestic situations that they cannot easily leave since the husband refuses to petition for their legalization. While it is legally possible for a woman to self-petition for herself and her children, this is a complicated process requiring documentation and police reports and is not easily available to everyone in this situation.

CONCLUSIONS

Regarding undocumented immigration, the situation in meatpacking is changing. Employers are more motivated to comply than in the past due to stepped-up INS enforcement and negative national publicity. In addition, the INS is opening up enforcement offices close to some of the larger employers.[10] At present most packing plants seem to have adequate labor, and given the relatively low educational levels of recently legalized immigrants, it is possible that they will continue to dominate the packers' labor force in the near future. On the other hand, legalized immigrants are apt to move out of meatpacking into more stable and less dangerous and debilitating work. The Basic Pilot, even if consistently implemented, is not completely foolproof. Some observers feel that packers will not have sufficient labor without using illegal immigrants and that fraudulent documents will still escape detection.

The case studies illustrate a complex situation; while many men have become legalized, women and children often remain undocumented. The absence of legal status means vulnerability to exploitation of various kinds and lack of eligibility for public services and benefits, including basic health care. While children receive education at lower levels, they will not be eligible for financial aid for college or technical training and cannot be legally employed.

Meatpacking will continue to attract new migrants from Mexico, regardless of legal status, through the social networks of present workers as well as deliberate recruiting (see Cohen 1998). Fewer of them will be retained in slaughter and processing plants, however, if employers systematically implement the new Basic Pilot system. The undocumented or those whose documents cannot be verified due to errors in the INS or Social Security databases will seek employment in less compliant plants, feed yards, construction work, cleaning companies, and elsewhere. Whether packers can continue to recruit sufficient legal labor under current wages and working conditions and to what extent they will comply with the law remain to be seen.

NOTES

Funding from the Kansas Agricultural Experiment Station (Project No. 839; contribution No. 98-498-B) supported my research on post-1990 immigration to southwest Kansas. Donna Sanchez-Jennings, Judie Brown, Jeannine Chapelle, and Donna Skinner helped arrange interviews, while Wilfredo Gutierrez provided Spanish-language translation services. Many thanks to Mark Grey for his initial suggestions and to Dave Schafer and Orlen Grunewald for information on the packing industry. INS officials and staff have contributed greatly to my understanding of the current situation and the new Basic Pilot program; I am particularly grateful to Elaine Schaming, Cassie Booth, Mike Heston, Albert Maldonado, Jerry Heinauer, and Mike Went. The assistance of Norma DeLao, Dora Falcon, Jose Olivas, Levita Rohlman, Penney Schwab, Donna Skinner, and John Mcloughlin is also very much appreciated. The public relations office of IBP, Inc. contributed background material for this chapter, though officials declined to be interviewed.

1. The year 1998 entry-level wages in southwest Kansas were about $8.00 per hour, up 5 percent within the prior two years and perhaps 15 percent within the prior five (John McLoughlin, personal communication 1998).

2. Salvadorans are the most common group, with 850,000 in the United States by 1985, but there are also undocumented immigrants from Guatemala, Nicaragua, and Honduras (Chavez and Flores 1988).

3. Some Lao and Vietnamese are still employed in meatpacking, but not in large enough numbers to provide packers with a sufficient workforce (cf. Grey 1995).

4. This includes the children of established Mexican Americans as well as recent, Spanish-speaking arrivals.

5. Between September 1990 and December 1991 I conducted forty-three systematic interviews with recent Latino, Lao, and Vietnamese immigrants and ten with established Anglo residents in Garden City, Dodge City, and Liberal as part of a study of services for newcomers. Immigrants were contacted through adult learning centers in their communities; participation was voluntary. Some interviews took place at respondents' homes, and others at the learning centers. Interviews, which averaged from an hour to an hour and a half in length, were taped and transcribed whenever possible. While we did not ask directly about legal status, and some individuals (who were probably undocumented) declined to be interviewed, others felt reasonably secure because they were in the legalization process or because of the "immigrant-friendly" atmosphere of the adult education centers. These interviews cannot be considered representative of the Latino worker population, but they do give insight into legalization issues affecting families.

6. Nicaraguans continuously in the United States since December 1, 1995, can adjust to permanent resident status. Salvadorans and Guatemalans who entered the United States before September 19 and October 1, 1990, respectively, and who applied for asylum *before* April 1, 1990, or were members of a class action lawsuit against the government can receive a hearing on claims for suspension of deportation and adjustment to permanent resident status (PL 105–100 1997). Simply the fact that unsuccessful asylees will be deported is likely to deter applicants.

7. INS records show that thirty-one companies and ninety-four sites were enrolled in this system, that is, that thirty-one companies signed memorandums of understanding (MOUs) between May and August 1996. IBP, Inc. participated at twenty-four sites, including its two (Emporia and Holcomb) in Kansas; Excel, whose corporate headquarters is in Wichita, listed ten sites; and National Beef entered its two sites in Dodge City and Liberal, Kansas. Other employers enrolled in the EVP included Hudson Foods (ten sites) and Farmland Foods, Inc. (eleven sites). These include processors as well as packers (United States INS 1998a).

8. The process of joining the Basic Pilot program is as follows. The company signs a memorandum of understanding (MOU) with the INS, usually faxing it to a Washington office. It is then signed by an INS official and a Social Security Administration official. After that the MOU is sent to the contractor, Lockheed Martin, which issues an access code, a user ID for the person who will be actually using the computer, and a password. The INS then sends what it calls a "pizza box" containing software and a training manual to the company. In the case of a large corporation, the corporate headquarters may do the verification for workers at all sites (plants fax the I-9 information to headquarters); otherwise, verification takes place at the individual sites. A sign warning workers about the Basic Pilot program should be posted in every participating plant (Schaming 1998).

9. If the family has working older children, they can help raise the household income so that it will meet guidelines. However, most immigrants tend to have young families.

10. The INS decided to open one in one of the southwest Kansas meatpacking towns.

REFERENCES

Baker, Susan Gonzalez
1997   The "Amnesty" Aftermath: Current Policy Issues Stemming from the Legaliza-

tion Programs of the 1986 Immigration Reform and Control Act. *International Migration Review* 31: 5–27.

Benson, Janet E.

1990   Households, Migration, and Community Context. *Urban Anthropology* 19: 9–29.

1993   [1994]   Staying Alive: Economic Strategies among Immigrant Packing Plant Workers in Three Southwest Kansas Communities. *Kansas Quarterly* 25 (1): 107–120.

1994   The Effects of Packinghouse Work on Southeast Asian Refugee Families. In *Newcomers in the Workplace*. Edited by Louise Lamphere, Alex Stepick, and Guillermo Grenier. Philadelphia: Temple University Press. Pp. 99–126.

1997   Vietnamese and Mexican Immigrants in Garden City, Kansas: The Changing Character of a Community. Paper presented at the annual meeting of the American Anthropological Association, November 19–23, 1997, Washington, D.C.

Bjerklie, Steve

1995   On the Horns of a Dilemma: The U.S. Meat and Poultry Industry. In *Any Way You Cut It: Meat Processing and Small-Town America*. Edited by Donald D. Stull, Michael J. Broadway, and David Griffith. Lawrence: University Press of Kansas. Pp. 41–60.

Broadway, Michael J.

1995   From City to Countryside: Recent Changes in the Structure and Location of the Meat- and Fish-Processing Industries. In *Any Way You Cut It: Meat Processing and Small-Town America*. Edited by Donald D. Stull, Michael J. Broadway, and David Griffith. Lawrence: University Press of Kansas. Pp. 1–40.

Chavez, Leo R.

1988   Settlers and Sojourners: The Case of Mexicans in the U.S. *Human Organization* 47: 95–108.

Chavez, Leo R., and Estevan T. Flores

1988   Undocumented Mexicans and Central Americans and the Immigration Control and Reform Act of 1986: A Reflection Based on Empirical Data. In *In Defense of the Alien*. Vol. 10. Edited by Lydio F. Tomasi. Staten Island, New York: Center for Migration Studies of New York. Pp. 137–156.

Cohen, Laurie P.

1998   Free Ride: With Help from INS, U.S. Meatpacker Taps Mexican Work Force. *Wall Street Journal*, October 15.

Donato, Katharine M., Jorge Durand, and Douglas S. Massey

1992   Changing Conditions in the U.S. Labor Market: Effects of the Immigration Reform and Control Act of 1986. *Population Research and Policy Review* 11: 93–115.

Fix, Michael, and Jeffrey S. Passel

1994   *Immigration and Immigrants: Setting the Record Straight*. Washington, D.C.: Urban Institute.

Gouveia, Lourdes, and Donald D. Stull

1995   Dances with Cows: Beefpacking's Impact on Garden City, Kansas, and Lexington, Nebraska. In *Any Way You Cut It: Meat Processing and Small-Town America*. Edited by Donald D. Stull, Michael J. Broadway, and David Griffith. Lawrence: University Press of Kansas. Pp. 85–107.

Grey, Mark A.

1995   Pork, Poultry, and Newcomers in Storm Lake, Iowa. In *Any Way You Cut It:*

Meat Processing and Small-Town America. Edited by Donald D. Stull, Michael J. Broadway, and David Griffith. Lawrence: University Press of Kansas. Pp. 109–127.

Griffith, David

1995   *Hay Trabajo*: Poultry Processing, Rural Industrialization, and the Latinization of Low-Wage Labor. In *Any Way You Cut It: Meat Processing and Small-Town America*. Edited by Donald D. Stull, Michael J. Broadway, and David Griffith. Lawrence: University Press of Kansas. Pp. 129–151.

Hedges, Stephen J.

1996   Job Fair: The Border Town Middlemen. In The New Jungle. *U.S. News and World Report.* September 23, 39.

Hedges, Stephen J., and Dana Hawkins, with Penny Loeb

1996   The New Jungle. *U.S. News and World Report.* September 23, 34–44.

Kay, Steve

1996   Twenty Billion by 2001. *Meat and Poultry* (July): 16–24.

Martin, Philip

1990   Harvest of Confusion: Immigration Reform and California Agriculture. *International Migration Review* 24 (1): 69–95.

Massey, D. S., R. Alarcon, J. Durand, and H. Gonzalez

1990   *Return to Aztlan: The Social Process of International Migration from Western Mexico.* Berkeley: University of California Press.

Nunes, Keith

1998   Twentieth Annual Ranking of Meat and Poultry Companies. *Meat and Poultry* (July): 17–50.

Passel, Jeffrey S., Frank D. Bean, and Barry Edmonston

1991   Assessing the Impact of Employer Sanctions on Undocumented Immigration to the United States. In *The Paper Curtain: Employer Sanctions' Implementation, Impact, and Reform*. Edited by Michael Fix. Washington, D.C.: Urban Institute Press. Pp. 193–213.

Portes, Alejandro, and Rubén Rumbaut

1996   *Immigrant America.* Berkeley: University of California Press.

Public Law 105–100

1997   D.C. Appropriations Act, 1998; Nicaraguan Adjustment and Central American Relief Act. (111 Stat. 2160; November 19, 1997; enacted H.R. 2607). Text from U.S. Code of Service Advance Legislative Service. Available from Congressional Universe (Online Service). Bethesda, Maryland: Congressional Information Service. http://web.lexis-nexus.com/cong.comp

Rural Migration News

1998a   *Rural Migration News* 4 (1), January 1998. http://migration.ucdavis.edu/mntxt.html

1998b   *Rural Migration News* 4 (2), April 1998. http://migration.ucdavis.edu/mntxt.html

Skaggs, Jimmy M.

1986   *Prime Cut: Livestock Raising and Meatpacking in the United States, 1607–1983.* College Station: Texas A&M University Press.

Stanley, Kathleen

1992   Immigrant and Refugee Workers in the Midwestern Meatpacking Industry: Industrial Restructuring and the Transformation of Rural Labor Markets. *Policy Studies Review* 11 (2): 106–117.

Stull, Donald D., Janet E. Benson, Michael J. Broadway, Arthur L. Campa, Ken C. Erickson, and Mark A. Grey

1990   Changing Relations: Newcomers and Established Residents in Garden City, Kansas. Report No. 172. University of Kansas: Institute for Public Policy and Business Research.

Stull, Donald D., and Michael J. Broadway

1990   The Effects of Restructuring on Beefpacking in Kansas. *Kansas Business Review* 14 (1): 10–16.

Stull, Donald D., Michael J. Broadway, and David Griffith, Editors.

1995   *Any Way You Cut It: Meat Processing and Small-Town America.* Lawrence: University Press of Kansas.

U.S.D. 457

1998   USD 457 Enrollment by School, Minority, Sex. 20.

U.S. General Accounting Office

1998   *Community Development: Changes in Nebraska's and Iowa's Counties with Large Meatpacking Plant Workforces.* Washington, D.C.: U.S. Government Printing Office.

U.S. Immigration and Naturalization Service

n.d.   *Basic Pilot Employment Eligibility Confirmation Overview.* Pamphlet.

1998   List of Meatpacking Companies Signed up to Participate in the EVP Program. SAVE Program, INS Headquarters. Washington, D.C.

8

Undocumented Latino Immigrant Workers: The Los Angeles Experience

Enrico A. Marcelli

The reemergence of restrictionist immigration policy sentiment in the 1990s has in no small measure relied on the presumption, real or imagined, that undocumented Latino immigrants threaten the labor market opportunities of lower-skilled, lower-income, U.S.-born workers and consume an undeserved share of public assistance.[1] For instance, three national surveys conducted during the 1980s reveal that from 48 to 71 percent of all respondents viewed undocumented immigrants as competing with variously skilled, native-born U.S. workers. Similarly, a majority of persons interviewed during the present decade saw them burdening, rather than strengthening, the U.S. economy fiscally (Espenshade and Belanger 1998). However, it is rarely doubted that "illegal aliens," a less flattering appellation, are an economic boon to those businesses that employ them directly or subcontract with other firms that do and to those who consume the arguably otherwise more expensive goods and services they help produce (Baker et al. 1998; Cornelius 1998; Smith and Edmonston 1997).[2] For reasons that shall only be hinted at in the concluding section of this chapter, the first and more pessimistic interpretation has become the dominant view as the twentieth century comes to a close.

Mostly as an artifact of the difficulty involved in estimating the number and demographic characteristics of undocumented immigrants, very few studies actually investigate the economic effects of undocumented immigrant workers on others. This may seem surprising given the confidence with which political leaders and immigration scholars alike have either asserted or implied the putative negative economic consequences of illegal immigration (Borjas 1995; Borjas and Hilton 1996; Briggs 1996).[3] Interestingly, analyses that have attempted to evaluate the economic effects of illegal or lower-skilled immigrants consistently report only negligible effects (Bean, Lowell, and Taylor 1988; Blasberg and Sorenson 1997; Chavez et al. 1997; DeFreitas 1991; Fix and Passel 1994; Hammermesh and Bean 1998; Lowell 1996; Marcelli and Heer 1997, 1998; Winegarden and Khor 1991). The separation of public opinion and policy from empirical evidence, what I shall refer to as the *sentiment-evidence mismatch*, implies that either the public's perception and recent policy changes are misinformed, or researchers have not uncovered the real economic effects of illegal immigration.[4] In truth there is probably some merit to both interpretations (Hammermesh and Bean 1998; Smith and Edmonston 1997).

The purpose of this chapter is to investigate the economic role of undocumented Latino immigrant laborers and their impact on businesses and other workers. More specifically, it focuses on the role of non-Cuban, Central, and South American undocumented immigrants in Los Angeles County during an era of rapid globalization and economic restructuring. Many places throughout the country provide similar evidence of the continued importance of undocumented and legal immigrant labor for certain U.S. businesses, but few offer the kind of insight into the economic effects of undocumented Latino immigrants and economic restructuring as does the "L.A. experience" (Soja 1996: 426). Still, Central and South American undocumented immigrants have been the focus of few studies.

The following section highlights some of the important economic changes that have occurred in southern California since the 1970s, defining the Los Angeles region as a unique economic domain in which undocumented Latino immigrant workers continue to play a prominent role. The succeeding section describes the two most frequently employed methods of estimating the number and characteristics of undocumented immigrants in the United States and describes the methodology and data used in this chapter. It is followed by estimates of the number of undocumented Latino immigrant workers in the 1990 Los Angeles County labor force and comparison of their demographic characteristics and labor market position by occupation and industry with those of workers in other ethnoracial groups. The final section juxtaposes the employment findings with recent restrictionist public opinion and policy changes. It illustrates how undocumented Latino immigrants continue to help meet certain industries' appetite for inexpensive and highly reliable labor and considers the possible noneconomic factors influencing recent antipathy toward immigrants regardless of legal status.

LOS ANGELES AS AN ECONOMIC DOMAIN

Most contemporary scholars investigating the effects of economic restructuring in the southern California region have emphasized the role of globalization, segmentation, deindustrialization, and reindustrialization (Davis 1990; Dear,

Hise and Schockman 1996; Joassart 1998; Scott and Soja 1996). In order to understand the continued importance of undocumented Latino immigrant labor in Los Angeles, it is essential to consider the occupational and income manifestations of both de- and reindustrialization—structural changes common to the sunbelt region but particularly important for Los Angeles County.

Deindustrialization and Reindustrialization

The United States has experienced major economic changes since the conclusion of World War II that have altered the structure—or character, if you will—of labor demand. Although the unemployment rate from 1946 to 1973 averaged 4.7 percent[5]—well below the full employment standard of 6 percent—this was not the case during the 1970s and 1980s. By 1982–1983, for example, the unemployment rate had approximately doubled as a restrictive monetary policy was used by Federal Reserve authorities to counter fears of inflation, and the general diffusion of computer-based technology and foreign competition in the goods market rose (Easterlin 1999). One result was that income disparity began to widen during the 1980s (Baker et al. 1998), a fact not unrelated to the diminution of the demand for labor in the manufacturing sector.

Accompanying this structural change in the demand for labor was a demographic change in the supply of labor. Although immigrants represented only a small component of the overall population in 1990 (8 percent), compared to earlier this century (fifteen percent in 1910), immigration is currently contributing more and more to population growth. Between 1980 and 1990, for example, it accounted for fully one-third of the estimated 20 million population increase in the United States. An often unrecognized reality, however, is that fertility declines among the American resident population contribute to this rising immigrant proportion (Easterlin 1999). Thus, the early 1980s began a period of moderate labor demand and rapid labor supply growth—in short, a weakening of the American labor market.

Unlike other areas in the United States, Los Angeles County has experienced not only a deindustrialization in certain manufacturing sectors (characterized by a declining share of automobile, furniture, and steel production) but a reindustrialization (characterized by a rise in both high-technology production and labor-intensive industries such as textiles, jewelry, motion pictures, and printing).[6] Hence, despite the fact that the proportion of manufacturing employment fell from twenty-two to twenty percent from 1950 to 1990 in the Los Angeles region, while the proportion of service employment rose from twenty-six to thirty-eight percent during the same period, both sectors experienced an absolute increase in the number of persons employed (see Figure 8.1). The absolute rise was less pronounced in manufacturing, however. For instance, while the service sector rate of employment growth was double that of the manufacturing sector from 1950 to 1990, the latter was still 200 percent. The

Figure 8.1

Change in Employment, by Major Industry Sector, Los Angeles Region, 1950–1990

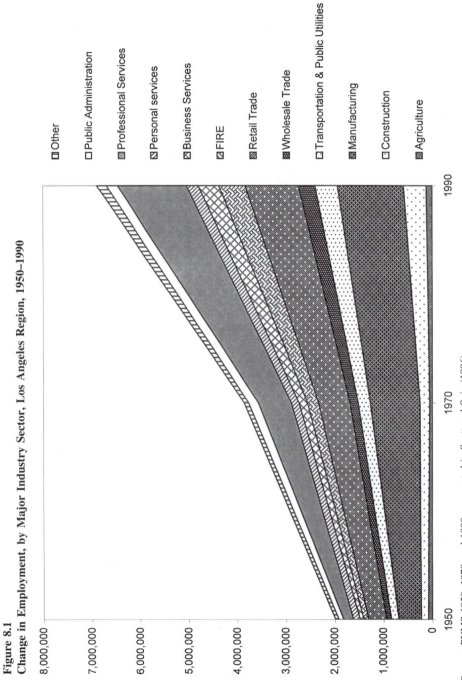

Legend:
- □ Other
- □ Public Administration
- ▨ Professional Services
- ▨ Personal services
- ▨ Business Services
- ▨ FIRE
- ▨ Retail Trade
- ▨ Wholesale Trade
- □ Transportation & Public Utilities
- ▨ Manufacturing
- □ Construction
- ▨ Agriculture

Source: PUMS 1950, 1970, and 1990 as reported in Scott and Soja (1996).

average for all industries was 250 percent. Importantly, as late as 1990, manufacturing and professional services were equally represented, with each accounting for 20 percent of all jobs.

These findings reveal, contrary to the general trend of deindustrialization throughout the entire country, that the Los Angeles region has not experienced a reduction in the number of jobs requiring fewer skills; rather, it has seen a rise in the demand for lower-skilled workers in both the manufacturing and service sectors (Levy and Murnane 1992). The decline of wages and the growth of income inequality that have accompanied economic restructuring, therefore, have resulted from something other than the supposed relative explosion of service sector jobs requiring few labor market skills. Baker et al. (1998: 90) suggest that the actual cause has been "manufacturing jobs increasingly resembling those in the service sector." In short, rather than the proliferation of less attractive jobs in the service sector, manufacturing sector jobs have increasingly lowered their skill standards and compensation for desired labor.

Reliance on Undocumented Latino Immigrant Labor

This changing "character of industry" (Commons 1967: 133) has impacted the "structure of employment" (Scott and Soja 1996: 220) demographically. For example, white representation dropped from 71 to 45 percent of all manufacturing jobs in the Los Angeles region from 1970 to 1990, African-American representation grew from six to ten percent, and Latino (native- and foreign-born) representation doubled from 21 to 40 percent (Scott and Soja 1996: 221–223). A less dramatic transition has been the continued feminization of the manufacturing labor force from the 1950s, when approximately one-quarter of those employed in manufacturing were women. From 1970 to 1990 female representation increased from 28 to 34 percent. While one might be inclined to argue that greater ethnoracial and gender diversity in the manufacturing workforce has been detrimental to those previously occupying the majority of manufacturing positions, most of these persons (e.g., white males) have obtained more desirable and better-paying jobs. Rather than the influx of immigrants or women into the workforce, it is more likely that the changing structure of manufacturing itself has had the larger influence on the character of labor demand and contributed to flat or declining wages.[7]

While the quest for inexpensive, reliable labor is consistent with the theory of unfettered or competitive markets, the foregoing analysis suggests that labor market outcomes for immigrants have been more than a response to Adam Smith's "invisible hand." Indeed, corporate investment in securing and maintaining a pliable workforce has precedence in American history. At the turn of the century one critic of liberal immigration policies wrote that "it is scarcely an exaggeration to say that even more important than the initiative of immigrants have been the efforts of Americans and ship-owners to bring and attract them" (Commons 1967: 107). Portes (1995: 21) notes when discussing the core-periphery analytical framework, for example, that "prior expansion of stronger nation-states into peripheral sending areas" resulted in "coerced labor extraction (slavery) beginning in the sixteenth century to the present self-initiated labor flows." "Throughout our history these efforts have been inspired by one grand, effective motive—that of making a profit upon the immigrants" (Commons 1967: 107–108). More recently, Martin (1986) and Waldinger (1997) explain how firms use Latino immigrant supervisors to lower labor search and management costs and how this institutional arrangement leads to immigrant concentration in certain industrial sectors.[8] Delgado (1993) provides convincing evidence, however, that the reliance on, or concentration of, undocumented workers does not necessarily imply docility and subservience. Nonetheless, recent legislative calls for a new agricultural guest worker program (Stern 1998; Taylor and Martin 1997) and for an increase from 65,000 to 115,000 in the number of H-1B visas for high-tech workers (Branigin 1998) amply illustrate the continued demand for immigrants in both lower-skilled and high-technology industries. As shown in the following section, this bifurcated labor demand has not been limited to only legal immigrants in Los Angeles County or in southern California in general (Cornelius 1998).

Before investigating the comparative labor market position of undocumented Latino immigrants, it is helpful to note that "push" factors, as well as the "pull" factors just reviewed, contribute to immigrant penetration into the U.S. labor market. The former may be usefully separated into international economic forces and public policy changes. For example, beginning in 1982, a year characterized as recessionary, Mexico abandoned its import-substitution industrialization model of economic growth for an export-oriented one. While the former was protective of dominant domestic industries, the latter embraced foreign investment, acquiesced to the General Agreement on Tariffs and Trade (GATT), and prepared for international trade competition. The subsequent adjustment was painful, especially for the working poor (Birdsall and Londono 1997). The Mexican economy grew only modestly and hardly at all in per capital terms during the subsequent five years, and the minimum wage fell by about 40 percent (Baker et al. 1998: 94). Unsurprisingly, the Mexican component of undocumented immigration rose briskly and was only momentarily interrupted by the Immigration Reform and Control Act (IRCA) of 1986. As shall be seen later, persons of Mexican origin continue to represent the largest proportion of undocumented immigrants in Los Angeles County. By 1990 this recession-restructuring-generated migration began to rise again, leading, eventually, to more recent benefits-based restrictionist efforts to discourage illegal immigration. Similar structural adjustments and unique political circumstances also contributed to a rise in immigration from Central and South American countries.

Disregarding the seemingly contradictory, simultaneous pursuit of restrictionist immigration and liberal labor-importing policies for the moment—as well as a consideration of whether push, pull, or individual-level factors best explain the continued entry and presence of both legal and undocumented labor in the

United States—the next sections investigate the contemporary role of undocumented Latino immigrant labor in Los Angeles County, turning first to methodological issues.

DATA AND METHODOLOGY

The data used for this research are from a 1994 University of Southern California and El Colegio de la Frontera (USC-COLEF) Los Angeles County Household Survey and the 5 percent Public Use Microdata Samples of the 1990 Census. The former was conducted in November and December 1994 and is a probability sample of those census tracts in Los Angeles County in which (according to the 1990 Census) 25 percent or more of the total population was born in Mexico. Adults from 271 households in which at least one person was born in Mexico were asked a series of demographic, migration, and legal status questions, from which information about 661 foreign-born Mexicans, aged eighteen and older, was obtained.[9] Given the sensitivity of the legal status information being collected, only Spanish-speaking (mostly Mexican origin) interviewers were employed.[10]

Research on the number and characteristics of undocumented immigrants began toward the end of the 1970s (North and Houston 1976; Fogel 1979) and was still in its infancy during most of the 1980s. The range of estimates, for example, remained relatively wide at 2–6 million, although having narrowed from the much wider 1–12 million that prevailed in the early 1980s (Woodrow-Lafield 1998). By 1990, leading scholars in the field concluded that "a more definitive assessment of the size of the illegal alien population is probably not possible at this time with available data" (Edmonston, Passel, and Bean 1990: 27). Although the pace of illegal immigration research has quickened since 1990, that which estimates the economic impact and integration of undocumented immigrants may still be characterized as inchoate. The United Nations recently reported, for example, that "by its very nature, undocumented migration remains difficult to quantify" (United Nations 1998: 207). Consequently, given these limitations and despite recent progress, the restrictionist public opinion that fueled the 1994 passage of California's illegal immigrant ballot initiative (Proposition 187) and recent federal-level immigration and welfare policy changes was premised on a firm, but unsubstantiated, belief in an illegal immigrant problem.

As various studies have noted, differences in demographic and economic characteristics illustrate the importance of distinguishing by legal status. For example, that levels of education and benefit eligibility criteria differ between undocumented and legal immigrants suggests probable differential economic effects. Indeed, while "both analysts and policymakers often draw conclusions regarding the impacts of regularly admitted legal immigrants based on the characteristics of all noncitizens" (Clark and Passel 1998: 3), they also draw conclusions concerning undocumented immigrants from similar research findings without separating by legal status.[11] The point here is that not separating the foreign-born resident population by categories correlated with their expected economic "quality" (e.g., admission or legal status, educational attainment, gender and country of origin) and impact prohibits one from systematically investigating how various groups of foreign-born persons influence business profitability, consumer prices, fiscal coffers, and other U.S. residents' labor market opportunities and outcomes. Regardless of the interpretive limitations of most current research, however, illegal immigration is on the rise (Heer 1996) and as of October 1996 reached an estimated 5 million persons (Warren 1997).

There have been two general methods of estimating the number and characteristics of the net resident undocumented immigrant population.[12] The most frequently used is an indirect, census-based procedure, or what has come to be known as the *residual methodology*. Estimates from this approach are obtained by subtracting from the foreign-born population counted in census data those who have become either legal permanent residents or naturalized citizens. A more costly alternative, the *survey-based methodology* obtains information about individuals believed likely to be undocumented directly from localized, nonsystematic or random samples and then weights these observations to produce estimates of the undocumented immigrant population—see Heer and Passel (1987) for a comparison of these two methods, Warren and Passel (1987), Warren (1994, 1997), and Woodrow-Lafield (1998) for examples of the former approach, and Clark and Passel (1998), Cornelius (1982), Heer (1990), and Marcelli and Heer (1997, 1998) for examples of the latter.[13]

Some survey-based methodologies, while not capable of producing national estimates, permit one to distinguish between individuals who are more likely to be legal and those who are not in a smaller geographical area. This latter method is used for this chapter. In previous research Marcelli and Heer (1997, 1998) separated those likely to have been legal from those likely to have been undocumented among the foreign-born Mexican population in Los Angeles County for 1990. This was done by measuring the relationship between reported legal status and various demographic variables (age, sex, years in the United States since first entering, and educational attainment) using data from the USC-COLEF survey, and then applying this information to adult, nonnaturalized, foreign-born Mexican individuals enumerated in the 1990 census.[14] Here this information is used to estimate who was legal and who was not among both foreign-born Mexicans and all non-Cuban Central and South American nonnaturalized, foreign-born adults residing in Los Angeles County in 1990.[15]

Specifically, however, the labor market position of undocumented Salvadoran, Guatemalan, and other non-Cuban, non-Mexican Central and South American immigrant workers is compared with that of members of other ethnoracial groups in Los Angeles County to estimate whether the former are more likely to be complements or substitutes in production for the latter.[16] This chapter focuses on undocumented Central and South American immigrants in Los Angeles County for two reasons. First, as noted before, most studies either investigate all immigrants collectively, regardless of national origin or category of entry, or focus only on immigrant ethnoracial groups purportedly most detrimental to economic welfare (Duleep and Regets 1996; Lowell 1996). As Ong and Valenzuela (1996: 179) suggest, however, "generalizing about all immigration is an exercise in misleading polemics." Second, California, more specifically, Los Angeles County, is home to the lion's share of undocumented immigrants, many of whom are not only from Mexico but from Guatemala, El Salvador, and various other countries (Fix and Passel 1994; Warren 1994; Warren and Passel 1987).[17] Although Warren (1994) estimated that there were 205,000 undocumented immigrants from El Salvador, 88,000 from Guatemala, and approximately 100,000 from other Central and South American countries in 1992 (totaling almost 400,000 undocumented Central and South American immigrants) using a composite estimation methodology,[18] no previous study, to my knowledge, has estimated the number of undocumented Central and South American immigrants in Los Angeles County. Lopez, Popkin, and Telles (1996), however, offer an estimate of undocumented Salvadorans and Guatemalans in the five-county Los Angeles region of 178,000 and 80,000, respectively.[19]

In addition to generating the first survey-based estimates of the number of this population in the Los Angeles County labor force, this chapter tests the hypothesis, following human capital theory, that there is a close, positive relationship between the amounts of human capital (educational attainment, language ability, etc.) with which the members of an ethnoracial group are endowed and their relative position in the labor force. To the extent that undocumented Central and South American immigrants are found to have relatively lower levels of educational attainment, less experience, and less familiarity with U.S. labor market institutions, they can be expected to occupy less beneficial and thus less desirable labor market positions than members of other ethnoracial groups with more human or social capital. Put differently, if undocumented Central and South American immigrants are found to be less formally educated and to have been in the United States for a shorter period of time than members of other ethnoracial groups, then they are more likely to be overrepresented in those occupational, industry, and class-of-worker categories requiring lower levels of human capital. One would not be surprised in this context, for example, to find male (female) undocumented Central and South American immigrants overrepresented in agricultural or construction (textile or private household) and underrepresented in professional services and public administration.

This does not imply that other factors, such as family (Ben-Porath 1980) or social (Pastor and Adams 1996) networks, do not significantly influence labor market opportunities and outcomes. Even if occupational or industry positions are highly correlated with human capital endowments, this does not permit one to conclude that structural-level factors are not as, or more, important in influencing individual labor market consequences, including how others are affected by an influx of undocumented or legal immigrants. Indeed, one must disaggregate individual-level (human capital) and structural-level (demand and supply of labor) factors and regress them on the earnings and employment of lower- and higher-skilled nonimmigrants separately in order to test the relative complementarity and (or) substitutability of undocumented immigrants. (This chapter does not include earnings or employment regressions, and hence no clear conclusions can be drawn regarding the impact of undocumented Central and South American immigrants workers on other workers' wages and employment. However, the findings do suggest what is likely to be the case in Los Angeles County.)

For now it is sufficient to note that while this research is similar in some respects to earlier work (Bean, Lowell, and Taylor 1988; Espenshade and Goodis 1988; Heer 1990; Marcelli and Heer 1997, 1998), it is unique in being the first to estimate the number of undocumented Central and South American immigrants in Los Angeles County in the 1990s, separating them from other Latino immigrants at the individual level and inquiring directly into the validity of contemporary restrictionist immigration sentiment based on antipathy toward undocumented Latino immigrants in the Los Angeles County labor market. Finally, no previous study has examined the over- and underrepresentation of undocumented Central and South American immigrants in specific occupational, industry, and class-of-worker categories in comparison with members of other ethnoracial groups.

UNDOCUMENTED LATINO IMMIGRANTS: CHARACTERISTICS AND EMPLOYMENT

Restricting the sample to those aged eighteen to sixty-four in the 1990 Los Angeles County labor force, 24.5 percent of the 4,233,717 labor force participants were of Latino origin, and 71.5 percent of these were foreign-born (Figure 8.2). While Mexicans constituted the largest share of undocumented Latino immigrants, other undocumented Central and South American immigrants represented fully thirty percent (Figure 8.3). The impact of this latter ethnoracial group of 146,838 (78,807 male and 68,031 female) persons is the focus of this chapter.

According to human capital theory, educational attainment of the various ethnoracial groups should determine who fills more or less desirable occupations and industries. An analysis of educational levels reveals that all foreign-born Latinos (both undocumented Central and South American immigrants and others) were less well educated than members of other ethnoracial groups (Table 8.1). For example, approximately 20 percent of the former had completed less than five years of schooling, while less than 2 percent of the latter had. This has been the source of the renewed debate regarding the rapidity with which newer immigrants (mostly Latino) can be expected to assimilate (Alba and Nee 1997; Duleep and Regets 1997). Although undocumented Central and South American immigrants were clearly less well-educated than all other ethnoracial groups except undocumented Mexican immigrants, there appears to have been

Figure 8.2

Nativity of Labor Force Participants, Aged 18-64, by Ethnoracial Group, Los Angeles County, 1990

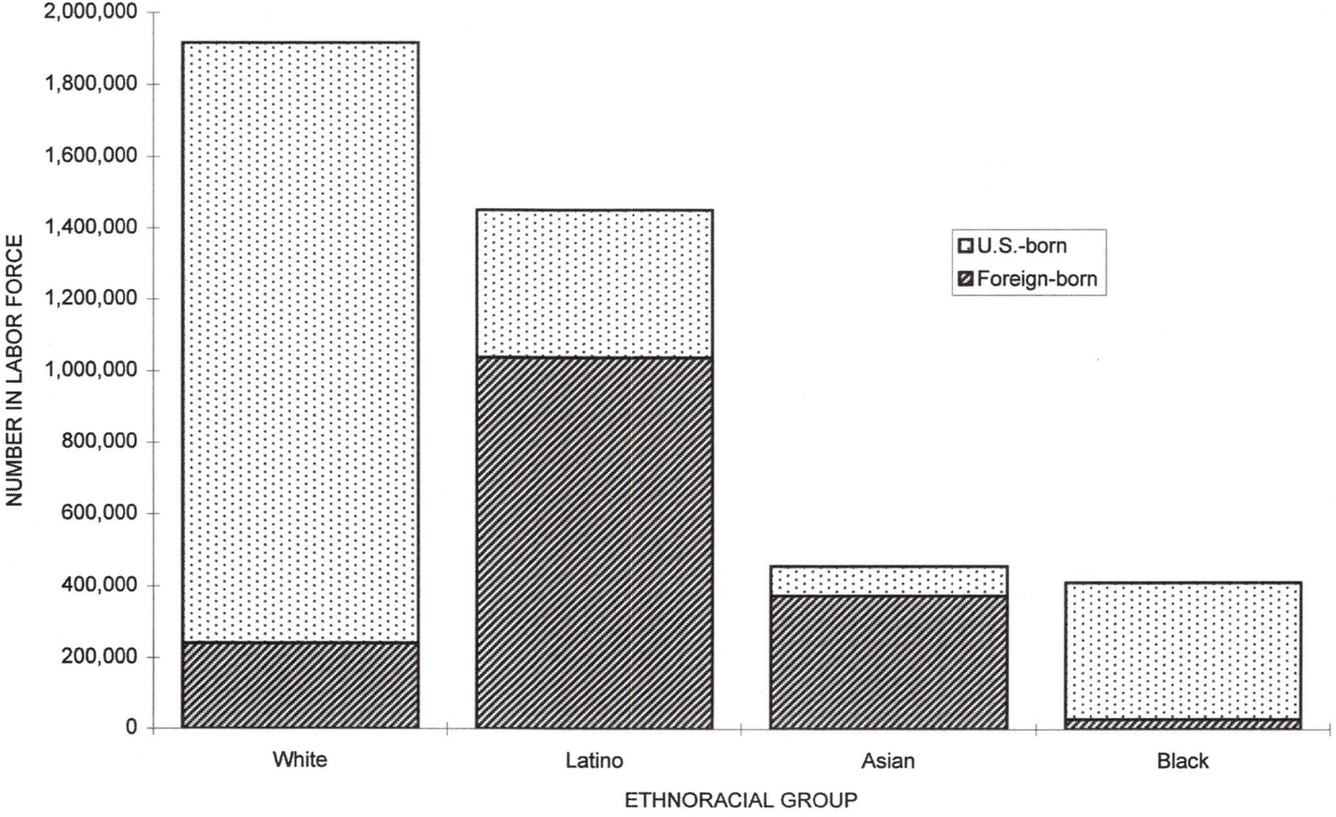

Figure 8.3
Undocumented Latino Immigrants by Country of Origin, Los Angeles County, 1990

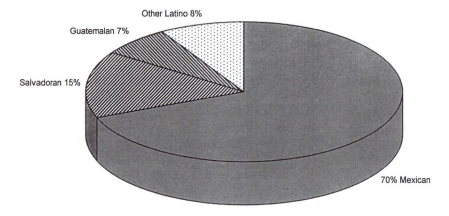

significant variation among the three different undocumented Latino groups (Table 8.1). Both undocumented Guatemalan and Salvadoran immigrants were less well educated than other Central and South American undocumented immigrants, with Salvadorans slightly better educated than Guatemalans.

Undocumented Central and South American immigrants also distinguish themselves by the fact that, on average, they have been in the United States for a shorter period of time than all other ethnoracial groups. For example, while no more than two percent of the former had arrived for the first time before 1974, over 30 percent of other immigrants had done so, except undocumented Mexicans (Table 8.2). On the other hand, undocumented Central and South American immigrants were similar to other foreign-born ethnoracial groups in terms of the proportion of immigrants who had been in the United States for no more than a decade. It is reasonable to suspect that English-language ability and familiarity with U.S. labor market institutions are highly correlated with time spent residing and working in the United States. Accordingly, we would expect undocumented Central and South American immigrants as a group to have filled slightly less desirable labor market positions than other foreign-born Latinos (except for undocumented Mexican immigrants) and significantly less desirable positions than all other ethnoracial groups. Furthermore, as indicated from analysis of educational attainment, one would expect undocumented Guatemalan immigrants to have been overrepresented in less beneficial positions than undocumented Salvadoran immigrants. However, no evidence suggests that undocumented Salvadoran immigrants were less familiar with U.S. institutions than were other undocumented Central and South American immigrants (Table 8.2).

Consequently, if average educational attainment and time spent in the United

States are good indicators of the average skill level of an ethnoracial group, then it is reasonable to suspect that undocumented Central and South American immigrants should have been overrepresented in less desirable positions and that among them undocumented Salvadoran and Guatemalan immigrants would have the less desirable positions.

How to interpret these findings is not immediately obvious. Agreement exists that undocumented Central and South American immigrants are less well prepared to compete with others in the Los Angeles County labor market. However, while some infer from this that they are less likely to progress economically over the course of their lives, others highlight the apparent complementarity of undocumented Central and South American immigrant characteristics with persons born in the United States and suggest they accept jobs that are unattractive to others.

Employment by Occupation

As suggested from the foregoing analysis, undocumented Central and South American immigrants were more highly represented in service-oriented, textile, and agricultural occupations and less highly represented in technical and professional occupations than other groups. This holds for all Latinos regardless of nativity. For example, although undocumented Central and South American immigrants represented only 3.5 percent of the labor force in Los Angeles in 1990, they filled more than 8 percent of service, 6 percent of nonfarm labor, 4 percent of precision workers, and 5 percent of farming occupations. Not surprisingly, they filled less than 2 percent of technical and managerial jobs (Figure 8.4).

A comparison of the occupations filled by the different undocumented Latino immigrant groups suggests that a greater share of ''other'' undocumented Central and South American immigrants filled technical and professional occupations, while a minority of undocumented Guatemalan and Salvadoran immigrants (as well as undocumented Mexican immigrants) did (Figure 8.5). Also consistent with what human capital theory would predict, undocumented Salvadoran immigrants had a slightly larger share of their members filling technical and professional positions than undocumented Guatemalan immigrants. It is interesting to note also that undocumented Central and South American immigrants did not have the same occupational distribution as undocumented Mexican immigrants. While the former were concentrated in service occupations, a greater proportion of the latter was found in operator, laborer, and farming occupations (Figure 8.5).

Comparing forty-two more specifically defined occupations, one finds that undocumented Central and South American immigrant males and females were underrepresented in most white-collar occupations and overrepresented in most others (Table 8.3).[20] For example, undocumented Latino immigrants occupied a substantially smaller proportion of administrative and technical positions and a substantially larger proportion of household and health care service positions.

Table 8.1
Educational Attainment of Male and Female Labor Force Participants, Aged Eighteen to Sixty-four, by Ethnoracial Group, Los Angeles County, 1990

Ethno-Racial Group	Sex	Number of cases	Total percent	YEARS OF SCHOOLING COMPLETED (PERCENT)				
				<5	5-8	9	10-12	>12
1a. Undocumented Salvadoran Immigrant	M	38,810	100	22.20	22.64	11.53	27.36	16.26
	F	34,216	100	20.95	24.64	9.68	31.34	13.39
1b. Undocumented Guatemalan Immigrant	M	19,245	100	23.09	30.41	9.06	22.55	14.90
	F	14,363	100	24.21	27.85	6.91	29.39	11.65
1c. Undocumented Other Central & South American Immigrant	M	20,752	100	14.27	14.84	3.77	26.12	40.99
	F	19,452	100	10.59	13.72	4.34	34.35	37.00
1. Undocumented Central and South American Immigrant	M	78,807	100	20.33	22.49	8.88	25.86	22.44
	F	68,031	100	18.68	22.20	7.57	31.79	19.77
2. Other Central and South American Immigrant	M	98,838	100	9.82	15.40	6.47	40.67	27.55
	F	69,118	100	11.42	17.87	6.24	33.86	30.61
3. Undocumented Mexican Immigrant	M	214,332	100	22.48	30.33	10.21	25.94	11.04
	F	112,513	100	24.60	27.28	7.90	28.99	11.23
4. Other Mexican Immigrant	M	271,644	100	18.28	25.43	7.22	35.05	14.01
	F	123,050	100	12.74	25.05	6.66	35.53	20.02

5. Latino, US-born	M	223,692	100	1.84	2.90	2.12	49.73	43.41
	F	190,324	100	1.11	2.35	2.10	47.39	47.06
6. Asian Immigrant^	M	199,111	100	2.76	2.30	1.08	21.49	72.36
	F	173,746	100	2.93	3.09	1.47	22.99	69.51
7. Asian, US-born^	M	43,791	100	0.43	0.56	0.48	20.89	77.65
	F	39,588	100	0.70	0.53	0.20	20.19	78.38
8. Black Immigrant^	M	14,784	100	1.40	2.76	1.52	31.20	63.12
	F	11,758	100	1.29	1.34	0.88	33.47	63.01
9. Black, US-born^	M	186,151	100	0.62	1.33	1.10	40.05	56.89
	F	198,373	100	0.52	0.61	0.51	32.98	65.37
10. White Immigrant^	M	140,992	100	1.84	3.12	1.42	26.25	67.37
	F	98,525	100	1.47	1.87	0.88	29.17	66.60
11. White, US-born^	M	930,102	100	0.21	0.61	0.63	25.24	73.31
	F	746,447	100	0.23	0.33	0.44	26.82	72.18
12. Total	M	2,402,244	100	5.80	7.96	3.00	30.21	53.03
	F	1,831,473	100	4.14	5.72	2.10	30.46	57.59

Notes: Percentages in "years of schooling" may not sum to 100 due to rounding. Group 1c includes other non-Cuban, and Group 1 includes Groups 1a through 1c. ^ excludes Latinos.

Table 8.2

Percent of Male and Female Foreign-Born Labor Force Participants Having Been in the United States for a Specified Period of Time, Aged Eighteen to Sixty-four, by Ethnoracial Group, Los Angeles County, 1990

Ethno-Racial Group	Sex	Number of cases	Total percent	YEARS SINCE FIRST ARRIVAL (PERCENT) <10	10-16	>16
1a. Undocumented Salvadoran	M	38,810	100	25.67	74.33	0.00
Immigrant	F	34,216	100	21.59	76.84	1.58
1b. Undocumented Guatemalan	M	19,245	100	41.55	58.30	0.15
Immigrant	F	14,363	100	38.17	60.91	0.92
1c. Undocumented Other Central &	M	20,752	100	29.86	70.06	0.09
South American Immigrant	F	19,452	100	30.31	68.84	0.85
1. Undocumented Central and	M	78,807	100	30.65	69.29	0.06
South American Immigrant	F	68,031	100	27.58	71.19	1.23
2. Other Central and South	M	98,383	100	54.47	10.78	34.75
American Immigrant	F	69,118	100	47.43	4.39	48.19
3. Undocumented Mexican Immigrant	M	214,332	100	30.86	68.96	0.19
	F	112,513	100	25.01	69.05	5.94
4. Other Mexican Immigrant	M	271,644	100	39.34	4.54	56.11
	F	123,050	100	28.03	1.43	70.54
5. Asian Immigrant^	M	199,111	100	39.24	35.48	25.28
	F	173,746	100	37.27	35.69	27.04
6. Black Immigrant^	M	14,784	100	29.00	33.23	37.77
	F	11,758	100	27.12	30.13	42.75
7. White Immigrant^	M	140,992	100	26.88	29.01	44.12
	F	98,525	100	21.50	24.26	54.25
8. Total	M	1,018,508	100	36.46	33.56	29.98
	F	656,741	100	30.96	33.55	35.49

Notes: Percentages may not sum to 100 due to rounding. Group 1c includes other non-Cuban, and Group 1 includes Groups 1a through 1c. ^ excludes Latinos.

Perhaps the most striking example is found in the case of private household occupations, which employed 16.93 percent of undocumented Central and South American immigrant females as opposed to 1.75 percent of other females (Table 8.3).

Employment by Industry

Although industrial patterns of representation are similar to those found in the occupational distribution analyses, industries are composed of various oc-

Figure 8.4
Ethnoracial Group Representation by Major Occupational Category, Los Angeles County, 1990

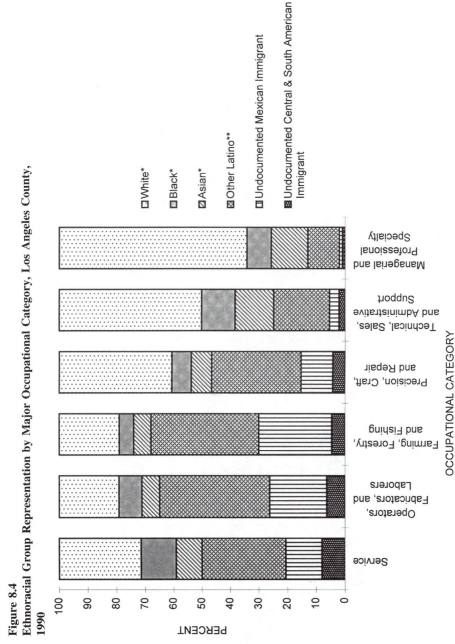

Notes: *non-Latino; **includes both other foreign- and U.S.-born persons.

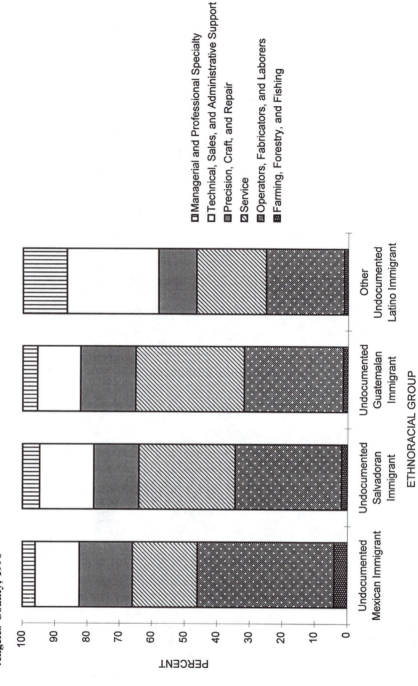

Figure 8.5
Major Occupational Category Distribution of Undocumented Latino Immigrants, Los Angeles County, 1990

Managerial and Professional Specialty
Technical, Sales, and Administrative Support
Precision, Craft, and Repair
Service
Operators, Fabricators, and Laborers
Farming, Forestry, and Fishing

PERCENT

Undocumented Mexican Immigrant
Undocumented Salvadoran Immigrant
Undocumented Guatemalan Immigrant
Other Undocumented Latino Immigrant

ETHNORACIAL GROUP

Table 8.3

Percentage Distribution by Occupation for Undocumented Central and South American Immigrant (UCSAI) and Other, Male and Female, Los Angeles County Labor Force Participants, Aged Eighteen to Sixty-four, 1990

Occupational Category	UCSAI Males	Other Males	UCSAI Females	Other Females
Officials & administrators, Public	0.02	0.23*	0.05	0.27*
Management related	1.43	3.35	1.07	5.05*
Officials & administrators, Private	3.00	9.49	1.97	8.09*
Engineers	0.52	2.89*	0.06	0.46*
Architects, surveyors, mathematicians, & natural scientists	0.09	1.28*	0.09	0.87*
Health diagnosing	0.14	0.99*	0.03	0.44*
Health assessment & treating	0.20	0.42	1.08	3.29
Teachers, elementary & secondary	0.29	1.06	1.09	4.11
Other teachers, librarians, & counselors	0.29	1.05	0.52	2.05*
Other professional specialty	1.60	5.41	1.01	4.78*
Health technologists & technicians	0.52	0.48	1.36	1.66
Technologists & technicians, except health	0.93	3.19	0.45	1.69
Supervisors & proprietors, sales	1.28	3.10	0.61	2.07
Sales representatives, finance	1.39	4.04	0.76	3.24*
Cashiers	1.70	1.11	4.64	2.99
Other sales	2.75	2.71	3.21	3.36
Computer equipment operators	0.25	0.44	0.39	0.69
Secretaries, stenographers & typists	0.11	0.28	2.77	8.29
Financial records processing	0.41	0.56	1.16	3.83
Mail & message distribution	0.32	1.09	0.33	0.71
Other administrative support	5.74	6.30	7.94	15.79
Private household	0.44	0.08*	16.93	1.75*
Police & firefighting	0.08	0.88	0.08	0.21
Other protective service	1.09	1.48	0.22	0.41
Food service	7.78	4.01	5.38	3.52
Cleaning & building	6.25	2.72	10.17	1.89*
Health service & personal service	1.08	1.18	8.77	5.73
Farm operators & managers	0.13	0.11	0.06	0.03
Farm workers & related	2.38	1.71	0.45	0.31
Forestry & fishing	0.02	0.06	0.03	0.01
Mechanics & repairers	6.34	5.34	0.36	0.35
Construction trades	9.95	7.02	0.37	0.29
Precision production	6.13	5.39	3.42	2.22
Extractive	0.06	0.04	0.01	0.02
Machine operators & tenders, except precision	11.98	5.73	15.98	4.85
Fabricators, assemblers, inspectors, & samplers	4.57	3.15	4.12	2.43

Table 8.3 (*continued*)

Occupational Category	UCSAI Males	Other Males	UCSAI Females	Other Females
Motor vehicle operators	7.20	4.56	0.56	0.62
Rail & water transportation	0.01	0.10*	0.01	0.02
Material moving equipment operators	0.61	0.89	0.03	0.06
Construction laborers	4.23	1.99	0.16	0.08
Freight, stock, & material handlers	6.06	3.85	2.25	1.46
Other handlers, equipment cleaners, helpers, & laborers	0.65	0.24	0.07	0.03
TOTAL	100	100	100	100

Notes: * indicates natural log of odds ratio is 1.39 or more, or -1.39 or less; percentages may not sum to 100 due to rounding.

cupations, and the differences are less extreme. This is consistent with the idea that the specific job one has corresponds more closely with one's skill level and that often a person with a certain level of education or experience can more easily move across industries than switch occupations. For example, a janitor may be working for the manufacturing, trade, or finance industry. Hence, although concentrated in specific occupations, undocumented immigrants may be found in various industries. It is revealing, however, that undocumented Central and South American immigrants represented over ten percent of the personal services industry category and approximately 5 percent of at least five other industries (Figure 8.6). Furthermore, although undocumented Salvadoran and Guatemalan immigrants were almost perfectly distributed among nine major industry categories, larger proportions of other undocumented Central and South American immigrants were employed in professional industries (Figure 8.7). Interestingly, undocumented Mexican immigrants were more likely to be employed in manufacturing industries and less likely to work in personal services than other undocumented Latino immigrants. That these differences are not as distinct as were those of the occupational categories is not surprising, however.

Comparisons of forty detailed industrial categories suggest that, in general, undocumented Central and South American immigrants are only moderately underrepresented in white-collar positions and moderately overrepresented in others (Table 8.4). Few industries were characterized by drastic under- or over-representation. For example, perhaps not surprisingly, while 0.01 percent of undocumented Central and South American immigrant males worked in the other educational services category, 0.29 percent of other males did. Conversely, although 17.36 (0.57) percent of undocumented Central and South American

Figure 8.6
Ethnoracial Representation by Major Industry Category, Los Angeles County, 1990

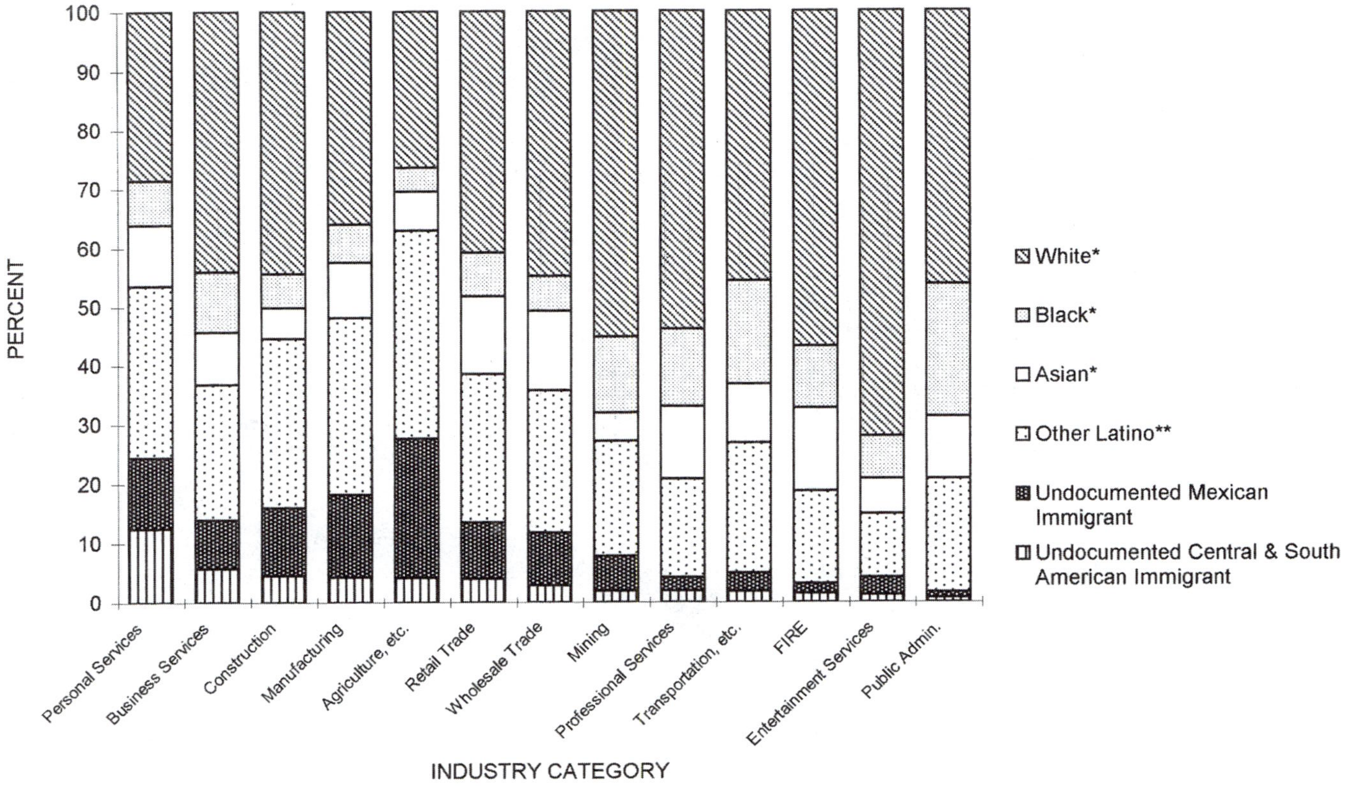

Legend:
- ▨ White*
- ☐ Black*
- ☐ Asian*
- ☐ Other Latino**
- ▦ Undocumented Mexican Immigrant
- ▥ Undocumented Central & South American Immigrant

Y-axis: PERCENT (0–100)

X-axis (INDUSTRY CATEGORY): Personal Services, Business Services, Construction, Manufacturing, Agriculture, etc., Retail Trade, Wholesale Trade, Mining, Professional Services, Transportation, etc., FIRE, Entertainment Services, Public Admin.

Notes: *non-Latino; **includes both other foreign- and U.S.-born persons.

Figure 8.7
Major Industry Category Distribution of Undocumented Latino Immigrants, Los Angeles County, 1990

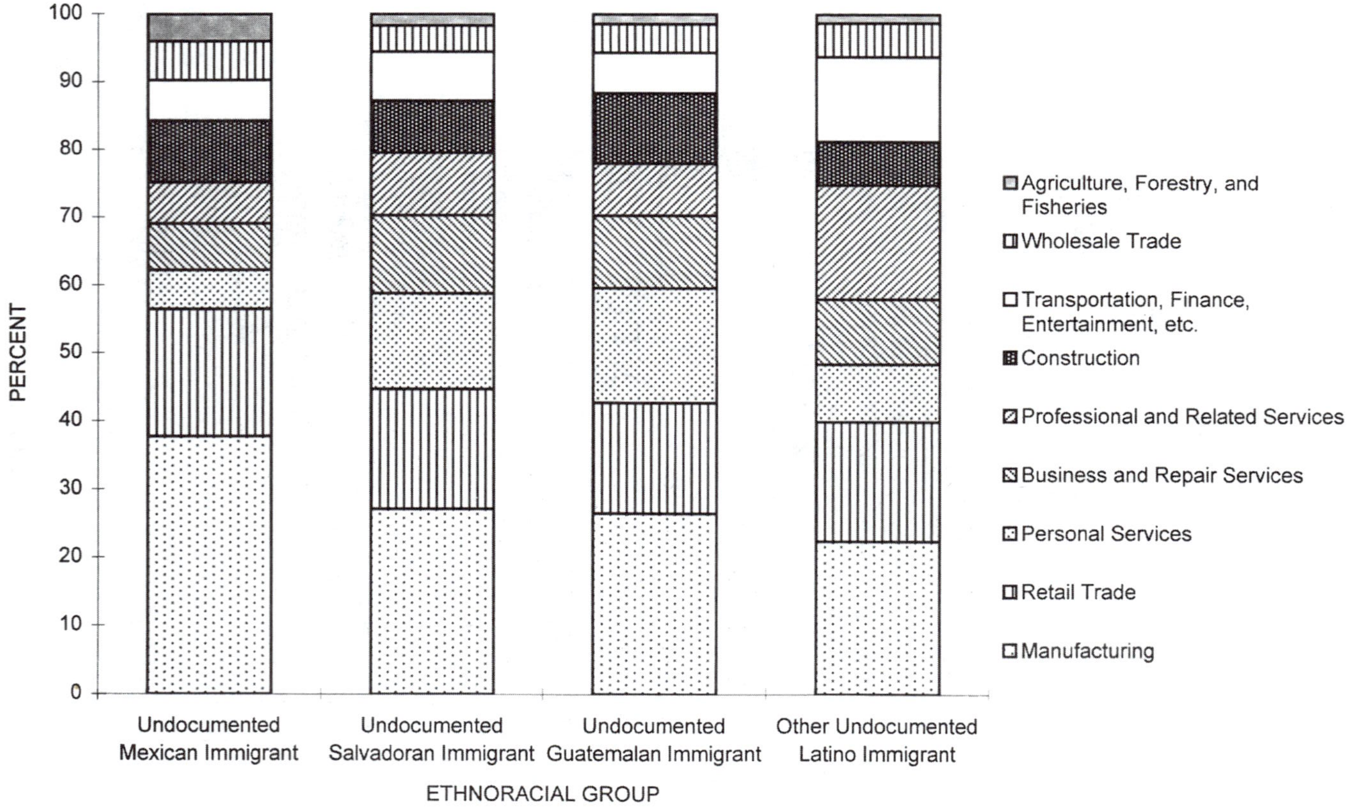

PERCENT
100
90
80
70
60
50
40
30
20
10
0
Undocumented Mexican Immigrant
Undocumented Salvadoran Immigrant
Undocumented Guatemalan Immigrant
Other Undocumented Latino Immigrant
ETHNORACIAL GROUP
Agriculture, Forestry, and Fisheries
Wholesale Trade
Transportation, Finance, Entertainment, etc.
Construction
Professional and Related Services
Business and Repair Services
Personal Services
Retail Trade
Manufacturing

Table 8.4

Percentage Distribution by Industry of Undocumented Central and South American Immigrant (UCSAI) and Other, Male and Female, Los Angeles County Labor Force Participants, Aged Eighteen to Sixty-four, 1990

Labor Force by Industry	UCSAI Males	Other Males	UCSAI Females	Other Females
Agriculture	2.48	1.77	0.40	0.49
Forestry & fishing	0.01	0.65*	0.01	0.04*
Mining	0.16	0.22	0.01	0.09*
Construction	14.30	9.80	0.70	1.29
Food manufacturing	0.85	1.21	0.98	0.80
Textile mill & finished textile products	6.15	1.90	11.84	3.64
Printing & publishing	2.18	1.86	0.83	1.54
Chemical & allied products	0.69	0.74	0.71	0.60
Other non-durable goods	1.40	1.45	1.15	0.93
Furniture, lumber, & wood products	2.33	1.46	0.55	0.51
Primary metal	0.28	0.60	0.14	0.20
Fabricated metal, including ordnance	1.66	1.38	0.51	0.59
Machinery, except electrical	1.94	2.24	0.85	0.86
Electrical machinery	1.81	1.97	1.53	1.78
Transportation equipment	2.64	5.76	0.64	2.97*
Other durable goods	5.18	3.13	4.24	2.38
Trucking service & warehousing	2.55	2.27	0.24	0.57
Other transportation	1.78	3.37	1.02	2.59
Communications	0.55	1.39	0.37	1.57*
Utilities & sanitary services	0.47	1.35	0.01	0.66*
Wholesale trade	4.76	5.96	3.37	4.00
General merchandise stores	1.55	1.44	1.60	2.41
Food, bakery, & dairy stores	2.75	2.37	1.87	1.96
Automotive dealers & gasoline stations	2.62	2.09	0.60	0.65
Eating & drinking places	7.95	4.70	6.13	4.13
Other retail trade	3.90	4.73	5.16	5.65
Banking & credit agencies	0.82	1.72	2.03	4.44
Insurance, real estate, & other finance	1.53	4.05	2.09	5.95
Business services	7.69	5.05	8.36	4.75
Repair services	4.99	2.32	0.19	0.31
Private households	0.57	0.14*	17.36	1.92*
Other personal services	3.91	1.93	5.92	3.07
Entertainment & recreational services	1.08	3.64	1.19	2.83
Hospitals	1.92	2.02	4.87	6.55
Health services, except hospitals	0.70	1.58	3.29	5.01
Elementary & secondary schools & colleges	1.20	3.71	2.70	9.88
Other educational services	0.01	0.29*	0.39	0.62
Social service, religious, & membership organizations	0.66	1.32	4.14	3.76
Legal, engineering, & other professional services	1.40	4.10	1.51	5.07
Public administration	0.59	2.92*	0.52	2.92*
TOTAL	100	100	100	100

Notes: *indicates natural log of odds ratio is 1.39 or more, or −1.39 or less; percentages may not sum to 100 due to rounding.

immigrants females (males) were employed in the private household industry, only 1.92 (0.14) percent of other females (males) were (Table 8.4).

Type of Employment

A final labor market classification distinguishes participants by the legal status of the company. Eight "class-of-worker" categories are used to analyze the comparative composition of undocumented Central and South American immigrants (Table 8.5). In general, they were not extremely different in terms of working for a private corporation or for government or in terms of being self-employed. Specifically, undocumented Central and South American immigrant males and females were only moderately overrepresented in for-profit companies. They were moderately underrepresented in six of the remaining seven (except that males were moderately overrepresented in the unpaid family worker category) and, as might be expected, extremely underrepresented in the federal government category. Perhaps surprisingly, undocumented Central and South American immigrants were slightly underrepresented in the self-employment category, with 4.63 percent of them being self-employed as opposed to 9.03 percent of other males.[21]

Do Undocumented Latino Immigrants Fill Similar or Dissimilar Labor Market Positions?

Two separate measures are used to estimate the relative distinctiveness of undocumented Central and South American immigrants and other ethnoracial groups as compared with other labor force participants. The Index of Dissimilarity (DISS) is computed for each ethnoracial group by (1) taking the difference between how a given ethnoracial group (distinguished by sex) and all other labor force participants (male or female) are proportionally represented in each of the forty-two occupational, forty industrial, and eight class-of-worker categories; (2) summing the differences for each group of occupational, industry, and class-of-worker categories; and (3) dividing each group in half. This measure gives disproportional weight to those categories in which the percentage frequency is larger. The Index of Differentiation (DIFF), alternatively, is computed by (1) taking the absolute value of the natural logs of the odds ratios and (2) summing them. This measure does not give more weight to those categories in which the percentage frequency is larger, and hence DISS and DIFF may rank the proportional differences differently (as seen in Tables 8.6 through 8.8).

Undocumented Central and South American immigrant males are found to be more dissimilar to other labor force participants in Los Angeles County according to the occupations they filled than every other ethnoracial group except for Mexican immigrants and U.S.-born white males (using DISS), but less dissimilar than other foreign-born Latino males according to DIFF (Table 8.6). Similarly,

Table 8.5

Percentage Distribution by Class of Worker of Undocumented Central and South American Immigrant (UCSAI) and Other, Male and Female, Los Angeles County Labor Force Participants, Aged Eighteen to Sixty-four, 1990.

Class of Worker	UCSAI Males	Other Males	UCSAI Females	Other Female
For-profit company worker	87.74	73.69	84.44	70.32
Not-for-profit company worker	2.89	3.84	4.29	7.10
Local government worker	1.92	5.72	2.73	9.39
State government worker	0.60	1.81	0.98	3.23
Federal government worker	0.37	2.26*	0.34	2.18*
Self-employed business, not incorporated	4.63	9.03	5.74	5.76
Employee of own corporation	1.33	3.33	0.94	1.45
Unpaid family worker	0.52	0.33	0.54	0.56
TOTAL	100	100	100	100

Notes: *indicates natural log of odds ratio is 1.39 or more, or −1.39 or less; percentages may not sum to 100 due to rounding.

undocumented Central and South American immigrant females are more dissimilar to other female labor force participants in terms of the occupations they filled except for undocumented Mexican immigrant females (DISS) or other Mexican immigrants (DIFF).

A similar pattern is found for industries (Table 8.7). While undocumented Central and South American immigrant males are the second (third) most dissimilar ethnoracial group according to DISS (DIFF), undocumented Mexican immigrant females are ranked most dissimilar, and undocumented Central and South American immigrant females are ranked second most dissimilar by both measures.

Regarding the class of worker, a more complicated picture emerges from the analysis (Table 8.8). Undocumented Central and South American immigrant males are tied for third most dissimilar with foreign-born white males, according to DISS, but are only less dissimilar than undocumented Mexican immigrant males, according to DIFF. Undocumented Central and South American immigrant females are ranked third most dissimilar by DISS and DIFF.

The story obtained from these analyses is that although undocumented Central and South American immigrants are very dissimilar in terms of the occupations, industries, and class-of-worker categories they fill, they are not the most dissimilar ethnoracial group. Other foreign-born Latinos, blacks, and whites sometimes occupy more dissimilar labor market positions. Undocumented Mexican immigrants are always more dissimilar than undocumented Central and South American immigrants.

Table 8.6

Occupational Indices of Dissimilarity (DISS) and Differentiation (DIFF), and Percentage Discordant Pairs (DP), by Ethnoracial Group and Sex, Los Angeles County, 1990

Ethno-Racial Group	Males			Females		
	DISS	DIFF	DP	DISS	DIFF	DP
Undocumented Central and South American Immigrant	28.87	38.49	-	43.70	41.41	-
Other Central and South American Immigrant	22.91	28.04	9.52	39.87	34.79	16.67
Undocumented Mexican Immigrant	40.73	56.19	14.29	53.83	59.87	14.29
Other Mexican Immigrant	38.50	47.67	14.29	40.57	44.33	11.9
Latino, U.S.-born	16.77	16.97	40.48	16.34	18.98	54.76
Asian Immigrant	24.60	27.52	66.67	16.57	27.51	52.38
Asian, U.S.-born	22.95	29.49	73.81	17.39	31.66	76.19
Black Immigrant	22.67	33.43	59.52	18.99	35.60	57.14
Black, U.S.-born	22.09	22.32	64.29	18.26	23.64	69.05
White Immigrant	21.55	21.51	64.29	14.62	28.07	69.05
White, U.S.-born	30.11	28.51	78.57	26.89	245.67	78.57

Table 8.7
Industry Indices of Dissimilarity (DISS) and Differentiation (DIFF), and Percentage Discordant Pairs (DP), by Ethnoracial Group and Sex, Los Angeles County, 1990

Ethno-Racial Group	Males			Females		
	DISS	DIFF	DP	DISS	DIFF	DP
Undocumented Central and South American Immigrant	25.55	30.23	-	34.87	33.01	-
Other Central and South American Immigrant	17.15	18.62	12.50	25.61	23.16	5.00
Undocumented Mexican Immigrant	32.97	35.04	27.50	42.40	38.86	27.50
Other Mexican Immigrant	29.48	28.64	25.00	28.16	27.34	27.50
Latino, U.S.-born	11.90	10.72	62.50	11.96	12.66	62.50
Asian Immigrant	18.76	18.64	52.50	18.27	15.92	45.00
Asian, U.S.-born	18.16	21.39	70.00	15.85	23.65	67.50
Black Immigrant	22.53	24.51	57.50	17.70	32.76	42.50
Black, U.S.-born	23.82	20.03	57.50	21.87	21.45	57.50
White Immigrant	11.92	12.45	67.50	11.99	14.06	60.00
White, U.S.-born	20.93	21.64	75.00	19.28	19.01	67.50

Table 8.8

Class of Worker Indices of Dissimilarity (DISS) and Differentiation (DIFF), and Percentage Discordant Pairs (DP), by Ethnoracial Group and Sex, Los Angeles County, 1990

Ethno-Racial Group	Males			Females		
	DISS	DIFF	DP	DISS	DIFF	DP
Undocumented Central and South American Immigrant	14.25	7.42	-	14.12	6.24	-
Other Central and South American Immigrant	8.80	3.83	12.50	9.36	4.15	12.50
Undocumented Mexican Immigrant	16.64	8.24	0.00	17.33	6.98	0.00
Other Mexican Immigrant	12.68	6.31	0.00	9.11	3.58	0.00
Latino, U.S.-born	7.37	3.39	50.00	5.62	3.61	50.00
Asian Immigrant	6.80	2.86	75.00	4.80	3.13	50.00
Asian, U.S.-born	5.81	2.37	87.50	7.75	2.61	50.00
Black Immigrant	7.79	3.57	62.50	6.10	7.83	50.00
Black, U.S.-born	14.70	5.49	75.00	17.55	5.87	62.50
White Immigrant	14.25	3.50	75.00	5.88	3.21	62.50
White, U.S.-born	8.33	2.70	100.00	5.41	2.04	50.00

A more direct measure of whether undocumented Central and South American immigrants occupy more (dis)similar positions than members of other ethnoracial groups is to compare them with the other ten ethnoracial groups directly in terms of the direction of dissimilarity (i.e., whether they are over- or underrepresented as indicated by the natural logs of the odds ratios). To accomplish this we use the percentage discordant pairs (DP), which reveals that they are most dissimilar (potential complements) to six of the remaining ten ethnoracial groups (both U.S.- and foreign-born Asian, black, and white groups) and most similar to (potential substitutes for) one (legal Central and South American immigrants).[22] The remaining three ethnoracial groups fall into the intermediate realm of similarity and dissimilarity (both undocumented and legal Mexican immigrants and U.S.-born persons of Latino origin). It thus appears from the foregoing analyses that undocumented Latino immigrants and the majority of other Los Angeles County residents occupy quite different labor market positions, with the exception of legal Latino immigrants. Whether this implies that undocumented Central and South American immigrants have displaced, rather than merely replaced, most other workers and have driven down their wages in the past, as suggested by Martin (1986) and Waldinger (1997), requires a more comprehensive analysis than is attempted here. But we may conclude with some confidence that if undocumented immigrant and other workers continue to be distributed throughout the labor market as they were in 1990, the former are likely to be complements rather than substitutes in production.

CONCLUSION

This chapter has described how the Los Angeles regional economy differs structurally from other regions in the United States. While deindustrialization has occurred nationally since the 1970s, Los Angeles has also experienced a reindustrialization that has maintained or increased the demand for both higher- and lower-skilled workers. Part of this demand has been met by the supply of undocumented Latino immigrant workers. By using a survey-based estimation methodology applied to the 5 percent Public Microdata Samples of the 1990 Census, a total of 146,838 (78,807 male and 68,031 female) undocumented Salvadoran, Guatemalan, and other non-Cuban, non-Mexican Central and South American immigrant workers were estimated to be in the Los Angeles County labor force in 1990. Undocumented Mexican immigrant workers, moreover, numbered an estimated 326,845 persons.[23]

Undocumented Central and South American immigrants were found to be "most dissimilar" to foreign- and U.S.-born Asian, black, and white ethnoracial groups in terms of the labor market positions they filled and "most similar" to other Central and South American immigrants. Three groups fell in the "intermediate" category of (dis)similarity. In other words, while undocumented Central and South American immigrants were potential complements in production to six of the ten ethnoracial groups examined, they were potential substitutes for one group only.

Although no previous study, to my knowledge, has estimated the number and relative labor market position of undocumented Central and South American immigrants in Los Angeles County, these results are consistent with a similar study of undocumented Mexican immigrants (Marcelli and Heer 1997). Moreover, this chapter's findings are not inconsistent with Lopez, Popkin, and Telles (1997) and are almost identical to those interpolated from Warren's 1992 estimates (Warren 1994).[24] The figures reported in this study are 13 percent lower for undocumented Salvadoran immigrants (73,026 vs. 83,923), .07 percent lower for undocumented Guatemalan immigrants (33,608 vs. 33,633), and 34.9 percent higher for other undocumented Central and South American immigrants (40,204 vs. 29,794)—but only .35 percent lower for all undocumented Central and South American immigrants combined (146,838 vs. 147,350). These comparisons show that this chapter's findings are exceptionally consistent with those derived from Warren's 1992 composite (components-of-change and residual methods combined) estimate of the number of undocumented Central and South American immigrants but that they are less consistent at the level of national origin. Overall, the extremely similar interpolated estimate of the number of all undocumented Central and South American immigrants from a very different estimation (composite) methodology executed on a national scale provides some confidence in the findings of this chapter. The similarity between the estimates of the number of undocumented Central and South American immigrants who were in the 1990 Los Angeles County labor force, however, does not necessarily mean that either estimation methodology is correct. Because the parameter estimates used here were obtained from census tracts in which at least 25 percent of the population was foreign-born Mexican, the estimates may be slightly biased in the upward direction.

Nonetheless, the foregoing analysis suggests that to the extent that antipathetic feelings toward immigrants emanate from the fear that undocumented Central and South American immigrants are filling labor market positions desired by others residing in Los Angeles County, they may be ill founded. Contrary to the accepted wisdom, it would appear that a continued flow of undocumented Central and South American immigrants into Los Angeles County would benefit, rather than harm, the majority of persons residing there by complementing their labor market positions instead of competing for them. This conclusion is consistent with the view that sees low-income, hardworking people as an abundant source of economic energy rather than a source of economic and social conflict (Pastor et al. 1999), but conflicts with the view that sees undocumented or lower-skilled immigrants as a source of worker competition (Hammermesh and Bean 1998; Martin 1986; Waldinger 1997).

While it is theoretically plausible that undocumented Central and South American immigrants compete with certain lower-skilled workers of some ethnoracial groups, it is not the case for the majority of those working in Los Angeles

County. Moreover, undocumented Central and South American immigrants, as is the case for their Mexican counterparts (Cornelius 1998; Marcelli 1997), represent a factor cost advantage for certain industries and firms that employ them. Their use of both public and private goods and services, finally, implies that undocumented Central and South American immigrants may actually increase the demand for what higher-skilled persons (lawyers, teachers, business owners, managers and foreman, etc.) produce. This higher demand by undocumented Central and South American immigrants and their employment may combine to augment earnings and employment opportunities for higher-skilled persons while simultaneously permitting them to compete more effectively. Because separate groups of undocumented Central and South American immigrants are distributed differently throughout the Los Angeles County economy, it would appear that more than human capital or immigrant initiative is at work in determining the labor market positions they fill—specifically that both macroeconomic or structural ''push'' (e.g., the globalization of trade and investment) and ''pull'' (e.g., employer preferences or ethnic-specific networks) factors contribute to determining where undocumented Central and South American immigrants work.

There is thus evidence that undocumented Central and South American immigrants are more likely to be complements to most labor force participants than competitors. In turn, that suggests that restrictionist illegal immigration policy, based on the presumption of such labor market competition, may not be justified. Further investigation into the earnings and employment effects of undocumented immigrants in Los Angeles County and elsewhere is required, however, before we can be more confident about the labor market effects on other U.S. residents. Likewise, research into undocumented Central and South American immigrants' use of welfare (Borjas and Hilton 1996; Marcelli and Heer 1998) and other public resources (Wallace et al. 1998) is necessary for a more complete understanding of their overall economic effect. To this end, future survey-based estimates of the number and economic effects of undocumented immigrant workers ought to be based, when possible, on demographic data obtained from the same ethnoracial groups. Another fruitful direction for subsequent research suggested by the present study's findings would be to investigate the causes of occupational and industry segregation among undocumented Central and South American immigrants and other immigrants.

To conclude that the apparent immigration *sentiment-evidence mismatch* is substantiated by results reported in this chapter concerning Los Angeles County, where the largest proportion of undocumented immigrants reside, is not to suggest that there may not be convincing humanitarian, legal, or political reasons for which both undocumented immigrants and other U.S. residents may benefit from a more restrictive illegal immigration policy. Nor does the L.A. experience necessarily reflect conditions elsewhere in the country. Nevertheless, the L.A. experience does suggest the need for great caution in constructing policy based on ''data'' that may reflect sentiment more than evidence.

NOTES

1. Johnson (1996) and Sanchez (1997) suggest that racial nativism in Los Angeles has also played an important role. This is not necessarily inconsistent with perceived negative economic effects.

2. Fully 70 percent of all respondents in another recent national survey indicated that they believe illegal Mexican aliens "mostly take menial jobs that American workers don't want" (Espenshade and Belanger 1998: 385) and that persons from a wide range of income groups, not only the wealthiest persons, consume goods and services that undocumented immigrants help produce (Smith and Edmonston 1997: 230–235).

3. Elton Gallegly (R-Simi Valley, California), for example, refused to read a recent immigration impact study because it did not distinguish between legal and undocumented immigrants and said that "the illegal immigrant takes a great deal more out than they [sic] put in" (Wilgoren 1998: A19).

4. The INS fiscal 1997 budget of $3.1 billion was twice that of 1993. Although this increase corresponds to rising restriction immigration policy sentiment quite well, it is a political exception given the present trend of government downsizing (Andreas 1998: 344) and disregards scholarly findings. The INS budget for fiscal year (FY) 1998 was $4.3 billion.

5. As of July 1998 the unemployment rate was 4.5 percent. Before the United Auto Workers' strike in Flint, Michigan, at General Motors began in June, it was 4.3 percent nationally.

6. See Scott and Soja (1996) and Joassart (1998).

7. In 1970 (using 1989 as the base year) average real manufacturing weekly earnings in the Los Angeles region were $607, and in 1990 they were $594 (Scott and Soja 1996: 223).

8. Similarly, Sassen (1995) argues that it is important to study the context (or process) as well as the moment of labor exchange. The process through which immigrants become effective rather than merely potential workers explains a significant portion of labor market reliance on immigrants.

9. Nine census tracts were randomly selected from 574 in Los Angeles County, and within each census tract a sample of census blocks and then of households (previously obtained by a project canvasser) was selected for interviewing. Of the 686 addresses visited, 271 were interviewed. Of the 415 that were not, 184 had no adult born in Mexico, 64 were housing units at vacant addresses, 68 had no one home or no adult present after three visits, 9 were inaccessible due to a dog or other obstacle, 14 addresses given to an interviewer did not exist, and 76 refused to be interviewed.

10. A series of eight legal status question was asked, and 9.6 percent of all persons interviewed refused to answer at least one of them. This rate, however, is more illustrative of two of the more technical questions, which asked respondents to distinguish either between which kind of amnesty they received or what kind of nonimmigrant visa holder they were. The highest nonresponse rate of the remaining six questions was 7.5 percent, but for the most important questions (which asked respondents to distinguish between being a citizen, naturalized citizen, legal permanent immigrant, or a nonimmigrant) they were less than 1 percent.

11. For example, it is not uncommon for researchers simply to consider the most recent, lower-skilled entrants as undocumented.

12. There are also those based on analyses of apprehension data, but these do not pretend to provide estimates of the number of resident undocumented immigrants (Espenshade 1995). Instead, they attempt to estimate the flow of undocumented immigrants.

13. It is worth noting that Heer and Passel (1987) show that 1980 estimates of the undocumented Mexican population obtained from the residual method (Warren and Passel 1987) and the survey-based method (Heer 1990) were surprisingly consistent. Also, the General Accounting Office (GAO) has recently referred to the type of estimates provided by Warren (1994, 1997) as "composite estimates" given that they are actually a mix of both residual and "component of change" methodologies.

14. The prediction equation used to distinguish between legal and undocumented Mexican immigrant adults generated a percentage concordant pairs of almost 85 percent—an estimate of the equation's predictive accuracy.

15. Two analytical concerns have been raised by others and require attention. First, one may object that applying parameter coefficients obtained from one year (1994) to another (1990) will produce erroneous results. However, data concerning undocumented immigrants are difficult to obtain, as explained earlier, and in all likelihood the characteristics of Latino immigrants did not change substantially from 1990 to 1994. Second, one may also oppose applying parameter coefficients obtained from one foreign-born group to another (e.g., from foreign-born Mexican to Guatemalan and Salvadoran persons). This may be a more appropriate concern. However, given that the ability to compute reliable, local-level estimates of the undocumented population was significantly diminished by the elimination of the INS I-53, we must work with the data we have (Heer and Passel 1987; Warren and Passel 1987). In an effort to check the relative appropriateness of applying Marcelli and Heer's (1997) coefficients to other non-Mexican, Latino immigrants residing in Los Angeles County, relevant demographic characteristics were compared with those of the foreign-born Mexican population. Foreign-born, non-Cuban and non-Mexican Latinos were significantly more similar to foreign-born Mexicans in Los Angeles County in terms of the predictor variables than other foreign-born groups such as Asians, blacks, and whites, to whom there is no suggestion of applying the generated coefficients. To the author's surprise, however, when coefficients generated from the USC-COLEF survey were applied to the entire 1996 California immigrant population, the estimated number of undocumented immigrant children was extremely close to the General Accounting Office's most recent estimates (Wallace et al. 1998).

16. In order to more definitely determine the extent to which any incoming migrant group substitutes for, or complements, other labor force participants, it is necessary to perform dynamic earnings and impact regressions, which the present study does not. Moreover, I do not discount historical replacement of nonimmigrant with immigrant labor (e.g., janitorial occupations in Los Angeles County over the past thirty years) as an institutional reality that shields certain groups from direct contemporary competition with immigrants (Briggs 1996).

17. The INS began compiling immigration statistics from El Salvador in the 1930s and from Guatemala in the 1960s (Popkin, Arguelles, and Rivero 1997).

18. A composite estimate is a hybrid methodology combining residual and component of change methodologies.

19. These researchers multiplied Warren's (1994) California estimates by a proportion equal to the five-county Los Angeles region's portion of the state's Salvadoran and Guatemalan population granted amnesty under IRCA.

20. The natural log of the odds ratio is completely symmetrical with respect to under- and overrepresentation and is used here to determine whether differences are substantial. For example, if the odds ratio is 4 (e.g., .80/[1−.80]), then the natural log of the odds ratio is 1.39. If the odds ratio is 1/4, then the natural log of the odds ratio is −1.39. When comparing the natural log of the odds ratio, whenever there were no cases, we added .005 to the number of persons reported in that category for both undocumented Latino immigrants (ULI) and other labor force participants. Highlighted are those "extreme" cases for which the odds ratio is 1/4 or less, or 4 or more (or when the natural log of the odds ratio is less than −1.39 or greater than 1.39) by the superscript "*" in Table 8.3 as well as in Tables 8.4 and 8.5.

21. It is sometimes assumed that immigrants, especially those unauthorized to work legally in the United States, work informally. It is further often assumed that working in the informal sector typically means that one is a self-employed entrepreneur (e.g., the street vendor selling oranges at a Santa Monica freeway exit ramp). Recent evidence from Los Angeles County (Marcelli, Pastor, and Joassart 1998), however, challenges these assumptions. See de Soto (1989) for a good example of the conventional neo-classical economic view.

22. An ethnoracial group is defined to be "most dissimilar" to undocumented Central and South American immigrants if in at least four of the six possible occasions where the percentage discordant pairs has been computed, the result is greater than 50 percent. Alternatively, an ethnoracial group is defined as "most dissimilar" to undocumented Central and South American immigrants if all DP measurements are less than 25 percent. An "intermediate" ethnoracial group would be one that does not meet either criterion.

23. This estimate is somewhat (16 percent) higher than Marcelli and Heer's (1997) estimate due to different estimation criteria, but the occupational, industry, and class-of-worker distributional patterns are almost identical.

24. Warren (1994) reported that there were approximately 305,088 undocumented Central and South American immigrants residing in California in 1992. Furthermore, he estimated that there were 155,595 Salvadoran, 69,696 Guatemalan, and 54,600 other Latino immigrants (other undocumented Central and South American immigrants) who were undocumented. Multiplying these figures by the proportion of each foreign-born group residing in Los Angeles County according to the 5 percent 1990 PUMS (64 percent, 65 percent, and 60 percent, respectively), there were an estimated 99,192 undocumented Salvadoran immigrants, 45,233 undocumented Guatemalans, and 32,667 other undocumented Central and South American immigrants residing in Los Angeles County in 1992. To adjust these so that they could be compared with the 1990 findings, I next subtracted from these numbers the average of Warren's estimated (by undocumented group) increase from 1988 to 1992 multiplied by two (for years 1990 to 1992). Accordingly, there would have been an estimated 83,923 undocumented Salvadoran immigrants, 33,633 undocumented Guatemalan immigrants, and 29,794 other undocumented Central and South American immigrants residing in Los Angeles County—or a total of 147,350 undocumented Central and South American immigrants.

REFERENCES

Alba, Richard, and Victor Nee
1997   Rethinking Assimilation Theory for a New Era of Immigration. *International Migration Review* 31(4): 826–874.

Andreas, Peter
1998   The U.S. Immigration Control Offensive: Constructing an Image of Order on the
       Southwest Border. In *Crossings: Mexican Immigration in Interdisciplinary Per-
       spectives*. Edited by Marcelo M. Suarez-Orozco. Cambridge: Harvard University
       Press. Pp. 341–356.
Baker, Susan Gonzalez, Frank D. Bean, Augustin Escobar Latapi, and Sidney Weintraub
1998   U.S. Immigration Policies and Trends: The Growing Importance of Migration
       from Mexico. In *Crossings: Mexican Immigration in Interdisciplinary Perspec-
       tives*. Edited by Marcelo M. Suarez-Orozco. Cambridge: Harvard University
       Press. Pp. 81–105.
Bean, Frank D., B. Lindsay Lowell, and Lowell J. Taylor
1988   Undocumented Mexican Immigrants and the Earnings of Other Workers in the
       United States. *Demography* 25(1): 35–52.
Ben-Porath, Yoram
1980   Families, Friends, and Firms and the Organization of Exchange. *Population and
       Development Review* 6: 1–30.
Birdsall, Nancy, and Juan Luis Londono
1997   Asset Inequality Matters: An Assessment of the World Bank's Approach to Pov-
       erty Reduction. *American Economic Review* 87 (2): 32–37.
Blasberg, Nikki, and Elaine Sorensen
1997   *Do Immigrants Use and Need JTPA?* Washington, D.C.: Urban Institute.
Borjas, George J.
1995   The Economic Benefits from Immigration. *Journal of Economic Perspectives* 9
       (2): 3–22.
Borjas, George J., Richard B. Freeman, and Lawrence F. Katz
1997   How Much Do Immigration and Trade Affect Labor Market Outcomes? Brook-
       ings Paper on Economic Activity 1.
Borjas, George J., and Lynette Hilton
1996   Immigration and the Welfare State: Immigrant Participation in Means-Tested En-
       titlement Programs. *The Quarterly Journal of Economics* (May): 575–604.
Branigin, William
1998   Visa Program, High-Tech Workers Exploited, Critics Say; Visa Program Brings
       Charges of Exploitation. *The Washington Post*, July 26: A1.
Briggs, Vernon M., Jr.
1996   Immigration Policy and the U.S. Economy: An Institutional Perspective. *Journal
       of Economic Issues* 15 (2): 371–389.
Card, David
1997   Immigrant Inflows, Native Outflows, and the Local Labor Market Impacts of
       Higher Immigration. NBER Working Paper No. 5927.
Chavez, Leo R., F. Allan Hubbell, Shiraz I. Mishra, and R. Burciaga Valdez
1997   Undocumented Latina Immigrants in Orange County, California: A Comparative
       Analysis. *International Migration Review* 31 (2): 88–107.
Clark, Rebecca L., and Jeffrey S. Passel
1998   Identifying Legal and Illegal Immigrants in the Census and Current Population
       Surveys: A New Technique Based on the Occupational Distribution of Illegal
       Aliens. Washington, D.C.: Urban Institute. Paper presented at the April 2–4, 1998,
       Population Association of America Annual Meetings, Chicago.

Commons, John R.
1967   *Races and Immigrants in America.* New York: Augustus M. Kelley.
Cornelius, Wayne A.
1982   Interviewing Undocumented Immigrants: Methodological Reflections Based on Fieldwork in Mexico and the United States. *International Migration Review* 16 (2): 378–404.
1998   The Structural Embeddedness of Demand for Mexican Immigrant Labor: New Evidence from California. In *Crossings: Mexican Immigration in Interdisciplinary Perspectives.* Edited by Marcelo M. Suarez-Orozco. Cambridge: Harvard University Press. Pp. 113–144.
Davis, Mike
1990   *City of Quartz: Excavating the Future in Los Angeles.* London: Verso.
Dear, Michael J., Greg Hise, and H. Eric Schockman, Editors
1996   *Rethinking Los Angeles.* Thousand Oaks, California: Sage.
DeFreitas, Gregory
1991   *Hispanics in the U.S. Labor Force.* New York: Oxford University Press.
Delgado, Hector L.
1993   *New Immigrants, Old Unions: Organizing Undocumented Workers in Los Angeles.* Philadelphia: Temple University Press.
de Soto, Hernando
1989   *The Other Path.* New York: Harper & Row.
Duleep, Harriet O, and Mark C. Regets
1996   Admission Criteria and Immigrant Earning Profiles. *International Migration Review* 30 (2): 571–590.
1997   Measuring Immigrant Wage Growth Using Matched CPS Files. *Demography* 34 (2): 239–249.
Easterlin, Richard A.
1999   U.S. Population Growth in the Twentieth Century: Trends and Differences. In *North American Population Growth.* Edited by M. Haines and R. Steckel. Cambridge: Cambridge University Press.
Edmonston, Barry, Jeffrey S. Passel, and Frank D. Bean
1990   Perceptions and Estimates of Undocumented Migration to the United States. In *Undocumented Migration to the United States: IRCA and the Experience of the 1980s.* Edited by Frank D. Bean, Barry Edmonston, and Jeffrey S. Passel. Washington, D.C.: Urban Institute Press. Pp. 11–31.
Espenshade, Thomas
1995   Using INS Border Apprehension Data to Measure the Flow of Undocumented Migrants Crossing the U.S.–Mexico Frontier. *International Migration Review* 29 (2): 545–565.
Espenshade, Thomas J., and Maryann Belanger
1998   Immigration and Public Opinion. In *Crossings: Mexican Immigration in Interdisciplinary Perspectives.* Edited by Marcelo M. Suarez-Orozco. Cambridge: Harvard University Press. Pp. 363–403.
Espenshade, Thomas J., and T. Goodis
1988   *Are Mexican Immigrant and U.S. Native Workers Substitutes or Complements in Production?: Lessons from Southern California and the American Southwest.* Program for Research on Immigration Policy. Washington, D.C.: Urban Institute.

Fix, Michael, and Jeffrey S. Passel
1994   *Immigration and Immigrants: Setting the Record Straight.* Washington, D.C.: Urban Institute.
Fogel, Walter
1979   *Mexican Illegal Alien Workers in the United States.* Los Angeles: Institute of Industrial Relations, UCLA.
Frey, William H.
1995   Immigration and Internal Migration "Flight." A California Case Study. *Population and Environment* 16 (4): 353–375.
Hammermesh, Daniel S., and Frank D. Bean
1998   Introduction. In *Help or Hindrance?: The Economic Implications of Immigration for African Americans.* New York: Russell Sage Foundation. Pp. 1–14.
Heer, David M.
1990   *Undocumented Mexicans in the United States.* New York: Cambridge University Press.
1996   *Immigration in America's Future: Social Science Findings and the Policy Debate.* Boulder, Colorado: Westview Press.
Heer, David M., and Jeffrey S. Passel
1987   Comparison of Two Methods for Computing the Number of Undocumented Mexican Adults in Los Angeles County. *International Migration Review* 21 (4): 1446–1473.
Joassart, Pascale M.
1998   Participation in Informal Labor Markets: Evidence from Undocumented Latina Immigrants in Los Angeles. Ph.D. diss., University of Southern California.
Johnson, Kevin R.
1996   Fear of an "Alien Nation": Race, Immigration, and Immigrants. *Stanford Law & Policy Review* 7 (2): 111–126.
Levy, F., and R. J. Murnane
1992   U.S. Earnings Levels and Earnings Inequality: A Review of Recent Trends and Proposed Explanations. *Journal of Economic Literature* (September): 1333–1381.
Lopez, David E., Eric Popkin, and Edward Telles
1996   Central Americans: At the Bottom, Struggling to Get Ahead. In *Ethnic Los Angeles.* Edited by Roger Waldinger and Mehdi Bozorgmehr. New York: Russell Sage Foundation. Pp. 279–304.
Lowell, B. Lindsay
1996   Skilled and Family-Based Immigration: Principles and Labor Markets. In *Immigrants and Immigration Policy: Individual Skills, Family Ties, and Group Identities.* Edited by Harriet O. Duleep and Phanindra V. Wunnava. Greenwich, Connecticut: JAI Press. Pp. 353–372.
Marcelli, Enrico A.
1997   Labor Market Impact. In *The Political and Economic Effects of Illegal Mexican Immigration to Los Angeles County.* Ph.D. dissertation, Los Angeles: University of Southern California. Pp. 41–98.
Marcelli, Enrico A., and David M. Heer
1997   Unauthorized Mexican Workers in the 1990 Los Angeles County Labour Force. *International Migration* 35 (1): 59–83.
1998   The Unauthorized Mexican Immigrant Population and Welfare in Los Angeles County: A Comparative Statistical Analysis. *Sociological Perspectives* 41 (2): 279–302.

Marcelli, Enrico A., Manuel Pastor, Jr., and Pascale M. Joassart
1998   On the Effects of Informal Sector Activity in Los Angeles County. Center for U.S.–Mexican Studies, UCSD. Paper presented at the 72nd Annual Conference of the Western Economic Association, Seattle.

Martin, Philip L.
1986   *Illegal Immigration and the Colonization of the American Labor Market.* CIS Paper No. 1. Washington, D.C.: Center for Immigration Studies.

North, David S., and Marion F. Houston
1976   *The Characteristics and Role of Illegal Aliens in the U.S. Labor Market: An Exploratory Study.* Washington, D.C.: Linton.

Ong, Paul, and Abel Valenzuela, Jr.
1996   The Labor Market: Immigrant Effects and Racial Disparities. In *Ethnic Los Angeles.* Edited by Roger Waldinger and Mehdi Bozorgmehr. New York: Russell Sage Foundation. Pp. 165–191.

Pastor, Manuel, Jr., and Ara Robinson Adams
1996   Keeping Down with the Joneses: Neighbors, Networks, and Wages. *The Review of Regional Studies* 26 (2): 115–145.

Pastor, Manuel, Jr., Peter Dreier, J. Eugene Grigsby III, and Marta Lopez-Garza
1999   *Growing Together: Linking Regional and Community Development in a Changing Economy.* Minneapolis: University of Minnesota Press.

Popkin, E., L. Arguelles, and A. Rivero
1997   *Constructing the Los Angeles Area Latino Mosaic: A Demographic Portrait of Guatemalans and Salvadorans in Los Angeles.* Claremont, California: Tomas Rivera Policy Institute.

Portes, Alejandro
1995   Economic Sociology and the Sociology of Immigration: A Conceptual Overview. In *The Economic Sociology of Immigration.* New York: Russell Sage Foundation. Pp. 1–41.

Sanchez, George J.
1997   Face, Immigration, and the Rise of Nativism in Late Twentieth Century America. *International Migration Review* 31 (4): 1009–1030.

Sassen, Saskia
1995   Immigration and Local Labor Markets. In *The Economic Sociology of Immigration.* Edited by Alejandro Portes. New York: Russell Sage Foundation. Pp. 87–127.

Scott, Allen J., and Edward W. Soja, Editors
1996   *The City: Los Angeles and Urban Theory at the End of the Twentieth Century.* Los Angeles: University of California Press.

Smith, James P., and Barry Edmonston
1997   *The New Americans: Economic, Demographic, and Fiscal Effects of Immigration.* Washington, D.C.: National Academy Press.

Soja, Edward W.
1996   Los Angeles, 1965–1992: From Crisis-Generated Restructuring to Restructuring-Generated Crisis. In *The City: Los Angeles and Urban Theory at the End of the Twentieth Century.* Los Angeles: University of California Press. Pp. 426–462.

Stern, Marcus
1998   Lobbying on Guest Workers Bears Fruit. *San Diego Union Tribune,* March 10: A1, A4.

Taylor, Edward J., and Philip L. Martin

1997 The Immigrant Subsidy in U.S. Agriculture: Farm Employment, Poverty, and Welfare. *Population and Development Review* 23 (4): 855–874.

United Nations

1998 *International Migration Policies.* New York: United Nations.

Waldinger, Roger

1997 Black/Immigrant Competition Re-assessed: New Evidence from Los Angeles. *Sociological Perspectives* 40 (3): 365–386.

Wallace, Steven P., Hongjian Yu, Carolyn Mendez, and E. Richard Brown

1998 *Adjusted Estimates of Uninsured Children and Program Eligibility, California 1996.* Los Angeles: UCLA Center for Health Policy Reseach.

Warren, Robert

1994 Estimates of the Undocumented Immigrant Population Residing in the United States, by Country of Origin and State of Residence: October 1992. Paper delivered at the California Immigration seminar sponsored by the California Research Bureau.

1997 Estimates of the Undocumented Immigrant Population Residing in the United States: October 1996. Paper presented at the Annual Meeting of the American Statistical Association, Anaheim, California.

Warren, Robert, and Jeffrey S. Passel

1987 A Count of the Uncountable: Estimates of Undocumented Aliens Counted in the 1980 United States Census. *Demography* 24 (3): 375–393.

White, Michael J., and Lori M. Hunter

1993 The Migratory Response of Native-Born Workers to the Presence of Immigrants in the Labor Market. Population Studies and Training Center (PSTC) Working Paper Series 93–08, Brown University.

White, Michael J., and Yoshie Imai

1994 The Impact of U.S. Immigration upon Internal Migration. *Population and Environment* 15 (3): 189–209.

Wilgoren, Jodi

1998 Immigrants Are a Boon to Economy, Study Says. *Los Angeles Times,* July 7: A3, A19.

Winegarden, C.R., and Lay Boon Khor

1991 Undocumented Immigration and Unemployment of U.S. Youth and Minority Workers: Econometric Evidence. *The Review of Economics and Statistics* 73 (1): 105–112.

Woodrow-Lafield, Karen A.

1998 Undocumented Residents in the United States in 1990: Issues of Uncertainty in Quantification. *International Migration Review* 32 (1): 145–173.

Salvadorans and Nicaraguans: Refugees Become Workers

Cecilia Menjívar

Until 1979, Salvadorans and Nicaraguans were relatively unknown to the American public despite the long and intimate relationship between the United States and El Salvador and Nicaragua. Two major and interrelated events occurred that year that contributed to the public's and policymakers' attention being focused on these immigrants. First, two long-standing dictatorships were ousted in this year, thus marking the beginning of what was going to become a long and tumultuous civil conflict in El Salvador and Nicaragua, with deeper U.S. involvement in both. This was linked to a second event—the unprecedented flow of U.S.-bound refugees from both countries. However, although the migratory flows that the political events in El Salvador and Nicaragua generated might have fitted the classic profile of refugees, the Reagan and Bush administrations refused to grant blanket refugee status to these immigrants. Thus, many of them automatically became undocumented immigrants, even though their situation resembled that of people from other countries who were formally designated as refugees. This meant that Salvadorans and Nicaraguans were ineligible for important government assistance for their resettlement. They were denied the "structure of refuge," as Rumbaut (1989) terms the government resettlement aid available to officially recognized refugees, and thus were left on their own to cope with the consequences of political flight. Moreover, because they were categorized as undocumented immigrants, they were unable to work legally in the United States. This situation brought serious consequences to the lives of these immigrants.

Although Salvadorans and Nicaraguans had been migrating to the United

States for decades, they had remained relatively invisible, "passing," or often being mistaken, for Mexicans. They constituted a relatively small group, and many arrived at a time when immigration laws were far more relaxed. Most of these earlier arrivals, therefore, faced a significantly different context, as they more easily obtained documents—including green cards and U.S. citizenship. For the Salvadorans and Nicaraguans who arrived after 1979, this situation changed dramatically. Many left their countries at a moment's notice or, in any case, under extreme situations of danger. The circumstances under which they migrated were far more precarious than for earlier immigrants; often they had to travel by land, which made their journeys quite costly and dangerous; their numbers increased, and U.S. immigration policies stiffened during this period. These factors conspired against the immigrants for whom this initial reception has hampered incorporation into the United States.

Despite the vicissitudes of their resettlement and their still uncertain legal status, Salvadorans and Nicaraguans actively continue to create communities and establish families and thus to reaffirm their presence in the United States— albeit often on the margins of society. This chapter examines the origins, transit, and resettlement of these immigrants. In discussing their resettlement, I focus on the complexities of their legal status and the implications for their socioeconomic incorporation, particularly employment and schooling, and then assess prospects for the future.[1]

ORIGINS

Salvadoran and Nicaraguan migration to the United States has a long history. Initially, these flows were directed to San Francisco and were rooted in the commercial trade between San Francisco and Central America. Early in this century, San Francisco became the chief processing center for coffee from Central America, fostering ties with the coffee-producing elites in that region. Initially, these contacts were limited to coffee growers and businesspeople traveling to and from Central America. During and after World War II, shipyards and wartime industries recruited Central Americans, mainly Nicaraguans and Salvadorans, to work in these labor-scarce industries. Salvadorans and Nicaraguans, who had been recruited to work on the Panama Canal, joined shipping lines that were operating in the canal and then continued to San Francisco. Many were attracted by these job prospects, which accounted for a significant increase of Salvadoran and Nicaraguan migration to San Francisco during the 1940s. In fact, by 1950, Central Americans outnumbered the Mexican-born population in that city (Godfrey 1988).

The migration of Salvadorans and Nicaraguans to the United States continued throughout the next few decades, but particularly in the last fifteen years, its size, composition, and geographical concentration have changed substantially. The specific characteristics of each group also differed.

Salvadorans

Massive Salvadoran migration to the United States during the 1980s cannot be entirely attributed to a sudden crisis fueled by external forces. The political strife associated with this migration was the culmination of a long history of political and economic decisions that maintained a structure closed to fundamental reform. By the 1970s, the socioeconomic problems of the country had escalated to critical levels, and changes in the political apparatus seemed inevitable (Menjívar 1993). Efforts were made to restructure the leadership of the country in late 1979, when a junta deposed then-president General Carlos Humberto Romero. But they failed because the two pillars most vehemently opposed to any reform—the military and the landed elite—were left untouched. In fact, the army was even strengthened—in spite of widely publicized human rights abuses—with a large aid package from the United States. This was a strategic response to the vociferous opposition that had united—and obtained international assistance—to instigate radical social reform. This foreign involvement, combined with the destabilization of the junta, triggered a wave of conflict that escalated into a generalized, twelve-year armed conflict that profoundly affected all sectors of Salvadoran society (Menjívar 1993)

As the Salvadoran conflict intensified from the early 1980s onward, migration from El Salvador to the United States increased exponentially. The composition of this flow was not only quantitatively but also qualitatively different than in previous decades, in particular, the newcomers' class background differed significantly from that of previous immigrants. In earlier years, U.S.-bound emigration had been the privilege of the middle and upper classes of El Salvador. In contrast, recent migrants represented all sectors of Salvadoran society, including the urban working and lower-middle classes, which traditionally did not tend to migrate. The Salvadoran population in the United States increased from approximately 100,000 in 1980 to over .5 million enumerated in the 1990 Census (U.S. Census 1993), approximately 48 percent of whom were women (Table 9.1). Independent estimates place at nearly 1 million the number of Salvadorans in the United States (Montes and Garcia 1988). Thus, conceivably, the Salvadoran population in the United States could have at least quintupled during the years of the conflict.

The increased presence of Salvadorans in the United States prompted the attention of researchers, who focused initially on explaining this sudden increase. Because the U.S. government did not accord these immigrants refugee status, some studies concentrated on resolving whether this migration was political (Stanley 1987) or economic (Jones 1989). But a combination of political and economic factors may better explain the reasons that so many Salvadorans left their country during the civil war (Hamilton and Chinchilla 1991; Menjívar 1993). For instance, a Salvadoran electrician in San Francisco explained the reasons he decided to emigrate from his country in the following words:

Table 9.1

Socioeconomic Characteristics of Salvadorans and Nicaraguans in the United States

	Salvadorans	Nicaraguans
Total estimate	565,081	202,658
Percent undocumented*	59.3	42.6
Sex ratio	48.4	51.4
Educational level		
Less than high school	51.7	34.7
High school graduates	16.6	22.2
Less than B.A.	12.4	20.7
B.A.	2.7	6.6
Median age	29.1	27.1
Under 18 years of age	20.4	34.3

Source: 1990 U.S. Census; Immigration and Naturalization Service (INS) for asterisked undocumented percentage.

I used to go to downtown San Salvador to get materials to do my job, but that was not always possible. Once the "guys" [guerrillas] stopped our bus, asked us to leave and then burned it down. Another time, the army stopped us, searched us and detained a few passengers. There were some days when I was not able to get even the little pieces of cable to fix the radios I worked on, so I could not get any money. I was not able to earn anything for days and I have a family, a wife and two children. I became truly desperate (Menjívar 1993).

Although many Salvadorans responded in similar ways when asked why they left their country, there were many others who had more immediate, life-threatening motives for emigrating that were directly related to the civil conflict. These Salvadorans did not necessarily have to be political activists. Anyone who was suspected of sympathizing with opposition groups or simply with social change could be branded a guerilla. An integral part of "low-intensity conflict," the strategy used in El Salvador to fight the opposition, was psychological warfare. This consisted of systematic threats of harassment and torture with the objective of demonstrating how dangerous it was to support the opposition

(Martín-Baró 1990). As Archbishop Rivera y Damas said in a homily delivered in San Salvador in August 1980, "Many people flee because they are stamped as collaborators with the guerrillas and their life is in danger; because being marked is enough to cause the worst to happen" (Americas Watch 1984: 34). Thus, for instance, a schoolteacher who eventually arrived in San Francisco had to abandon his home less than forty-eight hours after soldiers took him out of his house because he was accused of knowing someone who was suspected of being a guerrilla sympathizer. This climate of insecurity and fear led many, even people not directly involved with any side in the conflict, to abandon their country. In some cases, even when people did not directly point to the war as a reason for their migration, the conflict still deeply affected their lives and their decision to leave their country.

The conflict formally ended in 1992, when the Peace Accords signed the previous year went into effect. The effects of the civil conflict, including rampant violence, an exponential increase in criminality, and economic insecurity, continue to profoundly affect life in El Salvador.

Nicaraguans

Similar to the Salvadoran case, the events surrounding the conflict that triggered massive Nicaraguan migration during the 1980s cannot simply be attributed to immediately preceding circumstances. Like neighboring El Salvador, Nicaragua's history is plagued with instances of resistance and opposition, as this country's leadership also had been fervently closed to any reform. The United States' long-standing presence in Central America is nowhere more evident than in Nicaragua, where in 1850 a Yankee filibusterer named William Walker declared himself president of that country. Additionally, the U.S. Marines occupied Nicaragua for approximately two decades during this century (Walker 1997). Since then, the United States has remained deeply involved in Nicaraguan affairs and a staunch supporter of the Somoza family, who ruled the country for over four decades—allegedly the longest dynastic dictatorship in Latin American history. The Somoza presidents amassed a large fortune and created a regime so despicable that it managed to alienate most of its political base (Wickham-Crowley 1992). Thus, the government of Anastasio Somoza Debayle was successfully toppled by a mass-based insurrection led by the Sandinista National Liberation Front (FSLN) in 1979.

When the FSLN took over, one of its major goals was the creation of a "mixed economy" to correct the social and economic injustices of the past and an independent and "nonaligned" foreign policy to terminate the long-lasting dependence on the United States. These events corresponded with the arrival of the Reagan administration in Washington, which launched a multifaceted assault against the Sandinista government. This included a trade embargo, influencing international agencies to cut off normal lending to Nicaragua, and funds for training, equipping, and directing a counterrevolutionary army (or "Contras") in exile. The Sandinista government countered this attack by using up to fifty percent of the national budget, which brought to a halt the social programs instigated by the revolution. This combination of factors unleashed a profound economic crisis from which the Sandinistas never recuperated; their government lasted only a decade. By early 1990, the Nicaraguan electorate had voted in Violeta Barrios vda. de Chamorro, effectively ending the Sandinista revolution.

During the decade-long Sandinista government, many Nicaraguans made their way to the United States. Initially, it was mostly wealthy Nicaraguans whose interests did not coincide with those of the revolution who fled and went mostly to Miami, where they had long-established contacts. Soon, professionals and businesspeople followed, as they found it increasingly difficult to maintain their lifestyles within the constraints of the socialist leanings of the Sandinista government. Toward the end of the 1980s, the outflow of migrants encompassed a broader socioeconomic spectrum, as workers and peasants were fleeing a civil (or Contra) war, which had by then wrecked the Nicaraguan economy. It is estimated that approximately three-quarters of Nicaraguan-born immigrants in the United States entered between 1980 and 1990 (U.S. Census 1993). The 1990 U.S. Census showed slightly over 200,000 Nicaraguans in the United States, 51 percent of them women (Table 9.1).[2]

TRANSIT

The Long Journey North

For many Salvadorans and Nicaraguans, the journey to the United States is not a straight line from their country of origin to their place of arrival. It is instead an enterprise plagued with uncertainty and danger, as many of these immigrants undertake their trips by land. They cross at least three (for Salvadorans) or four (for Nicaraguans) international borders—often without documents—which make the journeys a long process of negotiation, filled with anguish and incertitude. Their trips take a long time to complete, usually a couple of months but sometimes longer. A Salvadoran woman interviewed in San Francisco spoke about this uncertainty when she described her husband's trip.

My mother told me that my husband left ten days ago. But I don't know when he will get here. It may take a week, a month, or longer. See, when people leave El Salvador, you just say, so and so left, but that's it. You cannot say anything else with any certainty. My brother also left, but after two months in Mexico, he showed up in El Salvador again. So who knows, really, only God knows if my husband will eventually reach the United States. (Menjívar 1992)

The reasons that Salvadorans and Nicaraguans travel by land are linked to the increasingly stiff U.S. immigration policies that make even a simple tourist visa very difficult to obtain. These policies have been designed to restrict the entry of the thousands of Central Americans who emigrated in the late 1970s and throughout the tumultuous 1980s. The requirements for obtaining a U.S. visa were (and still are) quite stringent—proof of hefty bank accounts, land and property titles, and letters from employers to guarantee that people would have a reason to return to their country—making a visa beyond the reach of many potential migrants. Thus, many Salvadorans and Nicaraguans opt to travel without a U.S. visa, which means that to enter the United States clandestinely, they have to travel by land at least part of the way. For instance, in a survey conducted among Salvadorans in San Francisco, 80 percent of the respondents mentioned that they had traveled by land at least part of the way, a number that coincides with those who did not travel with a U.S. visa (Menjívar 1998a). Ironically, it is at least three times more expensive to travel by land than by air, yet those people with more resources can secure a U.S. visa to travel north (by air) and thus pay less for their trips.

The governments of the countries through which Salvadorans and Nicaraguans travel north also influence their experiences. For instance, during the Sandinista government's reign, Central American countries—including El Salvador, Honduras, and Guatemala, which Nicaraguans needed to cross on their way to the United States—required a visa for Nicaraguan travelers. Salvadorans could travel freely to Guatemala, the only Central American country they needed to cross. But Mexico had aggressive tactics and stiffer immigration laws to control the inflow of immigrants from Central America, particularly those traveling to the United States. For the same reasons that keep them from obtaining U.S. visas, many of these immigrants also crossed these other international borders without documents. Thus, traveling by land from Central America to the United States often involves complicated arrangements with *coyotes* (smugglers), as well as robberies, assaults, and extortion by local authorities, mostly in Mexico. For instance, in the survey of Salvadorans in San Francisco mentioned previously (Menjívar 1998a), approximately one-third of the respondents mentioned that they had been assaulted or robbed at least once during their journey, with an additional one-third indicating that they had been victims of these crimes multiple times while traveling. One woman said that she was traveling with a large group that included people of different Central American nationalities. In one of the three instances when they were robbed—she still did not know if it was Mexican authorities or common criminals—everyone in her group was strip-searched, and at one point they were threatened with torture. Additionally, approximately 70 percent of the respondents indicated that they felt their lives were in danger at some point during the journey. A woman who was pregnant when she traveled described her trip in Mexico in the following words:

Somehow, our coyote miscalculated the amount of water that we needed, and we ran out of water. It was horrible. The sun was so strong and we were so thirsty. A man drank some sort of after-shave lotion. This other woman got very sick; I think it was tension, she was very young. Someone stayed with her because we had to continue. . . . That day I felt like staying there, to die, but I didn't want to die in the middle of nowhere, so I gained some strength to keep going. (Menjívar 1992)

The United States as a Place of Destination

The Salvadorans and Nicaraguans who undertook these often-perilous journeys had powerful reasons for doing so. Sometimes they sought to escape persecution, generalized violence, or the harsh conditions brought about by years of civil war in their countries—often a combination of these factors. These reasons shaped their decision to *leave* their countries, but they could not have influenced their motivation to migrate specifically *to* the United States. The reason so many Salvadorans and Nicaraguans crossed several international borders to reach a "safe haven" is linked to the social networks these immigrants had already established in the United States. These links had been forged over a long history of U.S. political, military, economic, and cultural influence in Central America, unparalleled by any other country except Spain during colonial times. Thus, when the conditions in El Salvador and Nicaragua deteriorated to the point where many sought refuge elsewhere, the United States emerged as a logical destination point. The families and friends already in the United States thus provided the important link between these immigrants' decision to leave their countries and the point where they eventually settled.

Even though both Salvadorans and Nicaraguans have a long history of migration to the United States and can claim San Francisco as their first "home," their present concentration spans several states. The thousands of Salvadorans and Nicaraguans who arrived in the 1980s settled across the United States, with some obvious concentrations. Salvadorans mainly concentrated in California; approximately 60 percent of the Salvadoran-born immigrants live in that state, and three-fourths of them have congregated in the Los Angeles area. There also are concentrations of Salvadorans in Texas (mostly in Houston), Washington, D.C., and New Jersey. The Nicaraguans' destination of choice is Florida, where almost one-half of all Nicaraguan-born immigrants in the United States live, the majority in the Miami area. California is another popular destination for Nicaraguans, but there are small communities in other states also, such as New Jersey and Illinois.

ARRIVAL IN THE UNITED STATES

The Issue of Legality

One of the most critical issues for the Salvadorans and Nicaraguans who arrived in the United States in the 1980s was that even though many left their countries for reasons linked to the political conflict there, neither group was officially recognized as refugees by the U.S. government. The reason for this discrepancy can be found in U.S. foreign policy toward El Salvador and Nicaragua while those countries were undergoing political upheaval. During the twelve-year Salvadoran civil war, for instance, the Salvadoran government fought leftist guerrillas with substantial U.S. support; thus, the U.S. government could not legally recognize the refugees generated by the conflict. Accepting that the Salvadoran government was persecuting its own people—with U.S. support—would have contradicted U.S. government policy toward El Salvador.

In the case of the Nicaraguans, who were fleeing a government the United States was intent on overthrowing, the U.S. government could have granted them refugee status in a symbolic gesture, as it had done with other groups fleeing communist regimes. However, the U.S. government applied a different logic in dealing with the Nicaraguan conflict. The Sandinistas were going to be fought in their own territory; the Contras were going to apply pressure to the Sandinista government, and thus, their base of operations was in Honduras, as close to Nicaragua as possible (Portes and Stepick 1993). Nicaraguans disenchanted with the revolution were needed as close to Nicaragua as possible, not in the United States. Granting these Nicaraguans refugee status—meaning a place to settle and aid to do so—would, therefore, have dissuaded them from pressuring their own government.

In spite of legal barriers, however, many Salvadorans and Nicaraguans entered the United States during this time of political upheaval in their countries. Once on U.S. soil, they could apply individually for political asylum. Salvadorans did not fare well, however; throughout the 1980s less than 3 percent of the applicants were granted such status. Immigrants' rights groups lobbied on the Salvadorans' behalf, and eventually Congress granted temporary protection from deportation to all Salvadorans who arrived prior to September 19, 1990. This special dispensation, known as temporary protected status (TPS), allowed Salvadorans to live and work in the United States for a period of eighteen months, during which time the Salvadoran conflict was supposed to be resolved. Given the intractable nature of the Salvadoran conflict, a series of government actions extended the provision; however, it finally expired in December 1994. To ensure a smooth transition, however, these Salvadorans' work permits were extended for an additional nine months. Although, originally, close to 200,000 Salvadorans applied for this dispensation, fewer submitted applications for the successive extensions. While some changed their status to permanent residents, many found the application procedure for the extensions confusing and reliable information hard to obtain. TPS did not require individual application (as in the case of asylum), and, although it was a blanket determination that included all Salvadorans who had arrived before a certain deadline (as it would be in the case of refugees), it did not confer amnesty on these Salvadorans. TPS was only a temporary status; thus, technically, it was neither asylum nor refugee status. The only privilege bestowed was the conferral of a work permit; refugee status and concomitant access to social services were still denied. The Salvadorans who continued reapplying and maintaining their TPS until this dispensation expired—approximately 60,000—were given the opportunity to submit asylum applications.

In addition to having been granted TPS, Salvadorans whose asylum applications had been unsuccessful could resubmit them under the *American Baptist Churches v. Thornburgh* (ABC) settlement. Initially, their success rate increased to 28 percent in fiscal year 1992 (National Asylum Study Project 1992) but has since leveled off and declined. According to the Immigration and Naturalization Service's latest estimates, the success rate for these applications (which by now mainly constitute new submissions) stands at about 3 percent (INS 1995), or identical to what it was throughout the 1980s.

Certain Salvadorans were included as beneficiaries of the 1997 Nicaraguan Adjustment and Central American Relief Act (NACARA). Designed for Nicaraguans, it also included Cubans and nationals of former Soviet-bloc countries. Salvadorans who entered the country before September 19, 1990 (the same cut-off date established for TPS) and registered under the ABC settlement or who had filed an asylum application before April 1, 1990, could be granted a "cancellation of removal." This is a special discretionary relief, which, if granted, permits an individual who is subject to deportation or removal to remain in the United States. Salvadorans who are already placed in deportation procedures and are therefore required to appear before an immigration judge, can request a cancellation of removal. If an individual is granted cancellation of removal, his or her immigration status will then be readjusted to that of a permanent resident (INS 1998). Immigrant rights groups were lobbying on behalf of the Salvadorans so that the benefits that NACARA confers to Nicaraguans and to other nationals included in this act—adjustment to permanent residence without a hearing on a case-by-case basis—would also be extended to Salvadorans. However, in October 1998, once again Congress denied Salvadorans and Guatemalans such benefits.

The reception given to Nicaraguan asylum seekers during the 1980s was as ambivalent as it was in the Salvadorans' case.[3] In the aggregate, during this decade about one-quarter of the Nicaraguan applicants were successful (National Asylum Study Project 1992). The U.S. government had been reluctant to grant Nicaraguans any special dispensation, but under pressure from the Cuban-American constituency in Miami—where the majority of the Nicaraguans lived—it stopped deporting Nicaraguans for a short period of time between 1987 and 1988. Nicaraguans were invited to apply for asylum, that is, given work permits but not access to the resettlement aid similar to that given to refugees from communist countries. But when Congress froze military support for the Contras in 1988, the number of Nicaraguans entering the United States increased substantially (Portes and Stepick 1993). To stem this flow, the U.S. government reversed its policy, and Nicaraguans—now without work permits or protection from deportation—once again were treated as undocumented immigrants.

The Nicaraguans are the intended beneficiaries of NACARA. Unlike Salvadorans, Nicaraguans are not required to appear before an immigration judge in order to be granted the benefit. Nicaraguans who can prove that they have continuously resided in the United States since December 1, 1995, can be considered for adjustment of status to permanent residency. This act, signed into law in November 1997, gave Nicaraguans until March 31, 2000, to submit their applications. But the guidelines to apply for this adjustment were slow to appear.

Salvadorans and Nicaraguans, lacking any protection as refugees and with few chances for obtaining political asylum, could have resorted to applying for amnesty under the 1986 Immigration Reform and Control Act (IRCA). Many Salvadorans and Nicaraguans who arrived in the United States prior to January 1, 1982—the cutoff point for amnesty applicants—did so. However, the thousands who arrived at the height of the political conflict in their countries (approximately three-quarters of the Salvadoran- and Nicaraguan-born population arrived between 1980 and 1990 [U.S. Census 1993]) were ineligible for this provision.

In spite of recent changes in immigration laws, the fact remains that throughout the civil unrest in their countries, Salvadorans and Nicaraguans were automatically categorized as economic migrants by the U.S. government (only a few successful asylum applicants could prove otherwise). This was the case even though research pointed to the detrimental effects of war trauma on these immigrants' lives (Aron et al. 1991; Guarnaccia and Farias 1988; Ward 1987). In particular, this situation was believed to have affected children, many of whom have been diagnosed with posttraumatic stress disorder (Espino 1991). Exposure to the war affected these immigrants' cognitive appraisal of their current life circumstances; and they were found to experience greater stress in their resettlement process than did Mexicans (Salgado de Snyder, Cervantes, and Padilla 1990). But in the absence of any form of legal protection that would have given them access to services available to officially recognized refugees—such as resettlement aid, job retraining, language instruction, and psychological counseling—Salvadorans and Nicaraguans instead arrived to swell the ranks of undocumented immigrants.

The INS has recently estimated that close to 60 percent of Salvadorans and approximately 40 percent of Nicaraguans in the country are undocumented (INS 1997; Table 1); Lopez, Popkin, and Telles (1996: 287) calculated this figure for the Salvadorans to be 49 percent. These authors depict Salvadorans (along with Guatemalans) as constituting "the most vulnerable national-origin group in the United States because they are among the most undocumented. . . . Their claim to refugee status has never been recognized; and they are about to lose what temporary protection against deportation they had" (Lopez, Popkin, and Telles 1996: 287). The Salvadorans' and Nicaraguans' uncertain legal status has reverberated through all aspects of these immigrants' lives.

Table 9.2
Employment Characteristics of Salvadorans and Nicaraguans in the United States

	Salvadorans	*Nicaraguans*
In labor force	76.2	74.0
Unemployed	10.7	10.7
Industries of concentration		
Manufacturing	21.7	20.7
Retail trade	20.3	23.5
Personal services	14.0	
Professional services		11.0
Occupations		
Operators, laborers	26.8	26.1
Tech/sales/admin support	15.0	25.9
Services	34.3	24.8

Source: 1990 U.S. Census—only three highest occupations and industries are noted.

Employment

These immigrants' legal status has limited their job opportunities. Furthermore, their generally low levels of education and skills—particularly among Salvadorans (see Table 9.2)—have contributed to their limited access to the better-paying jobs that provide security and mobility. The recession of the late 1980s and early 1990s has affected these immigrants' job prospects further as there are fewer and fewer jobs for which they can qualify. The labor force participation rate is about 76 percent for Salvadorans and 74 percent for Nicaraguans. The unemployment rate is nearly 11 percent for both groups (Table 9.2). In general, Salvadorans have found jobs in manufacturing, retail trade, and personal services industries; more than three-fourths of Salvadorans work as operators and laborers and in technical, sales, and service occupations (Table 9.2). Nicaraguans have concentrated in manufacturing, retail, and professional services, where they have worked as operators and laborers, in service, and in sales or administrative support occupations (Table 9.2). Even though immigration policies affect all immigrants regardless of where they live, the local economy shapes their experiences in very important ways since it determines what opportunities for work are present. Thus, Salvadoran and Nicaraguan employment experiences have varied depending on their settlement location. Also, important gender differences often cut across regions of the country.

In general, men have located jobs in gardening, construction, building cleaning, and restaurant services. For instance, Repak (1995) found that jobs in construction were plentiful in Washington, D.C., for Central American men— mostly Salvadorans. Wages in these jobs also were higher than in comparable jobs elsewhere, particularly in Los Angeles. In fact, one immigrant man traveled to D.C. every spring for the construction season and then returned to Los Angeles during the winter (Repak 1995: 99). These men also labored in restaurants as dishwashers and busboys, a pattern that Mahler (1995a) also found among Salvadoran men in New Jersey. Similarly, in California, Salvadoran male immigrants were concentrated in construction, landscaping, and restaurants, but the recession impacted these sectors greatly. With fewer of these jobs available, competition increased. Thus, many of these immigrant men turned to look for jobs at "corners," where day laborers congregate to look for jobs. But these men readily admit that this is the last resort in their struggle to find a job. One Salvadoran in San Francisco recounted his experiences as a day laborer as follows:

It's really tough. We have to be there by 6:00 A.M. everyday. Then, a person drives by, and asks a few of us if we want to go with him to help him build something, prune trees, or something. He sets the wage, and with luck, the guy standing right next to you won't agree to take the job for a lower wage; it's like an auction, you know. Then you go, you don't know where, everything is unknown, even your pay because often times you get cheated very badly. Sometimes they don't pay you what you have agreed or they give you checks without funds. Anyway, out of 100 men, maybe ten or twenty get those jobs. But we all go back the next day. (Menjívar 1992).

Regardless of the region where they have settled, Salvadoran women's jobs have mostly been concentrated in baby-sitting, cleaning, and elderly care. Some have also found jobs in fast-food restaurants, but, overwhelmingly, their predominant niche is domestic service, a sector that provides job opportunities for immigrant women even during recessionary times. Because these jobs are usually abundant, these women often are able to find jobs more easily than men (Menjivar 1998b), and, in some areas, Salvadorans (and other Central American women) seem to have taken over this sector. For instance, Salvadoran women in Los Angeles are twelve times more likely than the general population to work as private servants, as cleaners, and as child care workers; for Mexican women this factor is only 2.3 (Lopez, Popkin, and Telles 1996: 296). Interestingly, however, in spite of the relative ease with which these immigrant women find jobs (a situation observed in different settings, from San Francisco to Washington, D.C., to New Jersey), when men and women both work, men earn more than the women do.

The situation for Nicaraguans can be gauged more easily by examining their

Table 9.3
Economic Indicators for Salvadorans and Nicaraguans in the United States

	Salvadorans	*Nicaraguans*
Per capita income	$8,387	$8,517
Median household income	$23,546	$25,717
Percent in rental housing	83.0%	75.0%

Source: 1990 U.S. Census.

experiences in Miami, where most of these immigrants live. Similar to the experiences of Salvadoran men, Nicaraguan men in Miami also have found jobs in construction. Like Salvadoran men in California, these Nicaraguans also have become day laborers, huddling on street corners waiting for potential employers to drive by. Nicaraguans—men and women alike—also have found job opportunities in Florida's agriculture sector (Portes and Stepick 1993). In contrast to the Salvadoran women in other regions who have concentrated mostly in private services, Nicaraguan women have worked in the apparel industry, directly in factories, and for subcontractors at home (Portes and Stepick 1993). Nicaraguan immigrants in Miami have filled jobs that Cubans had occupied; the men have done so in construction, and the women in the garment factories.

These immigrants' earnings generally are, not surprisingly, very low. Time in the United States makes a difference, with immigrants who have been in the country longer earning more. But these foreign-born immigrants are still far from catching up with native-born Latinos and still farther from native whites (Lopez, Popkin, and Telles 1996). For instance, the 1990 Census reports that the per capita income of foreign-born Salvadorans was $8,387, and it was $8,517 for Nicaraguans; their median household income was $23,546 and $25,717, respectively (Table 9.3). But approximately two-fifths of the Salvadorans and close to two-thirds of the Nicaraguans live in households of five persons or more (U.S. Census 1993). Not only are these immigrants' incomes low, but they have to be stretched quite a bit and in different directions. For instance, even if these immigrants live in poor neighborhoods, their rents are high in relation to their earnings. A survey in San Francisco found that 75 percent of Salvadorans in San Francisco spent more than one-half of their incomes on rent (Calderón 1992). (Most Salvadoran and Nicaraguan immigrants were renters; over 80 percent of Salvadorans and 75 percent of Nicaraguans lived in rented housing [U.S. Census 1993; Table 9.3].)

Many of these immigrants are also financially responsible for families—often their own children and parents—still living in their countries of origin. Given the severely diminished employment opportunities in those war-torn economies, those families have come to rely on the immigrants' remittances for survival. Salvadorans and Nicaraguans send substantial remittances back to their countries of origin (Funkhouser 1995). Salvadorans have been found to remit regularly in spite of socioeconomic characteristics associated with lower incomes and low social standing (Menjívar et al. 1998). The high volume of remittances these immigrants sent back home has contributed to establishing important links between families in the sending communities and in the United States—links that have enveloped entire communities at both ends.

The undocumented status of these immigrants—together with their lack of access to job retraining and language instruction—has had a homogenizing effect on their job prospects. Professionals have not been able to find jobs commensurate with their skills and work experience. These professionals sometimes need only short-term job retraining and English-language skills, yet their unstable situation prevents them from looking for better job opportunities. For instance, a former mathematics and physics high school teacher and a woman with a degree in psychology and philosophy from the National University in El Salvador worked, respectively, as a clerk and housekeeper in San Francisco. They could not afford to look for a job commensurate with their skills or to obtain necessary language instruction because they did not have any other means of support (Menjívar 1998a). Fernández-Kelly and Schauffler (1994) depict a similar situation among Nicaraguans. In one case, a chemist with extensive work experience had been able to work only for an hourly wage and without any benefits, even though in his job, he performs the duties of a professional chemist. This immigrant pointed specifically to his uncertain legal status as the greatest impediment to getting ahead (Fernández-Kelly and Schauffler 1994: 672).

Schools and the Children

It is not uncommon for Salvadorans and Nicaraguans to leave their children in the care of an adult relative in their own country. For instance, the 1990 Census reported that only one-fifth of the Salvadoran and one-third of the Nicaraguan immigrants were under the age of 18 years (Table 9.1). Many, however, have brought their children to live with them, while others have borne children in the United States. In any case, there are Salvadoran and Nicaraguan children whose parents are still trying to cope with life in the United States. Given the general living conditions of these immigrants, these children are becoming American not in the suburbs but in the inner cities. Many Salvadorans and Nicaraguans have not been able to afford housing in middle-class neighborhoods and have instead moved into some of the poorest neighborhoods of the cities in which they live. The location where these immigrants reside has important repercussions on their lives.

One important area where the effects of their neighborhoods are manifested is in the schools these immigrant children attend. Many children of Salvadoran and Nicaraguan immigrants end up attending troubled schools with ever-more restricted budgets. There, these children are exposed to crime, gangs, and low academic standards. In the children's eyes, schools do not represent viable options for socioeconomic mobility because too many factors work against them, including their own uncertain legal status and a general lack of resources. In a recent survey, one-third of the Salvadoran respondents mentioned that the schools are the most important public service that they used. These respondents, however, identified deficient schools as the most important issue facing their children (NALEO 1998).

Some of these children, therefore, feeling the economic pressure under which their families live, start to work full-time at an early age, often dropping out of school. The jobs for which they are qualified, however, are not ones that provide mobility and security. For instance, a Salvadoran teenage girl dropped out of tenth grade so that she could work full-time at a fast-food restaurant, while another high school dropout mentioned that even if she continued in school, her prospects of getting a good-paying job were dim (Menjívar 1998a). Similarly, the prospects for the future of many Nicaraguan youths are not bright; in some cases, they cannot even get summer jobs because of their undocumented status (Fernández-Kelly and Schauffler 1994). Some of these children struggle in school, sometimes because war-related trauma still permeates their lives, a condition compounded by the conditions in which they now live (Espino 1991). For instance, research has found that among Nicaraguan adolescents greater acculturation stress is experienced than that experienced by Cubans (Gil and Vega 1996). In other cases these children do well in school and demonstrate potential to succeed, but the obstacles they face—including the uncertainty of their status, reduced economic opportunities, resource-poor schools, and anti-immigrant sentiments that have led to laws such as Proposition 187—are often too great to overcome. Research on Central American youth in the mid-1980s (Suarez-Orozco 1987) concluded that many, though not all, Central American children knew that the key to a better future in the United States for themselves and for their families was schooling. But studies of more recent Central American arrivals (Menjívar 1998a; Fernández-Kelly and Schauffler 1994) reflect the changing conditions that these immigrants have encountered in the communities they have entered and depict a far less confident attitude toward the benefits of education.

But the parents remain concerned with the children's schooling, as they place a premium on education. For instance, in the survey mentioned previously, Salvadoran immigrants, in spite of their generally low incomes, indicated that they were willing to pay higher taxes to improve service delivery in areas deemed critical, particularly the school system (NALEO 1998). These parents faced challenges with their children's rapid incorporation into the milieu they inhabited, which in these cases often means abandoning their native Spanish for English.

Immigrant children overwhelmingly demonstrate a preference for English (Portes and Schauffler 1994), and Salvadoran and Nicaraguan children are no exception. However, as has been observed in both of these groups (Menjívar 1998a; Fernández-Kelly and Schauffler 1994), often these children lose their fluency in Spanish while they do not yet have a good command of standard English. Because these children acquire English-language skills through interactions with their peers in inner-city schools, many do not gain the language proficiency necessary to qualify them for better-paying jobs.

The Immigrants Find Allies

To meet the great challenges faced in the United States, Central Americans—especially those who arrived in the past two decades—have organized in different ways to help fellow compatriots as well as forming groups to advocate for their rights. Organizing was hard, but these immigrants worked together and found important allies among some Americans. I do not imply that all, or even most, Central Americans have organized to rally for their interests; that would be a grave error.[4] At the same time, it would be a mistake to portray these immigrants as simply passively accepting whatever fate befalls them.

Salvadoran newcomers, for instance, joined efforts with "North Americans," as the mostly middle-class, white local residents who helped them were referred to in these Central American circles. These Central Americans and the "North Americans" with whom they worked tended to be critical of U.S. policy in Central America. Thus, opposing these policies and recognizing Central Americans (mostly Salvadorans and Guatemalans) as refugees—and providing them with support for resettlement—were important expressions of their political views. They set up community organizations that targeted the needs of the newly arrived and provided a wide range of services. These services ranged from legal defense and services for asylum applicants to job referrals, a free clinic, shelters, other emergency services, and psychological counseling. These organizations often worked in conjunction with churches—particularly established congregations such as the Catholic, Lutheran, and Presbyterian churches—to aid Central Americans. However, these organizations were not government-funded, and consequently, their budgets were always very constrained.

Though an important objective of these community organizations was to provide legal assistance, they also organized immigrant rights groups that actively pursued cases for Central Americans (again, mostly Salvadorans and Guatemalans). For instance, the mounting pressure from solidarity and immigrant rights groups was a major force behind the Justice Department's decision to provide temporary protected status to Salvadorans. In a related case, the Immigrant and Refugee Rights Project of the Lawyer's Committee for Urban Affairs in San Francisco filed (and won) a lawsuit against the federal government, arguing that fees demanded from Salvadorans applying for temporary protected status were far higher than for other groups. In both cases, the refugee organizations set up by the Salvadoran newcomers themselves played pivotal roles in these victories.

Nicaraguan newcomers also organized to help their compatriots, though their efforts were mainly concentrated on obtaining legal protection for them. As in the case of Salvadorans, these Nicaraguans united forces with local residents with whom they shared political ideologies to lobby on behalf of their compatriots. In the Nicaraguans' case, however, it was the powerful Cuban community in Miami that allied forces with them. These Nicaraguans and the Cubans shared important political affinities; their resettlement in the United States was linked to the establishment of Marxist regimes in their respective countries, and thus both were vehemently opposed to communist ideology. The alliance with the Cubans produced important victories for the Nicaraguans. For instance, they were able to temporarily reverse the practice of deportation of Nicaraguan nationals in the mid-1980s.

These Salvadoran and Nicaraguan community organizations continue to advocate on behalf of Central Americans' legal rights and, more recently, have organized responses to the current anti-immigrant backlash.

PROSPECTS FOR THE FUTURE

One of the most important factors that have affected the lives of Salvadorans and Nicaraguans—present and future—is their unstable legal status. For brief periods of time, they have been spared from deportation, but for the most part, particularly for Salvadorans, they have been unsuccessful in their attempts to gain any form of legal status. Often, their treatment has been harsh. The implications of their legal instability are far-reaching; it has affected the jobs they have been able to find as well as their prospects for mobility, the reunification of families, the reconstitution of informal social networks, and their children's future success. Although some of these immigrants have been able to regularize their status and have started making progress with regard to their socioeconomic advancement, this is not a general pattern for these immigrants. The fact remains that most still face harsh living conditions and marginalization; many do not anticipate great improvement in their conditions independent of their legal status. Their children also share gloomy views of the future as many, because of their legal status, are threatened with being cut off from benefits such as education, with serious repercussions for their future.

Salvadorans have lost their temporary protected status, and it is still unclear what their situation will be in the future. Some will have the option of appearing before an immigration judge to stop their removal from the country, but many others will remain in the country as unprotected as ever. Nicaraguans will have the opportunity of regularizing their status, but there is no way to estimate which immigrants or how many eventually will benefit from it. In essence, since immigration law has fluctuated and been rather ambivalent for these two groups, it may once again become restrictionist in the near future. The majority of

Salvadorans and Nicaraguans—their children and families—who arrived in the United States escaping from civil wars in their countries will likely continue to live on the margins of society for some time to come. They remain as vulnerable as ever to the ups and downs of the forces beyond their control that shape immigration law.

Salvadorans and Nicaraguans will also keep forging ever stronger ties with their communities of origin. Yet even as these immigrants seek to maintain and even strengthen ties with their home country and increase the frequency of their visits, the reality is that their primary economic commitment is to the United States. The future of the children of these immigrants (many of whom are U.S. citizens) is in the United States; thus, the parents will remain oriented to this country. That economic commitment to the United States provides regular remittances to El Salvador and Nicaragua that amount to close to (or at times even surpass) the national budgets of those countries, thus representing a vital contribution to war-ravaged economies that could not accommodate the immigrants if they were to return. Thus, for the foreseeable future, these immigrants will most likely live "here and there," as one Salvadoran in San Francisco put it.

NOTES

1. Given the paucity of information about Nicaraguan immigration to the United States, my discussion is based mostly on the Salvadoran experience, drawing, when possible, on research conducted on Nicaraguans.

2. I use 1990 Census data to delineate a general profile of the Salvadoran and Nicaraguan foreign-born population in the United States. But it must be kept in mind that there have been problems with undercounting Latinos in the census and that these figures are, by the time of this writing, eight years old. But they provide a good general estimate of the Salvadoran and Nicaraguan immigrants who arrived in the United States in the 1980s.

3. This inconsistency is perhaps best exemplified by the discrepancy in the implementation of policy between Miami and elsewhere in the United States. For instance, initially, only those Nicaraguans who lived in Miami were allowed to stay, whereas those living elsewhere were subject to deportation (Portes and Stepick 1993). Eventually, this provision was extended to Nicaraguans living elsewhere in the country, but only for a very brief period of time.

4. It would be particularly erroneous to make a general statement about ethnic solidarity, when recent research paints an image of dissension, friction, and tension in immigrant communities, including the Salvadoran communities (Mahler 1995b; Menjívar 1998a).

REFERENCES

Americas Watch
1984   *El Salvador's Other Victims: The War on the Displaced.* New York: Americas Watch.

Aron, Adriane, Shawn Corne, Anthea Fursland, and Barbara Zelwer
1991   The Gender Specific Terror of El Salvador and Guatemala. *Women's Studies International Forum* 14 (1/2): 37–47.

Calderón, Ricardo
1992   *Situación Socio-económica de la Communidad Salvadoreña en el Área de la Bahia de San Francisco*. San Francisco: Centro para Refugiados Centroamericanos/Asociación de Salvadoreños.

Espino, Conchita
1991   Trauma and Adaptation: The Case of Central American Children. In *Refugee Children: Theory, Research, and Services*. Edited by Frederick L. Ahearn, Jr., and Jean L. Athey. Baltimore: Johns Hopkins University Press. Pp. 106–124.

Fernández-Kelly, M. Patricia, and Richard Schauffler
1994   Divided Fates: Immigrant Children in a Restructured U.S. Economy. *International Migration Review* 28 (4): 662–689.

Funkhouser, E.
1995   Remittances from International Migration: A Comparison of El Salvador and Nicaragua. *The Review of Economics and Statistics* 77 (1): 137–146.

Gil, Andres G., and William A. Vega
1996   Two Different Worlds: Acculturation Stress and Adaptation among Cuban and Nicaraguan Families. *Journal of Social and Personal Relationships* 13 (3): 435–456.

Godfrey, Brian
1988   *Neighborhoods in Transition: The Making of San Francisco's Ethnic and Nonconformist Communities*. Publications in Geography, 27. Berkeley: University of California Press.

Guarnaccia, Peter J., and Pablo Farias
1988   The Social Meanings of Nervios: A Case Study of a Central American Woman. *Social Science and Medicine* 26 (12): 1223–1231.

Hamilton, Nora, and Norma Stoltz Chinchilla
1991   Central American Migration: A Framework for Analysis. *Latin American Research Review* 26 (1): 75–110.

Immigration and Naturalization Service
1995   *Statistical Yearbook of the Immigration and Naturalization Service*. U.S. Department of Justice.

1997   *INS Releases Updated Estimates of U.S. Illegal Population*. U.S. Department of Justice. (News Release, February 7).

1998   *Nicaraguan Adjustment and Central American Relief Act. 1997*. U.S. Department of Justice.

Jones, Richard C.
1989   Causes of Salvadoran Migration to the United States. *The Geographical Review* 79 (2): 183–194.

Lopez, David E., Eric Popkin, and Edward Telles
1996   Central Americans: At the Bottom, Struggling to Get Ahead. In *Ethnic Los Angeles*. Edited by Roger Waldinger and Mehdi Bozorgmehr. New York: Russell Sage Foundation. Pp. 279–304.

Mahler, Sarah J.
1995a   *Salvadorans in Suburbia: Symbiosis and Conflict*. Boston: Allyn and Bacon.

1995b *American Dreaming: Immigrant Life on the Margins*. Princeton, New Jersey: Princeton University Press.

Martín-Baró, Ignacio

1990   Political Violence and War as Causes of Psychosocial Trauma in El Salvador. *International Journal of Mental Health* 18 (1): 3–20.

Menjívar, Cecilia

1998a *The Ties That (Un) Bind: The Transformation of Social Networks among Salvadoran Immigrants*. Unpublished manuscript.

1998b   The Intersection of Work and Gender: Central American Immigrant Women and Employment in California. Forthcoming in *American Behavioral Scientist*.

1992   Salvadoran Migration to the United States: The Dynamics of Social Networks in International Perspective. Ph.D. diss., University of California, Davis.

1993   History, Economy and Politics: Macro and Micro-level Factors in Recent Salvadorean Migration to the US. *Journal of Refugee Studies* 6 (4): 350–371.

Menjívar, Cecilia, Julie DaVanzo, Lisa Greenwell, and R. Burciaga Valdez

1998   Remittance Behavior of Filipino and Salvadoran Immigrants in Los Angeles. *International Migration Review* 32 (1): 97–126.

Montes, Segundo, and Juan José García

1988   *Salvadoran Migration to the United States: An Exploratory Study*. Georgetown University, Center for Immigration Policy and Refugee Assistance, Hemispheric Migration Project.

NALEO (National Association of Latino Elected and Appointed Officials)

1998   *America's Newest Voices: Colombians, Dominicans, Guatemalans and Salvadorans in the United States Examine Their Public Policy Needs*. Claremont, California: Tomas Rivera Policy Institute.

National Asylum Study Project

1992   *An Interim Assessment of the Asylum Process of the Immigration and Naturalization Service*. Immigration and Refugee Program, Program of the Legal Profession, Harvard Law School. Cambridge: Harvard University Press.

Portes, Alejandro, and Richard Schauffler

1994   Language and the Second Generation: Bilingualism Yesterday and Today. *International Migration Review* 28 (4): 640–661.

Portes, Alejandro, and Alex Stepick

1993   *City on the Edge: The Transformation of Miami*. Berkeley: University of California Press.

Repak, Terry A.

1995   *Waiting on Washington: Central American Workers in the Nation's Capital*. Philadelphia: Temple University Press.

Rumbaut, Rubén G.

1989   The Structure of Refuge: Southeast Asian Refugees in the U.S., 1975–85. *International Review of Comparative Public Policy* 1 (1): 97–129.

Salgado de Snyder, V. Nelly, Richard C. Cervantes, and Amado M. Padilla

1990   Gender and Ethnic Differences in Psychosocial Stress and Generalized Distress among Hispanics. *Sex Roles* 22 (7–8): 441–453.

Stanley, William

1987   Economic Migrants or Refugees from Violence?: A Time-Series Analysis of Salvadoran Migration to the United States. *Latin American Research Review* 22 (1): 132–154.

Suarez-Orozco, Marcelo M.
1987   "Becoming Somebody": Central American Immigrants in U.S. Inner-City Schools. *Anthropology and Education Quarterly* 18 (4): 287–299.
U.S. Census
1993   Persons of Hispanic Origin in the United States. U.S. Department of Commerce: Economics and Statistics Administration. Bureau of the Census. CP-3-3.
Walker, Thomas W.
1997   Introduction. Historical Setting and Important Issues. In *Nicaragua without Illusions: Regime Transition and Structural Adjustment in the 1990s*. Edited by Thomas W. Walker. Wilmington, Delaware: Scholarly Resources Books. Pp. 1–19.
Ward, Thomas
1987   Price of Fear: Salvadoran Refugees in the City of Angels. Ph.D. diss., University of California, Los Angeles.
Wickham-Crowley, Timothy
1992   *Guerrillas and Revolution in Latin America: A Comparative Study of Insurgents and Regimes since 1956*. Princeton, New Jersey: Princeton University Press.

Illegal Europeans: Transients between Two Societies

Elzbieta M. Gozdziak

Current debates about illegal immigration have focused almost exclusively on undocumented migrants from Central and South America, who constitute the majority of the roughly 5 million illegal immigrants in the United States (Passel 1986, this volume; Bean, Edmonston, and Passel, 1990: 27). However, Central and South American undocumented workers are clearly not representative of all illegal groups. "Undocumented immigrants are not a monolithic group. They come from different countries, arrive in the United States via many different routes, and have very different social and economic characteristics" (Passel 1986: 192). Europeans constitute a considerable number of undocumented migrants seeking better life and opportunities in the United States. The U.S. Census Bureau estimated the number of illegal Europeans residing currently in the United States at 234,300 people, including 70,000 Poles, 30,000 Irish, 27,000 Portuguese, 25,000 Italians, and 39,000 individuals from the former Soviet Union and Yugoslavia combined (Fernandez and Robinson 1994). It is not surprising that they are coming illegally since the legal pathways for immigrants from Europe have dissipated.

This chapter focuses on two groups of undocumented Europeans—Poles and Irish—as they represent the largest groups of illegal migrants from Europe. Not easily distinguishable from Americans of European descent, the Poles and the Irish have suffered less discrimination than the Latinos. However, their existence is equally furtive. Without the "green card," they are unable to lead "normal" lives: obtain decent jobs, pay taxes, and participate fully in American society. Nonetheless, their inconspicuousness enables undocumented Europeans to carry on reasonably satisfactorily. They have acquired their own set of values and beliefs and formed organizations and lobbying groups trying to help them achieve legal status. Legal or not, both the Poles and the Irish have made important contributions to American politics, labor movement, arts and sports (Corcoran 1993).

POLES

The Exodus

Emigration became the latest vogue in Poland in the 1980s. Everyone was either emigrating or knew someone who did emigrate or was thinking about emigration or at least planning to travel to the West to earn some hard currency. Emigration and dollars seemed to be inseparable. Emigration reached an absolute peak in the late 1980s. In 1988, when the "passport for everybody" policy was implemented, 230,000 people emigrated (Korcelli 1992), and an additional 280,000 left the following year (*Migration News* 1996). It is estimated that during the 1980s about 2 million Poles left the country for one year or more, and about half of them stayed abroad permanently (*Migration News* 1996). More conservative estimates place gross out-migration from Poland during the period of 1981–1988 at 653,000 and the net out-migration at 641,000 (Korcelli 1992). According to Polish sources, the United States accounted for 12.3 percent of "permanent emigration" from Poland (Glowny Urzad Statystyczny 1989) and 17–20 percent or 110,000–125,000 "permanent" and "temporary" migrants combined (Korcelli 1992). American sources confirm the desirability of the United States as an immigration target among Poles. In 1989, the U.S. Consulate in Poland issued 80,000 visas to Polish citizens, but they also refused sixty percent of the visa applications. The sheer size of the emigration from Poland in the 1980s has created a situation in which virtually every second family in Poland has relatives abroad, primarily in Germany, the United States, and Canada.

The big change came in 1989, when the economy started to change in Poland. During the communist era, forty dollars bought enough *zlotys* for a family in Poland to live reasonably for a month, and with $5,000 one could establish a business and be set for life. Under those conditions, many Poles were coming to the United States to work for a while, save money, and go back. In the early 1990s, as a consequence of rapid political and economic change toward democracy and market economy, emigration from Poland decreased sharply, down to fewer than 50,000 people annually (Korcelli 1992). There are many incentives to stay, both political and economic. Since June 1989, all the basic institutions characteristic of a democratic, pluralistic society have emerged or reemerged in Poland. The system of parliamentary democracy and market economy is taken for granted by the overwhelming majority of the society and is not endangered. In addition, Poland offers many economic opportunities. Employment in privately owned enterprises is on the rise. Incomes comparable to those found in the West are earned by a relatively small, but expanding, category of entrepreneurs and employees of international firms. There are also examples of multimillion-dollar fortunes gained, often by quite young people, in commerce, banking, and real estate (Korcelli 1992).

Migration scholars predict that uprooting forces will continue to be somewhat weaker during the late 1990s in comparison with the situation in the 1980s. Disincentives to migrate are many. Poles are no longer eligible for political asylum or refugee status in the United States. The attractiveness of hard currency jobs has decreased as the purchasing power of the U.S. dollar went down to one-fourth of its initial level. There still remain, however, some incentives, including economic opportunities and kinship networks. For example, while the absolute numbers of emigrants will definitely decrease, the same might not be true about the share of highly educated persons within the total number of prospective migrants (Korcelli 1992). Substantial numbers of scientists, medical doctors, and teachers hold underpaid jobs in the public sector, where chances for improvement are minimal. This is in contrast to such professions as pharmacists and lawyers, whose prospects have suddenly improved due to new ownership rules and new market demands. In addition, the large size of emigration from Poland in the 1980s has created extensive kinship and friendship networks in the United States, and these networks will be conducive to successful streams of continued migration from Poland. The continual desire to immigrate to America is evidenced by the number of applications for U.S. diversity visas: Poles filed 50,000 applications for U.S. diversity visas in 1995 alone (*Migration News* 1996).

The Polish versions of illegal migrant workers are the so-called *wakacjusze*, or vacationers (officially classified as "temporary visitors for pleasure"). Many *wakacjusze* violate the restrictions of their visas by working in the United States and overstaying their six-month time limitations. While the annual admissions of temporary visitors from Poland averaged 12,000 in the 1960s, this number doubled to almost 24,000 in the 1970s and skyrocketed in the 1980s. In that decade, nearly 450,000 nonimmigrants arrived, and almost eighty percent of those came as temporary visitors for pleasure (Erdmans 1998). According to the Polish Welfare Association (PWA) in Chicago, approximately one-third of the *wakacjusze* overstay their six-month visas, so the number of temporary visitors from Poland in the United States is far greater than the annual number admitted. Using this one-third estimate, by the early 1990s there would have been about .25 million *wakacjusze* in the United States (Erdmans 1998), a number far exceeding the official Immigration and Naturalization Service (INS) estimate of 70,000 undocumented Poles (Fernandez and Robinson 1994).

Who Are the Undocumented Poles?

There are as many characterizations of undocumented Poles as there are sources of information about their lives in the United States. According to the Polish government, the "panic migrations" of 1980–1981 and 1987–1988 included large numbers of highly skilled professionals and scientists and posed a considerable brain drain on Polish society. The data collected by the Governmental Commission on Population (1989) indicate that university and high school graduates constituted 13.3 and 46.4 percent, respectively, of those who migrated abroad permanently or for an extended period of time during 1981–1988. Those who emigrated included some 19,800 engineers (with higher technical education), 8,800 scientists and academicians, 5,500 medical doctors, and 6,000 nurses. Most of the Polish emigrants during the 1980s originated in highly urbanized regions such as Katowice, Warsaw, Gdansk, Cracow, Wroclaw, Lodz, and Poznan. With the exception of Lodz and Poznan, these regions accounted for distinctly higher proportions of migrants than the national index of 1.71 percent, which denotes the relation between the number of emigrants, aggregated over the 1981–1988 period, and the total population as of 1989 (Korcelli 1992). This mass emigration worried both Solidarity and religious leaders. The Polish primate of the Catholic Church attempted to deter people from leaving Poland because of their moral duty to the nation. He argued that emigration diminished the supply of educated and skilled people (Erdmans 1992). Even Pope John Paul II "urged Poles to stay in Poland because of national duty" (Erdmans 1992: 11).

The Polish-language press in the United States and some publications in Poland described the "new Polish immigrants" as deplorable and disgraceful individuals (Mostwin 1989). Mostwin (1989) refers to this noticeable, but marginal, group as a "noisy minority" that does not represent all Polish immigrants to the United States. "Some of them come to work for a short time in America to earn dollars and return. But many of them stay longer. Away from family and community restraints, they may behave in a derogatory manner," she adds (Mostwin 1989: 26). "Every society has its marginal and deviant element. It is normal that it should exist in the Polish-American community. But it would be most unfortunate to generalize from the social ills of these persons, often creatures of circumstances, miserable and in need of help, to the majority of the new Polish immigrants" (Mostwin 1989: 26).

Polish-American scholars (Znaniecka Lopata 1994; Erdmans 1998; Mostwin 1971, 1991) provide a different characterization of undocumented Polish immigrants in the United States. Znaniecka Lopata, writing about a dramatic increase of Poles in America in the late 1970s and early 1980s, focuses on the so-called *wakacjusze*, or temporary visitors who declared their desire to be tourists while they actually came to earn money for a better life back home. Her research shows that out of the total number of nonimmigrants admitted to the United States between 1973 and 1979, the percentage of *wakacjusze* increased from 61 to 78 percent. In her estimate, *wakacjusze*, for the most part, were uneducated and did not know English and were thus dependent upon Polish Americans for their illegal jobs and life's necessities (Znaniecka Lopata 1994).

Mostwin conducted two studies of the newer cohorts of Poles in America, the "transplanted family" in 1970 (Mostwin 1971) and political émigrés in 1984

(Mostwin 1991). While both samples identified themselves as political immigrants, fifty percent of the latter group had come at the invitation of relatives and friends and presumably—at least for a time—lived as undocumented migrants. In fact as many as twenty-two percent identified themselves as being neither American citizens nor permanent residents. Many had gone to technical or vocational schools. Less than ten percent came from villages, and sixty-five percent listed large cities as their hometowns (Mostwin 1991: 50). The Poles in Mostwin's sample who came to the United States between 1974 and 1984 were young, under forty years of age. Sixty-eight percent did not speak any English (Mostwin 1991: 52). Erdman's (1992) sample of the post-1970 wave of Poles living in Chicago included a high proportion of professionals (23 percent) and skilled workers (45 percent). This was particularly true of permanent residents. More of the temporary residents, with valid or invalid visas, were in unskilled jobs mainly due to lack of English-language skills.

My own research and participant observation indicate that undocumented Poles are as diversified as—but not very different from—legal immigrants and refugees from Poland. They very much mirror the social strata of the Polish society in Poland. I found among them both highly skilled professionals—doctors, lawyers, engineers, economists, and anthropologists—and less educated tradesmen—carpenters, masons, and a variety of technicians. There is a considerable difference between resettlement experiences of Polish immigrants in cities like Chicago and New York that have had a long history of Polish immigration and cities like Dallas, Texas, Washington, D.C., and Atlanta, Georgia, that had virtually no Polish population prior to the 1980s.

The Chicago and New York Polonia are very similar in terms of living in historically Polish neighborhoods and being able to live and work, at least initially, using their native language. Conversely, Polish immigrants living in Dallas, Atlanta, and Washington, D.C., had to immediately adapt to the host society without the benefit or "interference" of the existing ethnic community. There is variation in educational levels by city. Poles in Chicago appear to have less education than those in New York City or Dallas (Gozdziak 1989, 1996). In one of my studies (Cichon, Gozdziak, and Grover 1986), almost all of the surveyed Poles had completed secondary or trade school, with a small percentage having completed college. In Dallas, however, about half were estimated to have completed college, the remainder secondary and vocational programs. In New York City, the clear majority had completed college, with over half having master's degrees or more. Consistent with these educational backgrounds, the native Polish work experience included some professionals and mostly skilled tradespeople in Chicago, but many college professors, engineers, accountants, lawyers, health professionals, teachers, and scientists in Dallas and New York City. Most seemed to be very ambitious, highly motivated to work and to move up the economic ladder, and, of course, anxious to find a way to adjust their immigration status.

How Do They Get Here?

The majority of Poles enter the United States legally, usually on tourist or business visas. They come to visit friends or family, attend a conference, participate in a student exchange or scholarship program. Only later, having overstayed their tourist or student visas, they find themselves undocumented. The INS estimates that of the 70,000 undocumented Poles currently in the United States, about 40,000 have overstayed their tourist visas (Murphy 1997; Zwick and Zwick 1998).

Some undocumented Polish immigrants arrive here without inspection by crossing the southern border illegally. Many Polish nationals cannot obtain a visa to the United States, but they get one to Mexico and then cross the border without authorization. Some go to Cuba first and once in Havana are easily granted permission to visit Mexico, where they are met by an English-speaking Polish American who drives them across the border for a price. The ride can cost between $3,800 and $5,000. It is often a case of Poles being exploited by Poles. According to the chief patrol agent for the McAllen, Texas, sector of the INS, 157 Poles were caught along the southeastern border of Texas in 1985, while three times as many have made it through the "Polish Pipeline" that extends from Warsaw to Havana then Mexico and across the border to the United States (Mulvihill 1986).

Others were smuggled across the northern frontier. In October 1992, a federal judge sentenced four individuals to prison for running a large-scale smuggling operation that brought illegal Polish immigrants into the United States from mid-1988 to spring 1991. The ring made at least sixty trips in a light airplane from a small airfield near Toronto to Du Page Airport in Chicago. The convicted ring leader was sentenced to three years in prison and fined $50,000. The ring made substantial money by bringing an average of three to five illegal immigrants on each of the sixty flights. Most passengers paid $2,000–$2,500. The director of the INS in Chicago called the operation the second largest non-Mexican smuggling ring ever apprehended in Chicago (O'Connor 1992).

Where Do They Settle?

Unlike their predecessors who left Poland "for bread" and established farming colonies in the Midwest or took over abandoned and worn-out farmlands in the East (Bukowczyk 1987) as well as settled in urban—primarily industrial—centers (Lieberson 1963; Wood 1955), the latest wave of immigrants from Poland, both legal and illegal, tend to settle almost exclusively in large metropolitan areas. They can be found both in Polish ethnic communities of Chicago, New York, and Philadelphia and in the suburbs of Atlanta and Washington, D.C.

At 47,000, Poles are the second largest—after Mexicans—undocumented group in Chicago (Passel and Clark 1998). According to Barbara Przezdziecka, the immigration supervisor at the Polish Welfare Association (PWA), there may be as many as 15,000 Polish immigrants in Chicago at any given time who are working illegally (Ungar 1995). *Jackowo* is the Polish ghetto of Chicago, surrounding the Roman Catholic Church of St. Hyacinth and the Polish businesses located along Milwaukee Avenue between Belmont and Diversity. Poles also live in other historically Polish neighborhoods on the northwest and southwest sides of Chicago, including Jefferson Park, Belmont-Cragin, Portage Park, and Archer Heights (Erdmans 1998).

Quoting INS and the Department of City Planning as sources, the *New York Times* (September 9, 1993) reported that there were 25,800 undocumented Poles living in New York City in 1993. While more than 600,000 people of Polish descent live throughout New York City, some 20,000 to 100,0000 Poles live in the Lower East Side in Manhattan. Little Poland, a fourteen-block-long, and five-block-wide area, is the largest Polish community in Manhattan. Here undocumented Poles live beside Polish refugees and legal immigrants, as well as first- and second-generation Americans of Jewish, Hungarian, Ukrainian, and Russian descent (Morehouse 1981). No one is sure how many illegal Poles live in Greenpoint, a large Polish community in Brooklyn (Kaufman 1992). Port Richmond, a classic working-class, white ethnic neighborhood in Philadelphia, is the Polish neighborhood in that city (Goode and Schneider 1994).

When it comes to Washington, D.C., Dallas, Texas, or Atlanta, Georgia, it is impossible to talk about Polish neighborhoods. While the Roman Catholic Church of Our Lady Queen of Poland in Silver Spring, Maryland, might by some be considered the center of worship for the Washington Polonia, only a handful of Polish families live in that neighborhood. There is always a crowd of Polish immigrants—nostalgic for the pageantry of the Corpus Christi procession, anxious to have their Easter eggs blessed on Holy Saturday, and ready to sing Christmas carols during midnight mass on Christmas Eve—at the church on major religious holidays, but few Polish newcomers attend that church on a regular basis. Many, particularly those representing Polish intelligentsia, prefer more liberal American Catholic churches such as Holy Trinity in Georgetown or St. John's in Silver Spring, Maryland. In 1996 only thirty-six families enrolled their children in the Polish language and religion education program at Our Lady Queen of Poland. Several of those families were members of the Polish diplomatic corps. Polonez, the local Polish deli, caters primarily to Americans. Most Polish immigrants are dispersed throughout northern Virginia and Maryland suburbs. A few families reside in the District of Columbia. By and large the Poles settled in the Washington metropolitan area are invisible. The only time when one hears Polish spoken in the streets of Washington is when the Polish National Symphony or another renowned ensemble plays at the Kennedy Center or when Poles flock to the Polish Embassy to cast their absentee ballots during parliamentary elections.

Between Here and There

Inconspicuous because of their race, undocumented Poles experience less discrimination than illegal migrants of color. On the other hand, lack of proper immigration status and work authorization does not make their lives easy. Most live suspended between here—America, the land of opportunity—and there— Poland, the motherland. Wherever they live, they are vulnerable to exploitation and forced to live lives of hustling and hassling. This is particularly true in the ethnic enclaves of Chicago and New York City, where competition with fellow compatriots is fierce, and exploitation by Polish Americans more pronounced than in other cities.

Living by their wits and coping with landlords and employers willing to exploit their uncertain status, undocumented Poles nevertheless bring energy and conspiratorial cunning to what used to be sleepy ethnic enclaves. Asbestos removal, dominated by Polish and Irish illegal workers, has been one source of prosperity in some Polish neighborhoods in New York City. However, the jealousy expressed by those who were unable to secure "lucrative" jobs in asbestos removal is misplaced. The work is hazardous and exhausting and not as well paid as people imagine. In the mid-1990s, the going rate was $10 an hour, but many had to kick money back to the subcontractor who hired them. Many Polish men reported that important safety equipment was missing and that they worked long hours without any lunch break. Some would get sick, but they did not dare to complain, knowing that they could be easily replaced with another illegal Pole. Given their tenuous situation, they take some of the most menial jobs and work ten to fourteen hours a day. The men work as dishwashers, janitors, restaurant workers, in construction or demolition, or as factory hands, while the women clean homes five or six times a week for cash payment only. They live frugally, three or four together in a tiny, one-bedroom apartment with no telephone, often heated only by small portable oil burners. They regularly send home most of their earnings and can be seen flooding local post offices with money and food packages for their food-short relatives and friends back home (Kaufman 1992).

Whatever their employment situation, most undocumented Poles live in constant fear of being caught and forced to leave. They pray that the lawyers they keep consulting will eventually find a way for them to become legal immigrants. Some men and women are so desperate to get a green card or find some other legal means of staying in the United States that they simply abandon their families back in Poland and start up new ones here. There are also quite a few fraudulent marriages taking place in the different Polish communities. For example, in Chicago undocumented Poles reportedly pay anywhere from $2,000 to $10,000 to marry an American citizen. According to the PWA in Chicago, some Polish women who marry U.S. citizens in an attempt to remain in this country may unknowingly buy their way into abusive relationships. Fearful that they will be deported if the fraud is revealed, some have no choice but to stay with husbands they hardly know and endure maltreatment until they can petition for a green card (Ungar 1995).

Agnes Kowalewicz of PWA (an association founded in 1921 to deal with the fighting between Irish and Polish gangs) provides a glimpse of an underside of Polish life in Chicago that is rarely visible to the public. The association maintains a daytime shelter for Polish men, with room for about twenty to twenty-five at a time, usually people afflicted with chronic alcoholism. "In Poland alcoholism is enabled, by employers, by coworkers and by family," says Kowalewicz. "I would not say that it is worse than in other ethnic groups. It's similar to the Irish. But our culture tends to sweep it under the rug. These men usually arrive from Poland with an alcohol problem, and it seems that the only place they can go to socialize here is the Polish tavern. They feel lonely and isolated; they don't participate in American culture. Many end up, in fact, on Chicago's Polish Skid Row" (Ungar 1995: 238–239).

"Tie Me Down with a Rope"

Realizing the transient nature of their migration, some undocumented sojourners are torn between staying in the United States and returning to Poland. In September 1987, a leading Polish weekly, *Tygodnik Powszechny*, ran a cover story on Polish immigrants in America dramatically entitled "Tie Me Down with a Rope" (Berberyusz 1987). One of the undocumented Poles interviewed for the story pleaded: "Tie me down with a rope, so I will not listen to the desperate urging of my heart and will not run back to Poland." According to the journalist, who talked with many undocumented Polish immigrants living and working in Chicago, this plea is shared by many Poles who came to the United States for a short time to earn money.

Danuta Mostwin, commenting on the article, wonders whether the sojourners are immigrants. She answers her own question negatively:

Not yet. The person described in this essay came to the U.S. for a short time to earn dollars. Women with professional degrees work as maids. Men, alumnae of Polish universities take jobs in asbestos plants. The majority of these people try to extend their stay from year to year until some of them are forced by the U.S. Immigration Office to return to Poland, and the lucky ones will become naturalized Americans. They are torn between "to have" and "to be." America as a state, a nation, a culture does not concern them much. (Mostwin 1989: 27)

My own research as well as personal experience indicate that many Polish newcomers, legal and undocumented, are determined to resist what some call "a Polish ghetto existence and the fate and mentality that go with it" (Ungar 1995) by settling in ethnically and racially diversified neighborhoods, starting their own businesses, joining professional organizations, and lobbying potential employers to sponsor them for their green cards—as well as joining Parent

Teacher Associations at their children's schools and being actively involved in their Neighborhood Advisory Councils. In short, they choose to actively participate in American civil society.

IRISH

The Exodus

The Irish have poured into America for more than two hundred years. According to the 1980 Census, over forty million Americans—eighteen percent of the U.S. population—trace their ancestry to Ireland (Lieberson and Waters 1988: Table 2.1). The pattern of Irish emigration throughout the twentieth century has been quite distinct. Generally speaking, there has been a new wave of Irish arriving on America's shores every thirty years (Carol 1998). "It is the striking thing about Irish emigration this century," says Niall O'Dowd, publisher of *Irish America* magazine. "Every thirty years you have another wave. In the '20s you had the Civil War emigrants to America. In the '50s there was economic emigration from Ireland, mainly composed of the sons and daughters of small farmers in the west. In the '80s there was the entirely new issue of emigration by young and well-educated Irish who arrived in America and became the illegals" (O'Hanlon 1998: 221). If that pattern holds, the next wave will arrive any time after 2010. That's certainly how Niall O'Dowd, whose publishing enterprises were based on the 1980s immigration tide, is inclined to view the future.

The 1980s exodus was precipitated by a deterioration in Ireland's economic fortunes and a resulting twenty percent unemployment (Corcoran 1993, 1996). However, it was *not* simply the absence of work that prompted many Irish to come to America. According to Mary Corcoran (1993), Great Britain is more likely to attract the terminally unemployed Irish, not the United States. The high level of destitution and homelessness among the Irish in London suggests that Britain is the primary destination for those at the lower end of the socioeconomic structure (Connor 1985). The New York Irish in Corcoran's study who described themselves as

economic refugees cited underemployment, seasonal unemployment, and business failure as factors precipitating the decision to leave. For many of the Irish illegals, however, years of dead-end, boring work; limited promotional and entrepreneurial opportunities; and an overextended taxation system were cited as factors that provide an impetus to leave. A sense of adventure and a desire to meet new challenges also serve as motivational factors. Finally some illegals treat their period away as little more than a working holiday, which can be terminated at any time. (Corcoran 1993: 34)

Between 1980 and 1990, net outward migration from Ireland totaled 216,000, or 6 percent of the population, with the majority of immigrants leaving after 1985. The annual average migratory outflow reached nearly 34,000 people between 1986 and 1990 (Corcoran 1996). Following the increase in Irish emigration in the 1980s, legal immigration to the United States rose steadily during the decade. Approximately 65,000 Irish immigrants availed themselves of two visa lottery programs aimed at increasing the flow of immigration to the United States from countries that had been adversely affected by the provisions of the 1965 Immigration Act. The NP-5 visa program (popularly know as the Donelly visas after the member of Congress who initiated the scheme) brought 16,329 Irish immigrants—randomly selected from a mail registration list—to the United States between 1987 and 1990. The Immigration Act of 1990 established a second lottery system—engineered by Representative Bruce Morrison—that distributed 16,000 visas a year to immigrants from Ireland over a period of three years, beginning in October 1991 and ending in October 1993 (O'Hanlon 1998; Corcoran 1996).

These statistics do not include the high level of illegal Irish immigration to the United States during the 1980s. It is impossible to provide an exact number of undocumented Irish residents in the United States. There is, however, evidence that "tens of thousands of Irish people entered the United States legally on temporary visitors' visas" in the 1980s, and when "the visas expired, the holders simply failed to return home, jeopardizing their legal status by seeking work without the proper documentation. Hence, they became 'illegal aliens' or 'undocumented workers' " (Corcoran 1993: 10). In 1987, the Irish Bishops Commission on Emigration estimated that as many as 136,000 Irish lived illegally in the United States (Corcoran 1993). The U.S. Catholic Conference set the number of illegal Irish at 44,000 (U.S. Catholic Conference 1988), while the Census Bureau estimated the number at 30,000 (Fernandez and Robinson 1994).

Who Are the Undocumented Irish?

The majority of the "new Irish" are young and single. Given the precarious nature of life as an illegal, it is uncommon for entire families to emigrate from Ireland without appropriate documentation. Unlike their predecessors, many have college degrees and professional careers (Barry 1997). The new Irish come as students and tourists and stay on as undocumented, enduring an underground existence marked by furtiveness, homesickness, and an uncertain future.

Mary Corcoran, who conducted an extensive study of Irish illegals in New York, distinguishes three categories of immigrants among the undocumented Irish: "1) Those who leave because of adverse economic circumstances—the *bread and butter immigrants*; 2) Those who leave to seek adventure because they are bored with the routine of their lives and poor working conditions—the *disaffected adventurers*; and 3) Those who simply desire a temporary change of scene—the *holiday takers*" (Corcoran 1993: 34–35). The gender distribution among these categories is interesting. Approximately one-half of the women in Corcoran's study saw themselves predominantly as holiday-takers, while the remainder was equally divided between the other two categories. Among the men, the configuration differed slightly, with approximately equal numbers falling into each of the three categories.

"Bread and butter" immigrants tend to have experienced unemployment, underemployment, layoffs, or business failure as factors precipitating the decision to leave. Unable to find work at home, they were willing to uproot themselves and emigrate. The decision to go to America was often made in the context of a familial or personal history of emigration. The chance to work and the promise of regular income generally outweigh their concerns about illegal status. In Corcoran's view, these immigrants are the most likely to make a permanent commitment to the host country (Corcoran 1996). Unlike the "bread and butter" immigrants, the "disaffected adventurers" have never experienced the economic hardship or psychological demoralization of unemployment. Disaffected by the lack of opportunity for advancement in Ireland, many of the immigrants use their time in the United States to work hard and accumulate capital in order to make investments in the years to come. However, given their illegal status, their desire for transnational existence seems to be unrealistic. Corcoran describes the third category of immigrants as "people who come from relatively well-off middle-class families, who stand to inherit a farm or a small business when they return home. They see their time in New York as an extended working holiday, before settling down to adulthood and its attendant responsibilities" (Corcoran 1996: 465).

Where Do They Settle?

The primary destinations of the new wave in the historic tide of Irish immigration to America include New York, Boston, Chicago, and San Francisco, where vibrant "new Irish" communities have emerged in recent years. Irish immigration to New York City is almost as old as the city itself. New York City continues to be a port of entry, temporary stopping point, and place of settlement for many Irish women and men (Bayor and Meagher 1996). The new Irish in New York are primarily located in three neighborhoods: Irishtown in Queens and Erinvale and Gaelside in the Bronx (Corcoran 1993). All three neighborhoods share the characteristics of "urban villages": there are concentrated networks and organizations among residents, strong kinship ties are maintained, there is a primary dependence on local institutions, and personal connections are used to secure employment (Yancey, Ericksen, and Juliani 1976).

Irishtown, a multicultural neighborhood located in northwestern Queens, has the highest concentration of new Irish in comparison with other New York neighborhoods in which the Irish have settled. The center of Irishtown is a twenty-block stretch traversed by three main thoroughfares, the central one overshadowed by the elevated subway line. Housing stock consists of one- and two-family houses and rental and cooperative apartment buildings. Average rent ranges from $700 to $900 for two-bedroom apartments. The ethnic composition of the neighborhood was historically European—Irish, German, Polish, and Italian—but in recent years there has been a significant influx of Latino and Asian immigrants. There are more than twenty Irish bars in the area. They compete for space with other establishments: American diners; Colombian coffee shops; Spanish, Chinese, and Cuban restaurants; pizzerias; Korean stores; various travel agencies; and real estate offices. Recently, a traditional Irish bakery, an Irish import store, a Celtic craft shop, and a couple of delis selling Irish produce have also opened along the main strip. There are also three Catholic churches that serve primarily Irish and Hispanic parishioners (Corcoran 1993).

Erinvale, located in northwestern Bronx, is a predominantly white, middle-class neighborhood. Erinvale has a very distinctive Irish identity. It is home to Gaelic Park, and many of the New York Gaelic football and hurling teams train in the adjoining parkland. Gaelside, in the northeastern part of the borough, is more heterogeneous. The local parish priest estimates that his parishioners are fifty percent Irish and fifty percent Hispanic. The large number of Irish bars, restaurants, and delis provides evidence of the presence of a significant number of Irish newcomers in the neighborhood (Corcoran 1993).

Other major areas of settlement exist, each with its own distinctive features, including South Boston, or "Southie," and Dorchester. Both still attract Irish newcomers, both legal and undocumented. There are no current figures on how many settle here, but those working with immigrants place the figure in the thousands. Recently made famous by the movie *Good Will Hunting*, South Boston remains insular, working-class, and Irish. Wood-frame triple-deckers dominate the residential landscape, some displaying plaques with family names in English and Gaelic. Many windows are adorned with shamrocks. Irish flags are common, and the question "Where are you from?" refers more often to Ireland than to other parts of the United States. Ice hockey is the sport of choice for children. For adults, it's politics (Conover 1998).

Generally speaking, among the new Irish, the illegals tend to settle in traditional immigrant neighborhoods, while the legally documented have settled in less ethnically homogeneous areas. Established ethnic neighborhoods offer the illegals work and leisure opportunities as well as the psychological assurance of safety in numbers. In contrast, legal immigrants live in neighborhoods that are not identifiably Irish and interact with people from a wide range of backgrounds.

The Old Guard and the New Irish

Does living in ethnic neighborhoods translate into good relationships with established Irish-American communities? There is a great deal of controversy regarding the relations between the established Irish-American communities and the new Irish. "Many Irish newcomers say they have not found the kind of immigrant network that has long been a cornerstone of Irish-American pride, a symbol of generosity and strong community. It is common today for Irish newcomers to keep their distance from Irish-American enclaves, see themselves as outsiders, and to identify more closely with recent immigrants from other countries than with Americans of Irish ancestry'' (Bennett 1993: 1). "It's a complete myth that people are coming into a network,'' says Lena Deevy, executive director of the Irish Immigration Center in Boston. "The majority of people coming in here have no ties in this country. They are totally on their own.'' Indeed, the center was established as a result of her research on undocumented Irish in Boston that indicated that young Irish newcomers needed the help and support required to adjust to a new land, economically, psychologically, and culturally. The center began in a small basement office in the Dorchester area of Boston in 1989 and has now grown into three offices, a full-time staff of six, and 100 volunteers to assist thousands of Irish immigrants daily (Shannon 1997).

Mary Corcoran (1993) argues the opposite. Her research among undocumented Irish in New York indicates a high proportion of people who came from families with a history of emigration. Indeed, well over half of the individuals in her sample had at least one relative in the United States. Corcoran emphasizes the heightened importance, virtually a prerequisite, of familial contacts for newly arrived Irish seeking work without proper documentation. Illegality, she contends, intensifies dependence on patrons and power brokers in the established Irish community. The Irish illegals Corcoran studied made maximum use of ethnic networks to improve their position. Upon arrival they relied primary on close relatives and friends, but soon they moved "beyond the obvious first-order contacts . . . to make use of second-order contacts: key brokers in the different employment sectors, who are ultimately more influential in the community at large. As undocumented workers, the Irish are dependent on employers that will not question their immigration status. Hence they gravitate towards Irish contractors and Irish-owned bars and restaurants. The new Irish, in turn, revitalized many traditional Irish neighborhoods inhabited by the old and less upwardly mobile trying to weather the problems of inner-city decline'' (Corcoran 1996: 471).

The illegal Irish immigrants and the established Irish Americans formed the most vigorous alliance in their struggle to increase the number of legal immigrants from Ireland and legalize some of those who had already crossed the Atlantic. A detailed account of this struggle as it was fought on the floor of Congress, urged on by the Irish Immigration Reform Movement (IIRM) from New York, can be found in Ray O'Hanlon's (1998) book *The New Irish Americans*. However, while the new Irish immigrants and their predecessors forged powerful alliances in the labor market and in the political arena, culturally, they remain quite different. "The older Irish tend to be more family oriented, better established and more upwardly mobile. The younger, single people are into a totally different lifestyle. Bars are their cultural center, and they tend to close in on themselves'' (Corcoran 1996: 475).

With the church's influence waning at home, the new Irish complain that Irish-American communities have lagged far behind on social issues. One young

Irishman pointed out that "gays and lesbians are free to march in the Dublin St. Patrick's Day parade—just not in Southie" (Barry 1997). The entrenched Irish Americans are similarly ambivalent about the cosmopolitanism of the new Irish. Some find fault with the sojourners for the ease with which they drift through the Irish-American support system and then move on to the next global hot spot.

Illegal in America or a Yank Back Home

The lives of Irish illegals in America revolve around work. Given their illegal status, the Irish are primarily dependent on the informal economy. Most find jobs in three different employment sectors: the construction industry, the restaurant and bar trade, and private child care and home care services. Only a small minority continue to successfully penetrate the formal economy, where wages and benefits are considerably better.

Newly arrived immigrants who previously worked "on the building," in farming or in other manual occupations generally seek work in the construction industry. White-collar workers and those who worked in the service sector at home gravitate toward jobs in restaurants and bars or work as care-givers in private homes. These distinctions are by no means definitive, and one will find teachers working as laborers and former laborers working as bartenders. The majority of men, however, work in construction, while most women work as nannies and home companions. A smaller proportion of both sexes work in the restaurant and bar trades. (Corcoran, 1993: 55)

The Irish illegals, who are white, generally well educated, and English-speaking, do not experience racial discrimination. However, they are not immune to exploitation by unscrupulous Irish employers and landlords. Given the fact that the supply of labor frequently exceeds demand, many illegals cling to their employers in a form of indentured servitude. Forced to work marathon hours for minuscule wages, they often don't complain out of fear of losing their only source of income. On the other hand, their ethnicity confers upon them privileged status in the labor market compared with other immigrant groups, both legal and illegal. Mary Corcoran argues that despite their illegality, more Irish workers than other European or Central American undocumented migrants have succeeded in penetrating the formal labor market, while those confined to the informal sector tend to occupy the higher-status, better-paid jobs (Corcoran 1993).

Not unlike other sojourners, many Irish immigrants continue to identify with their motherland and often think of returning home. Indeed, many are going back. With Ireland's economy having grown at a rate of 7 percent over the last three years—faster than any other economy in Europe—Irish immigrants are moving home from all over the world. In 1996, the number returning to Ireland from overseas surpassed the number leaving (Barry 1997). According to Noel

Waters of the Irish Department of Justice, Equality, and Law Reform, there is no indication that the economic miracle will stop anytime soon. Until it does, emigrants will be toying with the idea of going back. The returnees are coming primarily from the European Union, but the trend has extended to the United States. For example, in 1995–1996, 6,000 people left Ireland for America, and 6,600 left America to return to Ireland (Barry 1997).

The return traffic has changed demographically, too. In the past, longtime emigrants would return when they were ready to retire. Nowadays, the returnees are in the prime of their working lives, with young children born in the United States. Many of them have done well in America. They had moved here in the mid-1980s, made some money, got settled, and paid off mortgages, but now with small children starting school they feel they need to choose between the two countries. In many instances it is the desire to have their children grow up Irish, in Irish schools, that makes many immigrants go back. To immigrant parents, Ireland seems like the best of all possible school districts—a refuge from crime and drugs and the influence of pop culture. Some are anxious, however, about their children's accents. "When you come back, you're a Yank," says Mary, a thirty-three-year-old from County Kerry. "I worry about that" (Barry 1997).

For some it is hard to return to an Ireland that has been transformed during the Mary Robinson era: richer but also more expensive, less respectful of the church, more Westernized, faster-paced, and, some say, more sarcastic. Others are more enthusiastic: Dublin is bursting at the seams with new money, they report. University graduates, particularly in the high-tech sector, are a hot commodity. Most find jobs within a couple of weeks of return. Under a national agreement, computer programmers are assured a 20 to 30 percent increase in pay every year. With the housing market booming, there is also a market for skilled laborers, and Irish construction workers in Boston and New York are beginning to think that they could actually earn more working in Ireland.

CONCLUSIONS

Although the experiences of the Polish and Irish undocumented diverge in many ways, several crucial similarities between the two groups illuminate more general issues of illegal immigration and the lives of undocumented migrants in the United States. European, middle-class, and well educated, the Poles and the Irish are not easily distinguishable from other Euro-American groups that have long been a part of America's establishment; this gives them many advantages over other illegal immigrants, particularly people of color. If English-language ability is added, as it is for the Irish, the advantages are even more significant, just as they are for legal immigrants.

European and white, they are nevertheless illegal, and illegality has its consequences. It embarks people on a daily life of "hustling and hassling," and it subjects them to discrimination and exploitation both in the labor market and in housing—although not to the same extent as other ethnic and racial minorities. Illegality also intensifies their dependence on patrons and power brokers in the established Polish and Irish communities.

Compared to legal immigration, illegal movements are more readily subject to amendment as conditions in both sending and receiving countries change. As migrants assess whether there is an advantage to remaining in the United States—even illegally—because of economic conditions or familial development, the immigration of illegals can be more easily reversed than the migration of legal immigrants.

REFERENCES

Barry, Ellen
1997   *Boston Phoenix*, October 9–16.
Bayor, Ronald H., and Timothy J. Meagher, Editors
1996   *The New York Irish*. Baltimore: Johns Hopkins University Press.
Bean, Frank D., Barry Edmonston, and Jeffrey S. Passel, Editors
1990   *Undocumented Migration to the United States: IRCA and the Experience of the 1980s*. Washington, D.C.: Urban Institute Press.
Been, Bil
1989   Irish and Illegal in America. *Christian Science Monitor*, March 23: 14.
Benjamin, Rachel
1997   Green Card Lottery Requires Luck and Lots of Lobbying. *Bronx Beat*, March 17.
Bennett, Philip
1993   On Boston's Fringes. Lack of a Network Frustrates New Irish Immigrants. *Boston Globe*, October 27: 1:2.
Berberyusz, Ewa
1987   Przywiazcie mnie sznurami. *Tygodnik Powszechny*, September 30.
Bukowczyk, John J.
1987   *And My Children Did Not Know Me*. Bloomington: Indiana University Press.
Carol, Joe
1998   Letter from America. *Irish Times*, May 2: 15.
Cichon, Donald J., Elzbieta M. Gozdziak, and Jane G. Grover
1986   *The Economic and Social Adjustment of Non-Southeast Asian Refugees*. Falls Church, Virginia: Research Management Corporation.
Connor, Tom
1985   *Irish Youth in London: Research Report*. London: London Irish Centre.
Conover, Kirsten A.
1998   Shifts Begin to Appear in Boston's Venerable "Southie" Community. *Christian Science Monitor*, March 10: 10.
Corcoran, Mary P.
1993   *Irish Illegals: Transients between Two Societies*. Westport, Connecticut: Greenwood Press.
1996   Emigrants, Entrepreneurs, and Opportunists. A Social Profile of Recent Irish Immigration in New York City. In *The New York Irish*. Edited by Ronald H. Bayor and Timothy J. Meagher. Baltimore: Johns Hopkins University Press.

DeVries, Hilary
1982   Chicago's "Little Warsaw." *Christian Science Monitor*, February 4: B7.
Erdmans, Mary P.
1992   The Social Construction of Emigration as a Moral Issue. *Polish American Studies* 49 (1): 5–25.
1998   *Opposite Poles. Immigrants and Ethnics in Polish Chicago, 1976–1990*. University Park: Pennsylvania State University Press.
Fernandez, Edward W., and J. Gregory Robinson
1994   Illustrative Ranges of the Distribution of Undocumented Immigrants by State. Technical Working Paper No. 8. U.S. Bureau of the Census.
Glowny Urzad Statystyczny
1989   *Rocznik Statystyczny*. Warsaw.
Goode, Judith, and Jo Anne Schneider
1994   *Reshaping Ethnic and Racial Relations in Philadelphia*. Philadelphia: Temple University Press.
Gozdziak, Elzbieta M.
1989   *New Americans: The Economic Adaptation of Eastern European, Afghan and Ethiopian Refugees*. Washington, D.C.: Refugee Policy Group.
1996   Eastern Europeans. In *Refugees in America in the 1990s. A Reference Handbook*. Edited by David W. Haines. Westport, Connecticut: Greenwood Press.
Governmental Commission on Population
1989   *Demographic Situation of Poland. 1989 Report*. Warsaw.
Kaufman, Michael T.
1992   For Greenpoint's Poles, an Uncertain Prosperity. *New York Times*, October 3, A: 27:3.
Korcelli, Piotr
1992   International Migration in Europe: Polish Perspectives for the 1990s. *International Migration Review* 26 (2): 292–304.
Lieberson, Stanley, and Mary C. Waters
1988   *From Many Strands: Ethnic and Racial Groups in Contemporary America*. New York: Russell Sage Foundation.
Migration News
1996   Poland/Romania Emigration. Vol. 3 (5), May.
Morehouse, Ward III
1981   Out of Poland's Strife, a New U.S. Immigration Riddle. *Christian Science Monitor*, April 3: 6.
Mostwin, Danuta
1971   The Transplanted Family. A Study of Social Adjustment of the Polish Immigrant Family to the United States after the Second World War. Ph.D. diss., Columbia University.
1989   The Unknown Polish Immigrant. *Migration World* 17 (2): 24–30.
1991   *Emigranci polscy w USA* [Polish immigrants in the U.S.A.]. Lublin, Poland: Catholic University of Lublin Press.
Mulvihill, Kathleen
1986   U.S. Officials Review Plans to Make It Easier for People Fleeing East Bloc to Gain Asylum. *Christian Science Monitor*, April 4: 3.

Murphy, Dean E.
1997   NATO Invites Upset over U.S. Visa Rules. *Los Angeles Times*, August 11: A-11.
O'Connor, Matt
1992   4 Get Prison Terms for Smuggling Poles. *Chicago Tribune*, October 1, 2C: 3–5.
O'Hanlon, Ray
1998   *The New Irish Americans*. Niwot, Colorado: Roberts Rinehart.
Passel, Jeffrey
1986   Undocumented Immigration. *Annals of the American Academy of Political and Social Science* (487): 181–200.
Passel, Jeffrey, and Rebecca L. Clark
1998   *Immigrants in New York: Their Legal Status, Income, and Taxes*. Washington, D.C.: The Urban Institute.
Shannon, Elizabeth
1997   An Irishwoman's Diary. *Irish Times*, October 13: 17.
Ungar, Sanford J.
1995   *Fresh Blood. The New American Immigrants*. New York: Simon and Schuster.
U.S. Catholic Conference
1988   Undocumented Irish in the U.S. *Migration and Refugee Services Staff Report*. Washington, D.C.
Yancey, William L., Eugene P. Ericksen, and Richard N. Juliani
1976   Emergent Ethnicity: A Review and Reformulation. *American Sociological Review* 41 (3): 391–403.
Znaniecka Lopata, Helena
1994   *Polish Americans*. 2d ed. New Brunswick, New Jersey: Transaction.
Zwick, Mark, and Louise Zwick
1998   Who Are the Illegal Aliens? Laborers Arrested by Police. *Houston Catholic Worker*, June 25.

11

Migration from the Caribbean: Economic and Political Factors versus Legal and Illegal Status

Samuel Martínez

The Caribbean presence in the United States today is growing and becoming ever more salient. In large parts of New York City and Miami, one is never far from the sounds of Haitian Creole, Jamaican English, or Spanish spoken with a Dominican, Puerto Rican, or Cuban accent. Official statistics back up the anecdotal evidence concerning the continuous influx of people who call some Caribbean country their ''home.'' Two Caribbean countries, Cuba and the Dominican Republic, today stand among the top ten countries of origin of foreign-born residents of the United States (with approximately 913,000 and 632,000 immigrants, respectively, as of 1997) (U.S. Census Bureau 1997). Between 1986 and 1996, the leading sources of immigration from the Caribbean have been the Dominican Republic (405,239 immigrants admitted), Haiti (210,636), Jamaica (198,077), Cuba (195,215) and Guyana (106,276) (INS 1997: 33). The first four of these were also among the top eleven countries of birth of immigrants entering the United State during 1995 and 1996 (INS 1997: 22). Undocumented immigrants make up a large segment of this flow. The U.S. Immigration and Naturalization Service (INS) (1997: 198) estimates that 105,000 Haitians, 75,000 Dominicans, and 50,000 Jamaicans reside in the United States without legal authorization.

The socioeconomic profile of immigrants from the Caribbean has much in common with other immigrant groups today. Immigrants from the Caribbean generally have higher than average educational attainment and occupational status for their countries of origin (Portes and Grosfoguel 1994: 58–60, 65). Most of the immigrants are born in cities or migrated to them before coming to the United States (Duany 1994: 105). The majority are young adults who enter the United States singly, rather than in family groups (INS 1997: 55–56). With the notable exception of Haitian "boat people" (Conway and Buchanan Stafford 1996: 183), the immigrants generally have either a roughly equal gender ratio or slightly greater numbers of women than men.[1] In common with many immigrants from other parts of the world, many Caribbean people have experienced downward occupational mobility in the United States, even while earning higher incomes than at home (Duany 1994: 106–108). Very few studies have focused on the occupations, earnings, and socioeconomic mobility of undocumented immigrants from the Caribbean, but at least one case study (Grasmuck 1984) indicates that documented and undocumented migrants differ not so much in their earnings or occupational profile (both find work predominantly in the light manufacturing and service sectors) as in their levels of unionization and mode of remuneration (cash vs. check). This finding suggests that the undocumented are concentrated disproportionately in the smallest firms, "many of which appear to be clandestine or off-the-books operations" (Grasmuck 1984: 710). Other studies point out that Caribbean immigrants as a whole "are not solely unskilled workers but comprise a diversified lot that includes entrepreneurs, professionals, technicians, and skilled workers as well" (Portes and Grosfoguel 1994: 49; Foner 1987; Sutton and Chaney 1987; Grenier and Stepick 1992; Portes and Stepick 1993; Pessar 1997).

The social process of Caribbean migration also has much in common with migration in other world regions. Many early immigrants did not move spontaneously but were recruited by U.S. employers. Frequently, the jobs were for nurses and domestic servants, and it may be primarily for this reason that Caribbean women have, perhaps to an unusual degree, been the pioneers of family immigration chains (Foner 1987: 199–200; Woldemikael 1989: 25, 28; Sutton 1992: 246). Other early immigrants sought refuge from political upheavals in their home islands. Pioneer migrants assisted the immigration of kin and fellow villagers by sending home money to help pay for the trip and offering new arrivals a place to stay and contacts and information vital to finding their own employment and lodging (Laguerre 1984: 78; Basch 1987: 167; Foner 1987: 198; Georges 1990: 94–97).

Migration out of the Caribbean has assumed massive proportions only in the past forty years (Duany 1994: 99). From the North American perspective, the relative recency of immigration on a large scale may give the impression that there has been a sudden outburst of movement in the region. This appearance is deceiving. Migration from the Caribbean today grows out of much earlier flows of migrants *within* the region itself. Migration traditions were established very early. In most islands, freed people and their descendants began to move outward immediately after the abolition of slavery (Thomas Hope 1978; Marshall 1982; Richardson 1983: Chapter 1). Migration began, in part, as a reaction to political and economic schemes designed to perpetuate the privileges of race and great property enjoyed by former slaveholders on the migrants' home islands. Not least of the legacies of slavery is the region's general poverty and chronic external economic dependence. At its most acute, dearth of economic opportunity has left Caribbean islanders little choice other than grossly underpaid, physically debilitating field labor at home or the risks of travel on the open seas and uncertain employment abroad.

The combined economic and political causes of emigration from the Caribbean have only confused the U.S. public and policymakers about what attitude they ought to adopt toward these immigrants. Asking simple questions about immigration—Is it oppression or poverty that drives emigration from these islands? Are these migrants political or economic refugees?—has yielded only uncertain answers. Filling the void of this uncertainty has been an official policy seemingly guided more by political expediency, Cold War ideology, and racial prejudice than by verifiable evidence concerning the politics and economics of the region. The result has been shifting and at times contradictory official responses toward the region's immigrants.

My focus is on the intricate connections between economics and politics in the shaping of immigration flows from the Caribbean. I first review the historical background of human geographical mobility in the Caribbean. I then examine how both relative proximity and the presence of an ocean barrier between the Caribbean and the United States have influenced the immigrants' modes of transit and U.S. government policy. In the context of a case study of immigration from Haiti and the Dominican Republic, I also consider both U.S. responses to undocumented immigration and the criticisms leveled at this policy by immigrants' rights advocates and academicians. The academic studies point to the conclusion that neither political refugees versus economic migrants nor ''legal'' versus ''illegal'' immigrants form distinct, easily identified groups. Contrary to assumptions that have shaped both U.S. policy and public debate concerning immigration, political and economic concerns are intertwined in the determinants of migration from the Caribbean. Similarly, legal and illegal residents may be more closely linked to each other through ties of kinship and community than is commonly supposed.

HISTORICAL BACKGROUND

Historically, the Caribbean was largely populated through forced immigration, and its lands were put into production by labor bound to the land in chattel slavery or contracts of indenture. Hence, it is not surprising that after emancipation geographical mobility might very soon become a means for the newly freed to assert their freedom. Nor is it any wonder that freed people and their descendants might feel entirely justified in flouting any new legal restrictions placed on their freedom by former masters seeking to retain privileged access to their labor.

But it is not entirely obvious what ''freedom'' meant to those who had experienced chattel slavery. It seems not too much to infer that, for former slaves, freedom included not just legal personhood but *economic* well-being. As Gerald

Murray (1977: 54) surmises, concerning Saint-Domingue/Haiti, "The desires for freedom which must have been felt by the majority of the slaves were not desires for freedom in the abstract, but for freedom to dedicate all of their labor to their own economic pursuits." Even more clearly, freedom had to be *based on* successful economic adaptation. Winning freedom was one thing; keeping it, another, and for freedom to be preserved, former slaves had to establish autonomous livelihoods (Mintz 1985).

Persistent Unfreedom

After the abolition of slavery, a combination of legal and economic constraints on labor mobility remained an important part of the context of migration in the Caribbean. Agricultural workers, even though no longer legally bound to the land, found that poverty and the law placed severe limits on their freedom of economic maneuver. On most islands, even though the people were now legally free, the land remained firmly in the hands of a few leading families. Where planter-orchestrated scarcity of economic resources did not suffice to bring large quantities of labor to commercial agriculture at low wages, ruling elites were not above enacting legislation aimed at tying former slaves to the land. Where that failed to produce the needed cheap and compliant labor, migration itself became a focus of island government intervention, through the promotion of indentured immigration and the passage of laws discouraging emigration.

Even Haiti's early rulers enacted laws designed to favor plantations over small farms. In 1804, Haiti had become the world's first country to achieve independence from European colonial rule through a revolution that sought freedom not just for the local propertied classes but for all its people, including the enslaved. Yet Haiti's early leaders—Dessalines, Christophe, Pétion, and Boyer—placed limits on the minimum quantity of land that could be exchanged or inherited and enacted antivagrancy legislation to recruit labor for large agricultural estates and infrastructure projects by force, suggesting that they envisioned a state made strong by the same plantation exports that had enriched their former French masters (Lepkowski 1968: 122; Murray 1977: 77). Labor mobility was decisive in undermining this vision of Haiti's future. After the revolution, the freed people had one decisive advantage: the availability of large tracts of unused land in the interior. Having the option of clearing their own small holdings, few Haitians were content to work the land of others for wages or a share of the crop. Former slaves also moved away from the coastal plains to escape onerous taxes and forced military recruitment. Landowners who were loath to farm the soil with their own hands could find no one to work for them as day laborers or tenants. Many beneficiaries of large state land grants made the best of a bad situation by selling to people who had no legal title to land (Murray 1977: 102).

A more difficult climate for internal mobility prevailed on islands where the planters remained securely in political control. With the abolition of slavery in the British West Indies in 1838, planters generally repudiated rights of free access to housing and provision, grounds that previously had been customarily granted to slaves, imposing rents for use of dwellings and land that in many cases the inhabitants had built and improved with their own hands. The application of these "wage-rent systems" varied considerably, but everywhere their intent was to restrict the employment alternatives of former slaves by making access to housing, subsistence plots, and family burial plots conditional on continued supply of field labor (Bolland 1992: 121–122). Many freed people responded by moving away from the estates to settlements on the margins of the plantations (Hall 1978). In Jamaica, Trinidad, and British Guiana, especially, many were assisted in obtaining land for residences and small farms by the economic downturn that hit the British West Indian sugar industries in the 1840s (Bolland 1992: 126–127). As planters fell into financial trouble, many sold pieces of their land or entire estates, enabling those who could afford land to establish independent villages and peasant livelihoods and thus diminish their direct subordination to the plantation economy.

British West Indian legislatures were quick to enact legal measures aimed at repairing the fissures in planter control opened by the economic crisis. These included laws to restrict emigration and vagrancy, taxes designed to pressure people into wage labor, the use of wage-rent and debt-peonage systems to tie workers to the land, the enactment of a series of masters and servants laws placing binding contracts on labor, and the expansion of police, judicial, and penal systems to back up the new laws (Bolland 1992). Legislation was largely ineffective in curbing emigration, but, in Trinidad and British Guiana especially, massive government-sponsored *immigration* was perhaps the most ambitious and effective official measure taken toward reviving the plantation sector. Largely using tax money contributed by ex-slaves, immigrants were transported from India in the tens of thousands as indentured laborers, bound to plantation labor for a period of years, normally five (Williams 1970: 358).

Postemancipation Migrations

When freed people and their descendants emigrated, it was, in part, an effort to shake off lingering economic and political bonds such as these. As Bonham Richardson (1983: 6) remarks concerning the Commonwealth Caribbean, "Migrating away for wages, although the earliest destinations were often other plantation islands, was an assertion of independence. It was not a complete escape from the larger plantation sphere, but neither did it represent a docile willingness to accept local conditions dictated by former plantation masters." Across much of the Antilles, migrants' repatriated savings financed the purchase of residential, agricultural, and commercial properties. Even where it did no more than subsidize consumption at home, migrant money helped Afro-Caribbean people distance themselves from direct plantation control.

Until the middle decades of the twentieth century, many more Caribbean emigrants went to destinations elsewhere in the Caribbean than went to Europe or North America. The emigrants left islands where foreign capital was stagnating or being withdrawn and moved toward places into which European and North American capital had been freshly injected (Marshall 1982: 8). By the 1950s, when people from the Caribbean began to go in large numbers to Western Europe and North America, a migration tradition had already long been established. Migration from the British West Indies to Britain and from Puerto Rico to the United States was set in motion largely to supply needed unskilled labor, after World War II (Richardson 1992: 142). In 1965, the door to Britain was closing, but the United States began to accept many immigrants from the English-speaking Caribbean. Political refugees were also instrumental in starting large-scale migrations from Haiti, the Dominican Republic, and especially Cuba (Portes and Grosfoguel 1994: 57).

An important part of these migration traditions has been a strong ''return orientation,'' manifested perhaps less often via actual return than by actions aimed at retaining claims to homeland property and participating at a distance in the lives of people at home (Rubenstein 1982). Leaving home in order to return with enhanced means has become an accepted turn in the life course (and perhaps even an *expected* life experience) for millions of Caribbean people. The return orientation helps assure that the influence of the emigrants is felt in even the most remote villages, through gifts in-kind and in cash sent home from North America (Richardson 1992: 133). The life chances of many people in the Caribbean are now bound up with the fate of family members working in the United States.

TRANSIT

The ocean that surrounds each Caribbean state presents a significant barrier to be overcome in migrating to the United States. Immediately after emancipation in the British West Indies, seafarers from several islands began shuttling migrants to Trinidad and British Guiana, in small wooden sailing craft (Richardson 1983: 18–19). The voyage was risky, and uncounted migrants were lost at sea. Steamboat and air travel brought improvements in distance, speed, and safety. Yet, because these modes of transportation generally took the form of regulated commercial voyages, it became easier for officials, shipping agents, and labor recruiters to monitor and control migration at ports of departure and entry.

By the late 1960s, U.S. consulates began to exercise greater skepticism in the evaluation of requests for resident visas as well as demanding stronger proof of intent to return for tourist visas, in the form of assets held by the applicants at home. On the basis of ethnographic fieldwork in one rural area in the Dominican Republic, Eugenia Georges (1990: 85) reports that visa brokers responded to tightened official restrictions by channeling migrants along other paths, including travel by air to Puerto Rico and Mexico and stowing away on cargo ships.

Others obtained forged immigration documents or "rented" papers from genuine visa holders. Obtaining official or falsified documents added to the already high cost of travel by air. Georges also confirms the observation made by Vivian Garrison and Carol Weiss (1987: 248–249) that Dominicans rank different modes of entry along a continuum of desirability and approval but attach little or no stigma to undocumented migration per se. Similarly, Charles Carnegie (1983, cited in Richardson 1992: 145) concludes that "legal" and "illegal" modes of entry are viewed by Caribbean people more as bureaucratic obstacles to circumvent than as immutable law.

The "Boat People"

Beginning in the 1970s, increasingly restrictive INS policies and procedures led many of those who lived within reach of the United States to opt for the riskier option of sailing to southern Florida in small wooden boats. Since the 1960s, mainly rural Haitians had been migrating to the Bahamas in small boats and as stowaways on freighters (Marshall 1979).[2] The increased hostility of the Bahamian authorities might have been a factor redirecting boat emigrants toward the United States, but both the Bahamas and Cuba continued to be used as staging points on the long journey to southern Florida (Conway and Buchanan Stafford 1996: 178). Contrary to popular perception, the boat people have not been drawn from the poorest Haitians: as early as 1980, boat captains were charging sums of $1,000 or more per person for passage to Florida (Allman 1982: 11), which many people in Haiti could not possibly afford.

Simultaneously and largely unknown to the U.S. mainland public, clandestine migration in open wooden boats has brought tens of thousands of Dominicans to U.S. territory, not by crossing the Florida Strait but by traversing the Mona Channel, which separates the Dominican Republic from Puerto Rico. This migration was not set in motion by recruitment or even by the promise of work opportunities for Dominicans in Puerto Rico. It began, rather, as Dominicans became aware that neighboring Puerto Rico might offer a "back door" for entering the U.S. mainland. Undetermined numbers of Dominicans have made the surreptitious crossing by sea and obtained fraudulent documents that identify them as Puerto Ricans. If undetected by INS officials, these Dominicans posing as Puerto Ricans can freely travel to the mainland. Also, many Dominicans have stayed in Puerto Rico and found work mainly in low-income, nonunion jobs in construction, domestic service, and petty commerce (Duany 1987: 119–121; Iturrondo 1993; Duany, Hernández Angueira, and Rey 1995: 52–56). The crossing between the Dominican Republic and Puerto Rico is shorter (seventy-five miles) and less dangerous but, even so, has produced its share of tragedies at sea, and the Dominican boat people, too, have been targets of intensive U.S. Coast Guard surveillance.

The Haitians have been the major focus of critics of U.S. immigration policy, while the Dominican boat people have received little notice, but migration from both countries poses difficult questions about U.S. policy, questions to which I turn next.

IMMIGRATION FROM HISPANIOLA

Haiti and the Dominican Republic

After Cuba, Hispaniola is the largest island of the Antilles. It is one of only two Caribbean islands (the other being tiny St. Martin) to be divided between two sovereign states, Haiti and the Dominican Republic. The two nations are also set apart by distinct histories of European colonization and divergent paths of economic development. The French colony of Saint-Domingue (later to become Haiti) was founded in the seventeenth century, after Spain ceded to France the western part of the island. In the eighteenth century, the brutal exploitation of hundreds of thousands of enslaved Africans made Saint-Domingue the most profitable European overseas colony of its time. By contrast, the Spanish regarded the island chiefly as a way station on the route to Middle America, and Santo Domingo lagged far behind its western neighbor in trade and population. The Haitian revolution, beginning in 1791, overthrew European power across the island. In the decades following the revolution, Haiti was militarily and commercially the dominant power on the island.

The opposed destinies of the two nations took a new twist in the last quarter of the nineteenth century. At this time, global demand for tropical staples stimulated capital-intensive agriculture in the Dominican Republic, while Haiti's prohibition of land sales to foreign interests impeded large-scale investment. The establishment of each major plantation sent out ripples of migration, as displaced agriculturalists and herders avoided the sugar estates and moved on to claim land elsewhere as their own (Calder 1981: 19). To take the place of the local workers, the sugar companies recruited harvest workers from various Leeward Islands and eventually from Haiti (Castillo 1978).

For a complex set of reasons, most attempts at establishing plantation agriculture in Haiti failed dismally, and Haiti remained the preeminent "peasant" society of the Caribbean, in the sense that its land lay mostly in the hands of smallholders (Mintz 1989). Effective control of the land should have afforded the Haitian masses a long period of prosperity, yet Haitian leaders were not about to let the freed people prosper and the state go to ruin. In taxes, Haitian rulers found a foolproof way of getting revenue out of even the most remote rural areas. Throughout most of its history, the Haitian government has raised revenues primarily through taxes on basic consumer goods and duties on basic imports and exports. As Trouillot (1985: 13) remarks, "It is not too much to suggest that the peasantry, almost alone, was subsidizing the Haitian state." The hostility of the world's great powers and the greed of international merchants also played a part in pushing Haiti into poverty (Trouillot 1990: 50–80). But the poverty that was a necessary condition for rural Haitians to want to emigrate in large numbers was largely a product of regressive taxation and other forms of indirect exploitation imposed by Haiti's rulers. The Duvaliers, rulers of Haiti from 1957 to 1986, added nothing fundamentally new to the means of self-enrichment enjoyed by earlier Haitian heads of state, but they did use unprecedented brutality in repressing all political opposition and dissent (Trouillot 1990: 170).

In spite of the two countries' cultural differences and divergent paths of development, there are a number of important similarities in the development and composition of migration from Haiti and the Dominican Republic. Emigration from both countries may be said to have begun largely with people fleeing political persecution. Haitians fled the Duvalier dictatorship after 1957 (Conway and Buchanan Stafford 1996: 178), while a small number of Dominicans first sought exile from the Trujillo regime (until 1961), followed by larger numbers who were expelled during the political instability of the early 1960s (Torres-Saillant and Hernández 1998: 42–44). Both migrations spread to ordinary working people after 1965 and assumed mass proportions as pioneer migrants assisted relatives, friends, and fellow villagers in relocating to the north (Georges 1990: 92–97; Stepick 1998: 16–21).

Large Haitian colonies have developed in Miami, Boston, and Montreal, but New York City has been the area of destination for hundreds of thousands of immigrants from both countries (Portes and Grosfoguel 1994: 60). New York's Haitian and Dominican populations are now surpassed in number only by those of Port-au-Prince and Santo Domingo, respectively. Both Dominicans and Haitians have settled mainly in poor urban neighborhoods and have found employment mainly in low-income service and manufacturing jobs (Grasmuck and Pessar 1991: 164–65; Stepick 1998: 41). Since the 1980s, the primary sector of employment among Dominicans in New York City has shifted from manufacturing to trade, reflecting a decline in the city's manufacturing sector, as well as possibly a transfer of jobs to the rising Dominican enclave economy, centered in Washington Heights (Portes and Guarnizo 1991: 59–66; Torres-Saillant and Hernández 1998: 65–67, 76–80). By contrast, the first wave of Haitian immigrants, who settled mainly in New York City before 1980, had fairly high levels of schooling (64.4 percent high school graduates and 21.4 percent graduates of four-year colleges and professional schools) (Portes and Grosfoguel 1994: 65). The second wave of immigrants, who moved largely to southern Florida beginning in the 1970s, possessed far less human capital (Stepick 1998: 38). Media images of bedraggled Haitian boat people struggling to shore also contributed to a public perception of Haitian immigrants generally as "illiterate, impoverished individuals who would drain public resources" (Conway and Buchanan Stafford 1996: 179). Haitians were further stigmatized by U.S. government health officials and the press as carriers of tuberculosis and the human immunodeficiency virus (HIV) (Stepick 1998: 34–35). The Haitians who entered as boat people have had particular difficulty in obtaining steady, well-paid employment. This group has been held back largely by low levels of educational attainment (an average of less than elementary school), by their limited knowledge of English and Spanish, by a saturated unskilled labor market in southern Florida, and by the lack of a preexisting Haitian ethnic enclave economy such as Cuban entrants found in Miami (Stepick 1992; Stepick and Portes 1986).

U.S. Policy

It has been difficult for U.S. authorities to formulate an effective and humane policy toward the Haitian boat people. Until 1981, authorities made no systematic effort to prevent Haitian boat immigrants from reaching U.S. shores, but undocumented entrants who fell into official custody on land were generally detained and deported as fast as possible. The "immigration crisis" of 1980—when roughly 125,000 Cubans and 25,000 Haitians came by boat to southern Florida—precipitated a major toughening of U.S. policy. After losing a lengthy court battle to deport the Haitian detainees, the government permitted most to remain in the United States. This action went along with a new border policing initiative aimed at preventing any further massive influxes of boat people from Haiti. The U.S. Coast Guard began to intercept Haitian immigrants on the high seas, returning most to Haiti after perfunctory asylum screening procedures at sea (Mitchell 1994).[3] Even intensive Coast Guard patrolling of the waters off Haiti and southern Florida was not totally effective, but the new policy effectively curtailed further immigration by sea.

U.S. policy faced a new challenge beginning in 1991, when the freely elected government of Jean-Bertrand Aristide was overthrown by the Haitian military, setting in motion a massive new wave of boat emigrants. Press accounts of the brutal repression of Aristide's supporters and fear of provoking a storm of public criticism made it politically untenable to continue immediate repatriation of the detainees. Instead, the United States hurriedly set up a refugee camp for the Haitian detainees at its military base at Guantánamo, Cuba. From this staging point, almost one-third of the early detainees were permitted to apply for asylum. By January 1992, U.S. officials began to deport those who were deemed to be economic migrants. These measures failed to dissuade further migration by sea. On the contrary, the number of boat people grew to the point that 10,000 were intercepted during the month of May 1992 alone. At this point, the Bush administration in Washington implemented an even more draconian policy than existed before Aristide's overthrow, by deciding that detained boats would be escorted directly back to Haiti, without allowing any asylum screening at all. This policy drew criticism from many, including members of the U.S. Congressional Black Caucus and presidential candidate Bill Clinton. In spite of this, the policy of immediate and total repatriation of Haitian immigrants intercepted at sea was continued by the incoming Clinton administration and was upheld by the U.S. Supreme Court, by a vote of 8 to 1 (Mitchell 1994; Stepick 1998: 107–108).

The fundamental premise of U.S. immigration policy is that it is possible to distinguish immigrants who are fleeing political repression from immigrants seeking economic betterment. The U.S. policy opposing undocumented immigration by sea from Haiti is based on the assertion that these are economically motivated migrants, not refugees. The immigrants, on the other hand, have mostly contended that they are victims of political persecution in Haiti or have at least claimed to come seeking freedom as well as work in the United States (Mitchell 1994: 72–73).

Some critics of U.S. policy have implicitly accepted the possibility of distinguishing refugees from economic migrants, while stating or implying that Haitian boat people were, in the majority, direct targets of persecution at the hands of Haitian government agents (Lawyers Committee 1990; Americas Watch 1993) or were likely to become victims if returned to Haiti (Americas Watch 1992; Amnesty International 1993). These critics of U.S. policy have included human rights and immigrants' rights pressure groups and African-American politicians and civic leaders (Mitchell 1994: 76). From 1980 to 1982, the detention of undocumented Haitian entrants at the Krome INS facility in southern Florida was a focus of criticism. Haitians' rights advocates argued that it was unfair to hold the Haitians behind high fences while most of the Cuban "Marielitos" were rapidly set free. Similar criticisms were later directed at the detention of Haitian boat people in Guantánamo between 1991 and 1994 (Stepick 1998: 103, 107). Advocates of Haitian immigrants' rights have also fought for more humane treatment of detainees and more fair and thorough asylum screening procedures. "Haitians and their advocates have fought an unparalleled series of legal battles to ensure that claimants receive due process of law: fair treatment, including access to Creole interpreters and attorneys at INS hearings; and work authorizations on release from INS detention" (Conway and Buchanan Stafford 1996: 180). The immigrants have won a number of important legal victories, and the federal government has been repeatedly rebuked by the courts for intentionally discriminating against Haitians.

Economic and Political Factors behind Migration

Academic critiques of U.S. policy toward the boat people have questioned the validity of drawing a sharp line between political and economic factors among the root causes of emigration from Haiti. In a study done among Haitians in Quebec, Larose (1985: 30) found that migrants' motives for leaving home were complex, commonly combining political, economic, familial, and personal concerns. A more radical view had it that poverty and dictatorship were so inextricably linked under the Duvalier dictatorship that it was artificial and misleading even to draw a distinction between political and economic motivations in assessing Haitians' claims of asylum (Laraque 1979). According to Stepick (1998: 104), "Empirically distinguishing between economic immigrants and political refugees was fundamentally impossible." A similar argument held that poverty itself was the central political issue and source of unrest and repression in Haiti. That there was a considerable kernel of truth to this argument is borne out by the observation that saying "I am hungry" to an agent of the paramilitary Tonton Macoute could easily be interpreted as an act of political protest, leading to a beating, detention, or even torture or death (Stepick 1983: 177). Poverty itself was an inducement to abuses of power, as when low-level Macoutes availed themselves of other people's property through the use of force or threats of punishment.

Oddly, even the U.S. chief executive came around to the position that there was a large political component to the reasons Haitians were leaving home when President Clinton cited the desirability of stemming further flows of Haitian boat people as one justification for U.S. intervention in 1994 to reinstate Jean-Bertrand Aristide to power in Haiti (Jehl 1994). As U.S. congressional representative Major Owens stated in 1991, "The best way not to have the problem that has been placed on our doorstep by this current wave of Haitians trying to leave is to have a policy where we support unequivocally democracy and the democratic process in Haiti" (cited in Mitchell 1994: 78).

A broad range of actors and commentators has supported democracy in Haiti and hoped that the end of violent repression and the establishment of democratic rule there would bring clandestine boat emigration to an end. In favor of this opinion, it must be observed that both Aristide's election in 1990 and his restoration to power in 1994 were followed by near cessation of unauthorized immigration by sea. But recent upswings in apprehension of Haitian boat people at sea and in southern Florida may soon shake confidence that the restoration of procedural democracy alone can contain the desperation of many Haitians to escape from poverty. It seems that overthrowing the Duvalier dictatorship, dissolving the Haitian army and paramilitary death squads, and alternation of leadership via open elections are failing to produce hoped-for improvement in the economy and standard of living. The roots of social and economic inequality in Haiti reach much more widely into society and further back in time than the Duvaliers and their cronies. That the lifting of government sanctioned repression in Haiti has brought neither greater prosperity nor an end to harrowing attempts to migrate by sea suggests a need for further study of the links between politics and the development of a poverty so severe that it seemingly leaves people no choice but to emigrate.

There is also a need for empirical analysis of the meaning of such concepts as "rights," "freedom," and "democracy" for Haitians. In a conference paper, Jennie Smith presents evidence that ordinary Haitians perceive an important economic content in these ideas. She movingly recounts her experiences as an aid worker and member of the United Nations/Organization of American States (UN/OAS) International Civilian Mission to Haiti. Sent into the countryside to teach Haitian peasants about civil rights and democracy, she instead learned that "these illiterate peasant farmers did not *lack* an understanding of 'democracy,' but rather understood on a profound level the problems plaguing their society and the changes that were necessary in order to ameliorate those problems"

(Smith 1994: 5). Specifically, when asked what "democracy" meant to them, these ordinary Haitians included, alongside free speech, enough good food to eat, clean water to drink, putting their children through school, and access to quality medical care.

Illegal Immigration and the Family

A second set of academic critiques holds that INS policy more often hampers than promotes its stated goal of "family reunification." Faced with a system of preferences for admission based on a definition of "family" more narrow than their own, Caribbean migrants must at times bend or break the letter of the law to find ways for their most important loved ones to enter the United States. In a classic case study, Garrison and Weiss (1987) trace the strategies used by one Dominican family, the "Domínguezes," in reuniting on U.S. soil. Like so many other Caribbean immigrant families, the Domínguezes' relocation to the United States began in the early 1960s with the legal immigration of a woman, one of the family's daughters, to do paid domestic work.[4] This pioneer migrant set in motion a chain of migration that ultimately included her parents, five out of her six living siblings, the husband of her youngest sister, and several of her Dominican-born nieces and nephews, as well as her consensual husband's brother. The whole sequence of events is too convoluted to summarize here, but the legal and illegal mechanisms used by the Domínguez family include:

1. Papers for work arranged from the Dominican Republic;
2. Being "asked for," with residence visa arranged in the Dominican Republic;
3. A marriage of convenience contracted as a personal favor;
4. A marriage of convenience contracted for money;
5. Overstaying a tourist visa;
6. Switching passports between a U.S.-born great-grandson and a Dominican-born grandson, born at approximately the same time;
7. "Purchasing a passport" from a tourist visa holder (later returned to the owner for use by another customer).

The Domínguezes' story was, in the end, a happy one, because "immigration regulations did not prevent the entry of an expected number of kin based on what might have been projected on the basis of the family constellation in 1965" (Garrison and Weiss 1987: 248). In spite of this, Garrison and Weiss rightly point out that the process was not painless or risk-free and that the strategies involved, "while adaptive in the short run, cannot be conducive to the long-run stability and cohesiveness of the Dominican family." For the Domínguezes, the whole process took well over a decade to accomplish, largely because of the many months it took to obtain visas even for family members who belonged to the INS preference categories. Also, the need to make recourse to tactics such as marriages of convenience places strain precisely on the bonds that U.S. immigration policy intends to protect: the relationships between spouses and between parents and children. "Not only are parents and their adult offspring and siblings (not included in preference categories) separated, but spouses . . . and parents and their minor children (preferred) are frequently separated for long periods" (Garrison and Weiss 1987: 248). For example, a woman who enters the United States through a marriage of convenience cannot claim any children she leaves behind in her home country until she serves out the two-year probationary period for permanent residence and cannot claim a consensual husband left behind without the further delays of undoing her fictitious marriage and legally marrying her "real" husband. In the case of the Domínguez family, the separations between spouses and children averaged two and a half to three years. Studies among other Caribbean immigrant populations have confirmed these general findings (Fjellman and Gladwin 1985), while differing on the relative importance to migrant network formation of consanguineal ties versus families formed through the marriage bond (Matthei and Smith 1996).

Contrary to the widespread perception that there are easily distinguishable groups of "legal" and "illegal" immigrants in the United States, the line between authorized and unauthorized immigrants does not always fall between family groups but often cuts through a single family. Persecution and deportation of the undocumented may therefore produce an increased number of cases where husbands are separated from wives, and parents are separated from children. Anecdotal evidence, drawn largely from Spanish-language press sources, suggests that this effect may already be occurring, as the INS more aggressively inspects immigrants' workplaces and as criminal resident aliens are increasingly deported rather than imprisoned in the United States.[5]

ASSESSMENT

Recent scholarship has contributed a great deal to elucidating the complex of political and economic factors behind immigration from the Caribbean. Yet, in retrospect, academicians and lawmakers alike seem to have pinned exaggerated hopes on democracy's being the cure for both Haitian poverty and unauthorized migration by sea. That the exodus by boat has been renewed, in spite of four years of freedom from government-sponsored political repression in Haiti, suggests that it was also an exaggeration to claim that most of the boat people were direct targets of persecution at the hands of agents of the state.

It is my contention that politics and economics *are* indissolubly linked in the determinants of emigration from the Caribbean but that to understand this, it is necessary to reach deeper than the immediate past and the most obvious infringements of civil liberties. Today, poverty is not so clearly rooted in abuses of civil rights as it was in the immediate aftermath of chattel slavery. In most Caribbean societies, legal restrictions on workers' civil liberties gave way over the course of the nineteenth and twentieth centuries to systems of economic constraints, in which workers' consumption needs and aspirations, combined with market-based rewards and penalties, came to assume primary responsibility for mobilizing large surpluses of cheap labor for seasonal employment in commercial agriculture. Yet, during and after the era of slavery, the landed elites of most Caribbean societies sought to narrow the alternatives to field labor available to the masses of rural working people and used both political and economic pressures to keep their islands' working people down. Bodies of law and police and military forces protected large property and assisted in channeling workers in their thousands toward large commercial farms. Therefore, from the first, a *politically* managed scarcity of economic resources on these islands made it necessary for people hoping to expand their opportunities to travel to other countries for work.

Today, political and economic factors are still intertwined in the forces and motivations that set emigrants in motion. Haitian people know that having political rights is worth little without also having at least the food, potable water, medicine, and access to education needed to live with dignity in the modern world. It therefore comes as little surprise that geographical mobility might still be regarded by them as a road to greater freedom, as well as prosperity.

Similarly, it is an illusion to think that separate groups of "legal" and "illegal" entrants can be identified on the ground and that the undocumented can be deported without splitting nuclear families, extended families, and community networks. Many immigrants' families include both people with and without proper immigration documents. Also, individuals who entered the United States illegally have often ended up obtaining legal residence status. The notion that there are ("good") legal entrants and ("bad") undocumented immigrants who stand as discrete social groups may be as much an illusion as the idea that there are discrete groups of politically and economically motivated movers.

As evidenced by the contradictions and turnarounds in the treatment of Cuban and Haitian entrants, U.S. policy has been dictated more by political convenience and possibly racial prejudice than by the elusive and possibly spurious distinction between political refugees and economic migrants. It is time to reject the simple dichotomies (migrant/refugee and legal/illegal) that have, in principle, guided U.S. immigration and refugee policy and open up public debate to consider the more complex factors that are putting people in motion in the Caribbean.

NOTES

Monica van Beusekom read and commented on this chapter in draft form.

1. In 1996, the sex ratio among immigrants from the top five Caribbean source countries ranged from 57.1 percent male and 42.9 percent females (among Cubans) to 46 percent male and 54 percent female (among Guyanese) (INS 1997: 55–56).

2. It is testimony to the impact of the migration to the Bahamas on Haitian popular consciousness that by the 1970s the Creole term "*fè nasomân*" ("to do a 'Nassau-

man' '') had come to refer to any surreptitious, unauthorized entry, such as sneaking into a dance club without paying for a ticket.

3. In the ten years between 1981 and 1991, only 28 detainees out of 25,000 were ultimately found to have a ''well-founded fear of persecution'' and permitted to stay in the United States (Mitchell 1994: 73).

4. Among Dominicans, the pioneer migrants have more often been men than women (Pessar 1982: 359; Georges 1990: 94). Yet immigration has often readjusted the balance of power in the household, as women's status and worth within the home improve as an unforeseen by-product of their waged employment (Pessar 1986).

5. ''For 1996, the INS removed 36,909 criminals, an increase of 36.5 percent over the previous high in fiscal year 1995'' (INS 1997: 171).

REFERENCES

Allman, James
1982   Haitian Migration: 30 Years Assessed. *Migration Today* 10 (1): 6–12.
Americas Watch
1992   *Half the Story: The Skewed U.S. Monitoring of Repatriated Haitian Refugees.* New York: Americas Watch and National Coalition for Haitian Refugees.
1993   *No Port in a Storm: The Misguided Use of In-Country Refugee Processing in Haiti.* New York: Americas Watch, National Coalition for Haitian Refugees, and Jesuit Refugee Service/USA.
Amnesty International
1993   *United States: Failure to Protect Haitian Refugees.* New York: Amnesty International.
Basch, Linda
1987   The Vincentians and Grenadians: The Role of Voluntary Associations in Immigrant Adaptation to New York City. In *New Immigrants in New York.* Edited by Nancy Foner. New York: Columbia University Press. Pp. 160–193.
Bolland, O. Nigel
1992   The Politics of Freedom in the British Caribbean. In *The Meaning of Freedom: Economics, Politics, and Culture after Slavery.* Edited by Frank McGlynn and Seymour Drescher. Pittsburgh: University of Pittsburgh Press. Pp. 113–146.
Calder, Bruce J.
1981   The Dominican Turn toward Sugar. *Caribbean Review* 10 (3): 18–21, 44–45.
Carnegie, Charles V.
1983   If You Lose the Dog, Grab the Cat. *Natural History* 92 (October): 28, 30–34.
Castillo, José del
1978   *La inmigración de braceros azucareros en la República Dominicana, 1900–1930.* Santo Domingo: Centro Dominicano de Investigaciones Antropológicas (CENDIA), Universidad Autónoma de Santo Domingo.
Conway, Frederick J., and Susan Buchanan Stafford
1996   Haitians. In *Refugees in America in the 1990s: A Reference Handbook.* Edited by David W. Haines. Westport, Connecticut: Greenwood Press. Pp. 170–190.
Duany, Jorge
1987   ''Buscando ambiente'': Estratificación social y minorías étnicas en San Juan, Puerto Rico. *Revista de Ciencias Sociales* (Puerto Rico) 26 (1–4): 105–138.

1994   Beyond the Safety Valve: Recent Trends in Caribbean Migration. *Social and Economic Studies* 43 (1): 95–122.

Duany, Jorge, Luisa Hernández Angueira, and César A. Rey

1995   *El Barrio Gandul: Economía subterránea y migración indocumentada en Puerto Rico*. Caracas: Editorial Nueva Sociedad.

Fjellman, Stephen M., and Hugh Gladwin

1985   Haitian Family Patterns of Migration to South Florida. *Human Organization* 44 (4): 301–312.

Foner, Nancy

1987   The Jamaicans: Race and Ethnicity among Migrants in New York City. In *New Immigrants in New York*. Edited by Nancy Foner. New York: Columbia University Press. Pp. 195–217.

Garrison, Vivian, and Carol Weiss

1987   Dominican Family Networks and United States Immigration Policy: A Case Study. In *Caribbean Life in New York City: Sociocultural Dimensions*. Edited by Constance R. Sutton and Elsa M. Chaney. New York: Center for Migration Studies. Pp. 235–254.

Georges, Eugenia

1990   *The Making of a Transnational Community: Migration, Development, and Cultural Change in the Dominican Republic*. New York: Columbia University Press.

Grasmuck, Sherri

1984   Immigration, Ethnic Stratification, and Native Working Class Discipline: Comparisons of Documented and Undocumented Dominicans. *International Migration Review* 18 (3): 692–713.

Grasmuck, Sherri, and Patricia R. Pessar

1991   *Between Two Islands: Dominican International Migration*. Berkeley: University of California Press.

Grenier, Guillermo J., and Alex Stepick III, Editors

1992   *Miami Now!: Immigration, Ethnicity, and Social Change*. Gainesville: University Press of Florida.

Hall, Douglas

1978   The Flight from the Estates Reconsidered: The British West Indies, 1838–42. *Journal of Caribbean History* nos. 10/11: 7–24.

INS (U.S. Immigration and Naturalization Service)

1997   *Statistical Yearbook of the Immigration and Naturalization Service, 1996*. Washington, D.C.: U.S. Government Printing Office.

Iturrondo, Milagros

1993   "San Ignacio de La Yola" . . . y los dominicanos. *Homines* 17 (1, 2): 234–240.

Jehl, Douglas

1994   Showdown in Haiti. *New York Times*, September 16, Late Edition: A1, col. 6.

Laguerre, Michel

1984   *American Odyssey: Haitians in New York City*. Ithaca, New York: Cornell University Press.

Laraque, Frank

1979   Haitian Emigration to New York. *Migration Today* 7 (4): 28–31.

Larose, Serge

1985   De la Complexité des motifs de la migration: Le Cas haitien. *Revue Internationale d'Action Communautaire* 14 (54): 23–31.

Lawyers Committee
1990   *Refugee Refoulement: The Forced Return of Haitians under the U.S.–Haitian Interdiction Agreement.* New York: Lawyers Committee for Human Rights.

Lepkowski, Tadeusz
1968   *Haití.* Havana: Casa de las Américas.

Marshall, Dawn I.
1979   *"The Haitian Problem": Illegal Migration to the Bahamas.* Kingston: Institute of Social and Economic Research, University of the West Indies.

1982   The History of Caribbean Migrations: The Case of the West Indies. *Caribbean Review* 11 (1): 6–9, 51–53.

Matthei, Linda Miller, and David A. Smith
1996   Women, Households, and Transnational Migration Networks: The Garifuna and Global Economic Restructuring. In *Latin America and the World Economy.* Edited by Roberto Patricio Korzeniewicz and William C. Smith. Westport, Connecticut: Greenwood Press. Pp. 133–149.

Mintz, Sidney W.
1985   From Plantations to Peasantries in the Caribbean. In *Caribbean Contours.* Edited by Sidney W. Mintz and Sally Price. Baltimore: Johns Hopkins University Press. Pp. 127–153.

1989   *Caribbean Transformations.* New York: Columbia University Press.

Mitchell, Christopher
1994   U.S. Policy toward Haitian Boat People, 1972–93. *Annals of the American Academy of Political and Social Science* 534: 69–80.

Murray, Gerald Francis
1977   The Evolution of Haitian Peasant Land Tenure: A Case Study in Agrarian Adaptation to Population Growth. 2 vols. Ph.D. diss., Columbia University.

Pessar, Patricia R.
1982   The Role of Households in International Migration and the Case of U.S.-Bound Migration from the Dominican Republic. *International Migration Review* 16 (2): 342–363.

1986   The Role of Gender in Dominican Settlement in the United States. In *Women and Change in Latin America.* Edited by June Nash and Helen I. Safa. South Hadley: Bergin and Garvey. Pp. 273–291.

Pessar, Patricia R., Editor
1997   *Caribbean Circuits: New Directions in the Study of Caribbean Migration.* New York: Center for Migration Studies.

Portes, Alejandro, and Ramón Grosfoguel
1994   Caribbean Diasporas: Migration and Ethnic Communities. *Annals of the American Academy of Political and Social Science* 533: 48–69.

Portes, Alejandro, and Luis Guarnizo
1991   *Capitalistas del trópico: La inmigración en los Estados Unidos y el desarrollo de la pequeña empresa en la República Dominicana.* Santo Domingo: Facultad Latinoamericana de Ciencias Sociales (FLACSO), Programa República Dominicana, and Johns Hopkins University.

Portes, Alejandro, and Alex Stepick
1993   *City on the Edge: The Transformation of Miami.* Berkeley: University of California Press.

Richardson, Bonham C.

1983   *Caribbean Migrants: Environment and Human Survival on St. Kitts and Nevis.* Knoxville: University of Tennessee Press.

1992   *The Caribbean in the Wider World: A Regional Geography.* Cambridge: Cambridge University Press.

Rubenstein, Hymie

1982   Return Migration to the English-Speaking Caribbean: Review and Commentary. In *Return Migration and Remittances: Developing a Caribbean Perspective.* Edited by William F. Stinner, Klaus de Albuquerque, and Roy S. Bryce-Laporte. Washington, D.C.: Research Institute on Immigration and Ethnic Studies. Pp. 3–34.

Smith, Jennie

1994   ''Rocks in the Water Can't Know the Trouble of Rocks in the Sun'': Efforts of the International Community to Promote Human Rights and ''Restore Democracy'' in Haiti. Paper presented at the Annual Meeting of the American Anthropological Association, Atlanta, Georgia.

Stepick, Alex

1983   Haitian Boat People: A Study in the Conflicting Forces Shaping U.S. Immigration Policy. *Law and Contemporary Problems* 45 (2): 163–196.

1992   The Refugees Nobody Wants: Haitians in Miami. In *Miami Now!: Immigration, Ethnicity, and Social Change.* Edited by Guillermo J. Grenier and Alex Stepick III. Gainesville: University Press of Florida. Pp. 57–82.

1998   *Pride against Prejudice: Haitians in the United States.* Boston: Allyn and Bacon.

Stepick, Alex, and Alejandro Portes

1986   Flight into Despair: A Profile of Recent Haitian Refugees in South Florida. *International Migration Review* 20 (2): 329–350.

Sutton, Constance R.

1992   Some Thoughts on Gendering and Internationalizing Our Thinking about Transnational Migrations. *Annals of the New York Academy of Sciences* 645: 241–249.

Sutton, Constance R., and Elsa M. Chaney, Editors

1987   *Caribbean Life in New York City: Sociocultural Dimensions.* New York: Center for Migration Studies.

Thomas-Hope, Elizabeth M.

1978   The Establishment of a Migration Tradition: British West Indian Movements to the Hispanic Caribbean in the Century after Emancipation. In *Caribbean Social Relations.* Edited by Colin G. Clarke. Liverpool: Centre for Latin-American Studies, University of Liverpool. Pp. 66–81.

Torres-Saillant, Silvio, and Ramona Hernández

1998   *The Dominican Americans.* Westport, Connecticut: Greenwood Press.

Trouillot, Michel-Rolph

1985   *Nation, State, and Society in Haiti, 1804–1984.* Washington, D.C.: Latin America Program, Woodrow Wilson International Center for Scholars.

1990   *Haiti, State against the Nation: The Origins and Legacy of Duvalierism.* New York: Monthly Review Press.

U.S. Census Bureau

1997   *March 1997 Current Population Survey.* Washington, D.C.: U.S. Census Bureau (www.bls.census.gov/cps/).

Williams, Eric
1970   *From Columbus to Castro*. London: Andre Deutsch.
Woldemikael, Tekle Mariam
1989   *Becoming Black American: Haitians and American Institutions in Evanston, Illinois*. New York: AMS Press.

12

Smuggled Chinese in the Mountain of Gold

Ko-lin Chin

Since the mid-nineteenth century, hundreds of thousands of Chinese have immigrated to the United States (Tsai 1986). For many Chinese, the United States is *Jinshan*, or Mountain of Gold (Sung 1967). They see the United States as a country where the streets are paved with gold, and they believe that anybody who makes it to the United States is going to make a fortune. The latest of these Chinese immigrants are the smuggled Fujianese immigrants, and they, too, like earlier immigrants, fantasize about living in the United States. However, because of U.S. immigration quotas, only a limited number of Chinese whose family members are U.S. citizens or who are highly educated have the opportunity to immigrate to, or visit, America (Zhou 1992). Consequently, the Fujianese turned to human traffickers to be smuggled into the United States (U.S. Senate 1992).

According to various sources (Myers 1992; Kwong 1997), most smuggled Chinese in the United States come from Changle city, Tingjiang township, Mawei district, Fuzhou city, and Lianjiang County, all of which are in the region of Fuzhou in Fujian Province.

There are three main ways by which Chinese are smuggled into the United States (Smith 1997). One way is to travel to Mexico or Canada and then enter the United States by crossing the land border (Glaberson 1989). The second method involves air routes. The immigrants fly into major American cities via any number of transit points (Lorch 1992). The third route involves entering the United States by sea, a method that was popular between August 1991 and July 1993 (Zhang and Gaylord 1996).

When the smuggled Chinese arrive in the United States, some of them are confined in so-called safe houses by the smugglers until their smuggling fees have been paid (U.S. Senate 1992). Inside the safe houses, they are repeatedly abused and tortured by debt collectors who often use cruel and unusual measures to force their captives' families and relatives to promptly deliver their smuggling fees (approximately $30,000 in 1994 but up to about $45,000 in 1998).

This chapter focuses on the lives of these smuggled Chinese immigrants after their initial arrival in the United States. Following an overview of the Chinatown in which they settle and their general problems, the discussion moves to the work they find, the financial obligations they face, their involvement in crime as victims and as participants, and their mixed desires about whether to stay in the United States or to return to China.

The chapter is based on multiple research strategies: a survey of 300 undocumented Chinese in New York City[1]; interviews with key informants who know the lifestyle and social problems of illegal Chinese immigrants; a field study in the Chinese immigrant community of New York City; two research trips to sending communities in China; and a systematic collection of media reports.

CHINATOWN AND THE FUJIANESE COMMUNITY

New York City's Chinatown is the largest Chinese community in North America (Zhou 1992). It was established in the late nineteenth century by Cantonese immigrants who came from the Taishan area of Guangdong Province (Wong 1982). Initially, the community was made up of only three blocks. Now, it is an ethnic enclave that covers more than twenty blocks of the Lower East Side of Manhattan (Kinkead 1992).

Most Fujianese come to live in New York's Chinatown. As a result, Fujianese businesspeople and residents now dominate East Broadway, Eldridge, Allen, Forsyth, Delancey, Grand, Hester, and Broome Streets of Chinatown. The entrances of the Triple Eight Palace Restaurant and the Bank of China, both on East Broadway, are major gathering places for Fujianese. Most of the employment agencies that cater to Fujianese are located on East Broadway or on the corner of Eldridge and Forsyth Streets.

As the number of Fujianese in New York City increased in the early 1990s, the political economy of Chinatown changed dramatically (Kwong 1997). Before the arrival of the Fujianese, the largest community associations in Chinatown were mostly controlled by Cantonese from Guangdong Province. These associations were predominantly supportive of the Nationalist government in Taiwan and were vehemently anticommunist (Lyman 1974). The few procommunist organizations that existed were ostracized, and they could occupy only a marginal role in community affairs. Every year, Chinatown celebrated the national holiday (October 10) of the Nationalist government. The communist national holiday, October 1, was never celebrated in the community (Kwong 1987).

All this changed in the early 1990s as tens of thousands of both legal and illegal immigrants from China began to pour into Chinatown and developed their own community associations. Currently, there are four Fujianese umbrella organizations: the United Chinese Associations of New York, the Fukien American Association, the United Fujianese of America Association, and the American Fujian Association of Commerce and Industry. These organizations represent a dozen or so Fujianese associations.

Because most of the newer community organizations were established by immigrants from China, they are ardently pro-communist, even though members of these organizations may privately criticize the Chinese government. As the number of pro-communist community organizations began to grow, the first-ever celebration of the communist national holiday was held in Chinatown in 1994 (*New York Times*, September 26, 1994). Since then, the Cantonese celebrate the October 10 holiday in their territory, primarily Mott and Bayard Streets, and the Fujianese celebrate the October 1 holiday, mainly on East Broadway. The Bowery is considered the dividing line between the Cantonese and Fujianese territories.

The economic sector of Chinatown has also changed. Before the late 1980s, Chinatown's economy was under the control of the Cantonese (Kleinfield 1986). Even though many Fujianese arrived in the mid-1980s, they did not have the capital to start their own businesses. Many Cantonese business owners resented the arrival of large numbers of Fujianese (Tsao 1993). However, for their business interests, they had to change their business practices to attract Fujianese customers.

By the early 1990s, some of the Fujianese who had arrived in New York City in the mid-1980s had raised enough capital to start their own businesses. Many began to open take-out restaurants. Within a few years, the whole Chinese fast-food industry had come under the control of the Fujianese. As a result, there was a dramatic increase in the number of Fujianese-owned businesses that either directly or indirectly relate to the take-out restaurant industry, such as food wholesalers, renovation companies, accounting firms, real estate companies, and law firms (*World Journal*, January 10, 1998).

Some Fujianese-owned garment factories also began to appear. Initially, most garment factories in Chinatown were owned by investors from Hong Kong and Taiwan, and women from the Fuzhou region went to work in them (Gargan 1981; Reid 1986). As the Fujianese became familiar with the operations of the garment industry, some of those with savings opened garment businesses of their own and, as a result, became a strong presence in Chinatown's garment industry. Of the approximately 600 garment factories in Chinatown, 150 were believed to be owned by Fujianese (*Sing Tao Daily*, October 27, 1997).

As the Fujianese began to flex their economic muscle, many types of businesses in the service sector that cater to Fujianese workers and businesspeople began to emerge—such as employment agencies, florists, barber shops, clinics, immigration consultant offices, and driving schools. Even illegal enterprises such as massage parlors and gambling dens grew to accommodate the needs of Fujianese immigrants (Chin 1996).

PROBLEMS ENCOUNTERED BY SMUGGLED CHINESE

I asked my respondents what their main problems in the United States were. Almost all my respondents said their major problem in the United States was their inability to communicate in English. Because most worked long hours in places where most other employees were also Chinese and had only one day off per week, they did not have time to learn English.

The second most often mentioned problem was homesickness. A substantial number of my respondents said they missed their families in China, especially when they were not feeling well or during Chinese holidays and festivals. They often talked about how shallow their existence in the United States was and said they often felt lonely. A respondent said: "Life has no meaning for me now because I am so far away from my family and relatives. Every time I call home, my wife cries."

Another respondent, a forty-four-year-old male from Changle, described his existence in the United States this way:

Work in America is tough. I work in a restaurant for more than 12 hours a day and rarely have a chance to see the sunlight. It's like I am a cow or a horse. That's why America for me is like a prison. Besides, I am all by myself here, with no family or relatives. If I get sick, only my family and relatives will look after me. Who else will come see me? Also, people here care only about their own business. This is a utilitarian society where people have no compassion.

The third most often mentioned problem could be categorized as job-related. This includes difficulty finding jobs, long work hours, difficulty finding permanent employment, difficulty finding a satisfactory job, hardships at work, dissatisfaction with wages, and having to deal with abusive employers. They felt that they were constantly under pressure of being fired by their employers. They knew that their employers would have little difficulty in finding others to replace them. This type of pressure was overwhelming for those who were accustomed to *chidaguofan* (eating food from a huge bowl, referring to the socialist system) or jobs that were considered to be *tiefanwan* (an iron rice bowl, meaning a government job). In China, most people work for the government, and most government jobs are lax and provide maximum job security. For my respondents who were unaccustomed to getting fired or laid off from work, the job market in the United States, especially in the ethnic enclave with its free-wheeling style of hiring and firing workers, can be hard to adjust to.

A number of my respondents said they were under enormous financial pressure. For some, this means that they have to repay money they owed to their friends and relatives. For others, it means they have to pay loan sharks exorbitant interest charges. Still others may feel pressure to send money to their families in China.

Other problems they mentioned were dissatisfaction with living accommodations and the inability to adjust to a new environment. For example, according to one respondent:

I now live in an apartment near Chinatown with a bunch of illegal immigrants. You have to come see our apartment yourself to really understand how bad our living conditions are. If you look at the apartments in Chinatown from the streets, they may appear to be all right. But if you step into one of these apartments, they are like pigsties: small, filthy, and overcrowded.

Another respondent explained why it was so difficult for him to adjust to the United States and expressed his desire to go back to China:

For me, the most formidable obstacle is finding a stable job. Keep in mind that the main reason I am here is to make money. I like U.S. dollars. They're worth much more than Chinese yuan. Besides U.S. dollars, there's nothing I like about the United States. The living environment here is not as good as in Fuzhou. Actually, it is much worse than there. I was relatively rich back in China; I owned two business stores. After I got here, my family became a *meiguoke*'s [Guest from the Beautiful Country] family, and of course, they are very happy. Since I can't adjust here, I wish that after I clear my debts and save $10,000 to $20,000, I would return home. I regret I came. In China, I did not need to hustle for a living. Here, I cannot afford to stay idle even for a day. After all, I agree with the saying among the Fujianese, "After you see the whole world, you'll find that Fuzhou is the best place on earth."

Asked what they liked about the United States, the vast majority of my respondents answered "U.S. dollars," among other things. Of those who mentioned dollars as the thing they liked the most about the United States, more than half emphasized that it was the only thing they liked about the country. Their answer was consistent with their incentive to come to the United States, which was to make money. The second most often mentioned thing they liked about the United States was freedom.

A substantial number of respondents spoke about the opportunities in the United States. They believe there are more and better opportunities, such as jobs, and more equality and fair competition in the workplace. Some respondents were impressed with the transportation networks and facilities and the overall quality of the environment. Others talked about the people in their new environment. They thought of American people as civilized, polite, and very nice to women. They believed they were surrounded by people of a higher quality than was the case in China. Some liked the United States for its democratic political system and its protection of human rights. Several said they liked the casinos and shopping malls; others liked the stability of U.S. government policies and the fact that ability counts, not personal or political connections (*guanxi*) or political ideology.

Table 12.1
Employment Patterns among Smuggled Chinese in New York City

	N	Full-time employment	Part-time employment	Unemployed
Number	300	234	32	34
Sex*				
Male	238	74%	12%	14%
Female	62	93%	5%	2%
Year of arrival				
1988 or before	23	87%	0%	13%
1989	43	84%	5%	12%
1990	50	84%	10%	6%
1991	61	75%	13%	12%
1992	62	84%	6%	10%
1993	61	62%	21%	17%
Route				
Air	143	79%	13%	8%
Sea	35	77%	3%	20%
Land	122	77%	11%	12%
Region of origin				
Changle	146	77%	10%	13%
Fuzhou	62	69%	19%	11%
Tingjiang	56	86%	5%	9%
Lianjiang	23	82%	9%	9%
Other	13	92%	0%	8%

Note: * = $p < .05$.

WORK AND INCOME

At the time the interviews were conducted, most of my respondents were working either full- or part-time (see Table 12.1). Most respondents said they had been employed either all the time or most of the time since coming to the United States. Of the thirty-four subjects who were unemployed, only one was female.[2]

Immigration scholars have noted that most illegal immigrants in the United States are primarily involved in low-wage, low-prestige occupations (North and Houstoun 1976; Chiswick 1988; Mahler 1995). I also found that my respondents

Table 12.2
Occupational Patterns among Smuggled Chinese in New York City

	N	Garment factory	Restaurant	Construction	Other
Number	266	92	127	19	28
Sex**					
Male	205	22%	58%	9%	11%
Female	61	77%	13%	0%	10%
Year of arrival*					
1988 or before	20	25%	70%	0%	5%
1989	38	18%	68%	3%	11%
1990	47	36%	47%	13%	4%
1991	54	33%	48%	6%	13%
1992	56	36%	46%	5%	13%
1993	51	49%	26%	12%	14%
Region of origin*					
Changle	127	44%	37%	7%	12%
Fuzhou	55	24%	55%	11%	11%
Tingjiang	51	22%	63%	4%	12%
Lianjiang	21	29%	62%	10%	0%
Other	12	50%	42%	0%	8%

Notes: Part-time workers are included. * = p < .05; ** = p < .001.

were mainly employed in the food, garment, and construction businesses (see Table 12.2).

Occupation

Although my respondents were not asked what types of restaurants they worked for, I assumed they were most likely to be employed by take-out restaurants, which are smaller then eat-in restaurants and are more likely to cater to cost-conscious customers. In the tristate area of New York, New Jersey, and Connecticut, there has been a dramatic increase in the number of Chinese take-out restaurants since the late 1980s, presumably a result of the arrival of so many Fujianese in the area. More than 1,000 Chinese take-out restaurants were in operation in the New York metropolitan area in the early 1990s, and some believed that almost ninety percent of them were owned by Fujianese (*World Journal*, January 10, 1998).

Table 12.2 shows that almost six out of ten of my male subjects worked in restaurants. It also indicates that while seventy percent of those who came in 1988 or before worked in restaurants in the United States, only twenty-six percent of those who came in 1993 earned their living in the restaurant business in America. The decrease in employment in the restaurant sector has been offset by an increase in employment in the garment industry. Also, immigrants from Changle were less likely to be employed in the restaurant sector than those from either Tingjiang or Lianjiang.

Of those female subjects who were working at the time of the interviews, seventy-seven percent worked in garment factories. Working conditions in the garment industry are reported to be extremely poor (Kwong 1997). In the words of a journalist, "In these [sweat] shops, holes in warping floors are covered by plywood boards. Sprinkler systems, unmaintained, no longer work. Electrical wiring dangles dangerously overhead. . . . fire exits are covered by metal gates that are padlocked" (Finder 1995: B4).

Many small firms in Chinatown specialize in commercial renovation and construction and in making signboards. These businesses are also dominated by Fujianese. Many Chinese restaurants in the tristate area change hands quite frequently. Whenever a new Chinese restaurant opens, the owner invariably changes the interior of the restaurant or, at the very least, changes the name of the restaurant. As a result, there is a strong demand for renovation/construction services. Twenty-eight respondents were employed in sectors other than the restaurant, garment, and renovation/construction industries.

Working Hours

Most of my respondents said their jobs required long working hours. Of the 228 respondents who worked full-time, only 16 said they worked eight hours or less a day. About sixty three percent of them stated they worked twelve hours or more a day. Not only did they work long hours daily, but they also worked more than the normal five working days a week. Of the 243 full-time workers, only five percent said they worked five days or less a week. About eighty five percent of them worked six days a week. The average number of working hours per week was sixty-nine for those who worked full-time.[3]

Most restaurant workers in my sample averaged seventy working hours per week in six days. The garment workers among my respondents, who were paid by the type and quantity of their work, averaged seventy-two hours per week, over six to seven days, surpassing the hours of restaurant workers. Respondents employed by renovation/construction firms worked only fifty-two hours per week, comparatively, due to their work being dependent on the availability of projects. Subjects who did not work in those three types of businesses averaged fifty-six working hours a week (see Table 12.3).

A fourteen-year-old girl from a relatively rich family from Changle described how hard she worked:

Table 12.3
Respondents' Average Weekly Working Hours, Monthly Wage, and Hourly Wage by Type of Occupation in 1993

	Restaurant	Garment factory	Construction	Other	Total
Number	115	84	9	18	226
Work hours per week	72	70	52	56	69
Monthly wage	$1,520	$1,252	$1,740	$1,387	$1,359
Hourly wage	$4.70	$4.30	$7.10	$5.40	$4.70

Notes: Part-time workers are excluded. The minimum hourly wage in 1993 was $4.25.

I work almost 14 hours a day. Sometimes, I work from 8 in the morning to dawn. My mom begged me not to work too hard. However, since I had to pay so much money to be smuggled here, I have to make money. My mom wants me to eat well, get a green card [permanent resident status], and attend school. My mom frequently sends me plenty of beautiful clothes. You see, I am working in a garment factory almost seven days a week; why do I need all these nice clothes?

Income

Because no systematic study has ever been conducted to determine the wages of smuggled Chinese, policymakers have to rely on anecdotal material from the media and the law enforcement community to estimate the income level of smuggled immigrants. However, these accounts may be misleading. For example, a *New York Times* reporter conducted a field study by working in a garment factory. After working for a couple of weeks, she said she made about sixty-five cents an hour in the sweatshop (Lii 1995). Law enforcement authorities have also suggested that illegal Chinese are getting paid far below the minimum wage. Consequently, they assume that immigrants who have to pay about $30,000 in smuggling fees may never be able to repay their debts (U.S. Senate 1992).

My data do not support the contention that smuggled Chinese make very little money in the United States. The average monthly salary of the 234 full-time workers in my sample was $1,421. Of workers in the three main occupation categories, those in the renovation and construction business had the highest average monthly salary, which was $1,740, followed by restaurant workers (with an average monthly income of $1,520). The garment industry workers had the lowest average monthly income, $1,252 (see Table 12.3). At the time of my study, the U.S. federally mandated minimum wage was $4.25 per hour; thus, the minimum-wage U.S. worker was making $731 per month under the legally mandated maximum of forty working hours per week.

Because most of my respondents worked substantially longer hours than the average American worker, I need to take into consideration their working hours before I conclude that their average monthly salary is not exceptionally low by American standards. That is, I have to find out whether they make a decent income simply because they work many more hours than an average American worker. Table 12.3 presents their hourly wage by type of occupation.[4] The table suggests that the studied Chinese immigrants in all types of occupations made more than the 1993 minimum wage of $4.25 an hour. This finding is congruent with research on illegal Mexican immigrants conducted by Chiswick (1988: 98), who concluded that "the average hourly wages for aliens are substantially in excess of the federal legal minimum wage. . . . To the extent that exploitation is defined as payment of a wage below the federal minimum wage, it appears to be rare or nonexistent in these data." This money is actually worth more in real dollars because the $4.25 American earner is also paying taxes on that full amount. These illegals are not.[5]

Nevertheless, from the data in Table 12.3, it is clear that most workers, especially those in the garment and restaurant industry, make a relatively decent income mainly because they work long hours. As with all jobs, though, wage is dependent on occupation. For example, in the restaurant business, the average hourly wage was $6.12 for waiters and waitresses and $5.35 for cooks, $4 for food delivery workers, $3.65 for kitchen helpers, and $2.38 for dishwashers. Likewise, in the garment industry, pressers (mostly male) averaged $5.88 hourly, compared to only $3.71 for seamstresses (mostly female). Table 12.4 presents a detailed list of positions within the various industries and their relevant hourly and monthly wages.[6]

Impact on the Local Economy

What is the impact of illegal immigrants on the U.S. labor market for vulnerable native groups, such as youth, women, and African-American men, who may look for jobs in the same restaurant, garment, and construction industries in which many immigrants seek to earn a living? During the 1970s, when southern California took in more immigrants than any other part of the country, including many illegal ones, it also led the nation in the creation of new jobs and enjoyed an above-average increase in per capita income. Wayne Cornelius, an authority on international migration, proposed two decades ago, "There is simply not enough credible evidence to establish the existence of a cause-and-effect relationship—even an indirect one—between illegal migration and domestic unemployment" (Cornelius 1978: 60). Summarizing several studies of illegal immigration a decade later, *Business Week* concluded that "on balance, the nation benefits more from the increased economic growth and lower inflation

Table 12.4
Respondents' Average Hourly and Monthly Wage by Industry and Selected Position in 1993

	N	Hourly wage	Monthly wage
Restaurant	115	$4.70	$1,416
Waiter	6	$6.10	$1,775
Cook	40	$5.40	$1,598
Chef	4	$5.30	$1,725
Food preparer	2	$4.50	$1,450
Cashier	5	$4.40	$1,400
Food fryer	6	$4.30	$1,325
Delivery person	9	$4.00	$1,272
Kitchen helper	26	$3.60	$1,146
Dishwasher	2	$2.40	$800
Garment Factory	84	$4.30	$1,252
Cloth presser	18	$5.90	$1,530
Cloth distributor/matcher	1	$4.90	$1,400
Button installator	3	$4.60	$1,366
General helper	2	$4.20	$1,300
Ends sewer	10	$4.20	$1,200
Seamstress	41	$3.70	$1,121
Cloth hanger	7	$3.50	$1,193
Renovation/construction	9	$7.10	$1,600
Other	18	$5.40	$1,381
Warehouse supervisor	1	$8.70	$1,500
Food packer	3	$6.80	$1,066
Delivery driver	2	$6.40	$1,550
Mover	2	$5.30	$1,200
Store cashier	2	$4.10	$1,200
Bakery store worker	1	$3.20	$900

Notes: Part-time employees, business owners, and prostitutes are excluded. The minimum hourly wage in 1993 was $4.25.

stemming from illegal immigration than it loses in jobs, lower wages and welfare costs'' (Dowty 1987: 242).

Little is known about the impact of illegal Chinese on New York City's economy. As mentioned before, most of the smuggled Chinese in this study worked in restaurants, garment factories, and renovation/construction firms in the Lower East Side of Manhattan. Most of these businesses were owned by Cantonese or Fujianese. Therefore, I do not think that newly arrived Fujianese immigrants take away jobs that would have gone to non-Chinese minorities or to women. I do assume, however, that many recently arrived, legal Chinese immigrants would have slightly better job prospects or higher wages if it were not for the influx of illegal Chinese.

Many people, especially the Cantonese in New York City's Chinatown, believe that the recent arrival of large numbers of Fujianese has suppressed wages. According to one media account, the average monthly wage for garment workers in Chinatown was $2,000 in 1992, but it had been reduced to between $1,600 and $1,500 by 1994 (*World Journal*, September 10, 1994). In 1995, one of the largest restaurants in Chinatown was involved in a labor dispute because the owner replaced Cantonese workers with Fujianese workers after the Cantonese protested against unfair practices adopted by the employer, such as collecting a portion of the waiters' tips. The firing of Cantonese employees resulted in a major strike that continued for months and split the community into pro-immigration and anti-immigration forces (Jia 1995).

Besides taking away jobs from natives and suppressing wages, illegal immigrants are also thought to have cost their host society dearly in detention, health care, education, and so forth (Padavan 1994; Clark et al. 1995).[7] For example, according to the U.S. General Accounting Office (1993), California, Texas, New York, Illinois, and Florida estimated $2.9 billion in annual federal, state, and local costs for illegal aliens and their citizen children.

According to Cornelius (1989), the illegal immigrants in California most likely to use state health and education services are spouses and children of the 1.1 million immigrants who won legal status under the SAW (special agricultural worker) program. Because the program did not offer legal status to these spouses and children, they became illegal immigrants. According to a study conducted by the Urban Institute (Clark et al. 1995) welfare use among working-age (fifteen to sixty-four years), nonrefugee immigrants is very low. The major "cost" of immigrants is the education of their children.

Most of the smuggled Chinese in this study were married and had children, but their children were back in China with their spouses or parents. I do not know how common this practice is among all Chinese illegals. Thus, I do not know the impact on the education system. In my sample, only one female said she had received state benefits, by receiving Medicaid. Because my sample is not random, I have no way of estimating the potential financial impact of smuggled Chinese on the wider community. However, my data suggest that my respondents kept to themselves and did not use health or educational services available to legal immigrants and citizens. I can only guess that this is the more common practice among smuggled Chinese.

DEBTS AND REMITTANCES

Most of my respondents arrived in the United States with up to $30,000 in debt because of their smuggling fee. Although more than half of my respondents said they had not borrowed any money to pay the down payment, only one out of ten said they had paid the balance of the smuggling fee without borrowing. This means nine out of ten of my subjects were in debt when they started looking for a job in the United States.

Contrary to the popular belief that smuggled Chinese immigrants are exploited by loan sharks who charge them an exorbitant interest rate, most respondents said they borrowed money from either relatives or friends. Of the 264 subjects who said they needed to borrow money to finance their illegal passage, 164 sought help from relatives in China, 147 received financial aid from relatives in the United States, and 53 were supported by friends either in the United States or in China.[8] Only 11 respondents said they borrowed all or part of their smuggling fees from loan sharks in China. Approximately seventy percent of those who owed money to friends and/or relatives said their friends and/or relatives did not charge them interest. If their relatives or friends did charge interest, the most common rate was two percent per month. A few respondents had to pay monthly interest rates of up to four percent to their relatives or friends. Loan sharks normally charge monthly interest rates from three to four percent.

If most smuggled Chinese owe about $24,000 to friends and relatives, and most of them do not need to pay interest on their loans, how long does it take them to clear their debt? Many media reports and law enforcement reports assume that: (1) almost all the smuggling fees are borrowed; (2) almost all of the borrowed money is from loan sharks who charge up to five percent monthly interest rates (contrary to the findings of this study); and (3) most undocumented Chinese make as little as $600 a month in the United States. They therefore conclude that many smuggled Chinese may never be able to clear their debt (Hood 1993). According to a senior Immigration and Naturalization Service (INS) official, ''They can work in a dishwasher job for the rest of their lives to pay off that debt'' (Glaberson 1989: B3). My data suggest that this was not the case for my sample.

At the time of my interviews, 105 respondents said they had repaid their smuggling debts. It took them an average of twenty-six months to do so. Most were able to repay the debts within two years, although some took as little as six months, and others as long as four years. Regardless of whether they were still in debt, most (eighty-six percent) said they had not encountered any problem in fulfilling their financial obligations.

When asked whether they were sending money home at the time of the interviews, eighty-six percent of respondents said they were. They did it either through the Bank of China (in Chinatown), through the underground banking industry of Chinatown, or through friends and relatives returning to China. The purposes of these remittances were either to repay their smuggling debts or to provide living expenses for their families in China. According to a manager of the Changle branch of the Bank of China, more than $2 million in overseas remittances were handled by the branch in 1991. The amount of remittances skyrocketed to $24 million the following year. He projected that in 1993, there would be more than $30 million in remittances sent back to the area. He estimated about ninety-six percent of this money came from the United States (*Tai Kung Pao*, June 15, 1993).

MENTAL HEALTH

Little is known about the mental health of Chinese immigrants, although social workers in Chinatown have been alarmed by the increase in the number of smuggled Chinese who become mental patients (*World Journal*, February 27, 1990).[9] According to mental health professionals, many Chinese immigrants have problems adjusting to their new environment. The immigrants, especially those from rural areas, are particularly troubled by their inability to speak English, to understand Western norms and values, and to grow accustomed to the demanding working environment. Consequently, according to a Chinese doctor I interviewed, many develop depression, somatic disorders, and sleeping disorders. A few become dependent on alcohol or suicidal. Despite this, not many social service programs in Chinatown cater to illegal immigrants.

In comparison with legal Chinese immigrants, illegal Chinese immigrants are in a disadvantaged position. As mentioned before, my subjects normally have to work up to seventy hours a week. Smuggled Chinese males who were away from their wives and work in restaurants often sarcastically describe their lives in the United States as "living in a world of two *tou*." When asked what this means, they said: "During the day, we face the *lutou* (foyer). At night, we hug our *zhentou* (pillows)" (*World Journal*, January 11, 1998: E1). In a sense, they do not have a life here in the United States. Consequently, some viewed themselves merely as *huojiqi*, or machines made of flesh and blood.

According to my respondents, after they left their workplace, they went right back to their apartments because it was often late, and they had no place to go or friends and relatives to visit. After a long and grueling day, their apartments were by no means their sanctuaries; more often than not, they were crowded with many tenants who were, like them, trying to save as much money as possible by sharing a one- or two-bedroom apartment with as many as a dozen others.[10] Sometimes, these apartments were shared by both married men and women who were far from their spouses and children. Bunk beds were set up not only in bedrooms but also in living rooms and kitchens. Some apartments in Chinatown do not even have their own bathrooms, and all tenants on the same floor may share one. Some apartments have makeshift showers constructed in the tiny kitchen area. Most do not have air-conditioning, and in winter, the heat often does not work.

Many young adults in my sample were married and had children but came to the United States on their own. They said they missed their families and parents, and some were traumatized by rumors that their spouses in China were having affairs. Ironically, they said their spouses in China, in turn, suspected that they were forming new families in the United States. Some of my subjects were overwhelmed with smuggling debts. Those who were not complained of their spouses' insatiable demands for U.S. dollars and became disheartened by the conviction that they could never satisfy their families back home.

Finally, many respondents lived in fear in their own community. They were afraid not because they were here illegally. Rather, they were wary of their own countrymen in New York City because they were vulnerable to Fujianese criminals who preyed on them through kidnapping, extortion, and home-invasion robbery. Many moved frequently, trying to find a place where they felt secure away from their own countrymen. They also changed their phone numbers or beeper numbers often.

Since most smuggled Chinese in my sample did not speak English, they were isolated from mainstream society. For them, the Mountain of Gold was China-town. It was, indeed, an extremely small world in which they dwelled in the United States. The resulting stresses, which can lead to mental illness, may be grouped into three categories: financial, emotional, and job-related.

Financial Burden

Heavy financial burdens may force some female immigrants to turn to prostitution, and they also may cause serious psychological problems for both male and female immigrants (Chan 1993). According to a thirty-five-year-old male from Mawei:

A 33-year-old male from Tingjiang came here with me. Because he had no money to repay his debts and could not find a job, there were enormous pressures from the people he owed money to. Maybe he was overwhelmed; he had a mental breakdown. Also, my wife became very nervous the day I left, and she became mentally ill. The first time I called home, my family told me the bad news. I almost did not know what to do with my life here.

Another subject noted that a young man he was associated with became mentally ill: ''There was a twenty-year-old male from Tingjiang. Everyday, he looked nervous, but he smiled like an idiot. I believe he is now disabled. He stayed in his apartment all day long doing nothing.''

Smuggled Chinese overwhelmed with debts may also develop unrealistic expectations of their earning power. For example, a person may become progressively dissatisfied with the amount of money he or she is making and may constantly look for jobs that pay a higher salary, despite the fact that he or she may not have the credentials to acquire a better-paying job. A forty-year-old male from Changle said:

There is a male from Changle. Due to job pressure, he lost his mind. He spends most of his time wandering from one employment agency to another and yelling: "I want to have a job as a cook." He is only 20 years old, but I don't think he can work anymore.

A twenty-nine-year-old Tingjiang male also described the plight of an immigrant who was failing badly in the United States. In the words of the subject:

There is a person from my village who is 28 years old. After his arrival, he had a hard time finding a job, and his family owed a lot of money. Besides, he could not adjust to the new environment. Now he is out of his mind. He does not work. Every day, he wanders around and comes back to sleep. He cannot differentiate between day and night. He is still surviving simply because we are taking care of him. He is not willing to go home, and there is nothing we can do to persuade him to find a job.

Psychological Stress and Emotional Pain

Some immigrants may not be able to overcome the pain and anxiety associated with separating from someone they love dearly. A thirty-year-old male from Guantou had this to say about one of his countrymen:

He came to the United States in 1991 and is now sharing a place with me. After his arrival in America, he and his girlfriend, who remained in Changle, broke up. He became mentally disordered. He speaks incoherently, and he cannot work. Some people are sympathetic and give him some money. He immediately spends it in the massage parlors.

Some immigrants may become mentally ill after enduring traumatic events on the trip to the United States and in the safe houses once they arrive. According to a thirty-year-old male from Fuzhou city:

There is a male who suffered a lot on the trip, like being bitten by mosquitoes and sleeping in the open in the mountains. He often thinks of how comfortable he was back home. He can't overcome the suffering, and now he is crazy. Sometimes he cries; sometimes he laughs. He crawls, he sleeps wherever he feels like it, and he cannot take care of his personal hygiene. Now I see him often wandering in the streets, and nobody can understand what he is talking about.

Job-Related Anxiety

Those who endured few hardships in China may be ill equipped to withstand the harsh reality of being an illegal immigrant in the United States. For example, in my sample, those who had a *tiefanwon* (iron rice bowl, meaning a government job) in China were the least likely to be able to adjust to the capitalist labor market in the United States. Because they were so accustomed to the work habits that prevail in Chinese government agencies, they were less equipped to adapt and might be fired by their new employers in America. Many yearn for the lax working atmosphere of the state-run bureaucratic institutions in China. A thirty-two-year-old male from Changle described a former government official's predicament:

There is a male who lived quite comfortably back in China. He had a good political background and was a senior government official. Since his arrival here, his mental health has degenerated because of his inability to adjust to the new environment. He has become like a fool. He wanders in the street every day and asks anybody he meets for help. He's like a beggar now.

Another subject, a forty-four-year-old sailor from Changle, spoke about a roommate who could not withstand the pain of frequently being discharged from work:

Many people told me America is a prison. Here, human beings are exploited like animals. We have to go to work for more than twenty hours a day and then go home just to sleep. The next day, you go to work again. There is a person who is sharing an apartment with me. When he arrived here, he had a hard time finding a job. After he finally found a job, he got fired quickly. He has been dismissed from work several times. Later, he lost his mind. Now, he verbally and physically assaults people around him. As a result, he was incarcerated in a mental hospital for three months. Now, he appears to be recovering gradually.

People who cannot face going on with their lives because of enormous suffering and pressures may decide to commit suicide. A thirty-four-year-old male respondent from Fuzhou city said a young immigrant committed suicide because he was unemployed and worried about his debts. Another respondent said a person he knew killed himself because he was unable to repay even the interest on his debt. He thought that many more suicide cases among illegal Chinese immigrants go unnoticed.

VICTIMIZATION

Studies on clandestine immigration have found that illegal immigrants are vulnerable to crime in host societies because of their illegal status and inability to protect themselves (Haller 1997). The media have reported that smuggled Chinese in New York City are often victimized by both Chinese and non-Chinese (*New York Times*, December 3, 1993). For example, many Chinese immigrants are robbed in the subway by non-Chinese (Burdman 1993). Because immigrants who work in restaurants and garment factories tend to leave work late at night, they are likely targets for predators. Their reluctance to approach police authorities after being victimized makes them all the more vulnerable (*Sing Tao Daily*, May 7, 1992).

Of the 300 Chinese immigrants in this study, 139 (47 percent) said that they had been victimized at least once since their arrival in America. They were most likely to have been victims of robbery; 97 (32 percent) were robbed at least once in the subway. Home-invasion robbery has long been considered the trademark crime of Chinese and Vietnamese gangs (English 1995; Long 1996). In my survey, thirty-one respondents (about 10 percent) were robbed in their homes or apartments. Because smuggled Chinese are accustomed to cash transactions and reluctant to deposit their money in banks, they tend to keep a substantial amount of cash in their homes (*World Journal*, January 10, 1998).

Few of my respondents were victims of other forms of crime. For instance, three subjects said they had been subject to extortion or sexual harassment. A twenty-year-old female respondent from Guantou said:

The debt collectors often bothered me [even though the smuggling fee had already been paid]. They wanted me to go out with them. Once, when I declined their invitation, they used force. I was literally dragged out of the garment factory where I was working. In the process, I fell down the stairs and hurt my arms. I am trying my best to hide from them. They invited me to go to gambling places, bars, and nightclubs with them. They even demanded that I sleep with them. I am really scared, and I plan to move out of Chinatown soon. However, these people are resourceful and well connected; they can easily find me even after I leave Chinatown.

Another respondent said she knew a female immigrant who was raped:

I know a female immigrant who was my neighbor in China. After she arrived in America, she was cheated by a male who persuaded her to go out of [New York] state with him to work. After she followed him to another city, he did not help her find a job. But that guy raped her. After she returned to New York City, she went insane. Now, I know her relatives are looking for her everywhere. She has disappeared for almost six months.

Of the respondents who were victimized, only twenty-five (18 percent) contacted police.

PROSTITUTION

The existence of a large number of houses of prostitution in the Chinese communities of San Francisco and New York City has long been a major concern for U.S. law enforcement authorities (U.S. Senate [1877] 1978, 1992). Police authorities have been specifically concerned that Asian women were smuggled into the United States by members of Chinese crime groups and forced to work as prostitutes (Martin 1977). With the arrival of a significant number of smuggled Chinese women, police assumed that many of them, especially those unable to pay their smuggling fees or debts, would be forced by their snakeheads to work as prostitutes (Chan 1993; *New York Times*, July 23, 1993). Authorities also theorized that some women might voluntarily go into prostitution because they could not endure the hardships of working long hours in garment factories or restaurants.

It is not clear how many smuggled Chinese have been recruited into the sex industry. Of the sixty-two females in my sample, only one said she was a prostitute. Another respondent, an eighteen-year-old girl from Guantou, said she was urged by her snakehead to become a prostitute. She rejected the suggestion, even though the snakehead assured her that she would not have to pay for her passage if she agreed to do so. Five other subjects said they knew someone who came with them who became a prostitute. One respondent, a thirty-year-old technician from Fuzhou city, said:

There was a woman on the smuggling ship I was on. Back in China, she was a member of a *chaoshu* (overseas family), so she did not have to work hard to be able to live a comfortable life. That's why here in America she cannot withstand the pressure, nor can she endure hardship. So she went to work in a massage parlor voluntarily. She also hung out with members of the underworld society. She was also seen helping gangsters rob newly arrived immigrants. Because she's a woman, it is easier for her to make her way into the victims' apartments.

Another respondent, a twenty-five-year-old woman from Changle, also knew two women who became prostitutes because of debts and marital problems. According to her:

Two female passengers on the ship I was on are now working as prostitutes in Chinatown. They were involved in this type of activity because they did not have money to repay their debts. Besides, they had marriage problems. They rented an apartment in Chinatown, and they go out and find customers themselves. They are not interested in finding regular jobs anymore.

Some women who are prostitutes may have tried working in a garment factory. However, they may have eventually given up the factory work because they borrowed their smuggling fee from loan sharks instead of from their families and relatives. Because most loan sharks demand three to four percent monthly interest rate, those who borrowed $25,000 from a loan shark may have to pay approximately $750 a month just to cover their interest payments. As a result, they may be under enormous pressure to make money.

CRIME

One of the issues related to the impact of immigration on the receiving countries is the association between crime and immigration, especially illegal immigration (Marshall 1997). Some researchers have suggested that immigrants are more likely than nonimmigrants to be involved in illegal activities, although they may have different explanations for the connection. Scholars such as Thorsten Sellin (1938) have proposed that immigrants may have a higher crime rate than nonimmigrants mainly because the norms and values of the immigrants may not be compatible with the norms and values of their host society. Others, such as Francis Ianni (1974), have suggested that each wave of immigrant groups was responsible for the emergence of ethnic organized crime in the United States because the newly arrived immigrants needed to find an edge, even an illegal one, to establish themselves in their host society.

U.S. law enforcement authorities have suggested an association between crime and immigration (Wang 1996). They have proposed that immigrants, especially illegal immigrants, are disproportionately represented in correctional facilities (Lyall 1992). Some states have begun to sue the federal government for allowing a large number of illegal immigrants into the United States because they have overwhelmed state correctional facilities. These states argue that the government should reimburse them for its failure to prevent people from entering the United States illegally (Lyall 1992).

Other scholars have disagreed with this proposition and argue that the "overwhelming majority of illegal aliens do not engage in violence or crime in the United States, and if they skirt the law because of their status they do not necessarily commit violent acts of lawlessness" (James 1991: 62). Alex Schmid (1996) has also maintained that illegal immigrants are less likely to commit crime because apprehension by authorities could lead to deportation.

The media have reported extensively about the relationship between smuggled Chinese and heroin trafficking (Wren 1996), prostitution (Chan 1993), kidnapping (Burdman 1993; Faison 1993; Chan 1995), and murder (Kennedy 1995). Journalists and law enforcement authorities often depict illegal Chinese immigrants as people who are vulnerable to the temptation of turning to crime because of their heavy debts (Glaberson 1989). Alan Lau, former president of the Fukien American Association, also holds this viewpoint:

A small percentage of illegal Fujianese is involved in criminal activities because they don't have friends or relatives living in the United States. Before they were smuggled out of China, they told the smugglers that they had relatives in America so that the smugglers would think that they would pay the smuggling fees upon their arrival in America. However, when the smugglers found out later that these immigrants didn't have any relatives in the United States to take care of the smuggling fees, the smugglers would ask these newly arrived immigrants to work as enforcers, debt collectors, gambling den guards, drug couriers, and so forth. Sooner or later, these people working for the snakeheads would become hard-core criminals. Besides, some of them might have been street thugs in their homeland to begin with. (*Sing Tao Daily*, November 9, 1993: 28)

In my sample, however, most respondents repaid their smuggling fees through years of hard legal work rather than by relying on illegal gains or, as a senior INS official asserted, joining gangs. A thirty-seven-year-old male from Fuzhou city said:

After they [undocumented Chinese] have arrived here [in America], only a few turn into criminals. In fact, many of those who were involved in criminal activities back in China became law-abiding people. Why? Because they were isolated and powerless in America, and they, like everybody else, needed to work hard to repay the smuggling fees.

Another respondent also believed that most smuggled Chinese, including those who did not bother to work in China, became industrious after immigrating to the United States: "I observed many people change for the better. For example, many of those who were unwilling to work in China now work very hard because of the dire circumstances they are in now."

The preceding two respondents' perceptions about the relationship between crime and immigration are also supported by a respondent who was a gang member in China:

They [members of the Fuk Ching] asked me [back in China] to help them collect smuggling fees after I arrived here. However, when I got here, the Fuk Ching gang was history.[11] That's why I didn't join them. My main problem now is this: "People" [gang members] often come to where I work and look for trouble because of my past gang affiliation. I don't know how they found out where I work. It is very difficult for a person like me to go straight. I stay home and rest when I am not working. Today is the first time I have been in Chinatown since my arrival three months ago. I don't think the United States is better than China. I came here for my future. People like me who have been imprisoned before have no future in China. We were discriminated against everywhere we go. That's why I came here and have tried very hard to change myself into a law-abiding person.

A few respondents in this study did become involved in debt-collecting activities after having difficulty finding a legitimate job. A twenty-eight-year-old male from Changle said:

I was asked to help them [the snakeheads] watch the illegal immigrants. My main responsibility was to keep an eye on the immigrants. In fact, I didn't want this job, but I was having problems finding other jobs. I never beat anybody, but I did yell at him or her. The snakeheads paid me $1,500 a month.

Another person, a thirty-two-year-old male from Changle, was working as a debt collector for a massage parlor at the time of the interview. He described his job as follows:

I owned a beauty parlor [house of prostitution] in China, and now I am working as a debt collector for a massage parlor. I make about $1,500 a month. I don't like my job at all because, after a while, I got really sick of it. When I have to go collect money, there are problems. If the person who owes the massage parlor money is one of those powerful people in the society (meaning gangsters), then it's a very challenging task. If I can't collect the money, there will be pressure from my boss. That's why I don't like my job and I am looking for a legitimate job.

Some smuggled immigrants who work for the snakeheads may become the victims of gang warfare in Chinatown. One respondent stated that he knew a person who lost his life due to his association with human smugglers: "I know a guy who used to hang out with a gang because he needed money. He was involved in debt-collecting activities, and he was shot to death by a rival gang."

I believe that most illegal Chinese immigrants are unlikely to be involved in either violent or property crimes. However, because of their illegal immigration status, they may fall prey to criminals in their own community, thus creating and sustaining a large number of criminals in the community. I also think that the arrival of a large number of smuggled Chinese has resulted in the creation of an underground economy in which business transactions are not completely legal. Business owners and customers join together in compromising business regulations simply because it is cheaper or more effective to do so.

CONCLUSION

The first wave of Chinese immigrants who came to the United States in the mid-nineteenth century were called "sojourners" because they did not intend to settle here. Their main purpose was to earn enough money so that they could go back to China and live comfortably (Barth 1964). Their reluctance to settle in the United States made them easy targets for anti-immigration politicians and labor union leaders, who often portrayed the Chinese as people who could not be assimilated into American society (Saxton 1971). What about the current wave of illegal Chinese immigrants? Are they, like their predecessors, "sojourners," or are they here to stay?

Of the 300 immigrants in my sample, 190 (64 percent) said they plan to stay in the United States permanently; 85 (29 percent) said they plan to go back to China after they have earned enough money. Another 20 (7 percent) said they were undecided. Thus, my sample of respondents could not be called "sojourners."

Table 12.5 shows the characteristics of the respondents who wanted to stay. Subjects who had been living in the United States for a relatively longer period were more likely to have made up their mind about their future. Those who were not sure about their future were younger and had arrived more recently. Male respondents were more likely than female respondents to say that they planned to go back to China. Also, those who were still in debt were more likely to express their desire to go home than those who had paid off their debts. Finally, those who were employed full-time were more inclined to stay than those who were not fully employed. No other variables were statistically associated with a respondent's future plans.

Reasons for the Desire to Stay

Some of my respondents, notwithstanding their frustration over their working conditions or job prospects in the United States, were convinced that America

Table 12.5
Respondents' Future Plans

	Plan to stay in America	Plan to go back to China	Not sure
Number	190	85	20
Average age	32	32	27
Length of stay in U.S. (in months)	31	31	17
Percent male	73%	93%	80%
Percent who owe money	52%	69%	80%
Percent who are employed full time	84%	71%	60%

Notes: Thirty months was the average stay for the sample as a whole. The respective percentages for the sample were 79 percent male, 59 percent owing money, and 78 percent employed full-time.

is a better place to live than China. For example, a respondent from Minhou said:

I believe America is better than China, no matter how you compare the two countries. America is a free country with plenty of opportunities. Too bad I was fired five times in seven days. And I cannot adjust to the kind of frantic lifestyle here. Moreover, I need to work long hours. Nevertheless, I now realize that in order to be successful, you need to endure this kind of frustration. I am sure I made the right decision in coming here.

Others found solace in the thought that their families in China were enjoying the kind of status only a family with an overseas Chinese can achieve. A thirty-six-year-old male from Changle explained why it was so important for him to remain in the United States: "Since I came here, my family became rich. My parents are happy because they are respected by others. Now, my family members' sleeves are torn apart by others [meaning, many people in the neighborhood wish to be close to his family]."

Another subject, a twenty-one-year-old married male from Changle who was a factory worker in China, said he had decided to stay in the United States:

After all, I think I made the right decision in coming to the United States because there are so many opportunities to make money here. Although there is a lot of hardship, I only need to work a few years to repay the debt and then I can start saving. If I had remained in China, how much money could I have earned for the rest of my life? I wouldn't have had the opportunity to *fanshen* (to change one's social status).

A nineteen-year-old single woman from Changle who was earning $2,000 a month as a garment factory worker also said she intended to remain in the United States. She reasoned:

In general, I do not regret coming here. After all, for a long time, I was determined to improve my family's status, and now I have achieved that. Besides, I like what I am doing now, working as a seamstress in a garment factory. All I hope for is to repay the smuggling debts as soon as possible and then send money home to help my family enjoy a comfortable life. It's no big deal that I myself have to endure some hardship here. If a person's bitterness can bring happiness to so many people, it's worth it. However, once in a while, I feel like this kind of life is boring. You go to work every day from morning till night, and you can only have one day off.

Reasons for the Desire to Go Home

Eighty-five respondents (29 percent of the sample) said they planned to return to China after they earned enough money in the United States. I do not know how serious these respondents were about returning home. I assume they said they wanted to return to China mainly out of frustration and that if their conditions improved in the United States—especially if they became legal residents—they would stay.

A forty-five-year-old fisherman from Changle said he was extremely upset with his experiences in America:

After I was released from a safe house, I did not have a penny. I didn't have relatives or friends around either. I was wandering in the streets. At night, I slept underneath the vegetable stalls in Chinatown. I had no money to eat. I was starving for two days. Later, a Cantonese woman saw me, and she was very sympathetic. She gave me $10, a cup of coffee, and a Chinese rice cake. She basically saved a hopeless soul. A few hours later, I bumped into a friend, and he took me to his place and offered me food. How bitter it was! I have a never-ending story to tell about my experiences. So far, I haven't found a stable job. I regret that I came here. I am broke now. A lot of people from my neighborhood were sympathetic toward my experiences. I never thought America would be so difficult a place to make money. If you ask me now what happiness is, I will say it's my life back in China. Back there, I had two meals a day, and nothing else, but it was a most fortunate life. Here, people have no compassion. China is the best place to be. I have to cry out loud, "Give me back my wife!" She killed herself last month because she was overwhelmed with the amount of money we owe.

Other respondents were determined to go home because they came to realize that being a *meiguoke* (guest from a beautiful country) did not mean much after all. A thirty-nine-year-old male from Changle said:

My family is now poorer than ever before. Family members and my children are also getting lazier. Only the label *meiguoke* sounds very good. Whenever there is a new construction project in the village, people will come to us for a donation. Because I am a *meiguoke*, my family must contribute money for all kinds of construction projects.

Another respondent, a thirty-eight-year-old construction worker from Changle who was earning $1,800 a month as a cook in the United States, explained his frustration as follows:

Since I started to send money home, of course my family lives a much better life. Status? Well, I don't feel it has improved at all. To tell you the truth, I feel like garbage in the United States; there's no status at all. Besides, in my area, there are so many overseas Chinese, especially *meiguoke*, there's nothing special about being one. Before I came, I had no idea that America would be like this. Here, we sleep on the floor, and we work like slaves. I really regret coming here. At home, I lived and ate well, and work was light. Now, even though I have became a bit used to being here in America, I still want to go back as soon as possible. There's nothing appealing here. Although my job is stable, I see many other people like me having many difficulties. They get fired wherever they go. Those living with me in the same apartment cry all the time. That's why, for three years, I did not apply for any documents. I am going back in a few years; what's the point of applying for anything?

Other respondents who expressed their desire to go home emphasized other factors as their motives. A twenty-two-year-old single male from Fuzhou city who was working in a garment factory at the time of the interviews, said:

I regret I came. Here, people have no feelings for others. Everybody is so pragmatic. Life here is hard, and finding a job is difficult. Crime is a major problem, and it makes people feel unsafe. Once it's dark, we dare not go out of our apartment. We live in fear all the time.

Another subject, a forty-one-year-old male from Tingjiang who was unemployed at the time of the interviews, was perturbed by New York's Chinatown, which he thought was worse than his village in China:

I regret coming to America. It's hard to find a job; there is a lot of pressure here; and the environment is far worse than in Fuzhou. The hell with Chinatown! It's even worse than my village. It's really meaningless to be here!

Some respondents had become convinced that money is not the most important thing in life after all. They became philosophical about the shallowness of their existence in the United States, and even though they knew there were many good things about the United States, they simply could not see how they could take advantage of these benefits.

Such views capture the basic ambivalence that the Fujianese have about

America: on one hand, few would disavow the economic opportunities that the United States offers. On the other hand, actually gaining access to those opportunities is difficult—if not impossible. Furthermore, even if those opportunities can be grasped, converting the rewards into a satisfying life either in America or in China remains a far from certain process.

NOTES

This research was supported by grant SBR-11114 from the National Science Foundation. The views expressed here are solely those of the author.

1. I was aware that using purposive sampling techniques would limit the generalizability of this study's results in a statistical sense. However, due to the lack of information about the population of smuggled Chinese in New York City, a random sample was not feasible.

2. Workers in Chinese-owned restaurants and garment factories normally do not have paid vacations (Kwong 1997). In fact, they are not even allowed to take a vacation without pay. As a result, most workers have to quit their jobs if they need to take a break from work. When they are ready to resume work, they look for another job. During the interviews, respondents who were unemployed said that they were confident they would soon resume work. My multivariate analysis revealed no statistically significant factors about persons or their means of entry or length of stay in the United States that could explain unemployment.

3. In New York City, many people work long hours during the week and weekends. This is true among wage earners in various service and manufacturing industries as well as professionals in law, finance, and so on.

4. Before calculating the hourly and monthly wages of those who were working full-time, I removed six subjects (four restaurant owners, one construction/renovation business owner, and one gambling den owner/operator) from the sample because they were self-employed, and their wages were substantially higher than those of wage earners. I also did not include a female subject who was working as a prostitute. She said she made $4,000 a month and considered herself to be working part-time.

5. Although I did not ask the respondents whether they pay taxes on their income, it is no secret in the Chinese community that a substantial number of employees in the Chinese business sector are paid in cash by their employers so they can avoid paying taxes. To prevent being audited by the Internal Revenue Service, some employers pay their employees most of their income in cash and a small portion by check. Thus, both the employers and employees pay taxes on only a small portion of their income. In examining the monthly income of smuggled Chinese, the amount considered was the actual take-home pay, on which they probably would not pay taxes.

6. As mentioned earlier, my sample is not a random sample, and thus, there is some possibility of underrepresentation of the worst cases.

7. Most illegal Chinese immigrants, as well as many legal Chinese immigrants, who work for Chinese employers are denied benefits such as paid leave, health care insurance, and related medical coverage.

8. Because some subjects borrowed money from both friends and relatives, these three figures do not add up to 264.

9. In this chapter, when I discuss ''mental illness,'' I want to stress that these con-

ditions are not medically diagnosed but based on common understandings and observations of those in my sample and others I interviewed.

10. Rent for a two-bedroom apartment in Chinatown may range from $800 to $1,200 a month. Often, a person rents a unit and sublets it to a dozen or so people. This way, each tenant needs to pay not more than $100 a month for rent. Landlords are generally reluctant to see so many people living in their properties, but they tolerate it because they know they are not going to receive many complaints from their tenants even if the property is poorly maintained.

11. In the aftermath of the grounding of the *Golden Venture* human cargo ship near New York City, federal prosecutors in New York City indicted the Fuk Ching gang as a racketeering enterprise. More than a dozen core members of the gang were arrested, and most pleaded guilty to the charges brought against them. The primary leader of the gang was arrested in Hong Kong after he fled the United States. He was extradited back to the United States to stand trial for murder. That was probably why the respondent said the gang "was history," even though the gang is still active in Chinatown.

REFERENCES

Barth, Gunther
1964   *Bitter Strength: A History of Chinese in the United States*. Cambridge: Harvard University Press.
Burdman, Pamela
1993   American Dream Sours in N.Y. *San Francisco Chronicle*, April 29: A8.
Chan, Ying
1993   Forced into Sex Slavery. *New York Daily News*, May 17: 7.
1995   JFK Gangs Prey on Chinese; Victims Grabbed for "Easy Money." *New York Daily News*, April 10: 5.
Chin, Ko-lin
1996   *Chinatown Gangs: Extortion, Enterprise, and Ethnicity*. New York: Oxford University Press.
Chiswick, Barry
1988   *Illegal Aliens: Their Employment and Employers*. Kalamazoo, Michigan: W.E. Upjohn Institute for Employment Research.
Clark, Rebecca, Jeffrey Passel, Wendy Zimmermann, and Michael Fix
1995   *Fiscal Impacts of Undocumented Aliens: Selected Estimates for Seven States*. Washington, D.C.: Urban Institute.
Cornelius, Wayne
1978   *Mexican Migration to the United States: Causes, Consequences, and U.S. Responses*. Cambridge: Center for International Studies, Massachusetts Institute of Technology.
1989   Impact of the 1986 U.S. Immigration Law on Emigration from Rural Mexican Sending Communities. *Population and Development Review* 15 (4): 689–705.
Dowty, Alan
1987   *Closed Borders: The Contemporary Assault on Freedom of Movement*. New Haven, Connecticut: Yale University Press.
English, T. J.
1995   *Born to Kill*. New York: William Morrow.

Faison, Seth
1993   Kidnappings Tied to Fall of a Gang. *New York Times*, October 5: B1.
Finder, Alan
1995   Despite Tough Laws, Sweatshops Flourish. *New York Times*, February 6: A1.
Gargan, Edward
1981   Asian Investors Battle for Footholds in Chinatown. *New York Times*, December 29: A1.
Glaberson, William
1989   6 Seized in Smuggling Asians into New York. *New York Times*, May 5: B3.
Haller, Karen
1997   Shadow People. *Connecticut Magazine* (June): 54–61.
Hood, Marlowe
1993   The New Slaves of Chinatown. *South China Morning Post*, June 13: 1.
Ianni, Francis
1974   *Black Mafia: Ethnic Succession in Organized Crime.* New York: Simon and Schuster.
James, Daniel
1991   *Illegal Immigration—An Unfolding Crisis.* Lanham, Maryland: University Press of America.
Jia, Ling (in Chinese)
1995   Why Do People Have to Prey on Their Own? *Critical Magazine* No. 14 (April): 10–19.
Kennedy, Randy
1995   Five Men Face Charges of Murder in a Slaying. *New York Times*, September 21: B3.
Kinkead, Gwen
1992   *Chinatown: A Portrait of a Closed Society.* New York: HarperCollins.
Kleinfield, N. R.
1986   Mining Chinatown's "Mountain of Gold." *New York Times*, June 1: D1.
Kwong, Peter
1987   *The New Chinatown.* New York: Hill and Wang.
1997   *Forbidden Workers: Illegal Chinese Immigrants and American Labor.* New York: New Press.
Lii, Jane
1995   Week in Sweatshop Reveals Grim Conspiracy of the Poor. *New York Times*, March 12: 1.
Long, Patrick Du Phuoc
1996   *The Dream Shattered.* Boston: Northeastern University Press.
Lorch, Donatella
1992   A Flood of Illegal Aliens Enters U.S. via Kennedy: Requesting Political Asylum Is Usual Ploy. *New York Times*, March 18: B2.
Lyall, Sarah
1992   Albany Sues U.S. on Aliens Held in Prison. *New York Times*, April 28: B1.
Lyman, Stanford M.
1974   *Chinese Americans.* New York: Random House.
Mahler, Sarah
1995   *American Dreaming: Immigrant Life on the Margins.* Princeton, New Jersey: Princeton University Press.

Marshall, Ineke Haen, Editor
1997   *Minorities, Migrants, and Crime*. Thousand Oaks, California: Sage.
Martin, Mildred Crowl
1977   *Chinatown Angry Angel*. Palo Alto, California: Pacific Books.
Myers, Willard
1992   The United States under Siege: Assault on the Borders: Chinese Smuggling 1983–1992. Unpublished manuscript.
New York Times
1993   Voyage to Life of Shattered Dreams. July 23: B1.
1993   An Increasing Sense of Vulnerability: Mourning a Murder Victim, Chinese Express Frustration with Crimes at Restaurants. December 3: B1.
1994   Chinatown Holds Its First Parade to Mark Mainland Anniversary. September 26: B3.
North, D., and M. Houstoun
1976   *The Characteristics and Role of Illegal Aliens in the U.S. Labor Market: An Exploratory Study*. Washington, D.C.: Linton.
Padavan, Frank
1994   *Our Teeming Shore*. New York State Senate Committee on Cities.
Reid, Alexander
1986   New Asian Immigrants, New Garment Center. *New York Times*, May 10: A1.
Saxton, Alexander
1971   *The Indispensable Enemy: Labor and the Anti-Chinese Movement in California*. Berkeley: University of California Press.
Schmid, Alex, Editor
1996   *Migration and Crime*. Milan: International Scientific and Professional Advisory Council of the United Nations Crime Prevention and Criminal Justice Programme.
Sellin, Thorsten
1938   *Culture Conflict and Crime*. New York: Social Science Research Council.
Sing Tao Daily (in Chinese)
1992   Police Chief Urges Fujianese Immigrants Not to Be Afraid of Reporting Crime to Authorities. May 7: 28.
1993   Alan Lau Denies He Controlled Human Smuggling. November 9: 28.
1997   The Emergence of Fujianese Overshadows the Cantonese. October 27: A26.
Smith, Paul
1997   Chinese Migrant Trafficking: A Global Challenge. In *Human Smuggling*. Washington, D.C.: Center for Strategic and International Studies. Pp. 1–22.
Sung, Betty Lee
1967   *Mountain of Gold: The Story of the Chinese in America*. New York: Macmillan.
Tai Kung Pao (in Chinese)
1993   Foreign Remittance, Foreign Language, Long-Distance Phone Call. June 15: 2.
Tsai, Shih-shan Henry
1986   *The Chinese Experience in America*. Bloomington: Indiana University Press.
Tsao, Chang-ching (in Chinese)
1993   Illegal Migrants Had No Rights to Pursue Freedom? *World Journal Magazine* (July 25): S8.
U.S. General Accounting Office
1993   *Benefits for Illegal Aliens*. Washington, D.C.: General Accounting Office.

U.S. Senate

1978 [1877] *Report of the Joint Special Committee to Investigate Chinese Immigration.* Reprint. New York: Arno Press.

1992 *Asian Organized Crime. Hearing before the Permanent Subcommittee on Investigations of the Committee on Governmental Affairs, October 3, November 5–6, 1991.* Washington, D.C.: U.S. Government Printing Office.

Wang, Zheng

1996 Ocean-going Smuggling of Illegal Chinese Immigrants: Operation, Causation and Policy Implications. *Transnational Organized Crime* 2 (1) (Spring): 49–65.

Wong, Bernard

1982 *Chinatown.* New York: Holt, Rinehart, and Winston.

World Journal (in Chinese)

1990 Chinese Restaurant Workers Suffer from Poor Working and Living Conditions. February 27: 23.

1994 The Existence of Sweatshops Signifies a New Chapter in the History of New Migrants. September 10: A4.

1998 Fujianese Dominate the Chinese Buffet Restaurant Industry. January 10: E1.

1998 The Hefty Price of Illegal Migration. January 11: E1.

Wren, Christopher

1996 Heroin Indictments Link Drugs to Smuggling of Aliens. *New York Times*, March 13, 1996: B3.

Zhang, Sheldon, and Mark Gaylord

1996 Bound for the Golden Mountain: The Social Organization of Chinese Alien Smuggling. *Crime, Law and Social Change* 25: 1–16.

Zhou, Min

1992 *Chinatown: The Socioeconomic Potential of an Urban Enclave.* Philadelphia: Temple University Press.

PART III

THE RESPONSES

13

Refugees at Risk: The Sanctuary Movement and Its Aftermath

Victoria Rader

The treatment of refugees is both a religious and political concern; in fact, the Western legal practice of asylum is grounded in Judeo-Christian traditions of compassion and justice for the destitute and persecuted. This chapter traces the evolution of the sanctuary movement, a nationwide, grassroots movement of religious citizens in the United States who challenged state hegemony regarding refugee policy. Between 1981 and 1990, the movement passed through three stages, beginning with a small group of U.S. church people assisting undocumented Guatemalans and Salvadorans with their immigration problems, to an "evasion strategy" of quietly transporting and harboring new arrivals through an "underground railroad," to the defiant public declaration of churches and synagogues as sanctuaries from the U.S. government. In the process, the sanctuary movement evolved from a focus on hiding "illegal immigrants," to a platform from which to speak out against U.S. foreign policy. Ultimately, it posed a fundamental question that U.S. citizens rarely stop to ask: What are the moral responsibilities of privileged, First World people in relation to poor and oppressed people in the Third World? After examining the evolution of sanctuary, the chapter explores the internal structure of the movement in relation to race and ethnicity, nationality, gender, and class and then analyzes how the transformative experiences of those within the movement led to a new theology of accompaniment. The aftermath of the movement is also examined.

THE EARLY DEVELOPMENT OF THE SANCTUARY MOVEMENT: THE EDUCATION OF U.S. CHURCH WORKERS

Sanctuary members commonly locate the beginning of their movement with two precipitating events. The first occurred outside Tucson, Arizona, in the summer of 1980, when a group of middle-class Salvadorans from El Salvador were found in the blistering Sonoran desert. Thirteen had died by the time the Border Patrol found them; the other thirteen were arrested and jailed while awaiting deportation hearings (Cunningham 1995: 14). Widespread media coverage of the incident, including accounts of torture and death in El Salvador, generated concern within several liberal churches in the Tucson area. Reverend John Fife of the Southside Presbyterian Church arranged to meet with the survivors. Reverend Dick Sholin and writer Gary MacEoin persuaded the Tucson Ecumenical Council to become a funding umbrella for legal work on behalf of Central American refugees. A small group of Catholics, Presbyterians, Quakers, and Jews formed the Tucson Ecumenical Council Task Force on Central America (Cunningham 1995: 16).

At the same time, U.S. priests and nuns working in Central America were sending word that, "contrary to what American officials are saying, there is a bloodbath going on" (Crittenden 1988: 23). Immigration lawyers and social workers also were hearing accounts of atrocities from Salvadorans and Guatemalans arriving at the U.S. border (Cunningham 1995: 18). Task force members began assisting Salvadorans and Guatemalan detainees by posting bond, offering legal assistance at deportation meetings, and helping people prepare their asylum applications. In June 1981 the task force decided on a strategy of bailing out Central American detainees in El Centro, California, in a way that would attract as much media attention as possible. They notified the press and traveled five hours to the detention center, which housed 300–400 prisoners in very bad conditions and isolated from legal assistance. They found that many more Salvadorans than Guatemalans were arriving at the border. For two weeks, sixty rotating volunteers processed asylum forms and freed (on bail) ninety Central Americans (Cunningham 1995: 28). In an intense fund-raising campaign, the task force raised $ .75 million for bonds and legal expenses (MacEoin 1985: 16). In the process, they received a crash course on immigration and refugee law.

ASYLUM

U.S. refugee laws did not formally emerge until after World War II, when the United States, principally for humanitarian reasons, began to admit thousands of displaced Europeans. As the Cold War intensified, U.S. refugee practices began to favor individuals fleeing from communist countries. Not until 1980 did the United States adopt a comprehensive and permanent position on refugee determination, which brought the U.S. definition of a refugee more in line with the United Nations 1967 Protocol Relating to the Status of Refugees and indirectly addressed the political biases inherent in U.S. asylum and refugee policy. The new law, the Refugee Act of 1980, adopted the United Nations definition of a refugee as any person who, "owing to a well-founded fear of being persecuted for reasons of race, religion, nationality, membership in a particular social group or political opinion, is outside the country of his nationality and is unable or, owing to such fear, is unwilling to avail himself of the protection of that country." Central to both refugee and asylum law is the principle of *non-refoulement*—that people should not be forcibly returned to their countries if they are likely to be persecuted. This reform introduced procedures designed to provide unbiased, case-by case assessment of individual claims for refugee and asylum status (Mahler 1995: 175).

Nevertheless, the anticommunist bias of U.S. practices persisted. This was particularly salient in U.S. government treatment of Salvadoran and Guatemalan refugees in the 1980s. About 2 million Central Americans fled violence and civil war between 1980 and 1983, the largest human displacement in the Western Hemisphere in modern history (Lorentzen 1991: 13). Yet the State Department continued to argue that El Salvador and Guatemala had not suffered the same widespread levels of violence as other countries. These claims were contradicted by documented reports of human rights groups such as Amnesty International, Americas Watch, and the Washington Office on Latin America (Lorentzen 1991: 12). Still, the U.S. government considered Salvadorans and Guatemalans as "illegal immigrants" here for economic reasons and usually rejected their asylum applications. Sanctuary participants believed that if the U.S. government acknowledged "political" refugees from client states with high levels of human rights abuse, it would raise embarrassing questions about U.S. foreign policy. The refugees' presence, moreover, might bring unwanted public exposure of U.S. covert and overt military activities in Central America (Lorentzen 1991: 12).

The Tucson church workers processing claims in the El Centro detention center discovered quickly enough for themselves that the protection supposedly provided by the 1980 act was widely ignored. Salvadorans and Guatemalans were not even informed of their legal right to apply for political asylum. Instead, they were pressed to sign voluntary departure forms, thereby waiving the right that they might have to remain in the country and apply for extended voluntary departure (Golden and McConnell 1986: 41). Indeed, a national network of immigration lawyers documented violations of due process "so consistent as to constitute a policy," and the United Nations high commissioner for refugees claimed that the United States was failing to fulfill its international obligations to refugees. The U.S. administration also chose to disregard the Geneva Convention of 1949, ratified by the U.S. Senate in 1955, relative to the treatment of civilians during a time of war. The Geneva Convention prohibits all signatory nations from returning refugees to a war zone (Golden and McConnell 1986: 41). The U.S. government denied the existence of war in Central America.

Several months after Tucson church workers began educating themselves in asylum politics, the second defining moment occurred. A friend visited the ranch of Quakers Jim and Pat Corbett to recount a distressing incident in which he had picked up a young Salvadoran hitchhiker and, soon thereafter, was stopped at a roadblock by the Border Patrol, where the agents arrested the Salvadoran and took him away. Jim Corbett grew upset when he heard the story, knowing enough to fear that this young immigrant and others like him would face possible death if deported. The next day, he decided to try to track down the young man. He made some phone calls and drove south from Tucson, uncovering the hidden world of "holding tanks," desert detention centers, and desperate Central Americans awaiting deportation.

Finagling his way into the Nogales prison across the Mexico border, Corbett was faced with dozens of prisoners begging him to notify their families that they were being deported. Corbett stayed several days writing letters to relatives and strategizing with the detainees, who feared severe repression upon their return. He took down testimony of village massacres, torture, rape and murder of family members. Corbett left the prison shaken and outraged and immediately contacted Mexican church workers, offering to guide Central Americans through a hole in the border fence. Then he drove home to Tucson to urge the Ecumenical Task Force to take stronger action (Cunningham 1995: 23–25). There was already an established support network within the clandestine church in Mexico, Corbett argued. Now church people needed to extend that support into the United States by creating a network of "safe houses" reminiscent of the "underground railway" that Quakers played an important role in building prior to the Civil War (Cunningham 1995: 25).

After months of frustrated efforts, plowing through the ponderous legal and bureaucratic asylum process, Tucson task force members were amenable to Corbett's passionate stand. For one thing, they were running out of money: they had tapped all their friends, families, and coworkers for contributions, hocked their valuables, taken out loans, and gotten second mortgages on their homes. Even then, they had assisted only a tiny fraction of the huge new influx of Central Americans arriving at the border, while deportation planes flew hundreds of frightened detainees back weekly (Golden and McConnell 1986: 42). Church workers also faced a moral dilemma in encouraging detainees to apply for asylum: many Central Americans feared that applying for asylum would be seen as taking a political stance against their government and that, if deported, they could be targeted for retribution by the government—or even killed. Asylum applicants also feared that their statements would be used against family members still living in the country (Mahler 1995: 14).

It also was becoming obvious that those filing for asylum status, though buying a year or two of time, were losing their cases. Of 5,500 requests nationwide by Salvadorans for political asylum in fiscal year 1980–1981, only 2 were granted. Of 22,000 Salvadorans applying during 1982, only 74 were granted asylum. Of the 100 refugees the Tucson church workers bonded out, 95 percent of the cases eventually would be denied. The Immigration and Naturalization Service (INS) required that detainees produce written, "certified" proof of persecution, which was impossible to accomplish in the midst of civil war. In September 1982, Tucson lawyers filed a $30 million lawsuit against the federal government for unlawful deportations, and the task force quietly turned to "evasion services" (Golden and McConnell 1986: 42).

THE OFFER OF HOSPITALITY: DEVELOPMENT OF AN UNDERGROUND RAILROAD

It began small and quickly expanded. Along the Mexican–U.S. border at Nogales, people were sheltering Central Americans in homes and churches, where they were picked up by sanctuary workers and driven to Tucson. Jim Corbett was secretly harboring over twenty Central Americans on his ranch, while Southside Presbyterian elders were quietly taking refugees into the church. Gradually, a loose network of churches, synagogues, and families became temporary way stations for refugees heading north: Tucson's underground extended south to Mexico City and was developing lines to Chicago, Los Angeles, San Francisco, Seattle, New York, and Boston. Eventually, the underground spread along a network of religious affiliates into thirty-four states. The illegality of harboring and transporting undocumented immigrants prevents an accurate count of how many people were involved, but estimates are that about 70,000 North Americans and 2,000–3,000 Central Americans participated (Lorentzen 1991: 15). (This was a tiny fraction of the .5 million Guatemalans and Salvadorans entering the United States illegally each year.) Tucson lawyers Margo Cowan and Lupe Castillo viewed the creation of sanctuary as "primarily a tactic to educate middle-and-upper class American churchgoers on the Central American refugee issue . . . most refugees don't need gringos helping them across the border" (Crittenden 1988: 216). Many of the participating churches had a history of sheltering the homeless and feeding the hungry; some had assisted Indochinese refugees after the close of the Indochina War (Bau 1985: 13). Only this time, it was against the law.

The sanctuary movement spread through the social action committees of churches and synagogues. Some congregations chose to be part of an "overground railroad," assisting those with temporary legal status and providing legal services to undocumented Central Americans. Those groups willing to break the law offered transportation and provided food, shelter, and medical aid to undocumented families. Sometimes, a small core of dedicated activists in a social concerns committee would sidestep the whole issue of legal status when asking help from their congregation, withholding a family's actual legal status until the new immigrants could "became real" to the congregation (Lorentzen 1991: 64).

As Tucson church workers began organizing resettlement in 1981, they came into contact with Los Angeles and San Francisco Bay Area lawyers and churches doing the same thing. Berkeley pastor Gus Schultz, who had pioneered sanctuary for conscientious objectors to the Vietnam War in Berkeley a decade earlier, galvanized a coalition of Bay Area pastors to consider the idea of declaring their churches as sanctuaries for Central Americans fleeing violence. This action was prompted by an incident in which an INS agent had chased an undocumented man into a church and arrested him there (Lorentzen 1991: 29).

THE MOVE FROM HOSPITALITY TO DIRECT ACTION: DECLARING PUBLIC SANCTUARY AND OPENLY DEFYING THE LAW

In November 1981, members of the Tucson task force met to evaluate their strategy of evasion services. They concluded that they had assisted only a few hundred refugees, while thousands more were being picked up and deported or forced into hiding. Although the movement was expanding in numbers, it was failing to build strong pressure against U.S. refugee policy. Task force members were learning about the growing U.S. military support for the repressive regimes in El Salvador and Guatemala and for the Contras in Nicaragua. As long as the movement stayed hidden, they were handicapped in alerting the U.S. public to the plight of Central Americans (Golden and McConnell 1986: 46). Then, around Thanksgiving 1981, an INS attorney approached a movement lawyer and warned her that the INS knew "something was going on with Corbett, Fife and some Central Americans" and that they'd better stop, or the government would indict them. Now there was the additional worry that leaders might be jailed before they had the chance to make Central America a public issue. Fife suggested that they preempt the government by publicly declaring Southside Church a sanctuary for Central American refugees (Cunningham 1995: 31).

On March 24, 1982, the anniversary of the assassination of the beloved Salvadoran martyr Archbishop Oscar Romero, the members of Southside publicly proclaimed their church as sanctuary. Five Bay Area churches declared sanctuaries on the same day. Southside's pastor, John Fife, sent a letter to the U.S. attorney general:

We are writing to inform you that Southside United Presbyterian Church will publicly violate the Immigration and Nationality Act, Section 274(A).... We take this action because we believe that the current policy and practice of the United States Government with regard to Central American refugees is illegal and immoral.... We beg of you, in the name of God, to do justice and love mercy in the administration of your office. We ask that "extended voluntary departure" be granted to refugees from Central America and that current deportation proceedings against these victims be stopped. Until such time, we will not cease to extend the sanctuary of the church to undocumented people from Central America. Obedience to God requires this of all of us. (Cunningham 1995: xi)

For a church or synagogue to publicly declare itself as sanctuary was a bold move, in active defiance of the law. The harboring or transportation of an "undocumented alien'' was a federal felony punishable by a $2,000 fine and/or five years' imprisonment. Such a penalty could be imposed for each assisted "alien." Given the heavy punishment, churches and synagogues underwent an intense, *collective* process of moral discernment: they invited undocumented Central Americans to speak to them as well as members of other sanctuary churches; they informed themselves about conditions in Central America as well as refugee policies. Rather than a few activists within the church quietly hiding a new immigrant, entire congregations were required to come to a shared decision; they had to choose sides.

THE MINISTRY OF HOSPITALITY

Sanctuary churches claimed the biblical obligation of hospitality to strangers, particularly those in need. There are long-standing traditions of sanctuary in the church and synagogue, sharing in common the sense of covenant to obey God's law when it conflicts with the state. Yahweh, the God of the Old Testament, commanded Moses to set aside cities and places of refuge in Canaan, the Promised Land, where the persecuted could seek asylum. These cities of refuge were for the Israelites, ''as well as the stranger and sojourner among you'' (Num. 35: 15). The proclamation of sanctuary also draws inspiration from the centrality of the Exodus and its aftermath (Golden and McConnell 1986: 15).

Sanctuary is a civic as well as scriptural tradition, recognized in Roman law, medieval canon law, and English common law. In the 1600s every church in England could be a sanctuary from the throne. More recently, some European monasteries hid Jews fleeing the Holocaust. During the seventeenth century the whole North American continent was seen by many as a sanctuary from European political and religious persecution. Within the United States, Pennsylvania and Rhode Island sheltered the outcast. Sanctuary became a part of what it meant to be American: ''give me your tired, your poor, your huddled masses, yearning to breathe free.''

As the spirit of sanctuary took new birth in the United States in the 1980s, the Chicago Task Force on Central America offered to coordinate the expanding underground railroad. This group had organized in 1980 to protest U.S. policy in Central America after the murder of four North American churchwomen in El Salvador. Like the Tucson group, its steering committee included mostly nuns, priests, and ministers who were well informed through their churches about conditions in Central America. Far from the border, the Chicago group developed a closer connection with border issues when Sister Darlene Nicgorski, who had lived and worked with refugees in Guatemala, joined the staff. The Chicago group worked tirelessly, supporting the forty-five churches and synagogues declaring sanctuary by early 1983, along with 600 supporting congregations and religious organizations and fifty local organizational committees in the movement. By the autumn of 1983, at least twenty-four more churches had declared, bringing the total close to seventy, with up to 30,000 U.S. church and synagogue members involved. By summer 1984 the number of sanctuaries had grown to 150, with thousands more participants (Bau 1985: 12).

THE PUBLIC TRIAL OF SANCTUARY WORKERS

In the initial months after declaring sanctuary, no one knew how the government might respond. The Reagan administration decided to infiltrate the movement but not openly confront the church. Leon Ring, chief of the Tucson Border Patrol, said: "Certain arrests could have taken place if we would have wanted to, but we felt the government would end up looking ridiculous, especially as far as going into church property. . . . These church groups wanted publicity. They were baiting us to overreact. We have been deliberately low key" (Golden and McConnell 1986: 47). As the movement spread, the government secretly surveilled and wiretapped activists in Texas and Arizona, and finally in early 1985, they indicted sixteen sanctuary workers in Tucson (Lorentzen 1991: 16). In September 1985, the sanctuary workers were put on trial. As with other publicized trials of social activists, such as the Catonsville Nine and the Chicago Seven, the sanctuary trial became a highly visible, contested arena in which each side made its case to the public. Were sanctuary workers alien smugglers and criminal conspirators? Or were they religious Americans assisting bona fide refugees who were persecuted? Though eight of the defendants were eventually convicted, and one young woman, Stacy Merit, served some time, the government's attempt to suppress the movement with these indictments had the opposite effect. Media coverage created enormous new interest in sanctuary. The media treated defendants sympathetically, reporting widely on their motives, testimony the judge had refused to allow inside the courtroom. The media exposure of widespread government surveillance and wiretapping inside churches and synagogues also swayed public opinion against the state. Forty-seven members of Congress intervened in an unusual request for leniency in the defendants' sentencing, and Amnesty International vowed to declare them prisoners of conscience if they were imprisoned (Coutin 1993: 145). After the trial, the media continued covering sanctuary and related issues, prompting the movement's greatest period of growth (Lorentzen 1991: 17).

INTERNAL STRUCTURE OF THE MOVEMENT: RACE AND ETHNICITY, NATIONALITY, CLASS, AND GENDER

Sanctuary participants were overwhelmingly white, upper-middle-class North Americans who, in essence, chose to reduce their social distance from oppressed Third World people of color. Complexities of race and ethnicity, nationality, class, and gender relations inevitably influenced movement dynamics. The movement attracted considerable media attention precisely because of the institutionalized racism and nativism that judges newsworthy the actions of white, middle-class North Americans over the actions of poor Third World people of color. The U.S. corporate media ignored the plight—and the heroism—of Guatemalans and Salvadorans, both within the United States and in Central America. The media were, however, willing to focus on North American heroes. As sanctuary cofounder Jim Corbett explained, the "media are not interested in the indigenous martyrs of Central America, but they are fascinated with the willingness of U.S. citizens to go to some slight risk in order to help refugees avoid capture" (Golden and McConnell 1986: 60). One exception to this norm was media coverage of occasional stories of refugee *victimization*; the widespread coverage of the Sonoran Desert travesty and the arrest of a refugee inside the Bay Area church galvanized early involvement in Tucson and Berkeley. On the other hand, the media rarely reported on refugee accounts of persecution in Salvador or Guatemala by government forces or evidence of U.S. complicity in the slaughter that was occurring. When sanctuary organizers attempted to direct the media to Chiapas, Mexico, where 200,000 Guatemalan Indians were barely surviving in refugee camps, the media declined, preferring human interest stories of individual refugees and of individual churches and synagogues housing them (Golden and McConnell 1986: 60). Authors Golden and McConnell argue that the almost total blackout of media coverage of these larger issues—especially in Guatemala—had serious implications: "The result of this undetected racism is that the plight of the Guatemalan Indians has not reached national attention. Individual Salvadoran and Nicaraguan deaths still receive more attention than the attempted extinction of Native American nations of the Guatemalan highlands" (Golden and McConnell 1986: 60).

Another aspect of institutional racism in the media is reflected in the selective coverage of sanctuary workers. When 600 African-Americans of Operation Push in Chicago issued a declaration of sanctuary and welcomed a Salvadoran family of five, the media ignored the ceremony. Several Native American communities sheltered Guatemalan refugees, a fascinating story receiving little or no media attention (Golden and McConnell 1986: 5).

Clearly, one of the most significant privileges of white, middle-class allies is their ability to draw attention by actions of solidarity to the suffering and injustice of poor people of color, which is otherwise ignored. There is a rich U.S. tradition of this kind of racial and class alliance. In 1964, for example, almost 1,000 mostly white, upper-middle-class college students ventured south to support black civil rights workers in Mississippi Freedom Summer, capturing the nation's attention and helping to create conditions favorable to passing the Voting Rights Act. The historic parallel to which sanctuary members most often referred—for inspiration and legitimization—was the Underground Railroad developed to resist the Fugitive Slave Law, which Congress passed in 1850. White allies established "stations" in cellars, barns, attics, church towers, old mills, caves in the woods, and back rooms in reputable businesses. The U.S. government made arrests for illegally conducting slaves to safety, and the sentences of convicted conductors were much more severe than in the sanctuary movement (Golden and McConnell 1986: 57). Once again, while white allies received national attention and evoked change, poor people of color who took equal or more risk were ignored. The northern media consistently chronicled the heroism of white abolitionists, tokenizing the courage and ingenuity of activists like Harriet Tubman and the African-American community in general. In fact, the black community overwhelmingly harbored and supported fugitives at great risk to themselves. Golden and McConnell note that no underground railroad could have functioned without the assistance of black "vigilance committees," which functioned to absorb runaway slaves, purchasing clothing and medicine, giving money, and helping them find jobs. Like these vigilance committees, undocumented Central Americans in the 1980s, having barely established their own foothold in the United States and risking their freedom, harbored the overwhelming majority of their undocumented compatriots. Sanctuary accommodated a tiny fraction of the total number. Such acts of solidarity by poor Central Americans were not considered "news" by mainstream media (Golden and McConnell 1986: 60–61). The racial bias that made invisible the instrumental and heroic role of the African-American community in the initial Underground Railroad continued in this century to ignore the role of poor people of color in caring for one another. Adding to the racism is the ideological bias of Western individualism, which emphasizes individual heroism and overlooks the courage of a group of people. In the case of sanctuary, these biases were reinforced by nativism.

The media can be not only racist but sexist in their construction of news. Once again, this bias is inextricably embedded within the larger social structure—in this case, gender roles—as well as the ideology of individualism. Media accounts of sanctuary consistently focused on a few key male "leaders" of what was, in fact, a highly decentralized, grassroots movement in which women outnumbered men by about two-thirds (Lorentzen 1991: 3). Given the gender structure of Christian churches, it is not surprising that many of the individuals whom the media construed as leaders were male—priests, pastors, and elders—who occupied positions of authority within their church communities (Cunningham 1995: 15). What was consistently ignored in media accounts was the "hidden work" of women in the movement. Contrary to one leader's claim that the movement "runs by itself, on faith," women literally produced the movement through their organization and coordination of movement activities as well as attending to the multiple, everyday responsibilities of resettling refugees (Cunningham 1995: 15; Golden and McConnell 1986; Lorentzen 1991).

Though middle-class, white laywomen could not attract the same media attention as white male clergy, they could tap into the many social networks of which they were a part, acting as a bridge between refugees and church and synagogue members in the local communities. Women did the bulk of the work preparing for the refugees' arrival, including fund-raising, locating living quarters and cleaning them, and soliciting furniture, food, linen, clothing, and cookware. Lorentzen found considerable gender consciousness among women in the Chicago wing of the movement and interesting differences between laywomen and nuns. Catholic sisters tended to be more political in their orientation than laywomen, drawing upon their extensive travel and residence in Central America and firsthand knowledge of the issues. Many had experience at organizing and fund-raising, as well as access to a wide network of religious and professional organizations and social justice agencies. Laywomen tended to express more humanitarian motives for their participation. They relied on their positions in informal, woman-based networks through which they customarily channeled goods and services as volunteers in their communities (Lorentzen 1991: 80).

Ethnic differences also played a significant role within the movement. In the beginning, sanctuary members badly underestimated refugee needs: Salvadorans and Guatemalans with illegal status were totally vulnerable in their new, unfamiliar surroundings. This made them completely dependent upon the goodwill of sanctuary members. "When the first . . . refugees came," one movement member noted, "we didn't realize they wouldn't speak Spanish. They had long skirts, braids. They were Indians. We were really insensitive that way" (Lorentzen 1991: 38). Even when families spoke Spanish, they rarely spoke English. Many new arrivals came from the countryside and suffered extreme "culture shock" in the United States. Many were terrified, having only recently survived the traumas of both war and the passage north. When a family arrived at one Chicago church, a sanctuary participant recalled that "they were afraid they'd see tanks coming down the street. That's when we realized their level of fear" (Lorentzen 1991: 44). In fact, both refugees and sanctuary members initially were fearful of INS and the Federal Bureau of Investigation (FBI) "harassment."

As sanctuary members involved themselves in the everyday lives of the refugees, they became aware of their own Anglo, middle-class assumptions. There were different expectations about the length of time a refugee should remain dependent on the movement. Some members expressed concern about how slowly the refugees were learning English or assimilating into U.S. culture. Then, there was the surprise arrival of extended family members who also needed support. Some Anglo workers were disturbed when Central American women took lovers or got pregnant. "While they're here, they shouldn't have kids," said one Chicago worker (Lorentzen 1991: 65). Another worker described her experience: "She arrived pregnant. We thought, 'Oh oh, nobody even told us this.' She didn't know how far pregnant she was. . . . Nobody knew. She'd had minimal care. . . . We started hysterically trying to figure out where she'd give birth. . . . Everywhere we took her, she was either too high a risk or not in their region. . . . I asked a friend, 'What would happen if we just showed up at a hospital?' She said, 'We've turned in illegals before.' " Time ran out, and the birth took place at the refugee's apartment, attended by fifteen extended family members and a Spanish-speaking midwife whom someone knew. This event was perhaps the caretaker's and refugee's closest, least conflicted moment together. "There were very interesting things going on," the sanctuary worker explained. "Grandma . . . was praying out loud (in) her Guatemalan language. . . .

there was a sensation in the room. . . . I felt in touch with women since the beginning of time, delivering a baby. I felt the flow of womanness going across centuries of time. It was the strength of women doing what all women can do. It's a bond all women share'' (Lorentzen 1995: 69). Immediately after the birth, cultural differences resurfaced. The sanctuary worker was concerned that the relatives weren't handing the baby over to the mother so that the two could ''bond.'' Later, the worker was distressed that the mother preferred formula over breast-feeding (Lorentzen 1995: 70).

Thus, while sanctuary confronted the forces of inequality that permeated relations between the United States and Central America, the movement itself was pervaded by those same structuring forces: privileged sanctuary workers held the purse strings and the power, and their cultural norms of ''helping'' led to what many Central Americans referred to as ''paternalism.'' One sanctuary refugee commented: ''The Anglos sincerely believe that they are superior, a superior race to us, that they know everything, know everybody, and they are able to do everything. And we are like second-class citizens. . . . It's a type of racism'' (Cunningham 1995: 155). Another refugee gave her opinion: ''The majority of North Americans do not have frequent contact with other classes. I don't know if it is an educational thing or cultural but there are those who see us as less. There is racism. . . . And there are those who are very friendly, very good'' (Cunningham 1995: 155). It was an anguished process for North Americans to examine the cultural assumptions they were projecting onto refugees. Lorentzen found that those with less political involvement and more of a humanitarian orientation were more adamant about their expectations.

THE TRANSFORMATION OF SANCTUARY MEMBERS: ''CONSCIENTIZATION'' AND PROPHETIC POLITICS

Middle-class North Americans who opened themselves to the refugees also opened themselves to a new historical and political understanding of the world as voiced by poor, oppressed people from the Third World. The dramatic personal testimonies of refugees in public meetings were the movement's chief means of recruiting members and informing the public. Young men and women with kerchiefs hiding their faces were ushered inside church basements, synagogues, Quaker meetings, and college classes to tell their stories. They also spoke to high school students, community groups, and journalists. Those with ''good stories'' were asked to tell them over and over again. The testimonies of village massacres, systematic torture, murder, and rape shocked and galvanized middle-class North Americans. ''Once you spend time with the people who are coming here,'' said a Tucson minister, ''once you have heard their stories, then there's no turning back'' (Coutin 1993: 67). Many sanctuary participants shifted from seeing Central American violence as an aberration of a few ''sick'' torturers or ruthless dictators to an analysis of systemic violence against the majority poor. The search for the roots of the violence led many to judge the United States as complicit in the impoverishment and deprivation of the poor—a complicity that went back to the early nineteenth century. Marty Finn, a Berkeley sanctuary volunteer, said: "For Central Americans to meet with North Americans and just to talk and be friends and socialize is extremely important, because it shows people that when U.S. backed governments of various sorts brutalize people, they aren't brutalizing animals, they aren't brutalizing robots, they aren't brutalizing Communist flunkies. They're brutalizing real people" (Coutin 1993: 70).

Contact with politically committed refugees moved many U.S. participants to see sanctuary as the religious wing of the growing Central American peace movement, with the major goal to change the Reagan administration's Central American policy. This peace movement had a distinct advantage over others in the past, such as the movement against the Indochina War, because Central America is so much closer to the United States. For the first time in this century, the human beings at the other end of U.S. bombs, artillery fire, and covert actions were not a faraway, anonymous enemy that could be stereotyped and dismissed. Large numbers of Central Americans were fleeing *into the United States* during the conflict, with real names and faces and stories they were willing to share.

Often the refugees themselves pushed sanctuary members to focus more on Central American politics. They asked sanctuary to "reverse the railroad" and "make Central America a sanctuary" to which the refugees could return (Bau 1985: 25). Two sanctuary refugees, Alejandro and Raul, reflect these ideas in a public letter to the movement:

Sanctuary as a Christian movement has to be a movement that tells the truth. . . . You are working for charity only if you deny that a crime is being committed and that the guiltiest party is your government. . . . The number of refugees will continue growing in large proportion and no one will be able to help them. All of us want to live in our countries without the danger of death. Christian love must not only be charitable, but must understand the roots of the problem. To continue sanctuary only at the level of charity is to be deceitful. It is to deceive and be at the service of the powerful. It is treason to the gospel. (Golden and McConnell: 131)

The principle of "solidarity" was constructed in opposition not only to charity but also to imperialism. Many sanctuary groups had experience in the Black Freedom struggle and in movements against the Indochinese War and arms race, where they had developed a strong critique of U.S. imperialism. The constellation of events in late 1980 and early 1981, including the murder of the Salvadoran opposition party leaders, the rape and murder of four U.S. churchwomen, the murder of two U.S. labor advisers in El Salvador, the Salvadoran rebel offensive, and the Reagan administration's aggressive interventionist policy in Central America all sparked a new sense of urgency. The U.S. Catholic bishops and virtually all mainstream Protestant denominations issued statements expressing concern that the Reagan administration was preparing the country for a U.S. intervention in Central America that would become another Indochina war. The bishops issued a strong statement questioning the East–West paradigm being used to justify U.S. policies. They also called for a moratorium on the deportation of Salvadorans. Tucson writer and activist Gary MacEoin contrasted the Central America movement with the earlier anti-Vietnam War movement, whose natural constituency had been young people facing the draft. In the Central America movement the ''main focus of opposition'' was neither the ''traditional liberal lobby'' nor ''marginal leftist parties'' but groups within the Catholic and Protestant churches (Berryman 1994: 224). Many other groups developed outside the church. By 1985, the directory of Central American organizations compiled by the Central America Resource Center listed 850 organizations ranging from national networks to local chapters (Berryman 1994: 221).

Not only were refugees speaking inside the United States, but it was much easier than in past wars for North Americans to travel to the conflict. Several thousand members of the Central American peace movement, including sanctuary workers, traveled with Witness for Peace, the Institute for Global Education, and other organizations to witness conditions for themselves and speak out when they returned home. Others picked coffee in voluntary brigades in Nicaragua to support the Sandinista leadership. Others worked in development projects or as health workers. Statewide campaigns organized speaking engagements by Central Americans and U.S. citizens who had lived or visited in Central America to speak in classrooms, even to Rotary and Kiwanis meetings, involving audiences that totaled 114,786 people by 1986 (Berryman 1994: 225). Coalitions periodically organized large-scale demonstrations in Washington and elsewhere, but the strength of the movement lay in the hundreds of local groups across the United States, connected through national and international peace networks. Sanctuary (and the larger Central America peace movement of which it was a part) was one of the few genuinely grassroots movements dealing with a global issue—as were the antiapartheid and antinuclear movements.

Tensions gradually developed within the movement between those who continued to focus on refugee resettlement and those oriented to changing U.S. foreign policy. The more ''humanitarian''-oriented groups tended to support loose decentralization of the movement, while the politically oriented felt the need for national coordination. Differences also surfaced around criteria for selecting the refugees to be adopted by sanctuary churches. Some spoke of ''the big split'' when Chicago returned some refugees on a bus to Tucson because they ''had no understanding'' of the political conflict in Central America and were ''therefore not useful'' in educating North Americans (Lorentzen 1991: 16). The tensions between the Chicago and Tucson groups were picked up and exaggerated by the media during the Tucson trial.

The split reflected real differences in individuals' political and religious orientations. Some of this related to geography; those at the border were overwhelmed by the immediate needs of massive numbers of refugees, and their underground operations were riskier and, therefore, required more decentralized autonomy. Sanctuary groups farther from the border tended to have a history of social involvement with civil rights, antiwar, and other political causes. As previously mentioned, motives also evolved over time. Initial involvement for many was expressly humanitarian, but with more contact with Central Americans as well as secular and religious activists, participants tended to become more intentionally political.

TOWARD A THEOLOGY OF ACCOMPANIMENT

One of the most lasting contributions of sanctuary and other church-based groups acting in solidarity with Central Americans was the articulation of "a theology of accompaniment." In the course of their solidarity work, many church workers experienced a profound shift in faith. Movement participants termed this a "call to conversion" (Golden and McConnell 1986: 156). In this context, "conversion" signaled a radical break with mainstream religious thinking and action, with a deepened sense of religious commitment to social justice. Liberation theologian Gustavo Gutierrez writes: "Conversion implies that we recognize the presence of sin in our lives and our world. In other words we see and admit what is vitiating our relationship with God and our solidarity with others—what, in consequence, is also hindering the creation of a just and human society" (1984: 97).

It is not clear how many sanctuary members had this experience of conversion. Many had previously connected their religious faith with prophetic social action as conscientious objectors during World War II, civil rights activists in the South, antinuclear, antiwar, or draft resisters during the Vietnam War. Coutin found approximately one-fourth of nearly 100 East Bay and Tucson interviewees describing a conversion experience that, although resonant with other social movements, was specific to sanctuary. Crucial to the process was at least one crossing over the border to see reality from the perspective of the oppressed (Coutin 1993: 71).

When U.S. church people traveled to Central America, they witnessed the devastating poverty, repression, and bloodshed for themselves. Sanctuary members were especially moved by the small, Christian base communities—*la iglesia popular*. In desperately poor towns and villages, humble villagers were interpreting the Bible in revolutionary ways for themselves and courageously acting on their faith. North Americans also met with local clergy, service workers, and human rights activists. A Tucson sanctuary minister recalls his trip:

I guess the most extraordinary experience was to be with people who knew that they were not going to live much longer occupying the position that they were, doing human rights work, or working with the base communities. Their colleagues were killed right and left. They wouldn't last much longer. And we talked about it candidly. And I had never talked with people of faith before who were in that position. And I pressed them on it. The question that I asked all of them was, "Why are you doing this?" and to hear their responses out of faith: "Well, because Monsenor Romero would want us to." "Because God wants us to be here." (Coutin 1993: 69)

Such trips tended to shift the way U.S. church people viewed the global distribution of resources and their own role within such inequality. Central to this change in consciousness was the theology of liberation that North Americans were learning from Central Americans. Liberation theology rejects the traditional Christian arguments that poverty is God's will or judgment on the sinful. Said one sanctuary participant:

I think God is with the poor and the only hope that we have as people of this culture who have grown up with so much in terms of possessions and things, the only hope we have to understand God is to unite ourselves with the poor. To make a conscious decision to let go of our stuff and be with people who have less. (Cunningham 1995: 132)

Crucial to liberation theology was the belief that a person must take concrete action to remedy social injustice and suffering. Some sanctuary members responded with a "theology of relinquishment," leaving secure jobs and comfortable homes to decrease the careerism, materialism, and individualism in their own lives that they believed characterized the economy that was oppressing the poor. The theology of relinquishment concluded that the answer to a just redistribution of resources required the wealthy to let go of their excess power and resources (Neal 1977). Socially engaged, progressive Christians had been exploring relinquishment throughout the late 1970s and early 1980s, but the brutal repression in Central America heightened the visibility of the worldwide chasm between the haves and have nots.

Then, shortly before his death, Archbishop Oscar Romero called for people of conscience everywhere to "accompany" Central Americans in their struggle for liberation. This encouraged some church workers to reconsider relinquishment as an adequate middle-class response to liberation theology. Writes Marie Dennis, a U.S. Catholic activist deeply involved in Central American struggles:

Our response to liberation theology was a theology of relinquishment . . . yet . . . is it really possible to negate our identity as middle class North American people? . . . is relinquishment enough? We absolutely believe in the need for "letting go" of power and material wealth, but wonder if we are not called to a more creative and participatory, and even more challenging, role in bringing about change. (Dennis 1988: 1)

This more creative and participatory role was articulated in an evolving "theology of accompaniment" by U.S. participants in the religious wing of the Central American peace movement. Accompaniment requires more than material and spiritual support: it involves "walking" with people who struggle for their liberation, offering one's physical, emotional, and spiritual presence, without trying to take over. "Accompaniment—*acompanamiento*—means to walk with, to be with, to let go," writes Dennis. "This is an idea so radical and difficult for us to comprehend that its power and significance reveal themselves to our Western/Northern minds only slowly and with great difficulty" (1987: 1).

The act of providing sanctuary, especially by risking arrest and imprisonment along with the refugees, was considered one form of accompaniment. Other opportunities presented themselves through the 1980s. After the Arias Peace Plan in 1987, for example, thousands of Salvadorans and Guatemalans, who had been surviving for years in squalid, oppressive refugee camps in Honduras and Mexico, decided to return to rebuild their villages. Often considered by their governments to be guerrilla sympathizers, the refugees invited international church people to accompany them in order to decrease potential government repression. Some U.S. church workers made these dangerous journeys and developed long-term commitments to particular villages in Central America.

THE WINDING DOWN OF THE MOVEMENT

In 1985, a group of churches filed suit against the U.S. government for illegal application of domestic asylum laws. The civil suit, *American Baptist Churches et al. (ABC) v. Thornburgh*, involved more than eighty religious and refugee organizations and charged that the Reagan administration's policy of routinely denying Salvadoran and Guatemalan requests for asylum was in violation of the U.S. Refugee Act of 1980. At the time of the suit, the U.S. government was granting asylum to 3 percent of Salvadoran applicants and fewer than 1 percent of Guatemalan applicants. In 1990, the government realized that the Court was probably going to rule in favor of the plaintiffs and offered to settle out of court, revising INS asylum proceedings to allow all Salvadorans and Guatemalans in the United States who had been denied asylum since 1980 or who had not applied, to be reconsidered by a newly trained corps of asylum officers (Cunningham 1995: 205). In the two years following the *ABC* settlement, asylum approval rates for Salvadorans and Guatemalans rose dramatically, and, finally, deportation proceedings were halted against those immigrants whose cases had been denied (Mahler 1995: 17). The *ABC* settlement was preceded by a bill passed by Congress in October 1990 that provided for Salvadorans to receive temporary protected status (TPS). The granting of TPS culminated a decade-long lobbying effort by many individuals and groups. Temporary protected status signified that Salvadorans arriving in the United States before September 29, 1990, would be able to remain in the country and obtain work authorization until the civil war terminated. Nearly 200,000 Salvadorans applied. Finally, peace accords were signed in El Salvador in 1992 and in Guatemala in 1995. The number of refugees dwindled considerably, and the underground gradually became dormant (Cunningham 1995: 203). Some sanctuary participants turned to helping Central Americans within the United States; others created solidarity groups with particular Central American communities. Still others took what they'd learned in sanctuary to build new relations of solidarity within inner-city neighborhoods.

Even before the peace accords were signed in Salvador and Guatemala, a new protest movement was simmering around U.S. refugee policy when, during intense military repression in Haiti, the United States began turning away Haitian "boat people" without any chance for them to apply for asylum. Many sanctuary groups threw their considerable support behind this movement. North Americans who had visited Haiti began speaking in church basements where Central Americans once stood; church members wearily recalled it as "a déjà vu experience." First there were the racism and foreign policy bias: Cubans at that time were plucked out of the ocean and brought to Florida and within a year became eligible for citizenship. Black Haitians were summarily turned back, often to imprisonment or death. Then there was the long history of U.S. complicity in Haitian political repression and economic exploitation. Finally, in 1991, the Haitian people overwhelmingly elected a democratic president, Jean-Bertrand Aristide, but, after seven months, he was ousted in a military coup. The Bush administration failed to intervene, and, in the bloodbath that followed, the United States turned back thousands of "boat people." A coalition of African-American leaders, including Randall Robinson, director of TransAfrica, National Association for the Advancement of Colored People (NAACP) officers, and the congressional Black Caucus pursued a two-track strategy of public demonstrations and pressure for legislation aimed at the restoration of the Haitian democracy. Said Robinson:

I believed strongly that the refugee issue was the key to overall success. If we could bring the United States to screen and shelter endangered Haitian refugees, the White House would then, and only then, vigorously seek the downfall of Haiti's military dictatorship, solving the problem at its root. It was plain enough that the last thing the United States wanted was a large influx of black Haitian refugees. We would make their exclusion politically difficult to publicly explain and defend. (1998: 196)

Congressional Black Caucus members initiated legislation and committed acts of civil disobedience at the White House. Human rights organizations openly criticized U.S. Haitian refugee policy. In 1994, Randall Robinson began a hunger strike, and, after twenty-seven days of fasting and considerable media coverage, President Clinton agreed to end his Haitian policy of automatic repatriation: refugees would be screened on an individual basis (Robinson 1998: 203). Soon thereafter, in 1994, Clinton supported a U.N. Security Council vote in favor of military intervention, and Aristide returned to complete his term of office.

A different kind of asylum campaign developed around the same time, fought largely in the courts, promising to be significant in its precedent-setting capacity. In 1993, Fauziya Kassindja, a seventeen-year-old Togolese women, fled her homeland to escape female genital mutilation. When she arrived in the United States she was locked up in a U.S. prison under deplorable conditions for sixteen months, while her application for asylum was processed. A young Bahai law student in Washington, D.C., Layli Miller Bashir, took up Kassindja's case and enlisted the help of Karen Musalo, acting director of the American University International Human Rights Clinic. In a landmark decision that has given hope to many who seek asylum on the basis of gender-based persecution, Kassindja was granted asylum on June 13, 1996 (Kassindja and Bashir 1998).

CONCLUSION

The Central American sanctuary movement and the more recent campaigns for refugee rights have experienced only partial victory. For one thing, the 1980s and 1990s witnessed a horrifying increase in human displacement; it was not only Guatemalans, Salvadorans, and Haitians fleeing from persecution. Southeast Asian "boat people," Ethiopians, Afghans, Cambodians, Kurds, Tamils, Bosnian Muslims, Tibetans, Chinese, and many other groups have fled armed conflict and political repression. The number of refugees grew alarmingly, from 2.5 million in 1970 to 4.6 million in 1980, to more than 14 million by 1989. The United Nations (UN) high commissioner for refugees estimated 19.7 million refugees outside their country in 1994 (Cunningham 1995: 209). This total is likely to be an underestimation.

Meanwhile, U.S. political rhetoric and media images have taught citizens to disconnect from such widespread suffering and to fear new immigrants: people without documentation are regularly blamed for U.S. problems with unemployment, crime, education, overpopulation, and the environment. As a consequence, U.S. refugee policy became even more harsh. In the new "expedited removal" law enacted by Congress in September 1996, those who arrive in the United States without legitimate travel documents will not be permitted to apply for asylum unless they express a fear of persecution or an intent to apply for asylum to an INS officer immediately upon arriving in the United States. This may seem reasonable, but many refugees fear talking to the first INS officer with whom they have contact and asking for asylum (Kassindja and Bashir 1998: 307).

Yet, sanctuary movements have made a difference. They have changed specific refugee policies and laws. Because of broad public exposure, many citizens have transcended the conventional view of refugees as the hapless victims of floods, drought, starvation, the odd dictator, or "civil war." Many more North Americans now recognize the larger economic, political, and cultural forces producing refugees, including the actions of the U.S. government and corporations. Countering popular images of being overrun by "aliens," these movements put a human face on "illegal immigrants," challenging us to look more deeply into why people are seeking refuge and how we might respond.

Moreover, the sanctuary movement called into question conventional notions of the relationship of religion to economic and political power. It challenged religious believers to act on scriptural commands to attend to the poor and persecuted. In the process of raising these issues publicly, sanctuary introduced U.S. church and synagogue members to the theology of liberation and participated in the development of a First World theological response. The theologies of liberation and accompaniment will surely take new forms as global economic and political conditions evolve.

REFERENCES

Bau, Ignatius
1985   *This Ground Is Holy: Church Sanctuary and Central American Refugees*. New York: Paulist Press.
Berryman, Phillip
1994   *Stubborn Hope: Religion Politics and Revolution in Central America*. Maryknoll, New York: Orbis Books.
Corbett, Jim
1991   *Goatwalking*. New York: Viking.
Coutin, Susan
1993   *The Culture of Protest: Religious Activism and the U.S. Sanctuary Movement*. Boulder, Colorado: Westview Press.
Crittenden, Ann
1988   *Sanctuary: A Story of American Conscience and Law in Collision*. New York: Weidenfeld and Nicolson.
Cunningham, Hilary
1995   *God and Caesar at the Rio Grande*. Minneapolis: University of Minnesota Press.
Dennis, Marie
1987   Central America—October 1987: Is Peace Possible? *New Creation News* 8(5).
1988   Is Relinquishment Enough? Memo from Center of New Creation.
Golden, Renny, and Michael McConnell
1986   *Sanctuary: The New Underground Railroad*. Maryknoll, New York: Orbis Books.
Gutierrez, Gustavo
1984   *We Drink from Our Own Wells*. MaryKnoll, New York: Orbis.
Kassindja, Fauziya, and Layli Miller Bashir
1998   *Do They Hear You When You Cry?* New York: Delacorte Press.
Lorentzen, Robin
1991   *Women in the Sanctuary Movement*. Philadelphia: Temple University Press.
MacEoin, Gary
1985   *Sanctuary: A Resource Guide for Understanding and Participating in the Central American Refugees' Struggle*. San Francisco: Harper and Row.
Mahler, Sarah J.
1995   *Salvadorans in Suburbia: Symbiosis and Conflict*. Boston: Allyn and Bacon.
Neal, Marie Augusta
1977   *A Socio-Theology of Letting Go: The Role of a First World Church Facing Third World Peoples*. New York: Paulist Press.

Religious Task Force
1987   A Call to Accompaniment from the Church and the People of El Salvador. Washington, D.C.
Robinson, Randall
1998   *Defending the Spirit.* New York: Viking Press.

14

Labor at Risk: The Exploitation and Protection of Undocumented Workers

David W. Haines

The undocumented in the United States fall into several categories: asylum seekers for whom the United States is a refuge; laborers who illegally enter the country seeking low-paid work; or tourists, students, or temporary workers legally in the United States who overstay for a mix of economic, social, and political reasons. What unites all of these categories of people is that they must generally find work. For most, that work will pay relatively poorly by U.S. standards, and their jobs will frequently be at risk. The extent of that risk can be extreme: illegal workers promised jobs as domestic workers are forced into prostitution, deaf immigrants are forced into virtual slavery to sell trinkets on the streets of American cities, agricultural workers live in dug-out burrows near the fields and drink water from contaminated containers, recently arrived immigrants (whether from Mexico in San Diego or from China in New York) are imprisoned in "safe" houses until they can pay off, or have a relative pay off, the debt their captors decide they owe. The lucky ones find jobs that often pay below minimum wage, have little security, and offer few benefits. Their working conditions are unsafe, and their resulting injuries on the job may well go uncompensated.

Whether or not one condones the presence of undocumented workers in the United States (many of whom are "legal" in terms of international law, may well become "legal" in the next twist of U.S. immigration policy, and may well be part of households that include "legal" residents and citizens), those undocumented workers retain basic rights that no one would contest, for example, the right not to be enslaved, beaten, or forced into crime or prostitution or to have property taken by force. Some of these rights are established in international law, particularly the United Nations (UN) Declaration of Universal Human Rights, Convention and Protocol on Refugees, and various other conventions regarding the rights of women and the protection of children. Other rights are covered by the U.S. Constitution's emphasis, especially in the Fourth, Fifth, and Fourteenth Amendments, on the rights of all "persons" in the United States, not simply those who are citizens.[1]

More specific rights attach to people as workers. Again, many of these are covered by international law and covenants, particularly those of the International Labour Organization (ILO). The ILO's 1998 Declaration of Fundamental Principles and Rights at Work, for example, reiterated the need for "elimination of all forms of forced or compulsory labour"—a need that had been the subject of previous ILO forced labor conventions in 1930 and 1957. Specific worker rights also exist in U.S. law. Statutes against forced servitude and racketeering are pursued at least occasionally. Federal and state laws on employee rights to proper pay, safe working conditions, compensation for work-related injuries, and the right to organize are not restricted to those who are legally in the country.

This chapter addresses the situation of undocumented workers with emphasis on the ways in which they can be exploited and the attempts to provide protection and relief for them. The discussion begins with the most severe system of exploitation, the actual trafficking of people. It then turns to the work arrangements in which the undocumented are often caught because of their illegality, describing first the dangerous and debilitating jobs to which they are often relegated and, second, the problems of insecurity and lack of benefits that affect even the better jobs that they find. Jobs, for example, can always be taken away by employer actions or Immigration and Naturalization Service (INS) raids, and normal controls over the workplace (such as occupational safety, workers' compensation, and general employee rights) can be abridged. The chapter concludes with a discussion of the kinds of efforts being made to protect the undocumented as people and as workers.

TRAFFICKING IN PEOPLE

Trafficking in people appears to be on the upsurge. The ILO has taken increasing interest in migrants (e.g., ILO 1998a), and the International Organization for Migration (IOM) established a new Trafficking Task Force that by 1997 was estimating that traffickers were moving as many as 4 million illegal immigrants a year, earning up to $7 billion in profits (IOM 1997). The problem is a global one that includes all kinds of migrants, from asylum seekers willing to pay high prices for an escape to freedom to those sold or stolen into servitude. Although much of the trafficking is for raw physical labor by men, a major segment involves the trafficking in women for the sex industry. Children are not safe from traffickers; they are bought, stolen, and transported often—although not exclusively—for the sex industry as well (IOM 1998). A casual conversation with one of my immigrant students about "things at home," for example, yielded a case where a young woman from Laos was involuntarily working in a factory in northeast Thailand, with the threat that she would be sold into prostitution in Bangkok unless her family—with known connections to the United States—paid for her freedom. For those long involved in global crime, trafficking in people provides a useful sideline and one with relatively little risk for relatively high profit.

Case study material from the United States suggests that at least some of the undocumented in the country reflect this same global pattern of human trafficking. As in other countries, some trafficking involves the forced movement of people who may initially be enticed to migrate voluntarily but who are then locked into servitude. This can be particularly severe for women. In Florida and South Carolina in 1998, for example, police were informed of a case of forced prostitution. The women involved had been recruited in Mexico with promises they would get regular jobs in the United States. But once they arrived, they were told that they had to work off the costs of the travel. A fifty-two-count indictment accused sixteen Mexican nationals (all but one of them undocumented) of recruiting at least twenty women (largely from Veracruz) and forcing them into prostitution, maintaining control through beatings, threats, rape, and forced abortions. One woman who tried to escape was reportedly locked in a closet for fifteen days; another was kicked in the stomach and suffered a miscarriage; another twenty-six-year-old was hit when she tried to stop the rape of a fifteen-year-old (Leibowitz 1998; Lardner 1998; Navarro 1998; *Rural Migration News* 1998). In this case, the women were as young as fourteen, but ages can be even lower. A BBC report noted the apprehension of a twelve-year-old Chinese girl, already a prostitute in an Italian airport (IOM 1998). She was on her way to Miami.

Trafficking in people is a broad problem for diverse economic purposes. In 1997, for example, authorities were informed of the forced servitude of deaf Mexicans in New York City. Eighteen people were charged with smuggling them into the United States from Mexico. Some sixty deaf workers were kept in houses in Queens and put on the streets and subways during the day to sell key chains and other trinkets. One of the two ringleaders (a brother and sister) admitted to using stun guns to maintain control over one worker and chaining another to a bedpost to avoid escape (Fisher 1997; Ojito 1998). Noted one of the lawyers prosecuting the case: "Every case of slavery is terrible, but what's especially appalling about today's case is the double exploitation. . . . The victims were targeted both because they were aliens and because they were people with disabilities" (Fisher 1997). Similar cases appeared in other places, although on a smaller scale. In El Paso in 1998, for example, three people were arrested for enslaving a deaf and mute Mexican couple and their children for five years after luring them to the United States with promises of good work and living conditions. An INS spokesman noted that the couple and their children were allowed out only to sell trinkets, worked twelve hours a day, seven days a week, turned over all their money, were beaten during the period, and the mother was allegedly forced into acts of prostitution (Reuters 1998; Navarette 1998; Trejo 1998).

Even when there is a clearer understanding by the potential migrant of the situation, the mechanics of human smuggling are grueling. When the *Golden Venture* ran aground off the coast of New York in 1993, for example, the extent of human smuggling from China became clearer. As various people have described it (Kwong 1996, 1997; Smith 1997; Chin, this volume), the smuggling is costly—running upward of $30,000, places the migrants at considerable risk during the journey, does not assure them of success in gaining entry, and may subject them to enormous financial pressure if they do successfully land in the United States. Particularly in more recent years, those who reach the United States may be imprisoned until they can pay off the cost of the passage. Kwong (1997) notes cases in which workers were abducted and tortured to put pressure on their relatives to pay off the debt. He also wryly notes how one *Golden Venture* passenger was finally released from prison only to find a message that it was time to pay off his debt. In another case, a worker who had already paid off his debt was abducted so that his captors could collect again. With high debts to be repaid and decreasing wages, the tendency to lock up new arrivals in "safe houses" until they can pay off their debt increases, as does the harshness of measures—including rape, torture, and murder—to gather those funds (Smith 1997; Kinkead 1992; Dugger 1997; Sachs 1998a, b; Chen 1998). By mid-1998, "safe houses" were more common even for Mexican immigrants crossing into California as the smuggling costs for a simple border crossing rose to a reported $1,200 (Kerkstra and McDonnell 1998). The worst aspects of human trafficking are seen in those cases in which the entry into the United States is turned into virtual slavery. Sometimes the servitude is temporary; sometimes, indefinite. The length of servitude is subject to cost calculations. One man, for example, was found wandering in an outlying area of Washington, D.C. He had, it was reported, been held as a worker in a local Chinese restaurant that bought him from some other Mexicans for $450 (Ordonez and Pan 1998).

Even if the journey to the United States does not end in such involuntary servitude or in other kinds of victimization, the trafficking itself can have lasting effects. As those trafficking in people recognize its potential profits, the illegal migrants become part of a new kind of marketing and production. Thus, as crossing the Mexican border has become more difficult and more expensive, it has gained renewed interest from those already involved in the smuggling of drugs. Interdiction reports, for example, suggest that those entering for work often serve double duty as carriers of drugs.

As in other areas, illegal immigrants face many of the same problems as do other immigrants. The desire to migrate indicates an important initiative by people to better their lives, although at the same time it requires a separation from the known and familiar. If the work of Douglas Massey and his colleagues on Mexican migrants to the United States is a fair indication, that decision has much to do with the desire to stabilize financial resources and accrue capital

(Massey and Espinosa 1997). Whether it is for such stabilization of risk or simply a general desire for better income, migrants decide to move. Their decision is usually conditioned by the experience of others they know and often by their own previous experience crossing borders—both legally and illegally. As in earlier times in American history, that migration is not without dangers. Like other immigrants in American history, current immigrants find less-than-ideal jobs and living conditions in America. But for illegal migrants each of those stages is amplified in risk and danger. The journey may result in death or simply be unsuccessful and cost time and money, and their reception in the United States is constantly in jeopardy.

Recent policies have, in many ways, exacerbated the problem. Attempts to keep people from migrating are of limited success. Despite being caught at the border, despite the known hazards of treks through deserts and trips across oceans, people continue to breach the U.S. border. As the borders are tightened, the process becomes harder, more expensive, and more dangerous. Instead of ambles across a border in populated areas, illegal border crossers from Mexico now cross in desolate territory, are drowned in rivers or course ways, freeze to death in the mountains in the winter, or die of the heat in summer. A hot spell in the summer of 1998, for example, led to at least forty-three deaths of people crossing the Mexican border (Schiller 1998; Branigin 1999) and put many advocacy organizations in a difficult position: should they help the INS apprehend border crossers in order to save lives or maintain their usual distance from border control activities? Similar problems occur in the Caribbean, where the danger of death on the journey is also high. Those taking the journey across the Caribbean, whether from Haiti and Cuba north to Florida or east from the Dominican Republic to Puerto Rico, often lose their lives. In one case, forty Dominicans died as their vessel was flooded. Captains familiar with the area talk of human bones littering the shoals and inlets between the Dominican Republic and Puerto Rico (Fineman 1998).

As the border crossings become riskier, the migrants turn to others for assistance. They readily find people who see the potential profit in helping them and are often already involved in criminal activities along the border. Two very different kinds of people are thus united under a label of "illegal": on one hand, migrants willing to ignore the formalities of a border in order to work at low-wage jobs or to join their family and, on the other, cross-border criminals who simply see another commodity to be exploited for profit. The more the path of illegal immigrants matches that of trafficking syndicates and their other illicit cargos, the more the undocumented are indebted to them, drawn into their criminality, and defenseless to their ravages. Even the Immigration and Naturalization Service is clear that the results are deplorable and constitute violations of basic human rights.

DANGEROUS, DEBILITATING, AND UNPROTECTED WORK

Despite such dangers, the undocumented may reach the United States without great loss, avoid deportation or incarceration in prisons (see Kahn 1996; Hope 1998), be able to pay or repay the costs of passage, and, finally, find work. But that work is unlikely to pay very well, for the undocumented have a particular role in the economy: they provide at inexpensive wages work that is, by and large, not wanted by others. Efforts to limit illegal migration have thus always foundered because of the strong interest groups that need their labor. Whether to save garment industry contracts from going overseas, to avoid the loss of a harvest, or to keep production in a small company going, deals on both the small and large scale are quickly made. Thus, agricultural interests tacked on a special agricultural worker (SAW) provision to the 1986 Immigration Reform and Control Act that added roughly a million people to the amnesty provided by that legislation. Ad hoc arrangements are also possible at the local level. For example, after INS raids in 1998 resulted in the apprehension of some twenty workers in Georgia's Vidalia onion fields, a broad range of business and political interests combined to effect a truce in which INS agents would conduct no more searches during that harvest season (Henson 1998a, b, c). With an estimated one-half of that labor force being undocumented, it was politically impossible to continue the raids in the middle of the harvesting season. Local politicians wrote to the INS that the "apparent lack of regard for farmers in this situation and the intimidation tactics being employed by federal officials are completely unacceptable" (Henson 1998b). The INS agreed, in return for promises of better compliance, to "curtail operations" (Henson 1998a).

Because undocumented workers work without the benefit of legal residence, they are inevitably in a weak bargaining position with their employers. The work that they find is generally hard and dirty. It is also often dangerous in the short term, debilitating in the long term, and unprotected by the minimal safety net that applies to most jobs in America. This is perhaps most clear in agricultural labor. Although the specific arrangement varies with the particular crop and the region of the country, the work is seasonal, the pay is marginal, and the living conditions are rudimentary. Owners argue that they cannot stay in business without such labor—that their profit margins are so narrow that any increase in the price of labor would drive them into bankruptcy. The national portrait of agricultural labor is a bleak one. Federal government reports show that hired farmworkers are paid poorly and live in marginal conditions (Runyan 1996). In recent years, they have become increasingly male, young, single, foreign, and illegal. After the legalization of about 2.7 million undocumented workers in the late 1980s (including the million agricultural workers covered by the SAW provision), the percentage of farmworkers who were illegal dropped but then began to climb again. Mines, Gabbard, and Steirman (1997) note a proportion of undocumented workers climbing from 7 percent in 1989 to 16 percent in 1990–1991, 28 percent in 1992–1993, and 37 percent in 1994–1995. In that last time period, they found that nearly a fifth (18 percent) of all hired farmworkers were in their first year of farmwork, and, of those, 70 percent were undocumented.

A somewhat different picture emerges from the garment industry, one of the major urban industries benefiting from the efforts of undocumented workers. Here again, there is a standard argument by owners that without such low-cost labor, they would be driven out of business, and—a usual threat in these cases— the jobs would go overseas. Owners also argue that the combination of flexible hours, occasional homework (when workers take materials home to complete them), and flexible working conditions (e.g., women can sometimes bring in their children) is helpful to the workers. Furthermore, there is an argument that, generally unlike the situation in agricultural labor, there is the possibility of working one's way up the system by becoming an owner of a small operation. Indeed, for some legal immigrants, the garment industry has functioned in such a positive way, with ethnic ties between owners and workers, flexible working conditions, and the possibility of advance through ownership together creating a potential for immigrant economic success (see Kwong [1996] on the Chinese in New York City and Grenier et al. [1992] on Cubans in Miami). That positive picture has darkened in recent years. In New York, the Chinese ethnic apparel firms and the mixed ethnic firms, such as Korean-owned firms hiring Latino workers (Branigin 1997), seem to evidence more exploitation than opportunity. Indeed, the continuing decline in wages, the frequent abuse of workers even by coethnic owners, and the competition from new immigrants for ever-decreasing wages have made the garment industry a national eyesore. Even though much of the industry is unionized, advocacy organizations who track the industry find a continuing pattern of abuses. President Clinton even convened an Apparel Industry Partnership to develop a standard workplace code of conduct. That code details minimum standards for wages and benefits, regular and overtime compensation, freedom for collective bargaining and from forced labor and child labor, health and safety protection, and protection from harassment and abuse.

In other industries the situation is not as bleak. It has been argued, for example, that the wage differential in the aggregate between illegal and legal immigrants is not significant or at least wasn't until the increased criminalization of illegal immigrants that commenced with the 1986 Immigration Reform and Control Act (Borjas 1990). But even in better-paying jobs, there are problems. In meatpacking, undocumented workers from Mexico sometimes stepped in to replace other workers who had moved on. Those previous workers were often immigrants themselves; many Southeast Asian refugees, for example, were attracted to the meatpacking industry as a place in which to accrue capital before moving on. Wages in the meatpacking industry are relatively high. On the other hand, the work is difficult and extremely dangerous. The industry as a whole has an injury rate that is among the highest in the country, and the injuries are often serious. Although the work is constant and lacks the seasonality of agricultural field labor, the turnover is high. There is thus a need for labor. From an owner's perspective, undocumented workers have certain advantages: if they are injured on the job, the likelihood is that they will be unable to collect what may be sizable benefits. They are also unlikely to be involved in contesting management policies since their goal is to avoid scrutiny (Stull, Broadway, and Erickson 1992; Stull, Broadway, and Griffith 1995; Griffith and Runsten 1992; Benson 1994).

Despite such potential for abuse, the meatpacking industry is relatively regulated, as it involves very large, visible plants under the direct control of major corporations. Those corporations are subject to public opinion and, in recent years, have worked with the INS to reduce the number of undocumented workers (Benson, this volume). Things are less regulated in the poultry industry (Griffith, this volume), in which plants tend to be smaller and more spread out. As with meatpacking, the wear and tear on workers is high, with occasional loss of limb and frequent cumulative trauma injuries—particularly, carpal tunnel syndrome. Again, if workers are avoiding scrutiny, they are less likely to report problems that would risk their employment and less likely to be around to collect benefits for workplace injuries. With such a silent workforce, general safety standards are likely to decline.

As undocumented workers take these jobs and other less desirable work in industry, construction, and service work, they walk in the footsteps of many generations of immigrant laborers in America. Meatpacking today echoes Upton Sinclair's *The Jungle*; agricultural migrant labor echoes John Steinbeck; the garment industry today is reminiscent of the sweatshops at the turn of the last century. The groups have changed, but the need for low-wage, disposable labor remains. Nearly a century after the great surge in U.S. immigration, it is odd to see the extent to which automation has slipped past many areas of work. In what some people propose as a postindustrial world, undocumented workers are often in areas of limited mechanization (e.g., in field labor, in construction labor, and in garment assembly) or participating in a classic "Fordist" construction of advanced automation (as in the disassembly lines of meatpacking and poultry plants). Furthermore, undocumented laborers are re-creating those old patterns without even the rudiments of legal protection.[2] They are thus truly disposable labor. A quick call to the INS makes them not only disposable but self-disposing.

DISAPPEARING JOBS, DISAPPEARING WORKERS, DISAPPEARING BENEFITS

In most of the jobs in which the undocumented work, there are offsetting needs to have labor and to dispose of labor when it is no longer needed. In agriculture, this need is largely seasonal. Depending on the crop, larger numbers of people are needed during particular periods of the year. The ideal system is one in which labor arrives for the needed period, is capable of very hard, intensive work, will accept low wages, will demand or need few fringe benefits (such as running water, medical care, facilities for families), and will disappear when the work is over. The ideal system is thus one of temporary workers.

Formal programs to import such temporary labor have long existed in the United States and still continue to exist in abbreviated format.[3]

Lacking such a formal temporary worker program or frustrated by the administrative complexity of existing programs, the alternative mechanism for providing workers who can be readily recruited and as readily terminated is illegal immigration. With effective recruitment through a few known contacts, laborers arrive when needed, will often compete for lower wages, seek to avoid attention (and thus will demand little in addition to wages), and are likely to disappear when the work is over. Initially, at least, they are likely to be single young males, so that the employers (and the local communities) will be less taxed with the practical and moral concerns posed by women, by children, and by families (and their decided tendency to put down roots). The presence of a large number of single males presents its own problems, but those problems are likely to be temporary or seasonal and pose no central threat to the community's understanding of itself. Indeed, the activities of the men may fuel community stereotypes about immigrants and give the community usefully clear cultural and spatial boundaries through which to keep themselves and the immigrants separate. In other kinds of work, there is also an intermittency of employment. Construction has seasonal limits. Like much other labor, it also has weather limitations. The perfect solution, from the employer's point of view, is an arrangement for day labor with no commitment to the employees beyond the single day that they are picked up for work.

But there is also increasingly a more general temporariness in employment. Jobs are no longer construed to be indefinite. As the argument goes, changes in markets and in production constantly reshape an organization's options and constraints. Global competition requires that the organization adapt, and to do so it must be able to effectively recruit the labor it needs and to terminate the labor it doesn't need. (Capital, of course, seeks a frictionless allocation of labor to its needs.) As a tight job market causes companies to complain that they cannot recruit the labor they need, often concurrently, other companies—indeed, sometimes the same companies—are "downsizing" and returning other workers (usually older and more expensive ones) back into the labor pool to stay afloat as best they can.[4] A rawer version of the recruitment and termination game is played out in the meatpacking industry, in which workers are unlikely to maintain high productivity for a long period of time. If they don't leave of their own accord, injury—traumatic or cumulative—may force them off the job. It is then helpful if the workers disappear as completely as possible. The ties of employment must be effectively and completely severed, else the company may carry a cost (in benefits, compensation, pensions) on its books indefinitely. Once again, the undocumented appear as the ideal workers: disposable and self-disposing. Even in cases where workers retain some control over the conditions of their work, as Hondagneu-Sotelo (1994) describes for Mexican domestic workers in California, that potential volatility of employment remains.

The employment contract thus becomes increasingly narrow and hedged with indeterminacy. If workers wear out soon, then it is important not to invest too much in them, certainly not anything that will outlast the employment. If the work may disappear soon (e.g., a lost contract to produce some clothes for a designer label), then it is also important not to invest too much in a worker, certainly not anything that will outlast the employment. The result is a direct assault on basic employee benefits and rights. Health insurance, for example, can have significant costs—why not avoid it? Retirement benefits are an extra cost—why not avoid them or make them conditional on a relatively long period of employment that most workers won't meet? It would even be better to have the workers classified as subcontractors, therefore avoiding Social Security taxes. Finally, it would always make sense to pay at longer intervals with more delay from the period worked to the payment for that period. Any withholding of payment not only improves cash flow but, because of the likely disappearance of at least some workers during the delay, is a potential cash bonus for the employer. After one INS raid in Kentucky in 1998, for example, undocumented employees who were deported were told that they would be paid if they could return to Kentucky after their deportation—presumably by crossing the border once again without documents. Two women, both mothers of four and around fifty years old, actually did so. They went to a neutral organization, the Hispanic Association of Lexington, which had indicated they could pick up their checks without fear of arrest. But when they attempted to do so, an INS agent—apparently in the building by accident—arrested them again (Bennett 1998; Herron 1998).

The final indignity occurs when unscrupulous employers decide to extend this pattern by not paying employees at all. Peter Kwong (1997) describes how in New York City several garment sweatshop owners simply stopped paying the workers. The workers were uncertain what to do; if they demanded payment, they would be fired and then would probably have a lessened chance of ever collecting anything. On the other hand, if there really would never be any payment, they needed to find another job. They also faced the possibility of being undercut in wages by newer, more desperate undocumented workers. On the employer side, then, this possibility of simply not paying[5] opens up a variety of other options, for example, underpaying but claiming that the payment is correct. If the figure is relatively close, the worker is under considerable pressure to accept it. What legal recourse is available? Any action exposes the worker to the possibility of deportation. This is far from an isolated problem. Indeed, one of the central efforts in the unionization of garment workers in El Paso, Texas, by La Mujer Obrera was precisely this claim for payment of wages (Marquez 1995). Robert Smith (1998) notes that one employer he interviewed on the East Coast bluntly told him that "if the person is illegal, you don't have to pay them."

The narrowing of the employment contract also includes the dangers of the work. In the United States, a combination of occupational and safety laws (largely federal) and workers' compensation laws (largely state) aims to provide a workplace that is reasonably safe and health costs and income replacement should a worker be injured on the job. Workers who are illegal in residence retain such rights as employees, but these rights can be circumvented. Except for the highest-profile industries and the larger companies, routine occupational safety and health inspections are few and far between. Even when problems are noted, inspectors from the federal Occupational Safety and Health Administration (OSHA)—or state inspectors for states approved by OSHA—will often negotiate resolution of the problem and waive any fine. With such limited sanctions, the incentive to maintain safety standards is low. Furthermore, the employer knows that undocumented workers are unlikely to press a complaint with OSHA since that might well bring their illegal status to light—especially if employers know the source of the complaint.

The situation with workers' compensation is different. The mechanisms for workers' compensation vary among the states, from coverage through insurance policies, to approval to act as a self-insurer, to state funds, to special federal programs for certain workers. All of those programs have some up-front concern with worker safety but are created largely in terms of compensation after an injury. Workers' compensation can become a significant business cost—especially in high-risk industries. Even in lower-risk industries and low-cost states, employers often complain about the costs. Undocumented workers who are injured on the job are, indeed, entitled to recompense, but again these basic rights are easily circumvented. Undocumented workers, for example, are unlikely to report minor injuries since they know they risk being fired, as, despite protestations to the contrary, is true of many workers (as I learned when I worked for a workers' compensation agency and talked to people agonizing about whether to report an accident and risk losing their jobs). Furthermore, it is often several months (and in some states years) before cash benefits will be available in a contested case.[6]

Even if benefits are finally paid, they are likely to be paid to a U.S. address and may not be forwardable. If the worker disappears before then, there will thus be no payment. There is also a provision in many states' workers' compensation laws that an injured worker must try to find other suitable employment. That is a difficult task for an undocumented worker who risks apprehension with every contact with the wider society. In some states, the situation can be even more difficult: domestic workers and casual laborers, for example, are often not covered by workers' compensation. In many states, seasonal farmworkers are not considered ''regular'' employees and are thus not covered by workers' compensation. The seemingly simple act of receiving benefits for on-the-job injury thus becomes problematic. Employers—even well-intentioned ones—can compound the problem by paying workers' compensation benefits off the record. If the undocumented worker subsequently moves, or the employer simply ceases such payment, the worker must then begin again to make a claim for benefits. This becomes more difficult over time, thus weakening the employee's case.

HUMAN RIGHTS, WORKER RIGHTS

Undocumented workers are at risk throughout the migration process and in their lives in America. Their basic rights as human beings are threatened, and the rights they retain as workers in America are often abridged. The protection of this combination of human and worker rights is difficult because the population is limited in its rights of residence in the United States, hard to find, and also, partially as a result, limited in knowledge of English and U.S. practices. For those who are seen as refugees, a wide variety of organizations may be of assistance—at least if contact can be made. For those who migrate simply as laborers—even if they are forced to such a decision by very difficult circumstances—the resources are fewer.

In terms of basic rights, some organizations try at least to monitor conditions for illegal workers. Amnesty International (1998), for example, turned its usual internationalist gaze on the handling of border crossings in the United States and found what it considered a pattern of abuse by the INS (cf. Human Rights Watch 1995). Various lawyers' groups have been active in seeing that basic rights are not abridged, both for those who may qualify as refugees and for the undocumented per se. The U.S. government itself has expressed concern about the severe violations in human rights that accompany trafficking and forced servitude, although the governmental solution generally includes deportation. Such efforts at protection reflect four major emphases: legalization where possible, enforcement of existing laws, labor reform, and human rights advocacy.

Legalization.   Many of the undocumented are asylum seekers and, once granted asylum, are legal residents. In other cases, the simple length of residence of the undocumented has been the rationale for legalization. In 1986, the Immigration Reform and Control Act (IRCA) provided for the legalization of two major segments of the undocumented population: those who had been in the United States since January 1982 and (due to the pressure from agricultural business) those who had worked for a limited period of time in U.S. agriculture. In 1997, additional legislation provided for the legalization of many Cuban and Nicaraguan nationals and also provided a modified way of avoiding deportation for certain undocumented immigrants from El Salvador and Guatemala—an approach the Clinton administration attempted to extend to Haitians as well.[7] Such amnesties directly address the problems of undocumented status; they make sense when the groups reflect refugee-like situations or have such a long residence in the United States that deportation appears unreasonably disruptive to their lives and to their families, including children who may well be U.S. citizens. However, it is also clear that such amnesties do not resolve the problem of illegal immigration. Research on those legalized by IRCA, for example, has tended to show that such newly legalized immigrants themselves become anchors for other undocumented migrants. Furthermore, since the newly legalized have broader job opportunities, they may well move away from the work they have been doing, leaving business once again with a recruitment problem—the answer to which is the generation of more illegal border crossing. That is perhaps most clear in the data on agricultural workers (Mines, Gabbard, and Steirman 1997).

Enforcement. The second major approach is to increase enforcement. The Immigration Reform and Control Act of 1986 had exactly the intent of increasing enforcement while at the same time providing amnesty for many of the undocumented already in the country. Although the crucial element of employer sanctions (without which other enforcement is undercut) remained weak, other aspects of enforcement were, indeed, pursued. During the 1990s there was a sharp increase in funding for INS operations with emphasis on strengthening the land border with Mexico (with fences, patrols, and electronic surveillance), developing more restrictive procedures at airports (including the widely contested practice of "expedited removal"), increasing raids of businesses within the United States, and enhancing cooperation between INS and other law enforcement agencies. As a result, border apprehensions increased, illegal border crossings were deflected from major urban areas, and raids netted significant numbers of the undocumented and pressured some employers toward a more rigorous attempt to exclude undocumented workers.

However, the results have also increased risks to the undocumented. Those crossing the land border, for example, cross in more difficult and dangerous terrain with considerable loss of life. Raids of businesses expose both undocumented and legally resident workers to potential abuse by law enforcement. As businesses change their hiring procedures to avoid future inconvenience, they may come to question the credentials even of citizens and legal residents of foreign origin. Businesses may also decide to contract out functions further from their responsibility. The danger is that the attempt at enforcement not only puts the undocumented in more dire straits but also extends a web of discrimination from the undocumented to legal residents who resemble the undocumented in ethnicity or foreign origin. Perhaps most importantly, by increasing the sharpness of accusation from "undocumented," to "illegal," and then to virtually "criminal," the government forces the undocumented into a new category of culpability and into a more criminal set of social networks.

The increase in enforcement has had little apparent effect on the use of illegal labor, merely pushing undocumented workers into "irregular jobs that pay lower wages and offer fewer hours of work" (Donato, Durand, and Massey 1992: 94) and making them "more susceptible to exploitation by unscrupulous employers" (Arp 1990: 327). Even if workplace sanctions are strengthened—as is not the trend at the end of the 1990s—the effects may be limited. As Cornelius, a particularly seasoned observer of Mexican labor migration, notes: "Selectively targeting and heavily fining employers who do systematically violate minimum wage and other labor laws might reduce the demand for illegal workers in a few subsectors of the economy. However, eliminating these pockets of hyperexploitation would by no means dry up employment opportunities in most large U.S. cities" (Cornelius 1998: 408–409).[8]

Labor Reform.   The third major approach is to address the underlying labor issues, thus recognizing the dynamics of particular industries and the fact that a pattern of labor abuse in them is likely to include both the undocumented and the legally resident. There are both business and labor versions. From the business side, it is clear that some jobs can, indeed, be more fully automated. A Washington organization favoring more limited immigration, for example, published an analysis of options for automating raisin growing and harvesting (Mason, Striegler, and Berg 1997). The individual case is important in its own right, but the wider suggestion is that the undocumented are being used simply to avoid a continuing automation of work that would be no more costly in the long run than current nonautomated approaches. An alternative business approach is to recognize the need for temporary work and expand and formalize it as a legal form of temporary migration—thus expanding current programs for both low-skill and high-skill foreign workers. The question, of course, is whether such a program could be adequately controlled yet administratively simple enough that businesses wouldn't reject it.

From the labor side, the main call has been for unions to recognize the need to organize across the documented/undocumented divide. This is essential since the competition for low wages affects all workers in the industry, the legally resident usually being undercut by the undocumented, who are, in turn, often undercut by more recent and more desperate arrivals. All workers, in turn, may fall victim to a company's decision to move operations overseas or simply across the Mexican border. The unionization process is not an easy one if a large proportion of the workers are undocumented. Héctor Delgado's (1993) study of the successful attempt to unionize a waterbed factory in Los Angeles highlights the problems. In this particular case, a very strong unionizing effort, very effective organizers, and some workers (women first) who were willing to risk losing (and, indeed, lost) their jobs made success possible. However, the costs were high, and Delgado notes that only this unusual constellation of factors made this effort at all successful.

Even if workers are unionized, problems may remain. Many undocumented workers are, indeed, unionized. Much of the garment industry, for example, is represented by the Union of Needletrades, Industrial, and Textile Employees (UNITE). Yet the union has not been as effective at representing labor as critics claim it should be—its major predecessor, the International Ladies Garment Workers Union (ILGWU), for example, was reported as a distinct problem in the unionization of garment workers in El Paso (Marquez 1995). Despite such problems, many advocacy groups and academics continue to see the unions as the major alternative. Despite his own concern with how unions operate, including noting the "union from hell" epithet once directed toward UNITE, Peter Kwong (1997) concludes his book on undocumented workers by stressing the need for recognizing undocumented workers as part of the challenge to re-create a labor movement with stronger local links. Massey and Espinosa (1997) conclude their review of data from Mexican migrants on both sides of the border with a similar call for coherent labor organization. The central advantage to the emphasis on labor reform is that it unites both the undocumented and those who may be most affected or displaced by their willingness to work at low wages (Beck 1996; Stoll 1997).

Human Rights Advocacy.   Finally, instead of viewing the situation of undocumented workers as a general call for legalization, enforcement, or unionization, many people and organizations focus on the individual rights that undocumented workers have and how these can be protected within the existing web of international and national law. Many undocumented migrants, for example, have at least plausible cases for asylum. Whether the issue is timely adjudication of their claims, access to legal counsel, humane conditions when applicants are incarcerated, or new, temporary options for those in distress who may not meet formal refugee standards (see Martin and Schoenholtz [1998] for a variant version of temporary protected status), the fundamental need for protection of human rights and life is widely acknowledged.[9]

For those who are more clearly economic migrants, support is likely to be more limited. Yet as employees they have certain rights. They should be paid; they should work in a safe environment; they should have some medical protection and some coverage for on-the-job injury; they should not be abused. The Clinton-convened Apparel Industry Partnership and its code are a mechanism for that. The difficulty is that the undocumented tend to avoid the public light and are hard to find—whether in the city or the countryside. Cornelius' comments about the difficulties of workplace enforcement also apply to workplace protection since "it is difficult to find a single industry in which illegal immigrant labor is not amply represented at some level . . . [which] . . . greatly complicates the targeting of workplace enforcement efforts" (Cornelius 1998: 407).

PROTECTION OR CRIMINALIZATION?

The situation of undocumented migrants is not dissimilar to that of the general stream of immigrants who were building a new America a century ago. Many of the issues are the same: whether labor unions will incorporate the new arrivals or victimize them in favor of existing members, whether the new arrivals join their new society or are denied the right to legal status by virtue of race or origin, whether the state intrudes to establish workplace safety standards or leaves workers as potential victims, whether or not state governments provide some form of compensation for injuries at work. What is different for undocumented migrants today is that they remain outside any of the official categories of "legality," even though they may well become "legal" in the future or may step in and out of "legality" over time. The undocumented represent those who have not been incorporated into the process of formalizing U.S. borders and thus remain unprotected within those borders. They are thus the fully disposable immigrants.

Like immigrants in general, the undocumented represent diverse motivations ranging from the flight toward political refuge, to the search for economic advantage, to the simple desire to be with family and friends. They are the shadow of immigration to America. It is not that they are unwanted—business relies on them and often actively recruits them. It is not that they themselves generated the framework for their migration—U.S. policies are at the root of the movement of the undocumented to the United States: Central Americans reflect U.S. foreign policy, and Mexican migration has been shaped by the demand for labor and policies (such as legalization) that have established a strong cross-border network, much of it into the very territory that once belonged to Mexico.

The irony, then, is that although undocumented workers may be outside the legalities of border crossing, they are very much part of established international networks and very much part of the active economic and social structures within the United States. They are part of the system but are denied by the system. They are labor but are used against labor. They transgress by furtively crossing borders that business glories in crossing with utter impunity.[10] The undocumented worker is thus a paradox that reveals the structure of U.S. society and economy, provides a critique of its inability to rationalize immigration policy, and perpetually raises difficult questions about the nature of human—and worker—rights in America.

NOTES

1. The Fourth Amendment protects all "people" from unreasonable searches, the Fifth provides the right to trial for any "person," and the Fourteenth requires states to afford equal protection under the law to "any person within its jurisdiction."

2. Grasmuck and Pessar (1991) note for their sample of Dominicans in New York that the undocumented tended to work in small, more informal companies and were far more often paid in cash (43 percent to 19 percent) than legal immigrants.

3. The so-called bracero program was initiated in 1942 and continued until 1964. Today, a variety of programs allow for temporary workers: the largest are the H-2A program (which allows for temporary agricultural workers but is criticized by employers as administratively cumbersome) and the H-1B program (which provides for a variety of higher-skilled workers without whom technology companies claim they cannot operate). There have been proposals to create a simple version of the H-2A program and to increase the numbers under the H-1B program. In late 1998, Congress finally arranged a compromise to expand the H-1B program temporarily.

4. In the late 1990s, for example, strong pressure developed to allow in more immigrants to fill jobs in the so-called high-tech industries. Indeed, one Intel Corporation official suggested that a "green card" (permitting legal residence) be stapled to all Ph.D. diplomas given to foreign students in engineering (Simons 1998).

5. If they do happen to get "caught," they may be fined or required to pay overdue wages. At that point they can simply go out of business, disappear, and then reappear somewhere else.

6. The exact details vary by state. In some states, payment may be completely delayed until resolution of the case; in other states at least some benefits may be paid. Medical costs, however, are usually either paid by the employer/insurer or delayed.

7. At the end of 1998 similar provisions were indeed extended to Haitians in the Omnibus Appropriations Bill.

8. Cornelius, Martin, and Hollifield (1994: 4) suggest in talking about the advanced economies of North America, Europe, and Japan that there "appears to be a 'hardening' of employer demand for foreign labor in key sectors of these countries' economies— i.e., the hiring or continued employment of foreign workers, regardless of legal status, is increasingly insensitive to cyclical economic fluctuations, as measured by unemployment rates in the labor-importing countries."

9. Living without documents greatly complicates the experience of asylum seekers as opposed to refugees. In technical U.S. terms, refugees are people whose official status is determined before their arrival, assuring that although their adjustment to the United States may be difficult, they will be spared further concern about legal status and will receive some assistance (Haines, 1996). Asylees, however, must be in the United States first and then make a claim for "refugee" status, which is individually adjudicated. The process can be a long one, and most asylum applicants are thus for at least some time either "illegal" or in a very restricted legal status. Their lot is thus generally a more difficult one. Nevertheless, some refugees, because of their unfamiliarity with American society and the traumatic life experiences they have had, may end up in some of the same marginal employment as do the undocumented (Haines 1987).

10. Andreas (1994: 46), for example, notes the irony that "even as officials have moved to close the border (to the illegal flow of people), they have moved to open it (to the legal flow of goods through [the North American Free Trade Agreement])." There is the added irony that "illegal immigration has attained a symbolic importance that some might argue is out of proportion with the actual number of immigrants illegally crossing state borders" (Doty 1996: 172).

REFERENCES

Amnesty International
1998   *United States of America: Human Rights Concerns in the Border Region with Mexico*. New York: Amnesty International.
Andreas, Peter
1994   The Making of Amerexico: (Mis)Handling Illegal Immigration. *World Policy Journal* 11 (2): 45–56.
Arp, William III
1990   The Exclusion of Illegal Hispanics in Agenda-Setting: The Immigration Reform and Control Act of 1986. *Policy Studies Review* 9 (2): 327–338.
Beck, Roy
1996   *The Case against Immigration: The Moral, Economic, Social, and Environmental Reasons for Reducing U.S. Immigration Back to Traditional Levels*. New York: W. W. Norton.
Bennett, Brian
1998   86 Illegal Immigrants Arrested in Raid. *Lexington Herald-Leader*, May 20.
Benson, Janet E.
1994   The Effects of Packinghouse Work on Southeast Asian Refugee Families. In *Newcomers in the Workplace: Immigrants and the Restructuring of the U.S. Economy*. Edited by Louise Lamphere, Alex Stepick, and Guillermo Grenier. Philadelphia: Temple University Press. Pp. 99–126.

Borjas, George J.
1990   *Friends or Strangers: The Impact of Immigrants on the U.S. Economy.* New York: Basic Books.

Branigin, William
1997   Reaping Abuse for What They Sew: Sweatshops Once Again Commonplace in U.S. Garment Industry. *Washington Post,* February 16: A-1.
1998   Heat Turns Border Patrol into Saviors. *Washington Post,* July 21: A-5.
1999   As Crossings Grow Treacherous, More Aliens Are Dying to Get In. *Washington Post,* February 16: A-10.

Chen, David W.
1998   I.N.S. Moves to Deport Persistent Illegal Immigrant a 2d Time. *New York Times,* June 12: B-9.

Cornelius, Wayne A.
1998   Appearances and Realities: Controlling Illegal Immigration in the United States. In *Temporary Workers or Future Citizens?* Edited by Myron Weiner and Tadashi Hanami. New York: New York University Press. Pp. 384–427.

Cornelius, Wayne A., Philip L. Martin, and James F. Hollifield, Editors
1994   *Controlling Immigration: A Global Perspective.* Stanford: Stanford University Press.

Delgado, Héctor
1993   *New Immigrants, Old Unions: Organizing Undocumented Workers in Los Angeles.* Philadelphia: Temple University Press.

Donato, Katharine M., Jorge Durand, and Douglas S. Massey
1992   Changing Conditions in the U.S. Labor Market: Effects of the Immigration Reform and Control Act of 1986. *Population Research and Policy Review* 11 (2): 93–115.

Doty, Roxanne Lynn
1996   The Double-Writing of Statecraft: Exploring State Response to Illegal Immigration. *Alternatives* 21 (2): 171–189.

Dugger, Celia W.
1997   Chinese Immigrants from Stranded Ship Are to Be Released. *New York Times,* February 15: 1-1.

Fineman, Mark
1998   Dominican Bones Line Pathway to States. *Los Angeles Times,* Tuesday, May 12.

Fisher, Ian
1997   Indictment Describes Abuses of Deaf Mexicans. *New York Times,* August 21: A-1.

Gettleman, Jeffrey
1998   Sixteen Indicted in Sex Slave Smuggling. *St. Petersburg Times,* April 24.

Grasmuck, Sherri, and Patricia R. Pessar
1991   *Between Two Islands: Dominican International Migration.* Berkeley: University of California Press.

Grenier, Guillermo J., Alex Stepick, Debbie Draznin, Aline LaBorwit, and Steve Morris
1992   On Machines and Bureaucracy: Controlling Ethnic Interaction in Miami's Apparel and Construction Industries. In *Structuring Diversity: Ethnographic Perspectives on the New Migration.* Edited by Louise Lamphere. Chicago: University of Chicago Press. Pp. 64–93.

Griffith, David, and David Runsten
1992   The Impact of the 1986 Immigration Reform and Control Act on the U.S. Poultry Industry: A Comparative Analysis. *Policy Studies Review* 11 (2): 118–130.

Haines, David W.
1987   Patterns in Southeast Asian Refugee Employment: A Reappraisal of the Existing Research. *Ethnic Groups* 7: 39–63.
1996   Patterns in Refugee Resettlement and Adaptation. In *Refugees in America in the 1990s*. Westport, Connecticut: Greenwood Press. Pp. 28–59.

Henson, Lois
1998a   Punishment or Publicity? and Bittersweet Harvest. *Savannah Morning News*, May 17.
1998b   Debate Begins to Fix Migrant Problems. *Savannah Morning News*, May 20.
1998c   Onion Farmers, INS to Negotiate Migrant Agreement. *Savannah Morning News*, June 23.

Herron, Matt
1998   Hispanics Living in Fear in Wake of Raid by INS. *Lexington Herald-Leader*, June 5.

Hondagneu-Sotelo, Pierette
1994   *Gendered Transitions: Mexican Experiences of Immigration*. Berkeley: University of California Press.

Hope, Katie
1998   Special Issue: INS Detention. *Refugee Reports* 19 (6): 1–10.

Human Rights Watch
1995   *Crossing the Line*. New York: Human Rights Watch.

ILO (International Labor Organization)
1998a   Report of the Director-General: Activities of the ILO, 1996–97. Geneva.
1998b   ILO Declaration on Fundamental Principles and Rights at Work. Geneva.

IOM (International Organization for Migration)
1996   Organized Crime Moves into Trafficking. *Trafficking in Migrants Quarterly Bulletin* 11: 1–2.
1997   Trafficking in Migrants: IOM Policy and Activities. Geneva.
1998   Trafficking in Children: Prevention before Victimization. *Trafficking in Migrants Quarterly Bulletin* 17: 1–2.

Jaffe, Maureen, and Sonia Rosen, Editors
1996   *Forced Labor: The Prostitution of Children*. Washington, D.C.: U.S. Department of Labor, Bureau of International Labor Affairs.

Kahn, Robert S.
1996   *Other People's Blood: U.S. Immigration Prisons in the Reagan Decade*. Boulder, Colorado: Westview Press.

Kerkstra, Patrick, and Patrick J. McDonnell
1998   Three Charged with Smuggling Immigrants. *Los Angeles Times*, June 17: B-1.

Kinkead, Gwen
1992   *Chinatown: A Portrait of a Closed Society*. New York: HarperCollins.

Kwong, Peter
1996   *The New Chinatown*. Rev. ed. New York: Hill and Wang.
1997   *Forbidden Workers: Illegal Chinese Immigrants and American Labor*. New York: New Press.

Lardner, George, Jr.
1998 16 Charged with Forcing Mexicans into Prostitution. *Washington Post*, April 24: A-21.

Leibowitz, Larry
1998 16 Mexicans Indicted in Slave Prostitution Ring. *Sun Sentinel* (Ft. Lauderdale, Florida), April 24: B-1.

Marquez, Benjamin
1995 Organizing Mexican-American Women in the Garment Industry: La Mujer Obrera. *Women and Politics* 15 (1): 65–87.

Martin, Philip
1996 *Promises to Keep: Collective Bargaining in California Agriculture*. Ames: Iowa University Press.

Martin, Susan, and Andy Schoenholtz
1998 Fixing Temporary Protection in the United States. *World Refugee Survey*: 40–47.

Mason, Bert, R. Keith Striegler, and Gregory T. Berg
1997 *Alternatives to Immigrant Labor?: Raisin Industry Tests New Harvesting Technology*. Washington, D.C.: Center for Immigration Studies.

Massey, Douglas S., and Kristin E. Espinosa
1997 What's Driving Mexico–U.S. Migration: A Theoretical, Empirical, and Policy Analysis. *American Journal of Sociology* 102 (4): 939–999.

Masters, Brooke A., and Sylvia Moreno
1998 Fraud Flourishes as Immigrants Seek Help. *Washington Post*, July 21: A-1.

Mines, Richard, Susan Gabbard, and Anne Steirman
1997 *A Profile of U.S. Farm Workers: Demographic, Household, Composition, Income and Use of Services*. Washington, D.C.: U.S. Department of Labor, Office of Program Economics, Research Report No. 6.

Navarette, Ruben, Jr.
1998 Mexican Family Enslaved. *Arizona Republic*, March 13: A-1.

Navarro, Mireya
1998 Group Forced Illegal Aliens into Prostitution, U.S. Says. *New York Times*, April 24: A-10.

Ojito, Mirta
1998 U.S. Permits 49 Deaf Mexicans to Remain. *New York Times*, June 20: A-1.

Ordonez, Jennifer, and Philip P. Pan
1998 Man Says Restaurant Bought Him for $450. *Washington Post*, March 22: B-9.

Reuters
1998 Three Arrested in Texas for Enslaving Deaf Couple. March 12.

Runyan, Jack L.
1996 *Profile of Hired Farm Workers, 1996 Annual Averages*. U.S. Department of Agriculture, Economic Research Service, Agricultural Economic Report No. 762.

Rural Migration News
1998 Florida: Smuggling Workers. Vol. 4 (3). Http://migration.ucdavis.edu.

Sachs, Susan
1998a Chinese Men Are Queried in Jersey Shore Smuggling. *New York Times*, June 2: B-5.
1998b Seizure of Ship Helps Officials Trace Route of Illegal Immigrants. *New York Times*, June 13: B-2.

Salt, John, and Jeremy Stein
1997   Migration as a Business: The Case of Trafficking. *International Migration* 35 (4): 467–491.

Schiller, Dane
1998   Record Heat Claims the Lives of 43 Undocumented Immigrants. *San Antonio Express-News*.

Simons, John
1998   High-Tech Firms to Ask Congress for Easier Immigration. *Wall Street Journal*, February 24: B-8.

Smith, Paul, J., Editor
1997   *Human Smuggling: Chinese Migrant Trafficking and the Challenge to America's Immigration Tradition*. Washington, D.C.: Center for Strategic and International Studies.

Smith, Robert
1998   Closing the Door on Undocumented Workers. *NACLA Report on the Americas* 31 (4): 6–9.

Stoll, David
1997   The Immigration Debate. *In Focus* 2 (31).

Stull, Donald D., Michael J. Broadway, and Ken C. Erickson
1992   The Price of a Good Steak: Beef Packing and Its Consequences for Garden City, Kansas. In *Structuring Diversity: Ethnographic Perspectives on the New Migration*. Edited by Louise Lamphere. Chicago: University of Chicago Press. Pp. 35–64.

Stull, Donald D., Michael Broadway, and David Griffith, Editors
1995   *Any Way You Cut It: Meat Processing and Small-Town America*. Lawrence: University of Kansas Press.

Trejo, Frank
1998   Three Accused of Enslaving Deaf Mexican Immigrants. *Dallas Morning News*, March 13: 1A.

15

Rights at Risk: California's Proposition 187

Karen E. Rosenblum

Proposition 187, also known as the Save Our State Initiative (SOS), was passed by California voters on November 9, 1994. While largely invalidated by court decisions over the succeeding five years, ''Prop 187'' is nonetheless widely regarded as a watershed in the national consideration of immigration. Its requirement that the providers of public services verify the legal status of those who use the services, report violators to state and federal agencies, and ultimately deny services would have created an immigration monitoring system far more pervasive than any previously existing system.

This chapter provides an overview of the key provisions of Proposition 187, then discusses the origins of the proposition, the peculiar characteristics of California that made it possible, and the arguments made for and against the proposition's core social service and education provisions.

PROPOSITION 187: AN OVERVIEW

Proposition 187 required the creation of a state system that would verify the legal status of those seeking public education, nonemergency medical care, and social services—denying benefits to those who were not citizens, legal permanent residents, or legal temporary visitors. Composed of ten sections, the four that addressed social services, health care, and education were the core of the proposition. Much of the public debate and consequent litigation of the proposition hinged on the particulars of these sections, especially their requirement that social service providers report those they suspected to be illegally resident, including the *parents* of children enrolled in the public schools, even if those children were themselves U.S. citizens. The key sections of the proposition were these:

SECTION 5. Exclusion of Illegal Aliens from Public Social Services.

(a) In order to carry out the intention of the People of California that only citizens of the United States and aliens lawfully admitted to the United States may receive the benefits of public social services and to ensure that all persons employed in the providing of those services shall diligently protect public funds from misuse, the provisions of this section are adopted.

(b) A person shall not receive any public social services to which he or she may be otherwise entitled until the legal status of that person has been verified as one of the following:

    (1) A citizen of the United States.

    (2) An alien lawfully admitted as a permanent resident.

    (3) An alien lawfully admitted for a temporary period of time.

(c) If any public entity in this state to whom a person has applied for public social services determines or reasonably suspects, based upon the information provided to it, that the person is an alien in the United States in violation of federal law, the following procedures shall be followed by the public entity:

    (1) The entity shall not provide the person with benefits or services.

    (2) The entity shall, in writing, notify the person of his or her apparent illegal immigration status, and that the person must either obtain legal status or leave the United States.

    (3) The entity shall also notify the State Director of Social Services, the Attorney General of California, and the United States Immigration and Naturalization Service of the apparent illegal status, and shall provide any additional information that may be requested by any other public entity.

SECTION 6. Exclusion of Illegal Aliens from Publicly Funded Health Care.

(a) In order to carry out the intention of the people of California, that excepting emergency medical care as required by federal law, only citizens of the United States and aliens lawfully admitted to the United States may receive the benefits of publicly-funded health care. . . .

(b) A person shall not receive any health care services from a publicly-funded health care facility, to which he or she is otherwise entitled until the legal status of that person has been verified. . . .

SECTION 7. Exclusion of Illegal Aliens from Public Elementary and Secondary Schools.

(a) No public elementary or secondary school shall admit, or permit the attendance of, any child who is not a citizen of the United States, an alien lawfully admitted as a permanent resident, or a person who is otherwise authorized under federal law to be present in the United States.

(b) . . . each school district shall verify the legal status of each child enrolling in the school district for the first time. . . .

(c) . . . each school district shall have verified the legal status of each child already enrolled and in attendance. . . .

(d) . . . each school district shall have verified the legal status of each parent or guardian of each child referred to it. . . .

SECTION 8. Exclusion of Illegal Aliens from Public Postsecondary Educational Institutions.

(a) No public institution of postsecondary education shall admit, enroll, or permit the attendance of any person who is not a citizen of the United States, an alien lawfully admitted as a permanent resident of the United States, or a person otherwise authorized under federal law to be present in the United States.

The final section of the proposition stipulated that if passed by the voters, Proposition 187 could be changed only to "further its purposes" requiring a statute approved in both houses by a two-thirds vote or by another voter initiative. Because the sections of the proposition are separable from one another, 187 has moved in a somewhat piecemeal fashion through the courts.

Proposition 187 was supported by 59 percent of the ballots and, according to exit polls, a majority of the whites, Asian Americans, and African Americans who voted. Only Latino/a voters opposed the measure, with a 69 percent negative vote. White Californians were disproportionately represented at the polls. Seventy-five to 80 percent of those who voted were white, while the state's population is 57 percent white (Martin 1998: 898). Only eight California counties—all in the San Francisco Bay Area—failed to support the measure.

Initial reaction to the measure was swift. The day after its passage, suits were filed in state and federal courts by immigrant rights groups arguing that the law violated both the California and U.S. Constitutions. Simultaneously, Governor Wilson ordered implementation of Section 6 by barring state-reimbursed prenatal services and nursing home care of undocumented immigrants. Within a few days, the courts had enjoined implementation of almost all sections of the proposition pending a court decision.

The suits filed by immigrant rights groups contended, first, that the proposition was in conflict with the Supreme Court rulings establishing the primacy of the federal government in the establishment of immigration policy, second, that it would deny due process, and, third, that it violated the equal protection clause of the Fourteenth Amendment. Each of these arguments was illustrated in the major complaint, *Gregorio v. Wilson*. Gregorio T. was a seven-year-old receiving Medicaid for treatment of encephalitis, and in their brief the plaintiffs argued that

Proposition 187 creates a state immigration enforcement mechanism separate from the Immigration and Naturalization Service (INS) and employing standards different from those required under federal law. . . . States have no power to regulate immigration or the incidents thereof [primacy of the federal government in the establishment of immigration law]. . . . The initiative . . . violates due process by cutting off benefits without a hearing on mere "suspicion" by any one of tens of thousands of untrained state employees [due process]. It denies equal protection of the laws by creating classes and subclasses of aliens without any rational basis, and by encouraging rampant discrimination against persons who appear or sound foreign [equal protection].

In defense of the proposition, California's attorney general argued that the measure assisted, rather than supplanted, federal immigration laws, that due process issues would be resolved in the regulations that would be developed to implement the proposition, and that the equal-protection clause of the Fourteenth Amendment covered citizens but not undocumented immigrants.

Less than a month after its passage, a federal judge barred implementation of the verification provisions until the constitutionality of the proposition was affirmed by the courts. A year later, in November 1995, U.S. district judge Mariana Pfaelzer (presiding over a consolidated case of five of the challenges) issued a partial ruling that the ban on elementary and high school education for undocumented immigrants was unconstitutional because it violated a 1982 Supreme Court ruling, *Plyler v. Doe*, that guaranteed public education to all children irrespective of their legal status. In her final ruling on the cases in 1997, Pfaelzer concluded that Proposition 187 "is not constitutional on its face," because it presumed that a state could regulate immigration, which is the exclusive domain of the federal government: "California is powerless to enact its own legislation scheme to regulate immigration. It is likewise powerless to enact its own legislative scheme to regulate alien access to public benefits." As evidence that the federal government has primacy in the regulation of immigration, Judge Pfaelzer cited the 1996 congressional overhaul of welfare law, which, she concluded, "ousts state power to legislate in the area of public benefits for aliens."

Ironically, Proposition 187 was itself the catalyst for the 1996 welfare reform act. Thus, supporters of Proposition 187 argued that it was illogical for the Court to throw out the very initiative that had sparked welfare reform. While President Clinton had opposed the proposition in his 1996 reelection campaign, he had also promised that the federal government would do more to help states deal with the costs of illegal immigration. The 1996 welfare reform, which was affected by both the Personal Responsibility and Work Opportunity Reconciliation Act itself, and the Illegal Immigration Reform and Immigrant Responsibility Act, was in some ways even more broadly cast than Proposition 187. Most significantly, it denied nonemergency health care and public benefits (such as disability benefits and food stamps) to many categories of those *legally* admitted to the country, not just to illegal immigrants. Still, the welfare reform package did not bar undocumented immigrants from public primary and secondary education, nor did it require that officials be informed of suspected undocumented immigrants.

Judge Pfaelzer did let stand Section 2 of the proposition, which barred "the manufacture, distribution, or sale of false citizenship or resident alien documents." This section applied only to documents that would "conceal the true citizenship or resident alien status of another person" and not to documents used for other purposes, for example, by teenagers to buy alcohol (Martin 1995: 256).

That three years passed before Judge Pfaelzer issued her ruling raised considerable criticism from the proposition's backers, since during that period Proposition 187 could neither be implemented nor moved to the next level of judicial review. The delay prompted consideration of court reform by the U.S. Congress, which has proposed legislation requiring that federal challenges to state initiatives be heard by a panel of *three* judges (rather than one) and that courts complete their review within a year.

THE ORIGINS OF PROPOSITION 187

The authors of Proposition 187 were two former INS officials, Harold Ezell and Alan Nelson, and Republican assemblyman Richard Mountjoy, who had sponsored ten immigration bills in the state legislature. The chairman of the "Save Our State" Committee was an Orange County accountant, Ron Prince, who claimed to have lost "a half million dollars in a house construction project with a contractor who he later discovered was not a legal resident" (Jost 1995: 110).

Overall, Proposition 187 followed in the historic tradition of anti-immigrant, nativist backlash movements. The nativist theme—antagonism to internal minorities on the basis of their "foreignness" and threat to the American way of life—was clearly framed in the public statements of proposition drafters. One reviewer illustrates the phrasing:

Illegal aliens are killing us in California. . . . Those who support illegal immigration are, in effect, anti-American. [Illegal aliens should be] caught, skinned, and fried [because] the people are tired of watching their state run wild and become a third world country. . . . The militant arm of the pro-illegal activists [has] vowed to take over first California, then the Western states and then the rest of the nation. . . . You get illegal alien children, Third World children, out of the schools and you will reduce the violence. . . . You're dealing with Third World cultures who come in, they shoot, they beat, they stab and they spread their drugs around in our school system. (Johnson 1997: 178, 179).

California Voter Information pieces authored by proposition supporters were equally nativist:

We have to act and ACT NOW! On our ballot, Proposition 187 will be the first giant stride in ultimately ending the ILLEGAL ALIEN invasion. . . . While our own citizens and legal residents go wanting, those who choose to enter our country ILLEGALLY get royal treatment at the expense of the California Taxpayer. (1994 California Voter Information: Argument in Favor of Proposition 187)

Indeed, the first section of Proposition 187 declared that the people of California "have suffered and are suffering personal injury and damage caused by the criminal conduct of illegal aliens in this state." This equation of immigrants with criminals caused the Mexican ambassador to the United States to complain, "There is an equation now in California that goes: Illegal immigrants equal to Mexicans, equal to criminals, equal to someone who wants social services" (Johnson 1997: 178).

On the record in opposition to Proposition 187 were the presidents of the California Teachers Association, California Medical Association, California State Parent-Teacher Association (PTA), and American College of Emergency Physicians, California chapter, as well as the sheriff of Los Angeles County and the legislative director of the Congress of California Seniors, all of whom argued that the measure failed to address the key issues—border enforcement and employer regulation—and that the proposition would ultimately cost more than it saved. In response, the proposition's opponents were characterized as special, moneyed interests—a characterization that some have claimed contributed to the support of 187. The more that interest groups like the Teachers Association, the PTA, and the Medical Association opposed the proposition, the more popular support it garnered (Gabriel 1995: 571).

The real opponents of Proposition 187, the special interests who have pledged millions of dollars to defeat our initiative, have a deep financial interest in continuing the present policy. Remember, illegal aliens are a big business for public unions and well connected medical clinics. You pay the bills, they reap the benefits. . . .
THE SPECIAL INTERESTS ATTACKING PROPOSITION 187 INCLUDE THE CALIFORNIA TEACHERS ASSOCIATION AND THE CALIFORNIA MEDICAL ASSOCIATION. BOTH CONSTITUTE THE STATE'S BIGGEST LOBBYING GROUPS WHO OPPOSE US. THEY PROTECT THEIR OWN INTERESTS—NOT YOURS.
(1994 California Voter Information: Rebuttal to Argument against Proposition 187)

Proposition 187 started with strong support in the opinion polls. Four months before the election, it had a thirty-seven-point lead among likely voters, but by early November voters appeared evenly split, no major California newspaper had endorsed it, Hispanic students had walked out of high schools in large-scale protests, and most politicians and opinion leaders were arguing that "it was too blunt an instrument to deal with the complex issue of illegal immigration" (Martin 1998: 899).

Still, the measure was strongly supported by Governor Pete Wilson, who was up for reelection in a highly contested race with Democrat Kathleen Brown (daughter of one California governor and sister of another). Wilson had begun voicing his support of the measure a year earlier, although he did not formally endorse it until the week before the election (along with Attorney General Dan Lungren, who was also up for reelection). Wilson ran full-page ads in California papers, the *New York Times*, and the *Washington Post* demanding that President Clinton halt illegal immigration and reimburse the state for federally mandated services, and he assured voters that if he were elected, he would require state and local employees to report illegal aliens (Martin 1995: 258). His campaign sponsored what were to be the only pro-Proposition 187 television ads in the state. Throughout the campaign, however, Wilson was careful to distinguish illegal immigrants from those legally entering the country. "In his advertisements and public statements, he praised legal immigrants' contributions to society while accusing illegals of taking jobs away from Californians and consuming scarce public resources'' (Schuck 1995: 89). Getting only 55 percent of the vote, some characterized Wilson's victory as a stunning political comeback attributable, in large part, to his support of the proposition. Indeed, 40 percent of the voters in one exit poll said they voted primarily because Proposition 187 was on the ballot (Martin 1995: 259).

Wilson's support for the measure was an ironic contrast to the position he had taken as a U.S. senator in 1986 and to what he would say just ten days after his reelection. In 1986, he had proposed that a guest worker program (which would benefit agribusiness dependent on seasonal farm labor) be attached to the Immigration Reform and Control Act (IRCA). His lobbying helped produce a special agricultural worker provision (SAW) within IRCA that legalized over 1 million undocumented workers. Those workers then, inevitably, become magnets for the potentially illegal immigration of family members (Smith and Tarallo 1995: 666). Just ten days after the passage of Proposition 187, in a speech at the Heritage Foundation, Wilson argued that California needed to admit more temporary workers to meet harvest needs (Schuck 1995).

Some have argued that we should interpret the passage of Proposition 187 as more an effort to "send a message to Washington" than as a viable piece of legislation (Calavita 1996)—an interpretation supported by exit surveys and opinion polls at the time. One *Los Angeles Times* exit poll found 78 percent of those voting for the measure doing so because "it sends a message that needs to be sent" (*Los Angeles Times*, November 9, 1994: A22). In the final weeks before the election, even the sponsors of the initiative were describing it as purely symbolic—"Hesitant voters were told not to worry about any potential negative consequences of the initiative, because it was not likely to be enforced" (Calavita 1996: 299). Whatever voters' intentions, however, the effects of the proposition have been more than symbolic.

WHY CALIFORNIA?

There are several reasons that the initiative emerged in California. First, initiatives are an almost commonplace form of policy making in California, especially for policies that would otherwise not find support in the state legislature. In 1978 California voters passed Proposition 13, which reduced property taxes; in 1986 they passed Proposition 63, which amended the state constitution to declare English the state's official language; and in 1998 they approved Proposition 227, which substituted English immersion programs for bilingual education (interestingly, sponsored by a Republican activist who had campaigned *against* Proposition 187 [del Olmo 1998]). Court challenges to these initiatives are an equally regular outcome. As one reporter quipped, "When it comes to ballot measures, California has a tradition: Tuesday is election day, Wednesday is lawsuit day" (Bailey 1998). Most often the courts dismiss the initiative—rejecting almost half of the approved propositions between 1962 and 1992 and three out of four approved measures in recent years (Bailey 1998). Since the 1990s, California propositions have been most often challenged in the federal courts, where judges have lifetime appointments and are more likely to strike down such initiatives than are the elected judges of California state courts (Holman and Stern 1998).

Second, California had and continues to have the largest concentration of undocumented immigrants in the country. In 1995, 45 percent of the nation's undocumented workers lived in California (see Passel, this volume). As one of six states bearing a disproportionate share of illegal immigration (with Arizona, Florida, New Jersey, New York, and Texas), California had filed several suits against the federal government for reimbursement of the cost of services to illegal immigrants. The suits contended that the federal government was failing to control the nation's borders, thus forcing the affected states to spend millions of dollars on education, medical care, and corrections, and that this constituted a violation of state sovereignty (Jost 1995). One of California's suits claimed that the federal government had failed to protect California from a foreign "invasion" of immigrants.

Third, California—particularly southern California's Orange County and San Fernando Valley, which were home to the initiative—was gripped by ongoing recession and budget shortfalls. In the 1980s the state had experienced steady growth, with the addition of 2.6 million jobs and an 18 percent increase in real terms of average income per capita. But that had ended abruptly in the recession of the early 1990s. Between 1990 and 1992, 1.5 million jobs were lost; between 1990 and 1993 the official poverty rate grew from 12.5 percent to 18.2 percent; by 1993, unemployment was over 9 percent. By 1993, California was, according to some criteria, among the nation's ten poorest states (Campus Coalitions 1995: 54).

From 1989 to 1993, like victims of a deadly economic virus, the Valley's largest employers—Lockheed (Burbank), Hughes (Canoga Park) and General Motors (Van Nuys)—shut down their gates forever. Other major defense contractors, like Rocketdyne and Litton, slashed employment or transferred operations out of the Valley. As a consequence, the clusters of smaller aerospace subcontractors in Chatsworth and along San Fernando Road were devastated. . . . The collapse of the Valley's high-wage manufacturing base had grim multiplier effects on low-wage jobs in light industry, construction and services. . . . The supply of affordable rental housing, already tight, was devastated by the January 1994 earthquake, which also produced a new round of business failures and layoffs. (Davis 1995: 27)

These closings also had their ripple effect on state services: per pupil spending in public schools dropped from the highest rankings to thirty-eighth, school maintenance was deferred, and almost all the key functions of the state had been cut back by one-fourth to one-third (Campus Coalitions 1995). "By 1992 California was experiencing the worst economic downturn since the Great Depression: 4.9 million Californians (15.9 percent) lived in poverty, including one out of every four children'' (Zavella 1997: 141).

Not surprisingly, then, Proposition 187 and the debate it sparked focused on undocumented immigrants as a fiscal burden (Calavita 1996). In his 1994 gubernatorial campaign, Pete Wilson argued that in education, health care, social services, and incarceration, illegal immigrants cost California $2.9 billion a year (Jost 1995). The U.S. General Accounting Office estimated the net annual cost to California for elementary and secondary education, Medicaid, and incarceration at $2.35 billion (Bedrick 1996); others calculated the cost at $5 billion (Parker and Rea 1993). These calculations were challenged by an Urban Institute study (Clark and Passel 1993) showing that, at a minimum, such figures overestimated both the level of undocumented immigration and the use of social services. Whatever the specific calculation, ''To the federal government immigrants represent a net gain. Their state-level impact varies by state. At the local level the costs of immigrants—and of the native born—exceed taxes paid'' (Fix and Passel 1994).

THE KEY ISSUES: SOCIAL SERVICES AND EDUCATION

Four sections of the proposition were the subject of most of the attention: Sections 5 and 6 on social services and health care and Sections 7 and 8 on public education. The public education exclusion in the proposition was not so surprising, since public education is perhaps the most costly service used by undocumented immigrants (Martin 1995). The proposition's call for the exclusion of illegal immigrants from public benefits, however, made less sense since it affirmed what was already generally the case, at least at the *federal* level. The exclusion of immigrants on the grounds that they might become public charges had long been part of U.S. immigration laws, and that was even more straightforwardly the case with illegal immigrants.

When considering the vociferousness of the public debate over Proposition 187, one might be surprised to learn that undocumented immigrants are eligible for few of the major federal public assistance programs generally available to the poor in the United States. They are ineligible for major federally supported benefit programs, such as Aid to Families with Dependent Children (AFDC), Medicaid, food stamps, and Supplemental Security Income (SSI). Among the few major federal programs for which undocumented immigrants may be eligible are *emergency* medical care under Medicaid and the Women, Infants, and Children (WIC) nutrition program. (Johnson 1995: 1529)

On the *state* level as well, undocumented immigrants were not eligible for welfare grants, although they were eligible for some of the other benefits available to Californians. For example, any child in need could receive child welfare services or foster care, and unauthorized immigrants could receive some nonemergency health care services—such as county indigent health care for those who were poor, had no insurance, and were not covered by programs like Medi-Cal (1994 California Voter Information: Analysis of Proposition 187 by the Legislative Analyst). Proposition 187 would have discontinued these services.

Section 7 of the proposition required public elementary and secondary schools to verify status and bar those children who could not document lawful admission to the country. Most startling was the requirement that school districts also verify and report the status of parents and guardians *even if the students were themselves citizens*—which would be the case if they had been born in the United States (Johnson 1995: 1566).

Judge Pfaelzer ruled this section unconstitutional because it violated the Supreme Court's 1982 *Plyler v. Doe* holding. In that case, Justice William Brennan, writing for a five-to-four majority, argued that a Texas law withholding state funds for the education of children illegally entering the country would harm both the children and the nation, since those children would likely remain in the country and be "locked into the lowest socioeconomic class" even were they to become citizens as adults. The Court held that while

persuasive arguments support the view that a State may withhold its beneficence from those whose very presence within the United States is the product of their own unlawful conduct . . . they do not apply with the same force to classifications imposing disabilities on the minor *children* of such illegal entrants. . . . [Education] has a fundamental role in maintaining the fabric of our society. We cannot ignore the significant costs borne by our Nation when select groups are denied the means to absorb the values and skills upon which our social order rests.

Thus, Pfaelzer ruled, irrespective of the source of funds used for K–12 education, that is, whether those funds were state and/or federal, *Plyler v. Doe* required that states educate children whether or not they were legally admitted to the country. Only colleges and universities, she held, could deny entry or in-state tuition to illegal immigrants. In 1994, when the proposition was passed, the state university system charged undocumented immigrants in-state tuition; community colleges and the University of California system charged out-of-state tuition (Martin 1995, 1998).

In determining that the Texas law violated the equal protection clause of the Fourteenth Amendment, the Supreme Court had applied the "intermediate scrutiny standard" rather than either the "strict" or "traditional" standards. A "strict judicial scrutiny" standard is applied if the right affected is one guaranteed by the Constitution and thus fundamental. State action that denies or limits a fundamental right of one class of people but not another is presumed to be unconstitutional and must therefore undergo "strict scrutiny" to show that the action was specifically tailored to serve a compelling state interest. The Supreme Court had previously held that education is not a fundamental right under the U.S. Constitution (although it is a fundamental right under the California Constitution). The "traditional" standard of scrutiny is applied if the right affected is not fundamental and the classes of people created not "suspect," that is, if the class created is a product of "legislative rationality" rather than prejudice. The traditional standard "requires only that the state's system be shown to bear some rational relationship to legitimate state purposes" (Bedrick 1996).

In *Plyler v. Doe*, however, the Court used the "intermediate standard," which applies when the right is not fundamental and the class not suspect but when "the class affected has some similarities to suspect or semi-suspect classes . . . the right affected is very important, and the disability imposed is very severe." In such cases, "the state must show not only a rational relationship of its action to legitimate state purposes, but also that the resulting discrimination between classes 'furthers a substantial goal of the State' " (Bedrick 1996). Using the intermediate standard, Justice Brennan, writing for the majority,

acknowledged that the state had some leeway in such matters: Under equal protection principles, illegal alien status is not a "suspect class" like race or religion, and education is not a "fundamental right." Nevertheless, Brennan said, a law that denied children "the ability to live within the structure of our civic institutions . . . can hardly be considered rational unless it furthers some substantial goal of the State." (Schuck 1995: 87)

[In *Plyler v. Doe*], the Court recognized that, although "[p]ersuasive arguments support the view that a State may withhold its beneficence from those whose very presence within the United States is the product of their own unlawful conduct[,] they do not apply with the same force to classifications imposing disabilities on the minor children of such illegal entrants." (Johnson 1995: 1567)

It was precisely the absence of state interest that Texas had failed to demonstrate, Brennan argued. "The Texas law might save some money . . . but Texas failed to establish that unauthorized immigrants imposed a significant fiscal burden on state coffers or that their exclusion would improve the quality of education" (Schuck 1995: 87).

If the same "intermediate standard" is applied to the education section of Proposition 187, the Supreme Court would likely conclude that it is unconstitutional, since the California proposition is not significantly different from the Texas law, and both states have based their cases on the negative impact of undocumented immigrants on state economies. (The Texas law, however, did not require that school districts verify the immigration status of parents or guardians.) Yet, while the Court would likely rely on the same standard as it applied in *Plyler*, that standard is "vague and difficult to apply in practice" (Bedrick 1996). Is education so unique that it justifies a special constitutional protection for children? Does denying a child's education differ from denying the child's parents the medical care and social services that also contribute to the child's welfare? Is immigration so uncontrollable that we should assume, as Justice

Brennan did, that illegally entering children will become permanent residents? (Schuck 1995).

If the intermediate scrutiny analysis used in *Plyler* is followed, the courts must make difficult distinctions among various rights, all of which are non-fundamental. Equal Protection challenges to some non-fundamental rights will be assessed based on the traditional standard; Equal Protection challenges to other non-fundamental rights, such as public education, will require that the higher standard of intermediate scrutiny be met. (Bedrick 1996: 410)

Were the traditional, rather than intermediate, standard applied, some argue that Proposition 187 would likely be ruled constitutional (Bedrick 1996). Indeed, Proposition 187 drafter Alan Nelson has said that the purpose of the initiative was really to have the Supreme Court reconsider the *Plyler* decision (Johnson 1995: 1565).

ASSESSING THE SIGNIFICANCE OF THE PROPOSITION

Opinion about the significance of Proposition 187 varies. A comparison of the situation in California with that in Arizona and Texas would argue that there is a limit to how much we can generalize (Smith and Tarallo 1995). Even though they are also significantly impacted by illegal immigration, Arizona and Texas strongly repudiated similar measures. Unlike California, Arizona and Texas have nurtured interdependent business relations in the cities that span the Mexican border and have economies that are heavily dependent on exports to Mexico. In Arizona's case over a quarter of the state's exports go to Mexico, and in Texas that figure is 40 percent. By comparison, less than 10 percent of California's exports have that destination. All three states estimate that about a quarter of their population is Latino, but in California the percentage of the Latino population that is foreign-born is higher than in Texas and Arizona, the median age of Latinos is younger than that of other Californians, and their education is lower—all factors that reduce Latino/a political participation. Latinos in Arizona and Texas are more likely to vote than are those in California, and Arizona and Texas have better-established Latino political organizations. Finally, the economies of Texas and Arizona were healthier than California's, and business elites in those states were vocal in their opposition to Proposition 187-like grassroots organizations, unlike the relative silence of agribusiness in California.

Politically, passage of Proposition 187 has been hailed as a watershed event for Latino/a political participation, at least in Los Angeles. Voter registration has had a 30 percent increase in Los Angeles County since 1994, compared to 5 percent nationally (Tobar 1998). "A *Times* analysis of voter registration patterns in Los Angeles County shows that the local Assembly districts that are home to the largest numbers of immigrants have shown the fastest rise in registration, fueled by increased naturalization, opposition to Proposition 187 and strong Latino support last year for the Los Angeles school repair bond, Proposition BB'' (Tobar 1998). Proposition 187 also appears to have encouraged local immigrant activists to turn their attention to domestic issues instead of home-country ones. ''Typically, the *fraternidades*—formed by expatriates from a given town or province [e.g., El Salvador or Guatemala]—would help build medical clinics, schools and fire stations back in Guatemala. Now, [they] are channeling at least some of those resources to community empowerment in Los Angeles'' (Tobar 1998).

If implemented, health care professionals warn of the public health dangers created by denying nonemergency medical treatment, for example, the spread of diseases such as tuberculosis. The diminished use of health services has also generated concern about an escalating cost of health care, since emergency services would be used for conditions that might have been resolved with less expensive early intervention (Ziv and Lo 1995). Immediately following passage of the proposition, there appears to have been a reduction in the use of health and social services by illegal immigrants, with at least two deaths directly attributable to that (Johnson 1995: 1559).

Should the proposition be implemented, there remains the question of how an individual's status would be verified. Federal law protects the privacy of personal information in a student's educational record, and the Fourth Amendment prohibits the detainment of individuals on the basis of appearance (e.g., skin color, surname, or accent). ''So unless an alien volunteers her illegal status, due process principles almost surely require a hearing before the state may withdraw benefits previously granted'' (Schuck 1995: 89).

Sociologist Pierette Hondagneu-Sotelo argues that in origin and consequences there is a significant correspondence between the 1994 passage of Proposition 187 and the expulsion of half a million people to Mexico during the Great Depression:

There are at least four points of congruity between the present and the events of the Great Depression. First, the 1930s expulsion program came on the heels of the 1920s, a period of Mexican migration characterized by increased permanent settlements of families. Second, the ''draining public resources'' narrative was effectively used to rationalize expulsion, with social workers and relief agencies taking an active role in enforcement, targeting women and families. Third, the activism of civilian anti-immigrant groups, not just government agents, played a key role in the campaign. Last, the 1930s repatriation occurred during a period of national economic reorganization, just as contemporary events correspond to capitalist realignments at a global level. (Hondagneu-Sotelo 1995: 176)

Most importantly, Hondagneu-Sotelo argues that both ''initiatives'' were sparked by a change in the nature of illegal immigration, from the transitory migration of single males to the settled habitation of families. Insofar as families require services for the maintenance of everyday life—particularly health and education—the costs of unauthorized immigration rise. While some employers may encourage the illegal immigration of women (and thereby families), most prefer single males, who offer a much more "disposable" and inexpensive labor force. An increasing presence of women and children, then, makes evident that the undocumented population is no longer transitory, and it is that to which nativist impulses respond. Thus, grassroots nativist movements, such as the movement that produced Proposition 187, promote a "coercive" system of labor that denies or severely restricts family life for undocumented workers. Proposition 187 "mobilized support not against immigrant workers or illegal immigration" but against the *permanent* integration of *families* (Hondagneu-Sotelo 1995: 178). In all, Proposition 187 did not object to undocumented workers per se, only the social services that supported those workers (Ambruster, Geron, and Bonacich 1995).

The proposition's repercussions have been considerable. In addition to the increased activism of California's Latino/a population, it also appears that in California, applications for U.S. citizenship increased in the period immediately following passage of the measure (Smith and Tarallo 1995). Passage also spurred the Mexican government—which had actively opposed the proposition—to propose constitutional amendments allowing Mexicans outside the country to vote (Weintraub 1998). Certainly, Proposition 187 gave momentum to the anti-immigrant policies codified in the Personal Responsibility and Work Opportunity Reconciliation Act and the Illegal Immigration Reform and Immigrant Responsibility Act of the 1996 federal welfare reform. In all, Proposition 187 has become a political "line in the sand" legitimating a variety of anti-immigrant attitudes and policies, but also activating a more coordinated opposition to those attitudes and policies.

REFERENCES

Armbruster, Ralph, Kim Geron, and Edna Bonacich
1995 The Assault on California's Latino Immigrants: The Politics of Proposition 187. *International Journal of Urban and Regional Research* 19: 655–663.
Bailey, Eric
1998 Election Day Approval Just 1st Hurdle for Propositions. *Los Angeles Times*, June 8: A:1.
Bedrick, Benjamin N.
1996 The Equal Protection Clause: State Statutory Restrictions on the Education of Illegal Alien Children. *Dickinson Journal of International Law* 14: 403–410.
Calavita, Kitty
1996 The New Politics of Immigration: "Balanced-Budget Conservatism" and the Symbolism of Proposition 187. *Social Problems* 43 (3): 284–305.
Campus Coalitions for Human Rights and Social Justice
1995 California at a Crossroads: Social Strife or Social Unity? *Social Justice* 22 (3): 53–63.

Clark, Rebecca C., and Jeffrey S. Passel
1993   *How Much Do Immigrants Pay in Taxes?* Washington, D.C.: The Urban Institute (PRIP-UI-26).

Davis, Mike
1995   The Social Origins of the Referendum. *NACLA Report on the Americas* 29 (3): 24–28.

Del Olmo, Frank
1998   Perspective on Proposition 227. *Los Angeles Times*, February 15: M:5.

Fix, Michael, and Jeffrey S. Passel
1994   *Immigration and Immigrants: Setting the Record Straight.* The Urban Institute. May.

Gabriel, John
1995   Discussion: On Propositions, Racism and Democracy. *Discourse and Society* 6 (4): 570–572.

Hinojosa, Raul, and Peter Schey
1995   The Faulty Logic of the Anti-Immigration Rhetoric. *NACLA Report on the Americas* 29 (3): 18–23.

Holman, Craig B., and Robert Stern
1998   Symposium on the California Initiative Process: Judicial Review of Ballot Initiatives: The Change in the Role of State and Federal Courts. *Loyola of Los Angeles Law Review* 31: 1239–1265.

Hondagneu-Sotelo, Pierrette
1995   Women and Children First: New Directions in Anti-Immigrant Politics. *Socialist Review* 25 (1): 169–190.

Johnson, Kevin R.
1995   Public Benefits and Immigration: The Intersection of Immigration Status, Ethnicity, Gender, and Class. *UCLA Law Review* 42: 1509–1575.
1997   The New Nativism: Something Old, Something New, Something Borrowed, Something Blue. In *Immigrants Out: The New Nativism and the Anti-Immigrant Impulse in the United States.* Edited by Juan F. Perea. New York: New York University Press. Pp. 165–189.

Jost, Kenneth
1995   Cracking Down on Immigration: Should Government Benefits and Services Be Cut Off? *CQ Researcher* 5: 99–119.

Martin, Philip
1995   Proposition 187 in California. *International Migration Review* 29 (1): 255–263.
1998   Proposition 187 in California. In *Migration between Mexico and the United States.* Mexico City and Washington, D.C.: Mexico–United States Binational Migration Study. Pp. 897–901.

McDonnell, Patrick
1997   Decision Means Anti-Illegal Immigration Measure Won't Be Implemented, Barring Appeal. *Los Angeles Times*, November 15.

Mehan, Hugh
1997   The Discourse of the Illegal Immigration Debate: A Case Study in the Politics of Representation. *Discourse and Society* 8:249–270.

Parker, Richard A., and Louis M. Rea
1993   *Illegal Immigration in San Diego County: An Analysis of the Costs and Revenues.* Report to the California Senate, Special Committee on Border Issues.

Schuck, Peter H.

1995   The Message of 187. *The American Prospect* No. 21: 85–92.

Seib, Gerald

1996   Backlash over Immigration Enters Mainstream This Year. *Wall Street Journal*, September 27.

Smith, Michael Peter, and Bernadette Tarallo

1995   Proposition 187: Global Trend or Local Narrative? Explaining Anti-Immigrant Politics in California, Arizona, and Texas. *International Journal of Urban and Regional Research* 19 (December): 664–676.

Tobar, Hector

1998   American Democracy in Latino L.A. *Los Angeles Times*, April 13, A:1.

Weintraub, Sidney

1998   On the Unrenounceability of Mexican Nationality. In *Migration between Mexico and the United States*. Mexico City and Washington, D.C.: Mexico–United States Binational Migration Study. Pp. 1249–1250.

Zavella, Patricia

1997   The Tables Are Turned: Immigration, Poverty, and Social Conflict in California Communities. In *Immigrants Out: The New Nativism and the Anti-Immigrant Impulse in the United States*. Edited by Juan F. Perea. New York: New York University Press. Pp. 131–161.

Ziv, Tal An, and Bernard Lo

1995   Denial of Care to Illegal Immigrants. *New England Journal of Medicine* 332: 1095–1098.

16

Maintaining and Reunifying Families: Two Case Studies of Shifting Legal Status

Lucy M. Cohen

In recent decades policymakers and students of immigration have shown increased interest in examination of the impact of migrant and refugee resettlement on the health of adults and their children. Less attention has focused, however, on the children left behind and the processes of reunification with parents after periods of separation. This can span a period lasting from a few years to fifteen years or more, depending on the circumstances of migration. One of those "circumstances" is the legal status of the parents.

The report of the Canadian Task Force on Mental Health Issues Affecting Immigrants and Refugees in Canada (Beiser 1988) singles out the issue of prolonged separation of children from their parents as an area that needs to be addressed in order to prevent ill health and serious distress. In host countries, mothers and fathers often struggle for a number of years to earn enough money to make it possible for children to join them. Dependent on their particular immigration status, it may also take prolonged periods of time for parents to obtain the proper documents to bring about successful reunification with their children.

The task force further reports that for children "left behind" reunification can also have consequences. Their departure from a home country to join parents means a second separation, this time from parent surrogates. For some young people, separation from caretakers and the only homes some may have known during childhood and adolescence can be fraught with difficulties. An issue of interest is not the problems themselves but how young people manage these circumstances as they make accommodations in the country of birth and the site of resettlement.

Drawing on my research and advocacy work among immigrants and refugees from Latin America in Washington, D.C., I present two brief cases on the circumstances of separation and reunification of parents and children from El Salvador, followed by comments regarding the concepts of caretaking and child giving from the perspectives of the young people. Implications for health and mental health are discussed. In both cases, the parents were undocumented during at least some of their residence in the United States, even though the children themselves eventually came to the United States with ''proper papers.'' The case studies thus convey the secondhand effects of legal status on family reunification.

CONTEMPORARY SALVADORAN IMMIGRANTS IN WASHINGTON, D.C.

In the past three decades, the Washington metropolitan area has been one of the major regions of settlement for Salvadorans in the United States.[1] With the increased presence of Salvadorans and peoples of other Latin American heritage in this nation, researchers and practitioners interested in migration and health should examine reconfigurations of households and kinship that have impact not only on the newcomers and their settlements but on the circumstances of children left behind, some of whom may eventually join parents who have settled in the new country. The topic has practical as well as theoretical significance. Just prior to his tragic assassination, the well-known Salvadoran sociologist Segundo Montes conducted landmark research among immigrants and refugees. His work (Mozo 1987: 65–71) clearly showed that the circumstances of emigration, war, and exile of Salvadoran populations had contributed to the dislocation of households and the aggravation of problems of family disintegration. Under such conditions; the question of reunification of parents and children merits high priority in research.

Immigrants move across international boundaries and within regions and cities in host countries. Major changes take place in domestic units as families separate in order to facilitate migration. This focus is important since the household is the major context within which health is defined and problems of illness are managed. For some immigrants the requirements of social life and the guiding norms and values of the host region of resettlement call for fairly rapid reconfiguration of domestic units. Furthermore, the composition of a family changes with developments in the life cycle as children grow up and parents grow older.

There is an additional, important demographic aspect to consider. The families of immigrants do not move as a unit. Individual family members initiate the paths toward Washington followed by relatives and/or close friends. There is nothing particularly unusual about this ''chain'' migration of individual family members since the histories of immigration to the United States are filled with such cases from various world regions. However, in the context of present-day international migration, the movement and settlement of many immigrants of

Central American origin (as well as other regions in the Americas) are led largely by women. Moreover, most of these women had begun to establish their own households in their countries of birth prior to immigration, and thus they are separated from children, husbands, or other relatives for whom they had assumed responsibility. This growing proportion of women of Latin American heritage who lead transnational immigration movements and of their children has received limited attention in the literature about immigrants and their health.

Caretakers

Women immigrants and couples with young children left behind depend almost exclusively on the maternal grandmother or the child's aunts for child care. Children seventeen and under who remain in El Salvador are usually cared for by these grandmothers or other maternal kin.

This caretaking has often involved contact with a wider group of maternal kin than had been typical in the mother's household. The availability of support by these family members makes it possible for females to become initiators of immigration. This pattern of child care suggests that an immigrant's separation from children in the early or late phases of childhood serves to solidify the child's kinship ties with the maternal line.

In work I have conducted over a span of twenty years, the saliency of these dynamics of separation and reunification has become evident. In field trips to El Salvador, I have visited grandmothers, as caretakers, and the children for whom they have responsibility. Immigrant women in Washington have instructed me to report on the state of health of their absent children and to identify worries with which the caretakers at home need assistance. The questions that these visits raised for me concerned the impact of substitute parenting on the caretakers. Grandmothers, as caretakers of smaller children and youth, carry multiple responsibilities that are not easy for them to assume (Cohen 1979).

With the passage of time, parents in Washington, with or without "proper" immigration documents, arrange for reunification with children left behind. It seems important, therefore, to study the caretaking experiences for the young people involved. How do children look upon reunification with parents after periods of long separation? What is the meaning of caretaking to these young people?

Substitute caretaking is central to the processes of migration today in which women, as leaders of international migration, are forced to leave children behind. To illustrate selected issues associated with the health implications of resettlement, I present two cases in which the young women who had been left with caretakers in the home country discuss their experiences, following their resettlement in Washington. In both cases, their parents had come to Washington without "proper" immigration documents but eventually found employers who sponsored their entry to the United States. The process of requesting official entry to the country had begun. As this objective was set in motion, it eventually became possible to bring dependent children under twenty-one to Washington, with "proper" documents. Under immigration regulations, however, children over twenty-one could not be claimed. Adult children have to place their request for entry on their own.

Both young women resided in small towns in the eastern region of El Salvador which has sent many of its sons and daughters to Washington, D.C.[2] I met both of them at the time of their visits to a health center that serves the community of Spanish-speaking newcomers in Washington.[3] The two cases are a "sample of convenience." They are chosen to compare and to contrast their views concerning separation, caretaking, and reunification.

THE CASE OF RAFAELA HERNÁNDEZ

> Our parents are strangers. . . . To me, my grandmother *is* my mother.

When Rafaela Hernández first came to the Washington health center where I met her, she complained of headaches, palpitations, and chest pressures. The clinical evaluations were negative. Upon further assessment her symptoms were associated with periods when she recalled negative or tragic experiences in her life.

Rafaela and Her Caretakers

Rafaela, a twenty-four-year-old Salvadoran immigrant, had been reunited with her family in Washington three years earlier. She described separation from her mother in the following words:

My mother gave me away when I was ten months old. I did not live with her again till I was nineteen, when she brought me to the U.S. I grew up with my grandparents and with an unmarried aunt. This aunt got a special job which provided for my monthly expenses and school till I reached the ninth grade. To me, my grandmother *is* my mother. She taught me principles, morals, and responsibility. My grandparents are both people of strong character. They are solid people.

In addition to the care of Rafaela, the grandparents kept one of Rafaela's brothers. Five years after Rafaela arrived in this household the grandparents took in an additional child, the daughter of another of Rafaela's aunts who had emigrated to Canada, following her divorce in El Salvador. Although Rafaela's mother visited the grandparents' household intermittently, her two children continued to live with their grandparents.

Reunification

Eighteen years after her separation from her parents, Rafaela's mother arranged immigration papers to bring her and her brother to the United States. Since her mother had entered the United States without "proper papers," it had taken her a number of years to locate a *patrón* (boss) who was interested in sponsoring her entry to the country. Not until after these papers were processed and approved was her mother able to put in the request to bring her children to Washington.

Rafaela's early period in the parental household in Washington was strained. In her words, "Our parents are strangers." Nonetheless, she made the resolution to "move forward." She wanted to work and learn English so that she could fulfill a dream of mastering computer skills and working in an office.

However, her mother asked that she first repay the sum of $1,000.00, plus other expenses incurred to bring her to Washington. So Rafaela was not able to study until she repaid her mother for the expenses of this trip. She obtained a part-time job, and it took her two years to repay the money that her mother had claimed. In the meantime, her relationship with her mother was strained, so much so that upon completion of the repayment she decided to live independently, moving out to live with a family from whom she rented a room.

Her mother became upset about Rafaela's departure from the family home. As a consequence, she would not talk to her even when Rafaela visited other members of the family. Not until several months later, when Rafaela went back to her home country to visit her grandparents, did her mother contact her to send a parcel to the family.

Rafaela's visit to El Salvador was a fruitful experience. Both her grandfather and her grandmother expressed affection and sentiments of "welcome home." The visit reassured her of her continued positive sentiments toward the grandparents and their solicitous interest in her. During this trip she also visited her aunt to thank her for the many sacrifices she had made in providing for her education while she was a child. Rafaela told her that she would send her remittances as frequently as she could. This was not to be seen as "repayment" but as a token of appreciation.

Upon her return from this trip, Rafaela's mother met her at the airport. Since then, their telephone communication is more frequent, and Rafaela visits her periodically, when invited. Rafaela has also made some friends in her language school and at work. She recently met Roberto, a young man in her place of work. She values this particular friendship because they share common experiences. Roberto was also raised by his grandparents in El Salvador. When his father secured his entry to the United States as an adolescent, Roberto came to live in the family home, which consisted of his father and a new wife whom he had married following the death of Roberto's mother. The young man found it difficult to get along with his stepmother. Following completion of high school, he left the family home. Only recently did he reestablish communication with his father and stepmother.

Comments

From Rafaela's perspective, the caretaking offered by her grandparents was not substitute parenting. Rafaela states: "My grandmother *is* my mother." Her grandfather, who is "like a father," has been a source of wise advice. The aunt who paid for her early years of education in El Salvador now merits her remittances, a sign of her reciprocity for sacrifices made on her behalf.

Rafaela's sentiments of estrangement from her biological mother were heightened by her demand for repayment for the expenses of her trip and the paperwork involved. Not until she moved to an independent household, separate from her mother, did she feel that she could begin to establish her identity and experience a decrease of the physical symptoms that have burdened her since her arrival in the United States.

She has, in recent months, taken the initiative of calling her mother frequently and of accepting her invitations to visit on occasional weekends. She has found also that a sizable number of young friends who share like experiences of long separation from parents best understand her sentiments that her heart and identity as a daughter lie in the household left in El Salvador.

THE CASE OF MARLENE MOLINA

My mother's diabetes is caused by her sacrifices for all of us.

When I met Marlene Molina, a native of El Salvador, she had been in the United States for a year and a half. Marlene had come to the health center to seek relief for her headaches, nervous tension, and a skin rash. She wanted also to find health resources for her mother, who had been diagnosed as a diabetic.

Marlene, who is twenty-one years old, had been separated from her parents when she was six years old. Her mother first emigrated to the United States to join an uncle in search of improved economic resources for the family because Marlene's father, who was a heavy drinker, did not provide enough to support the family. Soon after her settlement in Washington, her mother made arrangements to bring over her husband and their son.

Marlene and Her Caretakers

Marlene and her four-year-old sister were left behind with their maternal grandmother and several aunts and the aunts' children, all of whom lived in the same household. Marlene's fourteen-year-old sister was away in school but came home every weekend. Although the grandmother and aunts were the designated caretakers, the fourteen-year-old sister became the de facto substitute parent to the girls. She offered advice and protection to her younger sisters. Indeed, the older sister's role as adviser soon expanded to one of protector and substitute parent due to the exploitative behavior of several aunts.

Remittances and Caretakers

Marlene recalls that when their mother's remittances arrived every month, the aunts would threaten to take the money away from them. They were said to have made up stories such as, "Your mother has abandoned you." Marlene believes that they tried to "put these ideas in our head so we could love them more than we loved our mother. They also wanted us to obey their orders which were usually to work harder than their own children."

Marlene countered the aunts' stories by such statements as: "A mother's love is different from all others. That is why our mother emigrated, so she could support us. She had to do this because our father has been very irresponsible about family support, and his relatives would not help her either." Marlene recalls that her aunts did not welcome her responses. As she states it: "They were afraid of me because I did not pay attention to them. They called me a rebel."

As Marlene maintained this positive image of her mother, her older sister continued to defend her younger siblings from the aunts' demands. The responsibility of protecting her younger siblings from adult demands was a constant source of worry. Marlene believes that for this reason this older sister developed a persistent headache problem.

When Marlene was eleven, their older sister sent an urgent message to their mother in Washington that their lives with the aunts had become increasingly difficult. In response, their mother returned from the United States and stayed with them until the older sister finished secondary school and was ready to go to San Salvador, the capital, to study pharmacy in the university. The mother helped to rearrange their caretaking arrangements so that the three sisters resettled in the capital, where Marlene and her younger sister attended high school, and the older sister studied in the university. Their older sister exercised her authority as needed, saying, "Obey me because I am the mother here. Our other mother is in Washington."

Reunification

Marlene's mother and father had entered the United States without "proper papers." Her mother was able to find an employer willing to sponsor her entry to the country. An immigration lawyer helped with her case. However, this process was interrupted when she returned to El Salvador to respond to her older daughter's call for assistance with caretaking. Marlene's father, who remained in the United States, found an employer who willingly served as his sponsor. His wife's attorney helped him with his papers. Both of Marlene's parents are grateful to this lawyer, who helped with all the steps involved and who seemed personally interested in the reunification of their family.

After their parents obtained the proper immigration papers, Marlene and her younger sister came to the United States to join their parents and their brother. Their older sister remained in El Salvador to complete her studies in pharmacy, with the support of her mother.

Marlene's early period of life in the United States was not easy. At first she did not feel comfortable placing her trust in her father and mother. They were like strangers. She missed her older sister. But her mother looked for ways to communicate effectively with them, and when Marlene said that she wanted to go back home, their mother said to her, "You'll get used to this new life." Marlene has, indeed, settled and felt more comfortable with new friends, a job, and classes in English.

When Marlene discusses the state of health of family members, she emphasizes that her mother's suffering with the struggles for her children and husband have been major contributors to her ill health and particularly the onset of diabetes. She summarizes these beliefs and sentiments with comments such as: "Our mother has suffered for our sake so we can launch our lives. She has worked hard so that we can overcome difficulties." Marlene worries about her mother and spends time helping her with needed medical resources. Her mother's recent diagnosis of diabetes has led Marlene to link her mother's sufferings with the onset of this illness. Narratives of past and present efforts to cope with family illness are drawn upon as examples of how her mother has overcome the difficulties of life.

For example, Marlene believes that one of her mother's early sources of suffering was with a life-threatening illness of unknown origin that her oldest daughter (Rafaela's oldest sister) experienced in El Salvador when she was a baby. For reasons unknown to her, the baby's body became swollen, and she was believed to be close to death. The mother's household employer offered to help, telling her that if she "gave her" the baby in a permanent caretaking arrangement, she would be cured. The employer also guaranteed provisions for future, lifelong medical care for the baby, when needed. Her mother responded that she would never give up her baby. She emphasized: "I would rather die than to give a baby away." Marlene believes that her sister is alive thanks to her mother's care. She placed the baby on a special diet and administered a series of sunbaths, until her symptoms disappeared.

Another of Marlene's mother's sources of suffering has been her husband's long-standing problems with alcoholism. After he emigrated to the United States, he worked, but his continued alcoholism made employment increasingly difficult. He finally stopped work altogether. Periodically, Marlene's mother has had to "rescue him" from the streets, where he slept among the homeless. All of this stopped a year ago after he was assaulted and beaten so badly that he lost all of his teeth. Since this incident, he has stayed at home and has abstained from alcohol. He is now beginning to work again.

With regard to her diagnosis of diabetes, one physician is reported to have told Marlene's mother that her problem is not due to heredity. Both Marlene and her mother are sure that this diabetes is associated with the suffering she has experienced throughout life.

Comments

Marlene's thirteen-year-long separation from her mother covered a different life span than Rafaela's. Moreover, she met the stresses of separation by actively drawing on the images of her mother and her motives for emigration. Her older sister, who assumed the role of protector of the younger siblings, maintained active communication with her mother in Washington. A network of active assistance offered moral support to the young girls left behind.

The linkage of illness with the burdens of suffering is part of a long tradition in El Salvador and in other Latin American societies. Suffering is not an explanatory concept for single incidents of illness. It is a core concept that reflects lifelong moral and physical pain. When Marlene's mother was asked by an employer whether she might not want to "give her child away" (*regalar la niña*), she touched on a deeply felt sentiment associated with the essence of motherhood. For the mother, there was a difference between "giving a child away" to her employer, a stranger, and the placement of children with her relatives, when the circumstances of migration forced the separation and dislocation of households.

DISCUSSION

In this chapter I have drawn on the cases of Rafaela Hernández and Marlene Molina to illustrate contrasting aspects of the lives of young members of immigrant populations that should receive increased attention in research concerned with vulnerability and resilience in child development. Four dimensions deserve consideration.

Age of Separation.   Children's ability to actively draw on the memories of parents during separation may be influenced by the age at which their parents left them with caretakers. Rafaela was ten months old at the time her mother placed her with substitute caretakers. She finds her relationship with grandparents and her aunt a major source of inspiration for her identity and ideals as a young woman in a new country.

Marlene was six years old at the time her mother left her with her grandmother and aunts. While residing with these caretakers, she actively drew on her mother's image and received protection from her older sister to deal with the aunts' demands. Since reunification, she has strengthened bonds with her mother and other family members. She has come also to a new understanding of the difficulties her mother endured and her continuous struggles. Daughter and mother interpret problems of health and illness within a framework that views suffering as a pervasive life force and a state of being.

Selection of Caretakers.   The mothers' selection of caretakers influenced the experiences of the children left behind. In Rafaela's case, both grandparents and the aunt assumed clear responsibility for her care and for that of her brother. In the case of Marlene, her aunts assumed an exploitative relationship. Her older sister became an informal caretaker as a "defense" against the aunts. Eventually, the older sister became the de facto caretaker.

Circumstances of Migration. Both Rafaela and Marlene entered the United States upon the approval of documents by the immigration offices. The length of time of separation thus depends not only on the resources parents put together to enable children to join the household but also on the policy and regulations of immigration agencies concerning conditions for reunification of families.

Since both sets of parents had entered the United States without "proper documents," reunification was initiated only after they had been able to find employers willing to sponsor their entry to the country. The paperwork involved in this process, in turn, had to be approved by several government agencies. Families involved in such processes appreciate the assistance of lawyers who demonstrate genuine interest in their clients.

Getting Along with Parents upon Reunification. During the early period of reunification, the daughters identified their parents as "strangers." Rafaela established her own independent household, but she has taken the initiative to nurture bonds with a mother from whom she has lived separately most of her life. Within the Salvadoran community of immigrants, she has found groups of young people in similar circumstances who seek each other's company and share common experiences.

In the process of reunification, Marlene has become a solicitous young adult, spending time in efforts to locate appropriate health resources for her mother's illnesses. She has witnessed her father's recent efforts to overcome another bout of alcoholism. Her older sister left in El Salvador continues to be remembered as a special caretaker who is a "pillar of strength."

Much research on the impact of immigration and refugee resettlement has focused on adult immigrants as they face the circumstances of new settings. Opportunities to listen to the voices of the young who have lived in caretaking contexts and are subsequently reunited with parents can contribute to a broadened understanding of the dynamic aspects of households as basic units of social organization among immigrant populations. The two cases present the perspectives of young women only. It is assumed that the viewpoint of young men would offer additional, complementary perspectives on the topic.

Processes of immigration are subject to a number of forces within larger institutional environments. The Salvadoran emigration waves that accelerated beginning in the 1960s have been influenced by demographic pressures and parental search for improved opportunities—especially for their children. The problems of a civil war that ravaged local communities in the early 1980s further contributed to these displacements. Newcomers arrived with or without "proper immigration documents." In communities such as the Washington metropolitan area, where women and men together with their children have carved new lives in reconfigured households, processes of separation and reunification need to be understood. Within these contexts the management of health and illness takes place. Furthermore, it is worth reiterating that the vagaries of legal status do, indeed, have effects on both individuals and their families. In the two cases here, for example, the ultimate ''legality'' of all the family members did not undo the effects of long separations partially caused by the uncertain and only slowly resolved legal status of the parents.

POSTSCRIPT

In late 1998, the author renewed contacts with Rafaela and Marlene. Their accounts illustrate the continued dynamics of settlement in the United States as these young women faced turning points in their lives and the challenges of continuous adaptation to the circumstances of changing societies in Washington and in El Salvador.

Rafaela Hernández has been married for a year, and she just gave birth to a baby girl. Her husband, José, is the son of a former schoolteacher in El Salvador. José came to Washington after an eight-year residence in Los Angeles. Although he had known Rafaela as a child in El Salvador, he renewed their ties after he saw her in the videotape of a *quinceañera* party in Washington, D.C.[4] José also entered without ''proper papers'' but found a ''boss'' who sponsored his entry. He is now a permanent resident.

Rafaela became a U.S. citizen earlier this year and proudly displays the U.S. flag, which she was given at the citizenship ceremony. Although she is on maternity leave, she plans to return to her regular job, where she has received a promotion. She is an active member of a labor union.

Rafaela points out that her parents have not come to see their new granddaughter. Her aunt in El Salvador offered to come to help her during the first month following the baby's birth, but, for reasons unknown to them, her request was turned down by the U.S. Consulate in San Salvador. So now, Rafaela and José hope to visit their hometown in El Salvador in six months. They want to have their baby baptized there in the presence of Rafaela's grandparents and her dear aunt, who had been so good to her when she was a child. To Rafaela, her aunt, who was also like a ''mother,'' has become the baby's ''real grandmother.''

Marlene Molina continues to live at home with her parents and brother. She has successfully completed the highest-level English course. She is considering studying at a university in a health science career or in computer science. Her mother encourages her to take advantage of the opportunities available to her as a young person before she assumes other responsibilities in life such as marriage.

Marlene's father had another bout of alcoholism, but he stopped recently and is back at work. Several months ago, her mother's health maintenance organization plan was dropped from her place of work. So Marlene is in the process of finding a way to enroll her in another plan. She is concerned because a private physician charges her $150 per regular office visit.

With regard to their immigration status, her parents have been told that they will be "called" to become U.S. citizens in one year. Marlene and a younger sister will be called next after them. However, their brother, who had come to the United States when the parents first established themselves in Washington, remains without "proper documents." He was over twenty-one years old at the time his mother and father obtained their papers. The family continues to hold the hope that someday he will find an employer willing to sponsor his entry to the United States.

NOTES

An abbreviated version of this chapter was presented at the Fourteenth International Conference on Social Science and Medicine in Peebles, Scotland, September 1996. The author acknowledges the suggestions offered by Professor Leila Calhoun Deasy of Tallahassee, Florida.

1. See Mozo (1990), Repak (1995), and Cohen (1979). Salvadorans constitute by far the largest proportion of students from foreign countries represented in the student population of the Washington, D.C., public schools. In 1995–1996 there were 135 foreign countries represented among students in the public school system (Moscoso 1996).

2. The waves of immigration from this region that began in the 1960s have continued to the present. In the 1980s, the ravages of the civil war accelerated these displacements.

3. This is the longest-serving community health center for Latin American immigrants in the Washington area. It is sponsored by the Catholic Archdiocese of Washington to meet the needs of newcomers, particularly those who do not qualify for public services or who are uninsured.

4. A *quinceañera* party honors a girl's fifteenth birthday. The celebration is a "rite of passage" and often has both a religious ceremony and a secular "coming-out" party. Rafaela had been a godmother to the girl whose birthday was videotaped.

REFERENCES

Beiser, Morton
1988   *After the Door Has Been Opened: Mental Health Issues Affecting Immigrants and Refugees in Canada.* Report of the Canadian Task Force on Mental Health Issues Affecting Immigrants and Refugees. Secretary of State—Multiculturalism and Welfare, Canada, and the Canadian Mental Health Association.
Cohen, Lucy M.
1979   *Culture, Disease, and Stress among Latino Immigrants.* Washington, D.C.: Smithsonian Institution, Research Institute on Immigration and Ethnic Studies.
Moscoso, Rebecca
1996   *Report, District of Columbia Public Schools.* Washington, D.C.: International Student Center for Orientation and Assessment.

Mozo, Segundo Montes
1987 *Salvadoreños Refugiados en los Estados Unidos*. San Salvador: Instituto de In-
      vestigaciones Universidad Centroamericana José Simeón Cañas.
1990 *El Salvador 1989: Las Remesas que Envían los Salvadoreños de Estados Unidos,
      Consecuencias Sociales y Económicas*. San Salvador: Universidad Centroameri-
      cana José Simeón Cañas.
Repak, Terry A.
1995 *Waiting on Washington: Central American Workers in the Nation's Capital*. Phil-
      adelphia: Temple University Press.

17

Border Crossings, Border Control: Illegalized Migrants from the Other Side

Duncan M. Earle

Despite the fact that undocumented persons come from nations all over the world, the near exclusive focus of governmental and public attention at the tail end of the twentieth century has been the undocumented immigration from Mexico. The racial impact of the recent push to crack down on "illegal aliens" is unmistakable.

Johnson (1998: 1137)

I believe new immigrants are good for America. They are revitalizing our cities. They are building our new economy. . . . [We] should share our country with immigrants, not shun them or shut them out. But mark my words: Unless we handle this well, immigration of this sweep and scope can threaten the bonds of our union.

President Clinton, June 13, 1998,
Portland State University

There is lots of discrimination against the illegal. That's one of the major things, because no matter where you are they call you "illegal" or "wetback." Wherever you go, at times you are humiliated because you are not legal. In all things you come last. Even our own race humiliates us.

Hector Gomez, cited in Chavez (1992: 182)

This chapter addresses some of the issues associated with official efforts to stop people from coming into the United States without proper authorization. It is not exhaustive and does not assess entry efforts by air and water, which, while a significant medium for entry attempts, pale next to the numbers associated with efforts to enter by land. The land focus is more than statistical, however, because the land border more completely embodies a political battleground for debates about immigration. This is because in the imagination of much of the general public and many of our elected and appointed officials, immigration has become synonymous with Mexicans crossing the border illegally to proliferate and profit within the United States. While there may be occasional efforts to step up patrols of certain sea routes and the discovery and interdiction of boats with Asians, Haitians, Cubans, and others seeking immigration, they are relatively brief blips on the radar screen of national news and commentary. By contrast, the level of conflictive public and political discourse regarding immigration that has focused largely on people coming from the south, at the state and national level, has had a sustained high volume in the 1990s. While to some degree this represents differences in numbers (at 5–7 million, Mexican migrants represent the largest single group and nearly half of all migrants in the last two decades, with at least 2 million cycling through yearly), it also represents much more. Migrants from Mexico represent very powerful political issues relating to the perceived future of the United States. They also serve to represent whom we think about and respond to as a nation when we think of ''illegal immigration'' and immigration regulation and law.

The political implications and rewards of immigrant bashing became dramatically evident in Governor Wilson's 1994 electoral victory, in which Proposition 187 served as an efficient means to defeat Democratic candidates by exploiting anti-Mexican sentiments. It also opened the door in California to later propositions against bilingual education, as well as other legal struggles associated with denying benefits and social assistance to unauthorized migrants, and renewed efforts for English-only laws. The beefing up of the Border Patrol and the launching of special operations (Operations Blockade, Hold the Line in El Paso and Gatekeeper in San Diego, as well as similar programs elsewhere along the border) have focused national attention on the border and ''the battle for access.'' Positive public response to these ''operations'' made for more legislative efforts, like further increasing the Immigration and Naturalization Service (INS) budget and fashioning of new laws of immigration. The Illegal Immigration Reform and Immigrant Responsibility Act of 1996 (IIRIRA) carried the debates to the national level, with even President Clinton supporting a bill that defunded services for legal, long-term immigrants who, for whatever reason, had not become citizens. Congress' doubling of the INS budget, largely for more Border Patrol agents to work on the southern border, responded to this national perception of a ''border out of control'' as the cause of too much immigration. The Border Patrol now is the largest armed organization after the military. The policy changes regarding the border have created conditions that have led to hundreds of deaths of people trying to cross in more remote areas; eighty people died in the first nine months of 1998 due to hypothermia alone, mostly in remote areas of Texas, Arizona, and California. These and related issues of the politics of border crossing and the real impacts these changes are having on mostly poor migrants from south of our border are the central themes of this chapter. In this focus I hope to capture the complexity of migration issues in a borderlands context and place migration studies in the light of it as well.

RECENT LEGISLATION AND LIFE ON THE BORDER

Recent legislation has created a three-tiered system: citizens, legal residents, and unauthorized, "illegal" migration workers. In the long hot summer of 1998, Mexican migrants died by the score in the desert. As a result of increasing Border Patrol activity and the Hold the Line/Gatekeeper border policy of lining armed men along the whole border where there are urbanism, roads, and infrastructure, only the deserts, mountains, and wilds provide unguarded routes. As a result, "coyotes," or people smugglers, have tripled their prices, and more and more migrants from Mexico are trying to cross in more remote and dangerous locations—which led to over 100 deaths in 1998 (AFSC 1998). Those without authorization to cross or remain in the United States have become a population "on the lam," a segment of the population that is increasingly hidden and "illegalized." In early September 1998, the INS began to deport legal immigrants under an IIRIRA provision that legal immigrants who commit certain crimes can be deported. Such crimes include driving while intoxicated (DWI). Deportation was not a possibility at the time the infraction occurred but now could be applied retroactively, even in cases where the subject had fully paid the penalty given at the time of the infraction. The practice of selective deportation, called "Operation Last Call," in its first days removed 114 people from the El Paso region alone, some 90 percent of them Mexican nationals, out of a borderwide total of over 500. It has broken up families (90 percent of the deported have dependents, 82 percent of them U.S. citizens) and caused distress, alarm, and outrage on both sides of the line. Of the ninety-one detainees surveyed by the Mexican Consulate, the average number of years in the United States is 2.6. One man, who at sixty-three had been riding buses for the last three years because his license was taken away for DWI, was among those deported. Even though the INS said (as quoted in the *El Paso Times*) the deportations were only of men, some women were deported, including a number of mothers taken from their children.

The INS acknowledged that the targeted group was Mexicans, admonishing these legal residents for not seeking citizenship so as to gain full protection under the law. The resulting fear and humiliation experienced by Mexican and other Latino people living here—legally or otherwise—work against their participation in the larger society. Mexico loves the millions in remittances sent back by migrant Mexicans in the United States but does not like the mistreatment of its citizens at the hands of the gringos. One aspect of maintaining patriotic loyalty to the government is for the government to work hard at criticizing the United States for abuses of migrants and the undiplomatic results of efforts to wall off Mexicans. The news of any slight of the Mexicans by the United States is major Mexican news, and there is active engagement with the consulates of Mexico and legal representatives for people charged with serious crimes to see them defended properly.

The Mexican border authorities, meantime, are applying the letter of the law in a form of tit for tat. One cannot escape the feeling that the law is deliberately misapplied to mock inflexible U.S. rules. Mexican authorities treat U.S. citizens who accidentally bring a weapon across the border in their cars and pickups as if they were full-fledged arms smugglers, giving them long prison terms for their oversight or ignorance (five years is typical). There was at first some talk of making exceptions for people who were clearly not attempting criminal acts, but so far there has been no agreement. While some U.S. citizens continue to languish in Juarez jails, many were released in prisoner exchanges with Mexico in August 1998. This is the latest skirmish in the ongoing conflict between these two nations, a struggle that seems like a smoldering war lived out at the border. The United States seeks ways to appear to arrest the politically unpopular influx of Mexicans. Meanwhile, the Mexican government attempts to protect and defend its citizens and attacks U.S. policy wherever it can. In this struggle, the policies of the nations are lived out on the border in ways not well understood by those who make these rules and regulations in far-off capitals. The border is, in this sense, a disfranchised colony of the respective nations and a staging ground for binational conflicts and ''border disputes'' either not relevant to the local people or misunderstood by the ''interiorites.'' Nothing about the border region can be understood without an understanding of the dynamics and politics of immigration/migration, and migratory issues and the politics of immigration cannot be understood without understanding Mexico and its northern border and its relations with the United States (Bustamante 1997: 245). That border is the great challenge, greater and greater each year, as the place to get through in order to have a life. At the same time, it is where the ''war'' against ''illegal aliens, drug smuggling, and violence'' is imagined by the United States.

THE NUMBERS GAME: WHO IS AN IMMIGRANT, WHO IS A MIGRANT, AND WHO IS ''LEGAL''?

Between 1970 and the present, the U.S. Census estimates that 20 million people have immigrated to the United States. Of those, half have been Spanish speakers, and over half of that group are from Mexico, with Central Americans second (14 percent), South Americans third (11 percent), and the rest from places in the Caribbean such as Cuba and the Dominican Republic. The vast majority of the first two continental groups, close to 7 million people (as calculated by the probably low census count), came by land and crossed the U.S.–Mexican border. So dominant has the Mexican influx become that for some people the term "illegal immigrant" is synonymous with Mexican or Central American. However, the issue is more complex because Mexico has by far the largest number of "circulatory" or temporary migrants, as well as the largest number of those who do take up U.S. residence. While the percentage of resident migrants has increased in the last two decades, it is still difficult to disaggregate the populations (Lozano Ascencio 1997). This is because some who have taken up residence at this time may not stay, depending on the national, regional, and even local circumstances of the place of origin and the conditions of life here. Others who have come and gone for years may settle down in one or the other or even both. Because we are often dealing with households and not individuals as the economic and social unit, they may have more than one locus. Moreover, in these households, some may be authorized workers, some may be legal residents, and some may be citizens (like children born here who become citizens automatically); the unauthorized residents may have authorization pending, while others have no legal status.

The INS estimated in late 1992 that somewhat less than 40 percent of the undocumented population was Mexican, which serves as a reminder that there are other "illegal aliens," many from Poland, Italy, and, of course, Canada. Mexicans and Central Americans are a more visible group, especially those who stand on street corners in search of work. I have heard estimates of numbers of noncitizen, extralegal Mexicans of upward of 4 million by INS officials off the record—the real numbers are very hard to come by. The range of estimates of unauthorized Mexicans in the United States has been 2–12 million (Anguiano Telléz 1997: 265). The reason for the focus on legal status and on the single-nation domination of the demographics of immigration is that unlike Europe or South and Central America, Mexico's contiguity facilitates both deportation and repeated attempts at reentry, all taking place at the border.[1]

Deportation is measured in miles or even blocks for those who are Mexican or can convince the Border Patrol and the INS they are. "Country of origin" determines how far you will be taken, and many Latin Americans have sought to pass as Mexicans when caught so as to be deported only to the far side of the bridge. As one local extralegal resident said to me from the doorway of his shack in borderlands Texas, "If they catch me before noon, I am home for dinner." It is thus pro forma for non-Mexicans to claim they are from Mexico if detained, so as to be deported only across the border. Some of the statistics to calculate migratory numbers come from suspect self-reporting and from counting people who cross and are detained multiple times. In sum, we cannot know how many Mexicans migrate permanently or temporarily, how many reported Mexicans are really Mexicans, or how many so-called illegals are really unauthorized or uncontestable cases.

IMMIGRATION AS INDETERMINATE MIGRATION: BORDER AS DOOR

The battle over immigration is, on one hand, a political one, but, on the other, it is part of a struggle taking place in the space of the borderlands. The border has been constructed in the national conscience as the ineffectual barrier to the unauthorized migrant. For border people, the border is not to blame for uncontrolled immigration, and there is resentment toward the "occupying troops" of the federal government, the long lines in which people must wait to cross the border into the United States, the lack of resources sent from the interior to pay for the problems the national policies cause for the border, and the general deprecatory attitude toward border people by those from the interior. The borderites feel they take so much of the costs and the heat but are not favored when it comes to help. For example, with all the added money from Congress for the Border Patrol, there has been very little money appropriated to expedite customs so as to handle the increases in traffic caused by the North American Free Trade Agreement (NAFTA) (e.g., truck traffic has more than tripled in El Paso since 1994, but inspection personnel has increased very little).

Migrants run from economic and political problems and run toward employment opportunity. Focusing on these factors would be more constructive than border bashing. To control migrants one needs only to control their illegal employment opportunities, that is, arrest the employers of cheap, unprotected, seasonal labor. It is estimated that forty percent of the farm labor in California is unauthorized (Immigration News Service). The promoting of community development and employment opportunities in Mexico would help lessen the push factors by helping to provide alternatives. Any of these would be more effective migration policy than increasing militarization of the border but is less in keeping with our imaginings of a border where militarization addresses a place that is out of control.

There is an important distinction between immigration as a single and definitive relocation from one country to another and migration, which includes temporary moves, multiple moves, and periodic relocation as part of the life cycle. This indeterminate migration includes such practices as transmigration (or transnational migration), in which there are an anchor community in the sending nation, one or more secondary anchors in the receiving one, and an aggressive movement both ways. Here we see border crossing not as a single event but as habitual. It is not the same as seasonal migration, which is the influx and outflow of workers in coordination with seasonal agricultural employment, or "circulatory migration" (Bustamante 1997). That is another form of migration that may or may not lead to "immigration" or transmigration patterns (such as with the Mixtecs studied by Kearney 1991). What constitutes immigration is the least clear with Mexicans and, to some extent, Central Americans, because of this transborder transnationalism. One must add to this the fact that many immigrants, regardless of their legal status, continue to return south to make family visits, shop, and tend to affairs they may still have there. A man who recently was found dead in the desert in Texas had gone back to Mexico from the United States just to be with his mother on Mother's Day. He was already a U.S. legal resident, but not one who was able to return legally due to U.S. residency rules that constrain departure. In other words, he was a legal immigrant illegally migrating who reentered without authorization by way of illegal means that led to his death. Immigration as a term has been borrowed from a previous era, when people came once and largely severed ties with the old country. Many of the Latin American immigrants do not cut ties to home, and for some the ties make migration possible. Two-thirds of those studied in one large survey of migrants had family members assist them in the process (Lozano Ascencio 1997).

BORDER AS AN "IMMIGRATION" PROBLEM: BEATING ON THE DOOR AND BEATING UP ON THE DOOR

From the perspective of the border, there is something very wrong with U.S. immigration policies. First if we can assume that the restrictions on entry have more to do with those planning to be permanent immigrants than those doing seasonal labor and leaving, then the focus is exactly backward. Second, making it difficult for those people to cross by "holding the line" and "keeping the gate" has the effect of making it more costly and dangerous for those who come across but is unlikely to impact numbers significantly until there is a lessening of demand or an improvement of the economies of the poor to the south. Further, this focus on the border as the source of the problem ignores that many of these border crossers are not new, potential immigrants but transmigrants and circulatory migrants for whom border crossing is an essential part of a binational strategy for economic survival. The effect of concentrating upon this sector of migrants is as follows:

1. Because those unable to get temporary visas tend to be poorer, the population targeted is the poorest and least able to find economic alternatives to migration. They are already the victims of economic crises.

2. The majority of the interdiction efforts focus on those less likely to be permanent immigrants and most likely to be regularly circling back to their places of origin.

3. The increase in difficulty in crossing tends to slow down the process of circulation, not so much in terms of arresting the arrivals as inhibiting their return or its frequency; ultimately, this will encourage more permanent immigration by unauthorized populations.

4. The higher hurdles in border crossing lead to a selection process in which the strongest are most likely willing and able to endure the hardships; this may decrease immigration by entire families or the sick, young, or old, but it will also constrain their return.

5. The arresting of circulation will tend to have the effect of cutting migrants off from

communication with their home communities, unless they acquire enough wealth to circumvent the border by other means.

Making the border harder to habitually cross suggests there is something profoundly disturbing to the interests of the nation-state (the national "project," as some scholars call it) about the idea of sustained circulation of unassimilated migrants. The maintenance of ties with countries of origin; modern, rapid forms of communication and travel; and the establishment of transnational enclaves all represent something of a repudiation of the ideology of "melting pot." By this I mean the widely held belief that in order to acquire American mainstream (or Anglo) culture, one must largely give up one's culture of origin, in a kind of exchange of this for that. The repudiation of this ideological concept comes in the form of widespread border biculturalism and bilingualism. On the U.S. side of the southern border, the majority of Mexican Americans speak both languages fluently and participate in numerous cultural activities that pertain to one or the other tradition. They have become acculturated but without much in the way of culture loss, and this is made easier in the borderlands, where crossing the culture/nation line is often a daily experience. The circulatory behavior of transnational migrants has a similar and ideologically threatening effect. The negative view of bicultural migrants and border people can be traced back to this repudiation of the melting pot ideology (see Earle in press).

Along with smuggling drugs and violence, the border has become a whipping boy for the failures of immigration policy to control the influx of people from Mexico. When a group of teenagers died in Denton, Texas, in 1997 from injecting a new kind of superrefined Mexican heroin, Senator Gramm used the opportunity to hold a press conference. Rather than refer to the problems of "family values" and the erosion of parental control that have so much to do with teen drug use or to make a call for more drug education and rehabilitation centers, he reiterated his demand for militarization of the border as a solution. Ohio congressman Traficant's bill to send 10,000 troops to the border to "help" the Border Patrol get the border under control dovetailed drug concerns with those of unauthorized migration. This bellicose suggestion was opposed by the Pentagon itself, fearing a repeat of a situation in Redford, Texas, where a local teenager was shot and killed in his own town, on his father's ranch, by marines out to "assist" the Border Patrol fight drug traffic. For the time being there are no plans to return to that policy, in part because of the killing and the attempts to prosecute the military (the U.S. government settled out of court for $1.9 million but denied blame). The perception, nevertheless, remains that the border allows the unwanted to pour into the country. The logic of border bashing in this instance is similar to blaming the door for the people who pass through it. Without addressing the pull forces or the push ones, the focus on the border is a displacement of attention from the forces at work creating the situation. Addressing these factors, however, might lead to politically unpopular positions and actions. It is easier to beat up the door.

UNREGULATED LABOR IN A GLOBALIZED ECONOMY: DISCIPLINE AND GLOBALIZATION

Every additional detention makes every employed migrant more loyal to the work she or he has managed to secure, no matter how poorly paid or how bad the work conditions. Blaming the border allows us to not blame the "illegal" employers, who, after all, include the Washington nanny-gate crowd and many other influential citizens and industries. Many conservative politicians enter into a contradiction, wanting to increase deportation and at the same time defending the businesses of their local district. So politically unpopular have the raids by the INS on workplaces become that they are now required to call the employers before the raid. In May 1998, the INS announced new procedures for inspecting workplaces in search of unauthorized workers, including such things as require- ments that an INS community liaison officer be present during all raids and that "a written operation plan" be prepared and submitted to the regional director for approval before each raid. The number of workers apprehended at work sites dropped from an average of 1,465 a month in 1997 to 368 in June 1998, ac- cording to published news sources (Immigration News Service). The Center for Immigration Studies has developed an Employer Sanctions Database (http: //www.cis.org/search.html), which lists the names of U.S. employers fined for the knowing hire or continued employment of unauthorized workers; violations of I-9 record-keeping requirements are not included, however.

The apparent hypocrisy of Washington politicians makes border people fu- rious, because the approach to unauthorized migrants parallels the approach to the border: blame them, for they have no lobby. Moreover, the failure to create meaningful sanctions continues to make the migration stream uncontrollable and, in turn, preserves the blaming of the door. The presence of migrants in the border region itself serves to suppress wages and increase unemployment, as it does everywhere else, but with unemployment in the U.S. borderlands three to five times the national average, and the majority of workers unskilled and un- dereducated, the impact is far worse. Those who live on the border have the lowest labor demand in the entire country (border unemployment in Texas hov- ers around 15 percent), yet they are the doorway to a huge level of labor demand, as underpaid, unauthorized labor becomes a significant part of the structure of a globalized U.S. economy. For a population in the millions, some form of migration is a way of life in Mexico and has been for generations. While it is an economic boon to labor-intensive interior industries, it is a burden on the labor-abundant borderlands.

This policy is not just a collision between the conservative ideology of anti- immigrant Republicans (such as those who were members of the 1994 House Republican Task Force on Illegal Immigration) and concern for one's own con- stituency or lobbyists. These seeming contradictions demonstrate the deeper, not-so-contradictory logic of immigration policy, which never intended to stop immigrants or prevent them from working for U.S. employers but only to more tightly manage the sociolegal conditions of their employment.[2]

Border scholars suggest that the function of the Border Patrol is to discipline rather than stop immigrants (Kearney 1991). In the post-Fordian conditions of economic globalization (i.e., without a fixed place or nation for production), the traditional forms of making robust profit have been largely discovered, exploited, and used up. The maturity of the process (some call this "late capitalism," meaning a mature system of market exchange and capitalist expansion) motivates new strategies for profit, such as investment in "emerging Third World markets" or, alternatively, finding some way to change the conditions of production profitability here at home. Some of the disastrous results of investing in these unstable locations include the peso crash of December 1994 and its brutal ripple effects in South America and Asia. This and the recent crises in Russia and parts of Asia have cooled investors in these emerging markets and redoubled efforts to find profits in places under better fiscal control. One basic way to increase profits at home involves lowering the cost of unskilled and semiskilled labor, which, by global standards, is currently high and as much as eight times higher than what it is in Mexico. Downsizing and subcontracting are strategies often employed by corporations and other businesses to effect this, as well as the increased use of temporary worker services. Another related strategy is the circumvention of labor unions with nonunion labor ("outsourcing") so as to pay less for the same work. Two-tiered pay systems cut labor costs by paying new workers at lower rates than the previously hired ones. Other strategies are "offshore" and border ("*maquilas*") plants where the labor-intensive parts of the manufacturing process can be done by cheaper labor without going too far from home.

It has been clear since Marx that labor organizing can be undercut by the presence of a large population of unemployed and underemployed people, unless they, too, are organized. One way of looking at U.S. immigration policy is that it creates this kind of "disciplined" (in the manner of a forced lesson) population. Repeated detainment by the Border Patrol and deportation as criminals create an awareness that when one crosses the border, while one may only be looking for honest work, one must learn to operate and behave as an "illegal" person. One is by definition not eligible for legal protection or rights under the law. Taught by such experiences that they are "illegalized," border crossers tend to keep away from any labor organization or any other collective effort that might create a political profile and, by that means, trouble. The vulnerability of such people to differential application of the law, as is already practiced extensively in Mexico, discourages these workers from complaining about conditions, pay, abuse, lack of benefits, and all the issues that might be at play in a labor strike. The Border Patrol and the other facets of immigration policy tend to create the conditions for increasing the exploitation of labor, suppressing wages for the low-end worker, undermining labor organizations, and dispensing with concern for paying benefits or, in some cases, Social Security. This boom in the ''informal'' and unregulated sector can lead to such abuses as child workers locked up in compounds and the Mexican deaf-mute slave rings found in several major U.S. cities. But these are just symptomatic of the larger trend— the citizen of the United States lives better because the low end of labor is a bargain carried out by the illegalized migrant who has learned from detention and deportation that she or he has no rights, no civil persona, and no recourse in cases of rape, injury, theft, summary dismissal, or nonpayment.

The recent changes in border policy increase the possibility of profit without alienating the Latino border citizens, who, with their political ascendancy, are increasingly dangerous to politically alienate. Removing the migrant to remote locations lessens the possibility of sympathy or solidarity. Profits come not only from the disciplines of illegalization but from the weeding out of those less capable of work and family members who might influence people to stay in the United States. The logic behind this is not to keep people out of the United States but to have them raised abroad (so as to avoid their production/ reproduction costs), import them for their most productive period, keep them in a fearful and insecure state, and then have them deported in their declining years so that the sending country absorbs the cost of retirement as well. The new immigration law, IIRIRA, narrows the definition of reunification to parents and children under twenty-one, and they must have an income 70–125 percent of the poverty level, depending on the case. Clearly, this part of the law works toward limiting the establishment of families within the United States and, in turn, encourages people who have extended family connections to return to their country of origin once the maximum surplus labor value has been squeezed out.

This explains the contradiction between employer sanctions in theory and practice. Even more than with illegal drugs, no one wants to actually address demand. It is too profitable. What this system does, then, is allow the United States to have de facto wage scales closer to those of the competing Third World countries, which, while illegal, are widespread. Through legislation, illegalization, and differential enforcement, the United States has created a shadow population of bargain-basement surplus labor value, which has helped to revitalize the U.S. economy in its transition to free market globalization by lowering the cost of low-end labor to be more internationally competitive. The cost has been a return to a nation where some people have almost no civil rights and live in constant fear and humiliation (Chavez 1992).

THE SOCIAL SPACE OF THE ILLEGALIZED

The disciplining of the Latino migrant does not end with escaping the borderlands, because migrants never leave the social space of the illegalized, no matter where they travel in the interior. This space is lived out in horrendous conditions with regard to law enforcement. The fear created by this space debilitates the application of the rule of law, which, in turn, makes migrants vulnerable to illegal acts without legal consequences. If people refuse to call authorities for fear of being deported, they fall deeper into the dangerous space of illegality, subject to all kinds of abuses. The more difficult the return from deportation becomes, the more reluctant people will be to seek legal recourse for crimes against them. Word gets around in the criminal element that migrants are targets without legal consequences.

There have been many efforts to keep the INS and Border Patrol from working together with the local police, for this very reason. While the courts vacillate about whether such cooperation is legal, practical problems arise with such collaborations. For example, in San Diego, such cooperation obstructed criminal investigations. Police would be in the process of investigating a crime in a Mexican population area, and the first thing they would do is ask for immigration papers. If people did not have them in order, the police called the INS. End of case. In order to avoid this obvious problem, a group of human rights groups made a pact in 1986 with the San Diego police department not to cooperate with the Border Patrol. This pact was in the police interest because they did not want people to be afraid to report a crime because of their immigration status (*In Motion*). With IIRIRA, such pacts have been made illegal. The law prohibits state and local governments from enacting noncooperation agreements with the INS.

Illegalization has numerous other negative effects. Lack of perinatal care, loss of education, and risk of permanent health problems from lack of acute health care are among its many side effects (Chavez 1992: 168). Further, the fear of being apprehended leads to people's wasting money on unscrupulous lawyers in hopes of gaining papers and makes people fearful of making visits back to Mexico (Chavez 1992: 170–172, 160–161). This isolation from Mexico tends to discourage the maintenance of cross-border ethnic solidarity and increases the division and alienation between the sides of the line. None of these effects are accidental. Illegalization is an unstated, but essential, aspect of "disciplining" Mexican migrants so they will behave in such ways as to maximize profit and minimize cost or risk. Even hiding at home (Chavez 1992: 158) serves to isolate people from each other and from the larger population, which, in turn, serves to minimize the possibility of organizing or taking part in the larger civil society. Isolation, both physical and social, so unlike the culture of Mexico, is a direct product of illegalization, serving as it does to minimize the possibility of a collectivity to challenge this harsh servitude.

Being apprehended is a nightmare for Mexican migrants not simply for the humiliation but because it risks erasing all the accumulated time that might have served toward gaining legal status (which used to be seven years and now is ten) if one voluntarily accepts deportation. The alternative, a hearing before an immigration judge, is also daunting in that the standard has also been raised. Before IIRIRA the standard was "significant noneconomic hardship," which meant one had to show reasons other than a negative economic impact or economic hardship to the family. After IIRIRA the language was toughened to "preponderant harm to a U.S. citizen," a standard much harder to attain. The loss of the initial hearing, made harder to appeal in the new law, means one is summarily deported and never again eligible for reentry into the United States. Unauthorized reentry is a crime for which one can be imprisoned. For this reason, the vast majority opt for voluntary departure, betting on the opportunity for reentry. The brass ring of legalization is held out so that people will accept the conditions of their servitude, while the daily practices of survival run the risk of apprehension and the loss of all the waited time.

CONCLUSIONS: BORDERING ON THE CRIMINAL

The focus on interdiction is still dominated by the U.S.–Mexican border, even though roughly half of those who enter the United States illegally do so by way of overextending their visas and other apparently legal means. The INS currently spends about $700 million a year on detention and deportation, twice what it spends on naturalization processing and far more than is spent chasing visa-jumpers. The INS detains an average 16,000 foreigners a day, two-thirds of them in local jails. The average INS detention stay is thirty-four days. If the number of foreigners slated for deportation continues rising at current rates, INS spending on detention and deportation will double (*Migration News*, October 1998).

According to the Mexican Consulate in Tijuana, 345 migrants have died during extralegal border crossing of the Baja California/California border since Operation Gatekeeper began in 1995, and those deaths rose by 52 percent from 1997 to 1998. The number of apprehensions has increased, but not in San Diego, where there was a 13 percent decline in FY 1997–1998. The interior and less developed Imperial County had an increase of 55 percent for the same time (cited in AFSC 1998). These figures are similar to the general trend along the rest of the border (Carter 1998). There is little credible evidence that the movement of immigration has become less because of the new technique of border blocking.

In their September 1998 report, "Locked Away: Immigration Detainees in Jails in the United States," Human Rights Watch maintained that the U.S. government is quick to accuse asylum applicants of being terrorists and detaining them. About 40 percent of those detained have no criminal record. At the same time, in some border areas the overflow of detainees in local jails forces the release of thousands of people each year (mostly Central Americans). There are occasional riots and protests in jails, as well as incidents of rape, child abuse, and other problems. The new laws, the increases in border patrols, the blockade "Operations" along the populated areas of the border, while not even slowing migration, make it far more dangerous, expensive, and fraught with opportunities for the abuse of migrants. Recent examinations of immigration and welfare reform, as well as migration patterns, have led to the conclusion that the effect is the reverse of the intention. There needs to be effective control of migration, but that can come only from workplace enforcement, not from stepped-up border patrolling and resident raids. Current policies and laws will only reduce legal immigration (Espenshade, Baraka, and Huber 1997). What many see as erroneous and ill-advised policy and legislation may thus be exactly appropriate for the desired effect. That desire is never to stop unauthorized entry. It is to make the conditions of labor most favorable for those who buy it.[3]

The current border migration policy is more than a failure; it is an illusion, a lie. Demonizing the border with Mexico and imagining a "war" with immigrants and smugglers to which we are to send troops, building triple fences (as has recently been done south of San Diego), and having large-scale INS "operations" will never stop unauthorized crossings. To do more, to really make a barrier to illegal entry, would be not only draconian and expensive but politically impossible as soon as the onion pickers were needed in Georgia. We do not really want to stop the flow of cheap labor. On the other hand, to open the borders would be to undermine the ideology of border control and expose the politics and profits behind it. Moreover, it would undo the political issue that bashing immigrants has come to be for many, dovetailing as it does with xenophobic inclinations of a nation becoming more Mexicanized and more in denial by the day. At the same time, effective employer sanctions are not politically feasible, as we have learned again and again. Nor are they financially attractive. Border migration policy remains in confusion, generating ideological irrationalities that consistently hurt the people of the borderlands, which begins to look like a war zone occupied by federal troops, looked down upon by the interior as out of control. Borderites pay for the sins of the nation, a nation that cannot live with the reality of massive migration and also cannot live without it.

NOTES

1. Because from a legal standpoint the status of immigrants must be adjudicated in order to issue a label that reflects full due process, I refrain from using the term "illegal aliens." Instead I prefer such terms as the "unauthorized," "inadjudicated," "extra-legal," "contested," or "contestable" migrants, depending on the case and context. "Aliens" is far too sinister, as Johnson notes in his article on the subject (1998). "Contestable" immigration suggests there is a question of whether it is or is not legal, only to be resolved case by case. Since there is considerable variation in the application of immigration laws by region and whim and even more in the ability of an individual to make a case when by rights she or he should be legal or a legal asylum seeker, the notion of legality itself remains murky.

2. Take the case of Chandler, Arizona. In what was dubbed "Operation Restoration," the INS, with the cooperation of local police, descended on the downtown area of this small borderlands town, checking everyone who looked "Mexican" for proof of citizenship. In the process, many citizens and legal residents were taken away to detention. As a result there were local protests, and a $35 million federal lawsuit was filed, alleging that Chandler police violated the civil rights of legal residents.

3. The colonias on the border deserve some mention. The Texas border alone has shanty settlements with .5 million residents, nearly half of them undocumented migrants. These are a heterogeneous group that includes former agricultural migrants, legalized residents, and out-migrants from the border cities. They live in what are called colonias, "substandard, unincorporated subdivisions, lacking basic services," as they are officially defined (Earle, in press). Like so many migrant settlements, they suffer from high unemployment, high incidence of health problems and disease, social isolation, lack of police, ambulance, garbage collection services, and educational opportunity. They are the creations of well-off land developers who took advantage of the absence of zoning in Texas counties (outside city limits) to divide up lots and sell them on a contract-for-deed basis without any amenities or services, oftentimes convincing the monolingual purchaser that as they built their own home, these services would come. For many, they never have. Colonias are where most migrants end up if they do not leave the borderlands. Many stay by the border because they can take advantage of labor opportunities on one side and prices on the other, without the risks of long-distance transmigration. As the border is marginal to the nation, the colonias are the margins of the borderlands. Here we are able to witness the same processes that plague migrants in the interior, especially illegalization and the fear and insecurity that come from being outside the protection of laws. The police do not usually patrol colonias, nor does the Border Patrol. The danger is when one leaves for work or for any purpose. Social as well as physical isolation is a severe problem in colonias, just as it is with unauthorized migrants. Most people do not get involved with community organizations, because they do not have papers, or their wife, brother, son, niece, or other family member lacks them. Or they have no insurance for their car and have a few unpaid tickets for their trouble. Or they are in trouble with one or another agency, the schools, the health department, the tax office. There are so many ways for the poor, ignorant of the outside system and at the mercy of it, to become illegalized. As a result they have been taken advantage of by the wealthiest land developers, as well as by the counties and social service agencies that have been able to get state and federal dollars to build infrastructure and offer services. There are many problems with the efforts at helping colonias because they often end up failing to address their need for work, education, and integration into the larger society (Earle 1997, in press). As the poorest mass of population in the United States, they are a caricature of the problems of border-crossing migrants, unable to prosper and oppressed by their legal status, hated by many of the other borderites for suppressing wages and crowding their schools and social services, while the developers who created the situation escape criticism and actually benefit from the aid for colonias.

REFERENCES

AFSC (American Friends Service Committee)
1998   More Border Deaths: A Report from the American Friends Service Committee U.S.–Mexico Border Project, on the Web: http://www.afsc.org/border98.htm, afscilemp@igc.apc.org.
Anguiano Telléz, Maria Eugenia
1997   Migracion laboral interna e internacional en la frontera norte mexicana. Diferencias por sexo y sector de ocupacion. In *Migracion y Fronteras*. Edited by Miguel Angel Castillo, Alfredo Lattes, and Jorge Santibañez. Mexico City: Colegio de México.

Bustamante, Jorge
1997   *Cruzar La Linea.* Mexico: Fondo de cultura economica.
Carter, Chelsea J.
1998   Mexicans in Slave Case Get Housing. *Associated Press*, July 20.
Chavez, Leo
1992   *Shadowed Lives: Undocumented Migrants in American Society.* New York: Holt,
        Rinehart, and Winston.
Duignan, Peter, and Lewis Gann, Editors
1998   *The Debate in the United States over Immigration.* Stanford: Hoover Institution.
Earle, Duncan
1997   Texas Colonias on the Border: Injustice by Definition. *Rio Bravo* 7: 23–34.
In press   The Borderless Borderlands; Texas Colonias on the Edge of Nations. In *New
        Perspectives on Migration.* Edited by Liliana Golden. Albany, New York: SUNY
        Albany Press.
Espenshade, Thomas J., Jessica Baraka, and Gregory A. Huber
1997   Implications of the 1996 Immigration Reforms. *Population and Development Re-
        view* 23 (4): 769–802.
Human Rights Watch
1998   *Locked Away: Immigration Detainees in Jails in the United States.* New York:
        Human Rights Watch.
In Motion
1998   Magazine interview with Roberto Martinez, 7/10/98 date on Web (http:
        //www.inmotionmagazine.com/border4.html).
Jacobson, David, Editor
1997   *The Immigration Reader.* Malden, Massachusetts: Blackwell.
Johnson, Kevin
1998   Race, the Immigration Laws, and Domestic Race Relations: A "Magic Mirror"
        into the Heart of Darkness. *Indiana Law Review* 73.
Kearney, Michael
1991   Borders and Boundaries of State and Self at the End of Empire. *Journal of
        Historical Sociology* 4 (1): 52–74.
Lozano Ascencio, Fernando
1997   Continuidad y cambios en la migracion temporal entre Mexico y Estados Unidos.
        In *Migracion y Fronteras.* Edited by Miguel Angel Castillo, Alfredo Lattes, and
        Jorge Santibañez. Mexico City: Colegio de México.
Magruder, Janie
1998   Activists Plan March on Anniversary of Chandler. *Arizona Republic*, June 13.
Stern, Marcus
1998   A Semi-Tough Policy on Illegal Workers: Congress Looks Out for the Employers.
        Washington Post, July 5.
Suarez-Orozco, Marcelo M.
1998   *Crossings: Mexican Immigration in Interdisciplinary Perspectives.* Cambridge:
        Harvard University Press.
William, Booth
1998   Immigrants' Hard Jobs Reshape the Economy. *Washington Post*, July 13.
Wilson, Janet
1998   Hermandad Must Repay $4.3 Million. *Los Angeles Times*, July 1:A3, A23.

PART IV

ILLEGAL IMMIGRATION
IN PERSPECTIVE

18

Vanishing Acts: Illegal Immigration in Canada as a Sometime Social Issue

Norman Buchignani and Doreen Indra

> Even in countries of immigration, illegal immigration will usually be regarded as undesirable. Politically it is unacceptable because it reveals a country as being unable to control its borders, and in a country of immigration governments will wish to demonstrate to the public that they are in control of the program, in terms of both overall numbers and selection.
>
> Cox and Glenn (1994: 284)

Canada has been profoundly formed by immigration. It is a country of 30 million people to which 5 million immigrants have come since the end of World War II. Roughly 17.5 percent of Canadians are now foreign-born (Statistics Canada 1998). Annual immigration rates have averaged 1 percent of the total population over the last decade, and similar rates are planned for the future. Toronto, Montreal, and Vancouver (Canada's three largest metropolitan areas) now have very large foreign-born populations: an astonishing 42 percent of people in Toronto and a third of those in Vancouver. Immigration has been an important part of government economic, social, political, and demographic policy since 1895–1914, when the west (now Alberta, Saskatchewan, and parts of Manitoba) was settled—within the living memory of some Canadians. It has also been actively debated for over a century and a half. Illegal immigration has played an important role in that debate.

In this chapter we identify some of the central narratives, themes, attitudes, activities, and social forces that determine how the public, interest groups, government bureaucrats, and scholars have characterized illegal immigration and caused it to rise and fall as a Canadian social issue. We also describe how representations of illegal immigration have shaped immigration policy and public perceptions of the Canadian nation and its borders, sovereignty, citizenship, and cultural diversity.

For the purposes of this discussion, we define *formally illegal residents* as those who establish themselves on Canada's physical territory in ways contrary to law and have not had their residence status regularized. As we demonstrate, the number of people at any given time who are or are about to become formally illegal residents and the strength and shape of the associated social issue of "illegal immigration" are not highly correlated. To the contrary, the salience of this social issue is a strong function of *reports and perceptions* of external and internal threat by individuals and groups considered by some to be *illegitimate* immigrants because of their perceived ethnicity or nationality. Most strongly impacting such perceptions are direct, newsworthy, "outsider" attacks on territorial and political borders, law and order, lifestyles, local cultures, putatively fair bureaucratic systems, and economic standards. Whether or not those evoking this threat response are formally illegal immigrants has always been secondary. Perceptions and assertions about illegal immigration have, instead, been tightly linked to the issue of *perceived immigrant desirability and legitimacy* and hence to often contentious ideas of Us and Them involving a changing, evaluative spectrum of imagined persons, classes, religions, ethnic groups, social races, and nations. Illegal immigrants are associated with the negatively evaluated end of this spectrum and hence to a constellation of ideas about how highly undesirable immigrants are thought to undermine Canadian society.

Notions of illegal immigration are also informed by public assessments of the effectiveness of government efforts to *control the nation's borders* and to administer an immigration program characterized by fairness, orderly management, choice, rationality, merit, and objectivity. In turn, many changes in immigration law and regulations affecting illegal immigration enacted over the last twenty years can be read as attempts by government to achieve and publicly demonstrate effective border control. In what follows, we show that narratives of direct assaults on territorial borders by unwanted migrant outsiders were an important component of nation-building ideologies during 1880–1960. Since then, most of the conflict-laden processes that keep out persons deemed inappropriate, undesirable, or illegal have become increasingly bureaucratized and have shifted away from Canadian territorial entry sites to source countries, countries of first asylum, Canada Immigration Centres, and quasi-judicial boards of refugee determination. One result has been a practical and conceptual merging of some forms of illegal immigration and in-country asylum seeking in complex ways we describe later—ways that have made sociological (and perhaps even legal) distinctions between illegal and legal immigration in Canada of dubious utility.

Many contemporary factors have kept the depth of public perceptions of border attack low, so that illegal immigration is not currently a major Canadian social issue. Some factors we consider are objectively low rates of long-term illegal residence; vigorous efforts by politicians, government bureaucrats, key interest groups, and academics to disguise, recharacterize, or mute discussion of illegal immigration, such that it "disappears" as a social issue[1]; the fact that illegal immigrants are primarily visa-overstayers rather than surreptitious border crossers; increasing public acceptance of national cultural pluralism, which confers greater legitimacy on once-stigmatized ethnic groups; and critically, a conflation in talk, practice, and public opinion between negatively viewed illegal immigration and refugee asylum seeking, which is typically positively associated with Canada's stance on human rights and international responsibilities.

While we concentrate on the last twenty years, so powerfully have notions of illegal immigration been informed by associated historical discourses on immigration and immigrants that we present a long-term historical review of the subject. We partition the chapter into four chronological sections, followed by a conclusion: up to 1895, 1896–1944, 1945–1977, and 1978 to 1998.

HINTERLAND OF EMPIRE: ILLEGITIMATE AND ILLEGAL IMMIGRATION BEFORE 1896

Notions of unwanted and undesirable immigrants have been around as long as immigration itself. Some greatly predate Canadian Confederation (1867), the development of coherent immigration policy and law (1896–1914), and effective border control (1910–1930). Until the early 1700s, the French Crown saw Protestants as inappropriate immigrants to New France, and few were among the 12,000 settlers ancestral to most of today's Quebecois. The conquest of New France by the British in 1760 marked the beginning of a long period during which the British and then local colonial governments lackadaisically used immigration to develop British North America and subordinate what initially was a large French majority. Further French immigration was strongly discouraged from the conquest to when Quebec began to exercise its constitutional powers over immigration in the 1980s. Excepting laws to control sedition among resident aliens and others (Legislature of Lower Canada 1794), the legal situation was laissez-faire, reflecting general European practice. The only other laws in place regulated conditions on immigrant ships and the spread of disease by arriving immigrants. There was nothing approaching an immigration act until 1869, and that sketchy act was not replaced by another until 1906. Hence, it is difficult to conceptualize what could be considered formally illegal immigration prior to Confederation. The forced removal of 16,000 Acadians from Nova Scotia beginning in 1755 is the sole early case of a large European-origin population being classed as formally illegal residents, though few were immigrants; instead of their moving across borders, they were rendered illegitimate by a border's moving across them (Voutira 1998). Many dispersed into the woods or surreptitiously returned as illegal immigrants in fact.

Imperial Ties and Preferred Immigrants

Early immigration to British North America was marked by a number of strong preferences for particular kinds of immigrants. These preferences were informed by deeply entrenched imperial views on peoples and their mobility rights. As in other British colonies where indigenous people were characterized as few and politically weak (such as Australia and New Zealand), emigration of the "right sort" from the home country or elsewhere in the empire was always desired to develop Canada, and it was episodically encouraged. Reciprocally, prospective British immigrants gazed on British North America with imperial eyes and felt that they had a privileged right to settle there. An illustrative example were the 40,000–50,000 United Empire Loyalists fleeing Civil War in the American colonies who immigrated with government assistance to Nova Scotia, Quebec, and what would become New Brunswick and Ontario.[2]

Episodic flows of Scots and Irish immigrants occurred during 1800–1840, beginning with Highlanders displaced by the enclosures. Some came through colonization schemes; many did not. The emigration of those of lesser means or those who were destitute was sometimes encouraged or supported by British speculators, charities, and other organizations. Large numbers of immigrants continued south across the uncontrolled border with the United States, along with many native-born. Indeed, not until this century did immigration consistently outstrip the flow of people from Canada to the United States.

Protests to the Crown soon arose over the arrival of unwanted types of individuals—individuals whom colonial administrators were often legally unable to keep out. An early instance was the Nova Scotia legislature's negative response to the immigration of "black" settlers from Bermuda in 1815 (Malarek 1987: 63). After the War of 1812, "white" American immigrants were viewed ambiguously for a long time as good for economic development and racially acceptable but also as politically destabilizing United States foot soldiers. Extremely negative reactions developed to the large flows of impoverished Catholic *and* Protestant individuals fleeing the devastating economic conditions of Ireland after 1846—an estimated 400,000 between 1846 and 1854 (Knowles 1997: 44); these reactions became a paradigm for later episodes. Poor immigrant Irish were seen as an economic threat, undermining the rights of native labor in economic hard times. Middle-class stereotypes imported from Britain also characterized the Irish as culturally backward, unassimilatable, immoral, penniless, subversive, and Catholic. Even so, only fitful attempts to restrict those deemed diseased were made. Negative attitudes were manifest not in heightened border control but in discriminatory treatment of immigrant settlers. Many Irish people moved on to the United States, particularly those who were Catholics.

In 1867 the British North America Act organized the modern Canadian state and established the basic relationships between the federal and provincial governments that exist today. It gave the federal government power over aliens and over immigration policy in general. However, most matters pertaining to immigrant settlement and immigration into specific provinces were under provincial control; the right of provinces to manage their own immigration was rarely used until the 1980s. Great power to manage immigration was placed in the hands of the federal Cabinet, which issued an increasing stream of binding regulations in the form of Orders-in-Council. The entry of criminals was banned in this way in 1872, followed by the destitute in 1879. Such Orders-in-Council did not require parliamentary assent or discussion and could be implemented quickly with low political risk. From the onset, they became the preferred method of changing immigration practice and continue to be extensively used today. As a result, Canada's immigration program has continuously evolved (Green 1995: 41), shifting with the issues and the philosophies of federal political parties.[3]

Immigration programming from Confederation to the 1890s was ill planned, poorly resourced, and ineffective. Government policy reflected narrow Conservative and British Imperial ethnic preferences for the "right kind" of Scots and English settlers (i.e., not Catholic and not poor), and immigration barely kept up with out-migration to the United States. Immigration rates averaged 33,000 a year in the 1870s, 85,000 a year in the 1880s, and only 28,000 a year during 1890–1896. While Canada's population increased from 3 million to 5 million from 1867 to 1901, this was chiefly through natural increase, not immigration.

One vigorous attempt to render a particular ethnocultural immigrant stream illegal dates from this period. Chinese immigrants had been coming to British Columbia since the Fraser River gold rush of 1858. As their numbers grew, and as large employers increasingly used Chinese men as cheap labor or to cheapen labor generally, an organized effort arose to have immigration from China banned. Anti-Chinese arguments of the day were much like those used against the Irish earlier. Immigrants from China supposedly undermined labor, took away economic opportunities for native-born and more appropriate British and American immigrants, and were unassimilatable, immoral, racially inferior, and a threat to local lifeways. The federal government eventually convened its first Royal Commission pertaining to immigration to address this rising social issue (Gray, Chapleau, and the Royal Commission on Chinese Immigration 1885). Cynically, the federal government imposed a fifty-dollar head tax on each Chinese immigrant in 1885 only after the completion of the transcontinental Canadian Pacific Railroad (CPR), upon which many Chinese men labored. This initial head tax barely slowed immigration, but in the next era considered it would be followed by legal exclusion and consequent illegal immigration.

NATIONAL DEVELOPMENT, IMMIGRATION, CLASS, AND CULTURAL DIVERSITY: ISSUES OF IMMIGRATION CONTROL DURING 1896–1945

The rise of modern immigration policies in Canada dates from the beginning of the Liberal government of Wilfrid Laurier in 1896 and arose out of the efforts of two successive ministers of the interior, Clifford Sifton and Frank Oliver. From the onset, this policy aimed at a different kind of development from that of the United States—of the still largely untouched western prairies. It was an economically oriented policy designed to attract farmers and farm laborers, eventually, those among them with means (Troper 1972). However, it did incorporate many of the British and Anglo-Canadian ethnic and racial preferences of the day: "white" Americans and British first, followed by their Germanic cousins: Germans, Dutch, and Scandinavians; then, when necessary, Ukrainians, Poles, and others from Eastern Europe. Southern Europeans needed not apply, and people of Asian and African origin were beyond the pale.

The American frontier was closed. With the transcontinental railroad completed, appropriate agricultural technology in place, and homestead land freely available, the Canadian government mounted the world's first big international marketing effort aimed at attracting immigrants. The result was wildly successful if gauged by sheer numbers: 4.7 million people arrived from fiscal year 1897–1898 to 1930–1931. Like all Canadian immigration policies thereafter, it less definitively achieved its intended economic goals. Immigrants played a key role in settling the west, but three out of four migrants did not enter farming.

The Rise of Immigration Control

With the rise of this actively managed immigration program came an increasing number of control issues, most of which were addressed through crude efforts to restrict the entry of individuals and groups the government deemed undesirable. Some of these restrictions created large classes of potential illegal immigrants for the first time. There were no overall annual or country quotas, but bans on paupers, the communicably ill, and the "immoral" were sometimes applied—often to keep out people deemed undesirable for other reasons such as ethnicity or political opinion. The government's episodic response to poor economic conditions was to use Orders-in-Council to impose financial requirements on prospective immigrants and to discourage immigrants from coming. With the rise of a strong, largely anti-immigration labor movement (whose leadership was ironically dominated by British immigrants), legislation barring some types of workers was occasionally passed but did little to keep out those deemed illegal; a key example was the Alien Labour Act of 1897 (amended in 1905), directed against Italian contract laborers and eventually applied to the entry of all overseas-born contract workers coming from the United States (Canada, House of Commons 1905).

Overseas, control over immigrant ethnicity was secured indirectly by not soliciting among unwanted groups or in particular countries, such as Italy. Responses to "racially" different immigrants appearing at Canada's borders were much more direct. African-American farmers were informally banned from crossing the U.S. border in the west during 1905–1911. In British Columbia, Asian immigration was probably the most persistent provincial social issue during 1890–1915. Subject to intense media coverage (Indra 1979a, 1982), immigrants from China, Japan, and India were represented as the vanguard of hordes of destitute, uncivilizable Orientals aggressively attacking barriers set up to ensure that this British bastion on the Pacific Coast remained "white." Responding to pressure from interest groups in British Columbia, the federal government increased the head tax on new Chinese immigrants to $100 in 1900 and then to an exclusionary $500 in 1904. The subsequent Oriental Exclusion Act banned almost all Chinese from immigrating between 1923 and 1947. Imperial considerations required that Japanese immigration be terminated through a formal agreement in 1907 between Canada and Japan. As subjects of the empire, Sikhs and other migrants from India stood in still another relationship to Canada and so were barred by the continuous journey regulation of 1908. To avoid inflaming nationalists in India, this regulation did not name Indians specifically. Instead, it required all immigrants to have purchased through tickets to Canada from their source country, which could not be done from India.

A wish to more selectively manage immigration as a matter of general policy led to the 1906 Immigration Act and its successor in 1910 (significantly amended in 1919 and 1923), which further increased the range of those who could be deemed inadmissible and which for the first time created a coherent system of border control with the United States. The 1910 legislation arose, in part, as a response to Asian challenges in British Columbia, the arrival of large numbers of destitute British, and western British Canadian concerns with high levels of Eastern European immigration. Section 38(c) of the act allowed the Cabinet to designate any racial or national group inadmissible because they were either "unsuitable" or "undesirable." Subsequent Orders-in-Council aimed at the destitute in general and Eastern Europeans in particular established a minimum dollar amount that immigrants must have in their possession at entry. The 1910 legislation also formalized a process through which certain classes of individuals could be deported, including immigrants who were on public relief or who advocated the overthrow or violent change of government in *any* British possession. In response to the depression, the Canadian immigration system was virtually shut down in 1931, not to be revived until 1946.

Illegal and Barred Immigrants

It is impossible to estimate the number of individuals who entered Canada illegally during 1895–1945. Immigration controls at seaports were effectively all-inclusive by 1900, and there are no indications that many people arriving by ship bypassed these controls. However, immigrant flows were large, and the resources of immigration officials were slender. Scrutiny of immigrants and their documentation was cursory, and so the application of economic and other legal immigration requirements remained erratic until the 1920s. Anecdotal evidence suggests that thousands of people illegally entered Canada via the still-porous American border right through the 1930s, either by misrepresenting their purpose in traveling to Canada or by avoiding border checkpoints altogether. Canadian resources devoted to controlling the U.S. border were so meager that the number of such illegal cross-border migrants was primarily restricted by U.S. immigration controls on those arriving from overseas by ship and by the general perception that there were more opportunities for urban immigrants and native-born Americans in the United States than in Canada. Our reading of the archival correspondence of immigration officials during 1900–1939 shows that even individuals from highly contentious groups whose entry had been restricted or banned (such as South Asians and Chinese) moved easily back and forth across the U.S. border as late as the 1920s and that some illegal entries were occurring during the 1930s (Canada, Board of Review [Immigration] 1938). At the same time, citizenship was routinely granted to everyone born in Canada, and with citizenship came the right of residence. Illegal residence status was never transmitted to the Canadian-born children of illegal immigrants.

A novel feature of standing legislation from 1910 on was a provision to render a destitute "landed immigrant" (a person with legal permanent residence status, synonymous with the contemporary term "permanent resident") deportable—and in essence, an illegal immigrant. During the depression of the 1930s, hundreds of thousands of individuals on relief thereby became legally deportable—even if the total number actually deported for being indigent and on relief was low.[4] Then as now, the Canadian government did not use deportation as a major immigration management tool.

Demands to limit the immigration of particular groups and types of individuals on the basis of ethnicity, class, or Canadian economic conditions frequently became significant social issues during this period. However, illegal immigration per se, separate and aside from such demands for exclusion, never itself became a significant social issue then—or even long thereafter. As an illustrative case, one of us (Indra) has developed a representative sample of 2,469 domestic news items addressing ethnicity from three ten-year eras and three British Columbia newspapers spanning 1905–1976. Coverage of Asians represented 60.1 percent of province-based news items involving ethnicity during 1905–1914. Most of the coverage was very negative, yet only 3.2 percent of news items on Asians had illegal immigration as the main topic, and only 2.1 percent more addressed it as a subsidiary theme. Indeed, just thirty-eight domestic news items for all eras and ethnocultural groups even mentioned illegal immigration at all, and only seven of these were from after 1931.

Many themes found in reactions to illegal immigration during the 1980s and 1990s were nevertheless already in place. "Invasions" by unwanted Asians in British Columbia, Catholics and Eastern Europeans in the prairie provinces, Italian laborers, British paupers, and others had set the groundwork: a sense of an externally sourced threat, of borders being attacked or besieged, of inadequate governmental control, and of the undermining, culturally subversive threat posed by such unwanted foreigners. One additional, modern element, the issue of fairness in access to immigration, had not yet arisen, as it appears that most saw immigration as a privilege that the government could arbitrarily extend or deny (save perhaps to prospective "white," well-off British immigrants throughout the empire), based on national and imperial considerations alone. Reactions to unwanted immigrants were often harsh by today's standards, for there were no human rights protections then in place against ethnic, national, racial, gender, or religious discrimination. Immigrant applicants had only those limited rights deriving from British common law such as habeas corpus—rights available to them only when they were in the country and had the resources to access them.

THE RISE OF AN URBAN-ORIENTED, "MERITOCRATIC" IMMIGRATION POLICY, 1945–1977

Canada came out of World War II much more urban and heavily industrial-ized. In support of this shift, the government made immigration a central part of its postwar economic strategy. In addition, the government wished to maintain an active international presence after the war through the United Nations (UN) and soon as a mediator, peacekeeper, and advocate for human rights overseas. This also immediately affected immigration policy, particularly concerning ref-ugees. A new immigration policy was announced in 1947, which was imple-mented entirely through Orders-in-Council. While the new policy highlighted economic development (as in the 1920s), it nevertheless inherited ethnic and national preferences for British and American immigrants and a limited range of racial and national immigration bans on immigration from Asia and the Carib-bean. The latter were replaced by restrictive country quotas during 1947–1951. A central new element of policy was a system of immigrant support, through which Canadian residents sponsored the applications of relatives, giving these prospective immigrants preference in the queue.

Political Refugees

The Immigration Act of 1952 still concentrated on identifying who should be kept out and on providing means to deal with unwanted immigrants who nev-ertheless slipped in. The exclusionary powers of Section 38(c) remained, with "race" changed to "ethnic group." As previously, the act said nothing about how immigrants were to be selected or about political refugees. Many political refugees arrived earlier through normal immigration channels, including 50,000 who escaped slavery in the United States during 1830–1865 (Dirks 1977: 23). Some special programs had also group-settled oppressed ethnoreligious minor-ities, such as Mennonites and Doukhobors from Europe and Hutterites from the United States. In contrast, many bona fide Jewish and other asylum seekers had been denied entry during the 1930s and World War II (Abella and Troper 1983).

Some early postwar political refugees secured permanent residence through Orders-in-Council after first arriving through illegal means, including 1,700 Es-tonians, Latvians, and Lithuanians, who arrived on the Maritime coast in small boats between 1948 and 1950. Others such as Polish soldiers and displaced Palestinians, were accepted under special programs. During 1947–1952, the Canadian government selected 186,000 displaced persons in Europe on a case-by-case basis—using decided ethnic, religious, and political preferences. This was followed by a general refugee resettlement program selecting 2,000–3,000 people a year and by special programs for 37,149 Hungarian political refugees (1956–1957) and 11,943 people fleeing the failed revolution in Czechoslovakia (1968–1969). The rise of this refugee resettlement infrastructure set the stage for many later developments concerning illegal immigration, for refugee asylum seeking and illegal immigration became increasingly intertwined from the 1970s on. Also in regard to later developments concerning illegal immigration, it is important to note that all postwar political refugees were given the same permanent resident status as other immigrants, rather than temporary asylum.

Illegal Immigration in the 1950s and 1960s

Canada's first decade of postwar immigration was a great policy success in terms of numbers: 1,666,000 people arrived between 1946 and 1957. Even so, by the late 1950s officials increasingly believed that sponsorship-facilitated chain migration was so extensive that the program could neither meet the economy's need for skilled workers nor be adjusted to meet temporally varying labor demands. Some prospective immigrants responded to a subsequent toughening of immigration standards and to delays in processing their applications (an enduring informal method of government immigration control) by legally visiting Canada, overstaying their visas, and applying for permanent residence in-country on compassionate grounds.[5] An unknown number simply stayed as illegal immigrants. The incentives to do this were particularly large for those who still faced restrictive immigration quotas. So many Hong Kong residents availed themselves of false identities and immigrated illegally that the government quietly declared an amnesty program for Chinese illegals in 1960 (Knowles 1997: 150). This followed a countrywide Royal Canadian Mounted Police (RCMP) raid on Chinatowns to accumulate evidence (Avery 1995: 213). While the RCMP commissioner was attacked for claiming that "11,000 Chinese of the 23,000 that have come to Canada since 1946 have entered the country illegally," 11,600 people were granted permanent residence through this amnesty before it was phased out in 1973 (DeMont and Fennell 1989: 91). As with subsequent amnesties in fact and in name, the consensus was that fewer than half of those who qualified availed themselves of it.

Immigrant Selection: From Culture, Nationality, and Race to Class

In 1962, Canadian immigration policy was made nondiscriminatory with respect to race, ethnicity, religion, and nationality, in order to be consistent with the Canadian Bill of Rights and UN treaties and goals. After funding several analyses of policy immigration (Canada, Department of Manpower and Immigration 1966; Sedgwick 1965–1966), the government instituted sweeping changes in immigration law and practice in 1967—again through modifying regulations and bureaucratic practice. A points system was established for selecting "independent immigrants" (those who applied on their own, without the sponsorship of relatives) that emphasized education, skills, employability, age, facility in English and French, and occupational demand. Sponsored relatives (excluding one's spouse, dependent children, and aged parents) thereafter also faced a less demanding points system. Administratively, increased resources were allocated to processing applications outside traditional source areas, especially in some Asian countries. These changes profoundly reduced the number of unskilled immigrants coming to Canada (Green 1995: 32). They also dramatically expanded the ethnic and national composition of Canadian immigration, establishing large, ongoing flows of immigrants from Asia and the Caribbean.

Canada's First Illegal Immigration "Crisis" in the Postwar Era

Two changes in policy had an immediate effect on illegal immigration, establishing some patterns that resonate today. Section 34 of the Immigration Regulations of 1967 allowed visitors to apply for permanent resident status while in Canada (North 1982: A-13). In addition, the Immigration Appeal Board Act of 1967 brought into being the Immigration Appeal Board (IAB) to review deportations and some denials of sponsorship (Knowles 1997: 155; Sedgwick 1965–1966). Thousands of individuals were soon applying in-country, knowing that if they were unsuccessful (for the normal rules of selection were supposedly no less relevant to them), they could appeal to the IAB and that their appeal would have greater poignancy and weight the longer they were in the country. There was a good basis for this expectation. The new IAB rendered positive decisions 20 to 40 percent of the time (Canada, Department of Manpower and Immigration 1974b: 35–37). Moreover, encouraged by travel agents (North 1982: A-14; Knowles 1997: 163), the number of new in-country applications rose exponentially. In October 1972, 4,500 would-be immigrants arrived at Toronto International Airport during one weekend alone. The whole system and the IAB in particular, were quickly overwhelmed.

In 1972, regulations were drafted to allow a quick disposition of the huge backlog of in-country applications through Project 80, using special inquiry officers who employed very liberal criteria for landing (North 1982: A-29).[6] The provision allowing landing in-country was canceled, and access to the IAB was further restricted. Visitor airport arrival statistics indicated that there then may have been 200,000 illegal immigrants in the country, the equivalent of 1 percent of the Canadian population. The government consequently established a massively publicized amnesty program (Project 97), which in practice granted permanent residence to almost all illegal residents who applied, subject to criminal and security checks. Those who did not come forward were liable to be deported, although the actual risk of deportation was very low (North 1982: A-22).

This amnesty produced two linked surprises, the first of which was how few actually applied: only 50,000, of whom 39,000 were from 150 countries, benefited.[7] Applicants from the United States (28.4 percent) and Hong Kong (22 percent) were most numerous, followed by Jamaica (5.5 percent), Trinidad and Tobago (4.1 percent), India (3.3 percent), Great Britain (3.3 percent), Guyana (3.1 percent), Greece (2.7 percent), and Portugal (2.7 percent). Virtually all applicants lacking legal residence were visa abusers, not covert arrivals. Second, only 61 percent of those who came forward were formally illegal immigrants. The rest were legal nonimmigrant residents, chiefly students completing courses of study in Canada. Some puzzling questions were never answered. Where were all the other supposed illegal immigrants? Where were all those visitors who had arrived by plane in the previous few years?

Increasing Canadian Cultural and National Diversity in the 1970s

Over the next few years policy and administrative changes further broadened the nationalities of immigrants and increasingly involved Canada in the resettlement of refugees. Establishing a trend that continued into the 1990s, immigration shifted from Western Europe and the United States to Asia and the Pacific. The latter supplied 9.4 percent of immigrants in 1967, 18.8 percent in 1972, 26.9 percent in 1977, 34.7 percent in 1982, 44.0 percent in 1987, and 55.4 percent in 1996 (Reimers and Troper 1992: 34; Canada, Employment and Immigration Commission 1996). Immigration from the Caribbean also increased significantly (to 6–10 percent of the annual total), as did that from South America (5–7 percent) and Africa and the Middle East (10–16 percent). During 1964–1978, 2.4 million people immigrated, averaging 157,000 a year—the equivalent of 1.5 million a year for the United States.

Special refugee programs were instituted for Ugandan Asians (7,069 during 1972–1973), "South Americans" (chiefly Chileans, 7,016 in 1973), Cypriots (700 in 1975), Southeast Asians (9,060 during 1975–1976), and Lebanese (11,321, 1976–1979). Although neither accurately tallied nor formally designated as refugees to minimize U.S. displeasure, as many as 100,000 Americans refusing participation in the Vietnam War were given permanent residence during 1965–1975 (Adelman 1995: 53). These initiatives led up to the second Southeast Asian program (1979–1982), through which 98,000 individuals were landed.

A critical change in the protections available to in-country asylum seekers was made during this period that has had profound implications for how illegal immigration thereafter has been perceived and managed. In 1969, the federal government finally signed the 1951 UN *Convention Relating to the Status of*

Refugees and 1967 Protocol. This committed it not to *refoul* refugees (not to expel asylum seekers or turn them back at the border if they might consequently come to harm). To that point, refugee selection and resettlement had been almost exclusively controlled *by* Canadian officials, not by asylum seekers, and selection usually occurred overseas. Within a decade, this commitment not to *refoul* asylum seekers provided another option for those seeking residence outside conventional channels: get to or into Canada and apply for asylum.

Anti-Immigration "Backlash" in the Late 1970s

Many negative ethnoracial attitudes that had earlier framed public immigration discourse moderated greatly between 1960 and 1985, despite a major recession and the arrival of 750,000 visible minority immigrants.[8] Even so, a rise in the number of "racial" incidents and attitudinal polling both suggest that rapidly increasing immigrant diversity threatened some Canadians, particularly in Toronto, Montreal, and Vancouver, the places to which most immigrants went. In the 1950s and early 1960s such reactions had been directed against so-called DPs (displaced persons), Italians, and Portuguese. This time, the focus was almost exclusively on "visible minorities." Voiced concerns and polling highlighted the classic Canadian immigration triad: preferred ethnicity, absorptive capacity, and economic demand (Dirks 1995: 10). As data from a careful national survey of the era showed (see the 1977 data in Table 18.1, derived from Berry, Kalin, and Taylor 1977: 106), the more recent the migration flow, the more a group was perceived to be culturally and physically different; the poorer and more disempowered their source country, the more negatively they were assessed. A restudy in 1991 (Kalin and Berry 1996, from which the 1991 data in Table 18.1 are derived) produced similar results, as indicated in the values achieved in a composite measure of how informants evaluated various ethnic groups.[9]

Two folk categories of immigrants were singled out, that were soon identified with illegal immigration. One was "blacks," the majority of whom were then either native-born or Afro-Caribbean immigrants. By 1980, Afro-Canadians typically were better educated than the Canadian average and were similarly positioned in society. However, stereotypes of them were informed by negative media portrayal of African Americans (Indra 1979a) and sometimes characterized Afro-Canadians as illegal migrants. The literature gives no indication that Caribbean illegal immigration was extensive. However, some women visiting Canada during the 1970s overstayed their visas and sought work as domestics and factory workers, and by the late 1970s, the ratio of deportation orders to visitor arrivals did become high for certain Caribbean countries such as Jamaica and Guyana (see later).

The others singled out were South Asians or "East Indians," a Canadian folk covering-term for the twenty-some groups like Sikhs, Pakistanis, and Ismailis with ultimate origins in India, Pakistan, Sri Lanka, and Bangladesh. Their stereo-

Table 18.1
National Attitudinal Ranking of Ethnic and Racial Groups 1977 and 1991

	1977 ranking	1977 score	1991 ranking	1991 score
English	1	0.52	1	0.46
Scottish	2	0.49		
French	3	0.47	3	0.30
Dutch	4	0.46		
Scandinavian	5	0.39		
Japanese	8	0.13		
Hungarian	9	0.10		
Polish	10	0.08		
Jewish	11	0.04	7	0.16
German	12	0.02	5	0.18
Ukranian	18	-0.13	4	0.25
Italian	19	-0.20	2	0.32
Portuguese	20	-0.25	6	0.17
Chinese	21	-0.26	8	0.15
Greek	23	-0.36		
Negro, West Indian	25	-0.52	9	-0.15
Arab		0.77	10	-0.38
East Indian	26	-0.95	11	-0.53
Sikh			12	-0.68

typic attributes were modeled on media representations of India and Indians (Indra 1979a, b) and also were associated with illegal immigration (Buchignani 1993; Buchignani and Indra 1985, 1989). Based on our own extensive involvement in South Asian Canadian research, it is our impression that while many South Asians pushed the limits of immigration law, proportionally few then became formally illegal immigrants.

Chinese immigration through normal channels and Southeast Asian (Vietnamese, Vietnamese Chinese, Khmer, and Lao) refugee migration were also high during this period. However, both benefited from a revised, positive stereotype of Chinese Canadians (T. Chan 1983; K. Chan 1987) that characterized them as "polite, economically self-sufficient, hard-working, and law abiding" (K. Chan 1987: 126), strongly familial, apolitical, quickly integrating, and not socially disruptive. In addition, the large, second Southeast Asian refugee program had active public support as "deserving" refugees, and tens of thousands of Canadians had been directly involved in sponsoring and resettling refugee individuals (K. Chan and Indra 1986; K. Chan, Dorais, and Indra 1988). Although both organized and individualized illegal Chinese immigration undoubtedly continued, it attracted little attention.

BORDER CONTROL AND HUMAN RIGHTS IN TENSION, 1978–1998

The Immigration Act, 1976 (formally, *An Act Respecting Immigration to Canada, 1976–77*) was preceded by sustained public debate over immigration policy (see Canada, Department of Manpower and Immigration 1974a; Special Joint Committee of the Senate and House of Commons 1975). The act gave the government several powers to limit illegal immigration, including sanctioning air carriers for not confirming that visitors had appropriate documentation. It also made it against the law to knowingly employ an illegal resident—a law that has rarely been applied. The act, however, did not (indeed, considering subsequent court cases, probably could not) change the fact that an illegal immigrant was a person with rights who could not be summarily deported by an administrative decision (Cox and Glenn 1994: 288, 292). Moreover, no new significant resources were given to enforcement, and immigration guidelines pertaining to compassionate landing—an option long used with illegal visa-overstayers—remained lenient (Robinson 1983a: 19). Deportations consequently remained low. Federal and provincial governments continued to extend most social and health benefits to illegal immigrants (Johnson and Williams 1981: 47).

Critically, the act unintentionally opened up a new avenue for prospective illegal migrants. It incorporated important language from Article 33 of the UN Convention and Protocol on Refugees that significantly limited Canadian sovereignty and border control powers. While refugees considered for resettlement by officials outside Canada's borders continued to have few procedural rights (Dirks 1995: 25), Section 4(2) of the act gave convention refugees and those applying for asylum *in* Canada the right of *nonrefoulement*—irrespective of their resident status or how they entered the country. A complex method of assessing in-country asylum claims was established to allow an individual charged with being illegally in Canada to interrupt the deportation proceedings with a refugee claim.[10] Three things guaranteed that vigorous attempts would be made to use the new system to secure residence outside normal channels: the extension of convention protections against *nonrefoulement* to all in-country asylum seekers; consequent *political* decisions that transformed this *nonrefoulement* obligation into virtually an individual right of asylum (Martin 1991: 31–32); and the slow, cumbersome, and unselective way internal asylum claims were assessed.

Illegal Immigration as a 1980s Social Issue

Illegal immigration soon arose again as a social issue. One small-scale amnesty was aimed at Haitian illegals in 1981 (Robinson 1983a; 18), while another allowed domestics in Canada illegally or on work permits—chiefly women from the Caribbean—to apply for permanent residence. Based chiefly on shaky statistics on detentions and deportations, in 1982 the Canada Employment and Immigration Advisory Council (CEIAC 1982) estimated that despite a series of amnesties, there were still 200,000 illegal immigrants in the country. In response, the government commissioned W. G. Robinson to generate an issues paper (1983a), hold public consultations, and write a final report (1983b). Robinson's two reports (1983a: 6–7, 24, 41, 1983b: 12, 16, 25) reached several important conclusions:

- 46,000–55,000 was the best available estimate of the number of illegal residents, based on government studies of enforcement cases. If accurate, we note that on a per capita basis Canada then had one-ninth the proportion of illegal residents as the United States. This was at a time when Canada's overall per capita legal immigration flow exceeded that of the United States by two and a half times.

- Deportation evidence indicated that "most illegal immigrants in Canada are young, single men and women who enter lawfully as visitors [by air] but over-stay to take advantage of better economic opportunities than are available in their home countries." Almost half had relatives in Canada, suggesting that illegal chain migration was extensive.

- Deportation case patterns at the time reflected either a high level of abuse from some countries (most notably, Guyana, Jamaica, the United States, India, Portugal, and Peru) or a very selective system of detection and deportation.

- There was little evidence that illegal immigrants abused social welfare systems and none that they had negative economic impact.

- Exit border controls to identify illegal overstayers (as currently exist in Australia; see Cox and Glenn 1994) were unworkable, in the light of the 40 million-person annual flow across the U.S. border. Robinson likewise rejected proposals that officials more vigorously seek out illegal residents, noting that the current system, which depended on informants and on illegal immigrants running afoul of government systems, was efficient and unobtrusive.

- A universal system of visitor visas (exempting the United States) should be established to control illegal immigration at its source. Eighty countries were then still exempt from such visas.

The government soon announced a "long term illegals program" (Malarek 1987: 174), through which those living illegally in Canada five years or more could be considered for permanent residence—anonymously, if they wished. During the two years it was in operation the program attracted fewer than 4,000 applicants, ninety-six percent of whom were accepted.

Thereafter, several factors contributed to an increasing public association among refugees, asylum seekers, and illegal immigration. One such factor was Canadians' long-conflicted views on immigration and immigrants (Howith 1988; Tienhaara 1974), which are marked by deep concern over the possible negative effects of immigration while simultaneously valorizing ideal immigrants (Howith 1988: 24; Tienhaara 1974; Gallup Poll of March 31, 1988, Ekos Research Associates 1992a: 8; Angus Reid-Southam poll of February 16–22, 1993). Many Canadians also "genuinely wish to provide haven for the persecuted" (Martin 1991: 34)—conditional on individuals' being "true," deserving, political refugees who have gone through proper procedures to secure refugee status. They must not be perceived to be "cheating," exploiting Canadian generosity, or manipulating the refugee selection process in their favor. Neither should they exhibit any negative behaviors historically identified with ethnic out-groups, even if these behaviors are unconnected to the oppression that made them refugees. In short, many Canadians conceive of refugee resettlement as a kind of charity (Indra 1993)—a perception that has generated widespread support for Canada's refugee program and for the resettlement of "deserving" refugee populations. Even so, viewing asylum as a kind of charity can easily delegitimate the claims of asylum seekers whose actions or group stereotypes bring forth images of illegality, external threat, or border assault.

The "Crisis" of 1986–1987

What if refugees or asylum seekers associated with more negatively perceived ethnic groups, categories, or countries *were* to appear to pose a threat of entering illegally in large numbers? What if they did so in an ideological climate unlikely to engender public support or their identification with positive public values? Ironically, in 1986 the people of Canada received the UN's Nansen Medal in recognition of their assistance to refugees, just as great concern arose over illegal immigration and a rising number of dubious in-country and border applications for asylum.

Until then, geographical isolation and explicit government policy had ensured that Canadians were insulated from refugee resettlement selection, which had gone on under controlled conditions elsewhere (Stastny and Tyrnauer 1989: 13; Richmond 1989: 9). But Canada's borders were strongly challenged in the 1980s as the availability of international travel and information on world immigration options increased. As Dirks (1990: 88) observes:

Following the promulgation of the Immigration Act in 1978, thousands of refugee claimants entered Canada either by posing as visitors or students, or by arriving at Canadian airports without any appropriate documents. Obviously, many of the claimants were not bona fide refugees. The crux of the quandary for the Canadian government and public was to determine how this country can continue to be a humane state where legitimate refugees can find a haven, yet have a vigorous, efficient screening process to identify fraudulent claimants.

About 6,000 in-country applications for asylum were made in 1983, and the number rapidly increased thereafter (Adelman 1991: 206). Government bureaucrats and politicians found that they had few legal, politically acceptable means of controlling either the type of individuals who entered the in-country system or the proportion of applicants that could "meet the refugee definition" (Martin 1991: 33) and secure permanent residence. The government therefore moved on the only other front it had available to reestablish control: to "block the establishment of a claimant's physical presence on [the] national territory" (Martin 1991: 33). A universal visa system was judged unacceptable, because of the financial implications of requiring visas of those arriving from the United States, Britain, West Germany, France, and Japan (Dirks 1995: 52). The government path, instead, was "one of undisguised incrementalism bordering, some might suggest, on opportunism" (Dirks 1995: 50). The government began imposing visa requirements on one country at a time—including *refugee-producing* countries—whenever self-selection by asylum seekers from those countries increased: Cuba, El Salvador, Ecuador, Ghana, and Uganda in 1978, Chile in 1979, Haiti in 1980, and India in 1981. Visa requirements were placed on Bangladesh and Sri Lanka in 1983 and on Jamaica, Guatemala, Peru, and Guyana in 1984. The Dominican Republic (Girard 1990: 115), Afghanistan, Egypt, Iraq, Syria, and Lebanon (Creese 1992: 132) were added in 1985. During 1981–1986, the largest numbers of in-country asylum seekers were, in fact, from Guyana, India, Sri Lanka, Iran, El Salvador, and Jamaica (Girard 1990: 118).

In 1985 the Supreme Court of Canada (in *Re: Singh and the Minister of Employment and Immigration* [1985] 1 SCR 177) ruled that Section 7 of the Canadian Charter of Rights and Freedoms applied to everyone in Canada, not just citizens. This confirmed the right of illegal immigrants and asylum seekers not to be detained without cause, to be promptly given the reason for their arrest and detention, to have the right of counsel and habeas corpus, and to appear personally before the IAB. It also ruled that any minimally credible in-country asylum claim must be duly considered by the government. As a result, the cost of dealing with inland asylum seekers dramatically increased; by 1993–1994, the overall annual cost of IAB operations alone was $90.5 million.

In 1986, 18,000 new asylum claims were made in-country. Many were generated through processes that were clearly illegal (Dirks 1995: 87; Hawkins 1991: 13), including those of 4,000 Portuguese, who had begun arriving the previous year through a scheme orchestrated by lawyers, immigration consultants, and travel agents (Malarek 1987: 152). Travel agents encouraged a further 2,000 to come from Turkey and 800 from Brazil. Large numbers of individuals from two other refugee-producing countries, Iran and Sri Lanka (some were from other countries traveling on forged Sri Lankan passports; see Foster 1998: 56–57), claimed asylum on dubious grounds. However, "blatant fraudulence could not be easily detected" by the inland asylum determination system (Dirks 1995: 88) and rarely led to deportation. The government's response was to require visitor visas from further source countries, including Portugal, Turkey, Tanzania, Sierra Leone, Mauritius, and Gambia (Malarek 1987: 168). With the system once more in gridlock, the government announced a program to administratively review the backlog of cases filed before May 1986. It was an amnesty in everything but name, and permanent resident status was again granted routinely, subject to security and medical checks.

Martin (1991: 34–35) has suggested that "[w]hen the number of asylum seekers increases sharply [as it did then], the ability to control appears increasingly threatened, at least in the absence of a convincing demonstration that the increase came from a real outbreak of implacable persecution—that is, evidence that most of the new arrivals are 'true refugees.' " However, there are two additional elements in this sequence: that the incoming immigrant flows be widely *perceived* to be threatening, inauthentic, and large and that such flows as a consequence generate a social issues discourse. As a countercase in point, none of the more dubious flows of asylum seekers listed earlier (such as Portuguese) received more than episodic coverage by the media, and little social issues commentary about illegal immigration was generated by them. In contrast, two widely publicized events in 1986–1987 became the paradigmatic Canadian examples of this threat response to possible illegal immigration—examples that probably initiated a significant shift in public views of immigrants and immigration (Creese 1992: 130; Foster 1998: 133).[11] Neither instance involved many asylum seekers or posed a significant threat to border control. However, both were from South Asian ethnocultural groups to which some Canadians had developed negative attitudes in the late 1970s, and both involved direct, highly symbolic attempts to breach Canada's physical borders.

A small flow of Tamil asylum seekers had been quietly in existence for several years when, on August 11, 1986, 152 Sri Lankan Tamils were rescued from two lifeboats off the coast of Newfoundland and requested political asylum. Their claim of coming from India by ship engendered positive public support for them as "deserving" refugees (Malarek 1987: 139), but it was soon established that a smuggling ring brought them from Germany, where most had been granted asylum while being considered for refugee status. This revelation produced a broad-based negative reaction, turning this into a symbolically potent "popular image of an assault on Canada's borders by dishonest and bogus refugees" (Creese 1992: 130). As Dirks (1995: 88) notes, the Tamil incident quickly "caused public anxiety and made the entire immigration and refugee policy areas appear to be out of control." News coverage was intense and unsupportive (Creese 1992; Buchignani 1993), as in the Dutch "press panic" following the arrival of Tamil asylum seekers there (van Dijk 1988: 177).[12] Illegality, fraud, and lack of immigration control were central themes, as were Tamils' not telling the truth, exploiting Canadian generosity, and "jumping the queue" in which other prospective immigrants and refugees patiently waited. Support for all three major federal parties fell sharply as a result of the perception that they were not acting sufficiently vigorously against these and other "illegal" immigrants (Gallup Polls of August 7–9 and August 14–16 1996).

The Tamil incident weakened public support for immigration just when in-country asylum claims once more swamped the system (Malarek 1987: 117;

Dirks 1995: 88). Soon there was a backlog of over 50,000 cases, and another expedited program to dispose of the backlog could not bring it below 36,000 by the end of 1987 (Dirks 1995: 26). The number of Latin American asylum seekers applying at the U.S.–Canadian border increased sharply (primarily from El Salvador and Guatemala), and for a while in 1987 the government instituted a heavily criticized requirement that asylum seekers presenting at the U.S. border remain on the "safe" U.S. side until their hearing (Malarek 1987: 118). Because of the powerful linkage between U.S. foreign policy and U.S. refugee policy (Zucker and Zucker 1991), critics argued that they risked being *refouled*. Transit visas were also instituted to limit the number of in-transit individuals deplaning and making asylum claims.

In 1985, a handful of Canadian Sikhs had been implicated in the bombing of an Air India plane (Buchignani and Indra 1989), in which many passengers were Canadian. Given this, prevailing attitudes toward South Asian immigrants, and reactions to the Tamil incident, 174 Sikhs could depend on little goodwill or sympathy when they appeared on the Nova Scotia shore on July 12, 1987, having come from Europe by ship to seek asylum. For months thereafter, whenever radio talk shows or the editorial pages of newspapers referred to immigration, refugees, multiculturalism, or "what it means to be Canadian," discussion inexorably turned to the un-Canadian, irrationally traditional, duplicitous nature of Sikhs.[13] Many news stories focused on illegal immigration and dwelt on "problems associated with refugees overwhelming Canadian society, often by linking the arrival of refugee claimants with climatic disasters through the use of pejorative metaphors such as 'floods,' 'tides,' 'swamping,' 'deluges,' 'torrents,' and 'stampedes' in headlines and accompanying text" (Creese 1992: 131). Their arrival further weakened support for all immigrants, asylum seekers and illegal immigrants in particular. Indeed, almost a year later only 31 percent of Canadians supported a general amnesty on illegal immigrants, down by *half* from before the Tamils and Sikhs arrived (Gallup Polls of July 4, 1988, and December 1983).

Bureaucratic Attempts to Reestablish the Appearance of Border Control and an Orderly System of Inland Asylum Determination

These incidents generated so strong a public response that on July 31, 1987, Prime Minister Mulroney took the unusual step of recalling Parliament to consider two bills. The Refugee Deterrents and Detention Bill (Bill C-84) was drafted in direct response to the Tamil and Sikh incidents and provided harsh penalties for those who facilitated influxes of asylum seekers. It also gave the government expanded powers of search and seizure and initially even included a provision to turn away ships carrying inauthentic refugees. The latter provision so strongly evoked notorious historical cases of the seashore rejection of immigrants such as the *Komagata Maru* in 1914 (Buchignani and Indra 1985) and the *St. Louis* in 1939 (Abella and Troper 1983) that it was dropped.

The government's Refugee Reform Bill (Bill 55) was meant to streamline how in-country claims for asylum were processed. It also gave the government the (as yet never used) power to establish a list of "safe" third countries and to deny entry to asylum seekers arriving from such places (Davis, Kunin, and Trempe 1997: 80). Met with great opposition, the bill did not come into effect until January 1989. By then, over 120,000 asylum claimants were in the backlog (Knowles 1997: 185; Adelman 1991: 184)—a number that remained roughly constant for years (Foster 1998: 93), despite several more quasi amnesties meant to address it. The largest numbers of claimants then in the backlog came from Trinidad and Tobago (14,787), Sri Lanka (11,045), Iran (9,217), El Salvador (7,933), Portugal (5,745), India (3,963), Nicaragua (3,732), Guatemala (2,992), Lebanon (2,626), Turkey (2,626), Jamaica (2,600), Fiji (2,599), and Chile (2,596) (Adelman 1991: 184). Most were from countries that already had significant ongoing immigration to Canada. Many came specifically in the (correct) expectation that if they arrived before the new legislation came into effect or soon thereafter, they would benefit from the government's inability to deal expeditiously with so many cases (Creese 1992: 139).[14] In practice, an asylum seeker's major obstacle to permanent resident status was to make it to a border or Canadian airport to establish a claim. About 20 percent of the total annual intake of immigrants by then occurred within Canada (Dirks 1995: 32), despite government intentions to reduce inland applications to a trickle.

Three things made it impossible for the complex determination procedure established by Bill 55 to distinguish authentic refugees from others in this flow any more consistently than the system it replaced (Foster 1998: 97–99). First, most were from countries with refugee-producing conflicts. Second, most asylum seekers destroyed their personal and travel documents prior to making a claim, making oral testimony the main direct evidence presented in support of their claims (and their identities). Currently, over 60 percent of claimants claim to have no documentation (Auditor General of Canada 1997),[15] and 50 percent may have destroyed their documents (Davis, Kunin, and Trempe 1997: 81). Finally, practice was changed to give claimants the benefit of the doubt in ambiguous cases, as is recommended by the United Nations High Commissioner for Refugees (UNHCR). This was done to lower the probability of authentic refugees' being *refouled* because they could not provide definitive evidence of having been politically oppressed.

Policy shifted again with Bill C-86 to amend the immigration act, which came into force in 1993 (Dirks 1995: 158). The bill reflected the Conservative government's frustration in dealing with immigration in an increasingly globalized world in which its classical notions of border-defined national sovereignty had become seriously challenged: a world where people were perceived to be on the move everywhere and where information, human rights practice, capital, citizenship, and labor rights spanned borders in complex ways.[16] The bill was predicated on the assumption that the asylum determination system was being widely abused and that public support for immigration was softening (Knowles 1997: 198–199; Ekos Research Associates 1992a, b). The bill also anticipated further pressures on the Canadian immigration system from growing European restrictionism in response to asylum seeker challenges there. Another motivation was to reduce the cost of the immigration program in general and inland determination in particular.[17]

Bill C-86 gave the government new powers to restrict illegal and unwanted immigration, just when it had committed to high overall levels of immigration to bolster the economy and maintain Canada's population. Among other things, it tightened visa and airline visa-checking procedures. It also legalized the fingerprinting and photographing of asylum seekers, both for security reasons and to discourage multiple applications under different aliases. In addition, Bill C-86 allowed the government to enter into bilateral "safe country" agreements with other countries in order to reduce "asylum shopping."[18] While the inland asylum determination procedure was simplified, the legislation also created a Deferred Removal Orders Class of immigrants to land those who had been ordered deported but had been deemed legitimately at risk if they were to return to their country of origin; 5,000 were accepted in this class before it was abolished in 1997.[19] Since then, there has been further "streamlining" of inland asylum determination to reduce costs and backlogs. However, a flow diagram of the full process still requires sixteen boxes and provides five different ways to become a permanent resident: three as convention refugees and two on humanitarian and compassionate grounds. An expedited process has been established for noncontentious cases, through which those with strong cases move almost automatically. So great is the caseload burden that many now secure refugee status chiefly not on individual grounds but as a result of assessments of prevailing *general* conditions in their source countries, as determined by IRB reports.

Inland Asylum Determination in the Late 1990s

The system was extensively investigated by the auditor general of Canada (1997) in 1996, when the primary source countries claimed by inland asylum seekers were Sri Lanka (2,964), Chile (2,646), India (1,485), Iran (1,725), Israel (1,221), Pakistan (1,082), Democratic Republic of Congo (1,129), Somalia (940), and Mexico (974). Overall, 60 percent of all individuals accepted as refugees in that year were landed in-country.[20] The majority of inland asylum seekers arrived from countries other than the one in which they claimed they faced persecution, and for the first time, the majority of claims were made by people applying at U.S. border ports of entry (Auditor General of Canada 1997). The auditor general estimated the overall cost was at least $100 million each to the federal government, Ontario, and Quebec.[21] Cost notwithstanding, the auditor general claimed that the asylum determination process remained unable to consistently distinguish refugees from others. Many claimants consequently achieved legal permanent residence status through illegally misrepresenting themselves as refugees. As the auditor general observed, entry into the asylum determination system continued to give one a very high probability of securing landing. "Canadian deportation is very problematic and tortuous" (Cox and Glenn 1994: 287), and few in the end are blocked from all routes to permanent residence. Moreover, there is at present no way to ensure that most who are ordered deported or who abandon their asylum claims before they are decided actually leave the country.[22] Someone currently applying for asylum and losing every decision thereafter can count on being in the country for two and a half years—and then not be forced to leave. Anecdotal evidence currently suggests that some may be coming to Vancouver from Honduras explicitly to deal drugs while their manifestly false asylum cases lumber through the system.

In early January 1998, a Legislative Review Advisory Group released its report (Davis, Kunin, and Trempe 1997), *Not Just Numbers: A Canadian Framework for Future Immigration*. A surprisingly harsh assessment for a government-initiated effort, some of its 155 recommendations are now before the House of Commons Standing Committee on Citizenship and Immigration. These include 3 recommendations to toughen penalties and law enforcement against those involved in smuggling illegal immigrants (Davis, Kunin, and Trempe 1997: 115–116); 8 others advocate new practices to facilitate the deportation of illegal immigrants and the selective detention of individuals illegally in the country who are likely to perform criminal acts or go underground. It proposed that those in the inland system complying with the system be given a provisional residence status that could be regularized after several years and that those who did not comply should be detained. The overall restrictionist tenor of the document appears to reflect a growing unease with increasingly frequent media reports in the late 1990s of immigrant resident and asylum seeker criminality. Its authors claim:

Some people coming into Canada have found that it may be in their interests not to comply because the system as presently designed will allow them to meet their own ultimate goals. Citizenship and Immigration Canada cannot control the large number of people coming into the country who are inadmissible or who become subject to removal during their stay here. The department lacks the resources, the means and perhaps the will to deal effectively with them. The entire enforcement system has become overwhelmed. Without an incentive to comply with removal orders or reporting conditions, people will continue to stay on and become lost in the system. (Davis, Kunin, and Trempe 1997: 102)

On June 11, 1998, the Standing Committee released a report to Parliament, Immigration Detentions and Removals (Canada, House of Commons 1998a, 1998b). In it, the Standing Committee rejected a number of the recommendations regarding detentions, removals, and asylum seekers made by *Not Just Numbers*, arguing that they are too draconian. Like Robinson fifteen years before, the committee rejected greater or more invasive enforcement efforts in-country, recommending instead "that Canada's overseas interdiction programs be increased" (House of Commons 1998b). For example, it recommended that scanning technology be installed at airports *abroad* to "scan the travel documents of all individuals on flights coming to Canada that have presented control problems" in order to reduce misrepresentation, the "loss" of documents, and the need for detention.

CONCLUSION

While the way in which the government deals with illegal immigration is occasionally controversial and always equivocal, it has produced three striking results. Two of these are noted by Garcia y Griego (1994: 119). First, Canada does not have a large population of illegal immigrants today, either in absolute numbers or on a per capita basis. There are still no firm estimates of how many residents have no legal permission to be in Canada. Neither is there any rational way to determine what proportion of those who *have* legal residence secured that status through an unfounded claim for asylum or through gross misrepresentation in another immigration channel. Per capita, there is no evidence whatever that the current undocumented illegal population is on the order of that of the United States—which would proportionately be 300,000 to 600,000. Undocumented migrants simply do not have sufficient presence to support such numbers, even in cities like Toronto where they are thought to concentrate. Moreover, no large demand for illegal immigrant labor exists to draw them in. It is even hard to support a number like 100,000 unless this includes very long-term residents who have regularized everything about their residence but its legality.

Ironically, the current number of illegal immigrants would be much larger if Canada's system of dealing with illegal residents and in-country asylum claimants had been more effective. Had the government systematically rejected the use of amnesties and quasi amnesties, determined that even an additional 20 percent of inland claims were unfounded, and denied rejected individuals access to alternative routes to permanent residence, this easily could have added 200,000 individuals to the illegal population.

Second, as also noted by Garcia y Greigo (1994: 114), the government has achieved this low number "by applying mostly moderate immigration control policies." We believe that these policies are informed by a few simple principles:

• Select immigrants while applicants are overseas, save in exceptional circumstances.

• Concentrate resources to keep internal application rates as low as Canadian and international human rights laws and conventions allow—chiefly by acting unilaterally on those outside the Canadian human rights umbrella.

- Develop a modified "insular" approach (Zolberg, Suhrke, and Aguayo 1989: 280–281) to limit the yearly number of asylum claims, involving the selective imposition of country-specific visas for source countries and the careful review of travel and personal documents prior to visitors' leaving for Canada.
- Depend chiefly on a reactive enforcement of legal residence rather than a proactive (and hence controversial) strategy of aggressive investigations and quick deportations.
- Perhaps most important, have the will to have a comparatively coherent immigration policy and the actual ability to change associated programs quickly when circumstances dictate.

As Garcia y Griego observes (1994: 120), "Canada has never lost control over its borders, but it has, on more than one occasion, lost control over its own admission process." There is no evidence that in the 1990s the government's control over illegal immigration is anything more than of the crudest sort—control over the gross number of people who secure entry through illegal means. As Garcia y Griego (1994: 121) claims, "[o]nce we strip away Canada's unique circumstances and account for the flexibility in the administration of immigration policies, we are left, in fact, with a liberal democratic state that cannot, because of its liberal and democratic character, respond effectively to large flows of unwanted immigrants." This may be an overstatement, for standing behind the 200,000–250,000 immigrants the government accepts each year are millions of unsuccessful candidates and many millions more who would immediately enter the system if they thought they had any chance of success. However, until recently, each time illegal immigration has become an issue, the *appearance* of control has been quickly reestablished by change in law, regulations, or practice. While this appearance of control is, in part, illusory, it has functioned to defuse the issue.

There is, nevertheless, an important additional sense in which we agree with Garcia y Griego's conclusion. In the postwar era, geographical factors have ensured that Canada has not yet faced large-scale *cross-border* movements of illegal migrants—the current bane of orderly systems of immigration control in the United States and European Union (E.U.). Migrants must either come by plane or across the U.S. border, and in order to accomplish the latter, they must have satisfied or circumvented U.S. immigration control. Few individuals try to make Canada a country of first asylum (Zucker and Zucker 1991: 226). The members of the Immigration Legislative Review (Davis, Kunin, and Trempe 1997: 2) claim that the "first and most stubborn myth" they came across was "that Canada is protected by impenetrable borders, which we can open or close at will." In reality, the 3,000-mile shared border with the United States remains highly accessible to potential illegal migrants on the American side determined to enter Canada. Moreover, as Canadian efforts to stem the flow of asylum seekers and others arriving by plane are increasingly effective (especially in comparison to U.S. airport controls; see Mehlman 1994: 34), and as visa requirements in Europe are harmonized, more and more prospective claimants *have* shifted their efforts to the U.S.–Canadian border. Few of these are as yet from Mexico, Central America, or South America. Indeed, no country from Latin America is currently represented in the top ten Canadian immigrant source countries.

Disappearing Acts: From Illegal Immigrants to Legal Immigrants-in-Waiting

We believe that there is yet another way the Canadian government and others have dealt with illegal immigration that has been remarkable: while there may currently be a general, low-level "crisis of [public] confidence" in the enforcement of immigration laws and regulations (Davis, Kunin, and Trempe 1997: 102), the government and a range of interest groups have kept illegal immigration from becoming a persistent Canadian social issue. Illegal immigration has had a high profile in the United States for a long time and now has one in Australia (Foster 1998: 221; Cox and Glenn 1994). Why not in Canada? Several reasons are identifiable. First, since World War II, the government has increasingly avoided publicly identifying flows of migrants or individuals as illegal or having illegal dimensions to them—even when formally true. So also have "pro-immigration" organizations and ethnic-based interest groups, which far outnumber and are far more influential than the handful of organized interest groups that actively oppose immigration. Jakubowski (1998: 43), citing Reeves (1983: 177), notes that government bureaucrats tend to deracialize situations that appear to others to significantly involve race. This involves "the attenuation of, elimination of, or substitution for racial categories in discourse, the omission or deemphasis of racial explanation and the avoidance of racial evaluation and prescription." In the sometimes strange evolving saga of illegal immigration in Canada, politicians, government bureaucrats, ethnic spokespersons, academics, human rights activists, and those without legal status have performed a similar vanishing act on the "illegal" dimension of illegal immigration. While the increasingly frequent media reports of criminal behavior among illegal immigrants and asylum seekers may now be starting to undermine the effort, to this point "illegal immigrants" have largely been transformed into legal immigrants-in-waiting, especially into asylum seekers.

Active governmental involvement in this transformation is found everywhere. Immigration policy has long been determined primarily by bureaucrats (Garcia y Griego 1994: 123) and politicians with little public consultation. New initiatives to head off or disguise illegal immigrant flows usually involve changes in regulations rather than in law, so that the issues do not have to be subject to parliamentary debate or aired by the media. Statistics on illegal migrants who attract the attention of enforcement officers, are ordered deported, or actually leave are hard to find and rarely highlighted. Amnesties are not characterized as such but rather as housekeeping efforts aimed at efficiently resolving bureaucratic backlogs. Since the early 1980s, almost no publicly available bureaucratic discourse on asylum seekers ever uses symbolically potent words such as "illegal" but, instead, uses terms of reference for which there is more public goodwill, such as "refugees." Even the sharply critical 13,000-word 1997 auditor general's (1997) audit of in-country asylum determination never uses the word "illegal." Profoundly limited by public opinion, possible political fallout, the law, liberal-democratic principles, and the sheer cost of any system that would further restrict criteria for asylum, the government, instead, directs its efforts increasingly offshore, to ensure that most potential asylum seekers do not get in. The government also continues to support positively valued liberal ideologies of immigration and nation-building, of multiculturalism, and of Canada's significant contribution to refugee assistance. Derided by some as superficial responses to Canadian cultural diversity, these ideologies have significantly broadened the sense of what it means to be a Canadian and continue to increase the perceived legitimacy of immigrant-origin ethnic groups.

Other government disappearing strategies abound: shift inland refugee determination to a quasi-judicial body at arm's length from the government; never solicit broad-based public input into immigration or refugee policy unless the range of options to be discussed is greatly constrained beforehand; do not publicize the high cost of inland refugee determination, which is now estimated to be $30,000–50,000 for each eventually rejected claim (Canada, Employment and Immigration 1992: 18–23: *Toronto Sun*, December 3, 1997); do not make extensive use of temporary asylum, which could generate large interest groups of unlanded individuals in-country; and critically, establish a system for dealing with border control in which a large proportion of individuals who are illegally in the country can eventually secure permanent residence, without making the public aware that to get physically into Canada remains the main barrier to being granted the legal right to stay.

Other government branches and departments (such as Citizenship and Multiculturalism), immigrant settlement nongovernmental organizations (NGOs), lawyers and immigration consultants, human rights advocates, and especially ethnic associations have vested interests in minimizing the visibility and salience of the illegal dimensions of migration and so usually highlight other dimensions: immigrants' risk of harm and vulnerability in their source countries, their rights and statuses as human beings, their deservedness and contributions, and their family ties to Canada. A strong and systematic liberal value bias in Canadian ethnic and immigrant research (to which we have amply contributed) likewise valorizes immigrants and immigration, advocates immigrants' rights and privileges, and, as in Belgium (Suárez-Orozco 1994: 242), continues to avoid illegal immigration as a subject of inquiry in order to avoid inflaming anti-immigration sentiment.[23]

Postscript: Ethics and Illegal Immigration

When it does surface, social issue discourse on illegal immigration now concentrates on the authenticity of inland asylum seeker claims, individual immigrant criminality, or the legitimacy of new immigrant-origin ethnocultural groups. This narrowness of focus backstages many world-spanning ethical questions, none of which are frequently discussed or have easy solutions. For example, is the most good for the most people—either people in Canada, asylum seekers, refugees worldwide, or people in the world—being provided by today's expensive and ineffective inland system of asylum determination? If the primary function of this system is to support the protection of individuals who face political oppression—which is itself an open question—one is tempted to weigh the current system against the net moral benefit of the same resources being directed toward effective international conflict resolution, peacekeeping, or enlightened aid to the displaced.

If considered at face value, this surface-level comparison fails to address several other important ethical dimensions of the present system, particularly those deriving from its support of *nonrefoulement*. It is hard to imagine the consequences if frontline countries of first asylum around the world routinely turned back refugees at the border or, by characterizing them as illegal immigrants, forced refugees home thereafter without any consideration of their fate. Yet why should such countries be asked to cede as much sovereignty as they do, if politically stable, well-off ones like Canada that so strongly espouse liberal values continue to base their own border control policies on classical ideologies of the autonomous, self-determining state? As Hathaway (1994: 49) stresses, most folk and academic analysis of migration and border control "assumes the legitimacy of the legal and political framework within which immigration is presently controlled. We are asked to assess the effectiveness of a system that has not been shown to have moral or political validity . . . in the light of the right to freedom of international movement." In regard to the ethics of sorting out immigrants from refugees and illegal immigrants from asylum seekers, the Canadian government's present stance is often paradoxical and inconsistent. On one hand, the system of inland asylum and immigrant residency determination so strongly highlights *nonrefoulement* and due process that most who get into the country are eventually allowed to legally stay. On the other hand, the government does all it can within the realm of the politically acceptable to bar the door to those overseas who try to self-select Canada as a country of asylum, with no individual consideration of their situation and with little due process. Similarly, general immigration policy remains strongly informed by meritocratic and economic development values, yet those who are now actually accepted as immigrants are chiefly the overseas relatives of legal Canadian residents.

Canada's objectively low rates of formally illegal immigration and the "disappearing acts" that keep illegal immigration out of the public eye have kept Canadians from developing a sustained dialogue about the ethics of border control—both directed against people who attempt to immigrate outside normal channels and those who make use of those channels. The unfortunate result suggested by polling is that most Canadians still strongly subscribe to the facile position that "unbridled immigration control is an inherent aspect of a state's sovereignty" (Hathaway 1994: 49) and that nations are concrete entities defined by territorial borders. At least in this sense, they may be ill prepared for any sharp increase in actual or perceived illegal immigration the future may bring.

NOTES

1. Most Canadian social scientists who research immigration and ethnic topics have been conceptually captive of, and sympathetic to, liberal views that are "pro-immigration" and supportive of Canadian cultural diversity. As a consequence, there has been almost no research done on illegal immigration characterized as such for fear of inflaming anti-immigrant sentiment: none at all before Grace Anderson's (1971) initial statement. Many studies of immigration-derived ethnic communities (Buchignani and Letkemann 1993) were carried out in the 1970s and 1980s, but few even mention illegal immigration. Overall, the voluminous literature on Canada's ethnocultural populations provides researchers wishing to understand illegal immigration with scarce pickings. For example, there is almost no research on how formally illegal migrants live their lives, and we therefore cannot address this important domain here.

2. Canadian founding myths and historical evidence frequently diverge. Often represented as the prosperous, "white," middle-class British founders of Anglo Canada, many Loyalists were German. A sizable number were native, and 3,000 were of African origin.

3. Some key parts of current immigration practice do not even derive from Orders-in-Council, but rather from administrative guidelines (Davis, Kunin, and Trempe 1997: 16).

4. 57,701 people were deported for all reasons during 1900–1935 (Roberts 1988: 38).

5. One could not then apply to be an immigrant through normal channels while physically in Canada. However, individual Orders-in-Council could grant residence to those for whom leaving Canada to apply would be unfair or unreasonable, such as the immigrant spouses of legal residents.

6. 13,106 individuals directly benefited from Project 80.

7. Almost all applicants who did not secure permanent residence withdrew before a decision was reached on their status.

8. For example, the Economic Council of Canada's analysis (Swan and the Economic Council of Canada: 111) of sixty-four national surveys shows a consistent increase in tolerant attitudes between 1975 and 1989. The 1996 Census indicates that 11 percent of the Canadian population are non-Aboriginal visible minorities (Statistics Canada, *The Daily* 1998).

9. A notable exception is the shifting position of Italians, most of whom either immigrated in the 1950s and 1960s or are their descendants. Italians have evidently become fully legitimate since then.

10. A statement would be taken under oath and forwarded to an oversight committee for consideration (Adelman 1991: 202–203). Negative decisions there could then be

appealed to the quasi-judicial IAB. If unsuccessful there, one could appeal points of law to a federal court.

11. Concern also surfaced somewhat later over possible abuse of the Business Immigration Program, particularly regarding those coming from Hong Kong, Singapore, Malaysia, and other Southeast and East Asian locales. The 1987 act provided an immigration channel for entrepreneurs and investors bringing capital to Canada or establishing businesses employing Canadians. Members of the well-established immigration lawyer and consultant infrastructure were soon offering to "facilitate" entrepreneurial migration for a fee. With the 1997 handover to China approaching, entrepreneurial migration was increasingly exercised by Hong Kong's well-off. By 1988 strong concerns were being expressed in Vancouver about the culturally and economically destabilizing effect of incoming Asian money (Cannon 1989); $1 billion a year may have been flowing into the city and environs during the late 1980s. It was also widely reported that many "entrepreneurs" were not developing businesses in Canada and were, instead, using the system to purchase passports (for $250,000 in prosperous provinces, as little as $150,000 in others). Others reportedly recycled their start-up money back home, so that relatives could also apply using the same funds.

12. Sixty items on Tamils appeared in the national *Globe and Mail* in the month after they arrived (Buchignani 1993). In 1986, half the articles on refugees in this paper concerned Tamils (Creese 1992: 131).

13. Creese (1992: 131) reports that one-third of all news items on refugees in the national *Globe and Mail* during 1997—the total itself two times that of 1996—focused on Sikhs. Refugee news items made the front page of one out of five issues of the *Globe and Mail* that year (Creese 1992: 131–132). In a national Gallup Poll carried out soon after (August 14, 1987), 81 percent thought that the government had not acted against these Sikhs in a tough-enough manner.

14. Foster (1998: 94) reports that "by the end of 1990, senior officials in Ottawa announced that only one-third of the [backlogged] cases had been heard and that less than two hundred fraudulent claimants had been removed, while costs rose to $179 million. At this point, a House of Commons committee estimated that it would take at least six years and at least $600 million to clear up the log-jam."

15. The auditor general's report on inland asylum determination (1997) was accessed as a Web document lacking page numbers, and so we have been unable to provide them here.

16. The government of the day was so concerned with immigration control that in 1993 it put immigration into a Public Security portfolio.

17. By then, the *overall* federal cost of administering all its immigration-related programs was $900 million (Dirks 1995: 159).

18. Negotiations with the United States are ongoing, but no such bilateral agreement has yet been established.

19. Because virtually all asylum seekers made it successfully through the first stage of the previous determination system (for credibility), this stage was abolished, save for security and criminality checks—itself an ineffective screening rejecting 0.6 percent of claimants in 1996–1997. Further constraints on the assessment of security risk and criminality appear forthcoming, for in June 1998 the Supreme Court ruled that a Sri Lankan who had served prison time in Canada for conspiracy to traffic in heroin and who thereafter tried to forestall deportation by making an asylum claim could not be deported without a refugee determination hearing (*Globe and Mail*, June 5, 1998).

20. Many who apply for asylum secure permanent residence without being designated a convention refugee. They therefore do not appear in the annual immigration statistics as refugees.

21. One estimate of the total cost to metropolitan Toronto for providing services to all refugees and asylum seekers in 1991 was $326 million (Avery 1995: 226).

22. Of 19,900 claimants awaiting removal during 1993–1997, the government could confirm only that 22 percent had actually departed the country. About thirty percent of asylum seekers abandon their claims before they are decided.

23. The only significant exception has been research on the economic impact of immigration, which now indicates "diminishing returns" from immigration (Swan and the Economic Council of Canada 1991; DeVoretz 1995), after three decades of studies giving more positive assessments.

REFERENCES

Abella, Irving M., and Harold M. Troper
1983   *None Is Too Many: Canada and the Jews of Europe, 1933–1948*. New York: Random House.

Adelman, Howard
1991   Canadian Refugee Policy in the Postwar Period: An Analysis. In *Refugee Policy: Canada and the United States*. Edited by Howard Adelman. Toronto: York Lanes Press. Pp. 172–223.
1995   The Concept of Legitimacy Applied to Immigration. In *Legitimate and Illegitimate Discrimination: New Issues in Migration*. Edited by Howard Adelman. Toronto: York Lanes Press. Pp. 41–54.

Anderson, Grace M.
1971   *Illegal Immigration: A Sociologically Unexplored Field*. Waterloo, Ontario: Dept. of Sociology and Anthropology, Waterloo Lutheran University.

Auditor General of Canada
1997   *Report of the Auditor General of Canada to the House of Commons*. Chapter 25: Citizenship and Immigration Canada and the Immigration and Refugee Board— The Processing of Refugee Claims. Ottawa: Minister of Public Works and Government Services Canada.

Avery, Donald
1995   *Reluctant Host: Canada's Response to Immigrant Workers, 1896–1994*. Toronto: McClelland and Stewart.

Berry, John, R. Kalin, and D. Taylor
1977   *Multiculturalism and Ethnic Attitudes in Canada*. Ottawa: Information Canada.

Buchignani, Norman
1993   Refugees and Ethnic Relations in Canada. In *The International Refugee Crisis: British and Canadian Responses*. Edited by V. Robinson, London: Macmillan. Pp. 35–56.

Buchignani, Norman, and Doreen Indra
1985   *Continuous Journey: A Social History of South Asians in Canada*. Toronto: McClelland and Stewart.
1989   Key Issues in Canadian–Sikh Ethnic and Race Relations, and Their Implications for the Study of the Sikh Diaspora. In *The Sikh Diaspora*. Edited by N. G. Barrier and V. Dusenbery. New Delhi: Manohar. Pp. 141–184.

Buchignani, Norman, and Paul Letkemann
1993   Ethnographic Research. In *Multiculturalism in Canada*. Edited by John Berry and Jean Laponce. Toronto: University of Toronto Press. Pp. 203–237.

Canada, Board of Review (Immigration)
1938   *Report on Charges concerning Illegal Entry of Aliens into Canada*. Ottawa: King's Printer.

Canada, Department of Manpower and Immigration
1966   *White Paper on Immigration*. Ottawa: Queen's Printer.
1974a   *Green Paper on Immigration: Reports of the Canadian Immigration and Population Study*. 4 vols. Ottawa: Manpower and Immigration.
1974b   *A Report of the Canadian Immigration and Population Study*. Vol. 2 of the *Green Paper on Immigration: Reports of the Canadian Immigration and Population Study*. Ottawa: Information Canada.

Canada Employment and Immigration Advisory Council and Canada, Employment and Immigration Canada (Dept.)
1982   *Illegal Immigrants: Report to the Minister of Employment and Immigration Canada by the Employment and Immigration Advisory Council*. Ottawa: The Council.

Canada, Employment, and Immigration Canada
1992   *Government Proposes Changes to Immigration Program*. Ottawa: Employment and Immigration Canada.

Canada, Employment, and Immigration Commission
1996   *Annual Immigration Statistics*. Ottawa: Employment and Immigration.

Canada, House of Commons
1905   *Report of the Royal Commission on Italian Immigration (Sessional Paper 36b, [4–5 Edward VII])*. Ottawa: King's Printer.

Canada, House of Commons Standing Committee on Citizenship and Immigration
1998a   Report on Immigration Detention and Removals [Web Page]. Available at *www.interparl.parl.gc.ca/InfocomDoc/CITI/Studies/Reports/citirp01-e.htm*.
1998b   News Report (June 11, 1998): Committee Tables Report on Immigration Detention and Removals [Web Page]. Available at *www.interparl.parl.gc.ca/ InfocomDoc/CITI/PressReleases/ PRESS-eng.htm*.

Cannon, Margaret
1989   *China Tide: The Revealing Story of the Hong Kong Exodus to Canada*. Toronto: HarperCollins.

Chan, Kwok
1987   Perceived Racial Discrimination and Response: An Analysis of Indochinese Experience in Montreal. *Canadian Ethnic Studies* 19 (3): 125–147.

Chan, Kwok, Louis J. Dorais, and Doreen Indra, Editors
1988   *Ten Years Later: Indochinese Communities in Canada*. Ottawa: Canadian Asian Studies Association.

Chan, Kwok, and Doreen Indra, Editors
1986   *Uprooting, Loss and Adaptation: The Resettlement of Indochinese Refugees in Canada*. Ottawa: Canadian Public Health Association.

Chan, Tony
1983   *Gold Mountain: The Chinese in the New World*. Vancouver: New Star Books.

Cox, David, and Patrick Glenn
1994   Illegal Immigration and Refugee Claims. In *Immigration and Refugee Policy: Australia and Canada Compared*. Vol. 1. Edited by Howard Adelman, Allan

Borowski, Meyer Burnstein, and Lois Foster. Toronto: University of Toronto Press. Pp. 283–309.

Creese, Gillian
1992   The Politics of Refugees in Canada. In *Deconstructing a Nation: Immigration, Multiculturalism and Racism in '90s Canada*. Edited by Vic Satzewich. Halifax, Nova Scotia: Fernwood. Pp. 123–144.

Davis, Susan, R. Kunin, and Robert Trempe (Immigration Legislative Review Advisory Group)
1997   *Not Just Numbers: A Canadian Framework for Future Immigration*. Ottawa: Citizenship and Immigration Canada.

DeMont, John, and Thomas Fennell
1989   *Hong Kong Money: How Chinese Families and Fortunes Are Changing Canada*. Toronto: Key Porter Books.

DeVoretz, Don, Editor
1995   *Diminishing Returns: The Economics of Canada's Recent Immigration Policy*. Toronto and Vancouver: C. D. Howe Institute, Laurier Institution.

Dirks, Gerald E.
1977   *Canada's Refugee Policy: Indifference or Opportunism?* Montreal: McGill-Queen's University Press.
1990   Regulating the Refugee Flow: Some Observations. In *Refuge or Asylum: A Choice for Canada*. Edited by Howard Adelman and C. M. Lanphier. Toronto: York Lanes Press. Pp. 88–97.
1995   *Controversy and Complexity: Canadian Immigration Policy during the 1980s*. Montreal: McGill-Queen's University Press.

Ekos Research Associates, Anderson Strategic Research, Canada, Employment and Immigration Canada (Dept.), and Public Affairs Division
1992a   *The Public Opinion Impact of the New Immigration Legislation*. Toronto and Ottawa: Ekos.
1992b   *Final Report: National Opinion Study on Changes to Immigration Policy*. Toronto and Ottawa: Ekos.

Foster, Lorne
1998   *Turnstile Immigration: Multiculturalism, Social Order and Social Justice in Canada*. Toronto: Thompson Educational.

García y Griego, Manuel
1994   Canada: Flexibility and Control in Immigration and Refugee Policy. In *Controlling Immigration: A Global Perspective*. Edited by Wayne Cornelius, Philip Martin, and James Hollifield. Stanford: Stanford University Press. Pp. 119–140.

Girard, R. A.
1990   Canadian Refugee Policy: Government Perspectives. In *Refuge or Asylum: A Choice for Canada*. Edited by Howard Adelman and C. M. Lanphier. Toronto: York Lanes Press. Pp. 113–119.

Gray, John H., Joseph-Adolphe Chapleau, and the Royal Commission on Chinese Immigration
1885   *Report of the Royal Commission on Chinese Immigration: Report and Evidence*. Ottawa: Printed by order of the commission.

Green, Alan G.
1995   A Comparison of Canadian and U.S. Immigration Policy in the Twentieth Century. In *Diminishing Returns: The Economics of Canada's Recent Immigration*

Policy. Policy Study 24. Edited by Don DeVoretz. Toronto: C. D. Howe Institute; Vancouver: Laurier Institution. Pp. 31–64.

Hathaway, James
1994   Commentary. In *Controlling Immigration: A Global Perspective.* Edited by Wayne Cornelius, Philip Martin, and James Hollifield. Stanford: Stanford University Press. Pp. 49–54.

Hawkins, Freda
1991   *Critical Years in Immigration: Canada and Australia Compared.* 2d ed. Montreal: McGill-Queen's University Press.

Howith, H. G.
1988   *Postwar Canadian Attitudes to Immigration.* Ottawa: Employment and Immigration Canada.

Indra, Doreen
1979a   Ethnicity, Social Stratification and Opinion Formation: An Analysis of Ethnic Portrayal in the Vancouver Newspaper Press. 1905–1976. Doctoral diss., Department of Sociology and Anthropology, Simon Fraser University, Vancouver.
1979b   South Asian Stereotypes in the Vancouver Press. *Ethnic and Racial-Studies* 2 (2): 166–189.
1982   The Production and Legitimation of Racial and Ethnic Stereotypes in the Vancouver Press, 1905–82. In *Perspectives on Race, Education and Social Development: Emphasis on Canada.* Edited by Vincent D'Oyley. Vancouver: University of British Columbia. Pp. 35–43.
1993   The Spirit of the Gift and the Politics of Resettlement: The Canadian Private Sponsorship Programme and Southeast Asian Refugees. In *The International Refugee Crisis: British and Canadian Responses.* Edited by V. Robinson. London: Macmillan. Pp. 229–254.

Jakubowski, Lisa M.
1998   *Immigration and the Legalization of Racism.* Halifax, Nova Scotia: Fernwood.

Johnson, K. F., and M. Williams
1981   *Illegal Aliens in the Western Hemisphere: Political and Economic Factors.* New York: Praeger.

Kalin, Rudolf, and J. W. Berry
1996   Interethnic Attitudes in Canada: Ethnocentrism, Consensual Hierarchy and Reciprocity. *Canadian Journal of Behavioural Science* 28 (4): 253–261.

Knowles, Valerie
1997   *Strangers at Our Gates: Canadian Immigration and Immigration Policy, 1540–1997.* Rev. ed. Toronto: Dundurn Press.

Legislature of Lower Canada
1794   *An Act Passed in the Second Session of the Legislature of Lower-Canada, in the Thirty-Fourth Year of His Majesty's Reign, for Establishing Regulations Respecting Aliens . . .* Quebec City: John Neilson.

Malarek, Victor
1987   *Haven's Gate: Canada's Immigration Fiasco.* Toronto: Macmillan of Canada.

Martin, David A.
1991   The Refugee Concept: On Definitions, Politics, and the Careful Use of a Scarce Resource. In *Refugee Policy: Canada and the United States.* Edited by Howard Adelman. Toronto: Centre for Refugee Studies, York University. Pp. 30–51.

Mehlman, Ira
1994   Illegal Immigration through U.S. Airports Is a Serious Problem. In *Illegal Immigration*. Edited by William Barbour. San Diego, California: Greenhaven Press. Pp. 32–40.

North, David S.
1982   *Amnesty: Conferring Legal Status on Illegal Immigrants: The Canadian Experience, the Western European Experience, and Some Comments on Its Possible Consequences in the U.S.* Washington, D.C.: Center for Migration Studies, New Trancentury Foundation.

Reeves, F.
1983   *British Racial Discourse: A Study of British Political Discourse about Race and Race-Related Matters.* Cambridge: Cambridge University Press.

Reimers, David, and Harold Troper
1992   Canadian and American Immigration Policy since 1945. In *Immigration, Language and Ethnicity: Canada and the United States.* Edited by Barry Chiswick. Washington, D.C.: AEI Press. Pp. 15–54.

Richmond, Anthony
1989   Resettlement: Refugees and Racism in Canada. Paper presented at the Refugee Crisis: British and Canadian Responses, University of Oxford. Mimeo.

Roberts, Barbara
1988   *Whence They Came: Deportation from Canada, 1900–1935.* Ottawa: University of Ottawa Press.

Robinson, W. G.
1983a   *Illegal Immigrants: Issues Paper.* Hull, Quebec: Employment and Immigration Canada.
1983b   *A Report to the Honourable Lloyd Axworthy, Minister of Employment and Immigration, on Illegal Migrants in Canada.* Ottawa, Ontario: Employment and Immigration Canada.

Sedgwick, Joseph
1965–1966   *The Sedgwick Report.* 2 parts. Ottawa: Department of Citizenship and Immigration.

Special Joint Committee of the Senate and House of Commons on Immigration Policy
1975   *Report to Parliament by the Special Joint Committee in Immigration Policy.* Ottawa: Queen's Printer.

Stastny, C., and G. Tyrnauer
1989   Canada as a "Sanctuary"? Paper presented at the Refugee Crisis: British and Canadian Responses, University of Oxford.

Statistics Canada
1998   Immigrant Population by Place of Birth . . . for Canada, 1996 . . . [Web Page]. Available at *www.statscan.ca/english/census96/nov4/imm2a.htm*.

Statistics Canada, *The Daily*
1998   1996 Census: Ethnic Origin, Visible Minorities [Web Page]. Available at *www. statscan.ca/Daily/english/980217/d980217.htm*.

Suárez-Orozco, Marcello
1994   Belgium and Its Immigrant Minorities. In *Controlling Immigration: A Global Perspective.* Edited by Wayne Cornelius, Philip Martin, and James Hollifield. Stanford: Stanford University Press. Pp. 237–268.

Swan, Neil M., and the Economic Council of Canada
1991   *Economic and Social Impacts of Immigration: A Research Report*. Ottawa: Economic Council of Canada.

Tienhaara, Nancy
1974   *Canadian Views on Immigration and Population: An Analysis of Post-War Gallup Polls*. Ottawa: Department of Manpower and Immigration.

Troper, Harold M.
1972   *Only Farmers Need Apply: Official Canadian Government Encouragement of Immigration from the United States, 1856–1911*. Toronto: Griffin House.

van Dijk, T. A.
1988   Semantics of a Press Panic: The Tamil "Invasion." *European Journal of Communications* 3: 167–187.

Voutira, E.
1998   Post-Soviet Diaspora Politics: The Case of Soviet Greeks. Unpublished abstract.

Zolberg, A., A. Suhrke, and S. Aguayo
1989   *Escape from Violence: Conflict and the Refugee Crisis in the Developing World*. New York: Oxford University Press.

Zucker, Norman, and Naomi Zucker
1991   The 1980 Refugee Act: A 1990 Perspective. In *Refugee Policy: Canada and the United States*. Edited by Howard Adelman. Toronto: York Lanes Press. Pp. 224–252.

19

Illegal Immigration in Europe: Balancing National and European Union Issues

Deborah R. Altamirano

Immigration is one of the most complex, divisive, and ultimately compelling issues facing the European Union and its member states today. In the past twenty years, global trends have created major shifts in population flows worldwide, resulting in the emergence of Europe as a major destination for migrants, refugees, and asylum-seekers.[1] Many of these are undocumented. European governments, caught unprepared to handle this rapid influx of immigrants, have been frantically revising or, in many cases, devising policies to control the flow of migrants across their borders. This chapter addresses these general European problems and then deals in more detail with two countries that are currently grappling with these issues: Greece and Italy. Both countries were traditionally "migrant-sending" countries with extensive diasporas. In the past twenty years, however, both countries have become hosts to large foreign immigrant populations and are now trying to forge their own immigration policies within the framework of the European Union.

IMMIGRATION TO EUROPE: AN OVERVIEW

Several issues dominate the discourse on immigration in Europe. First, while European governments are making efforts to restrict the flow of immigrants by tightening the controls at external borders, countries—within the European framework—are implementing parallel policies to remove internal border controls to facilitate the flow of people, goods, and services across the borders of the participating member states. This conflict thus complicates an already complicated situation.

Second, the creation of the European Union not only entails the economic integration among the member states but also fosters a shared "European identity" that embraces the common history and values among "Europeans" while emphasizing the differences between "Europeans" and "others." The most visible "others" in the current European context are immigrants, most of whom are from non-European origins (Cole 1997: 3). What impact will the efforts to create a "Pan-European identity" have on the reception and treatment of these new immigrants who are now entering the region at the rate of 2 million a year?

Third, the overall goals of the European Union are often in conflict with the national interests. How will the individual member states balance their national interests with European Union objectives, and how might these conflicts become apparent in creation of immigration policy? The challenge for the European Union and its member states is to implement enforceable immigration policies in accordance with the overall goals of the European Union (which are in compliance with the human rights issues put forth in the Geneva Pact of 1951) that are also responsive to the national interests of individual member states.

Immigration to Europe was not a major concern for European governments until the last half of the twentieth century. Throughout the nineteenth and early twentieth centuries, large numbers of Europeans left their countries and emigrated to the "settler societies" of the United States, Canada, Australia, and New Zealand (Freeman 1995; Brinker-Gabler and Smith 1997). During the 1950s and 1960s, immigration occurred primarily within Europe as people from the poorer areas in Southern Europe emigrated to the wealthier areas in the north and west (Boissevain 1994: 47).

The end of World War II and the collapse of colonial empires coincided with a change in the flow of emigration. Western European countries, such as Germany, Sweden, Belgium, France, Britain, and the Netherlands, were trying to rebuild after the war. However, their aging populations, low birthrates, and the loss of a large percentage of their workforce to war and emigration had greatly reduced the available labor force. European governments solved this problem by recruiting labor migrants primarily from Southern Europe but also from former colonial countries, Eastern Europe, and Turkey. Many of the labor migrants arrived in Western Europe as part of sponsored work programs. However, once the migration links between sender and receiver countries were established, many of the unskilled jobs in the informal economy were filled by illegal immigrants (Kushnick 1995: 184). These initial immigrants were joined by asylum seekers, the majority of whom went to Germany because of its very liberal postwar asylum policy.

The intention on the part of the host nations was that these labor migrants would be temporary and that once the need for their labor ceased, they would return home to their countries of origin. According to Freeman (1995), there was never a political or social consciousness that these labor migrants would become permanent residents, much less seek citizenship in their host countries. In other words, most European governments did not envision their countries as "countries of immigration" in which enclaves of resident foreigners would exist among the native populations, creating a multicultural, multiethnic society. Europe was already "densely populated." Therefore, labor migrants to Western Europe were not considered "immigrants" in the sense of participating in "nation-building" as they were in other countries of immigration like the United States (Freeman 1995).[2]

Castles and Kosack (1985: 490) estimate that between 1960 and 1970, the number of guest workers in Europe increased from 6 million to 13 million. These labor migrants became a "structural component" in the European labor market, filling low-paid and low-skilled jobs in construction, industry, and the service sector (Brochmann 1993: 106).

The early 1970s ushered in a "new phase" of mass population movements in which the original labor migrants to Western Europe were joined, first, by their families through reunification programs and, second, by the arrival of a new wave of immigrants from all over the world. However, as immigration was beginning to increase into Europe, the economic recession and the oil crisis in the mid-1970s prompted many European countries to impose restrictions on immigration to try to stop the flow of migrants into Europe (Cole 1997: 3; Werner 1994: 162). The restrictions on immigration in the mid-1970s slowed down the pace of immigration, particularly to Germany, Switzerland, and France. But by the late 1970s, immigration, both legal and illegal, began to pick up again. By the early 1980s, immigration was on the rise.

Scholars on immigration in Europe emphasize that the contemporary patterns of immigration must be viewed within a global context in which a number of "push-pull factors" have made Europe a major destination of immigration (Brochmann 1993: 100; Solomos and Wrench 1993). Miller (1994) characterizes the current wave of immigration as the result of a number of global factors that include changing labor markets, industrialization and transnational employment networks, the opening up of Eastern and Central Europe, civil conflict in the former Yugoslavia; and political and economic strife in Albania, the Middle East, North Africa, and sub-Saharan Africa. Europe has continued to be the destination for immigrants from postcolonial societies in the Caribbean, the West Indies, India, and Asia. In addition to labor migrants, large numbers of asylum seekers, especially from Turkey, Iraq, Albania, Africa, Asia, and the former Yugoslavia, have entered the region (Goddard, Llobera, and Shore 1996: 29).

The economic downturn in Europe in the 1970s and throughout the 1980s was accompanied by a rise in the rates of unemployment, especially among European youth. Immigrants began to be perceived by many Europeans not as an integral part of the labor force but rather as a "threat to receiving societies" (Cole 1997: 11) and even the cause for Europe's economic decline (Freeman 1995; Kushnick 1995: 193). Most targeted for anti-immigrant sentiment were the illegal immigrants, who were perceived as taking jobs away from citizens and relying on social services to which they do not contribute. This sentiment prevails. Brochmann (1993: 108) points out that, to a large extent, illegal immigration to Europe was and continues to be perpetuated and sustained by the labor market and by those employers who rely on illegal immigrants as cheap sources of labor to sustain their businesses in times of economic hardship. European governments responded to the "immigrant problem" with renewed efforts to enforce security measures to restrict further immigration, both legal and illegal. But now European governments must implement immigration policies, not just on a national level but also on a supranational level within the framework of the European Union. In fact, the changes in the flow of international immigration have put the immigration issue at the "forefront" of national and EU political agenda (Brochmann 1993: 101).

In 1993, *Migration World Magazine* (vol. 21, no. 4) reported that there were somewhere "in the neighborhood" of 2.8 million illegal immigrants in Western Europe, with new immigrants entering the region at the rate of 1–2 million a year. Cole (1997: 3) points out that the current flow of immigration to Europe is "characterized by more permanent immigrant communities of increasingly non-European origins." He estimates that by 1980, approximately 40 percent of the estimated 16 million immigrants in Western Europe had come from non-European countries; a large portion of these were undocumented.

THE EUROPEAN UNION

The Formation of the European Union

In 1985, a group of ministers representing the Federal Republic of Germany, Belgium, the duchy of Luxembourg, the Netherlands, and France concluded an agreement for the dismantling of internal checks at their common borders. The Schengen Group, as they came to be known, first signed the Schengen Agreement on June 14, 1985. These member states created the agreement outside the framework of the European Community. The agreement was enacted under international law, and not all community members were a party to it (Baldwin-Edwards 1997: 503). After the signing of the Schengen Convention[3] (regarding the application of the agreement) in 1990, other European Community (EC) members adopted the convention, including Italy (November 1990), Spain and Portugal (June 1991), Greece (November 1992), Austria (April 1995), Finland and Sweden (December 1996), and Denmark.[4]

The Schengen Convention included provisions for the control of the external borders of the Schengen area, visa policies and conditions for border crossing, and sanctions against air companies transporting people without proper documents into the Schengen area. It also included criteria for acceptance of asylum applications by member countries and for the mutual exchange of information on asylum seekers with the aim to prevent multiple applications (Baldwin-Edwards 1997: 503).

While Schengen allowed for ease of movement for citizens of the signatory states, the movement of non-Europeans remained problematic (King and Rybaczuk 1993: 203). In order to allow signatory states to retain control over the movement of non-Europeans within their borders, a provision allowed each member state to "take whatever measures they consider necessary" to control the immigration of non-Europeans to their countries and to "combat terrorism, crime, the traffic of drugs and illicit trade," thereby juxtaposing "immigrants with crime, terrorism and drugs" (King and Rybaczuk 1993: 203).

Immigration Policy within the Framework of the European Union

Following the adoption of the Schengen Convention in 1990, the twelve members of the European Community met in Maastricht, the Netherlands, in 1991 to draw up a treaty creating a monetary and political union to take effect in November 1993. The Treaty of Maastricht was signed in November 1992 and ratified on November 1, 1993 by all members of the EC, thereby creating the European Union. The EU[5] represents the union of fifteen member states, the creation of which is to "integrate the economies, coordinate social development, and bring about the political union of Democratic States of Europe" (Shore and Black 1996: 293). McDonald (1997: 219) notes that the creation of the European Union in 1992 brought about the need for a common policy toward immigrants, specifically those from "third countries" (i.e., those outside the boundaries of the EU). The primary concerns regarding immigration within the framework of the European Union are the conditions of entry and movement of immigrants, the conditions of their residence and employment, and the combating of illegal entrance, residence, and employment.

The actual policies that have been proposed or implemented with regard to immigration are extremely complex and often embedded in treaties and agreements that are continuously being revised. Baldwin-Edwards (1997) points out that the early attempts at creating a Pan-European policy were one-sided in the sense that the central concern was in controlling the flow of illegal immigrants and asylum seekers with few stipulations as to the treatment of immigrants and asylum seekers once they crossed the borders of the EU member states. The emphasis has been on preventing illegal immigrants or asylum seekers from ever reaching the borders of the member states and, therefore, according to Baldwin-Edwards (1997: 500), putting the burden of illegal immigration on those countries that border the EU member states. Baldwin-Edwards believes that the emphasis on illegal immigration within the EU policy reflects a presumption that the "phenomenon" of illegal immigration is "necessarily harmful and that the actors are not deserving of rights" (Baldwin-Edwards 1997: 500). This attitude, he finds, is even more evident in precursor organizations, the TREVI group and the Ad Hoc Group on Immigration. The TREVI group, formed in 1976, was composed of a group of interior ministers and charged with "interdiction of terrorism, radicalism, extremism, violence, and immigration" (Kushnick 1995: 187).[6] The Ad Hoc Group on Immigration was formed in 1986 in order to establish guidelines to curb the "threat" of illegal immigrants, to monitor the applications and entrance of asylum seekers, and to prevent the immigration of criminals (Baldwin-Edwards 1997: 498).

One major concern of the European Union is that the enforcement of any European Union-wide immigration policy will be possible only if the member states are able to control the flow of illegal immigrants and asylum seekers at their respective borders. While immigration has been a major concern throughout the creation of the European Union, it was not formalized in an explicit policy in the European Union treaties until the revision of the Maastricht Treaty in 1996, which resulted in the Treaty of Amsterdam (Baldwin-Edwards 1997: 498). The current state of immigration policy within the framework of the European Union is outlined in this treaty.

Immigration Policy under the Treaty of Amsterdam

The Treaty of Amsterdam was written in June 1997 and signed by the EU member states on September 21, 1997. The four main objectives as outlined in the Treaty of Amsterdam include the concern for citizens' rights and employment, the removal of the final obstacles to security and freedom of movement within the union, the increase of Europe's role in world affairs, and the strengthening of the institutional structure within the union, making way for possibly increasing the union in the future. Within five years of the signing of the Amsterdam Treaty, the Council of Ministers is to adopt measures that will assure the "free movement of persons and the absence of any controls on people, be they citizens of the Union or nationals of non-member countries, when crossing borders between the EU Member States."[7] This means that countries bordering the EU will have to increase the security at their borders so that the checks within the borders may be relaxed or removed. Therefore, the governments of countries that border the European Union have agreed to "joint measures in the fields of asylum, immigration, and controls at the Union's external borders" ("The Treaty of Amsterdam: A Comprehensive Guide").[8] In short, the Treaty of Amsterdam puts forth an agenda for the creation and implementation of a common EU policy regarding control of entry into the union and, in particular, the control of the movement of immigrants and those seeking asylum within the bounds of the European Union.[9]

This EU-wide policy entails a standardized procedure for the issuing of visas for residents of nonmember states (this includes a list of those nonmembers that require visas to enter the union and those from nonmember countries that are exempt from visa requirements). With specific regard to refugees and asylum seekers, the Treaty of Amsterdam outlines procedures in compliance with the Dublin Convention[10] for determining the member state responsible for reviewing asylum applications and the procedure for granting or denying refugee status. The Amsterdam Treaty also puts forth procedures for the control of illegal immigration and illegal residence and for the repatriation of illegal residents (see

Baldwin-Edwards 1997: 504–505). Thus, with the implementation of the policies put forth in the Amsterdam Treaty, the procedure for dealing with immigration, illegal immigration, and asylum applications will be streamlined and "harmonized" throughout the European Union. At the same time, while movement within the union and the control of external borders are outlined in the Treaty of Amsterdam, the granting of citizenship is left up to the determination of each member state.

Along with the stipulations regarding control of movement within the EU and the control of the external borders of the union, the Treaty of Amsterdam also puts forth statements regarding the creation of a "Citizens' Europe" and the promotion of a Pan-European identity. Many scholars (see Castles and Miller 1993; Kushnick 1995; MacDonald 1997; Mandel 1996) suggest that the fostering of a "Pan-European identity" may have greatest impact on immigration policy and the treatment of immigrants within the European Union.

The Construction of a "Pan-European Identity" and Its Implications for Immigrants

According to Article 8 of the Treaty of Amsterdam, a citizen of an EU member state is also a citizen of the European Union (Shore and Black 1996: 281). Therefore, individuals maintain their national citizenship while being incorporated into a citizenry of a broader, more inclusive "United Europe." The Amsterdam Treaty also promotes a mutual respect between all citizens of the union and calls on union members to celebrate the cultural diversity within the union. Article 128(1) states that the "Community shall contribute to the flowering of the culture of the Member States, while respecting their regional diversity and at the same time bringing their common cultural heritage to the fore" (see Shore and Black 1996: 284). This goal would be furthered by cultural exchanges and by the creation of new symbols of "Europeanness" (Adonnino 1985: 29–30). Symbols of Europeanness would include European passports, driver's licenses, a European anthem and flag, and Pan-European celebrations (Shore and Black 1996: 286).

In addition to provisions celebrating European unity and diversity, there are provisions within the Treaty of Amsterdam (outlined in Article 6A) to combat discrimination, racism, and xenophobia (Baldwin-Edwards 1997: 504). However, it is unclear if these provisions are meant to cover discrimination against citizens from "third countries" (be they legal residents or illegal immigrants) as well as citizens of the EU (Baldwin-Edwards 1997: 504). Several scholars of Europe (see Bossevain 1994; Castles and Miller 1993; Kushnick 1995; McDonald 1997; Shore and Black 1996) are concerned that the emphasis on a common European identity will result in the construction of barriers between those who are and those who are not "European" and that these divisions will become manifest in policies, attitudes, and treatment toward non-European immigrants.

In order to construct a common cultural identity, Shore and Black (1996: 294) suggest that the European council must emphasize the common "values and virtues" and common heritage that all Europeans supposedly share. They go on to point out that although fostering cultural diversity is one of the goals put forth in the Treaty of Amsterdam, the creation of a shared European identity necessarily emphasizes cultural sameness rather than diversity. They warn (1996: 296) that the emphasis on a shared European cultural heritage may fuel intense nationalism and xenophobia and foster a "new form of Euro-racism" or "White Continentalism." That is, in fact, what Kushnick (1995: 183) sees occurring. He finds that the construction of a "new European identity" is being created "along predominantly racial lines" and that this emphasis on race is reflected in the EU policies governing criminal justice, housing, and immigration. The danger in constructing a "European consciousness" in this way is that, lacking real areas of shared cultural heritage around which Europeans may unite, the one area in which they may find a common basis is against immigrants who are not European (Castles and Miller 1993: 26). In France, for example, anti-immigrant passion was fueled by Jean Marie Le Pen's National Front when Le Pen portrayed immigrants in France as a threat to European cultural identity (Cole 1997: 11; Kushnick 1995: 189). The reunification of Germany in 1990 was followed by increased violence by East German youth toward foreign migrant laborers, especially Turks, whom they perceived as a threat to their own economic viability. According to Mandel (1996: 113–124), East Germans, who had previously lived in a homogeneous society, were unprepared to deal with a competitive capitalist economic system and a multiethnic society. As with France's Le Pen, far right-wing groups characterize foreigners as a threat to "Germanness" and have demanded their expulsion from Germany (Mandel 1996: 118).

In 1993, Germany adopted one of the most restrictive immigration policies in Europe (*Migration World Magazine* 1993). In addition to implementing a restrictive immigration policy, the German government has revised Article 16 of the German Constitution regarding asylum. Today, Germany grants few asylum requests, and, in accordance with the Dublin Convention, unsuccessful asylum seekers may be sent back to the country in which they first entered the European Union.

IMMIGRATION TO SOUTHERN EUROPE

With immigration to Western and Northern Europe becoming more restrictive, Southern Europe has emerged as a major destination for immigrants, refugees, and asylum seekers. By 1980, immigrants from Africa, Asia, and the Middle East began to enter Southern Europe in search of work (King and Rybaczuk 1993: 177). After 1989, these new immigrants were joined by Eastern Europeans and those escaping the civil strife in the former Yugoslavia, Albania, and other areas of the Balkans. King and Rybaczuk (1993: 175–206) attribute the rapid

influx of immigrants to Europe to a number of causes, including the rapid economic growth in Southern Europe, lax immigration controls and tourism, which
created "ease of entry," and the development of a large, informal economic
sector largely supported by illegal foreign workers. The rapid increase in immigrants into Southern Europe was unpredicted, and most countries had few
policies in force to deal with their immigrant populations (Freeman 1995; King
and Rybaczuk 1993). As former "migrant-sending" countries, Spain and Italy
did not have procedures in place to deal with the rapid influx of refugees and
began to implement immigration policies in the 1980s. Spain implemented its
first comprehensive immigration law in 1985, Italy in 1986, and Greece not until
after 1990 (Baldwin-Edwards 1997).

The goal of the European Union, to remove completely the internal borders
within the member states, has put great pressure on those member states that
comprise the external border of the union, particularly in Southern Europe.
Greece and Italy, for example, have become "hot spots" of immigration in the
Mediterranean (Emke-Poulopoulos 1991) and are under pressure from the European Union to control their borders and thus prevent the entrance of illegal
immigrants into the European Union.

CASE STUDIES

Immigration to Greece

In Greece today, it is almost impossible to walk down a street, turn on the
television, or listen to the radio without being aware of the "immigrant issue."
Almost daily, public forums in the newspapers and on television discuss and
debate issues dealing with Greece's expanding foreign population. Discussions
of racism and discrimination, human rights, and social and economic issues as
they relate to the immigrant population are constantly at the forefront of popular
discourse.

These new immigrants present a challenge for Greece. On one hand, Greeks
have firsthand experience with the plight of the immigrant—Greeks have a long
emigrant history—and this is not the first time Greece has accommodated a new
population. In 1922, the country absorbed approximately 1.2 million ethnic
Greek refugees from Asia Minor. Furthermore, Greeks have always had extensive contact with foreigners through their shipping and tourist industries. In fact,
every summer Greece is inundated with millions of tourists. There have always
been small clusters of foreigners living in Greece, mainly other Europeans but
also Americans, Africans, Arabs, and a growing Asian population. There have
always been a small number of ethnic minority populations in Greece, such as
the Muslim communities in Western Thrace and the Gypsy communities. Yet
only within the past twenty years has Greece had to deal with an expanding
foreign immigrant population. How will Greece respond to the challenge of
transforming from a "region of mass emigration to one of mass immigration"

(King and Rybaczuk 1993: 176)? How will Greece confront the challenge of becoming increasingly multiethnic and culturally diverse? At a time when other host countries are passing increasingly restrictive immigrant laws, how will Greece respond to issues regarding immigrant access to employment, health care, and social services? What are the social-cultural factors that will guide Greece's immigrant policy?

Greece as a Migrant Receiving Country

Immigration has long been a part of Greek heritage. The Greek diaspora is one of the most extensive in the world. By 1910, approximately one-quarter to one-fifth of Greece's total labor force had emigrated—over 183,000—to the United States alone (Kessner and Caroli 1982: 263). Between 1951 and 1972, over 1.2 million Greeks had emigrated.

Now the flow of emigration has changed. In 1980, Greece was recognized by the United Nations as a country of immigration as well as emigration. By 1989 the UN high commissioner for refugees estimated that there were between 60,000 and 100,000 illegal immigrants in Greece (Emke-Poulopoulos 1991: 8). Currently, the Greek Ministry of Labor estimates that there are over 1 million immigrants in the country, over half of whom are undocumented (Davanelos 1998). Among the immigrants entering the country are ethnic Greeks from Albania and the former Soviet Union. It is estimated that over 40,000 Pontian Greeks have migrated to Greece from the former Soviet Union and continue to migrate at the rate of 10,000 to 15,000 per year (Emke-Poulopoulos 1991: 6).

The majority of immigrants to Greece, however, are labor migrants from Albania, Poland, Egypt, Russia, Ethiopia, India, Pakistan, Vietnam, and the Philippines. In fact, in some of the rural areas, it is estimated that illegal immigrants constitute approximately 30 percent of the local workforce. An economist with whom I spoke saw this as a positive force—attributing to the immigrant workforce the recent 2 percent rise in gross national product (GNP).[11] Some economists warn against repatriating the underground workforce, as it could result in an economic downfall. Typically, immigrants are employed in agricultural labor, in manufacturing, construction, fishing, and shipping, and in hotel and domestic work (King and Rybaczuk 1993: 194).

Although many immigrants do plan to repatriate, preliminary research indicates that approximately 27 percent of the illegal workforce has decided to remain permanently in Greece (Davanelos 1998). "Elena," for example, arrived in Greece from Poland almost six years ago, accompanied by her husband and thirteen-year-old son, "Jan." They all sought work in a village on one of the Kykladic Islands, where they knew other immigrants from Poland with whom they could stay until they could get their feet on the ground. Neither Elena nor her son or husband had work permits. Elena quickly found work as a domestic, cleaning the homes and shops of Greek and foreign residents in the village. Her husband and son found jobs working in construction. Their plan was to stay in

Greece for five years. They felt that would be long enough for the economy to stabilize in Poland and for them to save enough money to put down on an apartment when they returned home. But a year after they arrived in Greece, Elena's husband was hit by a car and killed while driving home one night on his motorcycle. Devastated by this turn of events, their plans changed. Elena and Jan would stay in Greece permanently. The new plan was that when Jan turned eighteen years old, he would join the Greek military. His military service would then make him eligible for Greek citizenship. Once he acquired citizenship, he could support his mother until she could get a legal work permit through him. It was a good plan except that when Jan was seventeen years old, just a few months before he was to go into the military, he became very ill and was diagnosed with diabetes. Physically, Jan will be fine as long as he watches his diet and stays on his medication. However, because of his medical condition, he is no longer eligible to join the Greek military. A Greek woman for whom "Elena" works was very concerned about Jan's and Elena's future. Jan, she explained, was a wonderful, hardworking, good-looking young man. He was very well regarded in the village and had the reputation of being a very good worker. But, a Greek friend explained, Jan will have a hard time. He is uneducated (he hasn't attended school since he left Poland at age thirteen), has no work permit, and has a medical condition. There are very few young Polish women on the island, and, given Jan's situation, she predicted he would have a hard time finding a Greek wife. That was in the fall of 1996.

As of January 1, 1998, the situation for illegal immigrants changed. A presidential decree allowed the regularization of illegal workers who had entered the country prior to December 31, 1997. In order to obtain a legal work permit, an applicant must go to the local Manpower and Employment Organization and submit his or her name, home and work address, and verification of good health. An applicant must also prove that he or she is not "persona non grata" in Greece or have any criminal charges pending. Immigrants are then issued a temporary "white card" with which they may legally reside and work in Greece. The second phase of the legalization process began in July 1998. Immigrants who can prove that they have forty days' worth of salary between January 1, 1998, and June 1, 1998, are eligible to receive a "green card." The green card is valid for one to three years with the possibility of renewal. Immigrants with green cards will have access to the same health care, education, social services, and pension plan as any Greek national. This regularization process has widespread support, including that of the Greek trade unions. In fact, the General Confederation of Greek Workers (GSEE), the largest union, is pressing the government to simplify the regularization process even more.

From the Greek perspective, the new regularization process paves the way for new immigrants to be assimilated into the Greek labor force and "into Greek society in general" (Davanelos 1998). Labor minister Miltiades Papaioannou stated that he considered the new law to be "one of the most progressive of its kind in Europe" (Davanelos 1998). The regularization process did not go as smoothly as hoped. The requirements for health documents strained the resources of designated hospitals and health practitioners to provide all the necessary examinations and test results. Designated police departments were overwhelmed by the number of immigrants seeking security checks. Employers were reluctant to provide documentation regarding length of employment since regularization would require employers to pay into the Social Security accounts of their employees and thereby make hiring regularized immigrants more expensive than hiring illegal immigrants. As of May 1, 1998, the unofficial number of immigrants who had submitted applications for regularization was 270,000.[12]

Anti-Immigrant Response

The Greek government, with the backing of the workers' unions, student groups, and antiracist organizations, has been implementing what it considers a progressive immigrant policy within the framework of the United Nations. Despite the support of immigrants from many of the public and the labor unions, there has been some anti-immigrant sentiment directed primarily at Albanians. Between 1991 and 1995, Greece reportedly spent over 6 billion drachmas (roughly $21.5 million) deporting over 1 million Albanians. However, the police reported that the deportations were of little deterrent value. Due to the problems of securing the mountainous border that Greece shares with Albania, as soon as deportees are dropped off at the border, they come right back into Greece.

Albanians have also been associated with the rise in crime in Greece. The Athens News Agency (ANA, January 28, 1998) reported that the increase in the number of illegal immigrants coincided with a 40 percent increase in certain categories of crimes, such as burglaries and armed robberies—the latter a rare occurrence in Greece. As a result of the rising crime figures, the minister of public order boosted police patrols in the hardest-hit areas of Athens and increased border patrols. But the minister emphasized that the new measure should ''by no means be construed as a generalized drive against immigrants'' (Athens News Agency [hereafter ANA], March 28, 1998).

When one community council allegedly imposed its own dusk-to-dawn curfew for immigrants working in the region, the newspapers condemned the action. The prefecture police declared the actions taken by the council illegal and unwarranted. Furthermore, a government spokesman condemned the move which he characterized as the result of ''racism and xenophobia'' (ANA, March 29, 1998).

While Greeks are victimized by crimes allegedly perpetrated against them by immigrants, immigrants have been victims of crime as well. An Albanian worker explained one problem to me. Prior to February 1997, illegal immigrants were not allowed to open bank accounts. Therefore, whatever money or valuables they acquired were kept in their homes, thereby making them easy targets for thieves. This worker went on to explain that Greek police patrols would often raid a house known to be rented by illegal Abanian workers. The Albanians would be loaded up in vans and deported back to the Albanian border. Meanwhile, their homes would be searched by the authorities, and all money and valuables hidden in the house would disappear. The Albanians would have no recourse. In February 1997, in response to this problem, the Bank of Greece lifted its restrictions prohibiting illegal immigrants from "opening and holding bank accounts" (ANA, January 17, 1998). Illegal immigrants may open an account with proof of identity (by showing a passport), but they do not need to prove legal status in Greece. According to a spokesman for the Bank of Greece, liberalizing the banking services to more than .5 million immigrants provides safety for those who have been subjected to criminal activities (ANA, January 17, 1998). Furthermore, the funds submitted by the immigrants will increase the bank resources "with a favorable impact on the Greek economy" (ANA, January 17, 1998).

The direction of Greece's immigrant policy still seems to be in flux as Greece confronts the challenges of incorporating a large foreign population into its legal and economic systems. Like Greece, Italy is also experiencing a similar influx of immigrants.

Immigration to Italy

Until the early 1970s Italy was a country of emigration—between 1876 and 1965 roughly twenty-five million Italians emigrated to other countries (Vasta 1993: 83–84). In the 1950s and 1960s, there were also migratory shifts within Italy, with southern Italians emigrating to the north in search of work. By the early 1970s, migration patterns started to change. Labor migrants from Africa and Asia began to immigrate to Italy at the same time that Italians from abroad began to repatriate. By the mid-1970s more people had immigrated *to* Italy than had emigrated out.

Similar to Greece, Italy initially served as a temporary stopover for immigrants on their way to the wealthier countries in Northern and Western Europe. But when the other European countries began to restrict immigration in the 1970s, Italy, with no comprehensive immigration policy in place, became the destination country for hundreds of thousands of immigrants (Lecchini and Barsotti 1991). According to Cole (1997: 4) by the early 1980s Italy was host to immigrants representing more than two dozen nationalities. In 1989, the total number of foreign immigrants in Italy was estimated at over 1 million (Lecchini and Barsotti 1991: 72; Cole 1997: 4). By 1990, King (1993b: 283) reports that Italy had replaced Germany as Europe's largest recipient of mass immigration. The number of illegal immigrants is roughly estimated at between 100,000 and 420,000 (Montanari and Cortese 1993: 290; Vasta 1993: 86).

Today labor migrants to Italy are from Tunisia, Morocco, Egypt, Senegal, Ethiopia, China, Iran, Poland, Latin America, and the Philippines. Most find low-paying, unskilled jobs in the informal sector. In the coastal and rural areas, immigrants work in the fishing industry and in agriculture. Others immigrate to the industrialized areas and find work in small businesses, in shops and work-shops, in tourism, sales, and construction (Lecchini and Barsotti 1991: 81). The majority of the labor migrants are male, but there are women migrants who find work in the service sector and as domestics and health care providers in middle- and upper-class Italian homes.

Overview of Immigration Policy in Italy

Italy did not have an immigration policy per se prior to 1986. Rather, control of borders and immigration was under the purview of the police (Freeman 1995). In 1986, in an attempt to comply with the 1985 Schengen Agreement, Italy passed Law #943, which was designed to "protect" the national labor market from uncontrolled immigration (Lecchini and Barsotti 1991: 71). At the same time, Italy offered amnesty to all foreigners in an attempt to legalize those immigrants who were already living and working in the country (King and Rybaczuk 1993: 186). However, the response to the amnesty offer was unex-pectedly low. According to Vasta (1993: 88), only about 14 percent of the estimated illegal immigrants applied for regularization. She points out that (as in Greece) immigrants had a hard time collecting all of the official documents needed to prove their eligibility (1993: 88). Furthermore, the process required that illegal immigrants present themselves at the police department—this served as a powerful deterrent. By 1988, it was clear to the Italian government that immigration was a growing national concern. About the same time there were increased expressions of xenophobia by some sectors of the Italian public. In response, antiracist organizations and immigrant associations began to form, and immigration became a central focus of social science research (Cole 1997: 5–6).

In 1990, under pressure to control their borders in accordance with the Schen-gen Agreement, Italy passed Law #39, known as the "Martelli law." In short, this law stipulated government policy toward the entrance, residence, and reg-ularization of illegal immigrants, including regulations aimed at the employers of illegal immigrants. The law provided guidelines governing the expulsion of illegal immigrants who commit crimes and outlined the legal working conditions for immigrants. Furthermore, the law expanded the geographical limits set by the 1951 Geneva Convention so that it applied to refugees from non-European countries (Vasta 1993: 88). According to Cole (1997: 6–8), the Martelli law represents Italy's "first comprehensive legislation regulating resident foreign-ers" and brings Italy "into conformity with the laws of other EU member States." Under the Martelli law immigrants who were residents in the country prior to 1989 could legalize their status. Furthermore, the law provides for the human rights of immigrants. However, the law is restrictive in that it bars the entry of new immigrants until "further laborers are deemed necessary" (Cole 1997: 8).

More immigrants have legalized their status under the Martelli law than under the previous regularization periods (Cole 1997: 15). However, Italian immigration law still does not reflect or address fully the complexities involving illegal immigrants, asylum seekers, and refugees (Lecchini and Barsotti 1991: 89–91; Vasta 1993).

Attitudes Toward Immigrants

As in Greece, immigrants in Italy have found strong support among some sectors of the Italian population and have confronted opposition and hostility from others. Some see the immigrants as making a vital contribution to the Italian economy and support attempts to regularize workers and improve immigrants' working and living conditions. Church organizations have been particularly active on the immigrants' behalf, providing initial services and disseminating information to immigrants upon their arrival. In addition, a number of organizations have been created to combat racism and xenophobia directed at immigrants, such as SOS Racism, a youth organization with counterparts in France, Greece, and other European countries.

Although they have enjoyed some strong support, immigrants have been victims of anti-immigrant hostility as well. Some sectors of the Italian population regard the immigrants, especially non-European immigrants, as a threat to the economy and to the "Europeanness" of Italian culture. Interestingly, most of the anti-immigrant sentiment is centered in northern Italy, which has been much less impacted by immigration than southern Italy (Cole 1997). In the north, foreign immigrants have been equated with immigrants from southern Italy, who have long been regarded by many northern Italians as an economic drain on the north as well as culturally inferior. In fact, most overt acts of hostility have been directed at immigrants from Africa and Asia or those considered by anti-immigrant groups as too culturally and racially different to be absorbed into Italian society (Cole 1997: 15–16).

Despite the fact that many immigrants have decided to remain permanently in Italy, many Italians still regard their immigrant populations as temporary (Lecchini and Barsotti 1991: 72). Consequently, although there has been concern for the well-being of the immigrants in general, there has been little concern, especially on the part of the government, for the long-term economic, social, and cultural integration of new immigrants into Italian society (Vasta 1993: 97–98). Vasta (1993: 98) suggests that Italy's reluctance to establish a clear immigrant policy may be due, in part, to the government's concern that a clear immigration policy would exacerbate the situation even further by encouraging more migrants to choose Italy as their destination. In the future, Vasta (1993: 98) suggests that until a clear policy is implemented, immigrants will continue to be treated arbitrarily and that any problems experienced by the immigrants will be blamed on the immigrants themselves.

CONCLUSIONS

In Greece and Italy many complex factors influence the reception and treatment of immigrants, both documented and undocumented. Although Greece may look to the European Union for guidance in developing its immigration policy, in contrast to Italy, it appears to be moving toward a more open, inclusive policy directed toward integrating immigrants into the Greek economy and Greek society. Italy, in adopting the more restrictive Martelli law, seems to be developing a policy more in line with its Western European Union neighbors. Both, however, reflect the potential conflict between European Union issues and member state interests. For the most part, Freeman (1995: 893) sees the member states embracing an "ambiguous mix of inclusive (state) and exclusive (EU) measures." The extent to which Greece and Italy will be able to comply with the stipulations put forth in the EU treaties is yet to be seen. However, given their respective socioeconomic structures and geographical locations, it appears that the "balance" between their respective national interests and the supranational objectives of the EU will be delicate indeed.

Both countries are under pressure to increase security at their borders to control the flow of people and prevent illegal immigration into the EU area. This is extremely difficult for a number of reasons. First, the borders of Greece and Italy include long, rugged coastlines, islands, and mountains, making these borders difficult, if not impossible, to secure. Second, both Greece and Italy rely on tourism to support their national economies. Therefore, they must retain open borders to facilitate the movement of tourists into and out of their countries. However, tourism provides an open door for illegal immigration in the form of visa-overstays (King and Rybaczuk 1993: 185). Third, Greece and Italy have well-developed, informal economies that rely on the cheap, unskilled labor provided by illegal immigrants. The revenue generated from the informal sector contributes 15–30 percent to their respective gross domestic products (GDPs) (Baldwin-Edwards 1997: 508). In this respect, illegal immigration is a benefit to the host society, and there will be little incentive to curb it.

In the future, as their immigrant communities become more established, both Greece and Italy will have to adjust their policies to address issues such as family reunification, citizenship, ethnic and cultural diversity, racism and human rights, and national and ethnic identity. There is little doubt, note King and Rybaczuk (1993: 203), that immigration has become a highly charged political and social issue in Southern Europe in the past few years. It appears it will continue to be so for some years to come.

NOTES

1. The chapter focuses on immigration; however, in the European context policies regarding immigrants, refugees, and asylum-seekers overlap.

2. Freeman (1995) points out that as a result of the Turkish guest worker program

in Germany there are now third- and fourth-generation Turks who have been born and raised in Germany, yet because of Germany's citizenship law based on "blood" rather than birth, few are able to acquire German citizenship.

3. The Schengen Convention may be viewed in its entirety at: http://www.stud.ifi.uio.no/~hennings/schengen/body2.html.

4. The European Union (EU) was preceded by the European Community (EC), which was created in 1957 with the signing of the Treaty of Rome. The initial goal of the EC was to create a political community through social and economic integration. The European Community created the common market to facilitate the ability of goods, services, capital, and labor to cross borders unimpeded. The signatory states were France, the Federal Republic of Germany, Italy, Belgium, the Netherlands, and Luxembourg. The EC was joined by the United Kingdom, Ireland, and Denmark in 1973, Greece in 1981, and Spain and Portugal in 1986. With the passing of the Single European Act of 1986, the stage was set for the formation of the European Union in 1993 (see Werner 1994: 147–164).

5. The fifteen EU member states are Austria, Belgium, Denmark, Finland, France, Germany, Greece, Ireland, Italy, Luxembourg, the Netherlands, Portugal, Spain, Sweden, and the United Kingdom.

6. TREVI is the acronym created by the first letter in each of the following: terrorism, radicalism, extremism, violence, and immigration.

7. Ireland and the United Kingdom did not want to dismantle their internal border checks and therefore did not sign the Schengen Agreement. Norway and Iceland are not members of the European Union but did become signatories of the Schengen Agreement.

8. As stipulated in "The Treaty of Amsterdam: A Comprehensive Guide," which is available on-line at: http://europa.eu.int/abc/obj/amst/en/qu.htm#1.

9. The United Kingdom and Ireland will continue to maintain checks at their borders under the Amsterdam Treaty.

10. The Dublin Convention was adopted in 1990 to determine which country is responsible for determining the status of an asylum application and to provide a system of monitoring the submissions of asylum applicants in order to prevent individuals from submitting multiple and/or "bogus" asylum applications.

11. Parts of this section are based on preliminary research conducted in Greece by the author in October and November 1996.

12. Information on the problems experienced by immigrants in obtaining necessary documents for regularization was obtained through personal communication. The number of immigrant applications submitted for regularization was obtained by the author through personal communication with SOS Racism, an antiracist organization located in Athens that works to protect the rights of immigrants.

REFERENCES

Adonnino, P.
1985   A People's Europe: Reports from the Ad Hoc Committee, Luxembourg, Bulletin of the EC, Supplement No. 7.
Baldwin-Edwards, Martin
1997   The Emerging European Immigration Regime: Some Reflections on Implications for Southern Europe. *Journal of Common Market Studies* 35 (4): 497–519.

Boissevain, Jeremy

1994   Towards an Anthropology of European Communities? In *The Anthropology of Europe: Identities and Boundaries in Conflict.* Edited by Victoria Goddard, Josep R. Llobera, and Cris Shore. Oxford: Berg Press. Pp. 41–56.

Bowser, Benjamin, Editor

1995   *Racism and Anti-Racism in World Perspective.* Thousand Oaks, California: Sage.

Brinker-Gabler, Gisela, and Sidonie Smith

1997   Introduction: Gender, Nation, and Immigration in the New Europe. In *Writing New Identities: Gender, Nation, and Immigration in Contemporary Europe.* Edited by Gisela Brinker-Gabler and Sidonie Smith. Minneapolis: University of Minnesota Press. Pp. 1–27.

Brinker-Gabler, Gisela, and Sidonie Smith, Editors

1997   *Writing New Identities: Gender, Nation, and Immigration in Contemporary Europe.* Minneapolis: University of Minnesota Press.

Brochmann, Grete

1993   Control in Immigration Policies: A Closed Europe in the Making. In *The New Geography of European Migrations.* London and New York: Belhaven Press. Pp. 100–115.

Castles, Stephen, and Godula Kosack

1985   *Immigrant Workers and Class Structure in Western Europe.* Oxford: Oxford University Press.

Castles, Stephen, and Mark J. Miller

1993   *The Age of Migration.* New York: Guilford Press

Cole, Jeffrey

1997   *The New Racism in Europe: A Sicilian Ethnography.* Cambridge: Cambridge University Press.

Davanelos, Antonis

1998   Greece Begins Registration, Legislation of Illegal Immigrants. *Hermes Magazine* (February 1998).

Emke-Poulopoulos, Ira

1991   Immigrants and Refugees in Greece—Statistical Evaluation and Causes of Entry in the Country. In *International Migration to Northern Mediterranean Countries: The Cases of Greece, Spain, and Italy.* Edited by I. Emke-Poulopoulos et al. Report #38. Pisa: Università di Pisa, Dipartimento di Statistica e Matematica Applicata All'economica. Pp. 3–43.

Emke-Poulopoulos, Ira, Vicente Gozàlves Peréz, Laura Lecchini, and Odo Barsotti

1991   *International Migration to Northern Mediterranean Countries: The Cases of Greece, Spain, and Italy.* Report #38. Pisa: Università di Pisa, Dipartimento di Statistica e Matematica Applicata All'economica.

Freeman, Gary

1994   Can Liberal States Control Unwanted Immigration? *Annals of the American Academy of Political and Social Science* 534: 17–30.

1995   Modes of Immigration Politics in Liberal Democratic States. *International Migration Review* 29 (4): 881–903.

Goddard, Victoria A., Josep R. Llobera, and Cris Shore, Editors

1996   *The Anthropology of Europe: Identities and Boundaries in Conflict.* Oxford: Berg Press.

Kessner, Thomas, and Betty Boyd Caroli
1982   *Today's Immigrants, Their Stories: A New Look at the Newest Americans*. Oxford: Oxford University Press.

King, Russell, Editor
1993a *The New Geography of European Migrations*. London and New York: Belhaven Press.
1993b Recent Immigration to Italy: Character, Causes and Consequences. *GeoJournal* 30 (3): 283–292.

King, Russell, and Krysia Rybaczuk
1993   Southern Europe and the International Division of Labour: From Emigration to Immigration. In *The New Geography of European Migrations*. Edited by Russell King. London and New York: Belhaven Press. Pp. 175–206.

Kushnick, Louis
1995   Racism and Anti-Racism in Western Europe. In *Racism and Anti-Racism in World Perspective*. Edited by Benjamin P. Bowser. Thousand Oaks, California: Sage. Pp. 181–202.

Lecchini, Laura, and Odo Barsotti
1991   Jobs, Projects and Migratory Strategies of the Third World Immigrants in Italy. In *International Migration to Northern Mediterranean Countries: The Cases of Greece, Spain, and Italy*. Report #38. Edited by I. Emke-Poulopoulos et al. Pisa: Università di Pisa, Dipartimento di Statistica e Matematica Applicata All'economica. Pp. 71–98.

MacDonald, Sharon, Editor
1997   *Inside European Identities: Ethnography in Western Europe*. Oxford: Berg Press.

Mandel, Ruth
1996   "Fortress Europe" and the Foreigners Within: Germany's Turks. In *The Anthropology of Europe: Identities and Boundaries in Conflict*. Edited by Victoria A. Goddard, Josep R. Llobera, and Cris Shore. Oxford: Berg Press. Pp. 113–124.

McDonald, Maryon
1997   The Construction of Difference. In *Inside European Identities*. Edited by Sharon MacDonald. Oxford: Berg Press. Pp. 219–236

Miller, Mark
1994   Strategies for Immigration Control: An International Comparison. *Annals of the American Academy of Political and Social Science* 534: 8–16.

Montanari, Armando, and Antonio Cortese
1993   Third World Immigrants in Italy. In *Mass Migrations in Europe: The Legacy and the Future*. Edited by Russell King. London: Belhaven Press. Pp. 275–292.

Shore, Cris, and Annabel Black
1996   Citizens' Europe and the Construction of European Identity. In *The Anthropology of Europe: Identities and Boundaries in Conflict*. Edited by Victoria A. Goddard, Josep R. Llobera, and Cris Shore. Oxford: Berg Press. Pp. 275–298.

Solomos, John, and John Wrench
1993   Race and Racism in Contemporary Europe. In *Racism and Migration in Western Europe*. Edited by J. Wrench and J. Solomos. Oxford: Berg Press. Pp. 3–16.

Van Amersfoort, Hans
1997   The Dilemmas of Migration Policy. *Identities: Global Studies in Culture and Power* 4 (1): 149–154.

Vasta, Ellie
1993   Rights and Racism in a New Country of Immigration: The Italian Case. In *Racism and Migration in Western Europe*. Edited by J. Wrench and J. Solomos. Oxford: Berg Press. Pp. 83–98.
Werner, Heinz
1994   Regional Economic Integration and Migration: A European Case. *Annals of the American Academy of Political and Social Science* 534: 147–164.
Wrench, John, and John Solomos, Editors
1993   *Racism and Migration in Western Europe*. Oxford: Berg Press.

20

Illegal Immigration in Asia: Regional Patterns and a Case Study of Nepalese Workers in Japan

Keiko Yamanaka

By the early 1990s Asia had become one of the most active sites of international labor migration in the world. This was primarily due to its rapidly developing economy and the increasing regional integration that resulted in growing economic disparity between a few rich countries and the many poor neighbors in their region. Illegal immigration, a significant contributor to regional economic development, has emerged as a volatile political issue since the late 1980s. The five developed countries with mature economies—Japan, Korea, Taiwan, Hong Kong, and Singapore—currently import labor, whereas the two recent developers, Malaysia and Thailand, import labor and simultaneously export surplus labor.[1] Most neighbors of these seven labor importers in East, Southeast, and South Asia suffer from stagnant economies and large populations and therefore export abundant surplus labor to the former.

By 1998, the dynamics of regional labor exchange were rapidly changing as the recent economic crisis hit most Asian countries. In many countries, such as Korea, Thailand, and Indonesia, much wealth that had been accumulated as a result of people's hard work during the period of prosperity was reduced overnight to a fraction of its former magnitude, and the once-plentiful employment opportunities abruptly disappeared. As a result, immigrant workers who were once welcomed in the labor-importing countries became scapegoats for their frustrated citizens. Conversely, emigration as an alternative means for economic survival appealed even more than before to desperate citizens in the poor, labor-exporting countries. Here I focus on illegal immigration in Asia up to 1997, when the economic crisis began to take a heavy toll of Asia's immigrants. Although the crisis has already exerted enormous impact on regional labor migration and will continue to do so (see *Migration News* 1998), these processes and their consequences are beyond the scope of this discussion.

This chapter comprises two major parts: an overview of regional patterns and a case study of illegal Nepalese workers in Japan. In the first part, following a brief review of economic development, integration, and disparity in Asia, I discuss economic, social, and political causes of regional migration since the 1960s. I then present three models of administrative policies and mechanisms of enforcement for controlling immigrants that have been adopted by the seven labor-importing countries: an "open door policy," a "loose door policy," and a "back door policy."

The second part is a case study of illegal immigration in Japan conducted in the mid-1990s, using a sample drawn from an estimated 3,000 Nepalese visa-overstayers. Although they are few in number and relatively inconspicuous, Nepalese illegal workers exemplify causes, patterns, and processes common to all illegal immigrant populations in Asia. These include integrated, but uneven, economic development within Asia, historical and cultural forces shaping migrants' information networks, increasing participation of women in the global labor force, dual industrial structures entailing chronic labor shortages, and the essential role of illegal workers in local labor markets.

REGIONAL PATTERNS

Economic Development and the Migration Transition

By the mid-1990s, there were five affluent countries with mature economies in Asia. Japan began its heavy industrialization in the early 1950s and by the late 1960s was one of the world's richest countries. Singapore, Hong Kong, Taiwan, and Korea pursued industrialization between the 1960s and the 1980s. These newly industrializing countries adopted liberal trade policies, encouraging labor-intensive manufacturing, attracting large foreign investment, and exposing domestic industries to global market competition. A salient result was full employment leading to higher wages, improved social services, and political stability within these decades (Lim and Abella, 1994; Kuwahara 1998). However, rapidly expanding industrial sectors, such as labor-intensive manufacturing, construction, and services, required massive, inexpensive, unskilled labor. Improved wages, increased occupational mobility, and lowered fertility quickly depleted the pool of domestic labor willing to take low-paid manual labor.

Facing an increasingly tight labor market, particularly in the unskilled sector, the five Asian countries chose a wide range of policies on, and timing of, labor importation. Singapore, which achieved independence in 1965, adopted a policy from the outset of its industrialization to import selected skilled labor and massive unskilled labor, mostly from Malaysia, in order to complement its small labor force (Wong 1997). Since then, the country has been the largest net labor importer in Asia. In the early 1990s, there were 200,000 immigrants, accounting for 13.5 percent of the total labor force, far exceeding the 7,500 Singaporean emigrants to North America and Australia (Wong 1997; Low 1994).[2] In contrast, Japan, with its long history of industrialization and large population, pursued capital-intensive industrialization following the depletion of its surplus labor in the early 1960s. Japan was once a country of immigration and emigration. It imported Korean colonial labor from 1910 until 1945, while exporting its own redundant labor from the 1880s until 1973 (Watanabe 1994). In the post–World War II period until 1990—the year Japan revised its immigration law—the country maintained a policy that excluded unskilled foreign labor from its market. In 1990 the country reluctantly opened its market to the global labor force in order to supplement its aging and dwindling labor pool.

By the early 1990s, Hong Kong, Taiwan, and Korea, formerly labor-exporting countries, had been transformed into major labor-importing countries as a result of their spectacular economic success (Abella 1994; Fields 1994)—success that led them to be frequently referred to as the "East Asian miracle" (World Bank 1993). Until the mid-1980s the three countries officially limited admission to highly specialized professionals crucial for upgrading their economies. In a reverse flow, hundreds of thousands of citizens from these countries went to the Middle East as contract workers and to North America and Australia as permanent settlers. However, the countries also faced labor shortages and by the early 1990s had become net labor importers rather than labor exporters (Skeldon 1994; Tsay 1995; Park 1994).[3] This exemplifies the final stage of the process termed "migration transition," which refers to the transformation of a country from being a net labor supplier elsewhere to being a net labor receiver locally (Abella 1998: 54).

A similar migration transition occurred in the 1980s and 1990s, when Malaysia and Thailand, with their abundant labor forces, underwent rapid industrialization (Vasuprasat 1994). Both countries quickly reached full employment and faced labor shortages in low-skilled and low-paid jobs. By the mid-1990s immigrant workers from poor neighboring countries, both legal and illegal, arrived to replace domestic workers who had moved to more desirable employment. In the meantime, rapid industrial and technological progress created a segment of the population thrown out of work or off their farms who sought employment elsewhere—in metropolitan sectors or foreign countries. Simultaneous, two-way labor migration—importing and exporting—thus characterized Malaysia and Thailand in the mid-1990s until the economic crisis of 1997–1998.

Rich and Growing Economies

The dramatic and prolonged economic progress in the seven Asian countries discussed earlier is clearly demonstrated by various economic and demographic measures shown in Table 20.1. This table classifies twenty Asian countries active in regional labor migration into three stages of migration: (1) labor-importing (Japan, Korea, Taiwan, Hong Kong, and Singapore); (2) simultaneous

Table 20.1

Economic and Demographic Indices of Asian Countries by Status of Global Labor Migration

Labor Migration Status by Country*	1995 GDP (Millions of 1990-dollars) 1	Growth in GDP 1985-1995 [annual %] 1	1995 GDP per Capita (1990-dollars) 1	Growth in GDP Per Capita (%) 1985-1995 1	1996 Population (millions) 2	Pop. Growth 1985-1995 [annual %] 3	1996 Pop. Age < 15 (%) 2	1996 Pop. Urban (%) 2	1996 Infant Mortality Rate 2
LABOR IMPORTING									
Japan	3,127,999	3.0	25,101	2.6	126.1	0.4	16	78	4
South Korea	363,191	8.8	8,087	7.8	45.9	1.0	23	74	11
Taiwan	218,955	7.9	10,268	6.8	21.5	-	24	75	5
Hong Kong	95,619	6.5	15,616	5.3	6.4	1.2	19	-	-
Singapore	52,540	8.2	17,590	6.2	3.5	1.8	23	100	4
LABOR IMPORTING & EXPORTING									
Thailand	127,867	9.4	2,195	8.0	60.1	1.5	30	19	32
Malaysia	64,688	7.7	3,212	5.0	21.0	2.5	36	51	11
LABOR EXPORTING									
China	658,625	9.7	549	8.2	1236.7	1.3	26	29	31
Philippines	51,820	3.4	764	1.2	73.4	2.3	38	47	34
Indonesia	149,015	6.6	755	4.9	204.3	1.8	34	31	66
Vietnam	9,347	5.8	127	3.6	75.1	2.2	40	20	38
Laos	1,201	5.5	246	5.5	5.1	3.0	45	19	102
Cambodia	-	-	-	-	11.2	3.0	46	13	111
Myanmar	32,701	2.0	725	0.2	46.8	2.2	36	25	49
India	376,218	5.2	405	3.3	969.7	2.0	35	26	75
Bangladesh	26,503	4.2	224	2.4	122.2	2.1	42	16	77
Nepal	3,756	4.8	175	2.0	22.6	2.1	42	10	79
Sri Lanka	10,359	4.4	578	3.3	18.7	1.4	35	22	17
Pakistan	48,936	5.1	359	2.0	137.8	3.1	41	28	91
Iran	112,095	1.4	1,640	-1.9	67.5	2.7	44	58	53

Note: Countries are listed by geographic location from east to west in each of the three categories.

Source: 1—UNIDO (1997); 2—Population Research Bureau (1997); 3—United Nationas (1997).

labor-importing and exporting (Thailand and Malaysia); and (3) labor-exporting (China, Philippines, Indonesia, Vietnam, Laos, Cambodia, Myanmar, India, Bangladesh, Nepal, Sri Lanka, Pakistan, and Iran).

During the decade 1985–1995, the average annual growth rate in gross domestic product (GDP) of each of the five labor-importing countries in Asia ranged from 6.5 percent for Hong Kong to 8.8 percent for Korea. Japan's economic growth was comparatively small, 3 percent, during this period, but the country's GDP accounted for 56 percent of the total GDPs of the countries listed in Table 20.1. As a result of such rapid growth, average annual growth rates in GDP per capita of these countries ranged from 2.6 to 7.8 percent, which doubled individual incomes for the decade 1985–1995. The nation with the highest GDP per capita in 1995 was Japan, with U.S. $25,101, followed by Singapore, Hong Kong, Taiwan, and Korea, in that order, with Korea the lowest at U.S. $8,087.[4] Demographic indices of these countries shown in Table 20.1 further demonstrate low population growth, rapidly aging populations, urban concentration, and improved quality of life (measured by the low infant mortality rate).

Malaysia and Thailand, the two countries in the midst of their migration transition, also showed impressive annual growth rates in GDP, 7.7 percent and 9.4 percent, respectively, between 1985 and 1995. The GDP per capita shot up accordingly in each country during the decade, yielding an average annual rate of increase of 5 percent for Malaysia and 8 percent for Thailand. The actual figure for the 1995 GDP per capita was U.S. $3,212 for Malaysia and U.S. $2,195 for Thailand, considerably lower than the GDP figures for the five labor-importing countries—for example, one-fifth to one-third of Taiwan's GDP per capita of U.S. $10,268. Part of these relatively low income figures is explained by the rapid population growth and the low productivity of their agricultural and informal sectors, which coexist with modernized formal sectors in these countries.

Poor and Stagnant Economies

The "labor-exporting" category of Table 20.1 reveals that China and Indonesia experienced rapid economic growth from 1985 to 1995. China, with the largest population in the world, turned to global trade and succeeded in expanding its domestic production by nearly ten percent annually. Similarly, Indonesia, the fourth most populous country in the world, kept up with neighboring Malaysia and Thailand in industrialization with an annual GDP growth rate of nearly seven percent during the decade. As a result, during this prosperous period both China and Indonesia increased the GDP per capita annually by 8.2 percent and 4.9 percent, respectively. Despite their rapid growth rates in GDP per capita, the actual figure for China's 1995 GDP per capita was U.S. $549, and for Indonesia it was U.S. $755, a mere fraction of the GDP per capita received by citizens of the five labor-importing countries.

Other countries in Table 20.1, the Philippines, Vietnam, Laos, Cambodia,

Myanmar, India, Bangladesh, Nepal, Sri Lanka, Pakistan, and Iran, did not achieve the Asian miracle. During the decade between 1985 and 1995, their economies expanded by small margins, with annual GDP increases ranging from 1.4 percent for Iran to 5.8 percent for Vietnam. The economic expansion in these countries, however, scarcely benefited the very large and growing segment of their populations that engaged in subsistence agriculture. As shown by the demographic indices of these countries (Table 20.1), in 1995 the majority of the populations of Vietnam, Laos, Cambodia, India, Bangladesh, Nepal, and Pakistan lived in poverty, with a GDP per capita of less than U.S. $300.[5] A feature of the underdevelopment of these societies is lack of good health care and adequate education for the increasing population of young children. Several of these countries, including Vietnam, Laos, and Cambodia, suffered devastating wars, internal conflicts, revolutions, and social disorganization in the 1970s and 1980s, as a result of which economic recovery was severely delayed, while political uncertainty drove many people to other countries in search of temporary refuge.

In these "poor" Asian countries, including China and Indonesia, unemployment and underemployment were widespread. Under the prolonged economic stagnation they experienced, many individuals and households from all social strata considered migration an attractive alternative to seeking scarce employment in their own countries. According to Abella (1998), such pressure to emigrate tends to increase in countries where fledgling industrialization has yet to absorb their growing labor forces but is nonetheless destructive to subsistence agriculture. Off-farm populations typically move to metropolitan areas, where they form massive urban squatter populations and contribute to the unproductive informal economy. Such societies are often divided rigidly along class lines between the few rich and the many poor. The Philippines and Indonesia, among many other "free market" economies, are examples of countries with high "emigration pressure." China and Vietnam, with "socialist" economies, are confronted with the potential for increased emigration pressure as a result of industrialization and participation in global capitalism (Liu 1995; Abella 1998; Jixuan and Gao 1998).

Rising Regional Migration

Since the late 1970s the Middle East oil fields have provided a convenient solution for those Asian workers seeking foreign employment. In 1991, for example, a wave of labor migration estimated at more than 550,000 flowed westward from India, Pakistan, Bangladesh, and Sri Lanka to take part in large construction projects in oil-rich Arab countries (Shah 1994). Workers from other Asian countries, including Korea, Taiwan, the Philippines, Malaysia, Indonesia, and Thailand, were also drawn to the Middle Eastern construction boom. The vast majority of migrants to the Middle East were unskilled males, but women increasingly joined them as domestic workers for affluent Arab households (Shah, Al-Qudsi, and Shah 1991).

Declining petroleum prices in world markets, together with heightened tensions in the Persian Gulf region, began to drive many immigrant workers out of work in the mid-1980s. Concurrently, the rising Asian economic power of Japan, Singapore, Hong Kong, Taiwan, and Korea generated a massive demand for inexpensive and tractable labor. As a result of their economic success, in 1985 these countries' currencies were revalued sharply upward against U.S. dollars, which drastically widened wage differentials between these countries and their less prosperous neighbors.[6] This policy redirected the flow of many migrants away from the Middle East to the rising economic powers of East and Southeast Asia. Meanwhile, China liberalized its emigration rules in 1985, which added to the pool of Asian migrant workers. By the early 1990s, Asia had become one of the most active international migration sites in the world, with a migrant population estimated at more than 3 million (Skeldon 1992; Stahl and Appleyard 1992; Lim and Abella 1994; Martin, Mason, and Tsay 1995). The restrictions placed on immigration by most Asian countries created barriers to the inflow of foreign labor, which increased the pressure at the gate and led to greater resort to illegal migration, which entailed clandestine labor trafficking (Lohrmann 1987).

Historical, Cultural, and Geographic Proximity

Because international labor migration is an economic activity arising from differentials in labor and wages across national borders (Borjas 1990), literature on international labor migration, particularly in Asia, has defined economic and demographic factors as being of primary relevance to causes and effects of migration (e.g., OECD 1996, 1998). Other important factors, often neglected in economic analyses, include historical and political contexts that have produced unequal patterns of transfer of labor and resources over time (Portes 1978; Sassen 1988; Portes and Böröcz 1989). Throughout the modern period, colonialism, foreign invasions, civil wars, revolutions, and natural disasters have frequently provoked spatial movements of people, either temporary or permanent, in many parts of Asia. In the post–World War II period, migration itself gave birth to a number of nation-states, which revised the regional map of East Asia (e.g., Taiwan), Southeast Asia (e.g., Singapore), and South Asia (e.g., Pakistan and Bangladesh). Moreover, the Cold War significantly influenced regional politics and economy until its demise in 1989, thus affecting national policies concerning emigration and immigration in some countries (e.g., Hong Kong, Taiwan, and Korea).

Such turbulent histories and politics within the region have resulted in extremely heterogeneous populations within and between nation-states often separated only by artificially drawn borders. Singapore, for example, depends heavily on the Malaysian labor force across and within its border, although political and social power resides in the dominant population of people of Chinese descent (Wong 1997). Malaysia shares close ethnic and linguistic ties with its large, but poor, neighbor, Indonesia, whose citizens once freely crossed the Strait of Malacca and the Java Sea to Malaysia for settlement and employment (Hugo 1993). Similarly, Hong Kong has been an integral part of southern Chinese culture and society, receiving hundreds of thousands of refugees at times of political upheaval on the mainland despite the fact that the border had been closed since the 1949 communist revolution (Lui Ting 1987). Korea faces the problem of an estimated 2 million people of Korean descent whose ancestors fled the aftermath of the 1951–1953 Korean War to northeastern China, now seeking better economic opportunities in Korea—their recently wealthy ancestral homeland—often as illegal immigrants (Park 1995). Thailand shares, with poor neighbors Myanmar, Laos, and Cambodia, a long land border cutting across dense jungles and rugged hills, which presents them with the impossible task of controlling widespread illegal immigration (Stern 1996). In each of these examples, geographic proximity reinforces cultural and linguistic ties connecting people across national borders.

Past studies have found that these international historical, cultural, and personal ties play critical roles in international migration because they greatly facilitate entry, employment, and settlement in the host country (Kritz, Lim, and Zlotnik 1992). Such "a complex web of social roles and interpersonal relationships" (Boyd 1989: 639) leads to a rapid development of extensive information networks linking migrants at their destination with one another and with their kinsmen at their place of origin. Once the migrants' networks are established in the host country, they tend to grow into small-scale ethnic communities with their own institutions and enterprises (Castles and Miller 1993: 25). Restrictive immigration policies, fluctuating business cycles, and public opinion hostile to immigrants and ethnic minorities can negatively affect the development of ethnic communities. However, ethnic communities tend to remain resilient and flexible because family and community ties sustain the flow of immigrants into the host country, while growing ethnic enterprises absorb incoming immigrants into the workforce. Until recently, illegal immigration in Asian labor-importing countries rarely became a serious political problem precisely because close ethnic and cultural ties absorbed migrants into the social and economic fabrics of the receiving country (Hugo 1993, 1995).

Immigration Policy and Control

Host governments have tolerated illegal immigration for other important economic reasons as well. Unchecked flows of unskilled foreigners alleviate labor shortages and fuel economic growth in the short run (Pillai 1995). They provide inexpensive, tractable labor much needed by industry to create competitive economic advantage in the global market. In the long run, however, the growing presence of these employees is often perceived as threatening harm to the host country's economy. Immigrant workers, by replacing domestic workers in low-skilled and low-paid jobs, raise the possibility that unemployment rates will rise, ineffective industries will be preserved, and exploitative work conditions will prevail. The growing number of low-paid foreign workers may be thought to contribute to ethnic conflict, rising crime, and disruption of the social fabric of the nation. Their presence is often used by politicians to arouse exaggerated fears not only of negative economic consequences but of threat to national security and sovereignty.

Policymakers, caught in the dilemma between the need to import labor and the consequences of doing so, typically respond in ad hoc fashion. That is, they first permit entry of a small number of unskilled workers to ameliorate an acute labor shortage. Then, as demand for labor increases, they allow greater numbers to enter. Asian governments have, in this process, repeated exactly what their American and European counterparts did in the 1950s and 1960s. By the mid-1990s, however, each of the seven Asian labor-importing countries had arrived at policy decisions regarding principles, legal codes, and contract labor schemes with which to deal with unskilled immigrants. The metaphor of a door is often used in international migration literature in describing a country's immigration policy as symbolic of the permeability of the country's borders to foreigners.[7] The policy decisions of these labor-importing nations reflect the historical experience, political ideology, and population composition of the host country. They can be classified into three distinctive models of principles and mechanisms for control of immigrants. Employing the door metaphor, these can be described as (1) the "front door" policy adopted by Singapore, Hong Kong, and Taiwan; (2) the "loose door" policy maintained by Malaysia and Thailand; and (3) the "back door" policy employed by Japan and Korea.

Here, a country is regarded as having a "front door policy" when it officially makes contract labor programs available to unskilled foreigners who are thereby permitted to enter the country for lawful employment under closely monitored controls. A country has a "loose door policy" when it makes available contract programs for unskilled foreigners but is unable to control its borders (for geographic, cultural, and/or political reasons), with the result that many immigrants are able to enter unnoticed. Finally, a country has a "back door policy" when it officially prohibits all unskilled foreigners from being employed and maintains effective enforcement mechanisms but in practice admits them under artificial "contract labor programs" designed to allow their entry when needed. In the "front door policy" countries, illegal immigration has been sharply curtailed. In the "loose door" and "back door" countries, however, large numbers of illegal immigrants enter, posing serious political and social problems (see Table 20.2).[8]

Front Door Policy. Singapore, Hong Kong, and Taiwan, the three major Asian countries that follow a "front door policy," import unskilled labor through a number of state-run programs for labor-short industries, including

Table 20.2
Unskilled Immigration Policy and Unskilled Immigrant Workers in Seven Labor-Importing Countries in Asia

Policy	Country (Yr)	Industries	Immigration Control	Types of Workers	Estimated N	Source Countries
Front Door	Singapore (1996-97)	Manufacturing, Construction, Domestic Service, Other Service, Marine	The Work Permit Scheme: Levy, Dependency Ceiling, Country of Origin, Industry, Security Bond; Violation: Criminal penalty on workers, employers and recruiters	Contract Workers Illegal Immigrants	350,000 11,400 (arrested)	Malaysia, Indonesia, Thailand, Sri Lanka, India, Bangladesh, Philippines, Myanmar, Hong Kong, Macau, Taiwan, Korea, China Malaysia, Indonesia, Myanmar, Thailand, China,
	Hong Kong (1996-97)	Domestic Service, Construction, Manufacturing, Other Service	Foreign domestic helpers: No quota, No levy; Labor Importation Scheme: No quota, Occupation; Violation: Criminal Penalty on employers	Contract Workers Illegal Immigrants	200,000 20,000	Philippines, Thailand, Indonesia, Malaysia, China China
	Taiwan (1994-95)	Manufacturing, Construction, Nursing & Domestic Service	Country of Origin, Industry, Penalty	Contract Workers Illegal Immigrants	173,000 23,000	Thailand, Philippines, Indonesia, Malaysia Thailand, Malaysia,
Loose Door	Malaysia (1996-97)	Plantation, Construction, Domestic Service, Manufacturing, Other Service	Temporary work pass system: Levy, Dependency Ceiling, Country Origin, Industry, Security Bond; Violation: Stiff penalties on all parties	Contract Workers Illegal Immigrants	700,000 1,000,000	Indonesia, Bangladesh, Thailand, Philippines, Pakistan Indonesia, Bangladesh
	Thailand (1996-97)	Agriculture, Construction, Service, Prostitution	No contract workers but 372,000 illegal workers were regularized in November, 1996.	Regularized Immigrants Illegal Immigrants	372,000 360,000	Myanmar, Laos, Cambodia Myanmar, Laos, Cambodia, Other

Back Door	Japan (1996-97)	Manufacturing, Construction, Service, Entertainment	No contract workers but people of Japanese descent, company trainees, students and entertainers are allowed to engage in unskilled labor. Violation: Criminal penalty on employers	Japanese Descent	200,000	Brazil, Peru, Other
				Company Trainees	20,000	China, Indonesia, Other
				Students	82,000	China
				Entertainers	17,000	Philippines, Thailand
				Illegal Immigrants	284,000	Korea, Philippines, Thailand, China, Peru, Iran, Other
	South Korea (1996-97)	Manufacturing, Construction	No contract workers but company trainees under the Foreign Training Co-operation Corps program can engage in unskilled labor. Violation: Criminal penalty on employers	Company Trainees	66,000	China, Philippines, Bangladesh, Thailand, Pakistan, Vietnam, Other
				Illegal Immigrants	130,000	China, Philippines, Bangladesh, Thailand, Pakistan, Vietnam, Nepal, Other

Source: See text.

manufacturing, construction, marine, and retail and domestic and personal services. By the 1990s all three countries had moved their labor-intensive production to other countries with low labor costs, while upgrading the domestic economy from manufacturing-based to service- and information-based. This industrial restructuring reduced significantly the dependence on foreign labor in manufacturing industries. Foreign workers, mostly from neighboring Asian countries, are still in strong demand by employers in large construction projects, small-scale manufacturing, nursing institutions, and private homes. Because a high proportion of female immigrants work as domestic helpers in the three countries, gender plays an important role in determining patterns of immigration and their employment. Domestic service providers are predominantly from the Philippines but increasingly include those from Thailand and Sri Lanka (Cheng 1996; Constable 1997).

Illegal immigration occurs, albeit small in volume, in these "front door policy" countries, despite stringent enforcement of controls. It most commonly takes the form of overstaying a valid work or tourist visa beyond its expiration (Sullivan, Gunasekaran, and Sununta 1992; Tsay 1992). A legal immigrant can also become illegal by changing an employer without authorization. Employers may violate immigration and labor laws by failing to register their foreign workers in order to evade the payment of expensive levies, security bonds, and other fees required by law. They may also ignore the ceilings set for the maximum proportion of foreign workers allowable by law in each industry ("dependency ceilings"), the purpose of which is to maintain a balance between the immigrant pool and the domestic labor force. Each state imposes criminal penalties on all violators—immigrants, employers, and their intermediaries. Penalties include steep fines, imprisonment, and, in the case of Singapore, three strokes of the cane.

Loose Door Policy.   Malaysia and Thailand, with their porous borders, are home to a large number of illegal immigrants, mostly from culturally similar and geographically adjacent neighbors of Indonesia, in the case of Malaysia, and Myanmar, in the case of Thailand. The Malaysian government permits more than 700,000 contract workers to labor in plantation agriculture, construction sites, manufacturing factories, and private homes. In the remote plantations of both peninsular and east Malaysia, however, illegal immigration is widespread. While accurate statistics are unavailable, it is estimated that they number at least a million. This significantly weakens the Malaysian government's ability to manage its economy. Therefore, the "loose door policy" is actually less a policy than a de facto consequence of the failure of the government to control its borders. Despite considerable monetary and physical risks, Indonesian migrants employ clandestine brokers to arrange illegal entry and employment in Malaysia and Singapore (and the Middle East) (Hugo 1993; Spaan 1994). Small-scale Malaysian employers are inclined to hire illegal immigrants rather than contract workers, because abiding by the law entails going through a bureaucratic quagmire and waiting several months for workers to arrive.

Thailand, whose labor importation began only in the early 1990s, has not yet developed contract labor programs for unskilled foreigners. The lack of legal procedures, together with ineffective border control, has left the country largely defenseless against illegal immigration. The Thai government estimated 525,000 illegal workers in 1994. Two-thirds of the immigrants were Burmese, many of whom were ethnic minorities fleeing persecution by the military regime in their homeland. In Thailand's southwestern, northern, and eastern border provinces, illegal immigrants arrive on foot or by boat in search of employment in farming, fishing, construction, textile and footwear manufacturing, domestic service, and prostitution (Stern 1996; Human Rights Watch 1993). Border control officers often extort bribes from illegal entrants. Moreover, the lack of effective enforcement, together with the low wages required, encourages Thai employers to hire illegal foreigners. The Thai government has failed to establish a contract labor program for unskilled foreigners such as those found in Singapore and Malaysia. In order to deal with the large, but unknown, number of undocumented immigrants in its country, the government introduced, between September and November 1996, an amnesty for illegal immigrants, of whom 372,000 reported and were granted two-year work permits. This number is believed to represent about half of the total estimated to have been—and still remain—in the country.

Back Door Policy. Japan and Korea, both wealthy Far Eastern countries with relatively homogeneous populations, permit foreigners to work only in selected skilled occupations. Despite this restrictive rule shutting the door against unskilled foreigners, both countries are home to hundreds of thousands of unskilled immigrants who have entered as legal residents, workers, and tourists. In 1990 Japan opened its doors to South Americans of Japanese descent up to the third generation, most of whom lived in Brazil. As a result more than 200,000 such people were in Japan in 1996 to enter its unskilled labor market, working on assembly lines in manufacturing industries (Yamanaka 1996). Japan also grants limited-term visas to company "trainees," mostly from other Asian countries, to work in similar jobs in order to learn new skills. In 1996, there were 21,000 trainees in Japan.[9] In addition, foreign students are allowed to work for twenty hours per week while pursuing their studies. Finally, female entertainers enter and work legally as singers and dancers in bars and cabarets for limited periods (Piquero-Ballescas 1992). Adding to the 300,000 such legal immigrant workers, an estimated 284,000 illegal immigrants, mostly tourist visa-overstayers from other Asian countries, were working in Japan in construction, manufacturing, and service jobs, long shunned by the majority middle-class Japanese.

Korea's immigration policy resembles Japan's in its restrictions on unskilled labor but for reasons of national security gives no exemption to Chinese of Korean descent to work legally in the country, as Japan does to South Americans of Japanese descent to work in Japan. Like Japan, Korea manages "company trainee" programs. In 1996, 66,000 Asians of diverse nationalities were in such programs.[10] Outside of this narrow legal channel, 130,000 illegal workers (twice as many as the number of company trainees) in the country had overstayed their tourist or trainee visas. Under mounting social pressure for normalization, the Korean government twice implemented an amnesty for illegal workers, in 1992 and 1998. Two-thirds of these were Chinese of Korean ancestry. Despite the chance for legal departure that the amnesty offered, a large number remained in 1998. Two-thirds of those who remained are reported to have been owed large sums of unpaid wages by firms that had gone bankrupt, which was probably an important reason for remaining in the country (*Migration News* 1998). The back door policy of these two countries accommodates the national concern for social homogeneity and the fear of potential massive immigration from China, even though it is deceptive in that it is ineffective in achieving its claimed purpose of controlling immigration. In short, these policies as administered in Japan and Korea are the product of political compromise by governments that prefer the illusion of immigration control to the reality of burgeoning immigrant populations (Cornelius 1994).

Political Manipulation.   Illegal immigration is thus widespread in two sub-regions within Asia: in Southeast Asia (Malaysia and Thailand) and the Far East (Japan and Korea). In other labor-importing Asian countries (Singapore, Hong Kong, and Taiwan) implementation of regulated, legalized immigration through contract labor programs has substantially reduced illegal entry and employment. As demonstrated by these examples, the amount of illegal immigration at any point in time is largely an artifact of a country's administrative manipulation whereby legality of categories of immigrant workers already in the country is redefined. Amnesty programs have a similar impact on immigration statistics. Such political manipulations of the distinction between legal and illegal immigrants are shortsighted and often disingenuous means to enable policymakers to appease public opinion in the short run. The actual causes of illegal immigration, as explained before, rest in economic inequalities between neighboring countries and the cultures and histories they share. The inequalities generate nationalistic isolation, while the shared traditions facilitate international migration. This suggests that the shortsighted response to such historical and structural processes will deepen the contradiction in the long run between national priorities and global realities.

The remainder of this chapter comprises a brief case study conducted in central Japan on a small and relatively unnoticed group of illegal workers from Nepal. An examination of their labor migration illustrates in microcosm many of the economic, social, and political issues relevant to regional migration in Asia at large. These issues include regional economic integration, wide economic disparity between sending and receiving countries, antecedent emigration histories of the communities of origin, global information networks developed by migrants, their strategies to circumvent laws designed to block their entry into the target country, an increasing presence of women in regional migration, concentration of employment opportunities in the peripheral industrial sector, economic roles played by illegal workers in local labor markets, and social marginality and denial of rights imposed upon illegal immigrants by host societies.

ILLEGAL NEPALESE WORKERS IN JAPAN: A CASE STUDY

Economic Disparity and Integration

Japan and Nepal stand at opposite ends of the world economic continuum. Japan's 1995 GDP was 833 times as large as Nepal's, and its per capita GDP was 143 times that of Nepal (Table 20.1). In 1993, Japan exported machinery and steel products worth U.S. $67.8 million to Nepal. Nepal in return exported to Japan U.S. $4.1 million worth of clothing, carpets, and craft goods. Japan was the top supplier of foreign aid to Nepal in 1994 at U.S. $1,815 million. In the forty-two-year period 1951–1993, it also invested U.S. $20 million directly into the Nepalese economy (Japanese Ministry of Foreign Affairs 1996). Cultural relationships between the two nations have been equally one-sided. Japanese have visited Nepal in significant numbers since the 1960s for mountain climbing, trekking, and jungle tourism. In 1995, for example, 26,510 Japanese visited Nepal, while 2,686 Nepalese visited Japan. The Japanese visitors were attracted not only by tourism and fascination with Himalayan mountains and peoples but by a growing concern with issues of health, education, economic development, and environmental preservation. By the mid-1990s interested Japanese citizens had formed more than eighty grassroots, nongovernmental organizations in Japan dedicated to such issues in Nepal.

Nepalese Entry to Japan

According to Japanese immigration records, until the mid-1980s, annual Nepalese entries into Japan were fewer than 1,000, mostly short-term visitors for business purposes (Japanese Ministry of Justice 1987–1996). The number shot up to an unprecedented 2,964 during the height of Japanese economic growth in 1989 (Table 20.3). More than two-thirds of the entrants that year were working-age males entering with short-term visas (equivalent to tourist visas). In 1990, immediately after this influx, the Japanese government implemented immigration reform restricting the entry of unskilled foreigners, particularly working-age males seeking short-term visas. Consequently, Nepalese admissions dropped to 1,671 in 1990 but rose to 2,154 in 1991, after which they remained stable at an average of 2,200 for five years. Most entrants exited Japan within the short period specified by their visas, but a small number remained after their visas had expired. The excess of entries over exits grew quickly each year between 1986 and 1995. As a result, in 1995 there were an estimated 3,000 Nepalese visa-overstayers in Japan (excluding 1,314 legal residents). Immigra-

Table 20.3

Nepalese Entry into, and Exit from, Japan: 1986–1995

Year	Entries All [1]	% Short-term Visa [2]*	Sex Ratio [3]**	% of Males 15-29 Yrs [4]***	Exits Voluntary Exits [5]	Involuntary Exits [6]	Excess: Entries Over Exits [7]****
1986	986	69.2	457	38.4	867	0	119
1987	1,292	69.4	595	40.4	1,089	1	202
1988	1,671	76.3	593	47.2	1,311	11	349
1989	2,964	83.0	818	52.9	2,020	37	907
1990	1,671	65.2	533	41.6	1,145	394	132
1991	2,154	66.4	492	42.3	1,127	93	934
1992	1,982	60.1	445	33.5	1,136	127	719
1993	1,837	59.4	420	28.8	1,178	209	450
1994	2,174	58.8	394	27.3	1,840	244	90
1995	2,686	58.3	355	26.7	2,025	269	392
Total	19,417	66.4	542	38.3	13,738	1,385	4,294

Source: Japanese Ministry of Justice (1987–1996).

* [2] and [6] show percentages of short-term visas among all entries and exits for the year, respectively.

** [3] shows the numbers of males per 100 females each year.

*** [4] shows the proportion of males, fifteen to twenty-nine years of age, to the total number of male entrants each year.

**** [7] = [1] − [5] − [6].

tion records also reveal a gradually shifting sex ratio of men to women among the Nepalese entrants between 1989 and 1995, from 8 to 1 in 1989, to 3.6 to 1 in 1995.

The estimated total of 3,000 Nepalese visa-overstayers is a mere drop in the ocean of the estimated total of 284,000 visa-overstayers in Japan in 1996 and therefore poses little threat to Japan's immigration control. Significant, however, is the fact that the population of Nepalese overstayers grew rapidly in the ten years following 1986. This pattern of Nepalese immigration growth contrasts sharply with Bangladeshi and Pakistani immigration. Both Bangladesh and Pakistan had established mutual visa exemption agreements with Japan, enabling their nationals to clear immigration checkpoints without difficulty. Many of these arrivals proceeded to overstay their visas and engage in unauthorized employment (Morita and Sassen 1994; Mahmood 1994). The Japanese government reacted immediately, canceling the visa exemption agreements with Bangladesh and Pakistan in January 1989. Whereas in 1988 there were 14,500 Bangladeshi and 20,000 Pakistani arrivals in Japan, in 1990 entries dropped drastically to 3,400 for Bangladesh and 7,100 for Pakistan and remained at the same, or even lower, level thereafter. In 1996, 6,500 Bangladeshi and 5,500 Pakistani visa-overstayers were reported in Japan, representing a significant degree of attrition in those populations between 1988 and 1996.

Unlike their South Asian predecessors, Nepalese have never enjoyed the privilege of visa-exempted free entry into Japan. Nevertheless, despite all governmental efforts to control their entry, Nepalese have sustained a steady flow of arrivals and an increasing visa-overstayer population since 1989. This suggests the importance of migrants' cultural values, antecedent information networks, and strategies to circumvent immigration laws blocking entry to the target country and to enable such migration patterns to endure over time.

The Gurkha Connection

Nepal is made up of many ethnic groups, each with distinctive history, language, and religion (Berreman 1963; Bista 1996). The 1991 Nepalese national census lists sixty ethnic and caste groups within Nepal's 18.5 million population (Nepalese Central Bureau of Statistics 1996). Despite this extraordinary ethnic heterogeneity, the country's economic resources and political power have been historically monopolized by upper-caste, Nepali (i.e., Indo-Aryan)-speaking Hindu elites (Brahmans and Chhetris), accounting for 29 percent of Nepal's 18.5 million population. As ethnic minorities lacking political clout in national politics, Tibeto-Burman-speaking, multiethnic, multilingual, Buddhist/"animist" groups, making up 35.5 percent of the total population, have relied for some 180 years on recruitment into "Gurkha Brigades" of the British and Indian armies for economic survival.

The British were mightily impressed by the skill and gallantry of their defeated adversaries in the Anglo-Nepalese War of 1814–1816. As a result, they were convinced that Gurkha recruitment to their own armies was essential to maintenance of their military supremacy in South Asia. Since then, Gurkhas have fought numerous wars and battles for the British in every corner of the world, as early as the 1817 Pindari and Maratha Wars in India and including the two world wars, the 1982 Falkland Island War with Argentina, and as recently as the 1991 Gulf War (Cross 1985; Des Chene 1993; Pahari 1991). After Indian independence in 1947, most Gurkha battalions were incorporated into the Indian army, but some moved to Southeast Asia with the British, where "insurgents" had become increasingly active in Malaysia, Singapore, Brunei, and Indonesia. In 1970 the British moved their Gurkha Brigades to Hong Kong, where its 8,000 soldiers were deployed primarily in Border Patrols to block illegal immigrants' entrance from mainland China (Pahari 1991: 12). More than 180 years of transnational experience has established the extensive social networks of Gurkhas, often called the "Gurkha Connection," linking soldiers and their families across national boundaries throughout the world (e.g., Banskota 1994).

Between November 1995 and February 1998, I conducted a study among Nepalese immigrants currently working in Hamamatsu and Toyohashi, central Japan, and Nepalese return migrants from Japan in Kathmandu and Pokhara in central and western Nepal, respectively.[11] Systematic interviews and survey data were collected from 159 men and thirty women, supplemented by informal interviews with an additional sixty informants who provided contextual information. An analysis of these data indicates that the majority of Nepalese immigrant workers are of Tibeto-Burman language-speaking ethnic groups from Nepal's western and eastern middle hills—such as Gurungs, Magars, Rais, and Limbus, the groups from which most Gurkha soldiers are drawn.

From Global Warriors to Global Workers

For the past 180 years, the tradition of military service in the British army has provided families and communities of such Gurkha soldiers with a steady source of cash to supplement their subsistence economy based on terrace farming and cattle herding in precipitous Himalayan pastures. Soldiers' remittances and retirees' pensions were for many years sufficient to enable sending families to enjoy higher living standards than nonsending families (Hitchcock 1966; Pignède 1966; Caplan 1967; Macfarlane 1976). Massive Gurkha recruitment, however, ended in the early 1990s, when Britain drastically reduced its Gurkha Brigades in anticipation of Hong Kong's return to China in 1997. In the next several years "redundant" Gurkhas were prematurely discharged before they became entitled to pensions. In 1991 there were slightly more than 7,400 Gurkhas serving in the British army in Hong Kong and Brunei, but after July 1997 British Gurkhas were reduced to 2,000 in London and 1,000 in Brunei.

While the number of British army Gurkhas is small, their legacy continues in the Asia-Pacific region. Twenty-two hundred ex-Gurkha soldiers serve as the sultan's security guards in Brunei, 1,000 Gurkha policemen are on duty in Singapore, and 600 Gurkha retirees supply high-end security on contract to business organizations and private homes in Hong Kong.[12] In response to the British government's granting of Hong Kong citizenship to some 7,000 children born of Gurkha soldiers through 1982 and the rights of their dependents to Hong Kong residency, an estimated 20,000 Nepalese have entered Hong Kong primarily to work as unskilled laborers in major public construction projects.

Calls for contract labor in the Middle East and other parts of the world, including Japan, had already reached Himalayan villages by the late 1980s. Rising inflation and soaring unemployment made it difficult for most Nepalese households, particularly in urban centers, to maintain incomes sufficient to provide for their members (*Spotlight* 1996). Among those who were educated but lacking in job experience and personal connection with Nepalese employers, emigration became an increasingly attractive way to cope with Nepal's economic crisis.

Migrants' Networks and Strategies

My examination of the Nepalese migration data (here called the "Nepalese data") indicates that immigrant workers in Japan, both men and women, had been relatively well educated in Nepal, many with a high school diploma or beyond. The majority are found, nonetheless, to have held relatively low-prestige occupations, such self-employment in service and agriculture, or were students prior to departure to Japan. An important finding relevant to their migration is that one-third of 124 male informants of Tibeto-Burman language groups reported previous service in the British/Indian army or employment in the Middle East, Asia, Europe, or the United States. Apparently, this extensive prior migration experience had given them an advantage in obtaining information regarding employment opportunities and immigration laws in other countries. By the late 1980s, when Japan was about to reach its peak of economic prosperity, it had already drawn massive numbers of arrivals from Asia and South America, including 2,964 Nepalese.

In 1990 the Japanese Embassy in Kathmandu tightened its visa issuance policy in response to immigration reform taking effect that year. Thereafter, some visa applicants, in order to evade increased scrutiny at that embassy, traveled to countries where fewer questions would be asked. At that time, Germany did not require Nepalese visitors to have visas for short stays, so many Nepalese flew there to apply for visas to Japan. Other such ''intermediary'' countries included England, the United States, Middle Eastern countries, Australia, Hong Kong, Korea, and other Asian countries. The Nepalese data indicate that more than forty percent of Tibeto-Burman respondents obtained visas in such intermediary countries. This highlights the power of networks that had grown out of the tradition of foreign employment as soldiers in British Gurkha service.[13] Such networks I call the ''Gurkha 'migration' connection.''

After a substantial population of Nepalese men arrived in Japan in 1989, a trickle of women began to follow. A few accompanied their husbands to Japan, but most arrived later as wives (sometimes sisters) of earlier male arrivals. Having established employment and housing, the men were able to use savings to send for the women, often through channels provided by well-established professional or clandestine recruiters. The data suggest that by the mid-1990s a new cycle of immigration had begun, whereby relatives, not only nonworking wives but also graduating brothers of Nepalese immigrants, were able to enter Japan. In the case of women, they have broken the custom of being left behind in Nepal by joining the regional labor force (cf. Aryal 1991).

Local Labor Market Characteristics

Within three months of their arrival, immigrants' short-term visas expire. Then, these Nepalese of diverse languages, ethnicities, and classes, and both genders are reduced by Japanese immigration law to a single category: ''illegal foreign residents.'' As such they become informally absorbed into the workforce as one of its most vulnerable labor categories, while working for the weakest, most unstable employers. In the local markets of Hamamatsu and Toyohashi in central Japan, the jobs least desired by Japanese are low-paid, labor-intensive manual work offered by small-scale employers in the manufacturing and construction industries. Hamamatsu, a city of .5 million in western Shizuoka Prefecture, is a center for Japan's lifeline automobile and motorcycle industries. It harbors the headquarters of several major companies, including Suzuki, Yamaha, and Honda. Near Toyohashi, a city of 350,000 in eastern Aichi Prefecture adjacent to Hamamatsu, is Toyota City, home of another giant automaker, Toyota.

Altogether, Hamamatsu and Toyohashi are home to tens of thousands of small- to large-scale subcontractors supplying the parts assembled by automobile manufacturing companies ("automakers") to become vehicles. The industrial structure connecting an automaker with its numerous parts suppliers has historically comprised a pyramidal hierarchy of dependency. Automakers—a few very large corporations that assemble automobiles—are at the top of the hierarchy. They obtain the components to be assembled from large, "first-order" contractors who, in turn, obtain constituent parts of the components from numerous "second-order" contractors. The process continues down to third- and even fourth-order contractors. In one instance, a single automaker drew upon 47,308 contractors in a three-level hierarchy (Ito 1993: 86). Statistics on Hamamatsu's manufacturing establishments confirm these unequal hierarchical relationships. An overwhelming eighty seven percent of the establishments in the automobile industry there have fewer than thirty employees, which suggests that most establishments are small, third-order or even "fourth"-order subcontractors (Hamamatsu City 1991).

Immigrant workers, both legal and illegal, find this area (referred to later as the Tokai region) attractive because of its chronic labor shortage among small-scale subcontractors. In 1997 more than 8,000 Brazilians of Japanese descent (called Nikkeijin, literally, people of Japanese descent) registered as long-term residents in Hamamatsu alone. The number of illegal immigrants in Tokai is difficult to estimate, but there are substantial numbers, mostly from Asia, including an estimated 500 Nepalese.[14] Following the 1990 immigration reform establishing the illegality of hiring unskilled foreigners, many Japanese companies, threatened by criminal penalties, replaced illegal workers with legal Nikkeijin workers. An important question arising from the newly emerging availability of foreign workers concerns the structure of the low-skilled labor force as it is stratified according to workers' collective characteristics: nationality (whether Japanese or not), ethnicity (whether of Japanese descent or not), and legality (whether legal resident or not). The relationships between these workers' characteristics and employers' characteristics (i.e., the industry in which the employer is engaged and the relative size of the employers' organizations) are the subject of the next section.

Employment and Wages

As might be expected from the existing hierarchical industrial structure, 75 percent of 150 Nepalese men and 77 percent of twenty six women work in factories manufacturing automobile parts of plastic and metal. Most of the rest are working in construction industries, building private homes and public roads. More than half are employed by establishments with fewer than thirty employees. Those who report being employed by larger establishments are hired by labor contractors who, in turn, dispatch them to their jobs in large factories. Despite employment in such peripheral sectors of the industries, Nepalese workers report wages comparable to those of Nikkeijin and even of Japanese co-workers. On the average, Nepalese men earn 1,125 yen per hour (roughly U.S. $11.25), and women earn 835 yen (U.S. $8.35). In Kathmandu, the average monthly income for a government official or university professor is about 5,000 Nepal rupees (roughly U.S. $100).[15] In Tokai, an illegal, unskilled male makes that amount in a single day.

A breakdown of their hourly wage data (unreported here) further reveals that, while workers' age, education, and ethnicity/caste have little relationship to their wage levels, the type of industry in which they are employed, the years spent in Japan, and the number of job changes all make small, but systematic, statistically significant differences in their earnings. This means that regardless of company size, workers' wages are higher in construction industries than in manufacturing or service employment and that they tend to increase as workers' work experience and Japanese cultural competence increase over time. Moreover, comparisons of average monthly wages (not reported here) among illegal Nepalese, legal Nikkeijin, and Japanese workers in the manufacturing industry demonstrate an important finding: differences in national, ethnic, or legal status do not appear to contribute to significant wage differences. This suggests that Japanese small-scale employers place a high value on Nepalese workers' willingness and physical capacity for intensive labor in construction and manufacturing. It should be noted, however, that research clearly shows that regardless of nationality, ethnicity, or legal status, gender divides and ranks workers in Japan according to well-established patterns of wage and social discrimination against women (cf., Brinton 1993).

Roles of Illegal Workers

Japanese employers, although willing to pay the Nepalese hourly wages nearly equivalent to those of other workers, save significant labor costs by not granting them the numerous expensive benefits, entitlements, and job security that are granted to Japanese and (to a limited degree) legal Nikkeijin workers. Clearly, the relatively inexpensive and flexible labor that illegal workers offer to peripheral employers motivates them to employ illegals at standard wages. For them, hiring illegal workers increases profits while costing little. Although criminal penalties for hiring illegal workers have existed since 1990, the Japanese government has rarely enforced them. This is a manifestation of the "back door policy." It suggests that the aim of the penalty code is to discourage employment of illegals rather than to eradicate the practice. The following statement from an interview with the president of a manufacturing factory with twenty-seven employees, including six Nepalese, illustrates the limited impact the criminal code has made on his decision to employ illegal workers, while demonstrating the economic gain he derives by doing so:

My Nepalese workers are smart and dedicated to their jobs. They have learned everything very quickly. They arrive here early in the morning before anyone else and go home late in the evening after everyone has gone. They are much younger than my Japanese workers, who are in their fifties and sixties. Their good eyesight is very helpful in inspecting the machine parts. Even though the law says I should not hire illegals, I see no reason to replace them. Because our products do not carry my company name, I do not have to worry about the company image. If I were caught by the police, the local newspaper would report it in only one line. That's all.

Workers with No Rights

For sojourning foreign workers, the ultimate goal of migration is to save a large sum of money and return home as soon as possible. Japan is a "heaven" for achieving this goal, according to one Nepalese immigrant. But its underground labor markets are far from heavenly in their treatment of illegal workers. The Japanese workplace is often ridden with labor exploitation and occupational hazards. Small-scale employers, lacking capital and credit, frequently neglect safety codes, postpone paying salaries for months, and sometimes go out of business without paying their employees. Illegal workers have no recourse but to seek a new employer. Verbal abuse and rude behavior by employers are other forms of mistreatment commonly encountered. Many illegal workers also find that the work to which they are assigned is too demanding or the wages are unacceptably low.

In addition to difficult working conditions, Nepalese illegal workers suffer severe social invisibility and personal isolation. As day laborers, their lives are spent working in factories or construction sites for ten hours a day, six days a week. The limited time and clandestine nature of their presence in Japan prevent them from making friends outside the Nepalese community. This remains true even after they have learned to speak and understand Japanese. Fear of apprehension is pervasive, inhibiting their social participation both publicly and privately. As illegitimate aliens, they are denied access to inexpensive medical care. This poses a serious threat to the many who perform hazardous jobs in workplaces often devoid of adequate safety measures.

A relatively few Japanese volunteers, nonprofit organizations, labor union activists, social workers, and medical personnel play critical roles in overcoming legal problems and providing professional services in cases of labor exploitation, serious bureaucratic problems, and social and medical emergencies.

CONCLUSION

This chapter has discussed causes, patterns, and processes of illegal labor migration in East and Southeast Asia in the context of the growing economic inequalities inherent in the rapid economic growth and integration that characterizes the region. Such economic circumstances are largely accountable for the rising waves of labor migration and the rapid emergence of integrated labor markets in Asia. Behind this massive transfer of labor, historical, cultural, and political forces determine the direction and duration of migration flows across national boundaries. Policymakers of labor-importing countries in Asia are confronted with severe challenges resulting from this structural inequality. The example of Nepalese migration to Japan vividly illustrates issues and processes characteristic of the region and the time. The two countries, historically and culturally separated until recently, are now firmly connected through trade, foreign aid, and tourism. The fact that there is a sustained flow of illegal migration from Nepal to Japan is an expectable consequence of the integrated, yet regionally drastically unequal, economies of Asia.

In the process of growing transnationalism, national borders have become sites of contestation, challenged by global migrants and those who seek them, defended by the sovereign states they define. Although the growing economic crisis may cause temporary disruption in patterns and processes of regional labor migration, the imbalance between supply of inexpensive and flexible labor and demand for it is likely to sustain migration flows over the long run. The concepts of migration transition and emigration pressure are useful in explaining gaps between the economic and demographic reality in Asia and the political and ideological ideals sought by the few, rich, labor-importing countries. In short, massive numbers of illegal immigrants are bound to continue to arrive at their doors, whether front, back, or simply loose, despite their efforts to barricade them against the uninvited.

NOTES

I thank Gerald Berreman for his editorial assistance. I also thank the many Nepalese friends in Japan and Nepal without whose cooperation this study would not have been possible but whose names cannot be identified.

1. In this article, Korea refers to the Republic of Korea (South Korea). North Korea is largely isolated from the processes described here. Since July 1997, Hong Kong has been reunified with China but is here still simply called Hong Kong.

2. In 1970 Singapore had 21,000 foreign workers, accounting for 3.2 percent of its 651,000 total labor force. The number of foreign workers grew rapidly over the next two decades, reaching 200,000, 13.5 percent of the 1,480,000 total labor force, in 1991 and 350,000, 20.7 percent of the 1,690,000 total labor force, in 1995 (Wong 1997).

3. Singapore, Hong Kong, Taiwan, and Korea continue to send emigrants to North America and Australia as permanent settlers. However, the numbers dwindled in the 1990s for all but Hong Kong, where the exodus continued as a result of anxiety about its reunification with China.

4. The figures in U.S. dollars are adjusted to those for 1990 for comparative purposes (UNIDO 1997).

5. It should be emphasized that GDP accounts primarily for domestic industrial pro-

duction and is therefore largely irrelevant and unrelated to quality of life for subsistence farmers and peasants in countries whose agricultural production is not directly linked to the national economy (see Nader and Beckerman 1978).

6. In September 1985 financial representatives of the Group of Five—the United States, Japan, West Germany, France, and the United Kingdom—convened in the Plaza Hotel, New York City, where they issued the "Plaza Agreement," devaluing the U.S. dollar in relation to other major currencies (Schaeffer 1997: 48). As a result, the conversion rate for Japanese yen, for example, rose from 254 to the dollar in 1985 to 185 in 1986, to 151 in 1987, and to 127 in 1988, having thus doubled in value over these three years (Japanese Statistical Bureau 1998: 430).

7. An example is David M. Reimers' *Still the Golden Door* (New York: Columbia University Press, 1992), referring to the United States as a destination attractive to Third World immigrants in the post-1965 Immigration Act era.

8. Information in Table 20.2 is drawn from many sources: for Singapore, Soon-Beng and Chew (1995), Wong (1997), Hui (1998); for Hong Kong, Skeldon (1995) and Levin and Chiu (1998); for Taiwan, Tsay (1995); for Malaysia, Pillai (1995) and Pillai and Yusof (1998); for Thailand, Sussangkarn (1995) and Chalamwong (1998); for Japan, Okunishi (1995), Iguchi (1998) and Japan Immigration Association (1997); for Korea, Park (1995, 1998).

9. Trainees are recruited through four channels: (1) governmental agencies and international organizations; (2) private corporations; (3) intermediary organizations; and (4) the Japan International Training Cooperation Organization. In many cases of private recruitment of trainees for subsidiaries or joint-venture companies overseas, Japanese employers treat trainees as substitute labor on the assembly line (Oishi 1995).

10. Foreign trainees in Korea come from fourteen selected countries through two channels: (1) foreign affiliates of Korean firms and (2) the Foreign Training Cooperation Corps (FTCO) under auspices of the Korea Federation of Small Business (Park 1998). The majority of foreign trainees arrive through the second channel and work as unskilled laborers in labor-short companies in the manufacturing industries.

11. For research methods employed in this study and findings from analyses of the Nepalese data, see Yamanaka (1998).

12. Information on the current numbers of Gurkha soldiers and ex-soldiers was obtained in interviews with Major Dipak Bahadur Gurung (December 17, 1997, Kathmandu) and the Singapore Gurkha Pensioners' Association (December 18, 1997, Kathmandu). See also Aryal (1997).

13. This finding was derived from comparison of the two groups of Nepalese migrants to Japan: (1) the "Gurkha group" (N = 131), comprising members of eight nonelite, Tibeto-Burman language-speaking peoples; and (2) the "non-Gurkha group" (N = 58), including three power elite groups: two Indo-Aryan (Nepali)-speaking castes, Brahmans and Chhetris, and one Tibeto-Burman-speaking group, Newars.

14. The remaining Nepalese workers are mostly in the Greater Tokyo Metropolitan Area laboring in restaurants, laundries, printing shops, and meat-processing centers.

15. Japanese yen were valued at 107 per U.S. dollar in 1994, 93 in 1995, and 106 in 1996 (Japanese Statistical Bureau 1998). The figure of 100 yen per dollar is used here for convenience. During this period the Nepalese rupee was valued at about fifty per U.S. dollar.

REFERENCES

Abella, Manolo I.
1994   Introduction. *Asian and Pacific Migration Journal* 3 (1): 1–6.
1998   Emigration Pressures in Selected Asian Countries: Some Preliminary Findings. In *Migration and Regional Economic Integration in Asia.* OECD Proceedings. Paris: OECD. Pp. 53–70.

Aryal, Manisha
1991   To Marry a Lahuray. *Himal* (July/August): 18–19.
1997   Gurkhas in the People's Republic. *Himal South Asia* (July/August): 28–29.

Banskota, Purushottam
1994   *The Gurkha Connection: A History of the Gurkha Recruitment in the British Army.* Jaipur, India: Nirala.

Berreman, Gerald D.
1963   Peoples and Cultures of the Himalayas. *Asian Survey* 3 (6): 289–304.

Bista, Dor Bahadur
1996   *People of Nepal.* Kathmandu: Bhotahity.

Borjas, George J.
1990   *Friends or Strangers: The Impact of Immigration on the U.S. Economy.* New York: Basic Books.

Boyd, Monica
1989   Family and Personal Networks in International Migration: Recent Developments and New Agendas. *International Migration Review* 23 (3): 638–680.

Brinton, Mary C.
1993   *Women and the Economic Miracle: Gender and Work in Postwar Japan.* Berkeley: University of California Press.

Caplan, Lionel
1967   *Land and Social Change in East Nepal.* Berkeley: University of California Press.

Castles, Stephen, and Mark J. Miller
1993   *The Age of Migration: International Population Movements in the Modern World.* New York: Guilford Press.

Chalamwong, Yongyuth
1998   Dilemmas of Rapid Growth: International Migration and Cross-Border Flows in Thailand. In *Migration and Regional Economic Integration in Asia.* OECD Proceedings. Paris: OECD. Pp. 167–173.

Cheng, Shu-Ju Ada
1996   Migrant Women Domestic Workers in Hong Kong, Singapore and Taiwan. *Asian and Pacific Migration Journal* 5 (1): 139–152.

Constable, Nicole
1997   *Maid to Order in Hong Kong: Stories of Filipina Workers.* Ithaca, New York: Cornell University Press.

Cornelius, Wayne A.
1994   Japan: The Illusion of Immigration Control. In *Controlling Immigration: A Global Perspective.* Edited by Wayne A. Cornelius, Philip L. Martin, and James F. Hollifield. Stanford: Stanford University Press. Pp. 375–410.

Cross, J. P.
1985   Introduction. In *Gurkhas.* Sandro Tucci. London: Hamish Hamilton. Pp. 8–34.

Des Chene, Mary
1993   Soldiers, Sovereignty and Silences: Gurkhas as Diplomatic Currency. *South Asia Bulletin* 13 (1, 2): 67–80.

Fields, Gary S.
1994   Migration Transition in Asia. *Asian and Pacific Migration Journal* 3 (1): 7–30.

Hamamatsu City
1991   *Hamamatsu-shi Tokeisho, Heisei 3 nendo*. Hamamatsu: Hamamatsu City.

Hitchcock, John T.
1966   *A Mountain Village in Nepal*. New York: Holt, Rinehart, and Winston.

Hugo, Graeme
1993   Indonesian Labour Migration to Malaysia: Trends and Policy Implications. *Southeast Asian Journal of Social Science* 21 (1): 36–70.
1995   International Labor Migration and the Family: Some Observations from Indonesia. *Asian and Pacific Migration Journal* 4 (2–3): 273–301.

Hui, Weng-Tat
1998   Labour Migration in Singapore: Trends and Policies. In *Migration and Regional Economic Integration in Asia*. OECD Proceedings. Paris: OECD. Pp. 155–165.

Human Rights Watch
1993   *A Modern Form of Slavery: Trafficking of Burmese Women and Girls into Brothels in Thailand*. Asia Watch and the Women's Rights Project. New York: Human Rights Watch.

Iguchi, Yasushi
1998   Labour Market Changes and International Migration: The Japanese Experience. In *Migration and Regional Economic Integration in Asia*. OECD Proceedings. Paris: OECD. Pp. 107–120.

Ito, Motoshige
1993   Nihonteki Torihiki Knko: Keizokuteki Torihiki no Kino to Hyoka. In *Nihon no Kigyo Shisutem*. Edited by T. Itami, T. Kagono, and M. Ito. Tokyo: Yuhikaku. Pp. 74–94.

Japan Immigration Association
1997   *Zairyu Gaikokujin Tokei*. Tokyo: Japan Immigration Association.

Japanese Ministry of Foreign Affairs
1996   Kingdom of Nepal. Printed Material.

Japanese Ministry of Justice
1987–1996   *Annual Report of Statistics on Legal Migrants*. Tokyo: Japanese Ministry of Justice.

Japanese Statistical Bureau
1998   *Japan Statistical Yearbook*. Tokyo: Management and Coordinate Agency, Government of Japan.

Jixuan, Zhang, and Guanjiang Gao
1998   China: From Labour Export to Sub-Regional Economic Development. In *Migration and Regional Economic Integration in Asia*. OECD Proceedings. Paris: OECD. Pp. 73–80.

Kritz, Mary M., Lin Lean Lim, and Hania Zlotnik
1992   *International Migration Systems: A Global Approach*. Oxford: Clarendon Press.

Kuwahara, Yasuo
1998   Economic Development in Asia and Its Consequences for Labour Migration. In

Migration and Regional Economic Integration in Asia. OECD Proceedings. Paris: OECD. Pp. 19–26.

Levin, David A., and Stephen W. K. Chiu
1998   Hong Kong: Labour Market Changes and International Migration of Labour. In *Migration and Regional Economic Integration in Asia*. OECD Proceedings. Paris: OECD. Pp. 81–96.

Lim, Lin Lean, and Manolo Abella
1994   The Movement of People in Asia: Internal, Intra-Regional and International Migration. *Asian and Pacific Migration Journal* 3 (2–3): 209–250.

Liu, Yunhua
1995   Labour Migration of China. *Asian Economic Bulletin* 12 (2): 299–308.

Lohrmann, R.
1987   Irregular Migration: A Rising Issue in Developing Countries. *International Migration* 35 (3): 253–266.

Low, Linda
1994   Migration and Singapore: Implications for the Asian Pacific. *Asian and Pacific Migration Journal* 3 (2–3): 251–263.

Lui Ting, Terry
1987   Undocumented Migration in Hong Kong (Specific Measures Taken to Reduce the Flow of Undocumented Migrants). *International Migration* 25 (3): 260–276.

Macfarlane, Alan
1976   *Resources and Population: A Study of the Gurungs of Nepal*. Cambridge: Cambridge University Press.

Mahmood, Raisul Awal
1994   Adaptation to a New World Experience of Bangladeshis in Japan. *International Migration* 32 (4): 513–532.

Martin, Philip L., Andrew Mason, and Ching-lung Tsay
1995   Overview. *ASEAN Economic Bulletin* 12 (2): 117–124.

Migration News
1998   Asia. *Migration News* 5 (1–7). Department of Agriculture and Resource Economics, University of California, Davis.

Morita, Kiriro, and Saskia Sassen
1994   The New Illegal Immigration in Japan 1980–1992. *International Migration Review* 28 (1): 153–163.

Nader, Laura, and Stephen Beckerman
1978   Energy as It Relates to the Quality and Style of Life. *Annual Review of Energy* (3): 1–28.

Nepalese Central Bureau of Statistics
1996   *Statistical Pocket Book*. Kathmandu: His Majesty's Government National Planning Commission Secretariat, Central Bureau of Statistics.

OECD
1996   *Migration and the Labour Market in Asia: Prospects to the Year 2000*. Paris: OECD.
1998   *Migration and Regional Economic Integration in Asia*. OECD Proceedings. Paris: OECD.

Oishi, Nana
1995   Training or Employment?: Japanese Immigration Policy in Dilemma. *Asian and Pacific Migration Journal* 4 (2–3): 367–385.

Okunishi, Yoshio
1995   Japan. *ASEAN Economic Bulletin* 12 (2): 139–162.
Pahari, Anup
1991   Ties That Bind: Gurkhas in History. *Himal* (July/August): 6–12.
Park, Young-bum
1994   The Turning Point in International Labor Migration and Economic Development in Korea. *Asian and Pacific Migration Journal* 3 (1): 149–174.
1995   Korea. *ASEAN Economic Bulletin* 12 (2): 163–174.
1998   The Republic of Korea: Trends and Recent Developments in International Migration. In *Migration and Regional Economic Integration in Asia.* OECD Proceedings. Paris: OECD. Pp. 121–132.
Pignède, Bernard
1966   *The Gurungs: A Himalayan Population of Nepal.* First English edition in 1993; translated by Sarah Harrison and Alan Macfarlane. Kathmandu: Ratna Pustak Bhandar.
Pillai, Patrick
1995   Malaysia. *ASEAN Economic Bulletin* 12 (2): 221–236.
Pillai, Patrick, and Zainal Aznam Yusof
1998   Malaysia: Trends and Recent Developments in International Migration. In *Migration and Regional Economic Integration in Asia.* OECD Proceedings. Paris: OECD. Pp. 133–143.
Piquero-Ballescas, Ma. Rosario
1992   *Filipino Entertainers in Japan: An Introduction.* Quezon City: Foundation for Nationalist Studies.
Population Reference Bureau
1997   *World Population Sheet.* Washington, D.C.: Population Reference Bureau.
Portes, Alejandro
1978   Migration and Underdevelopment. *Politics and Society* 8 (1): 1–48.
Portes, Alejandro, and Böröcz, József
1989   Contemporary Immigration: Theoretical Perspectives on Its Determinants and Modes of Incorporation. *International Migration Review* 23 (3): 606–630.
Sassen, Saskia
1988   *The Mobility of Labour and Capital.* London: Cambridge University Press.
Schaeffer, Robert K.
1997   *Understanding Globalization: The Social Consequences of Political, Economic, and Environmental Change.* Lanham, Maryland: Rowman and Littlefield.
Shah, Nasra M.
1994   An Overview of Present and Future Emigration Dynamics in South Asia. *International Migration* 32 (2): 217–268.
Shah, Nasra M., Sulayman S. Al-Qudsi, and Makhdoom A. Shah
1991   Asian Women Workers in Kuwait. *International Migration Review* 25 (3): 464–486.
Skeldon, Ronald
1992   International Migration within and from the East and Southeast Asian Region: A Review Essay. *Asian and Pacific Migration Journal* 1 (1): 19–63.
1994   Turning Points in Labour Migration: The Case of Hong Kong. *Asian and Pacific Migration Journal* 3 (1):93–118.
1995   Labour Migration to Hong Kong. *ASEAN Economic Bulletin* 12 (2): 201–218.

Soon-Beng, Chew, and Roslind Chew
1995   Immigration and Foreign Labour in Singapore. *ASEAN Economic Bulletin* 12 (2):
        191–200.
Spaan, Ernst
1994   Taikong's and Calo's: The Role of Middlemen and Brokers in Javanese Inter-
        national Migration. *International Migration Review* 28 (1): 93–113.
Spotlight
1996   Unemployment: Time-Bomb Is Ticking. *Spotlight* (January 5): 16–20.
Stahl, Charles W., and Reginald T. Appleyard
1992   International Manpower Flows in Asia: An Overview. *Asian and Pacific Migra-
        tion Journal* 1 (3–4): 417–476.
Stern, Aaron
1996   Thailand's Illegal Labor Migrants. *Asian Migrant* 9 (4): 100–103.
Sullivan, Gerald, S. Gunasekaran, and Siengthai Sununta
1992   Labour Migration and Policy Formation in a Newly Industrialized Country: A
        Case of Illegal Thai Workers in Singapore. *ASEAN Economic Bulletin* 9 (1): 66–
        84.
Sussangkarn, Chalongphob
1995   Labor Market Adjustments and Migration in Thailand. *ASEAN Economic Bulletin*
        12 (2): 237–254.
Tsay, Ching-lung
1992   Clandestine Labour Migration to Taiwan. *Asian and Pacific Migration Journal* 1
        (3–4): 637–655.
1995   Taiwan. *ASEAN Economic Bulletin* 12 (2): 175–190.
UN (United Nations)
1997   *Statistical Yearbook for Asia and the Pacific 1996.* Bangkok: Economic and So-
        cial Commission for Asia and the Pacific.
UNIDO (United Nations Industrial Development Organization)
1997   *Industrial Development: Global Report 1997.* Oxford: Oxford University Press.
Vasuprasat, Pracha
1994   Turning Points in International Labor Migration: A Case Study of Thailand. *Asian
        and Pacific Migration Journal* 3 (1): 175–202.
Watanabe, Susumu
1994   The Lewisian Turning Point and International Migration: The Case of Japan.
        Asian and Pacific Migration Journal 3 (1): 119–147.
Wong, Diana
1997   Transience and Settlement: Singapore's Foreign Labor Policy. *Asian and Pacific
        Migration Journal* 6 (2): 135–167.
World Bank
1993   *The East Asian Miracle: Economic Growth and Public Policy.* New York: Oxford
        University Press.
Yamanaka, Keiko
1996   Return Migration of Japanese-Brazilians to Japan: The *Nikkeijin* as Ethnic Mi-
        nority and Political Construct. *Diaspora* 5 (1): 65–97.
1998   Nepalese Labor Migration to Japan: From Global Warriors to Global Workers.
        Paper presented at the 1998 Annual Meeting of the Pacific Sociological Associ-
        ation, San Francisco, April 16–19.

21

An Introduction to the Literature

David W. Haines

The following selections provide an introduction to the extensive literature on undocumented immigration to the United States. As with this volume as a whole, the primary intent is to introduce the wide range of people (undocumented workers, trafficked workers, asylum applicants, illegal spouses and children of those who are documented—or the reverse) who together constitute "illegal immigration" in the contemporary United States. The selections also illustrate the various origins of illegal immigrants and the broad range of opinion about them: ranging from those interested in improving immigration policy, to those simply trying to understand the lives of people who necessarily live in the shadows, to those trying to monitor the abuses of basic human rights that occur when people lack the usual protections of law.

I have tried to avoid general information on immigration in favor of items that address the specifics of those who are undocumented. Yet this causes a problem for so-called visa-overstayers, since they tend to melt into the general population. Thus, to introduce Korean or Indian illegals, the only effective way would be to begin to cite some of the general literature on those groups that may have an incidental mention or two of people in an undocumented status but are unlikely (for a variety of reasons) to delve greatly into the issue of illegality. Much of the undocumented population is thus severely underrepresented in these selections, as it is, of course, in the general debate about illegal immigration. As stressed throughout this volume, illegal immigration is largely the shadow of regular immigration, and for many immigrant groups the line between the light and shadow is almost imperceptible.

A few specific warnings are in order. First, feelings run high on the issue of illegal immigration. I have not directly included the tracts that appear on the subject, but many of the authors noted here have strong views—both pro and con. Such strength of commitment can sometimes override the need for balanced analysis.

Second, the definitions of illegal migration are perpetually changing. The Immigration Reform and Control Act (IRCA) of 1986, for example, is a major watershed. The massive legalization of nearly 3 million people changed both the dynamics of undocumented border crossing and the relative proportions of "illegals" from different countries. IRCA made it much harder to view illegal immigration as solely an issue of the Mexican border. Subsequent legislation in the 1990s again changed U.S. immigration law and the features that both directly and indirectly affect the flow of undocumented migrants and their situation in the United States. While such changes often worked to make more of the illegal legal, they sometimes also made those who were legal illegal. For example, those fleeing Cuba were for decades treated presumptively as refugees, but now those leaving Cuba are a component of the illegal immigration population.

Third, I have not included references to the legal literature. That literature is extensive, particularly as it relates to people, such as asylum seekers, trying to establish legal status in the United States. Several law journals pay particular attention to immigration and many at least occasionally address the issue. This literature is, however, one of the first to be made consistently available through electronic access. Most university libraries and some public ones now have on-line access to these law journals, which is particularly helpful since currency is essential, given frequent legislative, regulatory, and case law developments. (By comparison, on-line access to the more general social science journals remains limited as to both journals included and extent of coverage—usually only with citations and abstracts and not full text.)

In terms of availability of materials, a moderate-sized public or university library should suffice. Increasingly, both public and private sector data, publications, and newsletters are available on-line. Relevant Web addresses are not included here, since they can easily change, and on-line materials may be partial rather than complete. However, lists of links are available through many on-line organizations and can be a useful point of departure. An introductory list of some sixty-five organizations identified in the development of this volume, for example, is available at the Web site of the American Anthropological Association's Committee on Refugees and Immigrants (http://mason.gmu.edu/~cori) and will be updated periodically.

Amerasia Journal
1992   Asian Pacific American Workers: Contemporary Issues in the Labor
        Movement. Vol. 18 (1): v–156.
Special Issue. There is a variety of descriptive and activist articles in this issue that, although not mentioning undocumented workers very often, address many

of the central labor problems that are likely to affect undocumented workers the most severely. In particular, there are two articles on the garment industry (in San Francisco and Los Angeles) and several on the difficulties of unionizing low-wage and replaceable workers.

Amnesty International
1998   *United States of America: Human Rights Concerns in the Border Region with Mexico.* New York.
Report on abuses, largely by Border Patrol agents. Amnesty International heard allegations of beatings, denial of food, water, and blankets, sexual abuse of both men and women, denial of medical attention, and a variety of abusive, derogatory treatment. Those subjected to the abuse included legal residents and citizens, as well as undocumented border crossers. The report also addresses the more general problems caused by increasing fortification of the border.

Andreas, Peter
1994   The Making of Amerexico: (Mis)Handling Illegal Immigration. *World Policy Journal* 11 (2): 45–56.
Readable review of illegal immigration from Mexico. Andreas argues that the "problem" of illegal immigration is largely the result of U.S. policies about Mexican development, low-skill and low-wage work within the United States, and border control. In each area, policies often directly aimed at decreasing illegal immigration actually increased it. Rising nativist sentiments and the governmental logic underlying escalation in control strategies are also discussed.

Armbruster, Ralph, Kim Geron, and Edna Bonacich
1995   The Assault on California's Latino Immigrants: The Politics of Proposition 187. *International Journal of Urban and Regional Research* 19 (4): 655–663.
Succinct review of the economics and politics underlying Proposition 187. The authors begin with a short review of conservative and liberal positions on the proposition and then provide their own more radical critique. They are most effective in showing the irony that those who benefited the most from the low-cost labor of illegal immigrants were also those favoring the end to assistance to them. For the future, the authors argue that unions must massively organize the now-emergent Latino community in order to resolve problems of working conditions and civil rights.

Arp, William, III
1990   The Exclusion of Illegal Hispanics in Agenda-Setting: The Immigration Reform and Control Act of 1986. *Policy Studies Review* 9 (2): 327–338.
Analysis of the process of legalization specified by IRCA. The author argues that the legislative process failed to include views of illegal immigrants themselves, resulting in lower-than-expected rates of legalization. Following a discussion of the agencies involved in the legalization process, he provides data from surveys of those who successfully legalized and those who didn't. The

results suggest that those who were paid in cash, were farmworkers, didn't understand the program, and couldn't document residence had the most problems. The data are from Arizona.

Arp, William, III, and Sherrie L. Beaver
1994   Implementation of Congressional Intent: A Study of Amnesty Policy and the Immigration and Naturalization Service. *International Migration* 32 (3): 425–443.
Analysis of IRCA with emphasis on the process of applying for amnesty. The authors suggest that the INS failed to address key practical issues in the application process, thereby keeping many undocumented immigrants from applying for amnesty. They characterize this as an INS "nondecision-making" strategy and then present data from Arizona and New York that indicate the specific problems that kept people from applying (high fees, extensive documentation requirements, fear of the INS).

Baker, Susan González
1997   The "Amnesty" Aftermath: Current Policy Issues Stemming from the Legalization Programs of the 1986 Immigration Reform and Control Act. *International Migration Review* 31 (1): 5–27.
Useful review of the implementation and results of the IRCA-mandated legalization program. The paper begins with a concise review of the two distinct portions of the program: the original program and the last-minute special agricultural workers (SAW) program. Baker then presents some interesting comparative information on the widely varying results of the program in major cities and concludes with reflections on the meaning of legalization for the migrants themselves. The importance of being "legal" for travel between the United States and the home country, for example, is stressed.

Baldassare, Mark, and Georjeanna Wilson-Doenges
1995   Residents' Attitudes toward Race and Ethnic Relations in a Changing Suburban Metropolis. *Sociological Focus* 28 (4): 383–397.
Review of a 1994 survey in Orange Country, California. The survey included questions on attitudes about whether increases in ethnic diversity had helped or hurt the quality of life and whether different ethnic groups were getting along. The survey included a specific question about whether people would vote for or against Proposition 187 that fall. The analysis of the responses includes both individual variables (race, age, etc.) and community context variables (crime rate, ethnic composition, etc.). The authors stress the shifting nature of racial issues in suburban areas.

Basch, Linda, Nina Glick Schiller, and Cristina Szanton Blanc
1994   *Nations Unbound: Transnational Projects, Postcolonial Predicaments, and Deterritorialized Nation-States.* Langhorne, Pennsylvania: Gordon and Breach. 344 pages.
Review of migrants from Haiti, Granada, St. Vincent, and the Philippines. Al-

though the book does not deal directly with the legalities of immigration, it does address the way in which migrants maintain footholds and identities in both "home" and "host" societies. Since both Haiti and the Philippines are significant sources of undocumented migration to the United States, the book provides a useful sense of the fluidity of the migration process. Despite the theoretical concerns evident in the title, the book provides much sound and accessible ethnographic information.

Bean, Frank D., Barry Edmonston, and Jeffrey S. Passel, Editors
1990   *Undocumented Migration to the United States: IRCA and the Experience of the 1980s.* Washington, D.C.: Urban Institute Press. 271 pages.
Assessment of IRCA's success in reducing illegal immigration. The nine papers (plus Introduction) in the volume are, despite different authors, quite tightly integrated around the specific question of IRCA's effect on the number of illegal immigrants, particularly from Mexico, although with some attention to other countries as well. Because of the purpose of the book and the caliber of the authors, the volume also serves as a primer on how to estimate the illegal population.

Bean, Frank D., Rudolfo O. de la Garza, Bryan R. Roberts, and Sidney Weintraub, Editors
1997   *At the Crossroads: Mexico and U.S. Immigration Policy.* Lanham, Maryland: Rowman and Littlefield. 332 pages.
Set of ten papers with Introduction and Conclusion by the editors. The authors collectively have a very broad range of experience and provide useful perspectives and data on economic and political aspects of the border. The volume provides a particularly good starting point for considering recent concerns about migration from both sides of the border. Illegal immigration inevitably emerges in the broader discussion of Mexican migration.

Beck, Roy H.
1996   *The Case against Immigration: The Moral, Economic, Social, and Environmental Reasons for Reducing U.S. Immigration Back to Traditional Levels.* New York: W. W. Norton. 287 pages.
Strongly argumentative book urging reduced immigration. Beck's case has a strong moral argument in that immigration primarily benefits a small minority of wealthy and powerful Americans at the expense of significant segments of the middle class and poor. He is particularly concerned about the negative effects of immigration on black Americans and, more generally, the social and environmental costs paid to achieve "cheap labor." The book's focus, unlike that of many others, is specifically on legal immigration since Beck believes that illegal immigration is both numerically far less important and an issue that would largely be resolved if legal immigration could be controlled.

Borjas, George J.
1990   *Friends or Strangers: The Impact of Immigrants on the U.S. Economy.* New York: Basic Books. 274 pages.

Early, accessible work by one of the major analysts of the impact of immigration. Borjas provides an overview of recent immigrants in four chapters, and then spends six chapters on their economic situation and the effects they have on the native-born. He concludes with two chapters on the overall nature of what he calls the "immigration market" and the implications for policy development. Chapter 4 (pages 56–75) provides a clear introduction to illegal immigration.

Briggs, Vernon M., Jr.
1984   *Immigration Policy and the American Labor Force*. Baltimore: Johns Hopkins University Press. 294 pages.
Historical review and policy analysis of migration to the United States, with emphasis on labor issues. A long chapter (pages 128–184) on illegal immigration provides a readable introduction to basic issues, including data problems, economic development issues, and the policy debates in the early 1980s as Congress struggled toward the eventual IRCA legislation of 1986. The book also provides a review of related temporary worker programs. Although somewhat dated by events, this remains a useful and accessible introduction.

Briggs, Vernon M., Jr.
1996   *Mass Immigration and the National Interest*. 2d ed. Armonk, New York: M. E. Sharpe. 283 pages.
Review of immigration to the United States with emphasis on periods when immigration reached massive numbers. The author's general argument is that the most recent period of mass immigration is inconsistent with the national interest and therefore should be changed—particularly with more control and lessened numbers. Issues of illegal immigration are dealt with at various points in the discussion and can be accessed through the serviceable index.

Brown, Timothy C.
1997   The Fourth Member of NAFTA: The U.S. Mexico Border. *Annals of the American Academy of Political and Social Science* 550: 105–121.
Informal review of the border region. Brown argues that the border area is an important unit in its own right, with 22 million people, a gross domestic product of $300 billion, and over $100 billion in total exports and imports—compared to which any costs of illegal immigration are minor indeed. Following some general comments on the border and especially its major cities, he provides some suggestions for better managing the area.

Burns, Allan F.
1993   *Maya in Exile: Guatemalans in Florida*. Philadelphia: Temple University Press. 208 pages.
Accessible review of Mayan refugees, focusing on Indiantown, the central point of exodus in Florida. Burns has extensive research and advocacy experience with the Maya and presents a mix of qualitative and quantitative data on them. The chapter on work provides a particularly clear review of the problems in assessing their status as asylum applicants, illegal immigrants, and applicants

for legal status under the 1986 IRCA legislation. A highly evocative and personal Introduction is provided by Jerónimo Camposeco.

Bustamante, Jorge
1997   Mexico–United States Labor Migration Flows. *International Migration Review* 31 (4): 1112–1121.
Succinct overview of the dynamics of undocumented Mexican labor migration to the United States. Bustamante has some twenty-five years' experience in the formal study of undocumented Mexican migration, and this is a concise introduction to his views. In this short paper, he reviews the long-standing patterns of U.S. use of low-wage Mexican labor but consistent refusal to recognize that the resulting illegal border crossings are a labor issue rather than a criminal issue. He then briefly sketches a framework for addressing illegal migration, including NAFTA as part of the context.

Byrd, Bobby, and Susannah Mississippi Byrd, Editors
1996   *The Late Great Mexican Border: Reports from a Disappearing Line.* El Paso, Texas: Cinco Puntos Press. 227 pages.
Series of republished papers on the Mexican–U.S. border. The volume is a thoughtful selection from a broad range of writers and an equally broad range of border issues. This is not an academic collection but rather gives a series of personal snapshots of the border, the ways the border can be crossed, and the interrelated social communities and agricultural and industrial systems on both sides of the border. The book is a very good initial foray to and across the border that dominates the discussion of illegal immigration in America.

Chavez, Leo, F. Allan Hubbell, Shiraz L. Mishra, and R. Burciaga Valdez
1997   Undocumented Latina Immigrants in Orange County, California: A Comparative Analysis. *International Migration Review* 31 (1): 88–107.
Interesting comparison of 160 undocumented Latinas, 311 legal Latina immigrants, 313 Latina citizens, and 422 Anglo women. (The Latinas were largely of Mexican origin.) The undocumented Latinas tended to be younger and more frequently "living together" than formally married. Their households were generally complex in structure, their labor force participation was relatively low, and the jobs of those who did find employment were often in domestic work. Their use of assistance, however, was also low, and many had considerable commitment to U.S. residence. The article also discusses use of health services.

Chock, Phyllis Pease
1991   "Illegal Aliens" and "Opportunity": Myth-Making in Congressional Testimony. *American Ethnologist* 18 (2): 279–294.
Interpretation of early congressional hearings on illegal immigration. Chock argues that the hearings were largely structured in terms of the central American myth of opportunity rather than as an analytic or even information-gathering effort. Although her argument is decidedly theoretical, there are numerous quo-

tations from the testimony that convey very well the scripted nature of the hearings—echoes of which remain in current discussions of illegal immigration.

Cohen, Robin, Editor
1995   *The Cambridge Survey of World Migration.* Cambridge: Cambridge University Press. 570 pages.
Comprehensive survey of world migration. The book includes ninety-five selections organized into fifteen sections, each with its own brief prologue. Various entries deal directly or indirectly with undocumented migrants, including asylum seekers. For the United States, there are pieces by Mark Miller and Norman and Naomi Zucker; there are also useful pieces on illegal migration in Asia in general (Graeme Hugo) and Japan in particular (Helmut Loiskandle). The selections are relatively short but provide a usefully quick orientation to the global scope of migration and its "illegal" components.

Conway, Frederick J., and Susan Buchanan Stafford
1996   Haitians. In *Refugees in America in the 1990s.* Edited by David W. Haines. Westport, Connecticut: Greenwood Press. Pp. 170–190.
Review of Haitian emigration to the United States. The authors provide a succinct historical and cultural background to Haitian emigration, with particular attention to the shifting politics and often desperate economic situations in the country. The hazards of exodus and the sharp changes in U.S. policy toward Haitian emigrants are also discussed. The frequent lack of refugee status has exacerbated the adjustment of Haitians to the United States, as has the difficulty in maintaining ethnic identity in a racially polarized America.

Corcoran, Mary P.
1993   *Irish Illegals: Transients between Two Societies.* Westport, Connecticut: Greenwood Press. 205 pages.
Review of illegal Irish in New York City in the late 1980s. Based on participant-observation and interviews, Corcoran provides an invaluable look at the illegal "new" Irish. As she points out, there is a dearth of information on all but a few undocumented populations, and the fact that the Irish are well educated, white, and English-speaking provides the opportunity to consider issues of legal status as separate from issues of race, language, and ethnicity. The illegal Irish thus avoid some, though far from all, of the problems usually faced by undocumented workers.

Cornelius, Wayne A., Philip L. Martin, and James F. Hollifield, Editors
1994   *Controlling Immigration: A Global Perspective.* Stanford: Stanford University Press. 442 pages.
Series of papers with an international comparative perspective. Following an Introduction by the editors, separate chapters address the United States, Canada, France, Germany, Belgium, Britain, Italy, Spain, and Japan. Each chapter is followed by one or more commentaries. The chapters on the United States are by Kitty Calavita and Philip Martin, with comments by David Martin, Mark

Miller, and Jeffrey Passel. Issues of illegal immigration appear sporadically through the book and can be accessed through a serviceable index.

Coutin, Susan B.
1993   *The Culture of Protest: Religious Activism and the U.S. Sanctuary Movement.* Boulder, Colorado: Westview Press. 250 pages.
Thoughtful analysis of the U.S. sanctuary movement in the Tucson and San Francisco areas. The author, an anthropologist, both participated with, and interviewed, people in the movement in the late 1980s. The book is divided into three main parts: (1) how the culture of the movement developed; (2) the interplay of power and resistance between the movement and the government; and (3) the broader way in which participation in the movement's culture "enacted participants' visions of a more just social order." The book includes a great deal of solid interview material mixed with sound observation and reflection.

Crittenden, Ann
1988   *Sanctuary: A Story of American Conscience and the Law in Collision.* New York: Weidenfeld and Nicolson. 410 pages.
Account of the Arizona sanctuary movement. The book is a journalistic one that traces the development of the movement from the beginning of the 1980s through the trial of the sanctuary workers. The reconstructed narrative of events is based on press accounts, trial transcripts, and the author's own interviews. The book is particularly valuable for its detailed attention to the government investigation and trial, including what materials were provided to the jury and how government informers were used.

de la Garza, Rudolfo O., and Louis DeSipio
1998   Interests Not Passions: Mexican-American Attitudes toward Mexico, Immigration from Mexico, and Other Issues Shaping U.S.–Mexico Relations. *International Migration Review* 32 (2): 401–422.
Review of Mexican-American attitudes based on ten surveys from 1988 to 1996. The data suggest that Mexican Americans are committed to the United States, although retaining attachment to Mexico (although not to its government). They are similar to other Americans in seeking reduced immigration levels and increased control over undocumented immigration. On the other hand, they oppose harsh measures such as the building of a wall along the border and the denial of services to the undocumented. The authors caution that these attitudes can be volatile, particularly when there is a perception of discrimination.

del Castillo, Richard Griswold, and Arnoldo De Léon
1996   *North to Aztlán: A History of Mexican Americans in the United States.* New York: Twayne. 237 pages.
Succinct history of Mexican Americans. Beginning with early Native American and Spanish settlements, the authors trace the history of Mexican Americans up to the present. Because of the clear structure and format of the book, it is particularly useful as a general introduction. A short bibliographic essay pro-

vides a helpful guide to the broad literature on Mexican Americans. Illegal immigration is noted at relevant points, but the value of the book lies more in the comprehensiveness of its coverage.

Delgado, Héctor L.
1993   *New Immigrants, Old Unions: Organizing Undocumented Workers in Los Angeles.* Philadelphia: Temple University Press. 186 pages.
Case study of unionization among undocumented Mexicans and Central Americans in Los Angeles in 1987–1988. As the author notes, unionization of the undocumented is extraordinarily difficult. Nevertheless, in this case it was possible due to a combination of strong union commitment and considerable courage on the part of the vulnerable workers. The book provides core chapters that detail the organizing campaign itself, the world of the workers, and the legal rights that the workers possessed despite their undocumented status.

Díaz-Briquets, Sergio, and Sidney Weintraub, Editors
1991   *Determinants of Emigration from Mexico, Central America, and the Caribbean.* Boulder, Colorado: Westview Press. 356 pages.
First of six volumes of studies and findings from the Commission for the Study of International Migration and Cooperative Economic Development (which was mandated by IRCA). The series editors stress that, despite its long-term course and extensive demands, economic development in the sending countries is the only viable resolution to illegal immigration to the United States. In line with that view, the twelve papers in the book focus, for the most part, on the development-related factors inducing emigration to the United States. The book includes a wide range of intriguing data from commission-related research.

Díaz-Briquets, Sergio, and Sidney Weintraub, Editors
1991   *The Effects of Receiving Country Policies on Migration Flows.* Boulder, Colorado: Westview Press. 303 pages.
Final of six volumes of studies and findings from the Commission for the Study of International Migration and Cooperative Economic Development. The nine chapters in the volume range from general policy impacts to specific migration patterns in Mexico. As in the other volumes of the series, there is a wide range of interesting analysis and intriguing data. This sixth volume also includes as Chapter 10 the commission's final report and recommendations and thus, with the first volume, just noted, is of particular interest.

Donato, Katharine M., Jorge Durand, and Douglas S. Massey
1992   Changing Conditions in the U.S. Labor Market: Effects of the Immigration Reform and Control Act of 1986. *Population Research and Policy Review* 11 (2): 93–115.
Review of the effects of IRCA on the working conditions for Mexican immigrants in the United States. Based on interviews on both sides of the border, the authors provide a statistical analysis indicating that although IRCA did not appear to stem the volume of illegal Mexican immigration, it did sharply lower

the prospects for those illegal workers as they were pushed out of their current work and into more irregular jobs, with fewer work hours and less frequent withholding of taxes. IRCA, they suggest, "appears simply to have spurred the growth of an underground economy."

Doty, Roxanne Lynn
1996   The Double-Writing of Statecraft: Exploring State Responses to Illegal Immigration. *Alternatives* 21 (2): 171–189.
Theoretical essay on how illegal immigration reflects statecraft in general. Doty begins by noting "the territorial trap" into which much analysis of statecraft falls, specifically, notions that states are fixed spaces that contain societies and that have clear divides between domestic and international arenas. She then discusses how immigration in general and illegal immigration in particular challenge those notions and simultaneously bring into play efforts to reassert the reality of borders and thus the authenticity of the states contained within them. The essay is particularly effective in suggesting why illegal immigration is an issue of greater symbolic import than the numbers seem to warrant.

Earle, Duncan M.
1994   Constructions of Refugee Ethnic Identity: Guatemalan Mayas in Mexico and South Florida. In *Reconstructing Lives, Recapturing Meaning*. Edited by Linda Camino and Ruth Krulfeld. Basel, Switzerland: Gordon and Breach. Pp. 207–234.
Overview of identity formation among Mayan exiles in Mexico and the United States. The emphasis is on different bases for ethnic identity among a varied group of Guatemalan Maya, including both localized community links and contrasts between themselves and outsiders. The contrasts between urban settlement, stable agricultural areas, and migrant labor are of interest, as are the various ways in which "refugee" is used as a marker of identity. There is also a specific discussion of the implications of undocumented status.

Engstrom, David W.
1997   *Presidential Decision Making Adrift: The Carter Administration and the Mariel Boatlift*. Lanham, Maryland: Rowman and Littlefield. 239 pages.
Review of the 1980 Mariel exodus with emphasis on the overall development of policy. Engstrom begins with two chapters that provide background on Cuban migration to the United States and the factors that gave rise to the exodus. He then turns to the two distinct efforts the administration made to stop the exodus and to the complex discussions of legal status that ultimately led to the new "entrant" status. The Carter administration does not fare well in his analysis due to its lack of attention to information and a structure of decision making that excluded lower-ranking and often more knowledgeable officials.

Espenshade, Thomas J.
1995   Unauthorized Immigration to the United States. *Annual Review of Sociology* 21: 195–216.
Succinct review of illegal immigration. The author sequentially discusses (1)

estimates of numbers of illegal immigrants; (2) public opinion about them; (3) factors underlying illegal immigration; (4) consequences for both labor markets and government expenditures; (5) policies—largely unsuccessful—for control; and (6) future prospects. He writes: "We may have to conclude that the current level of unauthorized immigration is a price that most Americans are willing to pay to maintain an open society."

Espenshade, Thomas J.
1995   Using INS Border Apprehension Data to Measure the Flow of Undocu-
        mented Migrants Crossing the U.S.–Mexico Frontier. *International Mi-
        gration Review* 29 (2): 545–565.
Review of the problems in estimating illegal border crossings from data on apprehensions. Espenshade reviews the way apprehensions data have been used in the past and suggests a simple way to estimate total flow from such data, based on the assumption that failed border crossers always try again and the availability of some data on border crossers who are apprehended multiple times. The resulting estimates are that roughly a third of border crossers are appre-hended each time they try to cross. The net result is a total flow roughly 2.2 times as great as the number of apprehensions.

Espenshade, Thomas J., and Charles A. Calhoun
1993   An Analysis of Public Opinion toward Undocumented Immigration. *Pop-
        ulation Research and Policy Review* 12 (3): 189–224.
Analysis of a 1983 survey in southern California. The authors review some of the existing research on American views about immigration and consider the likely sources of that sentiment: labor market competition; cultural affinity; ed-ucational levels; personal costs and benefits; and symbolic concerns (e.g., de-clining use of English). Separate statistical analyses are provided about general attitudes on illegal immigration and more specific attitudes on the potential ef-fects of illegal immigration on California. The comprehensiveness of the survey questions and the flexibility of the statistical analysis make this a particularly valuable article.

Espinosa, Kristin E., and Douglas S. Massey
1997   Determinants of English Proficiency among Mexican Migrants to the
        United States. *International Migration Review* 31 (1): 28–50.
Analysis of English-language proficiency among Mexican migrants who have returned to Mexico. The authors find clear evidence that English proficiency improves with exposure to U.S. society and that there is a general pattern of increased proficiency for men, for those with better education, and for those with children in U.S. schools. The importance of the study, however, lies more with its method: statistical analysis of interviews with migrants both in the United States and in their Mexican communities after return. Whether the mi-grants possessed legal documents is one variable used in the analysis.

Ferris, Elizabeth
1987   *The Central American Refugee.* New York: Praeger. 159 pages.

General overview of the patterns in Central American refugee origins and movements. The author introduces the policy context and the respective situations in El Salvador, Guatemala, and Nicaragua that generated the refugees. She then addresses in separate chapters the Mexican, Costa Rican, Honduran, and U.S. responses to the refugees. The section specifically on the United States is helpful, but brief.

Finch, Wilbur A.
1990   The Immigration Reform and Control Act of 1986: A Preliminary Assessment. *Social Service Review* 64 (2): 244–260.
Early review of IRCA implementation. Finch provides an overview of the 1986 legislation, its implementation (including the numerous legal shifts along the way), and the initial data on its effectiveness (incomplete though they were at that time). The article provides a useful reference point before the subsequent set of immigration law changes in the 1990s. There is a useful, short section on nondiscrimination provisions of the law.

García y Griego, Manuel, John R. Weeks, and Roberto Ham Chande
1990   Mexico. In *Handbook on International Migration*. Edited by William J. Serow, Charles B. Nam, David F. Sly, and Robert H. Weller. Westport, Connecticut: Greenwood Press. Pages 205–220.
Concise review of the dimensions and impact of migration to and from Mexico. The authors address the basic structure of Mexican migration policy, the data available to assess in-migration and out-migration, and the lack of any great demographic impact on Mexican society. Emigration to the United States receives the most attention, but there are also useful reflections on Mexican acceptance of refugees and immigrants from Central America.

Gimpel, James G., and James R. Edwards, Jr.
1999   *The Congressional Politics of Immigration Reform*. Boston: Allyn and Bacon. 342 pages.
Review of immigration legislation with emphasis on the details of the legislative process. The authors provide three useful introductory chapters and then turn to more detailed chapters covering the 1965–1982 period, the 1982–1994 period, and the 104th Congress (which passed the Illegal Immigration Reform and Immigrant Responsibility Act). Illegal immigration is a continuing thread in the legislative action. This is a useful source and often engaging—the authors, for example, include brief biographies of the key players.

Grasmuck, Sherri, and Patricia R. Pessar
1991   *Between Two Islands: Dominican International Migration*. Berkeley: University of California Press. 247 pages.
Important study of Dominican migration to New York. The study is based on a mix of quantitative and qualitative research in both the United States and the Dominican Republic. The authors address the basis in the Dominican Republic for emigration, rural emigration there, the importance of generation and gender in household migration, and Dominicans in the U.S. labor market. Undocu-

mented Dominicans are discussed at several points, particularly in a chapter section (pages 169–186) on their employment compared to that of documented Dominican migrants.

Green, Nancy L.
1996 Women and Immigrants in the Sweatshop: Categories of Labor Segmentation Revisited. *Comparative Studies in Society and History* 38 (3): 411–433.
Historical review of the alternating use of native-born women, immigrant men, and immigrant women in the garment industry. Green's central concern is with how the demands for low-wage labor in increasingly deskilled jobs were met and how the people doing the work were constructed as innately qualified categories of people (nimble-fingered women, strong men, etc.) who had reasons to do the work for low wages (e.g., women supplementing family incomes). Although not directly related to current issues of undocumented immigration, it is useful for bringing together the ways in which gender and immigration are used for similar purposes in particular industries—in this case one in which the undocumented have come to be very important.

Gutiérrez, David G.
1995 *Walls and Mirrors: Mexican Americans, Mexican Immigrants, and the Politics of Ethnicity.* Berkeley: University of California Press. 320 pages.
Historical review of Mexican Americans and Mexican immigrants. The author's aim is to provide a balanced account of both established Americans of Mexican descent and newer immigrants from Mexico—specifically, how notions of Mexican-American ethnicity have constantly had to account for these new arrivals, many of whom have been undocumented. Gutiérrez begins his account with the end of the U.S. war with Mexico in 1848 and then moves toward the present, concluding with a useful chapter on the contemporary debate on how the Mexican-American community should respond to immigration issues.

Hagan, Jacqueline Maria
1994 *Deciding to Be Legal: A Maya Community in Houston.* Philadelphia: Temple University Press. 200 pages.
Ethnographic case study of Maya from San Pedro (Totonicapan). Hagan reviews their emigration from Guatemala and the course of their settlement in Houston. The focus of the book, however, is the social process of deciding to become legal under the provisions of 1986's IRCA and the subsequent effects of such legalization on their lives. These particular Maya are less arguably ''refugees'' than many other Maya and thus provide a useful counterpoint to the experience of other Mayan groups.

Hailbronner, Kay, David A. Martin, and Hiroshi Motomura, Editors
1998 *Immigration Controls: The Search for Workable Policies in Germany and the United States.* Providence, Rhode Island: Berghahn Books. 230 pages.
Set of five papers on immigration control. In one paper, David Martin provides

a lawyer's accessible critique of the problems in enforcing laws. In two others, Stephen Legomsky and Kay Hailbronner address the problems in managing a large caseload of asylum applications. A final chapter by the editors suggests how controls over unwanted immigration could be improved. This is one of five volumes on comparative U.S./German immigration under the general editorship of Myron Weiner. All are published in association with the American Academy of Arts and Sciences, which sponsored a two-year project on immigration and refugee policies in the two countries.

Hamilton, Nora, and Norma Stoltz Chinchilla
1991   Central American Migration: A Framework for Analysis. *Latin American Research Review* 26 (1): 75–110.
Review of internal and international migration in Central America from an historical and theoretical perspective. The authors begin with an emphasis on capitalism and its effects on core and peripheral areas and then trace migration in the region from the nineteenth century on, with particular attention to the post–World War II period and El Salvador. They note that the political violence of the 1970s and 1980s created a change in the magnitude of migration but that migrants continued to move through quite traditional channels. The article is a useful introduction to the overall patterns of movement in the region.

Harmon, Robert C.
1996   Intergenerational Relations among Maya in Los Angeles. In *Selected Papers on Refugee Issues IV*. Edited by Ann Rynearson and James Phillips. Arlington, Virginia: American Anthropological Association. Pp. 156–173.
Review of the Mayan community in Los Angeles, the major West Coast location of the Kanjobal Maya. Harmon provides a succinct introduction to the community, including their reaction to the 1992 riots and the later passage of Proposition 187. The later portion of the article focuses on scaling techniques used to assess what words best characterize the role of the elderly. The inability of the elderly to conduct traditional activities is stressed. Although the Maya in Los Angeles originally came illegally, some were legalized under IRCA; others have sought legal asylum.

Heer, David M.
1990   *Undocumented Mexicans in the United States*. New York: Cambridge University Press. 232 pages.
Analysis of the undocumented Mexican population in 1980–1981. Heer's presentation is roughly in two parts. The first reviews the existing data, and the second presents his own data from a survey of Mexican-origin parents in Los Angeles. The survey data provide clean distinctions between the documented and undocumented population. Heer is careful to assess whether differences are specifically related to legal status or to other factors.

Heer, David M.
1996   *Immigration in America's Future: Social Science Findings and the Policy Debate*. Boulder, Colorado: Westview Press. 244 pages.
Overview of immigration geared toward future policy decisions. Unlike most books on immigration, this is as much concerned with the process of determining options as with what those options should be. Heer starts with the questions that need to be addressed (standard of living, equity, maintenance of existing American culture, ethnic and class conflict, international affairs). He then addresses to what extent and how social science can help inform those decisions. Only then does he review the specifics of immigration to the United States. Illegal immigration receives due attention (especially on pages 88–101).

Hondagneu-Sotelo, Pierrette
1994   *Gendered Transitions: Mexican Experiences of Immigration*. Berkeley: University of California Press. 258 pages.
Ethnographic study of largely undocumented Mexicans in the San Francisco area. The author provides succinct theoretical and historical reviews of undocumented Mexican migration, then focuses on the specific experiences of the forty-four main respondents. The book emphasizes the interaction of gender and immigration, with a useful delineation of how household structure and gender affect the nature of settlement in the United States (e.g., families vs. individuals, single men vs. single women). The work lives, family lives, and community lives of women are all clearly portrayed.

Hondagneu-Sotelo, Pierrette
1994   Regulating the Unregulated?: Domestic Workers' Social Networks. *Social Problems* 41 (1): 50–64.
Analysis of domestic work among undocumented Mexican women in the San Francisco area (see previous entry). In this article Hondagneu-Sotelo focuses on domestic work, starting with a concise review of the development of domestic work from its original live-in basis, to day work, and ultimately to "job work." The most recent versions of domestic work involve atomized working conditions, privatized employer–employee relations, and the need to maintain multiple employers. The emphasis is on how the networks of domestic workers both constrain and provide options to the individual workers.

Hope, Katie
1998   INS Detention. Special Issue of *Refugee Reports* 19 (6): 1–10.
Timely review of INS detention of legal and illegal immigrants. The author focuses on the efforts of a variety of religious, legal, and human rights organizations to assure that prison conditions are livable, that service and religious workers have full access to prisons, and that prisoners have access to legal information and legal counsel should they desire it. This issue of *Refugee Reports* also includes a section on the applicability of the torture convention to female genital mutilation.

Human Rights Watch
1995   *Crossing the Line: Human Rights Abuses along the U.S. Border with Mexico Persist amid Climate of Impunity.* New York: Human Rights Watch. 37 pages.
Report on abuses along the border. The report is the third in as many years by Human Rights Watch concerning serious human rights abuses by Border Patrol agents. The report not only repeats previous reports of shootings, rapes, and beatings but notes the ineffectiveness of INS efforts to resolve problems previously reported. The earlier reports are also of value.

Human Rights Watch
1997   *Slipping through the Cracks: Unaccompanied Children Detained by the United States Immigration and Naturalization Service.* New York: Children's Rights Project. 128 pages.
Report based on site visits to INS facilities in Los Angeles and Arizona. Human Rights Watch found a variety of problems in addition to their general objection to imprisonment itself: particularly length of detention, failure to inform the minors of their rights, and impeding their access both to legal counsel and to family. The general recommendation is to move responsibility for these children away from the INS to child welfare agencies.

Human Rights Watch
1998   *Locked Away: Immigration Detainees in Jails in the United States.* New York: Human Rights Watch. 84 pages.
Report based on a wide range of interviews and materials, including interviews with some 200 detainees placed in local jails. The problems found include the lack of INS oversight and the placement of these persons, whose offenses are more administrative than criminal, indiscriminately among a criminal population. The treatment of detainees is often poor, and their access to friends, family, and legal representation is limited.

Interpreter Releases
Weekly   Washington, D.C.: Federal Publications Incorporated.
Valuable newsletter. *Interpreter Releases* aims to be the most up-to-date and comprehensive information source available on immigration law. Each issue includes articles on key issues but also provides updates, notification of law review articles, and even full text of new immigration-related laws and regulations.

Jaffe, Maureen, and Sonia Rosen, Editors
1996   *Forced Labor: The Prostitution of Children.* Washington, D.C.: U.S. Department of Labor, Bureau of International Labor Affairs. 152 pages.
Set of papers from a symposium on child prostitution. The general focus is on international aspects of the problem, including the trafficking of children across borders, and is in two main parts: the first provides overviews of the problem

in Asia, Latin America, and the United States; the second describes governmental and nongovernmental responses. This is a good introduction to the global problem. Appendixes include the main UN, ILO, and U.S. laws and conventions on the subject. (This volume follows two earlier reports by the Department of Labor on child labor in general.)

Jonas, Susanne, and Suzie Dod Thomas, Editors
1996   Immigration: A Civil Rights Issue for the Americas in the 21st Century. Special issue of *Social Justice* 23 (3). 184 pages.
Special issue focusing on how to construct a progressive agenda for immigration. As a whole, the articles attempt to identify the ethical issues in immigration. Three articles (by Nestor Rodriguez, David Bacon, and Michael Welch and Sara Diamond) provide special focus on the undocumented, including an analysis of the right-wing, anti-immigration position seen in Proposition 187.

Jones, Richard C., Editor
1984   *Patterns of Undocumented Migration: Mexico and the United States.* Totowa, New Jersey: Rowman and Allenheld. 242 pages.
Set of twelve papers on origins and destinations of undocumented Mexican immigration. The editor notes in his introduction the tendency to view undocumented migration at a general level and his consequent desire to present the more focused case studies in this volume of specific migrant pathways. The result is an interesting sampling of such pathways. The editor is a geographer, as are several other contributors, and that helps give the volume a useful focus and some intriguing individual maps.

Kahn, Robert S.
1996   *Other People's Blood: U.S. Immigration Prisons in the Reagan Decade.* Boulder, Colorado: Westview Press. 265 pages.
Passionate review of the situation of Salvadorans and Guatemalans in the United States. Based on very extensive interviews and work as a legal assistant in four prisons, Kahn presents a harrowing portrait of what happened to Central Americans once they reached the United States. Prisons at Port Isabel, Laredo, Oakdale, Florence, and Brownsville each receive a chapter's attention. The presentation is often very personal, reflecting the struggles of both the Central Americans and those volunteers who attempted to extricate them from the prison system.

Kassindja, Fauziya, and Layl Miller Bashir
1998   *Do They Hear You When You Cry?* New York: Delacorte Press. 518 pages.
Personal account of an asylum seeker from Togo. This autobiographical account follows a Muslim women from her home country through transit and final arrival in the United States, where she was incarcerated but finally won political asylum in 1996. In the process, her case publicized issues of female genital mutilation,

the avoidance of which is now at least occasionally recognized as grounds for asylum. The book is an effective insider's view of incarceration and the complex judicial processes asylum applicants must face.

Kessner, Thomas, and Betty Boyd Caroli
1982   *Today's Immigrants: Their Stories.* New York: Oxford University Press.
          317 pages.
Readable introduction to immigrants in New York City. Although now some-what dated, this volume provides a useful portrait of New York as it was again becoming an immigrant city—as it had been at the beginning of the century. Chapter 2 (pages 71–104) deals directly with undocumented immigrants. The authors note the extent to which the undocumented in New York at that time were visa-overstayers rather than illegal border crossers and provide a variety of vignettes addressing why they came to New York and the way their legal status affected their lives.

Kinkead, Gwen
1992   *Chinatown: A Portrait of a Closed Society.* New York: HarperCollins.
          215 pages.
Accessible introduction to New York's Chinatown. Kinkead exposes a wide range of problems and crime in Chinatown, based partially on general data but mostly on her own interviews and observations. The general darkness of the portrayal is leavened by the continuing vitality of the community and its mem-bers—children in particular. The book includes useful information on econom-ics—especially the garment industry. One chapter directly addresses illegal immigration and the toll it exacts.

Kossoudji, Sherrie A.
1992   Playing Cat and Mouse at the U.S. Mexican Border. *Demography* 29
          (2): 159–180.
Analysis of undocumented migration from Mexico. Kossoudji bases her analysis on data extracted from a major Mexican government-sponsored survey in 1978. Although the findings predate the recent increase in U.S. border control, they suggest that increased apprehensions of border crossers do not reduce attempts to cross the border. Instead, border crossings may rise, and the time the migrants spend in the United States may increase.

Kwong, Peter
1996   *The New Chinatown.* Rev. ed. New York: Hill and Wang. 226 pages.
Troubling review of New York City's Chinatown. The book is largely a reprint of the original 1987 edition, but with a substantial new chapter addressing Chi-natown in the 1990s, especially the Fujianese illegal immigrants, who are ad-dressed more fully in Kwong's *Forbidden Workers* (in the next entry). Kwong is an astute observer of both labor and ethnic community issues and provides clear guidance on the way traditional Chinese kinship and locality organizations

were utilized yet transformed in Chinatown. The discussion of the garment and restaurant business is especially detailed.

Kwong, Peter
1997   *Forbidden Workers: Illegal Chinese Immigrants and American Labor.*
        New York: New Press. 273 pages.
Frank examination of illegal Chinese immigration. Kwong begins with the grounding of the *Golden Venture* in 1993 in New York Harbor. He then backtracks to describe earlier Chinese migration. The discussion of the specific mechanisms and people ("snakeheads") who manage the new trafficking in people is especially valuable. (A film entitled *Snakehead* covers some of the same material, including a trip Kwong took to China to discuss undocumented Chinese migration with families and the snakeheads themselves.)

Lamm, Richard D., and Gary Imhoff
1985   *The Immigration Time Bomb: The Fragmenting of America.* New York:
        E. P. Dutton. 271 pages.
Early, somewhat sensationalized warning about the perils of immigration. The authors provide the usual list of problems caused by immigration and often do so very effectively. Their statement that "the exploitation that is an integral part of illegal immigration offends and outrages us" (page 28) will strike a resonant chord with both pro- and anti-immigration factions. Perhaps their central point is that "the melting pot, like any pot, is finite" (page x). Lamm's status as a governor made this a well-known and controversial book.

Langewiesche, William
1992   The Border. *Atlantic Monthly* 269 (5): 53–92; 269 (6): 91–108.
Two-part review of the U.S.–Mexican border. Although journalistic, Langewiesche's account of his travels and interviews on both sides of the border with a wide range of people is solid and provides a good introduction to the border. He is particularly effective in conveying the shifting physical nature of the border along its nearly 2,000-mile course. Those interviewed provide effective voices on the nature of the border from the perspective of Border Patrol agents, businessmen, and those involved in worker protection and human rights activism.

LeMay, Michael C.
1994   *Anatomy of a Public Policy: The Reform of Contemporary Immigration
        Law.* Westport, Connecticut: Praeger. 203 pages.
Review of the 1986 changes in immigration policy as a case study of the more general policy process. LeMay adopts a standard set of steps for the policy process from James Anderson: problem formation, agenda setting, policy formulation, policy adoption, implementation, and evaluation. He then uses those steps to structure his discussion of the events leading up to and after the passage of IRCA. The analysis is based on the legislative record, additional materials

made available by the Rand Corporation, and questionnaires sent by LeMay himself.

Loescher, Gilbert D., and John A. Scanlan, Editors
1983   The Global Refugee Problem. *Annals of the American Academy of Political and Social Science* 467. 253 pages.
Set of thirteen articles on refugees and asylum seekers. Five of the articles deal directly with the United States: Loescher and Scanlan on the effects of U.S. foreign policy on Cuban refugee flows; Ronald Copeland on the Cuban boat lift of 1980; Naomi Zucker on the legal contest over Haitian refugees; Arnold Leibowitz on the Refugee Act of 1980; and Norman Zucker on U.S. resettlement policy. An understanding of the events described in these chapters is essential to a broader understanding of the shifting categories of legal entry at the time—and the inability of the U.S. government to draw clear lines between refugees and other immigrants—thus ultimately creating a new hybrid ''entrant'' status.

Lorentzen, Robin
1991   *Women in the Sanctuary Movement.* Philadelphia: Temple University Press. 229 pages.
Review of the 1980s sanctuary movement. The author provides a general overview of the movement and its internal tensions—particularly between humanitarian and political goals—and then discusses in detail women's roles in the movement. Chicago receives the most attention, but the twenty-nine interviews that are at the core of the book include eight local sanctuary sites.

Lowell, B. Lindsay, and Demetrios G. Papademetriou
1992   Symposium [on immigration]. *Policy Studies Review* 11 (2): 76–186.
Set of ten articles on immigration policy. Articles that focus on illegal immigration or attitudes about illegal immigration include Roger Waldinger and Michael Lapp on the New York garment industry; David Griffith and David Runsten on the effects of IRCA on the U.S. poultry industry; Hector Delgado on IRCA and unionization in Los Angeles; Richard Morales on IRCA and the southern California restaurant industry; and Teresa Sullivan on immigration reform and the Latino small service sector.

Mahler, Sarah J.
1995   *Salvadorans in Suburbia: Symbiosis and Conflict.* Boston: Allyn and Bacon. 137 pages.
Invaluable study of Salvadorans on Long Island. Mahler, an anthropologist, both studied and provided legal assistance to the largely undocumented Salvadoran population, thus greatly enriching her account. She deals sequentially with demographic, historical, economic, and community issues, concluding with an analysis of how Salvadorans provide important economic services but are nevertheless resisted as neighbors.

Marcelli, Enrico A., and David M. Heer
1997   Unauthorized Mexican Workers in the 1990 Los Angeles County Labour
       Force. *International Migration* 35 (1): 59–81.
Review of undocumented Mexicans with emphasis on whether they compete
with other groups in the labor force. Using the same data described by Marcelli
in this volume, Marcelli and Heer argue that generally there is not much competition. The article is helpful in making the specific case about Mexican undocumented workers.

Margolis, Maxine L.
1998   We Are *Not* Immigrants! A Contested Category among Brazilians in
       New York City and Rio de Janeiro. In *Diasporic Identity: Selected Pa-
       pers on Refugees and Immigrants VI*. Arlington, Virginia: American An-
       thropological Association. Pp. 30–50.
Analysis of Brazilian attitudes toward immigration. Margolis provides an overview of the increasing migration of Brazilians to the United States and their
frequent return migration. She notes the extent to which Brazilians reject the
notion of being immigrants and the historical and class-based reasons for that
view. Much of the migration to the United States is, or becomes, illegal, and
the legality of migration, in turn, relates to Brazilian attitudes toward any label
that implies the permanence of migration.

Marquez, Benjamin
1995   Organizing Mexican-American Women in the Garment Industry: La Mu-
       jer Obrera. *Women and Politics* 15 (1): 65–87.
Review of the political economy of the garment industry, with emphasis on a
local union in El Paso, Texas. Marquez provides a useful discussion of the
garment industry. La Mujer Obrera is a locally developed union that had significant success in mobilizing for worker rights, but the obstacles, including
attitudes of the ILGWU, were formidable. The analysis is balanced with appreciation of the marginal finances of owners and the trade-offs regarding further
automation of garment assembly. (The issue of undocumented workers is not
directly addressed but is relevant.)

Martin, Philip L.
1996   *Promises to Keep: Collective Bargaining in California Agriculture*.
       Ames: Iowa University Press. 416 pages.
Thorough and important review of California agriculture, focused on unions and
unionizing. The book is divided into three major sections: the first reviews the
development of California agriculture; the second focuses on the successes and
failures in collective bargaining; and the third addresses the constant interaction
between California agriculture and immigration policy. Illegal immigration is an
important part of that story, and the book is particularly effective in illuminating
the issue of labor protection for both immigrants and the native-born.

Martin, Philip L., and David A. Martin
1994 *The Endless Quest: Helping America's Farm Workers.* Boulder, Colorado: Westview Press. 258 pages.
Review of assistance programs for farmworkers. The authors begin by pointing out how proportionately small and how seriously deprived is the migrant labor segment of agriculture. They then proceed to an overview of the kinds of assistance that exist for migrant workers—and what kinds should exist. The discussion of different programs and different layers of government provide a cautionary tale of difficulties in service coordination. One of their central concerns is that assistance to individual migrant workers may simply help them obtain better jobs and leave their inevitable replacements (who are often undocumented) in even worse conditions.

Massey, Douglas S., and Kristin E. Espinosa
1997 What's Driving Mexico–U.S. Migration: A Theoretical, Empirical, and Policy Analysis. *American Journal of Sociology* 102 (4): 939–999.
Analysis of first and repeat migration of Mexicans to and from the United States. The authors begin with a review of major sociological theories on migration and then consider those theories in the light of data gathered in twenty-five Mexican communities. They conclude that migration derives largely from the social links that potential migrants have to the United States, the experience that they accrue here, and the desire to obtain capital in a period of market consolidation. The authors are especially clear about how misguided U.S. policies to control this migration are: they are unlikely to reduce the migration and thus only marginalize the migrants.

Mehan, Hugh
1997 The Discourse of the Illegal Immigration Debate: A Case Study in the Politics of Representation. *Discourse and Society* 8 (2): 249–270.
Analysis of the arguments made for and against California's Proposition 187. Mehan's basic argument is that in the post–Cold War period, there has been a shift toward creating internal ''enemies,'' of whom ''illegal aliens'' are a major contender. His emphasis is on the ways the discourse on these migrants was constructed: ''us'' versus ''them'' distinctions, appeals to a general inclusive community, the power of appeals to self-interest, the strength of anecdotes in shaping opinion, and the declining salience of ''expert'' views.

Melville, Margarita B.
1985 Salvadorans and Guatemalans. In *Refugees in the United States: A Reference Handbook.* Edited by David W. Haines. Westport, Connecticut: Greenwood Press. Pp. 167–180.
Overview of the migration from El Salvador and Guatemala up to the mid-1980s. Melville provides brief reviews of the two countries, then examines the reasons the migrants left, largely because of the extensive violence in both countries. Much of the remainder of the chapter focuses on the problems the migrants faced because of not being formally recognized as refugees. A brief section

discusses U.S. citizen responses, especially the sanctuary movement. The chapter provides a good introduction to this migration at that time and to U.S. government responses.

Menjívar, Cecilia
1994   Salvadoran Migration to the United States in the 1980s. *International Migration* 32 (3): 371–401.
Review of migration from El Salvador to the San Francisco area, based on a survey of 150 people and follow-up, in-depth interviews with 40 of them. Menjívar provides an accessible, reasoned analysis on three points: (1) the reasons for migration were both political and economic; (2) the existence of kin links in the United States was essential in the exodus through Honduras and Mexico; and (3) those same links come under pressure in the United States and sometimes are ruptured—due largely to the limited availability of adequate employment.

Menjívar, Cecilia
1997   Immigrant Kinship Networks and the Impact of the Receiving Context: Salvadorans in San Francisco in the Early 1990s. *Social Problems* 44 (1): 104–123.
Review of difficulties within Salvadoran kinship networks. Following on her previous article, Menjívar notes the triple problems of the early 1990s for Salvadorans: the inherent difficulties of exodus, negative response from the U.S. government, and restriction in economic opportunities in the San Francisco area. She cautions that ''supportive networks should not be taken as an attribute of an immigrant group itself, but as processes contingent upon the physical and material location within which they unfold.'' The paper is based on some four years of qualitative research with fifty Salvadorans around the Mission District.

Mexico–United States Binational Study on Migration
1997   *Migration between Mexico and the United States: A Report of the Binational Study on Migration.* 82 pages. Jointly published by the U.S. Commission on Immigration Reform and the Mexican Secretarìa de Relaciones Exteriores.
Final report of an extensive bilateral study. The chapters of the report deal sequentially with an overview of the Mexican-American population, characteristics of Mexican-born migrants, causes of migration northward, economic and social effects in both countries, and responses in both countries to migration issues. Unauthorized migrants are discussed at various points, with particular concern about the frequent violation of human rights.

Mexico–United States Binational Study on Migration
1998   *Migration between Mexico and the United States: Binational Study.* Mexico City and Washington, D.C.: Mexican Ministry of Foreign Affairs and U.S. Commission on Immigration Reform.
Three-volume collection of papers prepared for the previously cited binational

study. Unlike the formal report, the selections in these volumes are all authored (in various combinations) by the Mexican and U.S. scholars involved in the study. They are organized to match the chapters in the final report. At over 1,200 pages, these volumes provide an enormous amount of insight into Mexican–U.S. migration by many of the best researchers on the subject. Undocumented migration is a major subject throughout, including its causes, hazards, and scale.

Migration News
Monthly   University of California-Davis.
Newsletter. There are both printed (shorter) and electronic (longer) versions of this monthly newsletter, which covers all aspects of migration both to the United States and to other countries. Although there are occasional special features and book reviews, the bulk of the newsletter is a compilation of synopsized newspaper accounts. This may well be the single best source for tracking current events and politics in the area of immigration. (See also *Rural Migration News*.)

Miller, Mark J., Editor
1994   Strategies for Immigration Control: An International Comparison. *Annals
       of the American Academy of Political and Social Science* 534: 8–177.
Set of papers on both American and other countries' attempts to control immigration. The Preface by Miller and an introductory chapter by Gary Freeman provide an overview of issues. Four of the remaining eleven papers deal specifically with the United States: Rosanna Perotti on IRCA's employer sanctions; Philip Martin on the reillegalizing of agricultural labor; David North on the failure to enforce the minimum wage in Los Angeles; and Christopher Mitchell on U.S. policy toward Haitian emigrants (see separate annotation for that paper).

Mines, Richard, Susan Gabbard, and Anne Steirman
1997   *A Profile of U.S. Farmworkers: Demographics, Household Composition,
       Income and Use of Services.* U.S. Department of Labor, Office of Program Economics Research Report #6.
Analysis of 1988–1995 data from DOL's National Agricultural Workers Survey. The data suggest that the farmworker population is increasingly male, increasingly foreign-born, and increasingly illegal. The report's chapters address demographics, household composition, income, and legal status. The report was prepared for the U.S. Commission on Immigration Reform and deals only with crop workers.

Miralles, Maria Andrea
1989   *A Matter of Life and Death: Health-Seeking Behavior of Guatemalan
       Refugees in South Florida.* New York: AMS. 172 pages.
Study of Mayan refugees in a small Florida town. The author's emphasis is on Mayan medical beliefs and the refugees' use of health services, but she also provides background on the origins of this refugee group, the stresses of migrant work, and the way this particular group fits into an unusually complex local

community. Most of the refugees were undocumented, although some sought legalization under IRCA.

Mitchell, Christopher

1994   U.S. Policy toward Haitian Boat People, 1972–1993. *Annals of the American Academy of Political and Social Science* 534: 69–80.

Coherent review of U.S. policy on Haitian refugees. The author briefly sketches the origins of legal and nonlegal immigration to the United States. The article then focuses on the legal and political aspects of the interception of boat refugees. The analysis of the Bush and early Clinton administrations is especially helpful. Mitchell finds U.S. policy ''on balance a discreditable affair'' but also notes how policy on Haitians is becoming less an anomaly than an emerging and sharply restrictive standard for all refugee groups.

Perea, Juan F., Editor

1997   *Immigrants Out! The New Nativism and the Anti-Immigrant Impulse in the United States.* New York: New York University Press. 342 pages.

Set of papers examining the anti-immigration backlash. The papers, by a variety of well-known writers, examine both the historical antecedents and current directions of the backlash, with a generally critical view of the allegations made by the nativists. The issue of undocumented immigrants appears at various points. The volume as a whole is a good introduction to the cultural and organizational dynamics of the new nativism.

Pessar, Patricia R.

1994   Sweatshop Workers and Domestic Ideologies: Dominican Women in New York's Apparel Industry. *International Journal of Urban and Regional Research* 18 (1): 127–142.

Case study of two Dominican women. Although the two women described were legal immigrants, the ways in which their personal and work lives intersect help illustrate the even more vulnerable position of undocumented women in the New York garment industry. Pessar's concern is to show the complexity of the decision-making process of Dominican women regarding whether to work and why the informal sector of the garment industry is appealing.

Portes, Alejandro, and Rubén G. Rumbaut

1996   *Immigrant America: A Portrait.* (2d ed.) Berkeley: University of California Press. 369 pages.

Solid overview of immigration and immigrants in America. The specific issue of undocumented migration receives considerable attention, particularly in terms of the dynamics of low-skilled labor migration and governmental attempts to control its borders. More general discussions of immigrant adaptation, shifting patterns for the second generation, and linguistic pluralism are also of relevance. The book is a good balance of readability and sociological analysis—with extensive data.

Portes, Alejandro, and Alex Stepick

1993   *City on the Edge: The Transformation of Miami.* Berkeley: University
        of California Press. 281 pages.

Accessible analysis of Miami's transformation, with emphasis on the effects of
the Cuban exodus to the city. Although Cubans until recently were firmly in
the legal category, the book also addresses two groups (Nicaraguans and Haitians) that until very recently were often undocumented in their entry and unsuccessful in their applications for asylum. The book is particularly helpful for
its description of the Nicaraguans. There is useful information on Haitians, but
some of Stepick's other work (e.g., his 1998 *Pride against Prejudice*) is more
detailed.

Powers, Mary G., and William Seltzer

1998   Occupational Status and Mobility among Undocumented Immigrants by
        Gender. *International Migration Review* 32 (1): 21–55.

Analysis of data from a survey of newly legalized immigrants. Powers and
Seltzer provide a succinct review of theories and assumptions about the economic status of immigrants and then assess those ideas against the 1989 survey
of a sample of those formerly undocumented who were legalized under the
provisions of IRCA. They note a clear increase in earnings and occupational
status over time (and before legalization) for both men and women, although
women fare less well than men throughout. The concentration of the undocumented in relatively few occupations receives useful attention.

Reimers, David M.

1992   *Still the Golden Door: The Third World Comes to America.* New York:
        Columbia University Press. 362 pages.

Overview of immigration to the United States during the last fifty years. Reimers
provides a brief sketch of earlier immigration but picks up his story with World
War II. Chapter 2 provides a review of the so-called bracero program and the
undocumented migration for which it helped set the stage. A later chapter describes more recent issues of undocumented immigration, with attention to the
broad range of people who are undocumented and the complex political response
to them. Unrecognized (and thus "illegal") refugee groups such as Haitians and
Salvadorans also receive attention.

Repak, Terry A.

1995   *Waiting on Washington: Central American Workers in the Nation's Cap-
        ital.* Philadelphia: Temple University Press. 243 pages.

Important study of documented and undocumented Central Americans. Following an introduction to the sending countries (especially El Salvador) and to
Washington, Repak sequentially addresses initial patterns of employment (particularly, the early predominance of women), the types and wages of jobs, the
shifts in legal status options that came with IRCA, and the shifts in roles that
occur with life in the United States. The research included interviews with ser-

vice agencies and employers and two distinct sets of interviews with the migrants (one relatively open-ended and the other more structured).

Rivera, Mario Antonio
1991   *Decision and Structure: U.S. Refugee Policy in the Mariel Crisis.* Lanham, Maryland: University Press of America. 263 pages.
Review of the 1980 governmental handling of a major influx of Cubans and Haitians. Rivera provides a detailed review and analysis of how the Carter administration responded to the influx of nearly 125,000 Cubans from the port of Mariel and the less dramatic, but still sizable, number of Haitians. Ultimately, a special "entrant" status was created, thus blurring the distinctions of refugee and asylee status, which had only just been clarified in the 1980 Refugee Act. Rivera was himself involved in these programs and thus gives firsthand witness to the shifting, often muddled quality of the bureaucratic response to these events.

Rivera-Batiz, Francisco L., Selig L. Sechzer, and Ira N. Gang, Editors
1991   *U.S. Immigration Policy Reform in the 1980s: A Preliminary Assessment.* New York: Praeger. 145 pages.
Set of six papers from a 1988 colloquium at Rutgers University. The papers collectively provide useful analysis of the intent of the 1986 changes and of the data that were then available on their effects (particularly from legalization applications). The authors are mostly economists, and the analysis is at times quite technical, but Rivera-Batiz provides a clear introduction, including noting the limitations of the data available at that time.

Rodriguez, Nestor P.
1987   Undocumented Central Americans in Houston: Diverse Populations. *International Migration Review* 21 (1): 4–26.
Review of the estimated 100,000 undocumented Central American migrants in Houston. The author discusses the origins, settlement patterns, employment, and reasons for emigration, based largely on interview data. Issues emphasized include the recentness of this immigration, its cultural and racial diversity, and the dynamics of household formation. The largest segment of the population was Salvadoran and included the greatest proportions of politically driven refugees.

Runyan, Jack L.
1996   *Profile of Hired Farmworkers, 1996 Annual Averages.* Washington, D.C.: U.S. Department of Agriculture, Economic Research Service, Agricultural Economic Report No. 762. 23 pages.
Report on the approximately 1 million farmworkers employed each week. The data indicate that as a group, compared to all U.S. workers, they were more likely to be male, Hispanic, younger, less-educated, never married, and non-U.S. citizens. Data are derived from the Current Population Survey (CPS). Legality of residence is not directly addressed, but the information does provide a useful

snapshot of the background and income of hired farmworkers (who are often illegal). Differences between crop and livestock workers are noted and are significant.

Rural Migration News
Quarterly: University of California-Davis.
Newsletter. There are both printed and electronic versions of this newsletter. Like *Migration News* (also from UC-Davis), this newsletter is largely a compilation of newspaper accounts, but the knowledgeability of the editor in rural economics makes the overview often clearer than the original stories from which it is drawn. Undocumented migrants are greatly overrepresented in many rural sectors, so this newsletter is an important and essential source.

Salt, John, and Jeremy Stein
1997   Migration as a Business: The Case of Trafficking. *International Migration* 35 (4): 467–491.
General analysis of trafficking as a global business. Although the discussion is based largely on European material, it provides a lucid framework for understanding how trafficking is organized and how it sometimes blurs the conventional distinction between legal and illegal international migration. The description of the three stages in trafficking (recruitment in the sending country, transit, and insertion in the receiving country) is a particularly good checklist of how the business logic behind trafficking operates.

Schiller, Nina Glick, Linda Basch, and Cristina Szanton Blanc
1995   From Immigrant to Transmigrant: Theorizing Transnational Migration. *Anthropological Quarterly* 68 (1): 48–63.
Review of the significance of transnationalism based on the authors' collective experience with migrants from Haiti, Grenada, St. Vincent, and the Philippines. The authors' lucid discussion of transnationalism focuses on the paradox that as migrants increasingly have lives anchored in both the United States and their native countries, so also is the United States increasing its efforts to force them toward assimilation as Americans. Their argument is a general one about immigration, but, at the end, they note how the recent emphasis on illegal immigration serves precisely to force legal immigrants toward closer attachment to the United States.

Select Commission on Immigration and Refugee Policy
1981   *U.S. Immigration Policy and the National Interest.* Washington, D.C.: Select Commission on Immigration and Refugee Policy. 453 pages.
Final report of a commission established by legislation in 1978. The commission conducted a broad spectrum review of immigration, including issues relating to illegal aliens. Section II of the final report (pages 35–85) attempts to assess the volume of illegal immigration and its impact on American society. Major recommendations include stricter enforcement at the border, sanctions against employers who hire illegals, and an amnesty for illegal aliens already in the

country. A separately bound Appendix E provides more detailed background information on illegal immigration.

Simcox, David
1997   Major Predictors of Immigration Restrictivism: Operationalizing "Nativism." *Population and Environment* 19 (2): 129–144.
Largely statistical analysis of the factors that affect people's attitudes toward immigrants. The author notes the importance of such factors as crime, welfare use, and job competition as the basis for nativist views but concludes that the preference for restriction is most affected by the "perception of immigrants as a threat to the dominant culture and society's fiscal health."

Singer, Audrey, and Douglas S. Massey
1998   The Social Process of Undocumented Border Crossing among Mexican Migrants. *International Migration Review* 32 (3): 561–592.
Analysis of border crossings based on a particularly extensive set of detailed personal histories. The authors' general argument is that for initial trips, undocumented border crossers rely on social networks to find a guide but on later trips rely more on their own experience. With that increased personal experience, data suggest that having a guide no longer aids in avoiding apprehension. The analysis is largely statistical but with clear discussion of the central theoretical issues.

Smith, James P., and Barry Edmonston, Editors
1997   *The New Americans: Economic, Demographic and Fiscal Effects of Immigration.* Washington, D.C.: National Academy Press. 434 pages.
Exhaustive team effort to assess the effects of immigration. The study was conducted for the U.S. Commission on Immigration Reform by a joint panel of the Committee on Population and the Committee on National Statistics of the National Research Council (National Academy of Sciences). The panel included twelve well-known experts and also contracted for several additional studies. Although there has been subsequent dispute about the findings, this remains a balanced attempt to assess immigrant impact. Undocumented immigrants appear at various points in the analysis (see the book's index).

Smith, James P., and Barry Edmonston, Editors
1998   *The Immigration Debate: Studies on the Economic, Demographic, and Fiscal Effects of Immigration.* Washington, D.C.: National Academy Press. 458 pages.
Companion volume to *The New Americans* by the same editors. An Introduction and nine chapters provide a variety of data and analysis on immigrant costs and effects. One chapter (John Hagan and Alberto Palloni, pages 367–387) is on immigrants and crime, including a breakdown of legal and illegal immigrants. They do not find much evidence for increased crime by immigrants (or by illegal immigrants in particular), although they do note the pattern of illegal immigrants' being less involved in serious crime and more involved in petty theft.

Smith, Michael Peter, and Bernadette Tarallo
1995   Proposition 187: Global Trend or Local Narrative? Explaining Anti-Immigrant Politics in California, Arizona and Texas. *International Journal of Urban and Regional Research* 19 (4): 664–676.
Review of Proposition 187 with emphasis on the California-specific features that made it possible. The authors begin with a review of the development and passage of the proposition, with an emphasis on Governor Pete Wilson's use of it during his reelection campaign. They then provide a contrasting view of the economic and political situations in Arizona and Texas (e.g., strong cross-border economic links) that would make such an initiative unlikely in those states. The article thus provides a succinct introduction to the extensive variation in sentiment toward immigrants along the long U.S. border with Mexico.

Smith, Paul J., Editor
1997   *Human Smuggling: Chinese Migrant Trafficking and the Challenge to America's Immigration Tradition.* Washington, D.C.: Center for Strategic and International Studies. 207 pages.
Set of ten papers from a 1996 conference on smuggling of Chinese. The conference had its origins in security concerns about human smuggling as the joint product of illegal labor migration and organized crime. Issues addressed include the internal dynamics in China that give rise to emigration, the processes and routes by which the smuggling occurs, and (with a final chapter by Ko-lin Chin) the so-called safe houses in which smuggled Chinese find themselves when they arrive in the United States without having completely paid their fees to the smugglers.

Stanley, William Deane
1987   Economic Migrants or Refugees from Violence? A Time-Series Analysis of Salvadoran Migration to the United States. *Latin American Research Review* 22 (1): 132–154.
Statistical analysis of political versus economic motivations for the immigration of Salvadorans. Stanley describes several statistical analyses based on economic and political factors (e.g., the level of political assassination in El Salvador) and how they relate to the monthly number of Salvadorans apprehended as illegal immigrants. The results underline the importance of political motivations for exodus to the United States.

Stull, Donald D., Michael Broadway, and David Griffith, Editors
1995   *Any Way You Cut It: Meat Processing and Small-Town America.* Lawrence: University of Kansas Press. 269 pages.
Set of eleven papers on beef, pork, and poultry production largely in the Midwest (although also including an intriguing paper on crab processing in North Carolina). The processing work ranges from enormously dangerous in the short term (beef) to more disabling in the long term (poultry). Yet with moderate pay, these related industries draw immigrant labor—both legal and undocumented.

The authors are attentive both to the labor dynamics of the work and to the business side. The book presents a good range of localities and a balanced introduction to these industries in which immigrant labor is so important.

Suárez-Orozco, Carola, and Marcelo Suárez-Orozco
1995   *Transformations: Immigration, Family Life, and Achievement Motivation among Latino Adolescents.* Stanford: Stanford University Press. 266 pages.

Broad, comparative study of Latino adolescents. The authors combine anthropology and psychology and provide an invaluable assessment based on a fourfold comparison: white non-Hispanics, U.S.-born of Mexican origin, Mexican-born but residing in the United States, and Mexican-born in Mexico. The research design, coupled with an unusually balanced sensitivity to both quantitative and qualitative data, make this an important book. Undocumented immigrants appear throughout.

Suro, Roberto
1998   *Strangers among Us: How Latino Immigration Is Transforming America.* New York: Alfred A. Knopf. 352 pages.

Readable introduction to the broad range of Hispanic immigration to the United States. Suro, a journalist, provides a mix of overview data, personal observation, and interview material. The book includes a specific chapter on efforts to close the Mexican border and throughout is attentive to migration streams that are—at least at some times—branded as illegal. This is a good place to begin an acquaintance with the range of peoples in particular American cities who together constitute the growing U.S. Latino population.

Takaki, Ronald
1989   *Strangers from a Different Shore: A History of Asian Americans.* New York: Penguin. 570 pages.

General history of Asian Americans. Takaki's book includes some attention to illegal immigrants per se, but the great value of the book is its lucid portrayal of the way in which different Asian groups were welcomed for their labor but then rejected when that labor was no longer needed or when cheap, more tractable laborers were found. The pattern is especially clear for California agriculture, with a succession of Chinese, Japanese, Indians, Koreans, and Filipinos before agricultural employers settled on Mexicans as the ideal farm laborers.

Tanton, John, and Wayne Lutton
1993   Immigration and Criminality in the U.S.A. *Journal of Social, Political, and Economic Studies* 18 (2): 217–234.

Review of crime involving recent immigrants. The authors provide an alarming inventory of the extent to which crime and America's "promiscuous immigration policy" are interrelated. Overview of particular crime groups (Chinese, Japanese, Jamaican, Cuban, Haitian, Russian, Israeli, Nigerian) is followed by discussion of impacts on states and major kinds of crime. The emphasis is on the drug trade. In a few cases, separate data are provided for illegal aliens, but generally all kinds of immigrants, refugees, and their children are lumped together.

Tomasi, Lydio F.
Annual   *In Defense of the Alien*. Staten Island: Center for Migration Studies. About 250 pages.
Proceedings of an annual conference in Washington, D.C., organized by the New York-based Center for Migration Studies. Although contents vary by year, there is usually a good range of papers addressing recent changes in immigration law, including undocumented entry. The 1998 volume, for example, includes four pieces on detention of immigrants, three on agricultural labor, and four on related issues of deportation and asylum application. The 1997 volume includes nine papers dealing with refugee and asylum issues.

Um, Shin Ja
1996   *Korean Immigrant Women in the Dallas-Area Apparel Industry: Looking for Feminist Threads in Patriarchal Cloth*. Lanham, Maryland: University Press of America. 147 pages.
Sociological review based on seventy-four questionnaires and a few other interviews and observations. Although the study is narrowly constructed, it benefits from being conducted in Korean and in a city that received relatively limited attention for its immigrant-related industries: The author focuses on the nature of the industry and the women workers' familial roles, work roles, social roles, and perceived health and well-being. (Legal status was not a question in the survey—although national data suggest a significant number of undocumented Koreans are likely to be involved in exactly this kind of work.)

Ungar, Sanford J.
1995   *Fresh Blood: The New American Immigrants*. New York: Simon and Schuster. 399 pages.
Positive and readable review of recent immigration. Ungar begins by noting his own immigrant origins and his overriding hope that his account will convince the reader that immigration is still ''an extraordinarily positive feature of American life'' (page 24). This book is based largely on Ungar's interviews with immigrants over a four-year period, particularly the six case studies that constitute the longest section of the book. Illegal immigration receives some attention, both for the Mexican border and in an intriguing discussion of the Irish (pages 337–346).

U.S. Commission on Immigration Reform
1997   *Becoming an American: Immigration and Immigrant Policy*. Washington, D.C.: U.S. Commission on Immigration Reform. 232 pages.
Final report of the commission that was established by the Immigration Act of 1990. The report provides a comprehensive review of American immigration policy and incorporates recommendations from various of the commission's pre-

vious publications. A forty-three-page section is devoted to curbing unlawful migration. Major recommendations include tighter border control, reducing access to employment through tighter verification of work papers, restricted access of illegal aliens to public assistance, reduction of causes of out-migration in source countries, mechanisms to better respond to actual humanitarian crises, and improvements in the apprehension and removal of illegal aliens already in the country.

U.S. Commission on Immigration Reform
1997 *Appendices: Curbing Unlawful Immigration.* Washington, D.C.: U.S. Commission on Immigration Reform. 631 pages.
Supplementary information on the commission's analysis of illegal immigration. The volume includes (1) commission statements and testimony on illegal immigration; (2) overviews of fact-finding visits; (3) formal briefing papers; and (4) portions of research papers contracted out by the commission. The briefing papers are useful overviews—often in considerable depth—of issues such as work site enforcement, employer sanctions, unfair employment practices, border enforcement, deportation and removal, and detention. Two comparative papers on Europe by Mark Miller are included in their entirety, as is the summary of a report by Frank Bean and others on border enforcement initiatives in the El Paso area (Operation "Hold the Line").

U.S. Immigration and Naturalization Service
Annual *Statistical Yearbook of the Immigration and Naturalization Service.* Washington, D.C.: U.S. Government Printing Office.
Key source on immigration and naturalization. The annual report provides an overview of program operations, extensive supporting tables, and useful appendixes (e.g., listing of all U.S. immigration laws). Data on enforcement and asylum (applications and determinations) are directly related to illegal immigration, but other sections on immigration in general and refugee entry may also be of interest.

Vélez-Ibáñez, Carlos G.
1996 *Border Visions: Mexican Cultures of the Southwest United States.* Tucson: University of Arizona Press. 360 pages.
Personalized, anthropological account of the border region. Vélez-Ibáñez works from a mixture of information to provide an experiential understanding of the people who have moved for centuries through this region and across what became a border in 1848. The mix of observation and interpretation, general themes, and personal narratives makes this a good place to consider the way meaning is constructed by people who, he notes, have often been seen only as a labor commodity.

Waldinger, Roger, and Mehdi Bozorgmehr, Editors
1996 *Ethnic Los Angeles.* New York: Russell Sage Foundation. 497 pages.
Set of interrelated papers on Los Angeles, with extensive use of data from the

1990 Census. Given the importance of L.A. as a destination for undocumented immigrants, the volume's discussions of the city, its population, and its economy are of value. Separate chapters on Mexicans and Central Americans are of particular interest—the Central American chapter by David Lopez, Eric Popkin, and Edward Telles specifically addresses legal status.

Wallace, Steven P.
1986   Central American and Mexican Immigrant Characteristics and Economic Incorporation in California. *International Migration Review* 20 (3): 657–671.
Overview of Central American and Mexican immigrant differences based on the 1980 Census. Central American immigrants were better educated, more urban, and more frequently female than the Mexican immigrants. Earnings for men were about the same, but Central American women earned more than Mexican women. Wallace notes the disproportionately political nature of Central American immigration and its distinctive settlement patterns.

Warren, Robert
1997   *Estimates of the Undocumented Immigrant Population Residing in the United States, October 1996.* Washington, D.C.: U.S. Immigration and Naturalization Service. 29 pages.
Updated estimates of the undocumented population. Warren has long been involved with estimating the undocumented population, and he provides here an essential update to the mid-1990s—thus addressing both the drop in the net illegal population after the IRCA legalizations and the subsequent effects of new arrivals. This report is not as detailed in its methodological descriptions as some of his earlier work but does provide what is as close to being the "official" numbers as exists—but see Jeffrey Passel's chapter in this book for more detail on these estimates.

Weiner, Myron, and Tadashi Hanami, Editors
1998   *Temporary Workers or Future Citizens? Japanese and U.S. Migration Policies.* New York: New York University Press. 482 pages.
Set of papers from two symposia held in 1994 and 1995. The fifteen chapters are largely pairings of U.S. and Japanese overviews of particular aspects of immigration. Yasuo Kuwahara and Wayne Cornelius provide the pair of papers on illegal immigration. Peter Shuck's chapter on rights of citizens and aliens also includes a brief review of rights that illegal aliens retain as "persons" under U.S. law.

Wellmeier, Nancy
1994   Rituals of Resettlement: Identity and Resistance among Maya Refugees. In *Selected Papers on Refugees, III.* Edited by Jeffery MacDonald and Amy Zaharlick. Arlington, Virginia: American Anthropological Association. Pp. 9–28.
Review of the migration of Maya to the United States. An introduction to the

hazards of illegal border crossings is followed by a discussion of Indiantown, Florida, with its roughly, 7,000 Maya. Ritual events, leadership, ethnic revitalization, and transnationalism receive attention. There is also useful insight on the way Central Americans moved into the migrant labor stream abandoned by Mexicans as they were able to legalize under the provisions of IRCA.

Wells, Miriam J.
1996   *Strawberry Fields: Politics, Class and Work in California Agriculture.* Ithaca, New York: Cornell University Press. 339 pages.
Detailed analysis of a specific agricultural subsystem in central California. The research included participant observation, interviews, and existing data on strawberry growing. Much of the anthropologist-author's concern is theoretical, but her emphasis on qualitative methods also produces a clear, localized picture of the industry and the largely Mexican (and often undocumented) workers who pick the berries. This is a thorough look at one slice of California's agriculture and the immigrants who appear both as workers and as owners.

Woodrow, Karen A.
1992   A Consideration of the Effect of Immigration Reform on the Number of Undocumented Residents in the United States. *Population Research and Policy Review* 11 (2): 117–144.
Detailed attempt to estimate volume and flow of undocumented migrants. The author ultimately concludes that while IRCA's amnesty reduced the total number of the undocumented, it did not appear to affect the annual number of new undocumented border crossers each year (roughly 200,000). In the process of developing these estimates, the article provides a particularly useful (although detailed) indication of the difficulties in estimating the undocumented population. The SAW (special agricultural worker) provisions of IRCA receive special attention.

Woodrow-Lafield, Karen A.
1998   Undocumented Residents in the United States in 1990: Issues of Uncertainty in Quantification. *International Migration Review* 32 (1): 145–173.
Review of estimates of the undocumented population with emphasis on recognizing the range of plausible estimates. Woodrow-Lafield provides a general review of estimates of the undocumented population, particularly the so-called residual estimates, which take census (or CPS) data on the foreign-born and subtract the known legal, foreign-born population to leave the residual: the undocumented, foreign-born population. The article is effective in illustrating how the varied estimates of the legality and length of residence of the *legal* population can thus skew the residual estimate of the undocumented.

Zabin, Carol, and Sallie Hughes
1995   Economic Integration and Labor Flows: Stage Migration in Farm Labor Markets in Mexico and the United States. *International Migration Review* 29 (2): 395–422.

Review of agricultural labor migration to northern Mexico and the United States from southern Mexico. The authors' basic argument is that the development of export-oriented agriculture in northern Mexico has increased the level of migration to the United States through staging points that provide useful exposure, preparation, and contacts for moving across the border. These areas also provide stable, low-wage labor for family members who do not attempt the often perilous illegal crossing of the border. The data relate largely to Mixtecs from Oaxaca and include surveys in the United States (California and Oregon) and Mexico (Baja).

Ziv, Tal An, and Bernard Lo
1995   Denial of Care to Illegal Immigrants. *New England Journal of Medicine* 332 (16): 1095–1098.
Short review of the implications of California's Proposition 187 for physicians. The authors make three central points about the proposition: (1) it poses dangers to public health (e.g., tuberculosis may spread because of lack of treatment, and decreased prenatal care will affect the health of future Americans); (2) it will result in denial of care both to illegal aliens and to those who may inadvertently be excluded by new reporting requirements; and (3) it would involve serious breaches of confidentiality that, unlike other physician reporting requirements, do not pertain to public health.

Zolberg, Aristide R.
1990   Reforming the Back Door: The Immigration Reform and Control Act of 1986 in Historical Perspective. In *Immigration Reconsidered: History, Sociology, and Politics.* Edited by Virginia Yans-McGlaughlin. New York: Oxford University Press. Pp. 315–339.
Review of IRCA's effort to reform the "back door." Zolberg begins with a review of the political dynamics of illegal immigration and then provides a blow-by-blow account of the "wondrous career" of the Simpson-Mazzoli legislation that eventually became IRCA in 1986. He stresses the odd alliance of support for the bill from groups at opposite ends of the political spectrum and analyzes separately those motivated by economic concerns and those activated by political/cultural concerns.

Zucker, Norman L., and Naomi Flink Zucker
1996   *Desperate Crossings: Seeking Refuge in America.* Armonk, New York: M. E. Sharpe. 169 pages.
Review of U.S. refugee policy with particular attention to mass movements across U.S. borders. The authors begin with a general review of U.S. policy but quickly turn to the issue of mass escape to the United States, mostly from Cuba, Haiti, and Central America. Throughout, they focus on the often erratic attempts to define who is a legal refugee, who is technically undocumented but has a

clear right to apply for asylum, and who is to be classified as an economic migrant. The book is a very good introduction to the human and political dimensions of those ''illegal'' immigrants who may be bona fide refugees in terms of international law or who should at least have the right to refuge.

Appendix

Summary of Recent Immigration Legislation

Refugee Act of March 17, 1980 (94 Statutes-at-Large 102). Provided the first permanent and systematic procedure for the admission and effective resettlement of refugees of special humanitarian concern to the United States:

1. Eliminated refugees as a category of the preference system.

2. Set the worldwide ceiling of immigration to the United States at 270,000, exclusive of refugees.

3. Established procedures for annual consultation with Congress on numbers and allocations of refugees to be admitted in each fiscal year, as well as procedures for responding to emergency refugee situations.

4. Defined the term ''refugee'' (to conform to the 1967 United Nations Protocol on Refugees) and made clear the distinction between refugee and asylee status.

5. Established a comprehensive program for domestic resettlement of refugees.

6. Provided for adjustment to permanent resident status of refugees who have been physically present in the United States for at least one year and of asylees one year after asylum is granted.

Refugee Education Assistance Act of October 10, 1980 (94 Statutes-at-Large 1799). Established a program of formula grants to state education agencies for basic education of refugee children. Also provided for services to Cuban and Haitian entrants identical to those for refugees under the Refugee Act of 1980.

Act of June 5, 1981 (95 Statutes-at-Large 14). Supplemental appropriations and rescissions bill reduced previously appropriated funds for migration and refugee assistance, including funds provided for reception and processing of Cuban and Haitian entrants.

Act of August 13, 1981 (95 Statutes-at-Large 357). Federal appropriations bill for fiscal year 1982 also contained items restricting the access of aliens to various publicly funded benefits. Immigration-related provisions:

1. Precluded the secretary of the Department of Housing and Urban Development (HUD) from making financial assistance available to any alien unless that alien is a resident of the United States by virtue of admission or adjustment as a permanent resident alien, refugee or asylee, parolee, or conditional entrant or pursuant to withholding of deportation. Alien visitors, tourists, diplomats, and students were specifically excluded.

2. Severely restricted eligibility of aliens to Aid to Families with Dependent Children.

Immigration and Nationality Act Amendments of December 20, 1981 (95 Statutes-at-Large 1611). "INS Efficiency Bill" amended the Immigration and Nationality Act of 1952 and the Act of November 2, 1978:

1. Authorized INS to seize vehicles without having to establish whether the owner was involved in the illegal activity in question.

2. Eliminated the requirement that the government bear administrative and incidental expenses where an innocent owner is involved.

3. Eliminated the requirement that the INS satisfy any valid lien or other third-party interest in a vehicle without expense to the interest holder.

4. Eliminated the required annual notification by aliens of their current address.

Act of September 30, 1982 (96 Statutes-at-Large 1157). Allowed admission as permanent residents to certain nonimmigrant aliens residing in the Virgin Islands.

Act of October 2, 1982 (96 Statutes-at-Large 1186). Greatly limited the categories of aliens to whom the Legal Services Corporation may provide legal assistance.

Act of October 22, 1982 (96 Statutes-at-Large 1716). Provided that children born of U.S. citizen fathers in Korea, Vietnam, Laos, Kampuchea, or Thailand after 1950 and before enactment may come to the United States as immediate relatives or as first- or fourth-preference immigrants.

Immigration Reform and Control Act of November 6, 1986 (IRCA) (100 Statutes-at-Large 3359). Comprehensive immigration legislation:

1. Authorized legalization (i.e., temporary and then permanent resident status) for aliens who had resided in the United States in an unlawful status since January 1, 1982 (entering illegally or as temporary visitors with authorized stay expiring before that date or with the government's knowledge of their unlawful status before that date), and are not excludable.

2. Created sanctions prohibiting employers from knowingly hiring, recruiting, or referring for a fee aliens not authorized to work in the United States.

3. Increased enforcement at U.S. borders.

4. Created a new classification of seasonal agricultural worker and provisions for the legalization of certain such workers.

5. Extended the registry date (i.e., the date from which an alien has resided illegally and continuously in the United States and thus qualifies for adjustment to permanent resident status) from June 30, 1948, to January 1, 1972.

6. Authorized adjustment to permanent resident status for Cubans and Haitians who entered the United States without inspection and had continuously resided in country since January 1, 1982.

7. Increased the numerical limitation for immigrants admitted under the preference system for dependent areas from 600 to 5,000 beginning in fiscal year 1988.

8. Created a new special immigrant category for certain retired employees of international organ-

izations and their families and a new nonimmigrant status for parents and children of such immigrants.

9. Created a nonimmigrant Visa Waiver Pilot program allowing certain aliens to visit the United States without applying for a nonimmigrant visa.

10. Allocated 5,000 nonpreference visas in each of fiscal years 1987 and 1988 for aliens born in countries from which immigration was adversely affected by the 1965 act.

Immigration Marriage Fraud Amendments of November 10, 1986 (100 Statutes-at-Large 3537). Provisions:

1. Stipulated that aliens deriving their immigrant status based on a marriage of less than two years are conditional immigrants. To remove conditional status, the alien must apply within ninety days after their second-year anniversary of receiving conditional status.

2. Required alien fiancé(e)s of U.S. citizens to have met their citizen petitioner in person within two years of the date the petition was filed.

Amerasian Homecoming Act of December 22, 1987 (101 Statutes-at-Large 1329). An appropriations law providing for admission of children born in Vietnam between specified dates to Vietnamese mothers and American fathers, together with their immediate relatives. They are admitted as nonquota immigrants but receive refugee program benefits.

Act of September 28, 1988 (102 Statutes-at-Large 1876). United States–Canada Free-Trade Agreement Implementation Act:

1. Facilitated temporary entry on a reciprocal basis between the United States and Canada.

2. Established procedures for the temporary entry into the United States of Canadian citizen professional businesspersons to render services for remuneration.

3. No nonimmigrant visa, prior petition, labor certification, or prior approval required, but appropriate documentation must be presented to the inspecting officer establishing Canadian citizenship and professional engagement in one of the occupations listed in the qualifying occupation schedule.

Act of November 15, 1988 (102 Statutes-at-Large 3908). Provided for the extension of stay for certain nonimmigrant H-1 nurses.

Foreign Operations Act of November 21, 1989 (103 Statutes-at-Large 1195). An appropriations law; provided for adjustment to permanent resident status for Soviet and Indochinese nationals who were paroled into the United States between certain dates after denial of refugee status.

Act of December 18, 1989 (103 Statutes-at-Large 2099). The ''Immigration Nursing Relief Act of 1989.'' Provisions:

1. Adjustment from temporary to permanent resident status, without regard to numerical limitation, of certain nonimmigrants who were employed in the United States as registered nurses for at least three years and met established certification standards.

2. Establishment of a new nonimmigrant category for the temporary admission of qualified registered nurses.

Immigration Act of November 29, 1990 (104 Statutes-at-Large 4978). A major overhaul of immigration law:

1. Increased total immigration under an overall flexible cap of 675,000 immigrants beginning in fiscal year 1995, preceded by a 700,000-level during fiscal years 1992 through 1994. The 675,000 level to consist of 480,000 family-sponsored; 140,000 employment-based; and 55,000 "diversity immigrants."

2. Revised all grounds for exclusion and deportation, significantly rewriting the political and ideological grounds. For example, repealed the bar against the admission of communists as nonimmigrants and limited the exclusion of aliens on foreign policy grounds.

3. Authorized the attorney general to grant temporary protected status to undocumented alien nationals of designated countries subject to armed conflict or natural disasters.

4. Revised and established new nonimmigrant admission categories: (1) Redefined the H-1(b) temporary worker category and limited number of aliens who may be issued visas or otherwise provided nonimmigrant status under this category to 65,000 annually. (2) Limited number of H-2(b) temporary worker category aliens who may be issued visas or otherwise provided nonimmigrant status to 66,000 annually. (3) Created new temporary worker admission categories (O, P, Q, and R), some with annual caps on number of aliens who may be issued visas or otherwise provided nonimmigrant status.

5. Revised and extended the Visa Waiver Pilot program through fiscal year 1994.

6. Revised naturalization authority and requirements: (1) Transferred the exclusive jurisdiction to naturalize aliens from the federal and state courts to the attorney general. (2) Amended the substantive requirements for naturalization: state residency requirements revised and reduced to three months; added another ground for waiving the English-language requirement; lifted the permanent bar to naturalization for aliens who applied to be relieved from U.S. military service on grounds of alienage who previously were in the service of the country of the alien's nationality.

7. Revised enforcement activities. For example: (1) broadened the definition of "aggravated felony" and imposed new legal restrictions on aliens convicted of such crimes; (2) revised employer sanctions provisions of the Immigration Reform and Control Act of 1986; (3) authorized funds to increase Border Patrol personnel by 1,000; (4) revised criminal and deportation provisions.

8. Recodified the thirty-two grounds for exclusion into nine categories, including revising and repealing some of the grounds (especially health grounds).

Armed Forces Immigration Adjustment Act of October 1, 1991 (105 Statutes-at-Large 555). Provisions:

1. Granted special immigrant status to certain types of aliens who honorably served in the armed forces of the United States for at least twelve years.

2. Delayed until April 1, 1992, the implementation of provisions relating to O and P nonimmigrant visas. (See Act of November 29, 1990.)

Act of December 12, 1991 (105 Statutes-at-Large 1733). Miscellaneous and Technical Immigration and Naturalization Amendments Act amended certain elements of the Immigration Act of 1990. Revised provisions regarding the entrance of O and P nonimmigrants, including the repeal of numerical limits of visas for the P categories of admission, and made other technical corrections. (See Act of November 29, 1990.)

Chinese Student Protection Act of October 9, 1992 (106 Statutes-at-Large 1969). Provided for adjustment to permanent resident status (as employment-based immigrants) by nationals of the People's Republic of China who were in the United States after June 4, 1989, and before April 11, 1990.

Soviet Scientists Immigration Act of October 10, 1992 (106 Statutes-at-Large 3316). Provisions:

1. Conferred permanent resident status (as employment-based immigrants) on a maximum of 750 scientists from the independent states of the former Soviet Union and the Baltic states. The limit does not include spouses and children.

2. Stipulated that employment must be in the biological, chemical, or nuclear technical field or work in conjunction with a high-technology defense project.

3. Waived the requirement that workers with expertise in these fields were needed by an employer in the United States.

Act of December 8, 1993 (107 Statutes-at-Large 2057). North American Free-Trade Agreement Implementation Act (supersedes the United States–Canada Free-Trade Agreement Act of September 28, 1988):

1. Facilitated temporary entry on a reciprocal basis between the United States, Canada, and Mexico.

2. Established procedures for the temporary entry into the United States of Canadian and Mexican citizen professional businesspersons to render services for remuneration: (1) for Canadians, no nonimmigrant visa, prior petition, labor certification, or prior approval required, but appropriate documentation must be presented to the inspecting officer establishing Canadian citizenship and professional engagement in one of the occupations listed in the qualifying occupation schedule; (2) for Mexicans, nonimmigrant visa, prior petition by employer, and Department of Labor attestation are required in addition to proof of Mexican citizenship and professional engagement in one of the occupations listed in the qualifying occupation schedule; (3) for Canadians, non-immigrant visas are not required of spouses and minor children who possess Canadian citizenship; (4) for Mexicans, nonimmigrant visas are required of spouses and minor children who possess Mexican citizenship; (5) for Canadians, no limit to number of admissions; (6) for Mexicans, a limit was set for a transition period for up to ten years at 5,500 initial approvals per year.

Violent Crime Control and Law Enforcement Act of September 13, 1994 (108 Statutes-at-Large 1796). Provisions: (1) authorized establishment of a criminal alien tracking center; (2) established a new nonimmigrant classification for alien witness cooperation and counterterrorism information; (3) revised deportation procedures for certain criminal aliens who are not permanent residents and expanded special deportation proceedings; (4) provided for expeditious deportation for denied asylum applicants; (5) provided for improved border management through increased resources; (6) strengthened penalties for passport and visa offenses.

Antiterrorism and Effective Death Penalty Act of April 24, 1996 (110 Statutes-at-Large 1214). Provisions:

1. Expedited procedures for removal of alien terrorists.

2. Established specific measures to exclude members and representatives of terrorist organizations: (1) provided for the exclusion of alien terrorists; (2) waived authority concerning notice of denial application for visas; (3) denied other forms of relief for alien terrorists; (4) excluded from process aliens who have not been inspected and admitted.

3. Modified asylum procedures to improve identification and processing of alien terrorists: (1) established mechanisms for denial of asylum to alien terrorists; (2) granted authority to inspection officers to both inspect and exclude asylee applicants; (3) improved judicial review process to expedite hearings and removal (if necessary) of alien terrorists.

4. Provided for criminal alien procedural improvements: (1) provided access to certain confidential

immigration and naturalization files through court order; (2) established a criminal alien identification system; (3) established certain alien smuggling-related crimes as RICO (Racketeer Influenced and Corrupt Organizations [Act])-predicate offenses; (4) granted authority for alien smuggling investigations; (5) expanded criteria for deportation for crimes of moral turpitude; (6) established an interior repatriation program; (7) allowed for deportation of nonviolent offenders prior to completion of sentence of imprisonment; (8) authorized state and local law enforcement officials to arrest and detain certain illegal aliens; (9) expedited the process of criminal alien removal; (10) limited collateral attacks on underlying deportation orders; (11) established deportation procedures for certain criminal aliens who are not permanent residents.

Personal Responsibility and Work Opportunity Reconciliation Act of August 22, 1996 (110 Statutes-at-Large 2105). Provisions:

1. Established restrictions on the eligibility of legal immigrants for means-tested public assistance: (1) barred legal immigrants (with certain exceptions) from obtaining food stamps and Supplemental Security Income (SSI) and established screening procedures for current recipients of these programs; (2) barred legal immigrants (with certain exceptions) from entering the United States after date of enactment from most federal means-tested programs for five years; (3) provided states with broad flexibility in setting public benefit eligibility rules for legal immigrants by allowing states to bar current legal immigrants from both major federal programs and state programs; (4) increased the responsibility of the immigrants' sponsors by making the affidavit of support legally enforceable, imposing new requirements on sponsors, and expanding sponsor-deeming requirements to more programs and lengthening the deeming period.

2. Broadened the restrictions on public benefits for illegal aliens and nonimmigrants: (1) barred illegal, or "not qualified aliens," from most federal, state, and local public benefits and (2) required INS to verify immigration status in order for aliens to receive most federal public benefits.

Illegal Immigration Reform and Immigrant Responsibility Act of September 30, 1996 (110 Statutes-at-Large 3009). Provisions:

1. Established measures to control U.S. borders, protect legal workers through work site enforcement, and remove criminal and other deportable aliens: (1) increased border personnel, equipment, and technology as well as enforcement personnel at land and air ports of entry; (2) authorized improvements in barriers along the southwest border; (3) increased antismuggling authority and penalties for alien smuggling; (4) increased penalties for illegal entry, passport and visa fraud, and failure to depart; (5) increased INS investigators for work site enforcement, alien smuggling, and visa-overstayers; (6) established three voluntary pilot programs to confirm the employment eligibility of workers and reduced the number and types of documents that may be presented to employers for identity and eligibility to work; (7) broadly reformed exclusion and deportation procedures, including consolidation into a single removal process as well as the institution of expedited removal to speed deportation and alien exclusion through more stringent grounds of admissibility; (8) increased detention space for criminal and other deportable aliens; (9) instituted three- and ten-year bars to admissibility for aliens seeking to reenter after having been unlawfully present in the United States; (10) barred reentry of individuals who renounced their U.S. citizenship in order to avoid U.S. tax obligations.

2. Placed added restrictions on benefits for aliens: (1) provided for a pilot program on limiting issuance of driver's licenses to illegal aliens; (2) declared aliens not lawfully present ineligible for Social Security benefits; (3) established procedures for requiring proof of citizenship for federal public benefits; (4) established limitations on eligibility for preferential treatment of aliens not lawfully present on the basis of residence for higher education benefits; (5) provided for verification of immigration status for purposes of Social Security and higher educational assis-

tance; (6) tightened the requirement for an affidavit of support for sponsored immigrants, making the affidavit a legally binding contract to provide financial support; (7) provided authority of states and political subdivisions of states to limit assistance to aliens in providing general cash public assistance; (8) increased maximum criminal penalties for forging or counterfeiting the seal of a federal department or agency to facilitate benefit fraud by an unlawful alien.

3. Miscellaneous provisions: (1) recodified existing INS regulations regarding asylum; (2) provided that the attorney general's parole authority may be exercised only on a case-by-case basis for urgent humanitarian reasons or significant public health; (3) created new limits on the ability of F-1 students to attend public schools without reimbursing those institutions; (4) established new mandates for educational institutions to collect information on foreign students' status and nationality and provide it to INS; (5) tightened restrictions regarding foreign physicians' ability to work in the United States; (6) added new consular processing provisions and revised the visa waiver program.

Act of January 3, 1996 (Public Law 104–302). Provided for the extension of the authorized period of stay within the United States for certain nurses.

Act of August 8, 1997 (Public Law 105–38; 111 Statutes-at-Large 1115). Amended the Immigration and Nationality Technical Corrections Act of 1994 to eliminate the special transition rule for issuance of a certificate of citizenship for certain children born outside the United States.

Continuing Appropriations Act of September 30, 1997 (Public Law 105–46: 111 Statutes-at-Large 1153). Section 117 extended the authorities of the Immigration and Nationality Act during the period of the joint resolution.

Act of October 6, 1997 (Public Law 105–54; 111 Statutes-at-Large 1175). To amend the Immigration and Nationality Act to extend the special immigrant religious worker program, to amend the Illegal Immigration Reform and Immigrant Responsibility Act of 1996 to extend the deadline for designation of an effective date for paperwork changes in the employer sanctions program, and to require the secretary of state to waive or reduce the fee for application and issuance of a nonimmigrant visa for aliens coming to the United States for certain charitable purposes.

Departments of Veterans Affairs and Housing and Urban Development, and Independent Agencies Appropriations Act. 1998 (Public Law 105–65 of October 27, 1997; 111 Statutes-at-Large 1344). Section 108 amended section 214(1)(1)(D) of the Immigration and Nationality Act—as amended by the Immigration and Nationality Technical Corrections Act of 1994 and the Illegal Immigration Reform and Immigrant Responsibility Act of 1996—to clarify geographical areas of medical practice for aliens.

Act of November 12, 1997 (Public Law 105–73; 111 Statutes-at-Large 1459). Amended the Immigration and Nationality Act to exempt internationally adopted children ten years of age or younger from the immunization requirement in section 212(a)(1)(A)(ii) of the INA.

Departments of Labor, Health and Human Services, and Education Appropriations Act. 1998 (Public Law 105–78 of November 13, 1997; 111 Statutes-at-Large 1467). Section 604 amended section 414(a) of the Immigration and Nationality Act (8 U.S.C. 1524[a]) by striking "fiscal year 1995, fiscal year 1996, and fiscal year 1997" and inserting "each of fiscal years 1998 and 1999," to be effective on October 1, 1997.

National Defense Authorization Act, 1998 (Public Law 105–85 of November 18, 1997; 111 Statutes-at-Large 1629). Section 390 stipulated that work contracts for Guam military base operations should not be performed by any alien who is issued a visa or otherwise provided nonimmigrant status under section 101(a)(15)(H)(ii) of the Immigration and Nationality Act (8 U.S.C. 1101[a][15][H][ii]). Title X clarified details of the naturalization of certain foreign nationals who serve honorably in the armed forces during a period of conflict.

Nicaraguan Adjustment and Central American Relief Act (Public Law 105–100 of November 19, 1997; 111 Statutes-at-Large 2160). Provisions:

1. Cuban and Nicaraguan nationals who had been in the United States since December 1, 1995, were eligible to have their status adjusted to lawfully admitted, so long as they could document their residence and were otherwise admissible as immigrants. Any pending deportation action against them was suspended, and work authorization was available. Spouses and unmarried children also became eligible for adjustment of status, although unmarried children also had to prove residence since December 1, 1995.

2. Salvadorans and Guatemalans who either filed applications for asylum on or before April 1, 1990, or arrived later that year (on or before September 19 for Salvadorans and on or before October 1 for Guatemalans) but registered for benefits under the ABC settlement (*American Baptist Churches et al. v. Thornburgh*) were eligible for protection from removal.

3. A variety of nationals from Eastern Europe and Russia were also eligible for protection from removal if they entered the United States on or before December 31, 1990, and filed an application for asylum on or before that same date.

4. Provided a numerical limitation on the number of cancellations of removal and suspensions of deportation allowed in a particular year, excepting those mentioned specifically in this act.

Departments of Commerce, Justice, and State, the Judiciary, and Related Agencies Appropriations Act, 1998 (Public Law 105–11 of November 26, 1997). Sections 110, 111, 112, 113, and 125 provided authorities for INS salaries and expenses.

Technical Corrections to the Nicaraguan Adjustment and Central American Relief Act (Public Law 105–139 of December 2, 1997; 111 Statutes-at-Large 2644). Provided technical amendments to that law and a temporary reduction in diversity visas.

Act of December 5, 1997 (Public Law 105–141; 111 Statutes-at-Large 2647). Established a program in local prisons to identify, prior to arraignment, criminal aliens and aliens who are unlawfully present in the United States, and for other purposes. The plan includes the basis for selection of facilities and a continuing increase in such facilities through FY 2003. A study is also mandated.

Act of April 27, 1998 (Public Law 105–173; 112 Statutes-at-Large 56). Amended the Immigration and Nationality Act to modify and extend the visa waiver pilot program and to provide for collection of data regarding the number of nonimmigrants who remain in the United States after the expiration of the period of stay authorized by the attorney general.

Agricultural Research, Extension, and Education Reform Act of June 23, 1998 (Public Law 105–185). Extended the eligibility for food stamps for refugees from five to seven years and restored them to several other categories of immigrants who were in the United States on August 22, 1996, when such benefits were initially denied by that year's welfare reform legislation.

Omnibus Appropriations Bill, FY 99 of October 21, 1998 (Public Law 105–277). This massive combined appropriations bill included a wide range of bills and provisions relating to refugees and immigrants, most importantly: availability of permanent residence to an estimated 50,000 Haitians (Haitian Refugee Immigration Fairness Act), increases in the number of visas for high-tech, H-1B workers (American Competitiveness and Workforce Improvement Act), extension of the so-called Lautenberg Amendment (which relaxes the refugee standard for certain groups from Southeast Asia and the former Soviet Union), adjustment of status of some 7,000 Kurds processed through Guam (to resolve the pressure on quotas for asylees), better monitoring of incarcerated aliens, restriction of Department of State funding for forcible return of refugees, a broad prohibition on the forcible return of people fearing torture, and a delay in the requirement for an INS automated entry and exit tracking system.

International Religious Freedom Act of October 27, 1998 (Public Law 105–292). Among the provisions are increased attention to training for awareness of religious persecution in the refugee determination process and annual reporting by the Department of State on international religious freedom.

Noncitizen Benefit Clarification and Other Technical Amendments Act of October 28, 1998 (Public Law 105–306). Restored SSI benefits to an additional estimated 20,000 persons who had been receiving them on August 22, 1996 but whose benefits had not been restored by the Balanced Budget Act of 1997.

NOTE

This summary is drawn from the INS annual reports and more detailed INS documents on recent legislation. These are available in their entirety on-line at <www. usdoj.gov/ins>. See the Library of Congress's online ''Thomas'' system for recent and in-process legislation.

Index

About the Editors and Contributors

DEBORAH R. ALTAMIRANO received her Ph.D. in anthropology from the University of California at Santa Barbara and is currently an assistant professor of anthropology at the State University of New York at Plattsburgh. Her primary areas of academic research include social movements and transnationalism in the southern Mediterranean and Latin America. She has conducted extensive field research in Greece, including work with exile, immigrant, and refugee populations.

JANET E. BENSON is an associate professor of anthropology at Kansas State University. She has lived and conducted research in Africa, India, Sri Lanka, the Caribbean, and southwest Kansas. During 1988–1990 she participated in the Ford Foundation's Changing Relations Project in Garden City, Kansas (one of six sites throughout the United States)—one of the first national studies to apply ethnographic research methods to the analysis of relations between newcomers and established residents in American cities. Her research interests include immigrant labor in meatpacking, immigrant household economic strategies, and problems among the second generation.

NORMAN BUCHIGNANI is professor and chair of the Department of Anthropology at the University of Lethbridge, Canada. He has been involved in studies of immigration, ethnic diversity, and community-based systems of meaning in Canada and elsewhere for twenty-five years. He is the co-author of *Continuous Journey: A Social History of South Asians in Canada*.

REBECCA S. CARTER is a Ph.D. student at Louisiana State University and a research associate on the project "Health Consequences of Mexican Migration," funded by the Hewlett and Rockefeller Foundations. Her dissertation examines how household work and child care affect the wages of women and men.

KO-LIN CHIN received his Ph.D. in sociology from the University of Pennsylvania and is an associate professor at the School of Criminal Justice of Rutgers University–Newark. He is the author of *Chinese Subculture and Criminality* (Greenwood Press, 1990), *Chinatown Gangs* (1996), and co-editor of the *Handbook of Organized Crime in the United States* (Greenwood Press, 1994). He has recently completed a manuscript on smuggled Chinese immigrants in America.

LUCY M. COHEN received her M.S.W. and Ph.D. from the Catholic University of America, where she is now professor and chair of the Department of Anthropology. She has conducted a wide range of research on immigrants in the United States, from Chinese in the post–Civil War South to recent Central American immigrants in the Washington, D.C. area. Her work, often with an applied orientation, has focussed on issues of ethnicity, gender, family, and health, with publications in both English and Spanish.

KATHARINE M. DONATO is an associate professor in the Department of Sociology at Louisiana State University. Her major research areas are demography and stratification, with specific interests in the effects of changing U.S. policy on Mexican migration. Currently, she is engaged in two major projects related to U.S. immigration: one addresses the effects of migration on the health of Mexicans on both sides of the border (funded by the Hewlett and Rockefeller Foundations), and the other examines the experiences of new immigrants in Louisiana.

DUNCAN M. EARLE received his Ph.D. in anthropology from the State University of New York at Albany and is currently an associate professor at the University of Texas at El Paso. His main research interests are in the displacement of rural people in Guatemala and Mexico, particularly Maya affected by economic and religious change in Guatemala; Guatemalan refugees in Mexico and the United States; and Mexicans located in border *colonias* in the United States.

ELZBIETA M. GOZDZIAK, a cultural anthropologist by training, has taught at various universities and is currently head of a refugee mental health program funded by the federal government. Her academic work primarily relates to displaced populations, research methods, and various aspects of Eastern European society and politics. She has also worked in policy analysis and project development for refugees both in the United States and in Poland and Slovakia.

DAVID GRIFFITH is a senior scientist at East Carolina University's Institute for Coastal and Marine Resources and associate professor of anthropology. Throughout his career, he has balanced studies of work with studies of fishing communities, publishing in a wide range of academic journals. His books include *Jones's Minimal: Low-Wage Labor in the United States* (1993), *Working Poor: Farmworkers in the United States* (co-authored in 1995), and *Any Way You Cut It: Meat Processing and Small-Town America* (co-edited in 1995). His most recent work, *The Estuary's Gift: A Mid-Atlantic Coast Cultural Biography*, is to be published in 1999.

DAVID W. HAINES received his M.A. in Southeast Asian studies and his Ph.D. in anthropology both from the American University. A former policy analyst for the U.S. refugee program, senior manager in state government, and Fulbright fellow in Europe, he is now an associate professor of anthropology at George Mason University. He is the editor of *Refugees as Immigrants: Cambodians, Laotians, and Vietnamese in America* (1989) and *Refugees in America in the 1990s* (Greenwood Press, 1996; Praeger, 1997). Other published works focus on Vietnamese social history, American culture and society, refugee and immigration policy, and the structure of governance.

DOREEN INDRA is a professor of anthropology at the University of Lethbridge, Alberta, Canada. Her most recent work concerns environmentally forced migrants in Bangladesh and the construction and culture of disasters. She is co-author of *Continuous Journey: A Social History of South Asians in Canada*, editor of *Engendering Forced Migration: Theory and Practice*, co-editor of two volumes on refugees in Canada, and author of many academic journal articles in the area of forced migration.

ENRICO A. MARCELLI received his Ph.D. in political economy and public policy from the University of Southern California and is currently a research fellow at the Center for U.S.–Mexican Studies of the University of California at San Diego. He is the author of various articles on the undocumented and Los Angeles, with particular emphasis on the political economy of immigration in California. His *California in Denial: A Political Economy of Unauthorized Mexican Immigration* will be published in 1999.

PHILIP L. MARTIN is a professor of agricultural economics at the University of California at Davis and editor of both *Migration News* and *Rural Migration News*. He has long been involved in research on immigration, publishing a variety of works on the United States, Germany, Turkey, Egypt, and Mexico. He has been an associate of the Brookings Institution, a Fulbright fellow in Germany, an economist for the Select Commission on Immigration and Refugee Policy, and a member of the Commission on Agricultural Workers.

SAMUEL MARTÍNEZ is an assistant professor of anthropology and Latin American studies at the University of Connecticut at Storrs. He is the author of *Peripheral Migrants: Haitians and Dominican Sugar Plantations* (1995). His current research interests include Haitian-Dominican community organizations and civil rights activism, the social construction of "democracy" in the Dominican Republic, and the impact of poverty and social inequality on the labor and minority rights situation of Haitian immigrants in the Dominican Republic.

CECILIA MENJÍVAR received her Ph.D. in sociology and is an assistant professor in the School of Justice Studies at Arizona State University. Her research interests include social networks among immigrants, refugee migrations, immigrant families and children, gender and migration, and religious institutions and transnational politics in immigrant communities. Her publications have appeared in *International Migration Review, Journal of Refugee Studies, Social Problems, International Migration, International Journal of Comparative Sociology, Journal of Comparative Family Studies*, and the *Revista Mundial de Sociología*.

JEFFREY S. PASSEL received his Ph.D. in social relations from the Johns Hopkins University and subsequently worked at the Census Bureau before joining the Urban Institute in 1989. His research has focused on the impacts and integration of immigrants into American society and the demography of immigration, particularly the measurement of illegal immigration. He co-authored *Immigration and Immigrants: Setting the Record Straight*, and co-edited *Immigration and Ethnicity: The Integration of America's Newest Immigrants, Undocumented Migration to the United States: IRCA and the Experience of the 1980s*, and *The Coverage of Population in the United States*.

VICTORIA RADER, who received her B.A. in sociology from the University of California, Berkeley, and her Ph.D. from the University of Chicago, currently teaches at George Mason University. She is past president of the Association for Humanist Sociology, a national organization linking several hundred scholar-activists. Her book *Signal Through the Flames* was the first study of the contemporary homeless movement in the United States. She has also published on issues of social change in both the United States and Mexico in a variety of sociology journals.

KAREN E. ROSENBLUM received her Ph.D. in sociology in 1979 and has taught since 1980 at George Mason University, where she is currently Vice-President for University Life. She is co-editor of *The Meaning of Difference: American Constructions of Race, Sex and Gender, Social Class, and Sexual Orientation* (1996; second edition forthcoming in 1999). Her publications focus on gender, language, and the social construction of minority groups.

KAREN A. WOODROW-LAFIELD received her Ph.D. in sociology and is currently an assistant professor at Mississippi State University. Her principal research and teaching interests are international migration, immigrant incorporation, poverty measurement, demography, development, and social change. She has published several studies of authorized and unauthorized immigration to the United States, measuring emigration to other countries and decennial census coverage. She was a participant in the Mexico–United States Binational Migration Study over 1995–1997, and co-authored a chapter for that study's final report on ''The Quantification of Migration between Mexico and the United States.''

KEIKO YAMANAKA received her Ph.D. in sociology from Cornell University and is currently a lecturer in the Department of Comparative Ethnic Studies of the University of California, Berkeley, and a research associate of the Institute for the Study of Social Change. She has conducted a wide range of research on migration focussing particularly on Japanese-Brazilians and Nepalese migrants to Japan, with recent publications on those issues in *Ethnic and Racial Studies*, *Diaspora*, *Beyond Boundaries*, and *Coming to Japan*.

ISBN 0-313-30436-X

90000>

EAN

9 780313 304361

HARDCOVER BAR CODE